6/03

From
Spirituals
to
Symphonies

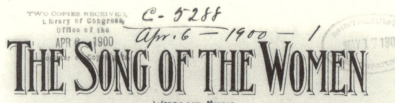

Cover sheet for *The Song of the Women* by Ida M. Yeocum, 1900. Courtesy of the Library of Congress, Music Division.

From
SPIRITUALS
to
SYMPHONIES

African-American Women Composers and Their Music

Helen Walker-Hill

GREENWOOD PRESS
Westport, Connecticut • London

Library of Congress Cataloging-in-Publication Data

Walker-Hill, Helen.
From spirituals to symphonies : African-American women composers and their music /
Helen Walker-Hill.
p.   cm.
Includes bibliographical references.
ISBN 0–313–29947–1 (alk. paper)
1. African American women composers—Biography.   2. Composers—United
States—Biography.   3. African American women composers—History and criticism.   I.
Title.
ML390.W16   2002
780'.89'96073—dc21   2001040600

British Library Cataloguing in Publication Data is available.

Library of Congress Catalog Card Number: 2001040600
ISBN: 0–313–29947–1

First published in 2002

Greenwood Press, 88 Post Road West, Westport, CT 06881
An imprint of Greenwood Publishing Group, Inc.
www.greenwood.com

Printed in the United States of America

The paper used in this book complies with the
Permanent Paper Standard issued by the National
Information Standards Organization (Z39.48–1984).

10 9 8 7 6 5 4 3 2

Copyright Acknowledgments

The author and publisher gratefully acknowledge permission for use of the following material:

Extensive quotes from Helen Walker-Hill's entries on Undine Smith Moore, Irene Britton Smith, Dorothy Rudd Moore, and Valerie Capers in Samuel A. Floyd, Jr., ed. *International Dictionary of Black Composers*. Chicago: Fitzroy Dearborn, 1999.

Excerpts from *The Collected Poems of Langston Hughes* by Langston Hughes, copyright © 1994 by The Estate of Langston Hughes. Used by permission of Alfred A. Knopf, a division of Random House, Inc.

Extracts from Langston Hughes. "Minstrel Man"; "Dream Variation"; "I Too." Reprinted by permission of Harold Ober Associates Incorporated.

Extracts from David N. Baker, Lida M. Belt, and Herman C. Hudson. "Undine Smith Moore." In *The Black Composer Speaks*. Metuchen, N.J.: Scarecrow Press, 1978.

Extracts from Undine Smith Moore. "Composer's Corner: My Life in Music." Transcribed by Jeannie Pool. In *International Alliance for Women in Music Journal* 3, no. 1 (February 1997): 9–15.

Extracts from Irene Britton Smith: undated letter to Stella Roberts and unpublished poems "My Song is His," "My People Laugh," and "When You're Away." Irene Britton Smith Collection, Center for Black Music Research Library and Archives, Columbia College, Chicago.

Excerpts from Patricia Sides: quotations from interviews with Helen Walker-Hill on July 13, 1994 and January 17, 1996; telephone conversations on April 24, 2000 and May 7, 2000; and correspondence on April 7, 1996 and April 10, 2000.

Excerpts from Piero Bellugi: quotations from correspondence and e-mail messages with Helen Walker-Hill on April 11, 2000, May 5, 2000, and May 15, 2001.

Extracts from Dominique-Rene de Lerma: quotations from letter dated January 21, 1975 to Julia Perry.

Extracts from letter dated May 10, 1967 from David Hall, President, Composers Recordings, Inc. to Julia Perry. Courtesy of Joseph Dalton, Composers Recordings, Inc.

Extracts from letters dated April 16, 1973 and April 30, 1973 from Edward N. Waters, Chief, Music

Division, Library of Congress to Julia Perry. Courtesy of Wayne Shirley, Music Division, Library of Congress.

Extracts from Margaret Bonds: quotations from letters to Langston Hughes, Carl Van Vechten, and Ned Rorem, dating from 1936 through 1967. Courtesy of Djane Richardson.

Extracts from Margaret Bonds: quotations from interview with James Hatch at the Inner City Cultural Center, Los Angeles, December 28, 1971. Courtesy of Djane Richardson.

Extracts from letters from Langston Hughes to Margaret Bonds dated April 27, 1960, March 25, 1963, January 27, 1964, March 4, 1966, and October 22, 1966. Courtesy of Craig Tenney, Harold Ober Associates, Inc.

Extracts from Ned Rorem: quotations from letter to Margaret Bonds dated July 1966 and from personal interview by Helen Walker-Hill on February 6, 1996.

Extracts from W.E.B. Du Bois. "Credo." *Darkwater: Voices from Within the Veil*. New York: Schocken Books, 1969. Published by arrangement with Shirley Graham Du Bois.

Extracts from Irene Britton Smith: taped interview dated July 7, 1989, correspondence dated July 28, 1989, August 20, 1989, September 4, 1989, October 1, 1989, October 9, 1989, October 31, 1989, July 15, 1990, and notes dated February 9, 1990. Courtesy of Circuit Court of Cook County, Illinois, Leon M. Despres.

Extracts from letter from Florence Price to Irene Britton Smith dated January 27, 1936. Courtesy of Vicki Hammond.

Extracts from Dorothy Rudd Moore: quotations from poems "The Sins of the Fathers," "Night Wanderer," "Dreams Unfurled," and "Mooning."

Extracts from Dorothy Rudd Moore: quotations from interviews with Helen Walker-Hill dated September 27, 1990, April 8, 1991, December 11, 1995, and December 3, 2000.

Extracts from James Weldon Johnson. "O Black and Unknown Bards." *The Poetry of the Negro 1746–1949: A Definitive Anthology*. New York: Doubleday, 1949.

Extracts from Valerie Capers: quotations from interviews with Helen Walker-Hill on October 12, 1990 and November 8, 1995; from interview with Walter Rudolph; from poetry for *Song of the Seasons*; and from libretto of *Sojourner*.

Extracts from Mary Watkins: quotations from unpublished memoirs, 1997; interviews and conversations with Helen Walker-Hill on February 23, 1998, February 23, 1999, October 1, 1999, and February 21, 2000; letter to Helen Walker-Hill dated April 1999; and e-mail correspondence with Helen Walker-Hill on October 13, 1999 and March 1, 2000.

Extracts from Regina Harris Baiocchi: quotations from stories and poems "Chromatic Interpolations," "A Few Black Voices," "Black with Pride," But for the Grace of God," "Ancestor's Medley," "What's in My Name," "Good News Falls Gently," "Say No to Guns," "Foster Pet," "Miriam's Muse," "Servants Muse," "Hell Hath No Fury," "Godmother's Lesson," "Louise's Prayer," "Ain't Nobody's Child," "Friday Night," "Hold Out for Joy," and "Hughes Man."

Extracts from Regina Harris Baiocchi: quotations from interviews and correspondence with Helen Walker-Hill.

To my coauthors, the composers whose words and music give this book its life

CONTENTS

Photo essay follows page xvi

ACKNOWLEDGMENTS

I acknowledge with gratitude the support provided for this book by a 1995 Aaron Diamond Resident Fellowship from the Schomburg Center for Research in Black Culture, and a 1998 Rockefeller Resident Fellowship from the Center for Black Music Research. Early phases of the research were made possible by a 1989 summer resident fellowship from the Newberry Library, a 1990 IMPACT grant from the University of Colorado at Boulder, and a resident fellowship during March 1992 at the American Music Research Center.

I am deeply indebted to Dorothy Rudd Moore, Valerie Capers, Mary Watkins, and Regina Baiocchi for their care and patience in answering questions, reading and correcting their chapters, and granting permission to use quotations from our conversations and from their writings. The encouragement and assistance of Undine Smith Moore's daughter, Mary Moore Easter, and Margaret Bonds' daughter, Djane Richardson, were more important than they can know. I also thank Dr. Carl G. Harris, Jr. for reading the chapter on his colleague Undine Smith Moore, and Patricia Sides and Kermit Moore for reading and correcting the chapter on Julia Perry. Angela Hammond's excellent research on Julia Perry was invaluable.

This book might still be unfinished were it not for the tireless assistance of Suzanne Flandreau, archivist at the Center for Black Music Research in Chicago, who answered innumerable questions, located elusive information, and supplied materials from the CBMR archives. Cassandra Volpe, archivist at the American Music Research Center at the University of Colorado at Boulder, was also helpful. I have Wayne Shirley, music librarian at the Library of Congress, to thank for guiding my research on the earliest black women composers.

I will always be grateful to Barbara Smith for her generosity of time and spirit, and for helping me stay grounded in truth. I am indebted to Dr. Deborah

Hayes for her detailed critique of a large portion of the book. Any defects are solely my responsibility. I acknowledge with appreciation the friends and family who read various chapters and gave encouragement, including Karoline Wolf, Karin Park, Donna Marburger, Christine Hamilton-Pennell, Lois Berry, and Kathleen Carlton. Eric Levy, my acquisitions editor and Lori Ewen, my production editor at Greenwood Press, responded promptly and kindly to my endless questions.

I am grateful to my friend and colleague Theresa Bogard for her readings of musical scores, piano performances of several of the works, and research assistance at the Beinecke Library of Rare Books and Manuscripts at Yale University, as well as her encouragement and support through the years. My heartfelt thanks go to my sons, Ian Walker and Gregory Walker, and my daughters-in-law, Andi Trindle Walker and Lori Wolf Walker, who have all provided ongoing encouragement and assistance. My grandson Grayson helped me keep my life in balance.

INTRODUCTION

I am tired of all our labels . . . I am not a black conductor . . . [I] am not a woman conductor. . . . The fact that I am in this physical costume does not describe my energy, does not describe my entity. My chosen purpose in life is to be a musician, a composer, a conductor. This is the way I am making my contribution to mankind.[1]

Tania León

When I invited Cuban-born Tania León[2] to participate in this study, she declined because of its narrow focus on black women composers. Although she had been involved through the years in numerous black music concerts and symposia, she had never been comfortable with labels and categories that separate people. The other composers in this study were sympathetic to the concerns voiced by Tania León. They, too, wish to be considered on the basis of their musical gifts, training, and craft rather than their race or gender. They are tired of having their works programmed chiefly during Black History Month or on Martin Luther King, Jr. Day.

The great majority of the composers, however, welcomed this study and were pleased to be a part of it. They see such categorization as a necessary step toward full participation in the larger musical world. They are proud to be identified as African-American women, and they are aware of the unique and highly politicized history of black women in the United States, a history that is not likely to have been absorbed or experienced by those who, like Tania León, have grown up outside this country. Almost all of them have their roots in a black American world that is unknown to most whites and common knowledge to most blacks. It has its own diversity and complexity, its own internal conflicts and antagonisms, class systems, churches, colleges, newspapers, heroes and leaders, writers and artists, history and historians, holidays and national anthem. It has its own musical traditions, genres, and styles, both vernacular and culti-vated. Although racial integration since the 1960s has given African Americans more access to the privileges of the larger world, and the two worlds interface more frequently, the black community is still the primary environment for the majority of African Americans. For black composers of either sex, who histor-ically have been ignored by the larger musical world, it has provided encour-agement, early training, financial support, performance opportunities, and audiences.

As females who are African Americans, these composers have been over-looked as a category because women composers are presumed to be white and African Americans are thought of as male. They are members of not one but two groups whose ability to write serious music was long denied by the dom-inant culture. They have struggled to be seen and heard, sometimes even within their own communities. They have had to combine and balance many roles and loyalties: they are both female *and* black, both wives and mothers *and* creative artists and professionals, both private and vulnerable *and* open and courageous, both unique individuals *and* members of the community.

As African-American women composers of concert music, often called "clas-sical" or art music, they are members of a marginalized group. They have had to reconcile their highly specialized calling (derided by many as bourgeois) with their loyalty to the whole black community. Often they have chosen to pursue careers in a highly competitive, sexist, and racist musical world. And they have had to decide whether and how to balance African-American and mainstream musical elements in their compositions.

Despite these hurdles, there have been scores of black women composers; they have been active in the United States since the late nineteenth century, and several have gained national and international recognition during their lifetimes. Many others remain unrecognized, content to create music for their own fulfill-ment, or for their churches and schools. They are part of a long African-American tradition of classical music. They come from a great variety of backgrounds and they write in a wide range of styles. They have composed works in many genres: songs, choral pieces, instrumental music, symphonies, and operas. Although the focus of this book is on concert or "serious" music, that category as used here crosses boundaries among styles and genres, and includes jazz compositions as well as music for film and musical theater.[3]

It is important to focus upon African-American women composers and their music for several reasons. First, their music deserves to be heard in the larger concert world. Second, the art music of African Americans still does not receive equal attention in the cultural mainstream. Third, knowledge of these composers and their music provides a more accurate sense of American music history and literature. There is also a need to correct the stereotyped concept of the "black experience"—in the words of bell hooks, "to move away from narrow notions of black identity, and [to] affirm multiple black identities and varied black experience."[4] And, most important, we owe it to ourselves to be aware of these significant musical contributions that can enrich our lives. As Barbara Smith observed, "For books to be real and remembered they have to be talked about."[5] For the compositions of African-American women composers to be "real and remembered," they need to be acknowledged and discussed.

This book is intended to be accessible and useful to a variety of readers, including nonmusicians as well as musicians. Each of the core chapters, focusing on eight representative individual composers, includes a separate section on social issues as well as a biography and a discussion of the subject's music. The composers chosen for individual chapters were selected either because they were accessible for interviews or because significant information was found: Undine Smith Moore (1904–89), Julia Perry (1924–79), Margaret Bonds (1913–72), Irene Britton Smith (1907–99), Dorothy Rudd Moore (b. 1940), Valerie Capers (b. 1935), Mary Watkins (b. 1939), and Regina Harris Baiocchi (b. 1956). There were many other worthy composers to choose from, and twelve core chapters were originally planned until a reduction was required because of length. An effort was made to represent a variety of backgrounds, perspectives, generations, geographical locations, and musical styles. Several of the composers are known, at least to black classical musicians, and others are more obscure. Some of the music described is available in recordings or scores, but much of it is not.

The opening chapter, a historical overview, provides a broad survey of African-American women composers from the perspective of their political and social context, with particular emphasis on their relationship to the history of African-American music.

The concluding section of the book correlates and summarizes the major themes revealed in the chapters, as well as in the study of other black women composers. It explores how issues of race, gender, and class operate in these composers' lives and music. It also examines the impact of other shaping circumstances, such as family of origin, marital status, motherhood, sexual orientation, and disabilities, as well as professional issues, such as access to training, performances, publication, and jobs.

The foundation for this study was the pioneering work on black women composers and musicians in the 1970s by Ora Williams, D. Antoinette Handy, Rae Linda Brown, Doris McGinty, Josephine Wright, Barbara Garvey Jackson, Kathryn Talalay, Eileen Southern, and especially Mildred Denby Green, along with earlier scholarship on black women and black music by Monroe Majors, Lawson Scruggs, Sylvia Dannett, and Maude Cuney-Hare. Original work included personal interviews with featured composers and also with Lena Johnson McLin, Betty Jackson King, Micki Grant, Jean Butler, Mable Bailey, Tania León, and Joyce Solomon, as well as colleagues and friends of Florence Price, Margaret Bonds, and Julia Perry; conversations and correspondence with over three dozen composers; visits to key locations; and extensive archival research on Florence

Price, Philippa Duke Schuyler, and other composers at the Library of Congress, the Moorland-Spingarn Research Center at Howard University, the Schomburg Center for Research in Black Culture, and Yale University's Beinecke Library of Rare Books and Manuscripts.

NOTES

1. Anna Lundy, "Conversations with Three Symphonic Conductors: Dennis DeCoteau, Tania León, Jon Robinson." *Black Perspective in Music* 16, no. 2 (Fall 1988): 218.

2. Tania León was cofounder and longtime musical director of the Dance Theater of Harlem, associate conductor of the Brooklyn Philharmonic Orchestra, and a former Revson composer in residence at Lincoln Center in New York, among numerous other positions.

3. This book deals only with composers who have written down their compositions, and who have composed in more than one genre. The many hundreds of black women who specialize in writing only songs, or gospel music, or blues, or who improvise jazz or folk music, are beyond the scope of this study.

4. bell hooks, *Yearning: Race, Gender, and Cultural Politics* (Boston: South End Press, 1990), p. 20.

5. Barbara Smith, "Toward a Black Feminist Criticism," in *All the Women Are White, All the Blacks Are Men, but Some of Us Are Brave*, edited by Gloria T. Hull, Patricia Bell Scott, and Barbara Smith (Old Westbury, N.Y.: Feminist Press, 1982), p. 159.

Florence Price. Formal Photograph of
Florence Price; (ASCAP photograph by
G. Nelidoff of Chicago). Florence Price
Papers (MC 988), box 1, folder 12.
Special Collections Division, University
of Arkansas Libraries, Fayetteville.

Philippa Duke Schuyler. Philippa Duke
Schuyler Collection, Photographs and
Prints Division, Schomburg Center for
Research in Black Culture, The New
York Public Library, Astor, Lenox and
Tilden Foundations.

Betty Jackson King. Courtesy of Arlene Sharp, Jacksonian Press, Inc.

Zenobia Powell Perry. Courtesy of the Composer.

Lena Johnson McLin. Courtesy of the Composer.

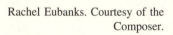

Rachel Eubanks. Courtesy of the Composer.

Ruth Norman. Courtesy of the Composer.

Jeraldine Saunders Herbison. Courtesy of the Composer.

Dolores White. Courtesy of the Composer.

Lettie Beckon Alston. Courtesy of the Composer.

Diane White. Courtesy of the Composer. Photo by Brad Elliott.

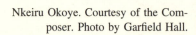
Nkeiru Okoye. Courtesy of the Composer. Photo by Garfield Hall.

From
Spirituals
to
Symphonies

Cover sheet for *Mother's Sacrifice* by L. Viola Kinney, 1909. Courtesy of the Library of Congress, Music Division.

1

HISTORICAL OVERVIEW

CHRONOLOGY

1619	Arrival of 20 African men and women as indentured servants at Jamestown, Va.
1626	Founding of New Amsterdam (11 African indentured servants arrived).
1630	Founding of Boston, largest colonial city until 1743.
1661	First "black codes" legally recognizing slavery, Virginia.
1664	British took New Amsterdam, renamed it New York.
1670	Founding of Charles Town (later Charleston), S.C.
1681	Founding of Philadelphia.
1688	Germantown Quakers protested against slavery in Pennsylvania.
1693	Founding of Society of Negroes in Boston.
1712	New York slave insurrection.
1729	First public concert in colonies: "Concert of Musick on Sundry Instruments" in Boston.
1730s	Great Awakening religious revival; hymns by Isaac Watts.
1735	First performance of an opera in colonies: *Flora: Or Hob in the Well*, in Charles Town.
1739	Stono Conspiracy near Charles Town by Angola Negroes.
1741	New York slave conspiracy.

1750s	" 'Lection Day" parades by blacks began in Connecticut; "Pinkster" celebrations later in New York.
1761	First published broadside poem by a black person, Jupiter Hammon, followed in 1770 by broadside poem by Phillis Wheatley (ca. 1753–84).
1773	Blacks petitioned for freedom in Massachusetts; Phillis Wheatley's volume of poems published in London.
1775	American Revolution (1775–83), in which 5,000 blacks fought; first Antislavery Society organized by Quakers in Philadelphia.
1776	Declaration of Independence.
1783	Slavery abolished in Massachusetts.
1787	Free African Society founded in Philadelphia; Negro Freemasonry in Boston.
1788	First permanent independent black church, First African Baptist Church in Savannah, Ga.
1790	First U.S. census: 750,000 blacks, including 59,000 free blacks.
1791	Ex-slave Newport Gardner (1746–1826) established music school in Newport, R.I.
1793	Eli Whitney invented the cotton gin, causing boom in cotton industry and slave trade.
1794	First independent black churches in Philadelphia: St. Thomas African Episcopal and Bethel African Methodist Episcopal.
1800	Second Awakening, camp meeting revivals stimulated growth of Negro spirituals; Gabriel Prosser slave revolt, Richmond, Va.
1801	Publication of first hymnal for blacks by Richard Allen.
1803	Louisiana Purchase.
1808	Congressional act abolishing the slave trade (but not slavery) in effect 1 January.
1821	African Grove Theatre established in New York (first black theater presenting Shakespeare and assorted entertainment).
1822	American colony of Liberia settled in Africa; Denmark Vesey insurrection, Charleston, S.C.
1827	Publication of first black newspaper, *Freedom's Journal* (1827–1829), New York, followed by *The Rights of All* (1829), *Weekly Advocate* (1837), and others.
1830s	Bandleader and composer Frank Johnson (1792–1844) inspired a "school" of black composers in Philadelphia.
1831	Nat Turner slave revolt, Virginia.

1833   Oberlin College established in Ohio (serving the Underground Railroad).

1840s   Concert tours by soprano Elizabeth Taylor Greenfield, the "Black Swan" (1824–1876).

1843   First white (blackface) minstrel show, Virginia Minstrels, New York.

1850s   First black women graduated from Oberlin College "Ladies Course" and Myrtilla Minor School in Washington, D.C.

1852   Publication of *Uncle Tom's Cabin* by Harriet Beecher Stowe.

1854, 1856 First Negro colleges established in Lincoln, Pa., and Wilberforce, Ohio.

1857   Dred Scott decision by Supreme Court: slave not a citizen.

1859   Raid on Harper's Ferry led by John Brown; Harriet Wilson's *Our Nig*, first novel by black writer.

1860   Census: 4,441,830 African Americans, of whom 488,070 were free; Abraham Lincoln elected president.

1861   Civil War (1861–1865).

1863   Emancipation Proclamation went into effect 1 January (only in Confederate states).

1865   Thirteenth Amendment abolished slavery in all the states; Freedmen's Bureau aided slaves and established schools (1865–70); first large migration of ex-slaves to cities; first black minstrel shows organized by Sam Lucas; founding of Oberlin Conservatory of Music.

1867   Founding of Boston Conservatory of Music, New England Conservatory, Cincinnati Conservatory, and Chicago Musical College; first published Negro spirituals: *Slave Songs of the U.S.*

1870   Fifteenth Amendment legalized vote for all black males.

1871   First tour by the Fisk Jubilee Singers.

1876   First black musical-comedy troupe, the Hyers Sisters Comic Opera Company.

1878   James Monroe Trotter's *Music and Some Highly Musical People* published in Boston.

1880s   Blues sung and played in several areas of the United States.

1886   Amelia Tilghman published first black music journal, *The Musical Messenger*.

1889   Harriet Gibbs Marshall the first black female graduate of Oberlin Conservatory of Music.

1890s   Jim Crow laws enforced segregation in transportation, public facilities, housing, education; disenfranchisement of blacks in the South under way; early coon songs and ragtime.

1892	Antonín Dvořák director of National Conservatory of Music in New York (1892–95), encouraged American nationalistic music utilizing Negro folksongs.
1893	Publication of Monroe A. Majors' *Noted Negro Women* (Chicago) and Lawson Scruggs' *Women of Distinction* (Raleigh, N.C.).
1894	Publication of Mrs. N. F. Mossell's *The Work of the Afro-American Woman* (Philadelphia); origins of jazz in, among other places, Storyville (New Orleans, 1894–1917).
1895	W.E.B. Du Bois received Ph.D. from Harvard; his *The Souls of Black Folk* published in 1903.
1896	U.S. Supreme Court decision in *Plessy* v. *Ferguson* legalized segregation.
1898	First black Broadway musical: Will Marion Cook's *Clorindy, or the Origin of the Cakewalk.*
1900	Cakewalk craze swept the nation; Johnson brothers wrote *Lift Every Voice and Sing.*
1904	First visit to United States by Afro-British composer Samuel Coleridge-Taylor.
1905	Niagara Movement; Scott Joplin completed opera *Treemonisha.*
1909	National Association for the Advancement of Colored People formed in New York.
1912	Helen Eugenia Hagan graduated from Yale University School of Music, received fellowship for study in Paris; her *Concerto* for piano and orchestra performed with the New Haven Symphony Orchestra.
1912–16	Four annual concerts of music by African Americans in New York; three annual "All Colored Composers" concerts in Chicago; first collection of gospel hymns published by Charles Tindley.
1914	First World War (1914–18).
1916–30	Great Migration to northern and western cities; rise of Garveyite movement.
1917–30	Harlem Renaissance of Negro art and literature; Langston Hughes' poetry published.
1919	National Association of Negro Musicians formed in Chicago; Prohibition (1919–33); "Red Summer" of race riots in Chicago and other cities.
1920s	Nineteenth Amendment gave women the vote; beginning of "race records" (jazz and blues for black purchasers); Chicago gospel era spearheaded by Thomas A. Dorsey, "Father of Gospel Music."
1925	Lillian Evanti (1890–1967) first black singer to sign contract with European opera company.

1929   Great Depression began.

1931   First performance by a major orchestra of a work by black composer (William Grant Still's *Afro-American Symphony* by Rochester Philharmonic Symphony); swing era began with Duke Ellington's *It Don't Mean a Thing*; Scottsboro trial of Alabama Nine.

1933   First performance by a major orchestra of a work by a black woman (Florence Price's *Symphony in E Minor* by Chicago Symphony Orchestra).

1935   Broadway production of Gershwin's *Porgy & Bess* with Eva Jessye as choral director; establishment of the Federal Arts Projects of the Works Progress Administration.

1939   William Grant Still music for Theme Exhibit at New York World's Fair; Marian Anderson sang at Lincoln Memorial to 75,000 after being denied the use of Washington's Constitution Hall by Daughters of the American Revolution.

1941–45   World War II; 1 million blacks in segregated military; another big migration to the North; jazz bebop era began around 1943.

1941   National Negro Opera Company organized in Pittsburgh by Mary Cardwell Dawson.

1945   First performance by a black singer, Todd Duncan, with major opera company, New York City Opera, followed by Camilla Williams in 1946.

1948   Harry Truman elected president, ordered end to segregation in military; appointed committee to investigate lynching.

1949   Apartheid began in South Africa; first major production of an opera by an African American, Still's *Troubled Island* by New York City Opera; "race records" category replaced by "rhythm & blues."

1950s   Korean War (1950–53); Senator Joseph McCarthy's Communist witch-hunt; mammoth all-gospel concert at Carnegie Hall featuring Mahalia Jackson; Ralph Bunche awarded Nobel Peace Prize; Gwendolyn Brooks first black poet to win Pulitzer Prize.

1954   U.S. Supreme Court decision in *Brown* v. *Board of Education of Topeka* desegregated schools in the South.

1955   Rosa Parks initiated yearlong Montgomery, Al., bus boycott; Emmet Till, 14 years old, lynched in Mississippi; Marian Anderson first black to sing at the Metropolitan Opera Company.

1957   President Dwight Eisenhower sent troops to Little Rock, Ark., to carry out the desegregation of Central High School.

1960–62   Civil Rights Act; sit-ins in Greensboro, N.C.; Freedom Rides on buses across South; James Meredith entered University of Mississippi; free jazz, "soul" music.

1963	March on Washington; President John Kennedy assassinated in November; U.S. involvement in Vietnam began.
1964	Race riots in many northern cities, continuing into the 1970s; Civil Rights Act and Equal Employment Opportunities Commission; Martin Luther King, Jr. awarded Nobel Peace Prize.
1965	Malcolm X assassinated; Voting Rights Act; Harlem School of the Arts founded by Dorothy Maynor.
1966	World Festival of Negro Arts in Dakar, Senegal, with African-American participation.
1967	Affirmative action in higher education; Thurgood Marshall first black appointed to U.S. Supreme Court.
1968	Martin Luther King, Jr. assassinated; Robert Kennedy assassinated; Chicago Democratic Convention demonstrations; Black Power and Black Arts movements; Afro-American Music Opportunities Association formed in Minneapolis; Black Music Center established by Undine Smith Moore and Altona Trent Johns at Virginia State College (became Virginia State University in 1979); Society of Black Composers formed in New York.
1970s	Beginning of women's studies and feminist musicology; school busing began; President Richard Nixon resigned; Vietnam War ended; Soweto massacre in South Africa in 1976.
1977	Second World Black and African Festival of Arts and Culture in Lagos, Nigeria.
1978	*University of California* v. *Bakke* Supreme Court decision setback affirmative action.
1979	National Black Music Colloquium and Competition at Kennedy Center in Washington; Sugar Hill Records' *Rapper's Delight* announces rap era.
1982	Civil Rights Act of 1964 and affirmative action program extended against strong opposition.
1990s	Annual Detroit Symphony Orchestra Unisys African-American Composers Competitions.
1991	Clarence Thomas/Anita Hill hearings; Gulf War.
1992	Rodney King verdict and Los Angeles race riot.
1996	Million Man March; George Walker first black composer to win Pulitzer Prize.
1997	Wynton Marsalis second black composer to win Pulitzer Prize.
1999	School busing ended despite continuing school segregation.

The gentler sex are only behind the other, in possessing a knowledge of music, to that extent which has been caused by those unreasonable, un-written, yet inexorable rules of society, that have hitherto forbidden women to do more than to learn to perform upon the pianoforte and guitar, and to sing.[1]

James Monroe Trotter, *Music and Some Highly Musical People*, 1878.

In one sentence Trotter tied together the elements of gender, class, and music in nineteenth-century black society, which took as its model the white society sur-rounding it. This statement from *Music and Some Highly Musical People*, his landmark survey of the musical accomplishments of "the race," also helps to ex-plain why he did not list a single woman composer, although fully a third of the approximately 180 musicians he named in his book were women. Why were so-ciety's rules regarding musical composition so powerful and why, in the decades following Trotter's declaration, did women begin to defy these rules publicly?

There is evidence of music by black women as early as 1870, but the first half-dozen surviving published parlor songs and piano pieces date from between 1885 and 1900. While is it not surprising, it is nevertheless a keen disappoint-ment to find so few actual scores of music from the nineteenth century when there are many examples of literary work by black women, as well as works of art and a multitude of other accomplishments.[2] After the turn of the century a steadily growing number of black women began composing seriously. Who were these women, and how many have there been? Where did they receive their training, and what kind of music did they write? How and when did a tradition of black classical music become established? How did a separate black society with an educated upper-middle class affluent enough to provide training for its daughters come about? The answers to these and other questions concerning the prerequisite social and economic conditions for musical composition by black women can be found in a review of their historical context.

THE SEVENTEENTH AND EIGHTEENTH CENTURIES

The economic and social conditions that led to the activity of African-American women composers were in formation from the earliest presence of Africans in the New World in the seventeenth century. During the first years of the colonial period, historical reference to specific black persons is rare. Therefore it is a singular satisfaction to find that the record of the first appear-ance of Africans in British North America (the arrival of 20 African indentured servants on a Dutch man-of-war in Jamestown, Virginia, on 10 August 1619) includes mention of two, Anthoney and Isabell, who formed a shipboard ro-mance and were married a few years later. Their son William, born in Elizabeth City, may have been the first true African American, the first person of African descent born on British-American soil.[3] In 1626, 11 African indentured servants were delivered to New Amsterdam (renamed New York in 1664, following the takeover by the British), and by 1636 the North American colonial slave trade had begun (it was already a hundred years old in South America) with the arrival of the slave ship *Desire* in Boston Harbor.

During the seventeenth century the most important historical developments were the settling of the coastal colonies and the founding of future major cities— New York (1626), Boston (1630), Charles Town (later Charleston) (1670), and Philadelphia (1681).[4] But the colonial population, both black and white, was still predominantly rural; only some 8 percent lived in villages or towns. The century saw the manumission of some of the earliest black indentured servants (first recorded in New Amsterdam in 1644, and in New Haven in 1646). It also saw the establishment of the institution of slavery (legitimized first in the "black codes" of Virginia in 1661), as well as the first organized protest against it (the Germantown Quaker protest of 1688 in Pennsylvania). A sense of black American identity and community was also in formation, as evidenced by the Society of Negroes, established in Boston in 1693. As the historian Ira Berlin demonstrates, at least three distinct regional black social systems were developing in British North America, corresponding to different economic conditions, religious and social backgrounds of the white settlers, climates, crops, and labor needs. One of these black social systems evolved in the northern states, another in the Chesapeake Bay area, and the third in the lowlands of the Carolinas and Georgia.[5]

In the eighteenth century the most important development for black Americans was the boom in the African slave trade, and the resulting growth of the black population. The new African slaves had a divisive impact on the plantations of the Chesapeake and lowland areas, and the distinction between the rural African plantation population and the urban African-American Creole[6] population became more pronounced. Since the planters often elected to leave their plantations under the supervision of overseers and to live for most of the year in mansions in the towns and cities, plantation blacks could preserve their African tribal speech, names, and ways of working the southern lowlands with traditional African methods. They had no desire to be part of the white population, and if they escaped, they ran away from population centers to form their own communities in the wilderness, often joining with Native American tribes. The Creoles, or African Americans, in the urban areas worked in close proximity to whites. As house slaves, black women were often seduced or raped by their masters, who considered this their right as owners. Sometimes these masters took special care of their mixed offspring, giving them vocational training, or property, or even freedom. In each generation more mixed individuals appeared, and they began to form an elite in African-American society, tracing their heritage to upper-class, often aristocratic, white ancestors. A strong class system, based on the rural-urban split and especially the African vs. African-American background and the attendant color variations, was in place well before the nineteenth century.

In the North, the African slaves quickly adapted to the European language and customs of the existing black communities and, in turn, enriched them with African traditions. Ignored by a complacent white majority, African customs could freely become part of the cultural landscape in such festivals as the famous 'Lection Day in Hartford, Connecticut, and the Pinkster celebrations in Albany, New York, in which the African penchant for pageantry was given free rein. Blacks would dress up in finery, form a parade, elect officials or pay homage to their royalty, and set up booths and carnival events amid much music and dancing. European costumes and instruments were featured in the parade, but African drums and dances took over in the ensuing days of the festival.

The use of the word "African" in names of self-help and fraternal organizations reflected this renewed consciousness of and pride in African heritage: the African Union Society of Newport (1780), the African Society of Boston (1796), the Masonic African Lodge of Boston (formed by Prince Hall in 1775), and the Bethel African Methodist Episcopal Church (formed by Richard Allen in 1795).

The new African imports of the 1700s produced some well-known black achievers. A few of them, like storyteller Lucy Bijah Terry, asserted their African identity and heritage.[7] Others, such as the poet Phillis Wheatley,[8] the artist Scipio Moorhead, and the music teacher Newport Gardner, demonstrated not only adaptation to, but mastery of, European culture.

Newport Gardner, born Occramer Marycoo (1746–1826) in Africa and bought at age 14 by Caleb Gardner in Newport, Rhode Island, showed an affinity for European music. Newport's mistress arranged for him to study with Andrew Law, a well-known musician and author of books on music. In 1791 Gardner won a lottery, bought his freedom, and opened a singing school in which his former mistress enrolled as a student.[9] He composed a number of tunes and anthems, was headmaster of a school for black children, and served as a deacon in the Congregational Church. In 1824 he helped found the first black church in Newport; two years later he sailed to Liberia as a missionary, and died there within a few months.[10]

Not only African but also American-born blacks achieved distinction in the colonial period. Benjamin Banneker (1731–1806) was a mathematician and astronomer who published almanacs and served as a member of the commission to plan the streets of Washington, D.C. James Derham (b. Philadelphia 1762–?), the first African-American physician, received his training from three different masters who were doctors. Massachusetts shipbuilder Paul Cuffee accumulated a small fleet and fortune in the 1780s and endeavored to take blacks to Africa on his ships, at his own expense.

The establishment of the first schools for black children was an important development of the 1700s. The first missionary school for slaves, organized by the Society for the Propagation of the Gospel in Foreign Parts, an offshoot of the Church of England, was opened in 1704 in New York's Trinity Episcopal Church by Elias Neau. It was followed by many others, and independent schools were also opened, such as Alexander Garden's in Charles Town in 1742, staffed by two black teachers who were his former students.

As the towns grew, cultural progress was rapid. The first public concert took place in Boston in 1729: "A Concert of Musick on Sundry Instruments." Boston was also the first city to boast a church organ, in King's Chapel in 1714. Charles Town, although considerably smaller, was nevertheless the cultural center of the South, and produced the first performance of an opera in North America: *Flora: Or Hob in the Wall* (1735). Charles Town also established a choral concert series and the first musical organization, the St. Cecilia Society (1762). Many European professional musicians arrived in the New World, and singing and dancing schools became common.

African Americans participated with whites in psalm singing, provided dance music for jigs and reels, and entertained their owners with European classical music played by well-trained instrumental ensembles. Music was also an important part of life among themselves: in African dancing and drumming, playing both European and homemade African instruments, and singing satirical songs about their masters. Blacks were able to play a variety of instruments and had skill in European music, either self-taught or through tutors paid by their masters; this is indicated by descriptions in newspaper advertisements for sales or escaped slaves: "TO BE SOLD: a young, healthy Negro fellow who has been used to wait on a gentleman and plays extremely well on the French horn" (*Virginia Gazette*, 1766); "RUN AWAY: Negro man named Zack . . . speaks good English, plays on the fife and German flute" (*Poughkeepsie Journal*, 1791).[11] The irony of such evidences of humanity and intelligence in enslaved chattel was apparently lost on their white owners. Women were mentioned rarely (and negatively) in connection with music skills: "RUN AWAY: girl fond of Liqueur and apt to sing indecent and Sailors' songs"; "WANTED: Sarah Knox, alias Howard, alias Wilson 'of brown complexion' " in Pennsylvania and Virginia, posing as, among other things, a dancing mistress under the name of Charlotte Hamilton.[12]

An important impetus to musical advancement was the religious revival of the Great Awakening in the 1730s, in which Methodist hymnody, particularly that of Isaac Watts, brought new life and expression to a previously feeble psalmody. These reforms reached the religious worship of slaves as well as whites. A missionary reported that he "heard the slaves at worship in their lodge, singing Psalms and Hymns in the evening, and again long before break of day. They are excellent singers and long to get some of Dr. Watts's Psalms and Hymns which I encouraged them to hope for."[13]

The eighteenth century was marked by major wars in which blacks both fought and played in military bands: the French and Indian War of 1756–63 and the Revolutionary War of 1775–83. The contradiction of slaves fighting for freedom from tyranny was recognized by Thomas Jefferson, who sought in vain to include a protest against slavery in the Declaration of Independence.[14] The early abolition movement was led by the Quakers and free blacks. Massachusetts was the first state to abolish slavery, in 1783; other northern states gradually followed, until by 1830 slavery in the North was gone.

THE NINETEENTH CENTURY BEFORE THE CIVIL WAR

By 1790 the population of the United States had grown to four million, of whom 750,000 were black. Of those 750,000, 89 percent lived in the South, with the heaviest concentration in Virginia. The changing demographics caused the three main regional black social systems to coalesce into two, North and South. In the southern lowlands, the cotton gin, a machine invented by Eli Whitney in 1793 that separated the seed from the fiber, revolutionized both the cotton industry and the slave trade. By 1830 the slave population had grown to two million. Slave prices rose from an average of $400 for a field hand in 1790, to around $700 in 1830, to an average of $1500 just before the Civil War, when the slave population stood at four million. A congressional ban on the slave trade from Africa in 1808 did little to stem the tide. The shortage was met by illegal importation, kidnapping and enslaving of free blacks, and most of all by the breeding of slaves, perhaps the nadir of the dehumanization of black women.[15] With the increase in slave population came white fear of retaliation. The slave codes, which restricted traveling and assembling in groups, were enforced by patrollers, and in Mississippi slaves were not allowed to beat drums or blow horns, both of which were suspected of being signals to conspirators. Many slaveholders prohibited religious services, leading to widespread secret worship at night in what has been called "the invisible church."

Nineteen percent of the black population in 1800 was free, and most free blacks were concentrated in the cities of Baltimore, Washington, Philadelphia, New York, Charleston, and New Orleans. They gained their freedom by several means: through birth to free blacks, by saving and purchasing their freedom, by running away, or through rewards or wills of masters who were often their fathers. Freedom enabled them to own property and open enterprises, and in some cases they became wealthy and respected: the grocer Solomon Humphries in Macon, Georgia; the hotelier Jehu Jones in Charleston; the sailmaker James Forten and the caterer Robert Bogle in Philadelphia; and the tycoon Thomy Lafon in New Orleans. Such men were the first Negro elite, sending their sons to colleges and universities to become doctors, dentists, lawyers, and teachers. They were also an embarrassment to white slaveholders whose rationale was based on claims of black inferiority, and efforts intensified to denigrate and vilify free Negroes. Between 1800 and 1860 the dangers and restrictions for free blacks steadily worsened, and their share of the black population fell from 19 percent to 13 percent. They were often kidnapped and sold as slaves, they had to carry papers proving they were free, they could not enter some states, they could not testify in court, they were forbidden to congregate in some areas, they were forbidden to marry whites, and they were banned from various trades in cities where their presence might upset the workforce. As a result, the separation of black and white worlds solidified. The historian John Hope Franklin summed up their situation: "In the nineteenth century, as the slave-holding class found it necessary to establish safeguards for effective control of the free blacks, a veritable wall was erected around the blacks who found it necessary to develop their own lives and institutions. There existed between them and the rest of the world a minimum of communication and even this communication steadily decreased."[16]

Self-governing black churches began to flourish, initially in Georgia, where itinerant slave "exhorters" went from plantation to plantation, preaching to groups of slaves. The earliest permanent congregation was the First Baptist Church in Savannah, Georgia (in 1788), led by Andrew Bryan. In Philadelphia two new black churches were dedicated in 1794: the African Episcopal Church of St. Thomas, led by Absalom Jones, and the Bethel African Methodist Episcopal (AME) Church, led by Richard Allen. Black churches in other cities quickly followed: New York's Zion Chapel Methodist Episcopal Church in 1796, Boston's African Baptist Church in 1805, the First African Presbyterian Church in Philadelphia in 1807, and the Abyssinian Baptist Church in New York in 1808.

MUSICAL DEVELOPMENTS IN THE AFRICAN-AMERICAN COMMUNITY

Two important developments in black music occurred in connection with the black church. In 1801 Rev. Richard Allen, founder of the Bethel AME Church, published *A Collection of Spiritual Songs and Hymns Selected from Various Authors by Richard Allen, African Minister*. This hymnal was the first to represent black worshippers' own choices. The hymns were sung by the congregation in a uniquely African style. A Russian traveler visiting Allen's church in 1811 described it thus: "At the end of every psalm the entire congregation, men and women alike, sang verses in a loud, shrill monotone. This lasted about half an hour. When the preacher ceased reading, all turned to the door, fell on their knees, bowed their heads to the ground and set up an agonizing, heart-rending moaning."[17]

Another religious phenomenon that was significant in the development of African-American music was the camp meeting, a custom that began around 1800. Middle-class Protestants gathered in the woods for periods of several days, worshipping in large tents, giving sermons, converting, witnessing, and singing. These camp meetings were interracial, although the Negroes had to sit or stand in a separate area. Their singing was noted by many: "Their shouts and singing were so very boisterous that the singing of the white congregation was often completely drowned in the echoes and reverberations of the colored people's tumultuous strains." Furthermore, after everyone else had gone to sleep, "On the black side . . . the tents were still full of religious exaltation. . . . At half-past five . . . the hymns of the Negroes, which had continued through the night, were still to be heard on all sides."[18] The details were noted by another observer: "short scraps of disjointed affirmations, pledges or prayers, lengthened out with long repetition choruses. . . . With every word so sung, they have a sinking of one or the other leg of the body alternately, producing an audible sound of the feet at every step, and as manifest as the steps of the actual Negro dancing in Virginia, etc. If some, in the meantime sit, they strike the sounds alternately on each thigh."[19] These are descriptions of the creation of the Negro spirituals, and also of the circling processional dance known as the "ring shout."[20] Such practices were brought from Africa, where communal musical creativity was common and dancing was a part of worship.

These customs were not approved by the more educated upper-class blacks, as demonstrated by the actions and comments of a later minister at Bethel AME, Daniel Alexander Payne (1811–93).[21] In 1841 he brought trained choirs into his church worship. He later wrote: "It gave great offense to the older members. . . . Said they 'You have brought the devil into the church and therefore we will go out.' "[22] Payne was not deterred; he encouraged the use of instrumental accompaniment of the choir in worship services,[23] and introduced another innovation, the fund-raising concert of sacred instrumental and vocal music. His antipathy to African religious customs was expressed in his report of a visit to a "bush meeting": "After the sermon they formed a ring, and with coats off sung, clapped their hands and stamped their feet in a most ridiculous and heathenish way. . . . These 'Bands' I have had to encounter in many places . . . to the most thoughtful and intelligent I usually succeeded in making the Band disgusting but by the ignorant masses it was regarded as the essence of religion."[24]

The African musical heritage survived mostly undocumented, in field hollers, work songs, call and response, dancing, drumming, and homemade instruments. The sound of black singing deplored by white observers was an African vocal style, less focused in pitch than the European, and with a wide variation in timbre and intensity (including shouting, moaning, etc.). Melodies were repetitive with many falling thirds, and rhythms were persistent and complex. Clapping, stamping, moving, and dancing were inevitable.[25] Communal participation, and audible give-and-take between performer and audience were essential. Dramatic presentation and colorful attire were frequently joined to music. Duration and form remained open-ended and timeless; a "piece" of music could last an hour or more. It is easy to see some of these traits in African-American blues, ragtime, jazz, and gospel music.

In the European tradition, pitch, timbre, and intensity were restrained and focused. Rhythms were square and rudimentary. Duration varied, depending on the genre, but was governed by a closed progression of musical events with a beginning, middle, and end: "becoming" as opposed to the "being" of non-Western musics. Movement was restricted to professional dancers trained in specific dance styles. Performer/audience interaction (indeed, any sound from the listener) was prohibited, and applause was approved only after the music was completed. The European manner of musical creation was particularly opposed to the African: music was composed by specially trained individuals and fixed in notation. In Europe during the nineteenth century, the vocation of the "serious" composer became associated with complex, abstract creativity and acquired an aura of revelatory intelligence that was considered the exclusive dominion of males. The mysterious and powerful psychological effect of music was believed to be too dangerous to be allowed in the control of women. The long delay in composition by females was largely due to this mystique.

Payne's conflict with his parishioners illustrates the conflict within the African-American community between the African and European heritages. Although both were truly African-American, acquired by birthright, the African heritage was associated with older generations, rural lifestyles, and less educated classes, and the European customs with younger, urban, educated, and aspiring African Americans.

The established black urban churches played an important role in the encouragement of a classical European music heritage. The church had become the center of African-American life, providing infant and Sunday schools and benevolent services, and organizing literary and debating societies, libraries, recreational programs, and singing schools. Many urban churches sponsored concerts of sacred vocal, choral, and orchestral music by such composers as Handel, Haydn, and Mozart (and frequently also by black composers) performed by local talent and guest artists. Occasionally these concerts were ambitious projects like the performance of Haydn's oratorio *Creation* in 1841 at Philadelphia's First African Presbyterian Church by a 55-piece orchestra and 150 voices. Such concerts had the longest and most developed history in New Orleans, where segregated sections were provided at the opera houses, black symphony orchestras were formed, black bands marched in the parades, and beautiful singing of the Catholic Mass by black nuns could be heard in the Convent of the Holy Family, founded in 1842.

The guest artists appearing in these sacred music concerts included accomplished black women who, long before they began to compose, achieved distinction as concert singers, studying in Europe and touring the United States. These singers also performed for white audiences attracted to the novelty of black women singing opera arias and art songs of European composers. A long list of celebrated singers began with soprano Elizabeth Taylor Greenfield (1824–76), Philadelphia's "Black Swan," whose Quaker owner financed her training and who sang a command performance for the queen of England.[26]

The music of black male musicians and composers of the nineteenth century reflected the stereotypical roles they were expected to play in white society. They had greater latitude for professional composition than women because a tradition had been established of male slave musicians providing dance music. Bandleader Frank Johnson (1792–1844), who brought the French promenade concert to America; Henry Williams (1813–1903); Joseph Postlewaite (1827–89); the child prodigy Blind Tom Bethune (1849–1909); and the minstrel James Bland (1854–1911) were composers of social dance music, sentimental and patriotic songs, programmatic pieces, and sacred anthems, some of which were published as sheet music for piano. The piano had become the prevailing instrument, essential to well-appointed middle-class homes, both black and white. In 1841 the author of *Sketches of the Higher Classes of Colored Society in Philadelphia. By a Southerner* described the prominent role of music: "It is rarely that the Visitor in the different families where there are 2 or 3 ladies will not find one or more of them competent to perform on the pianoforte, guitar or some other appropriate musical instrument."

Before the Civil War, black leaders, along with black and white abolitionists, worked to combat the doctrine of the genetic and intellectual inferiority of the Negro by publicizing black individuals who met European ideals of refinement and achievement, by establishing self-improvement and literary clubs, and by promoting the philosophy of racial uplift. Women figured prominently in this movement. The Afric-American Female Intelligence Society was formed in Boston in 1832, the Philadelphia Library Company of Colored Persons was established in 1833, and by the 1850s New York City had two black literary societies for women. The important role of women in racial uplift was emphasized by the prominent author Martin R. Delaney (1812–85), who wrote in 1852 that black women should be well-educated, because no black man could achieve equality as long as black women had to perform the "menial offices of other men's wives and daughters."[27]

Education was considered the most important avenue to equality, and the profession of teaching became the most desirable occupation for women. Schools were established by the black churches; the Presbyterian Church founded Lincoln University in Pennsylvania in 1854, and the Methodist Episcopal Church established Wilberforce University in Ohio, in 1856. Black female education was undertaken in Washington, D.C., by a white woman from New York, Myrtilla Miner, whose School for Colored Girls opened in 1851. It lasted only a decade, but its graduates were significant as teachers in the years to come.

Wealthy free blacks had been sending their sons to a few white colleges in the North since the early 1800s—Amherst, Bowdoin, Harvard, and others. Oberlin College, a center of abolitionist and Underground Railroad activity founded in 1833, was the first white college to admit black women. The first to graduate from "Ladies' Course" was Lucy Stanton in 1850, and by 1861, 10 more black women graduated and became teachers.[28]

Before the Civil War black women also distinguished themselves as authors: Ann Plato's (b. ca 1820) *Essays*, in 1841, and Harriet Wilson's (ca. 1807–70) novel, the autobiographical *Our Nig*, in 1858. More black women authors followed: Frances Ellen Watkins Harper (1825–1911), Anna Julia Cooper (1859–1964), Alice Dunbar-Nelson 1875–1935), and a host of others. While they utilized European and white American literary models, many wrote of their own experiences and argued the abolitionist cause.

In art, the remarkable affinity of black women for sculpture was first demonstrated by Edmonia Lewis (1843–1909?) in the 1860s.[29] In painting, Annie Walker (1855–1929) set early standards of excellence. At first, black women artists adopted the subjects and stylistic approach of European art, and (in contrast to authors and composers) many of them studied in Europe.

Through the abolition and Underground Railroad movements, more black leaders emerged, both male and female. Frederick Douglass (ca. 1817–95) was the most outstanding spokesman, writer, and activist, and the first major African-American hero. The militant abolitionist David Walker before him, and his contemporaries William Wells Brown, Martin Delaney, Robert Purvis, James Forten, and George Vashon, were only a few of the other distinguished black speakers, writers, and Underground Railroad agents. The names of black women stand out in the pantheon of heroes: the Underground Railroad agent Harriet Tubman, the orator Sojourner Truth, the writers and activists Maria Stewart, Frances Ellen Watkins Harper, Mary Ann Shadd, the Forten sisters, and the noted woman physician Sarah Parker Remond.

FROM THE CIVIL WAR TO THE 1920s

By 1860 the black population stood at almost 4.5 million. Several events immediately before the Civil War served to inflame public opinion either for or against slavery, among them the publication of the immensely popular antislavery novel *Uncle Tom's Cabin* by the white author Harriet Beecher Stowe (1852), and the *Dred Scott* decision of the U.S. Supreme Court that a slave was not a citizen and had no civil rights (1857). These were climaxed in 1859 by the raid on the federal arsenal at Harpers Ferry, Virginia, led by John Brown, with the intention of attacking Virginia slaveholders. It failed, and he was hanged, but he became a martyr especially beloved by African Americans. A popular camp-meeting tune was fitted with the words to *John Brown's Body* and became the theme song of the black soldiers of the Civil War.[30]

A year and a half into the conflict, blacks were reluctantly allowed to enlist. Some 186,000 black men in 166 regiments fought in the Civil War. After repeated appeals by Frederick Douglass and other abolitionists, President Abraham Lincoln finally saw that emancipation was in the best interest of the Union and proclaimed freedom for slaves in Confederate states on 1 January 1863. Crowds gathered all over the country, waiting for the stroke of midnight (even though freedom would not become a reality for all slaves until the war was over and the Thirteenth Amendment was passed in 1865). New Year's Day, formerly known as "Heartbreak Day" because big slave auctions that separated families were customarily held that day, now became an unofficial holiday in the African-American community.

In the chaos after the war many Confederate soldiers went underground in the Ku Klux Klan and other white terrorist secret societies, particularly after the Civil Rights Act of 1866 gave black males the vote and many were elected to state and national legislatures. The state of South Carolina elected eighty-seven blacks to office, the most of any state. In 1869 the U.S. Congress had twenty black representatives and two black senators, Hiram R. Revels and Blanche K.

Bruce, and P.B.S. Pinchback served as governor of Louisiana. Such advances, though important in black history, were cut off by a post-Reconstruction backlash in which many of the gains were lost.

During the war black and white educators, both men and women, had set up camps and schools for ex-slaves, and compiled and published the Negro spirituals and slave songs for the first time. The Freedmen's Bureau, set up by the federal government between 1865 and 1870 to provide services to the ex-slaves, organized job-training institutes and colleges. With the American Missionary Association it established Howard University in Washington, D.C.; Fisk University in Nashville, Tennessee; Hampton Institute, Biddle Memorial College, Atlanta University, and St. Augustine College. Later, Spelman College for women and Morehouse College for men, in Atlanta, were founded by the Rockefellers. Meharry Medical College in Nashville (1876), the first for blacks, gave impetus to the growth of the medical profession.

One school in particular was important in the evolution of the black concert music tradition. Soon after the establishment of Fisk University in 1866, the Fisk Jubilee Singers were organized by music instructor George L. White, a Union soldier from upstate New York. In 1871, in order to raise funds for the school, he took them on a concert tour to white schools and communities, a daring action at a time when the public was used to Negroes performing as minstrels. After a shaky start these living symbols of the success of emancipation began to find responsive audiences. The Fisk Jubilee Singers were soon singing in Europe before audiences of royalty, and they became the prototype for other Negro colleges' fund-raising, spiritual-singing jubilee choirs.

The Fisk Jubilee Singers' concerts included standard classical choir repertory and "their own music," the spirituals, which they had begun singing informally after rehearsals. The inclusion of the spirituals on concert programs was a historic moment in the evolution of African-American concert music, a first step toward the fusion of African-American and European traditions. Spiritual arrangements would become an art form, composed by virtually all black composers. The performances of the spirituals by the Jubilee Singers were described as "precise and disciplined with sudden changes in dynamics and careful alternation of the parts."[31] Their accompanist, Ella Sheppard, who was trained at the Cincinnati Conservatory, transcribed some of the choral arrangements of the spirituals. A published example, O I'm Going to Sing All the Way, shows the alternation of the choral parts, shifts in dynamics, a "pp" marked over the repeat of the refrain, and a piano introduction and accompaniment. It was just such carefully transcribed arrangements, together with the polished performances of the Jubilee Singers, that earned the spirituals a place in James Monroe Trotter's "higher reach and progress of the race." He explained, "It has been found that they are as subject to the laws of science as are others [songs]; that they were not, as many persons have supposed, merely a barbarous confusion of sounds."[32]

Another early black school stands out for its relevance to black women composers, although it is rarely mentioned in the history of black colleges: Western

University in Quindaro, Kansas. It provides a window into the middle-class African-American cultural life in the Midwest in the first decades of the twentieth century. It had its origins in the 1860s in the classes held in various homes for the children of slaves who had escaped from across the river in Missouri. In the 1870s and 1880s it was housed in an old brewery building and named Freedman's School. The AME Church took it over, and in 1891 the first building was dedicated. A theological course was added to the basic curriculum, and its first class of four ministers graduated in 1898. Soon after, a new president, William T. Vernon, changed its name to Western University, added several buildings, and hired a strong faculty including R. G. Jackson, the head of the music department. Jackson organized the Jackson Jubilee Singers, and they traveled around the country, attracting young people with musical ambitions. Western University was both a liberal arts and an industrial/agricultural training school, operating its own tailoring, blacksmithing, wheelwrighting, and printing classes; it was also affiliated with Douglass Hospital, with which it shared some buildings. The music department offered a rigorous four-year course of theory, harmony and analysis, and composition, as well as applied piano and voice, marching band (conducted in 1913–15 by the noted N. Clark Smith), orchestra, and the Jubilee Singers. At its peak in 1912 it had 153 music students.[33] They repeatedly won the composition competition held by the Interstate Literary Society, founded in 1891 by Langston Hughes' grandfather, Charles Langston, in Topeka, Kansas. Their winning compositions were then published and sold as sheet music by the school.[34] Printed on the back page of one published piece were testimonials given by Western University students that convey the flavor of upper-middle-class African-American attitudes. They said this music should be purchased "Because it shows the wonderful progress of the Negro race since slavery and our possibilities when given a chance" (William Lane); "Because it shows the world our appreciation of classical Music in preference to trashy ragtime Music" (Miss Fannie Toles); "Because it is a nice parlor ornament to beautify your piano, even if you can't play it" (Miss Alberta Kerr). In 1909 the winning composition was *Mother's Sacrifice*, a piano solo by Viola Kinney (see illustration preceding this chapter), who returned to her hometown of Sedalia, Missouri, after graduation, married an undertaker named Fred Ferguson, and taught music and English for 35 years at segregated Lincoln High School. The music graduates of Western University included several women who would become nationally known, among them the composers Nora Douglas Holt (who wrote the school song, *O Western University*, in 1907) and Eva Jessye, and the singer/actress Etta Moten. The school closed in 1943 because of political disagreements. The buildings are gone now, and all that is left is a statue of John Brown facing toward Missouri across the river, inscribed "Erected to the memory of John Brown by a grateful people." The statue, paid for by Western University students, alumni, and black residents of Kansas City, was unveiled at commencement in 1911.

During these years, the lives of black Americans were deeply influenced by two leaders, Booker T. Washington and W.E.B. Du Bois. Their contrasting philosophies of racial progress and education, including the different values they placed on music and the other liberal arts, had a significant impact on the black community. Born a slave around 1856 in Virginia, Washington was educated at Hampton Institute, a school established to teach trades and practical education. In 1881, inspired by what he learned at Hampton, Washington founded Tuskegee Institute in Alabama as an industrial and agricultural trade school to train blacks in skills for self-help and for services useful to the white community. In a famous speech at the Cotton State Exposition in Atlanta in 1895, he outlined his philosophy of accommodation to white supremacy and acceptance of segregation. The speech endeared him to the white power structure, and he soon became the exclusive conduit for white philanthropy and for government positions for blacks. In almost every town the National Business League, which he founded in 1900, had a chapter supporting black entrepreneurship and giving the black community strength and independence. He was immensely powerful, influential, and widely respected, even by the educated blacks who opposed him. One who challenged his influence was William Trotter of Boston, the son of author James Monroe Trotter.[35] William Trotter opposed Washington's views, heckled him at public speeches, was arrested and jailed, and eventually lost his fortune and his influence.

It was left to William Edward Burghardt Du Bois (1868–1963) to challenge Washington and to take up the mantle of Frederick Douglass as an advocate for first-class citizenship. Du Bois began his higher education at Fisk, then transferred to Harvard University, where he completed his Ph.D. in 1895. A man of aristocratic bearing and cultivated tastes, he taught Greek and Latin at Wilberforce University, sociology at the University of Pennsylvania, and economics and history at Atlanta University. He published numerous scholarly books as well as fiction and poetry. The most famous was *The Souls of Black Folk* (1903), a collection of essays in which he outlined his philosophy of race. Three main ideas stand out: his opposition to Washington's philosophy of accommodation; his advocation of higher education for leadership for the most intelligent and able African Americans, whom he called the "talented tenth"; and his concept of "double consciousness," the twofold experience of African Americans as members of both black and white worlds: "One ever feels his two-ness—an American, a Negro; two souls, two thoughts, two unreconciled strivings; two warring ideals in one dark body, whose dogged strength alone keeps it from being torn asunder."[36]

Du Bois and a select group of educated black men initiated the Niagara Movement in June 1905, which led to the formation in 1909 of the National Association for the Advancement of Colored People (some of whose founders were women), an interracial association whose goals included the promotion of job opportunities for blacks and the elimination of lynching. Its voice was the magazine *Crisis*, inaugurated in 1910 and edited by Du Bois. Outside the *Crisis* office in New York, a banner hung over the street for many years, announcing the current lynching toll. The NAACP organized meetings, rallies, and marches; published the book *Thirty Years of Lynching in the United States, 1889–1918*; and purchased full-page advertisements in the *New York Times* and other papers protesting the lynchings: "The Shame of America . . . 3,436 people lynched 1889 to 1922."[37]

Lynchings took place in almost every state of the union; the heaviest concentrations were in the South where the Ku Klux Klan was most active. Although most lynching victims were men, 76 black women and 16 white women were lynched between 1882 and 1927. The most frequent accusation against male victims of lynching was rape of or improper advances toward white women. One black woman in Tennessee was accused of poisoning her mistress. The white women presumably were thought to be in liaisons with black men. Very often lynching was threatened and/or committed in order to intimidate resourceful, successful, activist blacks.[38] Black women leaders like Ida B. Wells-Barnett (1862–1929) played an important role in the antilynching movement, and black women's clubs rallied behind them.

The peak years of lynching corresponded to the years when Jim Crow segregation was solidifying, legally in the South and unofficially in the North. Jim Crow laws first went into effect in 1875 in Tennessee, separating blacks and whites on trains, in depots, on wharves. Soon hotels, barbershops, theaters, restaurants, and schools were also segregated and in 1896 the U.S. Supreme Court upheld segregation in its "separate but equal" provisions of *Plessy v. Ferguson*. In the North, residential restrictions, de facto segregation, and racial discrimination hardened after 1890. Churches, professional organizations, and schools that had previously admitted blacks now closed their doors. Even Oberlin College made special arrangements for separate housing for black students. This situation lasted for some eighty years, and began to improve only in the late 1950s and 1960s. Many blacks coped by adopting the accommodationist policies of Booker T. Washington. Prosperous educated blacks either retreated into the safe haven of their own environment or, along with W.E.B. Du Bois, committed themselves to activism through the NAACP or the National Urban League. The effect of Jim Crow segregation was particularly devastating for black women, and one of their countermeasures was to band together in clubs for mutual support, enrichment and self-improvement, and social and political reform.

Although black women's clubs were in many respects parallel to the white women's club movement of the same era, there were significant differences. Regardless of their origins and education, black women were viewed by whites as all alike: crude, unlettered, immoral, easy, and deserving indignities including rape. Black women blamed not only white people, but also the lack of chivalry and protection by black men, for this situation. Their club life was directed toward educating the public; publicizing black women of culture, capabilities, and accomplishments; and working to elevate the lives and morals of lower-class black women. They recognized that their reputations and fates were inextricably entwined, and they could improve their own situations only by uplifting all black women. When black women's clubs formed the National Association of Colored Women in 1896, with Mary Church Terrell as president and "Lifting as We Climb" as its motto, Terrell acknowledged their special position: "We wish to . . . stop the ravages made by practices that sap our strength and preclude the possibility of advancement. . . . We refer to the fact that this is an association of colored women because our peculiar status in this country . . . seems to demand that we stand by ourselves." This position was confirmed at the 1900 national convention of the white General Federation of Women's Clubs, which voted against admission of the black New Era Club. The president, Rebecca Lowe, remarked, "It is the 'high-caste' Negroes who bring about all the ill-feeling. The ordinary colored woman understands her position thoroughly."[39]

THE FIRST AFRICAN-AMERICAN WOMEN COMPOSERS

By this time, the first documented evidence of music by black women composers in the United States had appeared. The earliest name is that of Annie Pauline Pindell (ca. 1834–1901), called the "Black Nightingale," a concert singer and songwriter who gave recitals in the far West and even in Hawaii. Her songs "Seek the Lodge Where the Red Men Dwell" and "Ah, Foolish Maiden" are listed in the *Complete Catalogue of Sheet Music and Musical Works, 1870*, published by the Board of Music Trade of the United States of America. However, no trace of the actual scores of her songs has been found. This fate most certainly befell the music of other, perhaps even earlier, black women composers whose names we shall never know.

The late appearance of black women composers corresponds to a similar tardiness among white women in the United States. Women composers in Europe had been systematically ignored by historians, in the belief that they did not possess the creative intellect necessary to produce significant works of art. In the United States, social conventions and prejudices regarding women were at least as strong, and the opportunities to overcome them more scarce, so it took much longer for women composers of significant music to emerge. It is true that black women were not as dominated by society's narrow view of women's functions, and many of them were able to overcome this obstacle to achieve in a number of fields of endeavor. However, as Trotter's observations on the "inexorable rules of society" indicate, this view did have its effect in the area of musical composition. It was not until the white composer Mrs. H.H.A. Beach (1867–1944) wrote her *Mass in E-flat Major, Gaelic Symphony*, and *Piano Concerto in C-Sharp Minor* during the last decade of the nineteenth century that American women composers began to claim their place alongside their male colleagues. Performances of Beach's music would have been heard by the black composer Florence Price while she studied in Boston, and may have inspired her own ambitions.

For that matter, white male composers in the United States were far behind their European contemporaries. Stephen Foster (1826–64) is universally recognized as the first truly American songwriter; his immensely popular "Ethiopian" and "Plantation" songs about black life were sympathetic rather than comic, unlike the typical minstrel tunes of his times. The composers Horatio Parker (1863–1919) at Yale and George Whitefield Chadwick (1854–1931) and Frederick Converse (1871–1940) at the New England Conservatory received their training abroad. Although they imitated European models, they were successful in laying the groundwork for future generations of American composers, including their African-American students Helen Eugenia Hagan, Florence Price, and William Grant Still.

The women's rights movement of the late nineteenth century caused a change in cultural values and a shift in roles for both black and white women and men. Women's independence and their entrance into the workforce and the professions slowly began to be accepted by society. The very first issue of *Crisis* magazine in 1910 commented on this development: "The restlessness of women the world over has led the female members of our population into activities never dreamed of . . . women have had to go into . . . work of a kind that in years gone by was looked upon as belonging by right to the stronger sex."[40] The newly "emancipated women" no longer believed the mystique that reserved the act of musical creation for men.

The 1890s saw books in print about the accomplishments of black women which illustrate this change. They described the range of activities in which black women excelled and gave short biographies of outstanding individuals.[41] Two were published in 1893 by black physicians: *Women of Distinction* by Dr. Lawson A. Scruggs and *Noted Negro Women* by Dr. Monroe A. Majors (the father of the composer Margaret Bonds). The year after the two men published their books, the journalist Gertrude Bustill Mossell joined their ranks with *The Work of the Afro-American Woman*. Though she lists only a few composers' names in one sentence, she does forthrightly name their occupation: "We have in the line of musical composers, Miss Estelle Rickets [*sic*], Miss Bragg, Miss Tillman [*sic*], Mrs. Yeocum and Mrs. Ella Mossell."[42] Of the approximately 360 or so women named in the books of Majors and Scruggs (there was a good deal of overlap), about 24 percent were musicians. Of that 24 percent, 60 percent were singers, 27 percent were pianists and/or teachers, 11 percent were organists, and six also composed. Although not admitted to many white institutions of higher learning,[43] they could obtain training at the Oberlin Conservatory of Music (opened in 1865) and four other music schools (all founded in 1867) that admitted blacks: the Boston Conservatory, the New England Conservatory of Music, the Cincinnati Conservatory, and the Chicago Musical College.

Both authors described the careers of Amelia L. Tilghman, Lucinda Bragg Adams, and Mrs. N.A.R. Leslie. Amelia Tilghman was born in Washington, D.C., and exhibited a talent for music at an early age.[44] She graduated from the Normal Department of Howard University in 1871 and continued music study at the Boston Conservatory of Music. She had an illustrious career as a teacher, author, and concert singer. In 1886 she began publishing the first Negro musical magazine, *The Musical Messenger*. Examples of her published music are in the Library of Congress and the Moorland-Spingarn Research Center at Howard University. Tilghman's assistant editor, Lucinda Bragg Adams, composed music that Majors described as "full of her soul."

Mrs. N.A.R. Leslie settled in Corpus Christi, Texas, to start a musical conservatory for young ladies. She is described by Majors as "not only talented as a reader and performer of her art, but a composer of some prominence." He goes on to say: "Hence the race, which has produced other great minds to shine forth proclaiming progress in various walks of life may feel proud of Mrs. Leslie who along with many more of her sex, is doing what she can to explode the doctrine of inferior music and the appellation, musical race in the rough."[45] Unfortunately, none of Mrs. Leslie's compositions have been found, nor has music by several other composers Majors mentions: May C. Reynolds Heyers, billed as "Actress, Singer, Musician, and Writer of Operas"; Mrs. Mary Le-McLemare Sinclair, "among the finest musicians in Tennessee . . . a composer of songs and many notable pieces of music"; and Mrs. J. E. Edwards of Washington, D.C., and Galveston, "a scholar in piano music, both a composer and a pleasing performer."

Both Edwards and Tilghman came from Washington, D.C., where women were prominent in the musical life of the city. Its many outstanding music teachers included Harriet Gibbs Marshall (1869–1941), the first black woman graduate of the Oberlin Conservatory of Music (1889), who founded the Washington Conservatory of Music and School of Expression in 1903. In 1905, Lulu Vere Childers (1870–1946) reorganized Howard University's music department, and under her guidance it became a conservatory of music in 1913, then a school of music in 1918.

In Boston, more than six dozen black classical women musicians active before 1900 have been identified. Most of them were singers, a few were instrumentalists, and a dozen were teachers, including concert pianist Rachel Washington, the first black graduate of the Boston Conservatory, who opened a music school and published a theory textbook. Well-known composers were Miriam E. Benjamin, one of whose marches was performed by the U.S. Marine Band under John Philip Sousa in the early 1890s, and Louisa Melvin Delos Mars, who wrote five full-length musical dramas that were covered in the Negro press.[46]

Most of the earliest surviving works of black women composers were sacred and secular sentimental songs.[47] The earliest purely instrumental music by a black woman to be found at the Library of Congress is Estelle Ricketts's solo piano *Rippling Spring Waltz* (1893).[48] Her waltz was followed by numerous similar piano pieces by other composers: the ubiquitous parlor music of sedate waltzes, marches, and two-steps.

None of the surviving solo piano music published by black women before 1910 displays black idioms. Negro idioms were not incorporated into published music by black male composers until the late 1890s, when Ernest Hogan (1865–1909), Blind John Boone (1864–1927), Scott Joplin (1868–1917), Thomas Turpin (1873–1922), and others began to introduce ragtime rhythms into the songs and dances of minstrel shows and ballrooms. Some black women collaborated with their husbands in composing "coon songs" (syncopated ragtime songs with lyrics that reflected white American stereotypes of black Americans) for the vaudeville circuits. In the case of Mrs. Ida Larkins (two of whose collaborations with her husband, John Larkins, were the coon songs *The Trolley Party in the Sky* and *Miss Hazel Brown)*, her solo piano piece *Wild Flowers*, composed under her name alone, was in a very conservative, ladylike style. The piano rags, which swept the country after the turn of the century, evolved through the dubious avenue of honkytonk pianos in bawdy houses and saloons. While numerous white women composed them with impunity, there were no known black women composers of ragtime piano music. Black women were more at pains to distance themselves from the lower-class origins of this exotic, popular craze. The black educated class seldom attended public entertainment and considered minstrel music, ragtime, and especially the cakewalk unacceptable.

The inclusion of African-American idioms in American classical concert music was instigated by Antonín Dvořák, the Bohemian nationalist composer who served as director of the National Conservatory of Music in New York City from 1892 to 1895. He was interested in America's folk music and asked one of his black students, Harry T. Burleigh (1866–1949), to sing Negro spirituals to him. This led to Dvořák's well-publicized view on the development of an American national school through the use of native materials and to his own use of Negro idioms in his *Symphony No. 9, From the New World*, and other works. Encouraged by Dvořák, the black composers Harry Burleigh, Robert Nathaniel Dett (1882–1943), and Clarence Cameron White (1880–1960) began to use black idioms in serious art music in the 1910s and 1920s.

Soon after Dvořák's departure, another visitor from abroad made a strong impact on black classical music in the United States: Samuel Coleridge-Taylor (1875–1912), the eminent Afro-British composer and professor at Trinity College of Music in London. He was invited to Washington, D.C. in 1904, and returned to the United States in 1906 and 1910, touring a number of cities. His works, including his arrangements of American Negro spirituals (inspired by a visit by the Fisk Jubilee Singers to England in 1899), were widely performed, and a crop of Coleridge-Taylor clubs, societies, and schools joined the flourishing black music clubs and schools in every city. His example as a black musician and composer, respected by whites in his own land, impressed the black audiences and communities and gave new impetus to their classical musical activities.

Among that generation of black composers were several who began as classical musicians in the 1880s and 1890s, but gained their reputations writing black Broadway musicals in the first decade of the twentieth century. Will Marion Cook (1869–1944) began as a violinist studying at the Berlin Hochschule für Musik and later at the National Conservatory of Music under Dvořák, and made his concert debut in Washington in 1889. His educated Washington family (his mother was an 1865 graduate of Oberlin College) was aghast when he began to compose Negroid music for *Clorindy, the Origin of the Cakewalk* (1898), *Swing Along* (1929), and many other musicals. However, his influence was widespread and long-lasting; among the many composers who acknowledged it were Duke Ellington and Margaret Bonds.

Another classically trained composer was John Rosamond Johnson (1873–1954), who studied at the New England Conservatory and in London. He, too, turned to musicals, collaborating with Robert Cole and his brother James Weldon Johnson. In 1900 the Johnson brothers wrote *Lift Every Voice and Sing*, which would become the *Negro National Anthem*, sung at every large formal gathering ever since.

No one fulfilled Dvořák's ideals more completely than Scott Joplin (1868–1917). Joplin received his early musical training from a German teacher in Texarkana, Texas, and later attended the George Smith School for Negroes in Sedalia, Missouri. He published his first ragtime piano piece, the famous *Maple Leaf Rag*, in 1899. But his work of genius was his second opera, *Treemonisha*, completed in 1905. He moved to New York and staged it himself in 1911 in a small hall in Harlem, without scenery, costumes, or orchestra. The audience was not impressed, and the work disappeared until 1972, when it received its first full performance at Morehouse College in Atlanta.[49] The theme and plot, as well as the music itself, pull together many strands of African-American experiences, conflicts, and yearnings, among them education as the salvation of the race, and rejection of superstition and conjuring (symbols of the African past). The opera is set on a plantation in Arkansas in 1884 and centers on a young educated heroine, Treemonisha, who illustrates the importance of women in the elevation and progress of the race. The European form of grand opera is followed, with 27 traditional numbers: overture, recitatives, arias, small ensembles, choruses, and ballets. Into this form Joplin pours African-American musical idioms: ragtime rhythms, dances such as the Slow Drag and the Dude Walk, a preaching scene with call and response, a spirituals-singing scene, even a blues scene. Not until William Grant Still's *Afro-American Symphony* in 1932 did a black American composer again attempt such an extensive fusion of European and African-American styles.

During these years Florence Beatrice Smith Price (1887–1953) was receiving her musical training at the New England Conservatory of Music. Price was to occupy a position in the front ranks of black classical music; she was the first black woman to achieve distinction as a composer nationally and abroad, and the first to compose symphonies. She was born in Little Rock, Arkansas, which, although a small city, had a cosmopolitan character unusual in the South, as well as a diverse population and a thriving black professional upper class. Florence's father, John Henry Smith, was a freeborn black dentist who moved to Little Rock from Delaware in the 1870s and had a large practice among wealthy whites as well as blacks. Dr. Smith was also a successful inventor, a talented artist, and a novelist. Florence's mother was an elementary school music teacher from Indianapolis. The Smith home had an extensive library, oil paintings, and a variety of musical instruments. Florence exhibited her musical talent early, with her mother as her first teacher. After she graduated as valedictorian from Capitol High School in 1903, she was sent to Boston's New England Conservatory (where she was registered as a Mexican, to avoid racism). Florence received her diploma in piano and organ in 1906, then returned to Little Rock to teach at Shorter College and to marry an attorney, Thomas J. Price. As her family grew, she continued to teach and compose, winning prizes in *Opportunity* magazine's Holstein competitions.[50] By 1926 the racial climate in Little Rock had deteriorated to the point of a lynching in a black middle-class neighborhood, and the Prices moved to Chicago. Upon her arrival in Chicago, Price was welcomed into a vital and nurturing black musical community. She took advantage of every opportunity to grow musically, attending Chicago Musical College, Chicago Teacher's College, the University of Chicago, Central YMCA College, and the American Conservatory of Music. A constellation of events that could have taken place only in Chicago at that time gave impetus to her steadily growing fame. Her *Symphony in E Minor*, which won the Rodman Wanamaker Prize in 1932, attracted the attention of the conductor Frederick Stock. He performed it with the Chicago Symphony Orchestra at the World's Fair in 1933, and that summer her works were featured on programs at the World's Fair Century of Progress exhibitions, the International Congress of Women, and the NAACP convention in Chicago.[51] This gave her national and international exposure because many visitors to the city heard her music. Price composed nearly 300 pieces, many of them large orchestral works that were performed in several American cities and as far away as England, where Sir John Barbirolli commissioned a work.

Price's musical style was conservative and late-romantic. Like Antonín Dvořák, she did not always quote actual folk melodies, but sought to imbue much of her music with characteristic black idioms, such as melodic falling thirds and the cakewalk and juba rhythms (see note 25). She alluded to this in her subtitles: the third movement of her *Symphony in E Minor* is called "Juba Dance," and her *Dances in the Canebrakes* carries the inscription "based on authentic Negro rhythms." In a letter of 1940 concerning her third symphony, about to be performed in Michigan under Walter Poole, she states, "It is intended to be Negroid in character and expression. In it no attempt, however, has been made to project Negro music in the purely traditional manner. None of the themes are adaptations or derivations of folk songs."[52] Her *Sonata in E Minor*, which took a first prize in its category in the 1932 Wanamaker competition, skillfully blends classical forms and techniques with Negro folk idioms. The third movement, titled "Scherzo" (meaning prank or joke), is a virtuoso parody of the long-winded European art music that early twentieth-century critics claimed black composers couldn't write. It demonstrates Price's affection for, as well as her wryly humorous ambivalence toward, the European composers and art forms in which she was trained.

Price never traveled or studied abroad. One early composer who did so was Helen Eugenia Hagan (1891–1964), born in Portsmouth, New Hampshire, and educated at the Yale University School of Music, where she studied with Horatio Parker. When she graduated in 1912, she performed her *Concerto in C Minor* with the New Haven Orchestra and received Yale's Sanford Fellowship for two years' composition study in France at the Schola Cantorum with Vincent d'Indy. She remained abroad until the outbreak of World War I, then returned in 1918 to entertain black troops in France. For some years she gave highly praised piano concerts and performed her concerto on several occasions. The *Concerto* is the earliest extant work in a large form by a black woman composer. In one movement, it adheres to the concerto-ritornello form in a late-romantic virtuoso and heroic style. It is the only work by Hagan that survives. Hagan's concert and composing career did not gather momentum, so she turned to teaching and choral directing.

Another musician who gave up composing was Nora Douglas Holt (1885–1974). A cultural pioneer, she was the first black person in the United States to earn the Master of Music degree in composition (Chicago Musical College, 1918). In 1919 she was one of the founders of the National Association of Negro Musicians, an influential organization still very active today. Holt was best known as a music critic for black newspapers, *The Chicago Defender* (1917–23) and *The New York Amsterdam News* (1944–52). She published and edited a journal, *Music and Poetry*, for a brief period in 1921.[53] Born in Kansas City, Kansas, she graduated as valedictorian from Western University in Quindaro, Kansas in 1916, and entered the graduate program of Chicago Musical College. Among her teachers was Felix Borowsky, president of the college and music critic for the *Chicago Sun-Times*. In order to pay her tuition, Nora began performing at elegant parties given by prominent Chicagoans, singing light songs, Noël Coward melodies, and spirituals. In 1918 she married hotel owner George W. Holt, forty years her senior, who died in 1921. For most of the 1920s and 1930s she traveled in Europe and the Far East, performing at private parties and exclusive nightclubs. After returning to the United States she settled for a while in Los Angeles, teaching in the public schools, then moved to New York City in 1944. In 1945 she began the annual "American Negro Artists" festival on radio station WNYC, and from 1953 through 1964 she was the producer and musical director of a weekly program, "Concert Showcase," on Harlem's WLIB radio station. Her music columns and radio programs influenced the musical tastes of several generations and encouraged countless young black musicians. Most of her compositions date from the early years in Chicago. She composed approximately 200 works, including piano and chamber music and a work for full orchestra, *Rhapsody on Negro Themes*. Among her art songs were several set to texts by Paul Laurence Dunbar, including *A Florida Night*, a favorite of the tenor Roland Hayes.

Nora Holt's years in Chicago point up the stimulating atmosphere and historic importance of that city in attracting and producing an unusual number of black women composers. Several factors contributed to the vigor of Negro cultural activity in Chicago: the large black population resulting from waves of migration from the South, the isolation and independence of the black community's economic and political infrastructure, the influence wielded by the *Chicago Defender* (founded in 1905), the "Golden Age of Jazz" in the 1920s, and the subsequent urban blues and gospel eras, the world's fairs and exhibits, and the institutions of higher learning which welcomed Negro musicians from all over the country.

In culture, black Chicago was not far behind its rival New York, and this rivalry did much to fuel artistic endeavor. The sociologist E. Franklin Frazier described the relative strengths of each city in 1929: "The feeling of rivalry between Harlem and Chicago has caused each to cast uncomplimentary epithets at the other. New York has charged Chicago Negroes with being a group of money getters, without any sense of the finer things in life, while Chicago has retorted that . . . [New Yorkers are] without any sound economic basis for their culture. . . . Moreover, Chicago held a Negro in Art Week in order to show her cultural rival what her artists could do."[54] New York's black population was scattered over its five boroughs, and was more diverse, with a large and influential West Indian contingent. With the blossoming of the Harlem Renaissance in the 1910s and 1920s, New York took a leading role in the intellectual and artistic New Negro Movement.

The large cities of the eastern seaboard had the advantage of longer history, bigger populations, more schools and colleges (including black schools), and larger black upper classes. When it came to a concentration of old names, wealth, light skin color, and professional elites, Washington, D.C., was the capital of black aristocracy.[55] The city had the largest concentration of black politicians and legislators; a history of great residents like Benjamin Banneker and Frederick Douglass; old families like the Syphaxes, Grimkés, Purvises, and Terrells; the excellent Dunbar High School, many of whose faculty had advanced degrees; and the presence of Howard University, the "black man's Harvard," with its surrounding group of intellectuals. The African-American upper class was affluent and cultivated highbrow tastes. A tightly knit group with connections to the upper class in other cities, they guarded their privacy closely to protect both their real lives and their public image.[56] Washington suffered from the same restrictive Jim Crow regulations, which respected no class distinctions, as did other Southern cities, but its privileged classes were able to protect themselves to some degree by living in their own isolated world. They avoided going downtown to use public facilities and restaurants, preferring to patronize black businesses and to have merchants bring clothes to their homes. Talk about segregation or discrimination was avoided, as if its existence might thereby be ignored, if not denied.[57]

While only a few black women composers of classical music came from the highest or wealthiest echelons of black society (which tended to reject anything that hinted of the entertainment world), they frequently came from well-educated, upper-middle-class and hardworking, aspiring middle-class families. Social class in black society was, and still is, a complex issue, and the usual criteria do not apply. The extreme wealth associated with the upper class in the dominant culture was not present in black society. Although a relatively affluent black aristocracy or upper class did exist, it was exceedingly small. Highly educated African Americans could seldom find employment commensurate with their qualifications, and often took jobs in the postal service or the civil service. Many occupations that in white society would be regarded as menial had status in the black community. House servants to the wealthy, Pullman porters, caterers, waiters, barbers, tailors, seamstresses, ice dealers, shopkeepers, and many others in the service trades were often political and cultural leaders.[58]

The educated upper-middle and upper classes, for all their snobbery and frequent indifference to the lot of the less fortunate, cultivated values that benefited and enriched all African Americans. Although they constituted less than 1 percent of the black population, most of whom struggled with poverty and blatant racism, their high regard for education and achievement produced leaders, scientists, writers, musicians, and artists. Their ideal of racial uplift for all Negroes contributed teachers, schools, and homes for orphans and the elderly; their historians and pride in Negro history preserved black heritage; and their loyalty to race bolstered Negro self-respect.

Emma Azalia Hackley (1867–1922) epitomized the upper-class black woman devoted to the service of her race. She worked tirelessly to promote black womanhood and black music. She obtained her basic training as a singer in her native Detroit and graduated from the University of Denver in 1901. After her debut concert in Denver, she toured extensively, raising money for music scholarships. She sponsored the European studies of several black musicians, opened the Vocal Normal Institute in Chicago, and organized mammoth community Negro folk song festivals in many large cities, gathering choirs of hundreds to perform classical music and spirituals. She also published *The Colored Girl Beautiful* in 1916 and gave inspirational talks at colored girls' boarding schools, counseling them to be "race missionaries," to take responsibility in their communities, to cultivate self-control, cleanliness, soft speech, conservative dress, and good manners.[59]

THE 1920s: THE HARLEM RENAISSANCE

Black class structure was changed by the newly rich business class produced by Booker T. Washington's principles of industry and self-help, and by large migrations of the poor from the South. The two world wars brought hordes of Southern blacks seeking the jobs they saw advertised in Northern black newspapers, and offending the established urban blacks with their rural lifestyles. Whites reacted to the influx with increased discrimination and rigid housing restrictions that created congested ghettos in which blacks of various back-grounds and classes, with no place else to go, lived side by side.

This social ferment stimulated the intellectual, artistic, and literary flowering known as the Harlem Renaissance (also called the Black Renaissance and the New Negro Movement). At first, the movement was dominated by "talented tenth" advocates such as Du Bois and Alain Locke. Although the desire to impress the white world with the Negro's intelligence and achievements put emphasis on upper-class European traits, African and American Negro folk cul-ture was embraced when presented by educated black anthropologists, artists, and writers such as Zora Neale Hurston.

The New Negro ideals in music were already flourishing, inspired by Antonín Dvořák and Samuel Coleridge-Taylor. In the 1920s the black concert artists Roland Hayes, Paul Robeson, and Marian Anderson embodied early Harlem Renaissance ideals, and were soon joined by the symphonic pioneers William Grant Still (1895–1978), William Dawson (1899–1990), and Florence Price (1887–1953). Still's *Afro-American Symphony* made history in 1931 as the first symphony by an African American to be performed by a major American or-chestra, the Rochester Philharmonic Symphony, conducted by Howard Hanson. It still stands as a milestone, the first successful fusion of the blues with a European concert form and genre. Through his symphonic, instrumental, and vocal works and operas, Still made important contributions to America's music that earned him the title "Dean of Afro-American Composers."

Even as black composers were proving their ability to write in large European classical forms and to contribute to America's musical nationalism by incor-porating Negro idioms, early twentieth-century developments in the larger mu-sical world were also having an impact. The foundations of Western music were being challenged by harmonic dissonance, atonalism, serialism, additive and irregular rhythms, and new kinds of sound were being explored. A new category of classical music emerged: the avant-garde, also called modernist.[60] William Grant Still studied with the traditionalist George Chadwick at the New England Conservatory of Music, and with the modernist Edgard Varèse in New York. He was skilled in traditional classical, as well as modernist and "racial" or jazz-inflected, composition, but eventually decided that modernism was not compat-ible with Negroid idioms. Black composers in the coming decades would also face such choices.

Harlem Renaissance writers soon responded to the dynamism and mobility of the migrations from the South with rebellion against upper-class European ideals and with affirmation of lower-class Negro art forms. The poet Langston Hughes was a chief spokesman for this reaction. Hughes condemned black upper-class society for its superficiality, sterility of thought, materialism, and especially class snobbishness. He affirmed jazz, which was taking the country by storm and drawing visitors to Harlem, as the emblematic music of the Harlem Renaissance in his essay "The Negro Artist and the Racial Mountain": "Let the blare of Negro jazz bands and the bellowing voice of Bessie Smith singing blues penetrate the closed ears of the colored near-intellectuals until they listen and perhaps understand. . . . We younger Negro artists who create now intend to express our dark-skinned selves without fear or shame."[61] Influenced by Hughes and his fellow writers, the educated black upper class slowly began to enlarge its idea of acceptable music to include jazz and blues.

Nothing illustrates the race/gender/class/music association as vividly as the phenomenon of the female blues singers, the "blues queens" of the 1920s and 1930s. The first body of music to be associated mainly with black women, urban blues was an outgrowth of Southern rural blues, an expression of the poor, oppressed, and dislocated blacks in the aftermath of the Civil War. Show business presented an alternative for young, attractive black women who hoped for more than domestic drudgery. The first major female blues singer, Gertrude "Ma" Rainey (1886–1939), began to perform in touring tent shows as early as 1903, and is credited with forging a link between rural and urban blues. Mamie Smith's (1883–1946) pioneer recording of *Crazy Blues* on the Okeh label in 1920 started the race-record industry on its way, and contributed immeasurably to the popularity of the women blues singers. Bessie Smith's (1894–1937) huge following epitomized the worship accorded singers whose sequined glamour was a welcome contrast to drab lives, and whose expressive, soulful lyrics and style empathized with the universal woes of the poor. Her powerful, distinctive voice and her earthy style influenced countless later singers. Blues singers toured on the vaudeville circuit, recorded, sang in clubs, performed in musicals, and were given royal titles by their fans: "Mother of the Blues" (Rainey), "Empress of the Blues" (Bessie Smith), and "Prima Donna of the Blues" (Alberta Hunter). But their theatrical life was considered sinful and the churchgoing black community did not approve. Among the tough, sexually suggestive lyrics were references to parental disapproval and social ostracism.[62]

Jazz swept the United States in the 1920s. It was a male-dominated field in which women were expected to "play like a man." Lil Hardin (1898–1971) was a classically trained musician, educated at Fisk University, Chicago Musical College, and New York College of Music. She crossed class and style barriers to enter the rough world of jazz, working as a pianist/arranger/composer with King Oliver's band and marrying Louis Armstrong (from 1924 to 1938). She is responsible for jazz hits from the 1920s through the 1960s: *Struttin' with Some Barbecue, Lonesome Blues, Jazz Lips*. Hardin also formed two all-female bands predating the remarkable all-girl bands of the 1930s and 1940s, Ina Ray Hutton and her Melodears, and the International Sweethearts of Rhythm.[63] The many women jazz singer/songwriters who followed the blues queens benefited from a gender-specific style in which attractive appearance and the female voice were part of the genre, and talent was more valuable than training or experience. Some wrote compelling, thought-provoking songs such as Billie Holiday's *God Bless the Child*. Although women jazz instrumentalists had a harder time, they gradually gained recognition. As they began to write down their music and tackled larger forms, jazz composers were eventually admitted to the world of classical music.

The most outstanding woman jazz composer of the century was the pianist Mary Lou Williams (1910–81). For more than six decades she absorbed and perfected each passing jazz style, performing, arranging, and composing for Andy Kirk, Benny Goodman, Louis Armstrong, Duke Ellington, Cab Calloway, and others. A child prodigy, Mary Lou began to play the piano at age two and a half. While still in grade school, she was earning money by performing at parties, and in her teens was touring with bands. Her mastery of stride piano, boogie-woogie, and swing was demonstrated in scores of recordings and several albums of piano music. Her extended work, the twelve-movement *Zodiac Suite*, was recorded in 1945 and several movements were performed by the New York Philharmonic in 1946. In 1956 Williams converted to Catholicism and began to compose religious jazz, completing three Masses in 1966, 1968, and 1970. The last Mass was choreographed by Alvin Ailey, renamed *Mary Lou's Mass*, and premiered in New York's St. Patrick's Cathedral in 1971. It encompasses many styles: blues, spirituals, Latin dance rhythms, lots of call and response, and even a mystical atonal choral movement, *Lamb of God*. Williams received two Guggenheim grants for her jazz compositions as well as several honorary degrees, and was a member of the faculty at Duke University from 1976 to her death in 1981.[64]

After the migrations of 1916–1930, the mixture and close proximity in Northern cities of African-American musical idioms from all over the country created a wealth of styles to choose from: blues, ragtime, jazz, European band music, opera and vaudeville numbers, and many others. The variety of black religious music had been expanded at the turn of the century by the emergence of holiness and sanctified churches, of which the Church of God in Christ became the largest. Participatory music was the primary form of worship in these folk churches; the African practices of spirit possession, holy dancing, ring shouts, and improvised praise songs were revived, and drums, guitars, piano, and other instruments were introduced. The slow, heavily ornamented "long-meter" hymns, named "Dr. Watts" after the eighteenth-century hymn writer, were common in all these churches. A new type of gospel hymn appeared, and women writers and singers were important in its evolution.[65] Lucie Campbell (1885–1963) was one of its pioneers, copyrighting her first gospel song in 1905. Campbell's *Something Within* was sung at the National Baptist Convention in 1919, three years before Thomas A. Dorsey, often called the "Father of Gospel Music," left his blues career to lead the Chicago gospel scene. Sallie Martin (1896–1988), Roberta Martin (1907–1969) and Willie Mae Ford Smith (1906–1994) were other well-known early gospel writers; they were followed by a host of other women, including Doris Akers (1922–95), Clara Ward (1924–73), and Dorothy Love Coates (b. 1928). Gospel style later influenced not only popular and soul music, but also stage and concert music.

The New Negro Movement of the 1920s and 1930s was a strong force in

Chicago, and Margaret Bonds (1913–72) grew up surrounded by its influence. Her mother, Estella Bonds, was a highly respected musician and a generous hostess. Writers, artists, and musicians from around the country visited her home and attended her Sunday afternoon musicales. As a teenager, Margaret studied composition with William Dawson and Florence Price, then attended Northwestern University. She was also a formidable pianist; in 1932 she became the first Negro to perform as soloist with the Chicago Symphony Orchestra. Few composers were as imbued as Bonds with the defiant Harlem Renaissance spirit of Langston Hughes' poetry, although the race-conscious ideals of the New Negro Movement were also expressed in the choral and stage works of the composers Eva Jessye (1895–1992) and Shirley Graham Du Bois (1904–78).

Eva Jessye graduated from Western University in Quindaro, Kansas, in 1914 and studied in New York with Will Marion Cook. She taught music at Claflin College in South Carolina and Baltimore's Morgan State University (1920) before she became the first black woman to gain international distinction as a professional choral director. She was asked to be choral director for Virgil Thompson's opera *Four Saints in Three Acts* (1933) and George Gershwin's *Porgy and Bess* (1935). She arranged spirituals for choir (*My Spirituals*, 1927), and composed and produced the folk oratorios *Paradise Lost and Regained* (broadcast on NBC radio in 1931), *The Life of Christ in Negro Spirituals* (1931), and the *Chronicle of Job* (1936).

Shirley Graham, who became the second wife of W.E.B. Du Bois in 1951, had a distinguished career as a writer and composer. The author of many plays, novels, and biographies, she wrote articles on music for *Crisis* and *Etude* magazines. Her first love was music, and she studied at Howard University and the Oberlin Conservatory, completing her master's degree in 1935. She taught music at Morgan State University from 1928 to 1931, and was a supervisor of the Negro Unit of the Federal Theater in Chicago (1936–1938), where she worked on the music and production of *Swing Mikado* and *Little Black Sambo*. Her most famous composition is her opera *Tom-Tom*, produced with elaborate staging at the Cleveland Stadium in 1932. She also composed stage music for *Garden of Time* and *Divine Comedy* by Owen Dodson, both produced at Yale University in 1939.

WORLD WAR II

More than 1 million black men and women served their country in World War II despite segregation in the military and exclusion from jobs in the defense industry at home.[66] As they returned to the United States they faced discrimination, segregation, and more lynchings. Their increasing frustration at home, together with increasing international scrutiny, convinced President Harry Truman to address these issues when he succeeded Franklin D. Roosevelt. He desegregated the armed forces in 1948 and appointed committees to investigate discrimination and civil rights violations.

The Great Depression and World War II had a sobering effect on American society. The severe economic situation turned black intellectuals' attention to workers' rights, and some Negroes were attracted to communism. The House Un-American Activities Committee investigated several members of the New Negro Movement, including Paul Robeson, W.E.B. Du Bois, and Langston Hughes. The "racialism" of the New Negro Movement began to be suspect, and black-oriented literature, art, and music went into decline. At the same time, hopes for integration were raised by signs of progress. Black Americans particpated in the formation of the United Nations, Ralphe Bunche won the Nobel Peace Prize, Gwendolyn Brooks won the Pulitzer Prize in literature (both in 1950), and in 1954 the Supreme Court *Brown* v. *Board of Education of Topeka* decision declared separate but equal educational facilities unconstitutional. Writers, artists, and musicians were encouraged by these prospects to join the mainstream. Many black composers embraced the current international musical trends: neoclassicism, atonal expressionism, serialism, and electronic music. Howard Swanson (1907–78) obtained his musical training at the Cleveland Institute of Music, then studied with the renowned teacher Nadia Boulanger at Fontainebleau, France.[67] His style is neoclassical but dissonant, and intensely lyrical. Ulysses Kay (1917–96) studied at the Eastman School of Music and abroad, and employed mid-twentieth-century techniques in dissonant but lyrical music for voice, instruments, orchestra, and opera. His works were performed by major orchestras and received many awards, including the coveted Prix de Rome, and election to the American Academy of Arts and Letters. George Walker (b. 1922) studied at Oberlin, the Curtis Institute of Music, and in France with Nadia Boulanger, then completed his doctorate at the Eastman School of Music. His music is deeply expressive, and uncompromising in its adherence to twentieth-century compositional techniques. Hale Smith (b. 1925) obtained his musical training at the Cleveland Institute of Music. Many of his compositions use modern compositional techniques, although he worked closely with the jazz artists Dizzy Gillespie, Horace Silver, and Ahmad Jamal, among others, and also wrote works in the jazz idiom.

One of the most distinguished black women composers of the century, Julia Perry (1924–79), established her career in Europe during the 1950s, organizing concert series, touring as a lecturer, and conducting performances of her orchestral and operatic works. Her music incorporates the neoclassic, dissonant, serial techniques typical of the twentieth-century international style, which she infused with an intense, dark lyricism. Since her reputation was based on a handful of early works, until now the only ones accessible, the full range of her stylistic expression has yet to be discovered (see chapter 3). Few black women composers embraced the international mainstream avant-garde as completely as Julia Perry. Little-known Irene Britton Smith (1907–99) distanced herself from her African-American roots and composed in European neoclassical forms, avoiding more modern techniques (see chapter 5).

In the 1940s and 1950s the boundaries between jazz and so-called serious music were more defined than they are today, and the prohibitions against jazz in many black churches were still strict. The pianists Mary Lou Williams (1910–81), Hazel Scott (1920–81), and Dorothy Donegan (1922–98) and the trombonist Melba Liston (1926–99) ignored these prohibitions and developed their jazz careers during these years. Other women composers pursued careers in church music and more conventional classical genres and styles. During the 1950s and early 1960s, continuity with black American choral traditions was maintained in the music of Evelyn LaRue Pittman (1910–92), Betty Jackson King (1928–94), Lena Johnson McLin (b. 1929), and Undine Smith Moore (1904–89), a major black woman composer of the century. Although the main body of Moore's work was choral and made extensive use of African-American idioms, she also composed instrumental music that incorporated many of the techniques of the twentieth century.

Evelyn Pittman studied with Kemper Harreld at Spelman College, graduating in 1929. She returned to her home state of Oklahoma to teach music and direct student choirs. Seeing a need for a way to teach black history through music, she wrote a collection of songs and short stories about famous black Americans, published as *Rich Heritage* in 1944. Her Evelyn Pittman Choir performed frequently in Oklahoma and was heard on local radio stations. She attended the Juilliard School of Music in 1948, studying with Robert Ward, and continued graduate work at the University of Oklahoma, completing her master's degree in 1954. In 1956 she traveled to Paris to study with Nadia Boulanger. Her master's thesis, the folk opera *Cousin Esther*, was completed and performed in Paris. It was performed again in New York to good reviews (broadcast over WNYC in 1963). The assassination of Martin Luther King, Jr. inspired her to write the opera *Freedom Child* in 1970; it, too, was widely performed in the United States and Europe. Another opera, *Jim Noble*, followed in 1978.

Betty Jackson King was a product of the early Chicago classical music tradition (much like Margaret Bonds). Her mother, Gertrude Jackson Taylor, was a highly respected Chicago musical pioneer, and her father was the founder and pastor of People's Community Church. At an early age Betty sang in the family trio with her mother and her sister Catherine, and their close harmonic style influenced her later compositions. She attended Wilson Junior College and received her bachelor's and master's degrees from Roosevelt University in Chicago. Later she did graduate work at Peabody Conservatory and Westminster Choir College, and taught at the University of Chicago laboratory school, Roosevelt University, Dillard University in New Orleans, and Wildwood High School in New Jersey. President of the National Association of Negro Musicians from 1979 to 1984, King served widely as a choral clinician and received numerous awards. Along with her choral works, songs, arrangements of spirituals, and a few instrumental pieces, she, like Pittman, showed a predilection for musical drama. Her biblical works include *Simon of Cyrene, My Servant Job*, and *Saul of Tarsus* (premiered in 1952 by the Chicago Musical Association). Her style, heavily infused with black idioms, is harmonically conventional but powerfully expressive.

Lena Johnson McLin comes from a background similar to King's. Her father was a preacher of the Greater Mount Calvary Baptist Church in Atlanta, Georgia, and her mother was a fine musician and community leader. As a child, Lena lived for several years in Chicago at the home of her uncle, Thomas A. Dorsey, one of the pioneers of gospel music. She was often called to the piano, when she was seven and eight years old, to accompany the lessons of gospel singers Sallie Martin and Mahalia Jackson. During that time she was cared for by her grandmother, whose reminiscences of family history and singing of slave songs made a deep impression on her. After graduation from Spelman she received a scholarship from the American Conservatory and moved back to Chicago, where she also attended Roosevelt University and studied voice with the noted teacher Thelma Waide Brown. In 1959 she began teaching in the Chicago public schools and became well known for her innovative high school music programs. She served on a Music Educator's National Conference commission, produced an educational film, wrote a music history textbook, and designed the pilot music program at Kenwood Academy High School. She formed the McLin Singers, a select touring concert group, and for several years she ran a small opera company, the McLin Ensemble. Much of her vocal and choral music is published and widely performed. Her cantata, *Free at Last, a Portrait of Martin Luther King, Jr.*, has been performed in New York's Carnegie Hall and in Europe. She composes in a wide variety of styles, ranging from gospel, popular, and rock to serious art songs, operas, and symphonies.

A striking exception to the more characteristic background and development of black women composers was Philippa Duke Schuyler (1931–67). A prolific composer and author, she was a child prodigy who began her concert career at age four, when she was already composing little piano pieces. Her father was George Schuyler, editor of the *Pittsburgh Courier*, and her mother was Josephine Codgell, a wealthy white Texas heiress. When she was 12 years old, Philippa's award-winning composition *Manhattan Nocturne* was performed by the Detroit Symphony Orchestra and also the New York Philharmonic Orchestra. At 14, she made her piano debut with the New York Philharmonic, and also played with the Boston Symphony the same year. Her Town Hall debut in 1953 received rave reviews, and in later years she made numerous guest soloist appearances with orchestras in the United States and abroad; she also made three world tours under the auspices of the State Department. She died in a U.S. Army helicopter crash while evacuating Vietnamese children from Hue to Danang, while she was on assignment as a news correspondent for the *Manchester* (N.H.) *Union-Leader*. Her approximately 60 compositions, many of them incomplete, are primarily for piano, although she also wrote orchestral and vocal music. They reveal no African-American influences but make extensive use of purely African materials within conservative classical forms, and show her fondness for occult numeric and intervallic codes. The *Nile Fantasy* for piano and orchestra, though repetitive and lengthy, demonstrates a gift for arresting, dramatically effective orchestration.[68]

CIVIL RIGHTS ERA: THE BLACK AESTHETIC

The 1960s was a decade of upheavals not seen since the Civil War and Reconstruction. Each advance in civil rights encountered white resistance; school desegregation was met with mobs and police dogs, and the voter's rights drive was met with violence and murder. Frustration lead to riots in city after city, summer after summer, leaving chaos and destruction. The assassination of Martin Luther King, Jr. on 4 April 1968 further fueled the disillusionment and rage of frustrated blacks. Faith in nonviolent protest gave way to the militant Black Power movement, and artistic expressions of patient hopefulness gave way to angry diatribes and rejections of European influence. Afrocentrism was ascendant as many African Americans adopted African garb, customs, and holidays, and discarded "slave names" for African names. A profound change in black class structure and attitudes occurred as a result of the civil rights movement. In Washington, Detroit, and other cities with many working-class blacks, resentment became intense against the upper-class African Americans, who were viewed as "Uncle Toms" currying favor from whites and indifferent to the plight of the poor. Well-kept black neighborhoods, where different classes had lived together, were destroyed and the inner cities were left to the poor as whites and affluent blacks fled to the suburbs. Class distinctions were now between church-going, strictly disciplined, hardworking families and those who were too disadvantaged or overworked to attend church or to care, often drifting into crime.

Despite the male-centered Black Power movement, black women continued to build on the strength of civil rights activists Rosa Parks, Septima Clark, Ella Baker, Fannie Lou Hamer, and countless others. They gained a voice of their own and national and international recognition, whether as black feminists—Barbara Smith, Gloria Hull, Barbara Christian, Toni Cade Bambara, and many others—or as authors of unprecedented virtuosity and vitality—Maya Angelou, Audre Lorde, Alice Walker, and Toni Morrison—or as musicians—the great opera singers Leontyne Price, Reri Grist, and Jessye Norman, and the all-women folk ensemble Sweet Honey in the Rock.

The much-needed antidote to European-dominated African-American culture unfortunately also turned into a new conformism to "politically correct" criteria. In art this took the form of devaluing abstract, complex, nonpolitical work in favor of realism and propaganda. In music, it took the form of devaluing concert music in favor of a jazz that negated its European components and emphasized African timbral and rhythmic characteristics. "Black music," whether in the black community or in the popular media, was equated only with blues, jazz, gospel, rock, and rap idioms. African-American classical or concert music was considered to be elitist or bourgeois by many blacks as well as whites, who forgot that "for a Black person, becoming a trained musician—one who could read and write music—has always been an anti-establishment act."[69]

But the momentum of black classical music was not checked, and it, too, was energized by the revolutionary spirit of the times. A number of black opera companies, including Mary Cardwell Dawson's National Negro Opera Company Guild, which operated in several cities, had been established in the 1940s, providing experience for the great singers, mostly female, who were admitted to major opera companies in the 1950s and 1960s. In the 1970s two new black opera companies, Opera/South in New Orleans and Opera Ebony in Philadelphia, were founded by, among others, Sister Elise of Xavier University in New Orleans and composer/conductor Margaret Harris. Harris (1943–2000) had been a child prodigy, performing a Mozart concerto with the Chicago Symphony Orchestra at age ten. She branched out into conducting in 1971, directing sixteen major orchestras as well as several Broadway musicals, including *Hair*. Her compositions include songs, piano pieces, and two concertos for piano and orchestra.

Classical composers in the civil rights era expressed a new affirmation of blackness, producing a harvest of works of top quality, skill, and sophistication: Margaret Bonds' *Three Dream Portraits* (1959), Ulysses Kay's *A Covenant for Our Time* (1969), Thomas Kerr's *Easter Monday Swagger* (1970), Dorothy Rudd Moore's *From the Dark Tower* (1970), Frederick Tillis's *Ring Shout Concerto* for percussion and brass (1973), Hale Smith's *Ritual and Incantations* (1974), and many more. The assassination of Martin Luther King, Jr., inspired many memorial works: David Baker's *Martyrs: Malcolm, Medgar, Martin*, Olly Wilson's *In Memoriam Martin Luther King Jr.*, Frederick Tillis's *Freedom: Memorial to Dr. Martin Luther King*, Carman Moore's *Drum Major*, Lena McLin's *Free at Last*, Evelyn Pittman's *Freedom Child*, and Undine Smith Moore's *Scenes from the Life of a Martyr*.

A number of institutions were formed for the advancement of black classical music. The Harlem School of the Arts was founded in 1965 by the celebrated concert singer Dorothy Maynor, and is still in operation. In 1968 the Black Music Center was opened at Virginia State College (later Virginia State University) by Undine Smith Moore and Altona Trent Johns (see chapter 2), and the Society of Black Composers was established in New York by young black composers including one woman, Dorothy Rudd Moore (see chapter 6).[70] The same year, the Afro-American Music Opportunities Association was founded by Edward C. Thomas in Minneapolis; it lasted until 1977. It published a newsletter, sponsored lecture-concert series, operated a job placement service, and produced an anthology series of 24 works by black composers (all male) in collaboration with Columbia Records between 1974 and 1978. The Black Composer Symposia project presented week-long conventions in Baltimore, Houston, Minneapolis, Detroit, and other cities during the 1970s.

The poor representation of women composers in some of these activities did not go unnoticed. In her essay for the book . . . *But Some of Us Are Brave*, Ora

Williams wrote, "During the 1960s, Black female composers have been further obscured as a trend developed to highlight a small group of Black male composers."[71] Attention to black women composers (as individuals and as a group) in the larger scholarly community began in the 1970s with the research of Ora Williams, Mildred Denby Green, Rae Linda Brown, and Barbara Garvey Jackson. By August 1985 women composers were well represented at the weeklong Black American Music Symposium at the University of Michigan, and since 1988 the Smithsonian Institution concerts of music by black composers have included women. The American Women Composers chapter in Chicago held a "Celebration of African-American Women Composers" in February 1987 at which works by Margaret Bonds, Betty Jackson King, Lena Johnson McLin, Undine Smith Moore, Dorothy Rudd Moore, and Florence Price (*Symphony in E Minor*) were performed.

MUSIC OF THE POST-CIVIL RIGHTS ERA

In the 1960s and 1970s new techniques appeared in the post-avant-garde mainstream, involving chance and improvisation, computer generation, and the new musical aesthetics of multimedia and minimalism. Many modernist composers were now considered to be conservative. In the music of black women composers it is not uncommon to hear European classical or even sixteenth-century techniques combined with serialism, atonality, Asian or Afro-American idioms, electronic music, and multimedia. Styles vary from the sensitive, cerebral, 12-tone constructions of Joyce Solomon (b. 1946) to the sophisticated blend of Hispanic, Afro-Cuban, and American elements in the music of Tania León (b. 1943) and the Balinese gamelan influences in the works of Gertrude Rivers Robinson (1927–95). Dorothy Rudd Moore (b. 1940), whose powerful dissonant statements of black pride stand apart from current trends, occupies an important place in the last half of the century (see chapter 6). Several others with widely different techniques and styles emerged in the decades following the civil rights era, among them Zenobia Perry, Rachel Eubanks, Ruth Norman, Jeraldine Herbison, Dolores White, Valerie Capers (see chapter 7), and Mary Watkins (see chapter 8), whose large orchestral works fuse jazz and classical idioms with skill, authority, and emotional impact.

Zenobia Powell Perry was born in 1914 in the all-black town of Boley, Oklahoma. Although she had been writing music since the 1950s, her composing career entered a more active phase in the 1980s after her retirement from teaching. She grew up at a time when some of the great black concert artists of the nineteenth century could still be heard on stage. When she was 13 years old, she heard the celebrated Blind John Boone (1864–1927) perform, and was taken to meet him after the concert. She recalled that he flawlessly repeated a piece she had just played for him. Perry was a student of Robert Nathaniel Dett at Tuskegee Institute, from which she graduated in 1938. She earned two master's degrees, one from the University of Northern Colorado and another from the

University of Wyoming, where she studied composition with Darius Milhaud. She taught at Arkansas Agricultural, Mechanical, and Normal College from 1946 to 1955, and at Central State University in Wilberforce, Ohio, from 1955 until her retirement in 1982. She has written an opera, *Tawawa House* (1987), a Mass, works for band and orchestra, and numerous songs and instrumental pieces. Her *Ships That Pass in the Night,* for winds, percussion, and narrator, premiered at West Virginia University in 1989, and her *Four Mynyms for Three Players* was performed at the Smithsonian Institution in 1988. The latter piece, a set of four miniature movements for flute, oboe, and piano, suggests medieval minstrels and illustrates her linear, contrapuntal, mildly dissonant, and whimsical style.

Rachel Eubanks wrote a good deal of choral music in the 1950s, but turned in the late 1970s and 1980s to larger forms and to the use of Far Eastern musical materials. She grew up in Oakland, California, and attended the University of California at Berkeley. She was a Mosenthal Fellow at Columbia University in 1946 and received a composition award from the National Association of Negro Musicians in 1948. In 1951 she founded (and still directs) the Eubanks Conservatory of Music and Arts in Los Angeles. She was inspired to write works based on Chinese, Korean, and Indonesian materials by the ethnomusicology courses at her school, which is affiliated with the Korean Philharmonic Orchestra and the Korean Opera Company. In the summer of 1977, she studied with Nadia Boulanger at the American Conservatory at Fontainebleau, France, and in 1980 she received her D.M.A. from Pacific Western University in California. Like Gertrude Robinson, Eubanks employs Indonesian traditions in her music: gamelan-style stratification, pentatonic scales, and a chanting vocal style. Indonesian instruments are combined with Western instruments and baritone voice in *Our God* (1984), based on a text by Khalil Gibran. Her 45-minute *Symphonic Requiem* (1980) makes use of Asian and African as well as European instruments and materials.

Jeraldine Saunders Herbison was born in 1941 in Richmond, Virginia. Like Zenobia Perry and Eubanks, she wrote music early in her career, but was particularly productive in the 1980s and 1990s. In 1963 she graduated from Virginia State University, where she studied composition with Undine Smith Moore, and she continued postgraduate work at several schools, including Hampton University, the University of Alaska, and the University of Michigan at Interlochen. She taught and directed ensembles in secondary schools in Maryland, North Carolina, and Virginia until her retirement in 1998. A violinist as well as a composer and teacher, she has performed with numerous orchestras and ensembles. Her works have been performed at the Kennedy Center in Washington and are frequently heard on radio programs and at college recitals. They include music for orchestra as well as chamber and vocal music, written in a basically tonal style freely combined with nontraditional harmonies and characterized by contrapuntal texture. Her *Trio No. 3 for Violin, Cello, and Piano,* Op. 22, No.

2 (1986) illustrates her command of complex forms through cyclic recall of spiritual melodies and other motives.

Ruth Norman, born in Chicago in 1927, grew up in Omaha, Nebraska. She received her bachelor's degree from the University of Nebraska and her master's degree in music from the Eastman School of Music. She was concert pianist for the U.S. State Department, and performed at the Kennedy Center and the Corcoran Museum, among other places, and has presented lecture-recitals on black composers at many schools, including Yale University, Tufts University, and Virginia State University. She received grants from the National Endowment for the Arts to make recordings of music by black composers (see discography). Her works include a large number of compositions for piano, a symphony, and choral, vocal, and instrumental chamber works, notably the *Prayer of St. Francis*, for mixed chorus, and *Golden Precepts*, for chamber ensemble and soprano. *Force Centres* is an example of her somewhat esoteric solo piano style: it has no key or time signature, and opens with a rising glissando on the inside-piano strings, which she instructs to be held by pedal while counting to 51. Its harmonies are based on fourths, minor sevenths, and tritones, and its indications refer to spiritual attunements and chakras.

Dolores White was born in Chicago. She attended Howard University and completed her bachelor's degree at the Oberlin Conservatory of Music. She earned her master's degree at the Cleveland Institute of Music and did postgraduate work at Ohio State University. She was a full-time faculty member at Cuyahoga Community College for over twenty years and is now an adjunct professor at Wooster College. She has traveled extensively in Africa, South America, Europe and the Caribbean. In the summer of 1999 she participated in an intensive music and dance program in Cuba that resulted in, among other things, her *Ritmo for Claves* for two pianos and drums. She is a member of the Cleveland Composers Guild, members of which present their works in concert and on the radio program *Not the Dead White Men Composers' Hour*. Her works include many songs, piano compositions, choral works, and instrumental arrangements of Negro spirituals. In *Crystal Gazing*, for orchestra (1994), outer sections by bells, harp, and solo violin in a high register frame a dissonant, intense middle section by full orchestra. The three sections correspond to the composer's program in which "three coloristic ideas are orchestrated: crystal-lium, solidification, and psychic state."[72]

Public and scholarly interest in black women composers increased in the 1990s. The third edition (1997) of Eileen Southern's *The Music of Black Americans* expanded its coverage of women composers, adding small separate sections on women in jazz and women in church music. In 1999 the two-volume *International Dictionary of Black Composers* listed 23 females among its 185 composers. In 1997 and 1999 Hampton University hosted the first and second Symposia of Black Women Composers, three-day sessions of concerts, lectures, and panels, at which the music of deceased composers was performed and discussed, and the music of living composers was introduced, often by the composers themselves: Valerie Capers, Jeraldine Herbison, Jacqueline Butler Hairston (b. 1938), Eurydice Osterman (b. 1950), Lettie Beckon Alston (b. 1953), Diane White (b. 1964), and many others.

Lettie Alston's music reflects her performing expertise on clarinet, guitar, organ, piano, xylophone, and electronic keyboard. Born in Detroit and trained at Bayley Temple School of Music and Wayne State University, she completed her doctorate in composition at the University of Michigan, where her composition teachers included Leslie Bassett and William Bolcom, and George Wilson in electronic music. She taught music in the Detroit public schools and at Wayne State University and Eastern Michigan University, and is on the faculty at Oakland University in Michigan. She directs two professional artists series in the Detroit area, Lettie Alston and Friends. Alston is among the few black women to embrace the composition of electronic music, with *Mandate* (1982); *Diverse Imagery*, for dancer and synthesizers (1995); *Spiritual Awakening* (1997); and *End Times* (1998). Her compositions also include orchestral, vocal, and chamber works, and encompass a variety of styles. Many of her works are atonal without employing serial techniques. One of these is her trio for violin, piano, and cello, titled *Memories* (1981), which uses a variety of contemporary string and piano techniques. Written in memory of her first piano teacher, the three movements "recall" and transform themes.

Diane White, a native of Washington, D.C., grew up surrounded by the music of the church where her father was pastor. She graduated in 1986 from Washington University in St. Louis, with an emphasis in composition, voice, and piano, and continued piano studies at the Ecole Normale de Musique in Paris on a Rotary scholarship. She performed as a solo gospel artist while in Europe and has directed numerous university and church choirs across the United States. She received her master's degree from the University of California at Santa Barbara, then served as artist-in-residence and assistant director of African-American student development at Appalachian State University in North Carolina before returning to Santa Barbara to complete her doctorate in 1998. Her compositions include works for solo voice, chorus, chamber ensembles, solo piano, and electronic tape, and range in style from gospel to avant-garde in a language that incorporates atonality, serialism, set theory, and both extended and traditional tonality. Her *Improvisatory Sketches of an Afro-American Spiritual* for solo piano, based on "Lord, I Know I Been Changed," encompasses a striking array of keyboard styles including gospel passages left open for improvisation, and inside-piano techniques.

Among the generation just starting to be heard in the 1990s, Nkeiru Okoye, born in New York in 1972 to a Nigerian father and an American mother, merits attention. She won her first award for composing at the age of 13, while a student in the Preparatory Division of the Manhattan School of Music. A recipient of a 1995 ASCAP grant for young composers, she has also received recognition from the NAACP, the Long Island Composers Alliance, and the New York State Martin Luther King Jr. Commission. She did her undergraduate work in piano

at Oberlin and completed her doctorate at Rutgers University, studying composition with Noel DaCosta. She was appointed to the faculty of Norfolk State
University in 2000. Her works include a song cycle, *The Heart of a Woman*; a
ballet, *Ruth*; and an orchestral piece, *The Creation*, which was performed by the
Richmond Symphony in March 2000 and later televised on the PBS program
Another View. Her cycle of eight songs, *Canciones Españolas (Spanish Songs
for Tenor and String Quartet)*, displays a sure, sophisticated technique, mildly
dissonant harmonic language, and wry humor.

This survey of African-American women composers has touched on just a
few significant factors in their evolution. I hope that it has conveyed some idea
of the complexity of black American history, the intricate counterpoint of seemingly unrelated events, and the wealth of information and details only hinted at
here. All have been important to the development of African-American women
composers, from the establishment of the first colonial urban centers in the
1600s, to the development of black social systems and divisions into Creole and
African cultural groups in the 1700s; the growth of independent social, educational, and cultural institutions in the 1800s; the racial uplift movement and the
important place of women in it; the turn toward practical, economic self-help
efforts in the early 1900s, together with the struggle for justice, equality, integration, and acceptance in the larger mainstream culture; and the renewal of
pride in African heritage and its integration with the European-American heritage in art, literature, and music. Since 1900, these composers have traveled an
immense distance, historically, politically, socially, psychologically, and musically. They have passed through a host of musical trends and "isms": traditional
classicism, nationalism, racialism, modernism, serialism, neoclassicism, chance
music, minimalism, electronic sound production, and multidisciplinary composition. They have incorporated African-American idioms to varying degrees,
from nonexistent to prominent. In the chapters that follow, the biographies and
music of eight composers from different times, places, and backgrounds will
provide a series of in-depth "soundings" of this broad overview.

NOTES

   1. James Monroe Trotter, *Music and Some Highly Musical People* (Boston: Author,
1878. Reprinted New York: Johnson Publishing, 1968), pp. 346–347. Trotter (1842–92)
was an amateur musician and a member of Boston's black elite, one of the first Negro
officers in the Boston post office and later a recorder of deeds for the District of Columbia. His book was the first to attempt a survey of a body of music in the United States.
It was followed in 1883 by white author Frederick Louis Ritter's *Music in America*.
   2. The Schomburg Library of Nineteenth-Century Black Women Writers, edited by
Henry Louis Gates, Jr. and published by Oxford University Press in the 1980s, runs to
30 volumes.

3. See Ann Allen Shockley, *Afro-American Women Writers 1746–1933* (New York: New American Library, 1988), p. 3.

4. The "cities" were very small. By 1700 Boston had only 12,000 people, of whom 2,000 were black; New York had 7,000, with 1,600 blacks; Philadelphia's population was 10,000; and Charles Town's was 3,500. See Eileen Southern, *The Music of Black Americans* (MBA), 3rd ed. (New York: W. W. Norton, 1997), p. 24.

5. See Ira Berlin, "Time, Space, and the Evolution of Afro-American Society on British Mainland North America." *American Historical Review* 85, no. 1 (February 1980): 44–78.

6. The term "Creole" has caused some confusion. It originally referred to a person of European descent born in the Americas, but also came to mean a person of mixed African and European descent. It is used here in the latter sense, as synonymous with "Creoles of color."

7. The African tradition of female oral historians was preserved in the New World by slave storytellers. Most of them remain anonymous, but a few names survive: Senegambia, of Narragansett, R.I.; Tituba, of Salem witch trial notoriety; and especially Lucy Bijah Terry (1730–1821), an African-born slave purchased by Ebenezer Wells of Deerfield, Mass. She married Abijah Prince, a former slave and large landowner in Sunderland, Vt., who bought her freedom. Her home was a gathering place where blacks came to hear her stories. Her ballad "Bar's Fight," about an Indian massacre in Deerfield in 1746, was preserved by oral historians and published in 1855.

8. Phillis Wheatley (1753?–1784) was sold at age seven to the family of John Wheatley in Boston. She was tutored by their daughter Mary, quickly learned to read and write English, and studied astronomy, geography, history, the Bible, and the Latin classics by Virgil and Ovid. By age fourteen she was writing poetry, and a collection of her poems was published in England in 1773, making her the first African American to publish a volume of poetry.

9. Another student of Law's, identified only as "Frank the Negro," taught music in New York, and a few years later the black musician John Cromwell operated a singing school in Philadelphia.

10. Liberia was an American colony in Africa founded in 1822 for the purpose of resettling ex-slaves. It became a Republic in 1847. The idea of returning blacks to Africa had the support of both white leaders (Thomas Jefferson, Abraham Lincoln, etc.) and some blacks; the last and biggest supporter was Marcus Garvey, born in Jamaica, who established the Black Star Steamship Line around 1918.

11. Southern, MBA, p. 26.

12. Southern, MBA, p. 27; Arthur La Brew, *Black Musicians in the Colonial Period: Preliminary Index* (Detroit: Author, 1977), p. 65.

13. Southern, MBA, p. 40. Two centuries later, long-meter hymns in the black church were referred to as "Dr. Watts."

14. Thomas Jefferson himself owned slaves, some of whom he fathered through his liaison with his slave Sally Hemings.

15. Jefferson considered "a woman who brings a child every two years as more profitable than the best man on the farm [for] what she produces is an addition to capital" (quoted in Berlin, p. 74).

16. John Hope Franklin and Alfred Moss Jr., *From Slavery to Freedom*, 7th ed. (New York: Alfred A. Knopf, 1994), p. 157.

17. Quoted in Southern, MBA, p. 79.

18. Frederika Bremer, *The Homes of the New World* (New York: n.p., 1853) quoted in Southern, MBA, p. 84.

19. John Fanning Watson, *Methodist Error*, quoted in Southern, MBA pp. 88–89.

20. Women participated prominently in this religious dance. A shout performed by two Georgia Sea Island women is described in Irene V. Jackson, "Black Women and Music: A Survey from Africa to the New World," *Minority Voices* 2, no. 2 (Fall 1978): 24: "Edith gives a stylized angular performance as though copying the poses of the figures in Egyptian decorations . . . Gertrude makes a pause with head and shoulders bowed slightly forward, arms held close to her body, elbows bent in a supplicating gesture."

21. Born of free Negro parents in Charleston, Payne operated a school there for Negroes (opened in 1829) until it was closed in 1834, when South Carolina prohibited education of all blacks. He went north, studied for the ministry, and had a long, distinguished career as minister, church historian, bishop, and president of Wilberforce University.

22. Daniel Alexander Payne, *Recollections of Seventy Years* (Nashville: Author, 1888) excerpted in Eileen Southern, ed., *Readings in Black American Music* (RBAM) (New York: W. W. Norton, 1983), p. 65.

23. St. Thomas Episcopal Church in Philadelphia was the first black church to install an organ (1828). The first organist there was Ann Appo (1808–28).

24. Payne, in Southern, RBAM, p. 69.

25. An African-derived dance called "juba" was widespread in the United States; it involved various combinations of foot tapping, hand clapping, and thigh slapping in precise and lively rhythm. Composer Nathaniel Dett included *Juba Dance* in his piano suite *In the Bottoms* (1913), and Florence Price used the genre several times.

26. Other famous singers were the sisters Anna and Emma Louise Madah Hyers (ca. 1850s), Nellie Brown Mitchell (1845–1924), and Marie Selika Williams (ca. 1849–1937). After the Civil War the talented Sissieretta Jones (1869–1933), known as the "Black Patti" (after the famous Spanish opera singer Adelina Patti), had a long career bridging the shift from concert performance to minstrel and vaudeville shows after the vogue for black prima donnas passed in the 1890s. From 1896 to 1915 she was the lead singer in Black Patti's Troubadors, a touring vaudeville company.

27. Martin R. Delaney, *The Condition, Elevation, Emigration, and Destiny of the Colored People in the United States* (Philadelphia, 1852; rep. New York: Arno Press, 1968), p. 42.

28. Mary Jane Patterson graduated from Oberlin's classical course in 1862, followed by the educator Frances Jackson Coppin in 1865.

29. Notable black women sculptors have included Meta Warrick Fuller (1877–1968), May Howard Jackson (1877–1931), Nancy Elizabeth Prophet (b. 1887), and Augusta Savage (1892–1962).

30. A version of the tune of *John Brown's Body* is also known as *The Battle Hymn of the Republic*, with words by Julia Ward Howe.

31. Dena J. Epstein, "Black Spirituals: Their Emergence into Public Knowledge," *Black Music Research Journal* 10, no. 1 (Spring 1990): 62.

32. Trotter, p. 327.

33. See Reginald Tyrone Buckner, "A History of Music Education in the Black Community of Kansas City, Kansas, 1905–1954" (Ph.D. diss., University of Minnesota, 1974), p. 53.

34. Several of these prize-winning compositions survive at the Library of Congress: *Farewell, Alma Mater* (1906), for piano, by Mable Harding; Kinney's *Mother's Sacrifice*; and *Nocturne* by Clyde O. Andrews

35. See note 1.

36. W.E.B. Du Bois, *The Souls of Black Folk* (1903; repr. New York: Gramercy Books, 1994), p. 5.

37. Advertisement, 23 November 1922, reproduced in Franklin and Moss, p. 357.

38. For example, the lynching in Little Rock that drove Florence Price's family to Chicago and threats against Margaret Bonds' father (see chapter 4).

39. Darlene Clark Hine, "Rape and the Inner Lives of Black Women in the Middle West," *Signs: A Journal of Women in Culture and Society* 14, no. 4 (Summer 1989): 917; Willard B. Gatewood, *Aristocrats of Color* (Bloomington: Indiana University Press, 1990), p. 240. The National Association of Colored Women brought together more than 100 black women's clubs. Its president, Mary Church Terrell, was a graduate of Oberlin, a Washington socialite, and an early member of the NAACP. This confrontation paralleled the rejection of their black sisters by the white women's suffrage groups, despite the early support from Frederick Douglass and Sojourner Truth, and the later suffrage activities by Mary Ann Cary, Frances Watkins Harper, and other black women.

40. Mrs. John E. Mulholland, "Talks About Women," *Crisis* 1 (1910): 1.

41. Of the women in these books, 40 percent were teachers, 12 percent writers, 7 percent elocutionists or speakers, 5 percent missionaries, 5 percent businesswomen, and 3 percent doctors (women often engaged in more than one profession, but these were the first listed).

42. Mrs. N. F. Mossell, *The Work of the Afro-American Woman* (1894; repr. Freeport, N.Y.: Books for Libraries Press, 1971), p. 27.

43. Ida M. Yeocum, one of the women listed by Mossell and the composer of *The Song of the Women* (see frontispiece), was "refused admission to the Philadelphia Musical Academy in 1890 on account of her color," and filed suit against the institution (*Detroit Plain Dealer*, 17 January 1890).

44. Bishop Daniel Payne heard Tilghman sing "Departed Days" at a memorial meeting and commented, "That child's parents had better spend a hundred dollars on her voice now than leave her a fortune when they die" (Lawson Scruggs, *Women of Distinction* [Raleigh, N.C.: Author, 1893], p. 212).

45. Monroe A. Majors, *Noted Negro Women: Their Triumphs and Activities* (Chicago: Author, 1893), p. 242.

46. One of Benjamin's marches is in the Library of Congress; none of Delos Mars' musical dramas survive. See Josephine J. Wright, "Black Women in Classical Music in Boston During the Late Nineteenth Century," in *New Perspectives in Music: Essays in Honor of Eileen Southern*, edited by Samuel A. Floyd, Jr. and Josephine Wright (Detroit: Harmonie Press, 1992).

47. Names of several of these composers appear in a file of Afro-American composers compiled by Walter Whittlesey, former head of the Library of Congress Music Division. From it Wayne Shirley, music specialist at the Library of Congress, has culled a list of over two dozen women composers whose works were published before 1920. Many of the works, though not all, are in the Library of Congress holdings or copyright files. The earliest are songs: *Forgive*, by Louise Smith ("sung with great success by Louis L. Brown of the Callender's Minstrels"), published in Washington in 1885, followed in 1886 by *Old Blandford Church*, by Lucinda Bragg ("dedicated to Hon. John Mercer Langston,

ex-minister to Hayti"), and *You Know*, by Mrs. Sam Lucas (Carrie Melvin Lucas, wife of the famous performer) in 1887.

48. She was listed in the 1900 U.S. census records as Stella D. Ricketts, born in 1871 in Darby, Pa., where her father operated a boarding stable. She was the only person in her family who could read and write.

49. In 1975 *Treemonisha* was performed by the Houston Grand Opera, recorded, and videotaped.

50. Casper Holstein was a black New York businessman who donated funds especially for Negro composers who competed in contests set up by *Opportunity* magazine (1925). Stimulated by the Harlem Renaissance, other competitions for Negro composers were established in the 1920s by Rodman Wanamaker and the Harmon Foundation.

51. More recent performances of Price's symphonies have been given by the Van Nir Community Orchestra in Chicago (1987), the North Arkansas Symphony Orchestra (1986), the Bay Area Women's Philharmonic Orchestra (1990s), the Atlanta Symphony Orchestra (1996), and at the William Grant Still Festival in 1998. See the appendix for locations of her scores and sources of more information.

52. Quoted in Barbara Garvey Jackson, "Florence Price, Composer," *Black Perspective in Music* 5, no. 1 (Spring 1977): 38.

53. *Music and Poetry* published a column by Helen Hagan, as well as articles by Kemper Harreld, Clarence Cameron White, and Maude Cuney-Hare. It also printed music by black composers, including two pieces by Holt. These two pieces thus survived the disappearance of Holt's other compositions, which were stolen along with her stored possessions in the 1930s, while she was abroad.

54. E. Franklin Frazier, "Chicago: A Cross-section of Negro Life," *Opportunity* vii (March 1929): 70–73.

55. The upper classes of Southern cities (Charleston, Atlanta, New Orleans, and many smaller cities) were the oldest and the most obsessed with class, lineage, and skin color, because many of them were descendants of white slave owners or enterprising antebellum free blacks. The cities of the Midwest had smaller black populations and fewer black colleges, but they, too, had their separate black worlds. Detroit was avoided by migrants because the city had a reputation for negrophobia and its early Negro population was small. Cleveland, on the other hand, had a reputation for egalitarianism and opportunity. It had an old black elite, and its black inhabitants were considered industrious and intelligent. The newer cities of the West—Denver, Los Angeles, San Francisco, and Seattle—were much smaller: in 1900 their combined black population was 7,191. California's black "pioneer" families (comparable in status to Eastern colored aristocracy, but with less emphasis on skin color and origins) were spread out rather than concentrated in black neighborhoods, and their lives were less segregated. In San Francisco, many blacks in the late 1800s were prosperous and educated; they established schools, newspapers, and cultural organizations, and campaigned for civil rights. Oakland's black influx began when San Franciscans fled there after the earthquake of 1906. Denver was settled as early as 1861, and the black women's club movement was active there well before 1900. In Colorado at the turn of the twentieth century there was more equal opportunity in education, housing, and employment than in many other states. More than half the cowboys in the West were black.

56. This concern for privacy is related to the "culture of dissemblance" which black women of all classes developed for self-protection. The masks of cheerful acceptance or genteel hauteur concealed the realities of hurt, humiliation, or anger (see Hine, note 39).

57. Public Broadcasting Service program *Duke Ellington's Washington*, 20 February 2000.

58. William Henry Hackney, who produced three "Annual All-Colored Composers" concerts at Orchestra Hall in Chicago (1914–16) at his own expense, drew this surprised comment by the white critic of the *Record Herald*: "The most interesting—certainly the most meritorious—feature of Mr. Hackney's connection with the music making is the fact that he is by profession—we trust that this is the right word—a waiter" (Felix Borowsky, "Colored Composers' Concert," *Record Herald*, 4 June 1914). Nora Holt and Helen Hagan were among the composers.

59. She urged them to be proud of their black skin (she herself was very light), their Negro hair, their beautiful eyes, strong, attractive teeth, and fine voices. She was also an occasional songwriter; one of her published songs, *Carola*, is in the Emma Azalia Hackley Collection at the Detroit Public Library, which also houses scores by Margaret Bonds, Florence Price, and other black composers.

60. The influence of ragtime and jazz on European music began as early as 1905 with Claude Debussy's *Golliwog's Cakewalk*, and can be heard in music by some of the composers who were challenging the foundations of Western music: Maurice Ravel, Igor Stravinsky, Paul Hindemith, and Ernst Křenek, as well as the American composers Aaron Copland and Ferde Grofé. When Still was playing oboe for the Broadway show *Shuffle Along*, George Gershwin liked to linger backstage and listen to the musicians improvise; one of Still's "licks" found its way into Gershwin's *I Got Rhythm*. Gershwin (whose works were composed in the 1920s and 1930s) was not the first white American composer to use jazz: John Alden Carpenter's *Concertino* for piano and orchestra was composed in 1916.

61. Published in *The Nation*, 23 June 1926.

62. *Caledonia*, by Sippie Wallace, deals with a hardheaded woman who did not heed her mother's advice. Along with Wallace, Edith Wilson and Helen Humes were other blues singers who crossed class lines from their well-educated families.

63. Black all-female bands were not new. They had their predecessors in groups such as the Julia Nickerson Ladies' Orchestra in New Orleans (ca. 1900), N. Clark Smith's eight-member Ladies Orchestra in Chicago (1905), and several others.

64. See the appendix for locations of scores and sources of information on Mary Lou Williams and the other composers described here.

65. Black women had been writing and publishing hymns since before the turn of the twentieth century: Elizabeth Marshall Smothers' hymnbook *The Heavenly Echoes*, published in Texas in 1900, included hymns by several women. A black woman composer even appeared in the Seventh Day Adventist hymnal (Eleanor Wright, Ohio, d. 1993).

66. These exclusions were relaxed after a march on Washington was threatened in June 1941.

67. Nadia Boulanger (1887–1979) was one of the most influential teachers of the twentieth century; among her many American students were Aaron Copland, Roy Harris, David Diamond, and Elliot Carter, as well as Julia Perry, Irene Britton Smith, Dorothy Rudd Moore, and at least three other black women composers (see Conclusion, note 4).

68. An indication of the high regard in which Schuyler was held was the national news coverage on radio and television at her death; the condolences of President and Mrs. Johnson and New York Mayor John Lindsay; the funeral cortège to St. Patrick's Cathedral, where 2,000 mourners attended the requiem Mass celebrated by Cardinal Spellman; and a memorial concert at Town Hall for which her *Nile Fantasy* was adapted

by Margaret Bonds. Schuyler's books include *Adventures in Black and White* (1960), *Jungle Saints, Africa's Heroic Catholic Missionaries* (1963), *Who Killed the Congo?* (1962), and *Good Men Die* (1969). The Philippa Duke Schuyler Middle School for gifted children is located in Brooklyn.

69. Ora Williams, with Thelma Williams, Dora Wilson, and Ramona Matthewson, "American Black Women Composers: A Selected Annotated Bibliography," in *All the Women Are White, All the Blacks Are Men, but Some of Us Are Brave*, edited by Gloria T. Hull, Patricia Bell Scott, and Barbara Smith (Old Westbury, N.Y.: Feminist Press, 1982), p. 298.

70. The society's confrontation with the tenets of the Black Arts movement is revealed in its May 1969 *Newsletter*: "The questions of a year ago—most often concerning which specific musical sounds and materials would be necessary to make black music—are no longer necessary. We know that because we are black, we are making black music" (Southern, MBA, p. 555).

71. Williams et al., p. 298.

72. Liner notes to CD *Cleveland Plays Music by African Americans* (see discography).

Undine Smith Moore. Courtesy of Mary Moore Easter.

2

UNDINE SMITH MOORE
(1904–89)

CHRONOLOGY

1904	Born 25 August in Jarratt, Va., to James William Smith and Hardie (Hattie) Turnbull Smith; youngest of three siblings.
1908	Family moved to Petersburg, Va.
Ca. 1911	Began piano lessons at age of seven; studied with Lillian Allen Darden.
1924	Received first Juilliard scholarship awarded for study at Fisk.
1925	Composed cantata *Sir Olaf and the Erl King's Daughter.*
1926	Graduated cum laude from Fisk; accepted position as supervisor of music in Goldsboro, N.C., public schools; composed songs *Uphill* and *Heart Have You Heard the News?*
1927	Began teaching at Virginia State College (name changed to Virginia State University in 1979).
1929–31	Commuted to New York to work on M.A. degree and professional diploma at Columbia University's Teachers College.
1930	Composed piano works *Valse Caprice, Scherzo for Piano.*
1932	Composed choral setting of spiritual *The Blind Man Stood on the Way and Cried.*
1935	Composed setting for men's voices of spiritual *No Condemnation.*
1938	Married Dr. James Arthur Moore.
1941	On 4 January gave birth to daughter, Mary Hardie.

1948	Composed choral setting of spiritual *I'm Going Home.*
1949	Composed choral setting of spiritual *Is There Anybody Here That Loves My Jesus?*
1950	Composed choral settings of spirituals *Fare You Well* and *I Just Came from the Fountain,* and choral work *Into My Heart's Treasury.*
1951	Composed solo voice setting of spiritual *Set Down.*
1952	Composed choral works *Daniel, Daniel, Servant of the Lord* and *Thou Hast Made Us for Thyself,* and piano works *Romantic Young Clown, Fugue in F Major,* two-piano *Romance,* and *Reflections for Organ and Piano.*
1953	Resumed composition study with Howard Murphy; composed *Before I'd Be a Slave* for piano, *Introduction and Allegro* for clarinet and piano, and choral works *Teach Me to Hear Mermaids Singing* and *Who Shall Separate Us from the Love of God?*
1955	Composed first setting of Langston Hughes' poems: choral *Mother to Son.*
1958	Composed choral spiritual settings and original choral works *I Would Be True, When Susanna Jones Wears Red, Striving After God, Sinner You Can't Walk My Path, The Lamb,* and *Hail Warrior,* and expanded *Introduction and Allegro* (1953) to *Three Pieces for Flute and Piano.*
1960	Composed choral works *Bound for Canaan's Land, Long Fare You Well, Let Us Make Man in Our Image.*
1961	Composed song *Love Let the Wind Cry.*
1963	Husband, Dr. James Arthur Moore, passed away.
1966	Composed choral works *Walk Through the Streets, O Spirit Who Dost Prefer All Temples, Lord Make Us More Holy,* and *How I Got Over.*
1967	Trip to France and Italy.
1968	Composed song *Second Spring.*
1968–72	Cofounded and codirected Black Music Center at Virginia State College.
1969	Composed *Afro-American Suite* for flute, cello, and piano.
1970	Composed choral *A Christmas Alleluia, Rise Up, Shepherd, and Follow.*
1971	Trip to France and Spain; composed choral *Lord, We Give Thanks to Thee.*
1971–72	Trip to West Africa.
1972	Retired from Virginia State College; visiting professor at Carleton College, Northfield, Minn.
1972–76	Adjunct professor of music theory and humanities at Virginia Union University.

1973   Composed solo settings of spirituals *Watch and Pray* and *To Be Baptized*, and choral *Tambourines to Glory*; gala Town Hall celebration 30 September; honorary doctorate from Virginia State College; awarded Humanitarian Award in the Arts by Fisk.

1973–75   Visiting professor at College of St. Benedict, St. Joseph, Minn., and St. Johns' University, Collegeville, Minn.

1974   Composed choral works *Benediction* and *Choral Prayers in Folk Style*, and the cantata *Glory to God*.

1975   Received National Association of Negro Musicians Distinguished Achievement Award; 13 April declared Undine Smith Moore Day by Petersburg Mayor Remmis Arnold; gala concert and reception by Beaux-Twenty Club; composed choral *Alleluia*, and songs *I Am in Doubt, Lyric for True Love*, and *I Want to Die While You Love Me*; began work on oratorio *Scenes from the Life of a Martyr*.

1976   Awarded honorary doctorate by Indiana University; composed choral *A Time for Remembering* and *O Come Let Us Sing unto the Lord*, also *Organ Variations on Nettleton, Two Easter Pieces for Mrs. Gamby*, and a *String Quartet; Afro-American Suite* selected to represent state of Virginia at the Kennedy Center for the Performing Arts during Bicentennial Parade of American Music.

1976–77   Artist-in-residence at Virginia State College; music consultant for arts in education seminars of Virginia State Board of Education.

1977   Participated in Celebration of Black Composers Week at Lincoln Center, New York City, in August; named music laureate of state of Virginia.

1978   Chair, National Honorary Advisory Board of Black Music Center of Indiana University; featured at seventh annual Afro-American Music Workshop at Atlanta University; scholar-in-residence at Richmond Community High School for the Gifted; composed solo setting of spiritual *Come Down Angels and Trouble the Water* and the *Three Bahai Prayers*.

1979   Composed choral *Be Strong I Will Fill This House with Glory, Alleluia, Christ Is Risen, and For My People Everywhere*; and *Ring Game II* for orchestra; songs *A Little Memory of Southside Virginia, My True Love Hath My Heart, Let No Flower of Spring Pass by You*; and *Organ Variations on There Is a Fountain*.

1980   Received National Black Caucus Award.

1981   Received Tufts University Distinguished Achievement Award; composed *On Imagination* for chorus and *Is There Anybody Here That Loves My Jesus?* for solo voice; completed oratorio *Scenes from the Life of a Martyr*; nominated for Pulitzer Prize for *Scenes*; delivered keynote address to first National Congress on Women in Music, 27 March at New York University.

1982   Composed *Three Centennial Pieces* for choir and instruments for Virginia State University centennial celebration.

1983–87   Appointed to board of directors, Richmond Symphony Orchestra.

1984–85   Participant in Virginia Women's Cultural History Project; Undine Smith
           Moore evening at Virginia Museum of Fine Arts.

1985   Three excerpts from *Scenes* performed by Brooklyn Philharmonic at Cooper
           Union in New York City; spoke at Black Music Symposium in Ann Arbor,
           Mich.; received Virginia Governor's Award in the Arts; *Scenes* performed at
           Oakland Symphony Calvin Simmons Memorial Concert.

1986   Composed *Many Thousand Gone* for piano.

1987   Composed piano trio *Soweto*, for piano, cello, and violin.

1989   Artist-in-residence at the University of Michigan for 10 days in January; died
           6 February at age 84 from a stroke, in Petersburg, Va.

> The power of things we heard when we did not know we were hearing, of
> the things we saw when we did not know we were seeing, is remarkable,
> a source of continuing wonder. . . . Such things heard and not heard, seen
> and not seen, are lodged deeply within us. . . . And the place where they are
> lodged is also the place from which our creativity comes. About five years
> ago, in the archives of the Library of Congress, I sat listening to a recording
> of early blues and hollers. Suddenly I found myself weeping, weeping al-
> most to the point of embarrassment. The timbre of the voices of Touse and
> Theandros . . . passing the farm at night, giving their special hollers . . . had
> come back to me from some place deep within myself which I did not know
> existed.[1]

The topic of memory appears frequently in Undine Smith Moore's spoken
thoughts as well as in her music. Her memories were vivid, and she commu-
nicated them eloquently. We are fortunate to have many of Moore's words and
memories in print, in published talks, panel discussions, and interviews. As the
opening quote demonstrates, Moore understood the importance of subconscious
memories in the creative process. She also considered memories to be a source
of strength in the struggle for survival. In the program notes for her trio *Soweto*
she wrote, "I would be happy if it [*Soweto*] was able to suggest the persistence
and value of memory. All of us human beings go through some terrible things.
Some of them look almost unbearable to an outsider. But in the middle of all
this, we have memories—memories that are beautiful to us; they are not always
heavy, not always of massive importance, but they remind us that we have a
spirit."[2] For Moore, art was a form of memory. She observed that "Art preserves
life in a very special way: our memories die with us, but art preserves the values
and experiences . . . not preserved by living memory or historical fact."[3]

Moore, a renowned educator, musician, and composer, was often referred to
as the "Dean of Black Women Composers." More than one generation of musicians and music educators owe their careers to her instruction, her inspiration,
and her personal interest in their lives. Since her death, neglect, so often the

fate of deceased composers, has not been her lot.[4] Her compositions continue to be widely performed, and festivals of her music are still being organized. The journey to this eminence was a long and eventful one.

BIOGRAPHY

Undine Smith Moore was born in 1904 in rural south Virginia, in Jarratt, "a little place between Zuni and Skippers," similar small towns inhabited mostly by African Americans. Her memories give us a picture of life in Virginia not only in the early twentieth century but also in the late nineteenth century. Ways of life changed slowly in the small towns, particularly those in isolated areas.

Though I left Jarratt when I was about three, I remember now songs and sounds that I had already absorbed—the singing at the Morningstar Baptist Church and the praying. . . . I remember the weeping as we went across the fields to see cousin Johnny—cousin Johnny dead—the mirrors covered, the clocks stopped. My aunts dressed in black with long veils, but dancing in a corner, dropping deeply and rising rhythmically from the floor, Aunt Sarah with her hair always corn-rowed.[5]

Moore's parents were not formally schooled but possessed fine minds, and gave their children an appreciation of education. Her mother, Hardie Turnbull Smith, was a music lover and a reader of cultivated tastes, and she instilled in Moore a love of books. In summers, she would order books by the case and read to her children, encouraging them to read on their own. Her father, James William Smith, was one of two black brakemen employed by the Norfolk and Western Railroad. This was a well-paying job for those times, and it enabled him to support his family in relative comfort. Moore had two older siblings, a brother, Clarence, and a sister, Eunice.[6]

The Smith family moved to Petersburg, Virginia, in 1908 to provide the children with greater educational opportunities and a stimulating environment. However, the family returned in summers to visit relatives, so her memories of Jarratt remained strong. Moore recalled:

What did Petersburg have? In the first place, the lives of black people in Petersburg were saturated with music of one kind or another. Barred from the theaters and all but the gallery of the Academy of Music, children went with their elders from church to church. . . . A child could not fail to observe the unrivaled status that a leading singer at church enjoyed. Besides, there was a veritable fascination with piano study. A person walking along the street carrying a music roll . . . walked proudly. This was clearly a person of culture. . . . There was never a lack of places to perform on whatever level one was able— the Sunday school, the church, the church socials and suppers. Petersburgers, in the days of my childhood, were deeply involved in what they called the "silver tea." Dramatic pieces were spoken, delectable foods were served, but above all else, music reigned. . . . The progress of children was inquired about in the community and noted with pleasure.

The favorite question asked to test advancement of children . . . was "You playing sheet music yet?"[7]

In Petersburg, Moore grew up on Harding Street and attended Gillfield Baptist Church with her family. At age seven she tagged along to the neighbor children's piano lessons given by a local high school girl, Miss Patty Campbell, who was paid a dollar a month for eight lessons. When Moore's parents bought an upright piano for her older sister, she was already able to sit down and play a piece, "Boat Song," to her parents' delight and surprise. Soon she began lessons with Lillian Allen Darden, the wife of a prominent physician and a graduate of Fisk University. She called Darden's arrival in Petersburg a major event in the town, "a proud day in my life and in the life of the community."[8] When she was eight or nine, Moore attempted to compose a canon, and became frustrated when it wouldn't "fit" all the way to the end. In fifth grade she was taken from her classroom and brought in to accompany the high school choir at commencement. During her own years at Peabody High School, Moore benefited from thorough and dedicated teachers. She gives the most credit for the firm foundation she received while growing up in Petersburg to her close-knit and loving family, but she also acknowledges the importance of the black community. She sums up her growing years in Petersburg thus: "To live in a society where one's favorite art is highly regarded, highly valued, where one's progress is a source of pride to the family and the entire community is enough to create in a child a fine sense of self-worth and a high level of aspiration."[9]

Although she was offered a scholarship to Petersburg's Virginia Normal Institute,[10] Moore was persuaded by Mrs. Darden to attend Fisk University in Nashville, Tennessee, because of its fine music department. Her father also encouraged her to make this decision, saying, "If Fisk is the best then that's where she's going."[11] At the end of her freshman year Moore was awarded the first scholarship given by the Juilliard School for study at Fisk, which enabled her to continue her studies there.[12] On hearing the news, her father was so proud that he walked into the Walter D. Moses music store in Richmond, still in his brakeman's uniform, and asked for "the best piano money could buy," a Steinway grand.[13]

At Fisk, Moore studied piano and organ with Alice M. Grass, a graduate of Oberlin and an inspiring teacher who expected perfection. At that time Moore's main focus was the piano, and she later looked back fondly on those years when she was considered a "real pianist." A thorough grounding in theory and composition was provided by Sara Leight Laubenstein, and Moore's talent as a composer was also recognized. Dr. Mary Hillman, then head of the music department, encouraged her writing and conducted the performance of her compositions, which included a large cantata for women's voices, *St. Olaf and the Erl King's Daughter*, based on a Scandinavian poem given her by Mrs. Laubenstein.

Moore's lifelong love of choral music began while participating in performances of large choral masterpieces and unaccompanied spirituals by the Mozart Society, conducted by John Wesley Work II.[14] Concerts by visiting artists and other rich cultural experiences were part of daily life. Moore also lists comparative literature professor Lillian Emette Cashin among the important influences on her life, and she spent many hours in the library, reading English literature. She later recalled that during stressful times she survived by reading the Greek Stoics, chiefly Epictetus. Having taken advantage of all the opportunities Fisk could offer, she graduated cum laude in 1926 with a major in piano performance.

Because of her talent as a pianist, her teachers at Fisk urged Moore to enter the Juilliard Graduate School in New York after her graduation. She chose instead to take a job as supervisor of music in the public schools in Goldsboro, North Carolina, in order to be self-supporting. A year later she accepted an invitation to join the music faculty at Virginia State College and returned to Petersburg. While hired ostensibly as a piano instructor and college organist, she soon found that her duties included teaching a wide variety of subjects. During her first year she was assigned to work with the chorus at the D. Webster Davis Laboratory High School on campus. Since money for the purchase of scores was limited and the vocal resources of the chorus were uneven, she found it expedient to write and arrange music specifically to show the singers to the best advantage. Thus began her hands-on training in choral composition.

Between 1929 and 1931 Moore commuted to New York City to complete the Master of Arts degree and professional diploma in music at Columbia University's Teachers College. Her most important influence at Columbia was her theory and composition teacher, Howard Murphy, and after her graduation he became a lifelong adviser and friend. During these years the Harlem Renaissance was in full swing, and although it had not yet acquired that title, she felt its energy: "Harlem as I recall it was a delightful place to be; one was not frightened to be on the streets. It had a quality of gaiety, of spontaneity, of zest for life."[15] The spirit of the Renaissance was not confined to Harlem; Moore had already felt its vitality at Fisk, where the emphasis on the musical and literary heritage of African Americans had long been a tradition. The great Renaissance poet Langston Hughes occasionally spoke at Virginia State College, and she began an association with him through her colleague Alston Waters Burleigh (son of the composer Harry Burleigh), by whom Hughes sent her an autographed copy of *The Weary Blues*.

Undine Smith married Dr. James Arthur Moore in 1938, the year he joined the faculty at Virginia State College as chairman of the physical education department. He was a fine tenor, and often appeared with his wife in recitals. He managed the college concert series, and the many celebrated artists he brought in, including Duke Ellington, were frequent guests at the Moore home.[16] On 4 January 1941 the Moores became parents of a daughter, Mary Hardie.[17] Moore credited her husband with being secure enough to permit her a freedom denied many wives of her generation. He died in 1963.

During the decades following her graduate work at Columbia, Moore's activities were many and varied. Although home and heavy teaching duties took precedence over composition, she continued to write music to meet the demands of specific situations in her work with rural schoolchildren, with church music ministries, and with her piano and organ students. For yearly high school performances at a small rural high school, she edited the Gilbert and Sullivan operettas. Her duties included at one time or another those of chairman of the theory department, supervisor of student teaching in music, coordinator of integrated courses in music and art, acting head of the department of music, and director of the college choir. Her theory classes became particularly renowned. She had always excelled in theory, and brought this enthusiasm to her classes. She was proud of a report by the National Association of Schools of Music on her theory classes that commented on her stimulating and inspiring teaching. Professor Carl G. Harris, Jr., her colleague at Virginia State for 13 years, described her presence in class as "electrifying."[18]

D. Antoinette Handy, who occasionally substituted for Moore, recalled her strict and thorough instruction and her formidable theory workbook.[19] This unpublished work, "A Recorded Supplement to Studies in Traditional Harmony," which used examples from both mainstream European composers and black composers, was highly praised by her former teacher at Columbia, Dr. Murphy, and was used in her courses for many years.

The testimonials to Moore's teaching and the successes of former students are legion: piano student James Pettis, who graduated from Yale University Music School and received the National Association of Negro Musicians' Young Pianist Award after his New York debut in 1974; Leon Thompson, educational director of the New York Philharmonic; Jewell Taylor Thompson, theory teacher at Hunter College; operatic soprano Roberta Alexander; Camilla Williams, the first black woman to sing with a major opera company; the composer Jeraldine Herbison; Phillip Medley, popular songwriter and founder of the Starflower Publishing Company; and jazz pianist Billy Taylor, who changed his major from sociology to music when Moore astutely judged his capabilities. He later said, "Dr. Undine Smith Moore was an important role model. A sensitive, compelling performing artist, a distinguished composer, a master teacher, a generous friend, she was always an inspiration to me."[20] Her former students populate the country's universities as heads of music departments and schools of the fine arts, and many have written dissertations and theses on her music.

Moore was also involved in designing a course integrating the arts—painting, sculpture, architecture, and dance—with music. For many years she was a coordinator of all sections of this course and a team teacher. She felt strongly that the potential artist or composer should be educated as a whole person, knowledgeable and sensitive to all the arts as well as to literature, history, and philosophy.

During the 1950s Moore renewed her composition activities, producing 22 works, of which eight were eventually published. In 1952–53 she commuted to New York to study further with Howard Murphy, who was then teaching at the

Manhattan School of Music; she also attended composition workshops at the Eastman School of Music in Rochester, New York. Murphy's influence may be detected in her more adventurous instrumental works employing dissonance. The 1960s were less prolific, but resulted in some of her most celebrated and challenging works, such as *Love Let the Wind Cry* (1961) and the *Afro-American Suite* (1969). This was the decade of intense civil rights struggles and the emergence of the Black Arts movement. Moore actively responded to its urgency with preparations for the Black Music Center at Virginia State College that she cofounded and codirected with Altona Trent Johns.[21] She considered the center to be one of the most significant activities of her career. It opened in 1968, assisted by a small sum donated by the Southern Education Foundation.[22] The purpose of the center was to disseminate information on the contributions of black people to the music of the United States and the world. To do this, a special three-credit-hour course, "The Black Man in American Music," was offered for graduate and undergraduate students; it has continued with large enrollments. Other important activities were a series of public seminars and three institutes including folk and popular black music, as well as "serious" music, literature, dance, and art, in which outstanding performers and lecturers, including Fela Sowande and Billy Taylor, were invited to participate.[23] A concert of works by black composers was organized, featuring the Richmond Symphony Orchestra under conductor Leon Thompson and a commissioned work by Hale Smith.[24] It was presented three times: at Virginia State College, at Hampton University, and in the city of Richmond. A collection was established of books, recordings, audiotapes, scores, the Johns-Moore Black Music Film Series, and African instruments. The center was in operation until 1972, when both Moore and Johns retired from teaching.

In 1971–72 Moore and Johns took a trip to West Africa, where they performed and lectured at the U.S. embassy in Nigeria; were given a special performance of the National Ballet of Senegal arranged by U.S. Ambassador Rudolph Aggrey at the Daniel Sorrano Theater in Dakar; and spent many hours observing and interacting with the ordinary people in both rural and urban areas in Senegal, Ghana, and the Ivory Coast. They were deeply moved by the historic slave trading centers of El Mina in Ghana and Gorree in Dakar, Senegal, where men were weighed in the underground chamber to determine their value while their families were separated. Moore noticed the resemblance of many Africans to her own relatives. She thought that had she been younger, she would have wanted to go to Africa to live, surrounded by people who looked like her. She was struck by the realization that each African child had grown up never knowing what it means to be a member of a minority and by the strangeness of seeing black people in positions of power, and in control. She also was impressed by the integration of the arts into daily life.

On Moore's retirement from Virginia State College in 1972, the honors flooded in. The next year, former students Leon Thompson, Billy Taylor, Camilla Williams, Phillip Medley, and Michael Gordon, together with other music teachers in New York, organized a Town Hall gala concert of her works at which she received a citation from Mayor John Lindsay of New York City and was awarded an honorary Doctor of Music degree by Virginia State College. Two years later, another gala concert and reception were held in Petersburg by the Beaux-Twenty men's club, with a proclamation and citation from Mayor Remmis Arnold of Petersburg. Indiana University awarded her an honorary doctorate in 1976. In 1975 she was honored as an outstanding educator by the National Association of Negro Musicians, and in 1980 the National Black Caucus acknowledged her contributions to black music. She received the Humanitarian Award from Fisk University in 1973. In 1977 she was named music laureate of the state of Virginia, and in 1985 she received the Virginia Governor's Award in the Arts. She delivered the keynote address at the first National Congress on Women in Music at New York University in 1981.

These are only a few of the many honors Moore collected, and she was by no means finished working. After her retirement she taught at Virginia Union University as a distinguished professor (1972–76), returned to Virginia State as artist-in-residence in 1976–77, and was a visiting professor at Carleton College, College of St. Benedict, and St. John's University, all in Minnesota (1972–75). She served as music consultant for the Arts in Education seminars sponsored by the Virginia State Board of Education. She continued to give workshops, and was the featured speaker and composer at the seventh annual Afro-American Music Workshop at Atlanta University in January 1978. She was a senior adviser to the Afro-American Arts Institute and chairman of the National Honorary Advisory Board at the Black Music Center at Indiana University (1978), and served on the board of directors of the Richmond Symphony (1983–1987).

Not surprisingly, the 1970s was Moore's most prolific decade of composition; she produced 27 works, many of them commissions. Moore had frequently said that she considered herself to be a teacher who composes, but after retirement she was just "a composer."[25] During the 1970s she began work on the oratorio *Scenes from the Life of a Martyr*, a mammoth project encompassing 16 pieces for large chorus, orchestra, four soloists, and narrator. Following its completion in 1981 and a premiere in Carnegie Hall, it was nominated for the Pulitzer Prize, and received many performances across the United States. The years from 1981 on were filled with travel and activities related to *Scenes*. Performances of *Scenes* in Atlanta, Cincinnati, Cleveland, Detroit, and Oakland involved speaking engagements.

On 6 February 1989, in Petersburg, only weeks after a 10-day artist-in-residency at the University of Michigan, Moore succumbed to a stroke at the age of 84. Her funeral, held at Gillfield Baptist Church, included several of her spiritual arrangements sung by the Virginia Union University Choir: *Bound for Canaan Land, Fare Ye Well, I Never Felt Such Love in My Heart Before*, and *I Will Trust in the Lord*. For the Meditation, her longtime friend and associate, Carl Harris, Jr., played her organ work *Variations on Nettleton*. She was buried in Eastview Cemetery in Petersburg.

SOCIAL ISSUES

Moore spoke eloquently on issues of race, drawing on her own experiences growing up and living as a black adult in Virginia, on the social patterns and events she witnessed during her lifetime, and on her vast readings in literature and philosophy. She pondered these experiences, observations, and readings deeply. Her conclusions were both strongly felt and clinically objective.

As a child she had experienced the Jim Crowism that barred blacks "from theaters and all but the gallery of the Academy of Music," and she acknowledged the "sharp and bitter memories, bitter experiences, particularly those related to the powerlessness of our race." She said, "It is a tribute to the determination of black parents, my parents, to create for their children, as far as possible at home and in the community, a haven so fortified with love and support that assault from the larger, dominant group could not pierce their armor."[26]

As she grew older, Moore recognized that a racist society "educated me to feel my 'otherness' . . . left me ignorant of that which was accessible to me." She said, "One of the most evil effects of racism in my time was the limits it placed upon the aspirations of blacks, so that though I have been 'making up' and creating music all my life, in my childhood or even in college I would not have thought of calling myself a composer or aspiring to be one."[27] As for publication, she automatically assumed that it was out of the question for her as a black person. Later in life, these patterns would continue to condition her expectations, so that she never thought of submitting her Gilbert and Sullivan operetta editions for publication (although similar editions appeared some years later), let alone her songs and instrumental music.

In addition to these personally experienced conditions, Moore observed and remarked on

the ability of Black people to live life with gusto in the midst of oppression, to survive, even flourish in situations that often were designed to humiliate them. [William] Faulkner's books and characters now run together in my mind, but I remember well a passage in which he comments on this. Black servants and white masters, having looked forward to the coming of the carnival, have at last arrived at the merry-go-round. Whites could pay, could ride, but Faulkner notes that the Blacks, not allowed to ride, stood on the ground outside looking with a quality of enjoyment never experienced by the riders.[28]

On a more abstract level of reflection, Moore concluded: "All liberation is connected . . . as long as any segment of the society is oppressed . . . the whole society must suffer. I believe that racism is the chief curse of American society and that there are few problems in American life upon which it does not impinge. The evil effects of racism are as injurious, at least spiritually, to whites as to blacks."[29] She considered one of the injurious effects on whites to be their self-imposed exclusion from the lives and culture of African Americans.

White composers, being a part of the dominant culture, do not know or participate in the culture of the black man. With a highly institutionalized racism, they have not shared the common memories, sufferings, aspirations, modes of dress and speech, styles of life characteristic of those they have educated to feel inferior....

Black people are aware of the qualities of the life of white people. As gardeners, cooks, nurses of white children ... in the educational world, the business world, black people know all their lives the inner workings of white life.

... the black composer has a more genuine and extensive participation in both cultures ... while whites have a *real* participation *only* in their own.... blackness does not limit his choices, it amplifies them.[30]

Moore felt strongly about inclusion of black music in both high school and college music classes. She pointed out that although American music is already imbued with black idioms, neither blacks nor whites are aware of the black elements. She cautioned, however, against using the same criteria for the study of black music as for the white European tradition, which approaches the study of music and literature through individual "great master" composers. This loads the dice against fair evaluation of the contributions of blacks (as well as women). "While a search for the individual Black composer is appropriate and overdue ... attention focused on the Black composer as an individual must always be given in a broader context."[31]

Along with this espousal of active inclusion of black music in the school curriculum, Moore chose a more subtle approach to social activism through music. She believed that the work of a gifted artist is a powerful agent for social change, and cited the artistry of the contralto Marian Anderson, the integrity of Paul Robeson, the perfection of the pianist Andre Watts, and many others who pursue excellence, as examples of such agents. In her own music she did not consciously try to express a social viewpoint, but was aware that personal philosophies cannot help being unconsciously involved in the creative process. She saw the role of the black artist in contemporary society in a similar light. "The primary function of *any* artist ... is to convey as honestly as he can his personal vision of life. Since the artist belongs to the most sensitive segment of any society, a black composer in contemporary America, aware of his own plight and that of his people, could scarcely avoid some expression reflective of these conditions.... he really cannot escape expressing his heritage somewhere in the body of his work."[32]

Moore was clear about the need to avoid stereotyping black people and their music. She emphasized that black music is a "house of many mansions ... blacks have many musics and some of them relate in an extremely universal way to the human condition." As for the concern over what constitutes "black music," she said, "black music ... is simply music written by a black man."[33]

She also rejected any tendency to avoid association with white musicians, advising young black composers to direct and perform in amateur groups including all races. Moore gave high praise to the musicians, all white, who gave the first performance of her oratorio *Scenes from the Life of a Martyr* in New Jersey in 1981: they performed the work "with all the empathy and depth of understanding anyone could wish." She acknowledged that not just black artists, but "*any*" artist is not highly valued in American society," and that considerations besides race can affect whether a composer's work gets performed or published.[34]

Moore also had something to say about the conditioning of gender. She observed that in her youth in Petersburg, little girls more often played piano than did little boys. She also observed the way in which race, gender, and musical inclinations interacted in her time at Fisk, where "girls like Sonoma Talley and Lydia Mason, who went on to Juilliard, played at a mastery removed from the false conception of music for a girl as a social grace designed merely to ornament the life of her husband. In music it must be said that in my experience, this concept of the woman pianist never seemed to dominate the Black community as it did more Anglo-Saxon groups."[35] In fact,

The rich musical and social life [of the community] . . . was largely initiated and nourished by women. They held power in the church and in the community. It was a power that was recognized and so commonly assumed that it was not even discussed. Nevertheless, this power was confined to certain areas that never even suggested the quality of authority enjoyed by men in running the affairs of church and the social group. Women could and did influence the building of a school, the choice of teachers, and the order and content of the church service, but there must have been a subtle etiquette that kept them in a particular place.

Further, so far as I know, the influence of women on the music and the culture in the life of the Black community, while known and applauded, was rarely, if ever, documented in any written form.[36]

She noted that the number of women poets and novelists, both black and white, appeared to be larger than the number of women composers.

The relative absence of women as conductors, women as composers, is of special interest to me . . . [they are] authority figures and as such it is not strange that opportunities for women as well as Blacks have been limited. This limitation includes the effect on the aspiration of women who have in their childhood and youth been able to observe few examples to inspire them with belief in their own power.

There is in addition the fiction of women's inability to deal with the abstract. Because music is an utterly non-verbal art, there is inevitably a certain quality of the abstract in the approach to the composer's art. Women, for a long time in the past, were indoctrinated with the widely held belief that the abstract is not their sphere. . . . Over and over, it has been held that the objective discipline which is necessary to transmute inner sources by giving them artistic form is a discipline suitable only to men.[37]

Moore spoke from personal experience when she noted, "They [women] have been forced to deal with the minutiae of life, often in a manner that freed men to be the creators." On another occasion, she returned to that issue when asked if she would choose to devote herself to composition on a full-time basis:

This question was surely written for men. Their wives assume those dreary responsibilities which make it possible for them to compose. . . . It would be fine to have a life so ordered that other everyday responsibilities did not impinge so heavily on my time. I am a widow of restricted means living in a fairly large house which must be managed in some way. The simple availability of a part-time typist or office assistant and a cleaning assistant would almost seem ideal as ways of making composing more possible.[38]

These observations border closely on the issue of class. Only affluent upper-class wives could afford to hire the kind of help Moore needed. Although she had little to say directly about class, her comments reveal much about her attitude. While she affirmed the aspects of what must surely have been upper-middle-class black life in Petersburg in her descriptions of silver teas and church socials, and the clear implication that a person carrying a music case was considered a person of culture "affluent enough to pay Miss Patty Campbell one dollar a month,"[39] her fond descriptions of "Touse and Theandros passing the farm at night, giving their special hollers" in Jarratt reveal her connection to, and respect for, other social strata.

In her arguments for inclusion of black music in the school curriculum, Moore emphasized that "the blues and the forms from the past which have emerged and mingled must be brought into the classroom. . . . Let us listen to blues, gospel, jazz with our own ears, our minds and hearts and not our inherited, unthought prejudices. . . . we must rid ourselves of the feeling that these musics are low and unworthy because of the social status of some of their creators. Social status has absolutely nothing to do with aesthetic value."[40] When she organized the Black Music Center at Virginia State College with Altona Trent Johns, she followed that principle. They did not focus attention only on the "serious" works of black composers, but included the music of the lowly, oppressed black masses. Moore pointed out that the events at the center were attended by persons of diverse backgrounds, and social status had no relevance to their participation.

THE MUSIC

Moore's compositions encompass many genres, from arrangements of spirituals, to solo art songs, instrumental chamber music, and multimovement works for chorus, soloists, and instruments. They number well over 100 compositions written between 1925 and 1987. More than 50 of these, including the three cantatas, are choral works. Another 21 compositions are for solo voice and piano or other instruments, and only eighteen are for instruments without voice. The preponderance of choral and vocal works is due not only to the type of opportunities and needs Moore encountered, to the commissions she received, or to the expertise that she developed as a result, but also to a genuine love for the genre. She openly declared her preference for choral writing, although she admitted that many composers disdain it and set their sights on large orchestral compositions. Of her favorites among her own works, she listed the choral *Mother to Son; Daniel, Daniel Servant of the Lord*; and *Lord, We Give Thanks to Thee*. Another favorite was the third movement of her instrumental trio, *Afro-American Suite*. A few years later she added to the list her oratorio *Scenes from the Life of a Martyr*, the cantata *Glory to God*, the choral works *Striving After God* and *The Lamb*, and the art song *Love Let the Wind Cry*. Thus, eight of her nine favorite works were vocal settings of texts, and seven of those were choral.

Moore is particularly well known for her many settings of spirituals, and they were dear to her heart. At least 22 of her choral works are spiritual arrangements, and several more incorporate spirituals as segments of larger works. Five of her solo songs are settings of spirituals, and three instrumental works—her *Afro-American Suite, Organ Variations on There Is a Fountain*, and solo piano *Many Thousand Gone*—have reference to spiritual melodies. Altogether, at least 33 works either arrange, or make reference to, spiritual tunes or texts. She said that her goal in setting the spirituals "was not to make something 'better' . . . [but] to have them experienced in a variety of ways." She remarked that the composition of these works "has given me much pleasure and has strengthened the memories of the people who loved and gave direction to my life."[41]

Some 26 of Moore's works were published and available during her lifetime. Twenty-four of them were choral works, most published between 1951 and 1979. Since her death eight works have been either reprinted or published for the first time, and several are included in anthologies.[42]

An evolution in style over the years is clearly discernible in Moore's compositions. Though she created music as a child, her first "serious" composing began while she was at Fisk University. Only three of those works survive. Although the African-American heritage was a strong and basic part of the education at Fisk, her tastes and styles at this stage were formed by her classically trained music teachers and did not include any African-American elements. The many pieces she composed for high schools, church choirs, and amateur choirs in her early years of teaching do not appear on any lists, let alone endure in scores. In fact, from her graduation from Fisk in 1926 to 1950, only four choral works (arrangements of spirituals) and two pieces for piano survive. Around 1953, when she returned to study composition with Howard Murphy, a marked change in style took place. Moore described the solo piano works of 1952, *Romantic Young Clown*, and *Romance* for two pianos as "Godowsky-like,"[43] that is, with the conservative harmonic palette and flowery style of the late nineteenth century. The next year she produced *Before I'd Be a Slave*, a powerful and dissonant piano piece characterized by tone clusters, bitonality, and quartal harmonies, all twentieth-century techniques. That year she also started a composition which began as a clarinet work, and ended in 1958 as *Three Pieces for Flute and Piano*. The portion she composed in 1953, the first and last pieces, *Introduction* and *Allegro*, are her first explorations of 12-tone serialism, which was extremely popular among avant-garde composers of that time. The middle piece, *March*, added in 1958, while not serial, is definitely not traditionally tonal, and features a fugal passage with a particularly disjunct melodic theme. The choral works of the late 1950s display more choral speaking, more attention to linear movement, and a greater use of imitative writing. These differences are apparent when comparing *Daniel, Daniel, Servant of the Lord* (1952) with *Teach Me to Hear Mermaids Singing* (1953), a three-part canon for treble voices, or *The Lamb* (1958), a two-part canon for treble voices. Traditional counterpoint was always important to Moore, but dissonant counterpoint is more in evidence from 1953 on. In speaking of the evolution of her style, Moore acknowledged that her concept of tonality was broadened by the 12-tone experiments of Arnold Schoenberg, Alban Berg, and Anton Webern. She said,

We live in a world that is constantly changing. It would be very strange if the events of the world about us did not affect us. There are those who hang on to the traditional, and there are those who want to make or speak the new language. . . . I should not want to be at the extreme end of either group. I do feel that, in any case, I must write with a sense of integrity; I must not write pseudo compositions, using the new language just to be in style.[44]

It was also in the 1950s that Moore began to make more use of her African-American musical heritage. She explained this late development:

Both in my home life and in my life as a student at Fisk University, I was surrounded by these great musical expressions of Afro-American people. As is frequently the case, that which is extremely familiar to us may temporarily escape our attention as the subject matter of creative effort. Thus, my early compositions at Fisk and later at Columbia University did not reflect my background with spirituals. After completing a master's degree, however, it suddenly dawned on me that the songs my mother sang while cooking dinner; the melodies my father hummed after work moved me very deeply. I began to write down the melodies they sang for some vague, undefined reason.[45]

She remembered: "I can see my mother resting in her bed, and I would draw up a chair with my manuscript pad to write as she sang."[46]

The 1950s was the period of the most dramatic growth in the evolution of Moore's style, but she continued to expand her style and explore new possibilities to the very end of her life. The *Afro-American Suite* (1969), for flute, cello, and piano, was a departure from her previous instrumental works in its use of spiritual themes together with highly sophisticated and often dissonant counterpoint. The style of the Song of Solomon songs (1975) in *Scenes* continues her rhapsodic late-romantic art song style, but in the late 1970s she wrote the more spare and contemporary solo vocal *Three Bahai Prayers*. By the mid-1980s Moore felt a need to make more use of instruments. This she did in *Many*

Thousand Gone, for piano (1986), and in *Soweto* for violin, cello, and piano (1987), which is uncompromising in its dissonance, and even returns to serialism to generate its melodic materials.[47] An opera-in-progress on Sojourner Truth yielded at least one addition to her art songs, the gripping *Sojourner Speaks*. Toward the end of her life, she was in the process of composing a cycle of art songs on texts by female writers.[48] She was even considering exploring the possibilities of other than conventional sound sources.

Moore may have been influenced in this consideration by her admiration for composer Olly Wilson's electronic works.[49] Her listening tastes covered a wide range of composers and performers. While she considered Bach to be the only essential composer, she also enjoyed Gladys Knight and the Pips, the Spinners, Gregorian chant, madrigals, Aretha Franklin, the French composer Gabriel Fauré, Béla Bartók, William Grant Still, William Dawson, Stravinsky (especially his *Symphony of Psalms*), Mozart, Vivaldi, John Coltrane, Brahms, Harry Partch, George Walker, and Beethoven. However, any influence from these composers is subliminal, and not readily apparent in her music, which has its own strong character. She acknowledged only black folk music and Bach as true influences.

Moore described her compositional style as freely tonal (that is, with a few exceptions, centered on a tonic note), sometimes strongly modal, often using twentieth-century techniques (tone clusters, bitonality, etc.), frequently using recitative or speechlike style, almost always strongly contrapuntal, and dominated by the black idiom. What she meant by "black idiom" was the use of elements from the Afro-American musical heritage: additive and syncopated rhythms, scale structures with gaps, call and response antiphony, rich timbres, melody influenced by rhythm, the frequent use of the interval of the third and, less frequently, fourths and fifths, nonhomophonic textures, and the "deliberate use of striking climax with almost unrestrained fullness." On a more philosophical level, she was concerned in her music with "aspiration, the emotional intensity . . . the capacity and desire for abundant, full expression as one might . . . expect from an oppressed people determined to survive."[50]

Moore's creative process began spontaneously with a "germ" of an idea which came to her after a period of gestation and often contained the possibilities for its own development. From that point, she made choices as to the technical considerations of unity, variety, balance, dominance, style, and form. She noted that when a text was required for a commissioned work, the length, medium, and mood were often predetermined, and she had read so extensively in many sources that she believed the words would come out of this past without her having to search for them. When the contralto Marie Goodman replaced a soprano in a scheduled concert, Moore wished to give her a song suited to the unique timbre of her voice. She slept on it and awakened with a line from a poem by Georgia Douglas Johnson, "I Want to Die While You Love Me," complete with melody and accompaniment. She went to the piano and finished the song in two hours. She had a similar experience with the composition of her trio *Soweto*. In her program notes she said, "Like almost everyone else, I am aware of some of the conflicts and confrontation there [South Africa], perhaps particularly the incident [in 1976 at the township of Soweto] where the people not only suffered the shooting murder of 22 of their number but were then denied the right to bury their dead." She thought the incident had been forgotten in the bustle of daily life over the next weeks. "Weeks later, very early in the morning, I awakened suddenly. I heard the single word 'Soweto.' I sat upright, astonished! And I knew then that my new piece would use the rhythmic motive 'Soweto' and it would inevitably have other overtones, some of conflict. There must have been deep internal turmoil to bring that word to me. I felt I did not choose the word. The word chose me."[51] This confirms the importance of the unconscious in her creative process, "things heard and not heard, seen and not seen . . . lodged deeply within us."

The many ingredients that mixed at this deep level included all of Moore's life experiences, as well as her love for art and literature. In art she cites the influence of the sculpture, masks, and jewelry of Africa, Picasso's *Guernica* for its fury and social relevance, John Biggers' *Celebration March* with its strong, determined black women, Van Gogh's *Self Portrait* and the human pain it distills, and Monet's *Water Lilies* at the Jeu de Paume in Paris, an entire pavilion of just water lilies.[52] Her love for literature was born when, as a child, she saved her money for a set of the works of Dickens. She read voraciously: the Bible, some philosophy, anthropology, psychology, and social science, the works of Paul Tillich, Ralph Ellison, Toni Morrison, Alice Walker, Anne Sexton, Margaret Walker, Gwendolyn Brooks, William Butler Yeats, Frederick Douglass, Benjamin Quarles, William Ryan, and particularly Langston Hughes. She was describing her own creativity when she advised an aspiring young composer to allow himself to be stimulated by painting, sculpture, dance, literature, drama, architecture, history and philosophy, and to stay in close contact with his roots, with the people who raised him and gave him inner strength.

Daniel, Daniel, Servant of the Lord (1952)

The unaccompanied choral piece, *Daniel, Daniel, Servant of the Lord* serves extremely well as an example of Moore's favorite medium. It has many hallmarks of her choral style: the opening unison expanding into several parts, the alternating male and female passages in quick succession, vigorous African-American rhythms and melodies based on gapped scales, division of parts for textural and dramatic contrast, imitative entries and contrapuntal details, and striking climactic chromaticism. It is possibly the best known of Moore's compositions, performed by church, student, and concert choirs across the country. Published by Warner Bros., it sold 10,000 copies a year for several years.

One minute and 45 seconds long, the work is scored for eight-part chorus. The key remains F-sharp minor,[53] and the meter is solidly duple. Moore preferred to call it a "theme and variations" rather than an arrangement, because of "the meager fragment from which it sprang."[54] The piece, dedicated to Moore's mother, grew out of a spiritual her mother used to sing while working around the house. The themes are a refrain (A) and verses (B) from the spiritual. These are enlarged by repetition and extension, and varied by voicing, harmonies, and counterpoint, resulting in a loosely strophic or double variation form: A A^1 B A^1 B^1 A^2 A^3. The refrain sections are choral, while the two verse sections feature tenor and bass soloists, respectively, accompanied by the chorus. The tempo is moderately fast, and rhythms are vigorous and strongly marked. The piece is dominated by a repeated rhythmic motive, short-short-long, corresponding to the syllables of "Dan-i-yul" and at times functioning as an ostinato, or underlying repeated pattern. Rhythmic syncopation occurs on the phrase "servant of the Lord" in the refrain as well as in the entire melody of the verses. The squareness of the regular phrase lengths is offset by added measures of held notes to prepare each solo, by overlapping of the end of the solo with the following chorus, and by dramatic pauses.

While the harmonies follow the basic implications of the melody with few added nonharmonic tones, the extended "Oh!" of the last variation presents a climactic stepwise progression upward through four parallel chromatic chords, pausing dramatically on the dominant C-sharp major chord before resolving upward to F-sharp in the tenor solo voice.

The scholar Augustus Pearson groups *Daniel* with Moore's "jubilee" spiritual arrangements, those set in a vigorous, happy mood, with markedly African-American rhythms, gapped scale melodies, duple meter, and regular four-bar phrases. However, the jubilance in this instance is in a minor key, tempered with seriousness, determination, and struggle; the victory of the closing phrases retains the shadow of adversity. *Daniel* could also be described as a "preaching" spiritual, with the tenor and bass "sermons" telling the story of Daniel in the lion's den in the verses. The chorus opens with the refrain: "Oh, the king cried, 'Oh! Daniel, Daniel, Oh! Daniel, Daniel, Oh! A that-a Hebrew Daniel, Servant of the Lord!" During the solos the chorus subsides into background support, like the traditional spontaneous group "basing" of the early black spirituals, first with the softly repeated "Dan-i-el" ostinato for the tenor solo: "Among the Hebrew nation, one Daniel was found. They put him in-a the lion's den. He stayed there all night long." Later the chorus, with expressively accentuated humming, supports the bass solo, "Now the king in his sleep was troubled, and early in the morning he rose, to find God had sent his angel down to lock the lion's jaws." The alternating exchange between solo and chorus is an example of the "call and response" typical of African-American preaching. The last phrase is marked fff, "broadly with great power," and the voices expand to eight parts on the closing chord. The work closes with the striking climax and "almost unrestrained fullness" so characteristic of African-American music.

Before I'd Be a Slave (1953)

The year after *Daniel* was composed, Moore wrote a piano piece titled *Before I'd Be a Slave*, which broke completely with the "Godowsky" sound of her previous keyboard works. Not only does Moore link an instrumental work to

African-American identity for the first time by naming it after a spiritual, but the style is starkly dissonant, using twentieth-century techniques and sounds: the piano played percussively (even harshly), tone clusters and blocks, polytonality, artificial scales, quartal harmonies, and nonfunctional chords extended with nonharmonic tones.[55] It is basically atonal, although the final reiterated clusters are built on C.

Neither the tune nor the text of the spiritual "Before I'd Be a Slave" appear in this work, although the resolute implications of the words are central to its meaning: "Before I'd be a slave, I'd be buried in my grave, and go home to my Lord and be saved."[56] Instead, Moore provides a "program" outlining the different sections and changing moods of the piece: "The frustration and chaos of slaves who wish to be free—In the depths—A slow and ponderous struggle—Attempts to escape—Tug of war with the oppressors—A measure of freedom won—Upward movement—Continued aspiration—Determination—Affirmation." Each section of the composition is different, with no recall or repetition of material. Since the work is short, only 69 measures, (about three and a half minutes) in length, these sections follow each other in fairly quick succession. That this work was commissioned by choreographer Barbara Hollis for the Modern Dance Group at Virginia State undoubtedly had a bearing on its program, length, and style. The composer played and taped the music for its first performance. It has since been performed numerous times. The reviewer of Selma Epstein's New York all-black composers piano recital in 1985 said of the piece, "[It] really seemed to say something about itself . . . [its] voice-like, often savage, directness conveyed anger and fear with great vividness."[57] It is included in the anthology *Black Women Composers: A Century of Piano Music 1893–1990*, edited by Helen Walker-Hill and published by Hildegard Publishing Company, and is also available on CD (see discography at the end of the chapter).

The music expresses the frustration and rage of its program, from the opening intense drummed tone clusters in the bass register to the furiously pounded tone clusters at the end. Many passages sweep from one extreme of the keyboard range to the other, and dynamics range from pp (very soft) to fff (very, very loud). It is the most violent of all Moore's compositions, although apparently it was not the only such work. In an interview in the 1970s, Moore told of another piano piece she had written that she considered her most interesting work for piano. Expressing her frustration and anger in a difficult personal situation, it was short and quite difficult, extremely dissonant and rhythmically irregular, and was never copied out or even titled, because she thought no one would ever want to play it. She thought of calling it "Warrior." This could almost be a description of *Before I'd Be a Slave*, and one can only imagine its ferocity.

Afro-American Suite (1969)

This suite for flute/alto flute, cello, and piano was commissioned by the flutist D. Antoinette Handy for her ensemble, Trio Pro Viva. It was first performed by this trio at the District of Columbia Teachers College in Washington, D.C., in April 1969, and later recorded by them on an LP album titled *Contemporary Black Images in Music for the Flute*. In his review of this recording, the work was described by Dominique-René de Lerma as "very freely based on traditional religious melodies . . . beautifully structured, harmonically imaginative, contrapuntally valid, and . . . primitive in the best sense of the word."[58] In 1976 it was chosen to represent the state of Virginia during the bicentennial music celebrations held at the Kennedy Center in Washington, D.C. It has not been published.

The suite is four movements long, with each movement based on a different spiritual. The last three movements, composed first, were completed in April 1969 and premiered the same month. At the suggestion of Handy, a first movement was added two months later, resulting in a work some 12 minutes long. This version was first performed at Hampton University by the Trio Pro Viva on 20 June 1969. The added first movement is the most dissonant, and employs the melody of the spiritual "Nobody Knows the Trouble I See" in the more rarely heard version that appears in James Weldon Johnson's *Book of American Negro Spirituals* (1925). The form is a type of strophic double variation very like that in the choral piece *Daniel, Daniel, Servant of the Lord*: A B A^1 B^1 A^2 B^2 A (where A is the refrain of the spiritual and B is the verse). The melancholy melody of the refrain is introduced by the cello against a steady, plodding chordal piano accompaniment in a high register, pianissimo, incorporating dissonance that, rather than jarring, creates a soft, bell-like, mournful effect. The next section, corresponding to the verses "Brothers [mothers, etc.] will you pray for me an' help me to drive ole Satan away," is played by the flute with cello counterpoint and sustained piano chords. Succeeding variations become increasingly dissonant in all instruments, which are used in various combinations, doubled in octaves, and in call and response. The markings "intenso" and "appassionato" indicate the growing emotional distress. The most striking moment is the third statement of the refrain, when the melody is shared by piano and cello in close alternation, with octave displacements, so that it sounds tortured and barely recognizable. After a climactic, fortissimo, "appassionato" statement of the verse, the movement concludes quietly, as it began, with a return to the refrain.

The second movement is based on the spiritual "I Heard the Preaching of the Elder." It is in D major, marked "Allegro molto e marcato" (very fast, with well-marked rhythm). There is an air of excitement and celebration, with exuberant, sudden passing modulations to other keys. The lively, syncopated spiritual melody is passed back and forth, in call and response, with frequent octave doublings. The style of a church choir is thus evoked by the instruments. The instruments each "preach" with commentaries on the melody in faster 16th-note counterpoint, as well as in solo improvisatory cadenzas that depart from the "text" entirely. These additions bring a gospel flavor to the simpler, basic spiritual melody. The movement culminates in a broad last statement of the melody in unison, marked "grandioso," again evoking Moore's choral style.

The third movement was among the composer's favorite works. It is an intensely personal setting of "Who Is That Yonder? (Oh, It Looks Like My Lord Coming in a Cloud)." The key returns to D minor with modal inflections. The soprano flute is replaced by the darker timbre of the alto flute. The style is declamatory. It is marked "Adagio appassionata" and opens with sustained chords in exhortatory dotted rhythms (short-long) played pianissimo by the piano. The rhythm and the sustained chords convey a sense of waiting, the expectancy muted by long-suffering patience. The melody is taken by first one, then another, instrument, expressively embellished, while the others interject with punctuating flourishes. The melody is stated more emphatically by the flute and cello in unison before the minor movement concludes with a D major chord, quietly plucked by the cello.[59]

The fourth and last movement in the suite is a setting of "Shout All Over God's Heaven." Marked, like the second movement, "Allegro molto e marcato," and also in D major, it opens with the jubilant, syncopated spiritual melody played by the solo flute in a high register, "shouting all over God's heaven." It is this movement that answers the question, "Who Is That Yonder?," a resolution only hinted at by the quietly plucked major chord concluding the third movement. The waiting is triumphantly rewarded with the sense of arrival, of announcement of the good news. The three instruments have a passage of intertwining, contrapuntal, cadenza-like improvisation in which they seem to "answer" one another. The movement finishes with a hocketlike[60] rendition of the melody in which the three instruments alternate in very quick succession.

Scholar/composer Yvette Carter views this work as an enactment of W.E.B. Du Bois' concept of double consciousness, the "two warring ideals" of the Euro-American and African-American cultures. Carter sees the Euro-American modernist ideal personified by the piano and its dissonances, while the African-American heritage, encoded in the spiritual melodies, is personified by the cello and flute and their more "vocal" consonant language.[61] It was, indeed, the first time that Moore used the actual melodies of spirituals in a purely instrumental work. As such, and as Moore's first trio and only work for this instrumental combination, *Afro-American Suite* occupies an important and pivotal position in her composition. For the first time she fully realized her wish: "I thought [the spirituals] so beautiful that I wanted to have them experienced in a variety of ways—by concert choirs, soloists, and by instrumental groups."[62] Both the instrumentation and the European origins of the form she chose, represent a striking reconciliation of traditions. The work as a whole follows the conventions of the classical dance suite in its uniform tonality in the key of D; it also follows the character suite of the romantic period, with its contrasting moods and variety of forms. It thus imbues traditionally European genres with an African-American spirituality and idiom.

Scenes from the Life of a Martyr (1981)

Moore's magnum opus is her oratorio for chorus, orchestra, narrator, and four soloists (soprano, contralto, tenor, and bass), *Scenes from the Life of a Martyr*, composed in memory of Martin Luther King, Jr. The three art songs on texts from the Song of Solomon, which form the second of the four main sections of *Scenes*, were completed as early as November 1975. Moore said that *Scenes* had been germinating since 1975, and actual work on the composition took about four years. The work was composed without a commission: "I began this in a personal way with no pressure at the beginning and not concerned about the ending. I wanted to write something for myself for this man." She had not known King personally, but had followed accounts of his actions with a personal sense of involvement. She wished the work to comment on the private life of King rather than the public life. In her imagination she pictured "a boy of spirit, a merry heart, a leader in childhood games; a youth capable of passion and devotion to his chosen mate; a man early dedicated to a ministry focused on love and necessity of bringing freedom for the captive."[63] She also wished to evoke memories of other martyrs, and the universality of the "lives of ordinary men and women who struggle against the tragedies of human existence."[64]

In 1979 parts of the work were performed at the Gillfield Baptist Church in Petersburg by the Harry Savage Chorale, accompanied by the composer at the piano. The orchestration was later done by Donald Rauscher, and the work was completed in 1980. Moore showed the score to the well-known scholar/composer Dr. Hugh Ross, who pronounced it "simply splendid, a fine work that ought to be performed."[65] Ross helped her contact the Carl Fischer Publishing Company, which accepted it for publication and nominated it for a Pulitzer Prize in 1981.

The premiere performance was to have been given by the Richmond Symphony in 1981, but due to scheduling difficulties their performance came after three previews, two in New Jersey in December 1981, and a third in New York at Carnegie Hall on 15 January 1982.[66] When the Richmond Symphony Orchestra finally gave it its "official" premiere on 19 April 1982, Jacques Houtmann was the conductor, with the participation of the Intercollegiate Chorus; Willis C. Patterson was narrator; and soloists were Cassandra Hayes (soprano), Marla McDaniels (mezzo-soprano), and Paul Spencer Adkins (tenor).[67] Subsequently, more than 20 performances have been given in New York City, Philadelphia, Boston, Wilmington, Detroit, Toledo, New Orleans, Cleveland, St. Louis, and Oakland, California. Among these, several stand out: the fifth performance in Detroit, in February 1983, when Moore received the key to the city and spent seven days seeing the city sights and visiting schools and colleges; the performance by the Oakland Symphony on 12 and 14 February 1985, in a Calvin Simmons Memorial Concert; the 1987 Cleveland Orchestra performance, conducted by Isaiah Jackson; and the Symphony Saintpaulia performances at

Carnegie Hall, the Apollo Theater in Harlem, and the Brooklyn Academy of Music two weeks before her death in January 1989.[68]

The work that had received such resounding response from the public received mixed reviews. Nicholas Kenyon commented in *The New Yorker* that it was "propaganda [rather than music]" (which reveals more about his resistance than about the music).[69] Will Crutchfield of the *New York Times* concluded that "the best passages made for a suitable stirring finale,"[70] and John Rockwell of the same newspaper observed, "This is in a conservative idiom, but its passing musical plainness was easily redeemed by its sincerity and fervor."[71] In the *Richmond Times-Dispatch*, Dika Newlin took a different view of its "passing musical plainness": "a monumental tribute. . . . The simplest of harmonic and melodic means produced an overwhelming effect. I wept—and so did many others."[72] Bernard Holland wrote in the *New York Times*: "The music spoke the simple, direct language of pre–World War II America—wide-spaced intervals, clean, hollowed out textures, with the deep influence of folk music, plus a few touches of jazz."[73] The most extensive critique came from Charles Shore in the *Oakland Tribune*: "supple, idiomatic choral writing. . . . Moore's musical idiom is traditional and conventional, combining the language of popular melody and familiar harmony with occasional dissonant gestures to express the libretto's points. Occasional references to gospel music and the spiritual never obtrude beyond allusion, and the musical style is well maintained. One moment is unforgettable—the chorus gradually moving from sung dissonance to individually shouted words, then reversing the procedure in a brilliant evocation of public grief."[74] That particular passage was noted by many. Some compared it to similar dramatic moments in Penderecki's *St. Luke Passion*, and others to Schoenberg's "Shema Israel" in *A Survival from Warsaw*.[75]

Moore's intent with this large work was to reach ordinary men and women. As in so many of her choral pieces, she chose a language accessible to all. She had no intention of writing other than "conservative," "conventional" music. But even so, she did not shrink from dissonance when it was appropriate to the drama of the moment. She says that from the beginning, she had no desire to achieve consistency of style, but tried, rather, to express in musical styles the different phases of the "life" of her subject. Indeed, almost all of her repertoire of musical language and resources—from African-American idioms and spirituals, to rhapsodic romantic arias, gospel-style elaborate vocal embellishments, speechlike recitative, and rugged dissonance—was employed in the service of the story she wished to tell. The story is told in Moore's own libretto, making free use of words and tunes from spirituals, and the King James Version of the Bible beloved by Martin Luther King, Jr. She adds excerpts from poets of "other times, places, and races" to reflect Dr. King's commitment to all people. These excerpts are taken from poetry by Stephen Spender, Claude McKay, and Robert Hayden.[76]

The oratorio is about 40 minutes long and consists of 16 movements grouped into four sections, corresponding to the different periods of Dr. King's life. A narrator provides a prologue, transitions from one period to the next, and commentaries within the movements. The first section begins with the narrator's three-part prologue, with texts from Stephen Spender ("What is precious is never to forget") and Negro spirituals ("O stay in the field, children" and "I know moon rise, I know star rise"). The first movement, for soprano and baritone (*Whenever a people is oppressed, they wait in hope*), continues in the spirit of the prologue. Its style is contemporary in its harmonic dissonance and disjunct vocal lines, and African-American in some of the rhythmic motives, especially the short-long dotted figure so characteristic of Moore's works. An orchestral interlude titled *His Mother Rocked Him Gently* continues the rhythmic motives from the first movement and provides a transition with gospel-like embellishments to the melody. This section then explores the beginnings of the life of a martyr in three *Songs at the Cradle* sung by the contralto soloist. The narrator follows with Claude McKay's line "have forgotten much but still remember . . . when we were so happy," which leads to the sixth and last movement of this section, a boisterous, syncopated, dancelike orchestral interlude, *Ring Game*, in which the folk tune "Cissy in the Barn" can be heard.

The narrator prepares the listener for the following section, on King's young manhood: "the time of the singing birds is come . . . the voice of the turtle is heard in the land." The three songs that follow are those composed in 1975, and feature Moore's lush, rhapsodic art-song style in texts from the Song of Solomon: *The Voice of My Beloved* for soprano; *Arise My Love My Fair One* for tenor; and *Set Me as a Seal on Thy Heart* for soprano and tenor. These songs, while tonal, employ dissonance expressively to illustrate the words.

The narrator again prepares for a new phase of the martyr's life: "the hour of his anointment is at hand." This third section opens with a pivotal movement for tenor and chorus, in declamatory recitative style. The text paraphrases a passage from Isaiah quoted by Christ in the gospel of Luke (4:18), which is a major scripture in liberation theology: "The Spirit of the Lord is upon me, because He hath anointed me to preach the gospel to the poor."[77] This is followed by one of the most memorable movements of the entire work, a contemplative choral piece in spiritual style, *I Never Felt Such Love in My Soul Before.* Bringing back the short-long rhythmic motive, it closes with the chorus humming very softly. The twelfth movement is an aria sung by the tenor that gives King's response to his people's love: "Lord, Thou knowest I have tried to do justly and love mercy and walk humbly before our God."

The narrator informs us that "Evil times came upon him," ushering in the fourth and final section. Martin Luther King's "voice" continues in the next two movements, *Martin's Lament*, sung by the tenor; *Oh God, How Many Are Them That Hate Me*, by the chorus; and the narration of a poem by Robert Hayden: "Know that love has chosen you to live his crucial purposes." The climactic choral piece, *They Tell Me Martin Is Dead*, begins with the voices in agitated fugal imitation, coalescing into frenzied screams and moans. (This passage is the one that drew comments from reviewers, quoted above.) In the hush that follows, muted drums and tolling bells are heard. A chorale, *Tell All My Father's People*, with refrain of sopranos and altos in a drooping, descending scale contour, and verses based on the spiritual "Angels Waiting at the Door,"[78] brings the oratorio to resolution and closure.

Although Moore continued to produce major works through the 1980s, *Scenes from the Life of a Martyr* was her most ambitious work and the culmination of her composing career. It is a fitting and enduring legacy from a composer whose music embodies so many of the central spiritual and musical characteristics of African-American music in the twentieth century.

LIST OF WORKS

(AMRC/CBMR) Checklist of scores in the Helen Walker-Hill Collection at the Center for Black Music Research, Columbia College, Chicago, and in duplicate at the American Music Research Center, University of Colorado at Boulder (16 manuscripts and published scores).

(IU and IU-USM) Catalog of scores in Indiana University Music Library (12 manuscripts and published scores) and Undine Smith Moore Collection at Indiana University (seven manuscripts).

(ME) Complete list of compositions by Undine Smith Moore compiled by her daughter, Mary Easter, from her personal collection. 1990. Unpublished.

References (see selected bibliography for complete reference)

(Allen) Allen, Simona. Program notes.

(Baker) Baker, David N., et al. *The Black Composer Speaks*. Times listed are from this source.

(IDBC) Music list compiled for "Undine Smith Moore" in *International Dictionary of Black Composers*.

Performing Medium Unknown

Awake, O North Wind (voice?). n.d. (ME)

Be Strong All Ye People (choral?). 1980. (ME)

The Church's One Foundation (choral?). 1984. (ME)

From the Southside (voice?). 1983. Same as *A Little Memory of Southside Virginia?* (ME)

If I Know (voice?). n.d. (ME)

It Was a Lover and His Lass (voice?). n.d. (ME)

Let No Flower of Spring Pass by You (voice?). 1979. (ME)

Let Us Sing (choral?). 1980. (ME)

A Little Memory of Southside Virginia (voice?). 1979. (ME)

A Little Spring Soliloquy (voice?) n.d. (ME)

Make Us a New Song (choral?). 1985. (ME)

O the Morning Stars Sang Together Children (choral?). n.d. (ME)

A Pretty Ducke (voice?). 1926. (ME)

Rededication (AKA *Song*) (choral?). n.d. (ME)

Set Down, Set Down (voice?). 1931. Same as *Set Down!* 1951? (ME)

A Street in Bronzville (voice?). 1984. (ME)

Think on These Things (choral?). 1970. (ME)

This Man Is a Good Man (choral?). 1980. (ME)

'Twas on One Sunday Morning (voice?). 1983. (ME)

Two Easter Pieces for Mrs. Gamby (voice?). 1976. (ME)

Truce (voice?). 1983. (ME)

Instrumental Music

Flute/Clarinet

Introduction and Allegro (clarinet, piano). 1953. Identical with first and last of *Three Pieces for Flute and Piano*. (IU; Baker, IDBC, ME)

Three Pieces for Flute (or Clarinet) and Piano. 1958. Contents: (1) Introduction—Pomposo; (2) March; (3) Allegro—Dance. Performed in September 1973 by Frank Wess, flute, and Garland Butts, piano, at the Town Hall gala concert in honor of Undine Smith Moore. 6 min. (IU-USM; Allen, Baker, IDBC, ME)

Trumpet

Conversation for Trumpet and Piano. 1978–84. (IDBC, ME)

Piano

Before I'd Be a Slave. 1953. In *Black Women Composers: A Century of Piano Music 1893–1990*, edited by Helen Walker-Hill (Bryn Mawr, Pa.: Hildegard Publishing Co., 1992). Commissioned by Barbara Hollis for the Modern Dance Group at Virginia State College. Taped for that performance by Undine Smith Moore. See discography. 3 min. 36 sec. (AMRC/CBMR; Allen, IDBC, ME)

Fugue in F Major (for piano or strings). 1952. 2 min. 30 sec. (AMRC/CBMR, IU-USM; Baker, IDBC, ME)

Many Thousand Gone. 1986. (AMRC/CBMR; IDBC)

Prelude. 1976. (IU-USM; IDBC)

A Romantic Young Clown. 1952. For Mary Hardie. First performed in 1952 by Undine Smith Moore at faculty concert, Virginia State College. 3 min. (AMRC/CBMR, IU-USM; Baker, IDBC, ME)

Scherzo for Piano (previously *Prelude*). 1930. First performed in 1930 by Undine Smith Moore at Columbia University Teachers College. 1 min. (AMRC/CBMR; Baker, IDBC, ME). Same as *Scherzo for Piano*, 1976? (ME)

Valse Caprice. 1930. First performed in 1930 by Undine Smith Moore at Columbia University Teachers College. 2 min. (Baker, IDBC, ME)

Organ

Organ Variations on Nettleton. 1976. Commissioned and first performed in 1976 by
    Mayme Maye at Christ and Grace Episcopal Church, Petersburg, Va. 3 min.
    (AMRC/CBMR; Baker, IDBC, ME)
Organ Variations on There Is a Fountain. 1979. (IDBC, ME)

Chamber Ensemble

Afro-American Suite (flute/alto flute, cello, piano). 1969. Contents: (1) Nobody Knows
    the Trouble I See; (2) I Heard the Preaching of the Elder; (3) Who Is That
    Yonder? (4) Shout All Over God's Heaven. Commissioned and first performed
    in April 1969 by D. Antoinette Handy and the Trio Pro Viva, Ronald Lipscomb,
    cellist, and Hildred Roach, piano, District of Columbia Teachers College, Wash-
    ington, D.C. (See discography). 11 min. 30 sec. (AMRC/CBMR, IU, IU-USM;
    Baker, IDBC, ME)
Fugue in F Major (string trio). 1952. Three-part eighteenth-century-style fugue. First
    performed in 1952 at Virginia State College. 2 min. 30 sec. (AMRC/IDBC, IU-
    USM; Baker, IDBC, ME)
Lamentosa (violin, cello, piano). 1987. Intended for use in *Soweto*. Incomplete. (IDBC,
    ME)
Reflections for Organ and Piano. 1952. First performed in 1952 by David Carroll, organ,
    and Undine Smith Moore, piano, at faculty concert, Virginia State College. 3 min.
    (Baker, IDBC, ME)
Romance (two pianos). 1952. First performed in 1952 by Undine Smith Moore and
    Garland Butts, pianists, at faculty concert, Virginia State College. 5 min. (Baker,
    IDBC, ME)
Soweto (violin, cello, piano). 1987. Two movements. Commissioned by and first per-
    formed in 1987 by the Nova Trio: Ray Pancarowicz, violin; James Herbison,
    cello; and Jayne Belkov Kaplan, piano, at the Chrysler Museum, Norfolk, Va. 7
    min. (AMRC/CBMR; IDBC, ME)
String Quartet. 1976. (IDBC, ME)
String Sentence (string quartet). 1975. Later arranged for SATB as *Alleluia*. First per-
    formed by students at Indiana University. (AMRC/CBMR as choral *Alleluia*, IU;
    ME)

Orchestra

Ring Game II. 1979. Originally for *Scenes from the Life of a Martyr* (?). (ME)

Vocal Music

Solo Voice

Change. n.d. Text: Undine Smith Moore. (IDBC, ME)
Come Down Angels and Trouble the Water (soprano, piano). 1978. In *Art Songs and
    Spirituals by African-American Women Composers*. Edited by Vivian Taylor
    (Bryn Mawr, Pa.: Hildegard Publishing Co., 1995). Spiritual. For Karen Savage.
    See discography. (Allen, IDBC, ME).
Heart Have You Heard the News? (soprano, piano). 1926. Text: Christina Rossetti. First

performed in 1926 by Anna Lois Goodwin, soprano, and Undine Smith Moore, piano. 2 min. (Baker, IDBC, ME)

I Am in Doubt (soprano, piano). 1975. In *Art Songs and Spirituals by African-American Women Composers*. Edited by Vivian Taylor (Bryn Mawr, Pa.: Hildegard Publishing Co., 1995). Text: Florence Hynes Willett. For Carolyn Kizzie. Companion to *Lyric for True Love*. First performed in 1976 by Carolyn Kizzie, soprano, and Carl Harris, piano, at Virginia State College. See discography. 2 min. 50 sec. (Allen, Baker, IDBC, ME)

I Want to Die While You Love Me (contralto, piano). 1975. Text: Georgia Douglas Johnson. For Marie Goodman. First performed in 1975 by Marie Goodman Hunter, contralto, and Clarence Whiteman, piano, at the Beaux-Twenty Club program in honor of Undine Smith Moore, Petersburg, Va. See discography. (Baker, IDBC, ME)

Is There Anybody Here That Loves My Jesus? (soprano, piano). 1981. In *Art Songs and Spirituals by African-American Women Composers*. Edited by Vivian Taylor (Bryn Mawr, Pa.: Hildegard Publishing Co., 1995). Spiritual. See discography. (Allen).

Love Let the Wind Cry. (soprano, piano). 1961. In *Anthology of Art Songs by Black American Composers*. Edited by Willis Patterson (New York: E. B. Marks, 1977). Also in *Art Songs and Spirituals by African-American Women Composers*. Edited by Vivian Taylor (Bryn Mawr, Pa.: Hildegard Publishing Co., 1995). Text: Sappho/T. W. Wharton/Bliss Carman. For Jewel and Leon Thompson. First performed at the wedding of Jewell and Leon Taylor Thompson, 10 June 1961. See discography. 3 min. (Allen, Baker, IDBC, ME)

Lyric for True Love (soprano, piano). 1975. Text: Florence Hynes Willett. For Carolyn Kizzie. Companion to *I am in Doubt*. First performed in 1976 by Carolyn Kizzie, soprano, and Carl Harris, piano, Virginia State University. 2 min. 30 sec. (Allen, Baker, IDBC, ME)

My True Love Hath My Heart (soprano, piano). n.d. (IDBC, ME)

Second Spring. 1968. Text: Audre Lorde. (IU-USM; IDBC, ME)

Set Down! (soprano, piano). 1951. Spiritual. See discography. 2 min. (Allen, Baker, ME)

Sojourner Speaks. 1984. First performed by mezzo-soprano Johnella Edmonds and pianist Buckner Gamby at the Virginia Museum of Fine Arts. (IDBC, ME)

To Be Baptized (soprano, piano). 1973. Spirituals: "Here Comes Another One to Be Baptized" and "Take Me to the Water." For Camilla Williams. Companion to *Watch and Pray*. First performed in 1973 by Camilla Williams at the Town Hall gala concert in honor of Undine Smith Moore. See discography. 2 min. 40 sec. (AMRC/CBMR; Allen, Baker, IDBC, ME)

Uphill (soprano, piano). 1926. Text: Dante Gabriel Rossetti. First performed in 1926 by Anna Lois Goodwin, soprano, and Undine Smith Moore, piano. 2 min. (Baker, IDBC, ME)

Watch and Pray (soprano, piano). 1972. In *Art Songs and Spirituals by African-American Women Composers*. Edited by Vivian Taylor (Bryn Mawr, Pa.: Hildegard Publishing Co., 1995). Spiritual: "Mama, Is Massa Goin' to Sell Us Tomorrow?" For Camilla Williams. Companion to *To Be Baptized*. First performed by Camilla Williams in 1973 at Town Hall gala concert in honor of Undine Smith Moore. See discography. 4 min. (Baker, ME)

Solo Voice and Instruments

Scenes from the Life of a Martyr, section 2. 1975. Text: Song of Solomon. Contents: (1)
   Arise My Love (tenor, orchestra), (2) *Set Me as a Seal on Thy Heart* (soprano,
   tenor, orchestra), (3) *The Voice of My Beloved* (soprano, orchestra). Altogether:
   5 min. New York: Carl Fischer rental. (Baker, ME)

Three Bahai Prayers. 1978. Contents: (1) *O God, Refresh and Gladden My Spirit* (voice,
   flute), (2) *From the Sweet Scented Streams of Thine Eternity Give Me to Drink,
   O God* (voice, 2 trumpets, oboe), (3) *He Is the Compassionate, the All Bountiful*
   (soprano, flute, cello). Commissioned by and first performed by soprano Janis
   Peri in 1979, Old Dominion University. (Allen, IDBC, ME)

Chorus

Alleluia (women's voices/SATB, optional organ). 1975. Dedicated to and first performed
   in 1976 by Clarence Whiteman and the choir of St. Stephen's Church, Petersburg,
   Va. Same as *String Sentence*. 2 min., 10 sec. (AMRC/CBMR, IU; Baker, IDBC,
   ME)

Alleluia, Christ Is Risen (SATB). 1979. (IDBC, ME)

Alleluia: For Women's Voices (six-part women's chorus, soprano solo, small chorus of
   light voices). 1970. (IDBC)

Be Strong, I Will Fill This House with Glory (SATB, piano). 1979. Composed for the
   dedication of the Wentz Memorial United Church of Christ in Winston-Salem,
   N.C. Text: Haggai 1: 4–9. (Allen, IDBC)

Benediction (SATB a cappella). 1974. Text: Donald Jeffrey Hayes. Dedicated to Dr. Carl
   Harris and the Virginia State College choir, and first performed by them at the
   1975 commencement exercises. 3 min. (AMRC/CBMR; Baker, IDBC, ME)

The Blind Man Stood on the Way and Cried (SATB a cappella). 1932. Spiritual. 2 min.
   (Baker, ME)

Bound for Canaan's Land (SATB a cappella, tenor solo). New York: Warner Bros.,
   1960. Spiritual. First performance in 1960 by the Armstrong High School choir
   (Richmond, Va.), Harry Savage, conductor, at the Virginia State Music Festival,
   Virginia State College. See discography. (IU; Baker, ME)

Celebration. See *Three Centennial Pieces*.

Centennial Fanfare and Heritage Procession. See *Three Centennial Pieces*.

Children, Don't Get Weary. Listed in IDBC, but not Moore's arrangement.

Choral Prayers in Folk Style (SATB a cappella). 1974. A Mass in folk style. Contents:
   (1) We Shall Walk Through the Valley (Augsburg); (2) O, That Bleeding Lamb
   (Augsburg); (3) O, Holy Lord; (4) Lord, Have Mercy (Augsburg); (5) I Believe
   This Is Jesus (Augsburg); (6) Glory to God in the Highest; (7) Come Along in
   Jesus' Name (Augsburg). 13 min., 25 sec. (Allen, Baker, IDBC, ME)

A Christmas Alleluia (SSA a cappella). 1970. Chapel Hill, N.C.: Treble Clef Music Press,
   1998. Based on spiritual "O Mary What Are You Going to Name That Pretty
   Baby?" Commissioned and first performed in 1970 by the Spelman College Glee
   Club, Aldrich Adkins, conductor. 2 min., 30 sec. (Baker, IDBC, ME)

Come Along in Jesus' Name (SATB a cappella). Minneapolis: Augsburg, 1977. Spiritual.
   From *Choral Prayers in Folk Style*. 30 sec. (Baker, IDBC, ME)

Daniel, Daniel, Servant of the Lord (SSAATTBB a cappella). 1952. New York: Warner

Bros., 1953. Spiritual. First performed in 1952 at a faculty concert, Virginia State College, Undine Smith Moore, conductor. See discography. 1 min., 45 sec. (AMRC/CBMR, IU; Allen, Baker, IDBC, ME)

Fanfare and Processional (SATB, optional brass and percussion). Minneapolis: Augsburg, 1985. Same as *Heritage Fanfare and Processional*, and part of *Three Centennial Pieces*. Dedicated to Dr. Carl Harris and the concert choir of Virginia State University in celebration of their centennial anniversary in 1982. (IDBC, ME)

Fare You Well (SATB a cappella, soprano and tenor solos). 1950. New York: M. Witmark and Sons, 1951. Spiritual. First performed in 1951 by Virginia State College choir, Robert Henry, conductor. See discography. 1 min. 30 sec. (IU; Baker, ME)

For My People Everywhere (SATB, piano ad lib). New York: Warner Bros., 1979. Text: Margaret Walker. For Nathan Carter and the Morgan State University choir. 2 min., 44 sec. (IDBC)

Glory Be to God Who by His Love Has Brought Us to This Day (SATB). 1982. (ME)

Glory to God. See Dramatic Music.

Glory to God in the Highest (SATB a cappella). Minneapolis: Augsburg, 1979. From *Choral Prayers in Folk Style*. 1 min. (Baker, IDBC, ME)

Hail Warrior (SATB a cappella). New York: M. Witmark, 1957. Spiritual. First performed in 1958 by the Virginia State College choir, Aldrich Adkins, conductor. See discography. 2 min. (IU; Baker, IDBC, ME)

Heritage Fanfare and Processional. See *Three Centennial Pieces*.

How I Got Over (SATB a cappella). 1966. Spiritual. 2 min., 50 sec. (Baker, ME)

I Believe This Is Jesus (SATB divisi a cappella). 1974. Minneapolis: Augsburg, 1977. Spiritual. From *Choral Prayers in Folk Style*. 1 min. 40 sec. (Baker, ME)

I Just Came from the Fountain (SATB a cappella, soprano solo). 1950. New York: Warner Bros., 1951. Spiritual. First performed in 1951 by the Virginia State College choir, Robert Henry, conductor. See discography. 1 min., 10 sec. (Baker, IDBC, ME)

I Never Felt Such Love in My Heart Before (SATB). 1981. From *Scenes from the Life of a Martyr*. (IDBC)

I, Too, America (SATB, piano). 1981. Text: Langston Hughes. Commissioned by James Kinchen, Jr., for the Winston-Salem State University choir. Companion to *On Imagination*. (Allen, IDBC, ME)

I Will Trust in the Lord (SATB). 1984. Minneapolis: Augsburg, 1986. For inauguration of D. S. Dallas Simmons as president of Virginia Union University. (Allen, IDBC, ME)

I Would be True (SATB/SAB/SSA, piano). 1958. Minneapolis: Augsburg, 1979. Text: Howard A. Walter. Written for choruses of Ruffner and Jacox Junior High Schools, Norfolk, Va. 2 min., 20 sec. (Baker, IDBC, ME)

I'm Going Home (SATB a cappella, soprano solo). 1948. Minneapolis: Augsburg, 1978. Spiritual. 2 min., 30 sec. (Baker, ME)

Into My Heart's Treasury (SATB/SSA). 1950. Text: Sara Teasdale. 2 min., 30 sec. (Baker, IDBC, ME)

Is There Anybody Here? (SSA a cappella). 1949. Spiritual. First performed by the women's symphonic choir of Virginia State College, Undine Smith Moore, conductor. 3 min. (Baker, ME)

The Lamb (SS or unison). New York: H. W. Gray, 1958 (in *Church Music Review*). Text:

William Blake. First performed in 1958 by the Gillfield Baptist Church children's choir, Altona Trent Johns, conductor. See discography. 2 min., 30 sec. (IU; Baker, IDBC, ME)

Let Us Make Man in Our Image (SATB a cappella, soprano solo). New York: M. Witmark, 1960. Text: John Milton. First performed in 1960 by the Virginia State College choir, Aldrich Adkins, conductor. See discography. 2 min., 20 sec. (IU; Baker, IDBC, ME)

Long Fare You Well (SATB a cappella). Minneapolis: Augsburg, 1960. Spiritual. First performed in 1960 by the Virginia State College choir, Aldrich Adkins, conductor. 3 min., 10 sec. (Baker, ME)

Lord, Have Mercy (SATB a cappella). Minneapolis: Augsburg, 1978. From *Choral Prayers in Folk Style*. 2 min. (Baker, IDBC, ME)

Lord, Make Us More Holy (two-part canonic treatment of spiritual with piano accomp.) 1966. 1 min., 30 sec. (Baker, IDBC, ME)

Lord, We Give Thanks to Thee (SATB a cappella). 1971. New York: Warner Bros., 1973. Text: Leviticus 25:9. Commissioned by and first performed in 1971 by the Fisk Jubilee Singers for their centennial celebration at Fisk University, Matthew Kennedy, conductor. See discography. 2 min., 55 sec. (Baker, IDBC, ME)

Mother to Son (SSAATTBB a cappella, alto solo). New York: Warner Bros., 1955. In *Contemporary Anthology of Music by Women*, edited by James Briscoe (Bloomington: Indiana University Press, 1999). Text: Langston Hughes. First performed in 1955 by the Virginia State College choir, Mozart Tevis Fraser, conductor. See discography. 2 min., 30 sec. (IU; Baker, IDBC, ME)

No Condemnation (TTBB a cappella). 1935. Spiritual. 2 min. (Baker, ME)

O Come Let Us Sing unto the Lord (SATB). 1976. (ME)

O, Spirit Who Dost Prefer Before All Temples (SATB unison, organ/piano). 1966. Text: John Milton. First performance by the Gillfield Baptist Church choir, Undine Smith Moore, conductor. 2 min., 50 sec. (Baker, IDBC, ME)

Oh, Holy Lord (SATB a cappella). 1974. Spiritual. From *Choral Prayers in Folk Style*. 2 min., 50 sec. (Baker, ME)

Oh, That Bleeding Lamb (SATB a cappella). 1974. Minneapolis: Augsburg, 1977. Reissued 1997. Spiritual. From *Choral Prayers in Folk Style*. 2 min. (Baker, ME)

On Imagination (SATB/SATB, orchestra/piano). 1981. Text: Phillis Wheatley. Commissioned by and first performed by James Kinchen, Jr., and the Winston-Salem State University choir, 26 April 1981. Companion to *I, Too, America*. (Allen, IDBC, ME)

Plenty Good Room (SATB, soprano and tenor solos). 1980? Spiritual. Commissioned by Virginia State University for its centennial celebration (1982). See *Three Centennial Pieces*. See discography. (IDBC, ME)

Remember Now Thy Creator (SATB). 1980. (ME)

Rise Up, Shepherd, and Follow (TTBB a cappella). 1970. Spiritual. Commissioned and first performed in 1970 by the men's choir of First Baptist Church, Petersburg, Va., Buckner Gamby, conductor. 4 min. 30 sec. (IU; Baker, ME)

Sinner, You Can't Walk My Path (SATB a cappella). New York: M. Witmark and Sons, 1958. Spiritual. First performed in 1958 by the Virginia State College choir, Aldrich Adkins, conductor. See discography. 1 min. 40 sec. (Allen, Baker, ME)

Striving After God (SATB a cappella). 1958. New York: Warner Bros., 1958. Text: Michelangelo Buonarotti. First performed in 1958 by the Virginia State College choir, Aldrich Adkins, conductor. See discography. 3 min. (IU; Baker, IDBC, ME)

Tambourines to Glory (SATB a cappella). New York: Warner Bros., 1973. Text: Langston Hughes. First performed in 1974 by the Virginia Union University choir, Odell Hobbs, conductor, at the Mosque Auditorium in Richmond, Va. 1 min. (Baker, IDBC, ME)

Teach Me to Hear Mermaids Singing (SSA, three-part canon). 1953. Text: John Donne. 30 sec. (Baker, IDBC, ME)

Thou Hast Made Us for Thyself (SATB a cappella). 1952. Text: St. Augustine. Choral fugue. First performed in 1952 by the Virginia State College choir, Undine Smith Moore, conductor. 5 min. (Baker, IDBC, ME)

Three Centennial Pieces. (SATB, 3 trumpets, 3 trombones, timpani, organ). 1982. Contents: 1) Fanfare and Processional, using spiritual "He Is King of Kings;" (2) Celebration, with text by Undine Smith Moore; (3) Spiritual, using "Plenty Good Room." Composed for the centennial celebration of Virginia State University and for the concert choir, directed by Dr. Carl G. Harris, Jr. (only Celebration at AMRC/CBMR; IDBC, ME)

A Time for Remembering (SATB, piano). 1976. Text: Undine Smith Moore. Commissioned by Virginia State Board of Education in memory of Dr. C. J. Heoch, supervisor of music. First performed in 1976 by the Southern University choir, Aldrich Adkins, conductor, at the Loyola University Bicentennial Choral Festival. 3 min. (Baker, IDBC, ME)

Two Pieces for Women's Voices and Clarinet. n.d. (IDBC, ME)

Walk Through the Streets of the City (SATB). 1966. Minneapolis: Augsburg, 1977. Spiritual. 3 min. (Baker, ME)

We Shall Walk Through the Valley (SATB a cappella). Minneapolis: Augsburg, 1977. Spiritual. From *Choral Prayers in Folk Style*. 3 min. (Baker, ME)

When Susanna Jones Wears Red (SATB a cappella). 1958. New York: Warner Bros., 1975. Text: Langston Hughes. 1 min., 10 sec. (Baker, IDBC, ME)

Who Shall Separate Us from the Love of Christ?(SATB, piano/organ). 1953. Text: Romans 8:35. First performed in 1953 by the Gillfield Baptist Church choir, Undine Smith Moore, conductor. 3 min. (Baker, IDBC, ME)

Dramatic Music

Glory to God (TTBB, flute, organ/piano, narrator, optional brass and percussion). 1974. Christmas cantata. Text: St. Luke, St. Matthew, and the Book of Common Prayer. Commissioned and first performed in 1974 by the men's chorus of First Baptist Church in Petersburg, Va., Buckner Gamby, conductor. 30 min. (Baker, IDBC, ME)

Scenes from the Life of a Martyr (SATB, orchestra, narrator, soloists). 1980. New York: Carl Fischer (rental), 1982. Oratorio. Based on life of Martin Luther King, Jr. Texts: Undine Smith Moore/King James Bible/spirituals/Thomas Hayden/Claude McKay/ Stephen Spender. First performed in December 1981 in Haddonfield, N.J., conducted by Arthur Cohn. 45 min. (AMRC/CBMR; IDBC, ME)

Sir Olaf and the Erl King's Daughter (SSA, piano). 1925. Cantata composed while student of Sarah Leight Laubenstein at Fisk. Text: Scandinavian folk poem. First performance at Fisk University by the Fisk University girl's glee club, Mary E. Hillman, conductor, Undine Smith at the piano. 25 min. (Baker, IDBC, ME)

Other

A Recorded Supplement to Studies in Traditional Harmony. n.d. (Workbook).

NOTES

Mary Moore Easter's assistance in supplying missing details and correcting this chapter is deeply appreciated.

Quotations from David Baker et al., "Undine Smith Moore," and Undine Smith Moore, "Keynote Address" (see selected bibliography) are used with permission.

Full references are given in the selected bibliography at the end of this chapter.

1. Moore, "Keynote Address," pp. 9–10. Touse and Theandros were field hands, friends of the family.

2. Allen.

3. Bustard, "Composer's 'King Work.' "

4. On 11 February 1990, the Virginia Union University choir dedicated its annual winter concert to Moore, naming it "A Time for Remembering," and on June 24 of that year "A Call to Remembrance Concert of Music by Undine Smith Moore" was presented by Winston-Salem Delta Fine Arts at the Stevens Center for the Performing Arts. The Archives of African American Music and Culture at Indiana University has named its collection of scores by black composers after her. Virginia State University held concerts featuring her music to raise funds in 1993, 1994, and 1995, and in March 1997 the Undine Smith Moore Scholarship Committee, headed by Dr. Ethel Norris, organized an Undine Smith Moore Festival including discussions, workshops, and a concert. Her choral works were selected for the "Witness" concerts by the Plymouth Music Series in Minneapolis, conducted by Phillip Brunelle. In February 1999 she was a featured composer at the second annual Black Women Composers Symposium at Hampton University.

5. Moore, "Keynote Address," p. 9. Dance as a religious practice, originating in Africa, is common among African Americans.

6. Moore's brother, Clarence William Smith died in 1955, and her sister, Eunice Smith (later Byus), became a public school principal in Petersburg.

7. Moore, "Keynote Address," p. 10.

8. Moore, "Keynote Address," p. 10.

9. Moore, "Keynote Address," p. 10.

10. This school soon became Virginia State College, where Moore was to spend so many years teaching. In 1979 it was renamed Virginia State University.

11. Wakeland. Fisk made musical history in 1871, its fifth year, when its choir, the Fisk Jubilee Singers, under the direction of George L. White, a white teacher from Massachusetts, began touring to raise funds for the school. This started the tradition of touring "Jubilee" singers at several black schools.

12. Numerous sources erroneously state that Moore studied at the Juilliard School of Music, probably a misunderstanding of her Juilliard Scholarship for study at Fisk. This was awarded by the Juilliard Graduate School, which opened in 1924. The Juilliard

School of Music was not formed until 1946, from a merger of the Juilliard Graduate School with the Institute of Musical Art, founded in 1905.

13. Bustard, "Composer's 'King Work.' "

14. Professor John Wesley Work II (1873–1925) taught history and Latin at Fisk, but was best known as the first black collector and arranger of Negro folk songs. From 1898 on, he organized touring student choirs at Fisk and elsewhere, following the model of the Fisk Jubilee Singers.

15. Beckner.

16. Their beautiful house in Ettrick, Va., was designed by F. T. Hylan, a student of Frank Lloyd Wright, and was featured in the *Virginia Architectural Record* in 1953.

17. Mary Hardie Moore Easter became a professional dancer and professor of dance at Carleton College in Minnesota, and presented the Moores with two granddaughters, Allison and Mallory.

18. Mobley. Dr. Carl G. Harris, Jr. served as professor and chairman of the department of music at Virginia State University from 1971 to 1984, and also taught in the Department of Music at Norfolk State University and Hampton University. Professor Harris has written numerous articles on Undine Smith Moore, and recorded her works with the Virginia State College choir in *The Undine Smith Moore Song Book*.

19. D. Antoinette Handy, interview with the author on 21 November 1990 in Washington, D.C. Handy is the niece of famed blues composer W. C. Handy; she had a career as a concert flutist, and later became head of the Music Division of the National Endowment for the Arts. She is the author of several books on black women musicians.

20. Program of Billy Taylor Trio concert, Norfolk, Va., 30 March 1990.

21. Altona Trent Johns (1904–77) was a fine pianist and highly regarded music teacher who also composed. She taught at Virginia State from 1952 until she retired in 1972. Moore called her "my most inspiring friend" (Harris, "Conversation," p. 88).

22. It was later supported by three grants from the National Endowment for the Humanities, and three from the Southern Educational Foundation and Title III.

23. In the first two years of the center's activities, 27 seminars and 3 institutes included participation by such groups as the Sea Island Spiritual Singers of St. Simon's Island in Georgia, Brownie McGhee and Sonny Terry on the blues, Pearl William Jones and The Voices Supreme (directed by Robert Fryson) for gospel music, and Dr. Samuel DeWitt Proctor, lecturer on black folk sermons. The course "The Black Man in American Music" was taught jointly by Moore and Johns until 1972, and by Dr. Carl Harris, Jr., from 1972 to 1984. It was still going strong in 2000 as "Blacks in American Music," taught by Ethel Norris and James Holden, Jr.

24. The work was *Concert Music for Piano and Orchestra*, and the soloist on that occasion was Jewell Thompson. The other composers featured included William Grant Still, William Dawson, Ulysses Kay, and George Walker.

25. Church.

26. Moore, "Keynote Address," p. 10.

27. Baker et al., p. 180.

28. Moore, "Keynote Address," pp. 10–11.

29. Baker et al., pp. 178–179.

30. Baker et al., p. 177.

31. Moore, "Black Music," p. 66.

32. Baker et al., pp. 178–179.

33. Baker et al., pp. 176–178. She also observed that there are some interesting exceptions: the paintings of El Greco were the epitome of Spanish art, and Joseph Conrad, born and raised a Pole, mastered English prose.

34. Waller, "Being in a Different Place." However, Moore also notes that the black artist is usually at the bottom of this group, less likely to be performed, published, included in texts, or recorded, and that others who imitate or use his work often reap the fame and fortune that should have been his. She also observed that many publishers seem to treat blacks on a token quota system: commitment to one black composer at a time.

35. Moore, "Keynote Address," p. 11.

36. Moore, "Keynote Address," p. 10.

37. Moore, "Keynote Address," p. 11.

38. Moore, "Keynote Address," p. 11; Baker et al., p. 191.

39. Moore, "Keynote Address," p. 10.

40. Moore, "Black Music," pp. 59–61.

41. Harris, "Conversation," p. 81.

42. *Love Let the Wind Cry* was reprinted from Willis Patterson's *Anthology of Art Songs* (1977) in *Art Songs and Spirituals by African-American Women Composers*, edited by Vivian Taylor, along with four of her spirituals for solo voice and piano. The piano piece *Before I'd Be a Slave* was included in the anthology, *Black Women Composers: A Century of Piano Music 1893–1990*, edited by Helen Walker-Hill. Her choral work *Mother to Son* is in *Contemporary Anthology of Music by Women*, edited by James Briscoe (Bloomington: Indiana University Press, 1999).

43. Leopold Godowsky (1870–1938) was a legendary Lithuanian-born American pianist and composer known for his difficult piano etudes and transcriptions. When Moore was asked by a piano duo in the 1980s for permission to perform the *Romance*, she told them, "No, because it is filled with too many diminished seventh chords." She went on to say, "It was a perfectly honest piece when it was written in 1952, but it is no longer of worth in the 1980s" (Harris, "Conversation," p. 85).

44. Harris, "Conversation," p. 85.

45. Harris, "Conversation," p. 81.

46. Moore, "Keynote Address," p. 13. Professor Harris, in a conversation with the author on 17 February 1999 in Hampton, Va., pointed out that Moore had other favorite sources for the spirituals she set: *The Story of the Jubilee Singers with Their Songs*, by J. T. Marsh (Boston: Houghton Mifflin, 1880), and *The Harp of Zion*, by W. Henry Sherwood (Author, 1893).

47. For a more detailed analysis of *Soweto*, see Helen Walker-Hill, "Moore, Undine Smith" in *International Dictionary of Black Composers*.

48. Goldsmith. Unfortunately, no trace of these songs has been found, and the identity of the writers is not known. The aria *Sojourner Speaks* is the only extant part of the unfinished opera.

49. Especially Wilson's *Cetus*, which won the first International Contest for Electronic Music in 1968, and his *Sometimes*, performed in 1977 at Lincoln Center in New York at a Black Composers Symposium concert with her *Love Let the Wind Cry*.

50. Baker et al., p. 178.

51. Allen.

52. Moore visited the pavilion when she traveled to Paris and Italy in the summer of

1967 with her sister and niece, and to France and Spain with her daughter in the summer of 1971.

53. Or rather, F-sharp pentatonic (G-sharp and D do not appear in the melody, resulting in the gapped scale).

54. Harris, "Conversation," p. 84.

55. See the more detailed analysis of *Before I'd Be a Slave* by Thomas R. Erdmann.

56. First published by William Barton in *Old Plantation Hymns* in 1899, it became a favorite during the civil rights movement of the 1960s as "Oh Freedom."

57. Holland, "Music: Black Writers."

58. De Lerma.

59. This device, the "Picardy third" (raising the third of the chord to major), which dates back to the sixteenth century, was used frequently by J. S. Bach and other baroque composers to bring pieces in minor keys to a bright final conclusion.

60. Hocket was a popular medieval vocal device of the thirteenth and fourteenth centuries in which two or more voices pass the notes of the melody back and forth in very quick alternations, like a hand-bell choir.

61. A detailed analysis of the work appears in Yvette Moorehead Carter's master's thesis, "The *Afro-American Suite* (1969) of Undine Smith Moore: A Study in Identity." I am indebted to Carter for the "preaching" concept of the second movement.

62. Harris, "Conversation," p. 82.

63. Wakeland.

64. Moore, "The Composer's Thoughts."

65. Wakeland.

66. The 1982 New York performance was by the Collegiate Chorale under the direction of Robert Bass, with William Warfield as narrator and soloists Esther Hines, Arthur Woodley, Vinson Cole, and Isola Jones, all from the Metropolitan and New York City opera companies.

67. The official Richmond premiere by the Intercollegiate Chorus included choirs from Longwood College, Virginia Union University, Virginia State University, Norfolk State University, Hampton University, and Virginia Commonwealth University.

68. The 1989 Saintpaulia symphony performances were under the direction of Julius Williams, with Julian Bond, narrator, Lynda Elliot, soprano, Gregory Hopkins, Grace Hackett, and John Anthony, soloists.

69. Kenyon.

70. Crutchfield.

71. Rockwell.

72. Newlin.

73. Holland, "Concert."

74. Shore.

75. Holland, "Concert"; Olivia Mathis, "Undine Smith Moore," unpublished paper, p. 6.

76. Moore, "The Composer's Thoughts." Sir Stephen Harold Spender (1909–95), English poet, literary critic, and editor, born in London and educated at Oxford, was a champion of the radical labor movement. Claude McKay (1890–1948), poet and writer prominent in the Harlem Renaissance, was born in Jamaica and died in Chicago. Robert Hayden (1913–1980), born Asa Bundy Sheffe in Detroit, was the first black American to be appointed as consultant in poetry to the Library of Congress (1976) and was associated with the Bahai religion.

77. Liberation theology is a Latin American Catholic theology (also shared by some other denominations) which holds that the church should stand with the poor and oppressed.

78. Dr. Carl Harris, Jr., informed me that this spiritual was found in Marsh, p. 189 (see n. 46).

SELECTED BIBLIOGRAPHY

Not all the sources consulted in this study are listed, only those useful to readers or cited in notes.

Allen, Simona. Program notes for "A Concert of Music by Undine Smith Moore" presented by Winston-Salem Delta Fine Arts, 24 June 1990.

Baker, David N., Lida M. Belt, and Herman C. Hudson. "Undine Smith Moore." Chapter 7 in *The Black Composer Speaks*. Metuchen, N.J.: Scarecrow Press, 1978.

Beckner, Steve. "Composer and Teacher—Mrs. Undine Smith Moore."*The Progress-Index* (Petersburg, Va.), 5 January 1975.

Bustard, C. A. "Composer's 'King Work' Gets Premiere." *Times-Dispatch* (Richmond, Va.), 18 April 1982.

———. "Undine Smith Moore." *Black History: Virginia Profiles*. 1996. http://www.gateway-va.com/pages/bhistory/moore.htm

Carter, Yvette Marie Moorehead. "The *Afro-American Suite* (1969) of Undine Smith Moore: A Study in Identity." M.A. thesis, University of Virginia, 1995.

Church, Francis. "Composer's Evening Filled with Warmth." *Richmond News Leader*, n.d. (from the files of Carl Harris, Jr.)

Cohen, Aaron I. *International Dictionary of Women Composers*. 2nd ed. New York: R. R. Bowker, 1985.

Crutchfield, Will. "The Voices in Honor of Dr. King." *New York Times*, 19 January 1989.

De Lerma, Dominique-René. Record review of *Afro-American Suite* on *Contemporary Black Images in Music for the Flute* by Trio Pro Viva. *The Black Perspective in Music* 1, no. 2 (Fall 1973): 192.

Easter, Mary. "Complete List of Compositions by Undine Smith Moore." 1990. Unpublished.

Erdmann, Thomas R. "The Formal Structure of Undine Smith Moore's *Before I'd Be a Slave*." *Women of Note Quarterly* 5, no. 2 (August 1997): 13.

Goldsmith, Diane. "U.S. Moore: Classical Composer of Life's Sweet Song." *Virginia Pilot*, 16 February 1984.

Harris, Carl, Jr. "A Study of Characteristic Stylistic Traits Found in Choral Works of a Selected Group of Afro-American Composers and Arrangers." Ph.D. diss., University of Missouri at Kansas City, 1971.

———. "Conversation with Undine Smith Moore, Composer and Master Teacher." *The Black Perspective in Music* 16, no. 1 (Spring 1985): 79–88.

Holland, Bernard. "Concert: Collegiate Chorale Offers Premiere and Revival." *New York Times*, n.d. (from the files of Carl Harris, Jr.)

———. "Music: Black Writers." *New York Times*, 20 February 1985.

Jones, John R. D. "The Choral Works of Undine Smith Moore: A Study of Her Life and Work." Ed.D. diss., New York University, 1980.

Kenyon, Nicholas. "Carnegie Hall Review: *Scenes from the Life of a Martyr.*" *The New Yorker*, 1 February 1982, 43.

Mathis, Olivia. "Moore, Undine Smith." In *New Groves Dictionary of Music and Musicians*. Edited by Stanley Sadie. New York: Macmillan, 2000.

Mobley, Mark. "Composer Leaves Behind Legacy of Spirit, Optimism." *The Ledger Star*. (Norfolk, Va.), 8 February 1989.

Moore, James Edward. "The Choral Music of Undine Smith Moore." D.M.A. thesis, University of Cincinnati, 1979.

Moore, Undine Smith, with Johnnie V. Lee, Portia Maultsby, and John A. Taylor. "Black Music in the Undergraduate Curriculum." In *Reflections on Afro-American Music*. Edited by Dominique-René De Lerma. Kent, Ohio: Kent State University Press, 1973.

————. "Keynote Address." Delivered at the first National Congress on Women in Music, 27 March 1981 at New York University. Cambria Historical Archives Cassette C142. Cambria Records and Publishing, Box 374, Lomita, Calif., 90717. Transcribed and published as "Composers' Corner: My Life in Music." *International Alliance for Women in Music Journal* 3, no. 1 (February 1997): 9–15.

————. "The Composer's Thoughts About the Composition." Program notes for "The 'Dream' Concert . . . Concert for a King." Symphony Saintpaulia, January 1989.

Newlin, Dika. Music review: *Scenes from the Life of a Martyr. Times-Dispatch* (Richmond, Va.), 20 April 1982.

Pearson, Augustus J., Jr. "Afro-American Characteristics in the Choral Works of Undine Smith Moore." D.M.A. diss., University of Kansas, 1982.

Pendle, Karin. *Women and Music: A History*. Bloomington: Indiana University Press, 2001.

Roach, Hildred. *Black American Music Past and Present*. 2nd ed. Malabar, Fla.: Krieger, 1992.

Rockwell, John. "Concert: Five Works by Black Composers." *New York Times*, 7 November 1985.

Ryder, William Henderson. "Music at Virginia State College, 1883–1966." Ph.D. diss., University of Michigan, 1970.

Scott, Sandra Cannon. "Undine Smith Moore." In *Black Women in America: An Historical Encyclopedia*. Edited by Darlene Clark Hine. Brooklyn, N.Y.: Carlson, 1993.

Shore, Charles. "Symphonic Elegy to Simmons, King."*Oakland Tribune*, 14 February 1985.

Southern, Eileen. *Biographical Dictionary of Afro-American and African Musicians*. Westport, Conn.: Greenwood Press, 1983.

————.*The Music of Black Americans*. 3rd ed. New York: Norton, 1997.

Stephens, Robert W. "Undine Smith Moore." In *Notable Black American Women*. Edited by Jessie Carney Smith. Detroit: Gale Research, 1992.

Taylor, Vivian, ed. *Art Songs and Spirituals by African-American Women Composers*. Bryn Mawr, Pa.: Hildegard Publishing Co., 1995.

Wakeland, Jeanier. "King Tribute at Memorial Concert." *West County Times*, 8 February 1985.

Walker-Hill, Helen. *Black Women Composers: A Century of Piano Music 1893–1990*. Bryn Mawr, Pa.: Hildegard Publishing Co., 1992.

————. *Piano Music by Black Women Composers: A Catalog of Solo and Ensemble Works*. Westport, Conn.: Greenwood Press, 1992.

————. *Music by Black Women Composers: A Bibliography of Available Scores.* CBMR Monographs no. 5. Chicago: Center for Black Music Research, 1995.

————. "Moore, Undine Smith." In *International Dictionary of Black Composers.* Edited by Samuel Floyd, Jr. Chicago: Fitzroy Dearborn, 1999.

Waller, Buddy. "Being in a Different Place Moves Composer." *Progress-Index* (Petersburg, Va.), n.d. (from the files of Carl Harris, Jr.)

————. "Composer Perfects King Tribute." *Progress-Index* (Petersburg, Va.), n.d. (from the files of Carl Harris, Jr.)

DISCOGRAPHY

Afro-American Suite. Performed by Trio Pro Viva: D. Antoinette Handy, flute; Ronald Lipscomb, cellist; and Gladys Perry Norris, piano. *Contemporary Black Images in Music for the Flute.* Eastern LP ERS 513, 1969.

Ah, Love but a Day. Performed by Louise Toppin, soprano; Jay Pierson, baritone; and John O'Brien, piano. Albany Records CD Troy 385, 2000. Album includes *To Be Baptized, Set Down, I Want to Die While You Love Me,* and *Come Down Angels.*

Before I'd Be a Slave. Performed by Helen Walker-Hill, piano. *Kaleidoscope: Music by African-American Women.* Leonarda Records CD LE 339, 1995.

Daniel, Daniel, Servant of the Lord. Included on following LPs: (1) *Undine Smith Moore Songbook.* Vol. 3 of the Afro-American Heritage Series. Virginia State University choir directed by Carl Harris, Jr., Richsound 4112N10A, 1974. (2) *The Oberlin College Choir.* Oberlin College choir, Daniel Moe, conductor. Oberlin College Choir Recordings, series B, vol. 2. (3) *The Oberlin College Choir 1961 Concert Program.* Oberlin College choir, Robert Fountain, conductor. Empirical EM 17–18. (4) *The Fisk Jubilee Singers.* Fisk Jubilee Singers, John W. Work III, conductor. World Records W-4007:L. (5) *Les Plus Beaux Negro-Spirituals par les Fisk Jubilee Singers.* Philips P76145R.

Lord We Give Thanks to Thee. Included on following LPs: (1) *The Undine Smith Moore Songbook.* Virginia State University choir, Carl Harris, Jr., conductor. Richsound 4112N10A. (2) *Lord, We Give Thanks to Thee.* Virginia Union University choir, Odell Hobbs, conductor. Eastern ERS-549. (3) *Festival of Music—Virginia Music Camp.* Massanetta Chorus, John Motley, conductor. Mark MC-8568C. (4) *The Eye of the Storm.* Fisk Jubilee Singers, Matthew Kennedy, conductor. Fisk University.

Love Let the Wind Cry and *How I Adore You.* Performed by Odikhiren Amaize, voice; David Korevaar, piano. *The Negro Speaks of Rivers: Art Songs by African-American Composers.* Musicians' Showcase CD 1011, 2000.

Undine Smith Moore Songbook. Vol. 3 of the Afro-American Heritage Series. Virginia State University choir, directed by Carl Harris, Jr. Richsound LP 4112N10A, 1974. Contains *I Just Came from the Fountain, Let Us Make Man in Our Image, Hail Warrior, The Lamb, Striving After God, Daniel, Daniel, Servant of the Lord, Bound for Canaan's Land, Sinner You Can't Walk My Path, Fare You Well, Lord, We Give Thanks to Thee,* and *Plenty Good Room.*

Watch and Pray: Spirituals and Art Songs by African-American Women Composers.

Performed by Videmus: Pamela Dillard, soprano; Robert Honeysucker, baritone; Vivian Taylor, piano. Koch International Classics CD. 1994. Includes *Watch and Pray, Is There Anybody Here That Loves My Jesus?, I Am in Doubt, Love Let the Wind Cry*.

Julia Perry. Snapshot taken by Irene Britton Smith at Tanglewood, Summer 1949. Helen Walker-Hill Collection, Center for Black Music Research Library and Archives, Columbia College, Chicago.

3

JULIA PERRY
(1924–79)

CHRONOLOGY

1924   Born 25 March in Lexington, Ky., to Dr. Abe Perry and America Lois Heath Perry; the fourth of five sisters.

1934   Moved with family to Akron, Ohio.

1934–39   Attended Spicer Elementary School; studied voice with Mable Todd in Akron; also studied piano and violin.

1939–42   Studied at Central High School; won a music contest in violin and voice in Wooster, Ohio.

1940   Julia's older sister America Lois died in late July.

1942–43   Attended the University of Akron.

1943   Received Knight Scholarship to attend Westminster Choir College; studied composition with Henry Switten.

1946   Summer in Birmingham, Ala., with a group from Westminster Choir College; composed *Prelude for Piano*.

1947   Completed B.M. degree at Westminster; choral piece *Carillon Heigh-Ho* published by Carl Fischer in New York; composed choral works *Is There Anybody Here?* and *The Lord Is Risen Today*, and songs *Deep Sworn Vow, King Jesus Lives*, and *To Elektra*; piano pieces *Pearls on Silk* and *Suite of Shoes*.

1948   Completed M.M. degree at Westminster; master's thesis cantata *Chicago*; attended National Association of Negro Musicians convention in Columbus, Ohio, in August and won first place in voice, tied for first place in composition.

1948–49   Taught at Hampton Institute: voice, theory, orchestration, composition.

1949   At Berkshire Music Festival in Tanglewood in summer: studied choral con-
          ducting with Hugh Ross; song *Lord, What Shall I Do?* published by Mc-
          Laughlin and Reilly in Boston; songs performed by concert artists Nan
          Merriman and Ellabelle Davis; won Marian Anderson Award in New York
          City.

1949–51   Lived at International House in New York; was assistant coach and participant
          in the Columbia Opera Workshop; cantata *Ruth* performed at Riverside
          Church on 16 April 1950; attended Juilliard School of Music Extension Di-
          vision in fall of 1950, took class in operatic conducting with Emanuel Bala-
          ban; song *By the Sea* and choral work *Our Thanks to Thee* published by
          Galaxy.

1951   Attended Berkshire Music Center at Tanglewood in summer on scholarship,
          studied composition with Luigi Dallapiccola; *Woodwind Trio* and *Stabat Ma-
          ter* performed at Tanglewood; benefit concert in October in Akron; departed
          for Florence, Italy, in November to study with Dallapiccola.

1952   Performances of *Stabat Mater* in Milan; Perry in Salzburg, Austria, on 26
          June 1952 for performance of *Stabat Mater*; attended American Conservatory
          in Fontainebleau, France, in July, studying composition with Nadia Boulan-
          ger; *Viola Sonata* won Prix Fontainebleau; returned to Florence for further
          study with Dallapiccola; *Short Piece for Orchestra* premiered by the Turin
          Orchestra conducted by Dean Dixon; solo voice *I'm a Poor Little Orphan
          Girl* and choral *Ye Who Seek the Truth*, published by Galaxy.

1953   Returned to New York in August; attended Berkshire Music Festival at Tan-
          glewood; *Stabat Mater* performed at Aspen Music Festival by Herta Glaz and
          New Music String Quartet; received first Guggenheim Fellowship for use from
          1 October 1954 to 10 September 1955; choral *Be Merciful unto Me* and *Song
          of Our Savior* published by Galaxy; composed *Frammenti dalle lettere di
          Santa Caterina* for soprano, chorus, and small orchestra.

1954   *Stabat Mater* performed by soprano Virginia Shuey and conductor Howard
          Shanet in New York on 20 February; *Stabat Mater* published by Southern
          Music Company; at the MacDowell Colony in New Hampshire in July–Au-
          gust; composed *String Quartet*, solo vocal *Parody, A Short Service* for so-
          prano and trumpet; opera *Cask of Amontillado* performed at Columbia
          University, 20 November; solo voice *How Beautiful are the Feet* published
          by Galaxy.

1955   *Short Piece for Orchestra* performed 21 February in Town Hall, New York,
          by The Little Symphony, conducted by Thomas Sherman; *Cask of Amontil-
          lado* performed at the University of Delaware Summer Festival; departed for
          Italy in November; engaged by the U.S. Information Service to give lectures
          in southern Italy.

1956   Second Guggenheim Fellowship awarded for use from 1 October 1956 to 30
          November 1957; composed *Three Negro Spirituals for Soprano and Orches-
          tra.*

1956–58   Summers in Siena, Italy, on scholarship for study at the Accademia Chigiana
          with Emanuel Balaban, Alceo Galliera, and Adone Zecchi.

1957   Engaged by the U.S. Information Service to tour European cities, lecturing
          and conducting orchestras, including BBC Orchestra in London.

1958   *Stabat Mater* performed in December in a Clarion Concert in New York, sung
          by Betty Allen and conducted by Newell Jenkins.

1959   Returned to New York on 9 February; attended performance of her *Requiem
          for Orchestra* conducted by Howard Shanet at Cooper Union on 13 March;
          at MacDowell Colony in May–June and November; composed *Pastoral* for
          flute and strings; began composing *Mary Easty*, opera on Salem witch trials.

1960   In Akron, Ohio; composed *Homunculus C.F.; Stabat Mater* recording released
          by CRI.

1961   Returned to New York on 11 August; taught piano privately; composed *Sym-
          phony No 1, Seven Sutures for Orchestra, Suite for Brass, Ballet for Orches-
          tra; Short Piece for Orchestra* recording released by CRI.

1962   At MacDowell Colony at some time; composed *Symphony No. 2, Symphony
          No. 3*, and *Dance for Chamber Orchestra*.

1963   Returned to Akron by 6 January; offered private lessons; taught at Akron
          Conservatory of Music; wrote to Library of Congress requesting commission
          from the Coolidge Foundation in December; composed choral *Hymn to Pan,
          The Beacon* for winds, *Contretemps for Orchestra, Liberation for Orchestra,
          Solstice for Strings, Four Pieces for Wind Quintet, Five Songs for Soprano
          and Piano*.

1964   Berg Street home razed for Akron University expansion; Perry resided at
          Akron YWCA; returned to New York by 3 February; *Contretemps* performed
          28 April by the Akron Symphony Orchestra; received National Institute of
          Arts and Letters grant for recording of *Homunculus C.F.* by CRI; composed
          Symphony No. 4, Ariel for Orchestra, Composition for Orchestra, three-act
          opera *The Selfish Giant*; expanded from *Three Negro Spirituals for Soprano
          and Orchestra* to Five; completed *Concerto No. 2 for Piano and Orchestra*;
          at MacDowell Colony October 1964–January 1965.

1965   Performance of *Homunculus* at Manhattan School of Music 14 January; per-
          formance of *Study for Orchestra* by the New York Philharmonic Orchestra,
          conducted by William Steinberg, in May; wrote poem *Graves of Untold Af-
          ricans*.

1966   Applied to National Council on the Arts for grant to write music dictionary
          in March; completed *Symphony No. 6* for concert band.

1967   Lived on Euclid Avenue in Akron; at MacDowell Colony in July–August;
          composed *Symphony No. 5* ("Integration"), *Symphony USA* (7th) for chorus
          and orchestra, *Module for Orchestra*, and three more Negro spirituals for
          orchestra without soloist; wrote translations of 78 African fables from Italian
          to English.

1967–68   Taught at Florida A&M University; completed *Concerto for Violin and Orchestra*.

1969   Visiting lecturer at the Atlanta University Center for a week in September–October; *Homunculus C.F.* released by CRI; won Honorable Mention in ASCAP Awards to Women Composers of Symphonic and Concert Music; wrote three-act play *Fisty-Me*, two essays, a three-act "dramatic ritual," completed *Symphony No. 8*.

1970   First stroke paralyzed Perry's right side sometime between March and May; performance of *Stabat Mater* by Betty Allen and Fine Arts String Quartet in Chicago in March; completed *Symphony No. 9*.

1970s   Perry's father, Dr. Abe Perry, died sometime in the early 1970s.

1971   Composed marching band pieces; right hand still paralyzed.

1972   Submitted works to conductors Paul Freeman, Henry Lewis, Zubin Mehta, and Georg Solti; completed *Symphony No. 10* ("Soul Symphony") and *Symphony No.11*, *Two Easy Piano Pieces*, *Marching Band Symphony*, *Panorama*, and *Tom Thumb* snare drum pieces.

1973   In Lakeside Hospital in March; composed *Symphony No. 12* ("Simple Symphony").

1974   Composed *Divertimento for Five Wind Instruments*, completed opera *Symplegades* (formerly *Mary Easty*).

1975   Several admissions to Edwin Shaw Hospital in Ohio from May to July; composed *Space Symphony*, and 3rd movement for *Concerto for Piano in Two Uninterrupted Speeds*.

1976   Applied to NEA for grant; composed *Quinary Quixotic Songs*.

1977   Composed *Bicentennial Reflections*.

1979   Died 24 April in Akron, Ohio, at the age of 55; buried at Glendale Cemetery in Akron.

> Music is an all-embracing, universal language. Music has a unifying effect on the peoples of the world, because they all understand and love it. In music they find a common meeting ground. And when they find themselves enjoying and loving the same music, they find themselves loving one another. . . . Music has a great role to play in establishing the brotherhood of man.[1]

The brotherhood of man was still a dream in the United States when Julia Perry made this statement in 1949. Her remarkable career began before the civil rights era, while de facto segregation was still the norm in the North as well as the law in the South, and black performers had difficulty gaining access to opera houses or concert stages. At midcentury she was acknowledged as one of a handful of significant American composers, whether black or female, whose music not only was performed frequently in Europe and the United States, but also was published and recorded. She drew on the strengths and musical traditions of her African-American heritage, competed successfully in the white mainstream musical world, and gained an international reputation as a composer of undisputed talent and skill in an eclectic twentieth-century musical language. This achievement was not only impressive but also subversive, a challenge to the status quo without being intentionally political.

The most striking aspect of Julia Perry's story is her extraordinary early success and its ensuing erosion by illness and public neglect. By her thirtieth birthday her most famous work, perhaps her major opus, the *Stabat Mater*, had been composed, published, and widely performed in Europe and the United States, and she had received the first of her two Guggenheim fellowships, one of the most prestigious awards available to composers. In her 40s, she strove thereafter to match her early success and to find a voice in tune with the changing times. Her tenacity and perseverance in continuing to compose and to pursue performances and publication, despite ill health, social and political upheaval, public ignorance, and rejection, is deeply moving and inspiring.

BIOGRAPHY

In Glendale Cemetery in Akron, Ohio, lies a neat marble tombstone inscribed "Julia A. Perry 1927–1979." The birth date is three years too late. Graven in stone, this information would seem to be irrefutable. Indeed, even before her death some references gave her birth year as 1927, leading one to suspect that she herself may occasionally have supplied the later date. Julia's passport states her date and place of birth as 25 March 1924 in Lexington, Kentucky. In the 1990s, her one surviving sister confirmed that this was correct, and speculated that her mother, confused and in poor health, provided the wrong information. This discrepancy illustrates a recurrent obstacle in researching Julia Perry's story: the difficulty of determining the truth among contradictory, often misleading fragments, clues, and erroneous published information. Perry, an intensely private person, revealed herself only obliquely through her music and texts. Many puzzles and mysteries concerning her life and her music are still unsolved.

The brilliant, courageous, resolute, and increasingly difficult life of Julia Amanda Perry began in Lexington, Kentucky, on 25 March 1924. Her mother had been a schoolteacher. Her father, Abe Perry, was a distinguished, well-spoken physician and an amateur pianist. The facts of her early years are little known.

In 1934, when she was 10 years old, the family moved to Akron, Ohio, a small industrial city with good schools and a cordial racial atmosphere. They settled on Berg Street near the University of Akron, in an excellent neighborhood where white and black families lived side by side. Julia and her sisters took violin lessons, and she also studied voice with Mable Todd. Todd had been

a pupil of John Finley Williamson at Westminster Choir College, and was a
strong presence in the musical life of Akron. Julia attended the Spicer Observation
School for talented children run by the University of Akron, not far from her
home. The eminent musician Kermit Moore, who was five years younger, grew
up one block away. He recalled her as an outgoing, cheerful, aggressive tomboy
who would suddenly ride off on his bicycle, then leave it unceremoniously
at the playground while she played baseball. She was athletic, excelling in
track and baseball. They both sang in the Moore Junior Singers, a select group
formed by Kermit's mother. This group of children performed in elegant blue
and white robes at church teas and other affairs, and they were also heard on
WTAM radio. Moore remembered Perry as an excellent sight reader and a
"fine dramatic soprano" who was confident and uninhibited in performance.
She also played the violin well, performing with Kermit in chamber music
concerts for the Akron Liedertafel. Their families were friends, and he knew
the Perry sisters well.[2] The oldest was Clara, the alluring "black sheep" of
the family; she danced in places of which her parents did not approve, such
as the Coconut Grove in Boston. The next was Lois America (named after
her mother), a talented pianist who also played cello. The third was Lucie, a
quiet, thoughtful girl and good pianist who later taught school for over 30
years. Then came Julia and after her, Alycia, who married a physician and
settled in Shaker Heights, Ohio. They were a refined, educated family, members
of the Negro upper middle class.

In 1940, Julia's sister Lois died tragically in a train accident at the age of
20.[3] She had been a promising pianist, and taught in the preparatory division of
the Cleveland Institute of Music. Barely four months before her death, she presented a benefit recital sponsored by the Cleveland Panhellenic Association and
broadcast by radio station WHK, assisted by her sisters Julia and Lucie. Lois's
body was shipped back to Lexington, Kentucky, for burial, and her existence
has never been acknowledged in any biographical material; Perry rarely spoke
of her, even to close friends. Julia was 16 years old at the time, and must have
been deeply affected by her sister's death.

By then Julia was in Central High School, where her sisters had also been
students. News of her participation in school musical events appeared in the
Akron Beacon Journal. In her freshman year she and another student attended
a musical contest in Wooster, Ohio, where she won prizes in both violin and
voice. Her experience in school must have been good because, after her graduation, she was invited by the principal to return to visit.

On graduating from Central High School in 1942, Julia won a scholarship to
the Cleveland Institute of Music. Since her parents felt it was too far from home,
she attended the University of Akron for a year. Then a Knight Memorial Scholarship, established by the president and editor of the *Akron Beacon Journal* in
memory of his father, enabled her to transfer to Westminster Choir College in
Princeton, New Jersey. There she studied composition with the renowned Henry
Switten, as well as voice, piano, violin, dramatics, and conducting. She was

"pitch giver"[4] for the Westminster College Choir, and sang solos in their concerts at Carnegie Hall. She was also concert mistress of the Westminster College Orchestra. In the summer of 1946, a group of students led by President John Finley Williamson traveled to Birmingham, Alabama, to work with young people. Julia served as minister of music at Birmingham's Cumberland Presbyterian Church and conducted a youth choir in a performance of a cantata by Alfred Gaul as well as a choral piece of her own.[5]

In 1947, Perry's choral piece *Carillon Heigh-Ho* was published by Carl Fischer. She graduated with her bachelor's degree that year and completed her master's degree at Westminster Choir College in 1948. Her master's thesis was *Chicago*, a cantata for narrator, male chorus and orchestra, based on a text by Carl Sandburg.

The summer after leaving Westminster Choir College, Perry was in Columbus, Ohio, attending the annual convention of the National Association of Negro Musicians. In their competition for young musicians, she received first prize in voice and shared first prize in composition. That fall Perry was on the faculty at Hampton Institute in Virginia, teaching voice, theory, orchestration, and composition. Two of Westminster's most distinguished faculty members also went to Hampton that year. Henry Switten became chairman of the music department and the musicologist Boris Nelson taught music literature. Perry stayed at Hampton for only one year.

In the summer of 1949, Perry went to the Berkshire Music Center Festival at Tanglewood, Massachusetts, to study choral singing and conducting with Hugh Ross. By this time she was beginning to attract wider attention, and was featured as a "Promising Negro Composer" in an article in the *Christian Science Monitor*. Her recently published song *Lord, What Shall I Do?* was on sale in the local store. Concert artists such as Nan Merriman and the Negro soprano Ellabelle Davis were including her songs in their concerts.

In September 1949 Perry took up residence in International House in New York City. That year she was one of five winners in the Marian Anderson Award competition,[6] and took voice lessons from Madame Eugenia Giannini Gregory, who was on the voice faculty at the Curtis Institute. In early 1950 Perry had a scholarship as assistant coach and participant in the Columbia University Opera Workshop, and in the fall she was attending classes in the Extension Division of the Juilliard School of Music in literature and materials of music and in orchestral conducting with Emanuel Balaban (with whom she would study later in Siena, Italy). In the fall of 1950 she met the young Italian conductor Piero Bellugi, who came to live at International House. He was immediately drawn to the "slim tall girl with a bunch of music paper under her arm. . . . She showed me the beginning of a *Stabat Mater* she was composing and I was amazed at her musicianship."[7] Bellugi wrote to his former teacher, Luigi Dallapiccola, in Florence, and persuaded him to accept Perry as a student at Tanglewood the next summer.

Thus began what was to become an extended apprenticeship with Dallapiccola. At Tanglewood, Perry also formed friendships, which would bear fruit in years to come, with the conductor Howard Shanet, the scholar Darius Thieme, and the mezzo-soprano Betty Allen. She completed the *Stabat Mater* for solo voice and string orchestra, and performed it with Bellugi conducting the student orchestra. Bellugi recalled that "afterwards she cried so much: it had all been so beautiful, the teaching of Dallapiccola, the admiration from everyone."[8] With Bellugi's encouragement, Perry made plans to go to Florence, Italy, as soon as she could raise funds. She gained the support of an anonymous benefactor and patron of the arts in Akron, and supplemented it with the proceeds from the benefit concert of her own works (including *Stabat Mater* with herself as soloist) at her alma mater, Central High School, in October 1951.

In November she was on her way to Europe on board the *Independence*.[9] In Florence, she stayed for a while with Bellugi's family, who welcomed her like a daughter and called her "Giuliettina Nera" (Little Black Julie). That winter she performed her *Stabat Mater* to enthusiastic audiences in Milan, Naples, and Rome, and it was recorded for broadcast on Radio Italiano. She wrote to her Akron benefactor, "The Milanese critics are most caustic. However, they were favorable and, more important, the public liked it. They cheered, yelling, 'brava, brava, brava.' I was quite nervous."[10] The next summer Perry traveled to Salzburg, Austria, and Fontainebleau, France. There she studied with Nadia Boulanger at the American Conservatory, winning the prestigious Prix Fontainebleau with her *Viola Sonata*. In the fall she resumed studies with Dallapiccola in Florence, and was by now a familiar sight riding her bicycle in Oltr' Arno (left bank of the Arno River). The journalist Patricia Sides, then doing research in Florence, met her through mutual acquaintances and they became good friends. She described Perry in those days as tall, dignified, gracious, serious, but also often very funny. Well-read and intellectual, Perry spoke perfect Italian and was verbal and articulate, conveying complex ideas without "talking down." She was affectionate, humorous, and made others feel important. People were fond of her as well as respectful, and Sides reported that she was called "Maestra" by everyone.[11]

Perry returned to the United States in August 1953, after performing her *Stabat Mater* in Germany and Austria. By now the fame that had blossomed in the summer of 1949 at Tanglewood was in full flower. *Musical America* reported her Milan success in glowing terms: "Miss Perry sang the soprano part in her *Stabat Mater*. . . . Not since the war has any serious American work received so enthusiastic a reception in Italy."[12] In her absence the work had been performed in New York in Carnegie Recital Hall, at the Juilliard School of Music, and at the Aspen Festival by Herta Glaz and the New Music String Quartet. This success was capped by the first of her two Guggenheim Fellowships, awarded in the fall of 1953.

With such affirmation, Perry felt confident that she could succeed and support herself as a composer. In the 1957 renewal of her passport she struck out her previous occupation[13] and entered "Composer" in bold print. (In her late letters, she often signed herself "Composer Julia Perry," a poignant self-affirmation at a time when her success had been all but forgotten.) This confidence was confirmed by a remark she made in a postconcert forum interview in February 1954, after a performance of *Stabat Mater* at Columbia University by her good friend Virginia Shuey and the Columbia University Orchestra conducted by Howard Shanet. In response to a question about whether she planned to teach, she replied rather wryly, "If I can get around it, no." This was to prove ironic in later years when she was looking for teaching jobs.[14]

In this interview Perry addressed another mystery without providing an answer: the complete cessation of her singing career by 1953. When questioned why she no longer sang the *Stabat Mater* herself, she replied, "Because I am not a singer." In view of her extensive vocal studies, the singing competitions she had won, and the good reviews her performances had received in Europe, this statement is obviously untrue. Ten years later, she also ignored a request to sing her own works for a Composers Recordings (CRI) album. Yet, long after her death, what many musicians recalled most vividly about her was the beauty of her rich and powerful mezzo-soprano voice.

In the summer of 1954 Perry was in residence at the MacDowell Colony in Peterborough, New Hampshire. Patricia Sides visited her there, and the two of them began collaborating on a song cycle of poems Sides had written about the Greek islands near her birthplace, Cyprus. Only one song has survived, *Parody*, which Sides had originally entitled *The Phoenician*. That fall, Perry was preparing for a performance at Columbia University of her one-act opera composed in Italy, *The Cask of Amontillado* (formerly titled *The Bottle*).[15] It, too, received favorable reviews and had a repeat performance the next summer at the University of Delaware Summer Festival.

For the next two years, Perry remained in the United States, traveling occasionally to Akron. She returned to Florence in November 1955. In December she wrote to the Library of Congress requesting information for a series of lectures the U.S. Information Service asked her to give in southern Italy on "Musical Activities on the American College Campus."[16] The following year she received another Guggenheim Fellowship which supported her to the end of 1957.[17]

During this time Perry was also studying composition in Florence with noted composer/conductor Roberto Lupi.[18] In 1956 she had begun spending summers in Siena, where she attended the Accademia Chigiana on scholarship, polishing her skills in conducting under the tutelage of Emanuel Balaban, Alceo Galliera, and Adone Zecchi. Conducting remained her most rewarding musical expression, second only to composition. This skill was put to use in a tour of concerts and lectures she made in 1957, sponsored by the U.S. Information Agency, in which she conducted orchestras throughout Europe in performances of her own works. These engagements took her as far afield as Greece and Norway, and to conducting engagements with the Vienna Philharmonic and the BBC Orchestra in London.[19] Her photo appeared in a *Life* magazine article on women abroad,[20] and her works continued to be performed in both Europe and the United States.

It may have been around this time that the first symptoms appeared of an ailment called acromegaly, chronic hyperpituitarism causing enlargement of bones in the hands, feet, and face, as well as other symptoms. This condition commonly has its onset in the late twenties to late thirties. Although external symptoms were not obvious, friends began to notice a change in Perry's personality during these years. Piero Bellugi reported that when he saw her again in 1956, he found her different: religious in a rather obsessive way, and very taken with St. Catherine of Siena (whose letters she had set in *Frammenti dalle Lettere*).[21] By the time Perry returned to New York in February 1959, Patricia Sides noticed a marked change in her demeanor. The formerly outgoing, cheerful "Maestra" now appeared distracted and withdrawn, "peculiar, difficult, and quick to take offense." This change was also noted by Howard Shanet, who conducted her *Requiem for Orchestra* in a concert in March 1959.[22]

In the summer of 1959 Perry was again in residence at the MacDowell Colony. The following year she was living in an apartment above her father's medical office in Akron, Ohio, "well-equipped except for a piano." This is where she composed *Homunculus C.F.* for 10 percussionists. In the liner notes to the CRI recording of this work, she wrote, "These clinical surroundings evoked memories of the medieval laboratory where Wagner, youthful apprentice to Faust, made a successful alchemy experiment, fashioning and bringing to life a creature he called homunculus." This fascination with alchemy and potions was to surface again in her opera *Symplegades* (formerly *Mary Easty*) on the Salem witch trials. That year her *Stabat Mater* was released by Composers Recordings Inc., and the next year her *Short Piece for Orchestra* (1952) was issued. In the summer of 1961, she wrote to CRI, offering them the "priority" of a third LP recording consisting of *Homunculus, Chicago*, and other works including *Seven Sutures for Orchestra* (a title with a decidedly clinical sound to it, recalling the laboratory inspiration of *Homunculus*). She stipulated that she would be conductor and narrator for *Chicago*. The reply from CRI has been lost, but nothing came of her proposal.

The letter to CRI also announced that Perry would be arriving in New York in August 1961. Patricia Sides remembers her apartment on Riverside Drive with a sign in the window, "Piano Lessons." Perry was doing some lecturing in universities and she may have enrolled in the graduate school of New York University as a Ph.D. candidate in musicology.[23] Friends continued to notice that she was more retiring and frequently in ill health. She would sometimes call singer Adele Addison, who had been a classmate at Westminster Choir College, when she had a specific request, such as needing a letter of recommendation for her application to the National Institute for Arts and Letters. But she never visited Addison, who described her as a loner. She did invite Kermit Moore to visit her on his return from Europe. They talked "for hours," catching up on their lives, although he noted that she was not well at that time. Howard

Shanet was concerned that he didn't hear from her, but was reluctant to be intrusive and call her. Another person who knew and admired Perry, Leon Thompson, then educational director of the New York Philharmonic, told Shanet that Perry was in poor health.

A dwindling of financial resources must also have strained Perry's health and state of mind. In January 1963 she was back in Akron, offering private music lessons and writing CRI with another list of compositions for possible recording. Added to the list of 1961 were three symphonies and a second *Ballet for Orchestra*. Whatever the state of her health, she had obviously kept busy. Although she included scores for several of the works, again there was no result from her request.

Some encouraging news arrived at the beginning of 1964 from William Steinberg, conductor of the Pittsburgh Symphony Orchestra. He was planning to include her *Short Piece for Orchestra* on their European tour that fall, and to conduct it with the New York Philharmonic that winter season. He asked her to change the title and suggested she call it "Study."[24] Since a performance with the New York Philharmonic was at stake (rare for a work by a black woman), Perry complied.

In what started as another positive turn of events that year, the American Academy and National Institute of Arts and Letters awarded Perry a grant to support another recording by Composers Recordings Inc. This time, CRI was obliged to cooperate, and their committee unanimously approved *Homunculus C.F.*, which was recorded in January 1965. But the remaining minutes and other side of the LP, for which she had provided her grant funds, proved to be a problem. Of the many other scores she submitted (including some of her best works), only the *Five Songs for Soprano and Piano* were approved on condition she sing them, which she declined to do. Numerous letters were exchanged and proposals made. In the end, *Homunculus C.F.* was the only piece by her on the LP.

Sometime in 1966 Perry left New York City and was back in Akron, now on Euclid Street. The old home on Berg Street had been razed to make room for the expansion of the University of Akron. She continued her prolific production of compositions: in addition to *Module for Orchestra*, she was writing *Symphony No. 5*, ("Integration"), *Symphony No. 6* for concert band, and more "Negro spirituals for orchestra without soloists."[25] She also embarked on, or perhaps returned to, another occupation as lexicographer of a music dictionary, and requested a letter of recommendation from CRI's David Hall to support her application to the National Council on the Arts for this project. In 1967 she applied to the Eastman School of Music doctoral program,[26] but apparently did not pursue it. She taught French and German as a substitute teacher in the Akron public schools. When she was engaged to teach for a year at Florida A&M University that fall, it must have been a welcome relief from financial strain.

Perry had always been drawn to words as well as music, writing the lyrics to several of her early songs and the libretti for her operas. In the absence of direct information from Perry, one turns to these writings for clues to her thoughts. They yield a variety of themes clothed in fantasy, some of which recur: loneliness, disillusionment with established authority, fascination with magic and alchemy, and concern with injustice. The opera she began in the late 1950s, titled originally *Mary Easty*, then *Gallows Hill*, and finally *Symplegades*, concerns the Salem witch trials. The themes that predominate in this libretto are the evils of public authority (ministers and magistrates who think they speak with divine authority) and the powers of "science" (alchemist Ezekiel Hibbens' potion, rejected by the authorities). In the libretto for another opera, *The Selfish Giant* (1964), loosely adapted from a story by Oscar Wilde, innocence and love triumph over selfishness and ignorance. The play is populated with fairy tale figures, the Selfish Giant, Frost, Snow, North Wind, and a Linnet bird, along with schoolboys and schoolgirls. Inserted by Perry are scenes from the stock exchange and passages on feminism and education. In the end, the innocent little girl/boy who wins over the lonely Selfish Giant ascends to Paradise, displaying "love wounds," stigmata on hands and feet (a reminder of St. Catherine of Siena).

The poem Perry wrote in 1965, *Graves of Untold Africans*, extols the grandeur and superiority of ancient African kingdoms. Perry's writing after her year at Florida A&M continued to explore the racial theme: translations of African fables from Italian to English and a "contemporary American play." This was *Fisty-Me*, the title a play on the word Mephistopheles, (another name for the devil and, like *Homunculus*, a reference to the Faust legend). It addresses the theme of racial injustice along with the evils of capitalism and the generation gap. The disparate elements in this play are even more surreal than in *The Selfish Giant*. Speaking roles include, besides the orphan boy "Fisty-Me" and his friends, a talking Blackboard, Church, State, University Faculty, a Negro Faculty Member, a Female Professor, and other representatives of groups of people (Ghetto Folk, etc.).[27] While they may not have literary value or exhibit significant creativity, Perry's writings do show that she felt strongly about ideals, social issues, beauty, love, loneliness, suffering, and redemption, and wanted intensely to communicate these feelings in some way.

After her year at Florida A&M, Perry resumed efforts to generate income. In September–October she was engaged for a weeklong lecture series as a music consultant for the colleges in the Atlanta University Center. That December Southern Music Company returned the score of her *Symphony No. 8*, saying they were unable to accept it for publication. Perry received one more award in 1969, an Honorable Mention in the ASCAP Awards to Women Composers of Symphonic and Concert Music. Sometime in the spring of the next year, she put together a typed announcement for a six-week course in composition to be offered privately that summer in Akron. The announcement included an invitation to colleges to place the course in their summer programs.[28] One can only assume that this class was planned before April/May 1970, because it was during that period that Perry suffered the first of the strokes that were to paralyze her right side, rob her of speech, and confine her to a wheelchair until the end of her life nine years later. The approximate time is known because of a letter that Perry typed and sent to Ronald Freed at Southern Music Company on 30 April 1972, offering more compositions for publication and expressing amazement that two years had passed in her paralytic condition.[29] In the same letter she expressed optimism that her ordeal was almost over and that she would soon be able to walk and talk.

Although Perry taught herself to write with her left hand, most of her letters and scores are barely legible. In letters she wrote from 1970 to 1979, her hand-writing, typing, references to her health, and return addresses at hospitals provide clues to the course of her illness. After a partial recovery in 1972,[30] she suffered further strokes, probably in early 1973 and late 1974. She made some improve-ment from July 1975 through 1977, because she spoke of coming home, getting a leg brace, exercising, and beginning to walk and talk.

All this time she was composing and promoting her music, despite formidable physical obstacles. In March 1971 Perry sent the score of *Soundout* for marching band to Southern Music, apologizing for her illegible manuscript and explaining the addition of letter names to notes. In November 1972 she wrote to the Library of Congress, announcing more compositions,[31] commenting on the difficulty of composing in a wheelchair, and asking for a commission. The most poignant letters are perhaps those referring to conducting, which had always been ex-tremely important to her. In 1975 she declared to musicologist Dominique-René de Lerma (then teaching at Indiana University) that she had once prided herself on her "Toscanini precision" and "Stokowskian grace." And in 1977 she wrote to him that she was getting a knee brace and exercising her conducting arm.[32]

This indomitable will continued to Perry's last days, and focused particularly on promoting her compositions. She tirelessly sent out scores to her publisher and to conductors, and composed many smaller band pieces. Those who spoke with her by telephone (I found no one who actually saw her in those years) reported that she was mentally confused and spoke with difficulty. One of the lowest points was reached in 1973 when, probably having suffered a second stroke, she wrote to the Library of Congress Division of Music in agonizingly shaky handwriting, asking them to send $500 for medical expenses. Librarian Edward Waters replied that such assistance was out of their power, saying "You have my sympathy and my admiration for your courage and determination."[33]

In May 1976 Perry asked conductor Paul Freeman and Professor de Lerma if there might be an opening on the Columbia Artists Black Composer Series for the second movement of her 8th ("Simple") symphony. De Lerma's reply is significant in that it acknowledges the injustice of the neglect she suffered in her last years. He said, "I am sensitive to the fact that you are among those established figures who have not been included thus far in the AAMOA's[34] projects, and I am hoping that the opportunity to involve you will develop before too much longer." Sadly, the opportunity apparently never did develop. In that letter De Lerma also made a suggestion that she did not heed: "Might I . . .

suggest that . . . you consider deposition of copies of your works with an institution which has an ongoing dedication to Black culture, such as the excellent libraries of Fisk or Howard. Scholars would then not face the frustration experienced with regard to Florence Price, Margaret Bonds, or Azalia Hackley—to mention three figures (coincidentally women) on whom dissertation research has been recently terminated for lack of data."[35]

Perry continued to compose sporadically, sending Southern Music Company scores for her *Quinary Quixotic Songs* for baritone and five instruments, her *Symphony No. 13 for Woodwind Quintet*, and a third movement (lost) for her *Piano Concerto*. In January 1979 she resubmitted several pieces although they had already been turned down, saying she preferred publication to deposition of her music at Fisk University.[36] In March 1979, a month before her death, she asked Southern Music to reconsider her pieces. In what may have been the last letter received by Perry, they replied that they were too busy doing inventory and thanked her for her patience; they added that they "trusted" in her good health and her ability to enjoy the high esteem and affection directed to her from her admirers all over the country.[37]

On 24 April 1979 Julia Perry died in Akron General Medical Center of a cardiac arrest. She was 55 years old. After a service at St. Phillip's Episcopal Church, she was buried in Glendale Cemetery. Her mother, who had cared for her through the years of illness, died three years later and was buried beside her. In the years following Perry's death, no systematic attempt was made to catalog or preserve her music, and by the 1990s many works were gone.[38]

SOCIAL ISSUES

Although race, class, and gender were powerful shaping conditions in her life, Julia Perry said little that we know of on these subjects until the mid to late 1960s, when she expressed her views through her writing of opera libretti, plays, poetry, and her music. The 1950s, 1960s, and 1970s were decades of tremendous change and upheaval in the social and political climate of the United States, and Perry traversed an equally great distance in her consciousness and attitude toward race, gender, and class. It is hard to say how much this turmoil may have affected her health. She was very aware of the events in the United States while she was in Europe. Even so, the normal culture shock of returning to the United States in 1959 after more than three years abroad must have been exacerbated by the difference not only of racial attitudes between Italy and America, but also by the new attitudes in the United States and the growing civil rights activism.

More than most other black women composers, Perry pursued her career in a largely white musical world. Her first music teacher, Mable Todd, was white, and her years at Westminster Choir College (Adele Addison, Lillian Hall, and she were the only black students[39]) prepared her for her years in Europe where even her American friends were white. A clue to her experiences and attitude in early adulthood in the 1940s can be gleaned from a quote in a 1949 article in the *Christian Science Monitor* titled "Promising Negro Composer Lauds Peace Role of Music." She claimed to have "enjoyed remarkable freedom from prejudice and misunderstanding" and believed that "music, coupled with her own fearless state of thought" was responsible. If this statement is true, one can only guess that Perry's confidence had also been conditioned by the protection she enjoyed as a member of the Negro upper middle class, which could often avoid public situations that might be unpleasant. They preferred not to speak about the hurts and humiliations they were unable to avoid, especially to white Americans. In her years of growing up, Perry would have absorbed not just the manners and speech of the upper middle class, but also their dismissal of lower-class Negroes as not of their element. The importance of propriety would have been indelibly etched by her family's reaction to the adventures of her older sister Clara. In Perry's life, issues of race were inseparable from class.

As Perry went through her years at Westminster Choir College, some of the idealism of her white professors may have influenced her, especially the summer they organized for their students in Birmingham, Alabama. Her year teaching at Hampton Institute may also have made an impact. It is noteworthy that the choral piece she wrote for the Hampton Institute choir employed African-American musical idioms not found in her later works. At no time, either then or in subsequent years, did she reveal awareness of the Harlem Renaissance ideals advocating a return to Negro roots and heritage, nor did she set the poetry of Langston Hughes, Paul Laurence Dunbar, Countee Cullen, or any other black writers to music.

By the 1950s, Perry's musical style was in the mainstream of contemporary European compositional techniques. She had left what traces her music had of Negro idioms behind her, and had gained entrance into the most prominent musical circles. According to the façade presented by the musical establishment at that time, race and gender were irrelevant to musical excellence. Other female composers, among them Louise Talma and Ruth Crawford Seeger, considered their sex unrelated to their craft, and they would have been insulted by the label "woman composer" (especially because they knew that their sex was an obstacle to being taken seriously). Like other Negro musicians before and during her time who attained such status, Perry was outwardly accepted by many other musicians as a composer who happened to be black. In behavior, dress, speech, intellectual attainment, and musical language, she was indistinguishable from other musicians. Regardless of the headline of the *Christian Science Monitor* article, Perry would not have asserted her identity as a woman composer or a Negro composer.

That is not to say that in casual conversation, Perry totally avoided the subject of race. In her early years in Italy she would joke with Patricia Sides that "Down South they'd drop dead to see us together," and in reference to the mother of a mutual friend: "If she saw us together, I'd grab a broom and say, 'jes' a cleanin' up'.".[40] Such exchanges remained lighthearted, avoiding more serious and painful discussions of injustice.

Within a year or two, Perry's attitude began to change. She was in the United States for two years (1953–55) at the time the U.S. Supreme Court overturned segregation in public schools and the Montgomery bus boycott was just beginning. After she returned to Italy (1956–59), Sides, now in New York, received a packet in the mail containing a fragmentary diary with instructions not to read it. Annoyed, Patricia did glance in it before sending it back to Julia. On the opening page Perry had written in capital letters, one beneath the other: THE NAME, THE FACE, THE RACE, next to her initials, JP. Sides said, "I was surprised by the sense of implied militancy. In Italy, Julia was well aware of what was going on in the U.S. with the advent of the Civil Rights movement and all it was likely to mean, but she—to my knowledge—had never expressed herself so strongly before."[41]

In the 1960s, Lorraine Hansberry's award-winning play about ordinary working folk, *Raisin in the Sun*, was a tremendous success. Harlem Renaissance poet Langston Hughes' iconoclastic writings on the pretensions of class resurfaced. Thanks in great measure to the prestige and eloquence of Martin Luther King, Jr., upper-class Negroes could no longer ignore racial inequality or the plight of poor, rural, and uneducated blacks. Every day, headlines carried news of lawsuits, sit-ins, school desegregations, and riots. After King was assassinated in 1968, men who would never have left home without coat and tie were seen (temporarily) in overalls, expressing their solidarity and their rage.

This change for a person like Perry was profound. Not only was her past fame beginning to fade, but all she had striven for—the approval of the white mainstream—was under question. In 1966–67 she was making overt references to race in the titles and materials of her music; she began incorporating Negro folk songs in works like *Module for Orchestra* and *Symphony No. 5* , (*"Integration Symphony"*), and it is likely that *The Suite Symphony* (with its movements titled "Bass-Amplification in 'Rock and Roll' Style," "Rhythm and Blues," etc.) dates from these years. Perhaps the most significant is *Symphony No. 10*, or *Soul Symphony* (1972); the title, musical materials, and accessibility of this work demonstrate a desire to be relevant to both race and class. The most explicit expression is Perry's 1969 "contemporary American play," *Fisty-Me*. Among the themes she touches on are the greatness of black heroes (Martin Luther King, Jr., Harriet Tubman, Dr. Ralph Bunche, the writer Douglas Turner Ward, and the artist Lois Mailou Jones), racial equality, educational relevance, and a special peeve of hers: the ignorance and prejudice of calling black and American Indian culture "ethnic." Perry refers in the play to the new vogue of the term "Afro-American," but continues to use the term "Negro." She expresses a lot of her own anger through the epithets and violence of the street folk in the play. Here the connection of racial awareness to class is most evident. Perry shows an acquaintance with lower-class street customs and mannerisms: the Negro prostitute "undulates" in amazement ("huh . . . huuh . . . huuuh . . ."), and a Negro street person retaliates against his Caucasian counterpart in a passage reminiscent of the rhyming insult contest called "the dozens."

Perry's awareness of gender discrimination and unfairness was expressed even earlier. In her opera *The Selfish Giant* (1964), the schoolboys are "dictatorial and free," while the schoolgirls argue the pros and cons of marriage and domesticity. Perry's own single state and professional choices are represented by one girl who extols the independence of the female "cosmonaut." In *Fisty-Me* the depiction of gender issues is more visceral and emotional. Her frequent references to sex and rape have an angry tone of protest, a sense of being overwhelmed by male dominance. She refers to the sexual revolution in a comment on the contraceptive pill, while entreating the listener to allow women the chance to be known as persons rather than sex objects.

In depending upon these artistic expressions for an understanding of Perry's views on race, class, and gender, one receives only a somewhat oblique perception. Perhaps the clearest indications of her position on these issues were her life choices and actions. She decisively pursued career and creative expression rather than marriage and family, effectively affirming a woman's right to do so. Her early racial ambivalence was revealed in her social contacts and choice of residence during the 1950s, and the Eurocentric titles, references, and techniques of her best-known compositions. But she taught at African-American schools (quite likely because of bias at other institutions) and affirmed her racial identity in her late music. She also demonstrated an awareness of lower-class customs, music, and language, and even expressed her own anger through them in her writing, while remaining solidly within her upper-class milieu.

Powerful as the issues of race, class, and gender were, Perry's life and the fate of her music demonstrate the importance of other factors. It is hard to imagine the frustration of her last nine years. Trapped in a body that could not move or communicate, Perry became irrelevant and invisible to the world. Many forces operate to shape not only a composer's music but also how it is perceived, how the composer is treated by history, what gets remembered, and what gets lost or discounted. In Perry's case, she had to contend with physical and mental ill health, sibling rivalries and family relationships, class values, and the social and political climate of the times and places in which she worked.

THE MUSIC

Forty-six out of Perry's 54 surviving scores were available for this study. The others are in archives where they may be seen but not borrowed or photocopied. Seventeen of the 54 existing scores were either incomplete, or only in instrumental parts, or illegible due to her shaky left hand notation after her stroke. Seven of these have been reconstructed and are now in computer editions made by Christopher Hahn and myself in 1995 and 1999.[42] There are 54 more titles of works still not located or verified, cited either by Perry herself in letters and lists, or by scholars. The works not yet located include significant compositions such as the *Viola Sonata* which won the Prix Fontainebleau in 1952, her cantatas *Chicago* and *Ruth*, six of her symphonies for full orchestra, and many songs and Negro spirituals for solo voice. Despite every effort to be accurate, the list of works (totaling 108) probably contains duplications and other errors because Perry often changed the titles of her compositions or revised them under new titles.

The publication of Perry's works began in 1947 with the choral piece *Carillon Heigh-Ho*, published by Carl Fischer. Within the next six years nine more songs and choral works were published, most by Galaxy, and one by McLaughlin & Reilly. Southern Music Company took up her major opus *Stabat Mater* in 1954, followed by six more major works. In 1968 Carl Fischer signed a contract for the *Symphony No. 6* for band and her violin concerto. Like several of those at Southern, these remain in manuscript facsimile and are for rental only. The total of published works by Perry remains 22, of which 14 are in print as of 2000.[43] Recordings are limited to those listed in the discography: *Stabat Mater, Short Piece for Orchestra, Homunculus C.F., Carillon Heigh-Ho, Prelude for Piano*, two songs, and the two solo vocal spirituals.

The performance history that is documented is sparse: assuming that the 10 early published songs and choral pieces were all performed at some time, only 14 other works are known to have received performances. The *Stabat Mater* holds the record, with probably more than two dozen performances in the United States and abroad, and *A Short Piece for Orchestra* has received almost as many. The opera *Cask of Amontillado* and *Homunculus C.F.* were each performed in public three times.[44] All the performed works were early compositions; there is no documented performance of a work composed after 1963.

Perry's compositional style was summarized in her obituary in the journal *Black Perspective in Music*: "in the neo-classical tradition, with rich, dissonant harmonies, and an intense lyricism along with rhythmic complexities." Other scholars also cited her eclectic musical language and her use of contrapuntal textures. Most of these assessments are based on her three well-known and recorded works of the 1950s and early 1960s. Michelle Edwards describes Perry's style in more specific terms covering a wider range of compositions: "Her works favored expressive restraint and concise manner. Rhythmic complexity, which varies among compositions, is sometimes created through shifting subdivisions, syncopations, and use of ties across pulses. Her melodic-harmonic language draws on chromatic as well as diatonic dissonance and makes frequent use of major sevenths with interior thirds. Pitch centers emerge through reiteration rather than from functional tonality. . . . Some works . . . utilize almost no melodic lines, relying instead on short repetitive patterns, alternating textures, and rhythmic drive."[45] These various characteristics become successively apparent in a survey of the evolution of Perry's musical style.

The first surviving composition by her, the short *Prelude for Piano*, composed in 1946 while Perry was a junior at Westminster Choir College, exists only in a revised version of 1962.[46] Its sophistication and its complex, dissonant harmonies are surprising in a first effort, or even an early one. A subtle, expressive blues idiom pervades this short but powerful piece of only 29 measures. Critical response to the 1995 recording on *Kaleidoscope: Music by African-American Women* was consistently positive. Vivian Taylor praised its "distinctive harmonic language, subtle rhythmic irregularities, and rich pianistic color achieved through Perry's chordal voicings."[47] In June 2000, critic Frank J. Oteri included her *Prelude for Piano* in his list of outstanding works of the century, calling it "a fascinating piano miniature by a too little known mid-century composer which defies pigeon-holing and stereotyping."[48]

The other works we have from before 1951 are songs and choral pieces that were published, and they show a more conservative harmonic language with straightforward rhythms. These works range from the full harmonies of the choral *Our Thanks to Thee* (only one or two quartal chords within the solidly triadic fabric) to the spare and exquisite solo setting of *I'm a Poor Little Orphan Girl*. The latter is one of only two vocal spiritual arrangements which survive, although Perry's listed works indicate a few more spiritual settings, both solo and choral. The other surviving setting, the jubilee *Free at Last*, uses traits of the black choral tradition more prominently: syncopations, climactic chord expansions and broadening tempo changes in the piano accompaniment.[49] Even more interesting are the two original pieces she wrote in "spiritual style." The choral *Song of Our Savior*, written for the Hampton Institute Choir, is reminiscent of spirituals in its modal melody, syncopated repetitive motives, layered hummed ostinatos in the manner of choral basing, antiphonal call and response between men and women, and interjections of "Glory Hallelujah" in shout style. The song *Lord, What Shall I Do?* is subtitled "A Spiritual by Julia Perry." The words and melody are striking in their improvisatory style. The refrain repeats the same three-note motive over and over, expressing growing desperation, and the verse stays within a narrow range except for climactic exclamations.

In 1951 Perry became less conservative with the appearance of *Stabat Mater*, the work which brought her national and international attention. The source of the composer's new skill and confidence poses a mystery because *Stabat Mater* was well under way before her lessons with Dallapiccola began, and her composition teachers just before that time are unknown. This composition strikes out into new territory in its length, instrumentation, dissonant harmonic language, and contrapuntal complexities. Although she was the first to sing the work, Perry wrote *Stabat Mater* not for her own voice, as is widely supposed, but with contralto Marian Anderson in mind. (Anderson never sang it.) Critical acclaim began with the first performances abroad. The *Corriere della Sera* critic said, "I have heard an outstanding 'Stabat Mater' by a young Negro American composer."[50] *Musical America*'s critic wrote of the Italian premiere: "Miss Perry has a great gift for the setting of words to music and a delicate sense of the meaning of the Latin Text. . . . Perhaps her idiom is not yet completely individualized, but the great line is there. She shows a thorough technical knowledge and one can readily forgive the extraneous contemporary influences."[51] In his review of the CRI recording, Eric Salzman was both enthusiastic and discerning: "Perry's *Stabat Mater* proves to be one of those extraordinary surprises that American musical life occasionally provides. The work, for mezzo-soprano and strings, is spare and sensitive, lean and expressive. It is one of those pieces that manage to say a lot in just a few tones. Every sound and motion is set forth with care and poetry. This is not a perfectly realized piece by any means, but its biggest weakness is almost turned into a plus mark. There is a disparity between diatonic (or even modal) ideas and a rather severe chromaticism but the resulting inequalities are carefully and effectively exploited."[52]

The conflict between diatonic and chromatic dissonance about which Salzman complained was a deliberate choice for Perry. This seminal work served as a laboratory for working out a wealth of ideas. Many of them never appeared again in her later compositions, but others became hallmarks of her later style: dissonant seventh, ninth, eleventh, and thirteenth chords; sustained homophonic quartal chords in parallel motion; the dichotomy between sections of driving rhythmic regularity and others of free mixed meters and durations; the importance of spacing and octave displacements; fondness for ostinato patterns; and a declamatory vocal style with sparing use of melismata. Perry never surpassed *Stabat Mater* in creativity and imagination. Edith Boroff summed it up: "A work of authenticity and authority . . . from its poignant cello opening to its vital harmonic sections, dramatic declamations, statistical climaxes, and its colorations— from misty layered sounds to vibrant interchanges, [*Stabat Mater*] creates its own world."[53]

This confident command of modern techniques and harmonic language was quickly confirmed in *Short Piece for Orchestra* in 1952, the first work to appear after she began to study composition with Dallapiccola. The works that followed were influenced by Dallapiccola's 12-tone techniques, his emphasis on motivic unity, rich orchestration, and expressive melodic lines combined with austere contemporary practices.

The one-act opera *Cask of Amontillado*, adapted from the story by Edgar Allan Poe by Perry and Virginia Card, makes use of modified 12-tone serialism in its orchestral score, but more frequently employs three-note cells, reiterated (often as an ostinato), inverted, and manipulated in various ways. Its vocal lines are predominantly declamatory, even in passages marked "Arioso." The only departure from syllabic vocal treatment comes in a prolonged duet melisma on the word "Amontillado." The opera closes with a quote of the *Dies Irae*, a part of the Roman Catholic requiem liturgy. At the Columbia University performance, the set design by Richard Mason was a metal structure resembling a giant spider, reminiscent of Alexander Calder's mobile sculptures. The structure could be rotated from an open to a closed position, simulating the entombment of Fortunato. Reviews were favorable, with one critic commenting, "From the first bar, it became apparent that Miss Perry was a composer of real originality. The macabre, almost psychotic tale of Poe, on which the libretto was based, called for music that would depict the mind of a madman, and that was what we heard. It was breathless, disconnected and grotesque, but dramatically true. ... Colorful and expressive orchestration was characteristic of the work as a whole."[54] Another reviewer wrote, "Miss Perry's way with an orchestra is extremely imaginative, and in this case, suspenseful, to fit the story. And her vocal lines were paced to help the human voice, not hold it back."[55]

Perry's use of serial techniques became distilled in a work for soprano (or tenor) and trumpet of 1954, *A Short Service from "The Mystic Trumpeter"* (text by Walt Whitman). Its four short movements are titled Prelude, Ricercar, Scherzo, and Postlude, and each begins with the same rising five-note motive outlining a minor ninth chord; the melodic line then continues with the other seven notes of a different row for each movement. The vocal line is expressively lyrical, while the trumpet part is idiomatically trumpetlike, with its repeated notes and chordal fanfares. The combination of lyricism with modified serialism continued in *Frammenti dalle lettere di Santa Caterina* for solo soprano, chorus, and small orchestra, begun by Perry in 1953, and in the lovely, meditative *Pastoral* for flute and string quintet composed at the MacDowell Colony in 1959.

On her return from Italy in February 1959, Perry brought the score of *Requiem for Orchestra* (later renamed *Homage to Vivaldi*). It was to be premiered the next month at a Music in the Making concert conducted by Howard Shanet at the Cooper Union. Its motoric patterned ostinatos are natural outgrowths of the themes by Vivaldi on which it is based. It would also seem to be a forerunner of Perry's works of the 1960s, many of which relied on repeated patterns and rhythmic drive in the absence of melodic interest. The work received a favorable review from the *New York Herald Tribune*, "[one of two] thoroughly viable works expressing sentiment worthy of communication," and the *New York Times* critic found it "conservative, tenuous and chromatic and [it] did not seem to get underway until it was half over."[56]

The next watershed composition was the *Homunculus C.F.* for ten percussionists (including xylophone, vibraphone, harp, and piano), which Perry began in the summer of 1960 in the apartment above her father's medical office, and completed in 1961. In her record liner notes, she explained, "Having selected percussion instruments for my formulae, then maneuvering and distilling them by means of the Chord of the Fifteenth (C.F.) this musical test tube baby was brought to life." Perry called this a "pantonal composition," and as such it is beyond progression; there is nowhere to go. The work is in four sections, each of which adds instruments, rhythms (some serially constructed), and notes from the fifteenth chord.[57] The accumulation of pitches, variation in dynamics, increasing rhythmic complexity, and thickening of texture would imply a sense of progression leading to completion. In listening to the work, however, the impression is, rather, of a series of terraced static sections. As used by Perry, the chord of the fifteenth is nonmelodic, without expressive content. The critic for *The New Records* disagreed, however, saying, "It has a rather lovely, lyrical flow to it, a feat difficult to achieve when working only with percussion instruments"; in another review, Bernard Jacobsen heard "a sensitive ear and purposeful rhythmic sense."[58] *Homunculus* is a pivotal work, setting the pattern for many of the compositions to follow.

In the 1960s Perry began the practice of referring to movements as "Speeds" (First Speed, Second Speed, etc.), and indicating tempos by English words (Fast, Slow, etc.) rather than the conventional Italian terms (Allegro, Adagio, etc.). Dynamics were indicated by letters L, S, ML, and so on (for Loud, Soft, Medium loud, etc.) instead of f, p, mf (for forte, piano, mezzo-forte, etc.).[59]

The *Concerto for Piano in Two Uninterrupted Speeds* relies upon three-note cells or motives and repeated patterns (many of them outlining seventh chords) in ostinatos or extended passages of sequences. The texture of the meditative first movement is extremely sparse: widely spaced three-note cells, often single notes exchanging hands on an identical pitch. In the second movement, ostinato patterns are sometimes doubled at the second or ninth between the hands, increasing the dissonance.

The *Miniature* for solo piano, published in 1972, offers another example of the kind of themeless patterning of dissonant solid seventh chord passages, alternating with broken ninth and eleventh chords in contrary motion. The same lack of melody is true of *The Beacon* for wind octet (1963) and *Symphony No. 6* for band (1966).[60] This was evidently Perry's intent, because in her program notes for *Symphony No. 3*, Perry speaks of "unary thematic material" and "introductory sequential patterns which appear throughout the first movement." Her attention was on other things besides melody: she explains that its two-dimensional texture is a dichotomy between horizontal and vertical structures with diagonal relationships as intermediaries. Her three-note cells, which she calls "chord kernels," are also subject to a dichotomy, close position alternating with widely spaced vertical structures. In her notes for *Symphony No. 4* Perry also speaks of pervasive five-note patterned figuration. Two other terms in her program notes for these symphonies stand out significantly: "taut passivity" and "immobility."[61] It is exactly the tense, static effect produced by her seventh, ninth, and eleventh chords with superimposed seconds, her narrow pitch cells, and constant repetitive patterns. A choral composition from this period, *Hymn to Pan* (1963), although devoid of patterning, conveys a kind of primitive, pagan friezelike immobility through its slow-moving dissonant minor ninth intervals and syllabic treatment of words on repeated notes. In contrast to such slow-moving, often arhythmic works and movements, sections of her other works of this period "maintain rhythmic propulsive excitation."

The avoidance of melody is carried into Perry's operatic works as well. *The Selfish Giant* ("A Sacred Musical Fable," 1964) relies on recitative-like vocal lines, the singers speaking syllabically on repeated notes, changing pitch infrequently. The orchestra provides the traditional recitative accompaniment of long-held intervals (seconds, ninths) and chords (sometimes quartal, with many added seconds). In the interludes it builds atmospheric color through its choice of instruments and the range, rhythm, and tempo of its repeated patterns. The few surviving fragments of the opera *Symplegades* (1959–74) indicate an even more restricted pitch range, with very sparse instrumental support.[62]

One of the more interesting works of the 1960s is the *Concerto for Violin and Orchestra*, begun in 1963 as *A Piece for Violin and Orchestra*, and completed in 1968. A sectional one-movement work, it opens with a long violin cadenza, beginning with three dramatic two-note phrases in double stops. This is the thematic material for the entire concerto, developed by extension, ornamentation, and inversion. Perry's own violin background and her knowledge of violin possibilities are evident in the variety of effects she produces with harmonics and other devices. Although the sequential repetition of patterns is still extreme, there is slightly more variation here than in other works, and perhaps a stronger sense of direction.

In some works of the late 1960s and 1970s—*Module for Orchestra* (20 variations on a Negro folk song, 1967–75), and the *Fifth ("Integration") Symphony*[63] (1966–67)—one might be tempted to see a return to ethnic musical roots.[64] In *Suite Symphony* (ca. 1969) and the *Tenth, ("Soul") Symphony* (1972), however, this is a return not to the same African-American musical heritage with which she began her composing career, but rather to more contemporary urban genres. The seven short programmatic movements of *A Suite Symphony* include "Bass-Amplification in 'Rock and Roll' style" and "Rhythm and Blues," and the socially relevant titles "Global Warfare," and "Coal-Miners Sealed in a Condemned Coal Mine." The brevity of the movements can sustain the reliance on short motives (often three-note cells) and repetitive patterns (aided by heavy backbeats). Perry divides rock and roll patterns among the sections of the orchestra, one or two notes each. The harmonica is featured in the instrumentation for "Wagon Train," but surprisingly, there is no electric bass in "Bass-Amplification."

The last musical compositions of the 1960s, her Symphonies Nos. *5, 7, 8,* and *9*, have not been located and may well be lost. In the early 1970s, after her stroke, Perry wrote several short marching band pieces, vainly hoping to have them published and performed by university bands. Another short piece which survives is the *Divertimento for Five Wind Instruments* (1974–76), dedicated to her mother. Like the *Suite Symphony*, it also imitates other instruments and combinations. The flute, oboe, saxophones, and bassoon are used as a rhythm section, sometimes very much like a bass electric guitar. The flute has a long solo before the piece closes with another rhythm section passage. Here she indicated "tap heel on floor" but later struck it out.

In 1976 Perry wrote *Quinary Quixotic Songs*, a set of five short pieces scored for bass baritone voice and five instruments. The texts, by Perry, are by turns poignant and nonsensical, sung in a recitative style with melodic interjections. Although the familiar three-note cells and dissonant sevenths reappear, the harmonic language is more varied. The last surviving piece, *Bicentennial Reflections*, is short, only one minute long. It was composed in 1977 for tenor soloist, two clarinets, three percussionists, and electric bass. The three percussionists are to be black, Chinese, and Jewish (or "Aryan"), dressed in red, white, and blue. Pictures are to be hung above the stage. The text by Perry poses and answers riddles about freedom in America.

In some ways it would appear that in her last years, Perry broke out of some of her more restrictive patterns of the 1960s. Despite the frustration of her physical and mental deterioration and the painful slowness of notating her ideas, she brought forth some last proofs of her creativity and skill, a parting musical testament from the woman who signed herself "Composer Julia Perry."

A Short Piece for Orchestra (1952)

The title started as *Piece for Orchestra*, but was soon changed to *A Short Piece for Orchestra*. It was performed as *Study for Orchestra* (at conductor William Steinberg's request) in 1965 by the New York Philharmonic Orchestra and the Pittsburgh Symphony Orchestra on tour in Europe. However, it was published as *A Short Piece for Orchestra* by the Southern Music Company in 1962, and recorded under that title.

It began as a work for chamber orchestra and was premiered by the Turin Symphony Orchestra, conducted by Dean Dixon, in 1952. It undoubtedly received more European performances on Perry's U.S. Information Service tours. In 1955 the instrumentation was expanded to full orchestra for its U.S. debut by The Little Orchestra Society conducted by Thomas Scherman. Of that performance, critic Ross Parmenter wrote, "This is a piece that is gentle and spirited by turns. It has plenty of material and perhaps could have been longer to its own advantage, for Miss Perry is both gifted and individual in her style."[65] When William Steinberg conducted the piece with the New York Philharmonic in May 1965, Harold Schonberg of the *New York Times* was disappointed: "It starts out in a buoyant manner and then bogs down, never fulfilling its initial statement. The harmonic idiom is neutral-modern but not too modern, lacking punch and personality."[66] It was recorded by the Imperial Philharmonic Orchestra of Tokyo, conducted by William Strickland, and released by CRI in 1961. One reviewer chose it as his favorite on the LP for its "compactness of form and sheer joie de vivre."[67] *Hi Fidelity*'s critic pronounced it "a very brilliant affair," and the *American Record Guide* admired its "excellent cohesion" and "differing concepts of a terse logical fundament."[68]

The work continued to be performed after Perry's death. In the summer of 1979, soon after she died, *A Short Piece for Orchestra* was chosen by composer/ conductor Kay Gardner for her performance in the National Adult Conducting Competition held in Wisconsin. *Short Piece* has been performed twice by the Bay Area Women's Philharmonic Orchestra in San Francisco, once in 1983, conducted by Antonia Brico, and again in 1989, conducted by JoAnne Falletta. The Atlanta Symphony Orchestra included it in an outdoor concert for the National Black Arts Festival in 1992.[69] A performance in February 2000 by the New York Virtuosi under Kenneth Kline drew this *New York Times* comment:

"rugged and powerful . . . an appealingly chromatic piece full of lovely orchestral details."[70]

Short Piece is the earliest of Perry's compositions for orchestra that is available to us, although she had written for orchestra previously.[71] It is also the first composition to appear after she began composition studies with Dallapiccola, and shows his influence in its rich, colorful instrumentation, its economy of thematic material, and the development of pitch cells. Like *Stabat Mater*, this work astonishes with its seemingly sudden authoritative command of this medium.

I agree with Michelle Edwards' assessment that "Although *Short Piece for Orchestra* has an overall structure of distinct sections, its organizing principle is organic development."[72] My perception of the form is A B A^1 C A^2 D A^3, with episodes B and D in contrasting slower tempos and moods, and C remaining strong and driving (although it is marked "Meno mosso"). The A^3 is abbreviated, in the nature of a coda. Almost all of the material in all sections is derived from three interrelated generating cells or motives that appear in the first four or five measures: (1) a group of half-steps, either rising, as in the opening grace group B, C, C-sharp, D, or descending G, G-flat, F, etc.; (2) a chord structure consisting of two minor thirds plus a fourth: C, D-sharp, F-sharp, B (this structure contains other intervals including the tritone, used by the timpani as a closing punctuation to the A sections); (3) a melodic contour of rising half-step and fifth, plus descending half-step and fourth: G-sharp, A, E, E-flat, B-flat. These three motives constantly reappear in continuous variation or development, modified through rearrangement of intervals, fragmentation, diminution (faster note values), augmentation (slower note values), and extended in long sequences or ostinato repetition.

While these permutations are not always obvious to the ear, they lend a powerful underlying cohesion to the work. Thus, after the bright, brassy fanfare-like opening section, marked "Allegro sostenuto e drammatico," with its distinctive syncopated chords, the B section's contrasting cantilena phrases (passed from flutes to clarinets to horns to violins) each begin with a version of the third generating motive, while the cellos repeat the second motive in a quiet background ostinato. The gentle, quiet mood is broken by a return to the opening brassy chords and driving tempo; this time the A section elaborates on motive 3 in overlapping repetition. The C section extends motives 2 and 3 in continuous sequences, while the following A^2 return of the fanfare ushers in extended driving passagework on the first motive. In an especially skillful transition, this motive is repeated successively more slowly in an expanding interval progression, leading into the meditative, mysterious D section marked "Molto lento." Here the motive expands from half-steps to whole steps, slowly widening to fifths to sevenths to ninths. Next comes a sustained, lyrical version of motive 3 in retrograde (backward), passed from solo flute to solo bassoon, to solo violin. All through this section a slowly syncopated pedal point on B is sustained by the cellos, contrabass, and harp, increasing the mystery and suspense. Finally the celesta and violas outline motive 2 in slow motion, doubled in sevenths. The quiet reverie reaches a still point just before the driving, continuous first motive brings the work to a brilliant close in a brief and final outburst. For all its dissonance and harmonic ambiguity, the work is firmly tonal, beginning with a loud unison D and ending with a unison D only slightly veiled by its surrounding tone cluster.

Symphony No. 4 (1964–68)

In late October 1964, Perry wrote from the MacDowell Colony to the American Music Center to say that she was revising and adding a string section and copying the parts to her fourth symphony, adding in parentheses, "The Selfish Giant Symphony." A perusal of the score of her opera *The Selfish Giant*, completed in 1964, does not reveal any connection, thematic or otherwise. In program notes found in the Carl Fischer Company files, Perry does not mention *The Selfish Giant* but subtitles it "Choreographic Symphony." Be that as it may, the symphony must be evaluated on its own merits as "pure," rather than programmatic, music.

The symphony exists in the PeerMusic archives in instrumental parts only, dated 1964–1968 (there is no record of it having been performed). Although the handwriting is legible, the transparent tape holding the extensive revisions together has crumbled and most of the onionskin parts have disintegrated. A further difficulty is that not only is the tenor saxophone part missing (noted by Perry on the folder holding the parts), but the bassoon part is missing for movements II and III. Nevertheless, an attempt was made by Christopher Hahn and myself to reconstruct the score, and it is now possible to see it and to hear a Musical Instrument Digital Interface (M.I.D.I.) computer realization sound recording of it in the Helen Walker-Hill Collection at the American Music Research Center at the University of Colorado (AMRC), the Center for Black Music Research at Columbia College, Chicago (CBMR), and the PeerMusic Publishing Company in New York (PM). Incomplete as this score is, it does provide clues to the direction of Perry's compositional evolution during the 1960s.

The work is in three speeds and lasts approximately 15 minutes. Despite a full orchestral complement of instruments, the texture is generally sparse. The first speed ("Moderate") rarely has more than two or three parts going at any moment. The harp is tacit throughout this speed. The second speed ("Fast") has a somewhat fuller orchestral texture. The harp is now present, and the piano/celesta gets more attention. The third speed ("Very slow") has the fullest orchestration, even without the missing tenor sax, timpani, and piano/celesta parts. Thus an intentional progression in thickness of orchestral texture is evident.

The first speed has two main ideas: a four-note zigzag motive consisting of a minor third up, major third down, minor third up, and tritone down, which appears in various note durations. The second motive is a slow, undulating motive in 5/4 meter that meanders in a somewhat random pitch progression. Other recurrent features are minor third tremolos (frequently doubled, adding up to seventh chords) and major seventh intervals in slower motion. As Perry states in her program notes, the form is roughly sonata form, and she alludes to the importance of instrumentation as a formal device: instead of the traditional thematic development, the B section of the first speed emphasizes the presence of "a newcomer, the baritone horn."[73]

The second speed presents an effective contrast to the outer speeds. The faster tempo, 7/8 meter, fuller instrumentation featuring piano/celesta and harp, and a four-note eighth note motive in perpetual motion combine for a striking effect. Another unusual feature is the alternating of the steady eighth notes among sections of the orchestra in a hocketlike technique, together with octave displacements and a counterpoint of long sustained notes by the horns. As Perry notes, the repetitive figuration is finally silenced by the percussion in the last few measures.

The third speed is the hardest to assess because of the missing parts, particularly the bass drum, whose "resolute eighth notes contribute immobility," according to Perry's notes. This quality is still apparent, along with the evocation of desert spaces, or lunar eclipse, or infinity in space that Perry describes. This is accomplished through the instrumentation of string harmonics, celesta and harp, the constant 5/4 meter in slow tempo, and the static harmonic effect of a pervasive underlying fifteenth chord. Each note of the chord (in its place in a recurrent rhythmic pattern) is played by a different section in constantly, slowly shifting timbres and colors. The form is A B C with a short A coda. The four main melodic motives consist of parts or all of the fifteenth chord, in different rhythms and repetitions of pitches.

Perry's *Symphony No. 4* provides a good idea of her compositional style in the 1960s. It carries forth features of *Homunculus C.F.*: the fifteenth chord and the division of its parts among different instrumental groups. Even though the motives and materials in this symphony are varied, the work has the static quality and avoidance of progression characteristic of *Homunculus* and her later works. It also displays other hallmarks of her style: the use of small pitch cells, repetition in ostinato-like patterns, a kind of passive immobility alternating with contrasting propulsive driving rhythms, and the sparse coloristic use of a large and varied orchestral palette.

Symphony No. 10, "Soul Symphony" (1972)

The manuscript of this work is known to exist in two places: Fisk University Special Collections, and the archives of the PeerMusic Publishing Company, each of which has two movements in score and two only in parts. The handwriting is extremely shaky, and Perry has added letter names to many notes. An edition of the entire score (with a sound tape of the M.I.D.I. computer realization) was made in 1999 by Christopher Hahn and myself. This edition can be seen and heard at AMRC, CBMR, and the PeerMusic Publishing Company.

Although the *Soul Symphony* is listed in most of the main reference materials on Perry, there has never been a discussion or description of the work. Perry's own program notes, which she had sent to Peer-Southern, have been lost. The only extant references to this work by Perry herself are in a 1972 letter to Paul Freeman, then conductor of the Detroit Symphony. She enclosed the first two movements "with trepidation," asking him to peruse them with performance in mind. She said she was also sending the music to the conductors Henry Lewis, Zubin Mehta, and Georg Solti, and that the parts, available at Peer-Southern, had been carefully checked against the score. The next year she wrote to Peer-Southern, urgently asking them to send the *Soul Symphony* to the conductor Claudio Abbado in Milan, Italy.[74] Nothing came of these efforts, and the work has never been performed.

The *Soul Symphony* was, for Perry, a radical departure in aesthetic philosophy. She had not previously devoted such a large effort to communicating clearly and accessibly with ordinary folk; everything about it is designed to be noticed and grasped instantly by the listener. The title and musical references to black idioms—jazz, rhythm and blues, gospel—are current for the 1970s. The closest precedent in her oeuvre is the programmatic *Suite Symphony*, probably completed just before her stroke. In *Soul Symphony* she was able to extend and combine such simple ideas on a larger scale with imagination and creativity.

In all movements of *Soul Symphony*, the rhythms are straightforward and obvious. The fast movements have strong, driving rhythms with heavy downbeats, often aided by strong backbeats. Harmonically, the entire work is strongly tonal with a minimum of dissonance, just enough to dispel monotony. The modal and jazz harmonies also provide interest and variety. Melodically, the themes are short and simple, but more well-defined than in many earlier works, with variety among them. In the second movement she uses some serial techniques, varying the eight-note row (similar to a jazz riff) through retrograde (backward), inversion (upside down), and a combination of retrograde and inversion, thus combining academic with popular elements. The narrow range of most of the themes is offset by the third movement's wide-ranging melody. As in her previous orchestral works, instrumental contrast in timbre and texture is used to delineate form.

The symphony's four speeds have strong and contrasting characters. Each speed has distinctive themes or motives which remain relatively unchanged, or are easily identified when they do change. The first speed, marked "Robust," opens with a sequence of deliberate fanfare-like two-note phrases, rising thirds, that combine to spell out the Perry signature seventh chord. After six measures, a faster second theme enters, a jazzy, blueslike riff in eighth notes which is repeated over and over in call and response by different sections of the orchestra. The steady 4/4 beat is interrupted briefly but repeatedly by a contrasting third theme in 13/8, just two measures long. Unlike the preceding concise eight-note theme, this one consists of repeated notes and rising, then falling, chromatic scale fragments. Alternating with sections of variations on themes 1 and 2, this two-measure 13/8 theme recurs five more times, and each time it is played by a different instrumental group: first by clarinets, the second time by bassoons, then violas, xylophone, and oboes. It finally closes the movement, extended into a 12-measure coda in which it combines violas, violins and saxophones, trumpets, clarinets and flutes. The opposing textures of full orchestra versus a single group (also reminiscent of jazz alternation of solo and ensemble sections), the contrast among the three themes, and the rhythmic interruptions operate to keep our attention.

The second speed, marked "Perpetual repetition," takes the jazzy eighth-note riff of the first speed and speeds it up, introducing it by the piano, celesta, and harp (all were absent in the first speed). This insistent, driving pattern is now a full-fledged ostinato, tossed back and forth among sections eight times. It is interrupted by a brief slower, contrasting theme before returning in different forms (retrograde, then inverted, etc.). The contrasting theme with its nine-beat combination of 4/4 and 5/4 parallels the irregular contrasting theme in the first speed. The coda consists of the last half of the contrasting theme (three descending steps), repeated in lengthening augmentation. This momentum comes to a halt in the next speed.

The third speed, marked "Very slow," presents an enigma. It may be that Perry was experimenting with minimalism (and the attendant preference for consonance), which was in vogue in the 1960s and 1970s. The movement consists of the same (or nearly the same) four-measure rising and falling melody, repeated five times by different solo instruments. The repetitions are separated by two measures of slow, repeated notes by the harp. The solo instruments are clarinet, then bassoon, tenor saxophone, trumpet using a straight fiber mute, the human voice (a bass baritone vocalise using falsetto on the high notes), and finally the string bass. The melody rises slowly in a major triad arpeggio from low G up to a long-held B-flat three octaves above, falls back to G, then finishes a fourth down on D (G B D G B D F A B-flat, down to F G D B G D). The third, fourth, and fifth repetitions vary slightly; the third and fourth end with a minor descending triad, and the fourth and fifth finish on G instead of falling to D. The slow tempo and melismatic melody are somewhat reminiscent of long-meter gospel hymns. At the beginning Perry wrote "Improvisation," then struck it out. Improvisation would make sense, because the melody is extremely repetitive as written. Improvisation would be easy since the instruments are solo, and the "Soul" title of the symphony begs for some personal, individual interpretation. A kettledrum pattern that Perry cut out might also be restored, to support the repeated harp note. This unusual movement has the potential to be an arresting interlude to the other rhythmically driving movements.

The final speed, marked "Raucous," uses all the instruments (except the voice), including an expanded percussion section, and remains solidly in duple time, with a heavy backbeat. It opens with just the percussion "boom-chick" rhythm, then quickly brings in all the instruments in a truly raucous tutti, exploiting Perry's penchant for repeated patterns to the fullest. Each time the tutti returns, the patterns are varied in rhythm, intervals, and instrumentation. Alternating with them are three different themes, each of which employs jazz idioms: lowered thirds and fifths (as in the descending progression G-flat, F, E-flat, C), triplet-eighths, triplet-quarters, and syncopations.

Soul Symphony displays a side of Julia Perry's music that is not usually associated with her, and it deserves to be performed and heard. It might revive interest in this important twentieth-century composer, and dispel the notion that her compositions are all difficult to understand and irrelevant to contemporary lives and tastes.

Quinary Quixotic Songs (1976)

This score is almost the last extant work by Perry (followed only by the *Bicentennial Reflections* of 1977). She referred to it in a letter to Peer-Southern in March 1977, when she reported that she had finished copying the parts for it. There she calls it *Five Quixotic Songs*. In September she asked the company to return the score to her, only to send it to them again in January 1979, remarking that it was being considered by a bass-baritone on the faculty at Eastman School of Music. The manuscript is so illegible that it is hard to believe it was seriously considered. This score has also been reconstructed, and can be seen (and heard in M.I.D.I. computer realization) at AMRC, CBMR, and PeerMusic.

Quinary Quixotic Songs was the first vocal work by Perry since 1964 (*The Selfish Giant*). The words by Perry are surrealistic, by turns poignant and nonsensical, with juxtaposition of seemingly unrelated ideas, and a terse, elliptical delivery. The text for each song is brief, only two or three lines. There is no continuity of subject, or images, or moods, although a sense of alienation and suffering does recur in different contexts.

Musically, the forms and materials sometimes reflect the text, and at other times contradict the surrealism of the words with their conventionality. Three-part A B A forms, repetition of melodic and rhythmic motives, a steady beat in many sections, a minimum of dissonance, simple harmonic structures, and a strong sense of tonality provide a sense of stability at odds with the mysterious text. Melodically, there is a dichotomy between declamatory passages and more lyrical vocal lines in which the familiar three-note cells and sevenths reappear. Rhythmically, sections of steady beats contrast with changing meters and free, varying durations. Harmonically, the familiar Perry hallmarks of seventh, or eleventh, or thirteenth chords and astringent minor seconds spice up stretches of otherwise blandly consonant harmonies. The instrumentation of flute, B-flat clarinet, viola, baritone horn, and piano provides a wide and variegated palette. Generally only one or two instruments have a continuous thematic function, the others being used sparingly for coloristic contrast. The choice of baritone horn is rather curious; it doubles the range of the bass baritone voice, and is most often used to prepare or bridge the vocal phrases.

The first song, "A Monodic Prologue," frames its two sentences, delivered by the unaccompanied voice, with instrumental sections of flute, clarinet, and viola. The viola's part consists of an odd rhythmic phrase on one note, repeated six times in all. The two-line text compares souls "abandoned in jail" with those "forgotten in Hell" (with a dramatic downward leap of a minor ninth to "Hell").

In the second song, "Ballad," the text extols the virtues of diamonds as opposed to other gems. This time it is the voice that repeats a rhythmic phrase while the flute, clarinet, horn, and viola sustain seventh chords against this recitative. The middle section breaks loose into instrumental trills and a series of short, descending vocal phrases rejecting the other precious stones, before returning to the recitative on the subject of diamonds, and concludes with the sustained diminished triad of A C E-flat by viola, clarinet, and flute.

The third song, mysteriously titled " 'Rock' Soliloquy," has neither reference to rocks or a steady "rock" beat, but protests "stifled sounds" which "mame" [sic] the soliloquy and "sawtooth wave forms" which "crush the tune" in a vocal line with the indication "quizzical." The second line shifts the subject to spaceships and outer space, with a recitative-like vocal line against instruments reiterating an A-major triad in triplets. The third line intones an absolution of (not by) God, and finishes ("hysterically") with a cry "Must I go insane?" at the very top of the baritone range. The pitches are almost all part of the major eleventh chord on D.

The fourth title is also mysterious: "Fortune Cookies." The text is an exhortation to maintain faith, hope, and courage while enduring the disgrace of poverty (lack of "fortune"?). The song is introduced by the piano's repeated seventh intervals (A G-sharp) against F-sharp. The vocal line leaps back and forth between the notes A and G-sharp, and in the second line of the text, both baritone horn (marked "fanfare") and voice outline the major seventh chord on E. This tonality closes the song as the piano reiterates a major third interval on E over a low sustained F-sharp.

The final song, "Fiesta," changes the mood dramatically with furiously strummed open strings of the viola in a quasi-fandango rhythm. This alternates with an instrumental melody outlining the minor ninth chord. In a declamatory vocal style, the text contributes images of bullrings, blood, the sounds of tambourines and castanets, and Morroccan and Tunisian visitors squabbling, interspersed with the refrain "What a day, Olé."

Despite the spare, simple words and musical materials, this is not a straightforward, obvious work. It is crafted with skill and imagination. The repetition of materials is always subtle and varied. Its economy and transparency are sophisticated, and its meaning elusive. As Perry's last available work, it provides an intriguing and worthy musical epitaph.

LIST OF WORKS

Archives Holding Scores

(AMC) The American Music Center in New York City (four works in manuscript)

(AMRC/CBMR) The Helen Walker-Hill Collection for scores by black women composers, in duplicate at the American Music Research Center at the University of Colorado at Boulder, and the Center for Black Music Research at Columbia College, Chicago (30 unpublished manuscripts, 15 published scores).

(Fisk) Fisk University Special Collections, Nashville, Tenn. (seven manuscripts)

(IU) Indiana University Music Library, Bloomington (eight published works)

(PM) PeerMusic archives. PeerMusic (formerly Peer-Southern Music Inc., Peer-International Corp., and before that, Southern Music Publishing Company) (eight works available for sale or for rent, 16 unpublished manuscripts).

References (listed only if they add or corroborate information)

See selected bibliography for complete citations.

(Ammer) Christine Ammer. *Unsung.*

(Cohen) Aaron Cohen, ed. *International Encyclopedia of Women Composers.*

(de Lerma) Dominique-René de Lerma. Bibliography of scores by black composers. Publication in progress. (Professor de Lerma cautions that entries are based on Perry's communications with him, and need to be verified).

(Green) Mildred Denby Green. *Black Women Composers.*

(IDBC) *International Dictionary of Black Composers.*

(JP) Julia Perry. Titles and descriptions from her correspondence, biographical material, and lists[75] at PeerMusic, Composers Recordings Inc., Library of Congress, American Music Center; from Dominique-René de Lerma (on file at Fisk University and the Center for Black Music Research); also from a tape of her New York City postconcert forum interview of 22 February 1954.

Unless a publisher is indicated, the music is unpublished. Only those works listed in archives have been seen and verified. The large number of footnotes is due to the problems in identifying Perry's works.

Instrumental Music

Violin

Sonatina (violin and piano). 1953[76]

Violin Solo. 1947. First performed 26 May 1947 by Alma Jean Work at Westminster Choir College. (JP[77])

Viola

Piece for Viola and Piano. Ca. 1968.[78] 1 min. (JP)

Viola Sonata (listed in some sources as *Violin Sonata*). Prix Fontainebleau in 1952. (JP, etc.)

Clarinet

Piece for Clarinet and Piano. ca. 1968. 2 min. (JP)
Serenity (B-flat clarinet, optional piano). 1960s, transposed for clarinet in 1972. Same as
    Composition for Oboe. 1 min. 50 sec. (Clarinet part only at AMRC/CBMR, PM)

Oboe

Composition for Oboe. 1960s. Same as *Serenity* for clarinet. 1 min. 50 sec. (Oboe part
    at AMRC/CBMR, PM)
Piece for Oboe and Piano. ca. 1968. 3 min. (JP)

Piano

Lament. 1947. Probably same as *Prelude for Piano.* First performed 26 May 1947 by
    Wil Russell at Westminster Choir College. (Green, etc.)
Miniature. n.d. (1960s). In *The New Scribner Library* 11, compiled by Howard Hanson.
    New York: Charles Scribner's Sons, 1972. (AMRC/CBMR)
Modern Piano Pieces. n.d. (IDBC, de Lerma)
Pearls on Silk. 1947. First performed 26 May 1947 by Wil Russell at Westminster Choir
    College. (Green, etc.)
Piano Pieces for Young and Older Citizens (?) (de Lerma)
Prelude for Piano. 1946, rev. 1962. In *Black Women Composers: A Century of Piano
    Music 1893–1990*, edited by Helen Walker-Hill (Bryn Mawr, Pa.: Hildegard Pub-
    lishing Co., 1992). See discography. (AMC, AMRC/CBMR, Fisk[79])
Suite of Shoes. 1947. *Soldier's Boots* from *Suite of Shoes* first performed 26 May 1947
    by Wil Russell at Westminster Choir College. (Green, etc.)
Three Piano Pieces for Children. n.d. (Green, de Lerma)
Two Easy Piano Pieces. 1972. (1) Spreading Peanut Butter; (2) Popping Corn. (AMRC/
    CBMR, PM)

Ensemble (see also Band)

The Beacon (2 English horns, 2 tenor sax, 2 bassoons, 2 trumpets). 1963. One movement:
    Allegro, quarter=126. (AMC, AMRC/CBMR)
Divertimento for Five Wind Instruments (flute, oboe, E-flat alto sax, B-flat tenor sax,
    bassoon). 1974. "To my mother." 4 min. 45 sec. (Ms. and computer sound tape
    and printed edition by Helen Walker-Hill and Chris Hahn at AMRC/CBMR, PM)
Four Pieces for Wind Quintet. 1963. (JP) Probably same as *Quartette for Wind Quintette.*
Homunculus C.F. (percussion ensemble, harp, piano). 1960–61. New York: Southern,
    1966. In *Historical Anthology of Music by Women*, compiled and edited by James
    Briscoe. (Bloomington: Indiana University Press, 1987). First performed on 14
    January 1965 by the Manhattan Percussion Ensemble, conducted by Paul Price,
    at the Manhattan School of Music. See discography. 5 min. (AMRC/CBMR, IU,
    PM)
Pastoral (flute, 2 violins, viola, 2 cellos). 1959. New York: Southern, 1962. Formerly
    Flute Septet or *Septet for Flute and Strings.* Composed at the MacDowell Colony.
    4 min. (AMRC/CBMR, IU, PM)
Quartette for Wind Quintette (flute, oboe, B-flat clarinet, E-flat alto sax, bassoon). 1963.
    Four movements: (1) Moderate, quarter = 72; (2) Fast, quarter = 138; (3) Slow,

quarter = 44; (4) Fast, quarter = 120. May be the same as *Four Pieces for Wind Quintet*. See also *Symphony No. 13*. 8 min. (AMC, AMRC/CBMR)

Septet for Flute and Strings. See *Pastoral*.

String Quartet. 1954. (JP)

Suite for Brass (2 French horns, 2 trumpets, 2 trombones, tuba). By 1961. Same as *Three Pieces for Brass Septet*, 1960? (JP)

Suite for Brass and Percussion. 1978. Same as *Suite for Bass and Percussion*, 1978 (IDBC)? (Ammer)

Symphony No. 1 (2 or more violas, 2 or more string basses). 1961. Same as *Symphony in One Movement*. Dedicated to sculptor Henry Moore. 7 min. (AMC, AMRC/CBMR)

Symphony No. 13 for Wind Quintet (flute, oboe, B-flat clarinet, E-flat alto sax, bassoon). 1963, revised 1976. The same as *Quartette for Wind Quintette* except for some revisions in the last two movements. 8 min. (Ms. and computer sound tape and printed edition by Helen Walker-Hill and Chris Hahn at AMRC/CBMR, PM)

Three Pieces for Brass Septet. 1960. May be *Suite for Brass*. (JP)

Triptych (violas and basses). Ca. 1961. Same as *Symphony No. 1*? 7 min. 15 sec. (JP[80])

Woodwind Trio (flute, clarinet, bassoon). 1951.[81]

Orchestra (large and small orchestras, and string orchestra)

Ariel for Orchestra. 1964. (JP)

Ballet for Orchestra (chamber orchestra). 1961. Same as *Portraits* from the ballet *Crossroads*? 4 min. 30 sec. (JP[82])

Ballet for Orchestra. See *Dance for Chamber Orchestra*.

Chicago (male chorus, narrator, orchestra). See *Chorus*.

Composition for Orchestra. 1964. (JP[83])

Concerto for Piano and Orchestra in Two Uninterrupted Speeds. 1964–69.[84] Second movement formerly *Concerto No. 2 for Piano and Orchestra* (1964). Another movement/speed was composed but has not been located.[85] An arrangement for two pianos of *Piano Concerto No. 2* was also made but has not been located. 11 min. (AMRC/CBMR, PM)

Concerto for Violin and Orchestra. 1963–68. New York: Carl Fischer, 1968 (rental). Formerly *Piece for Violin and Orchestra*, 1963. (Violin and piano reduction at AMRC/CBMR)

Concerto for Violin No. 2. (?) 1975. (de Lerma)

Concerto No. 2 for Piano and Orchestra. 1964. This one-movement concerto appears separately under this title but predates *Concerto for Piano and Orchestra in Two Uninterrupted Speeds*, of which it is the second movement. It raises the question of a concerto no. 1, perhaps the *Piece for Piano and Orchestra* (1963)? (AMRC/CBMR, PM)

Contretemps for Orchestra. 1963. Commissioned by the Greater Akron Musical Association. "In memory of Mable Todd" (Perry's teacher). First performed on 28 April 1964 by the Akron Symphony Orchestra, conducted by Louis Lane. Same as *Equation for Orchestra*. 6 min. (Chicago Symphony Orchestra, Margaret Hillis Collection; AMRC/CBMR)

Dance for Chamber Orchestra. 1962. Formerly *Ballet for Orchestra*. 13 min. (AMRC/CBMR, PM; JP)

Episode for Orchestra. 1973? (Green, Cohen, de Lerma)

Equation for Orchestra. 1963. Same as *Contretemps.*[86] (JP)

Four Spirituals for Orchestra. 1965–67. (1) I Couldn't Hear Nobody Pray; (2) Who Dat Comin' Ovah Yondah; (3) De Blin' Man Stood and Cried; (4) Unidentified. (Parts in memorabilia, printed edition of score by Chris Hahn at AMRC/CBMR; JP[87])

Frammenti dalle lettere di Santa Caterina (small orchestra, SATB, soprano). See *Chorus.*

Homage to Vivaldi. 1959, revised 1964. New York: Peer-Southern, 1964 (rental). Same as *Requiem for Orchestra* and *Vivaldiana.* First performed as *Requiem for Orchestra* on 13 March 1959 by the Music in the Making Orchestra, conducted by Howard Shanet, at Cooper Union, New York City. 7 min. 30 sec.[88] (AMRC/CBMR, PM, JP)

Liberation for Orchestra. 1963. 7 min. 30 sec. (JP)

Module for Orchestra (piccolo, flute, 2 oboes, 2 B-flat clarinets, 2 bassoons, E-flat sax, 3 horns, 2 trumpets, 3 trombones, harp, string section). 1967–75.[89] Twenty variations on a Negro folksong. (Piano reduction at Fisk; parts, no score at PM)

Prelude for Strings. 1946, revised 1962. Same as *Prelude for Piano.* 1 min. (JP)

Requiem for Orchestra. 1959. See *Homage to Vivaldi.*

Seven Sutures for Orchestra (woodwinds, brass, percussion, violas, string basses). 1961. 5 min. (JP)

A Short Piece for Orchestra (arranged for both small and large orchestra). 1952, revised 1962. New York: Southern, 1962 (rental). First performed in 1952 by the Turin Symphony Orchestra, conducted by Dean Dixon. See discography. 7 min. 30 sec. (AMRC/CBMR, PM)

Solstice for Strings. 1963. 5 min. (JP)

Study for Orchestra. See *Short Piece for Orchestra.*

A Suite Symphony (large orchestra). N.d. (late 1960s). Seven movements:[90] (1) Bass-Amplification in "Rock and Roll" Style; (2) Wagon Train and Indians After Sundown; (3) Global Warfare; (4) Sonic "E" in Space; (5) Slums; (6) Rhythm and Blues; (7) Coal-Miners Sealed in a Condemned Coal-Mine. May be *Symphony No. 9.* 17 min. (AMRC/CBMR, PM)

Symphony No. 1. See *Ensemble.*

Symphony No. 2 (large orchestra). 1962. 36 min. 30 sec. Three movements. (JP, de Lerma[91])

Symphony No. 3 (large orchestra). 1962.[92] Parts in C. Fischer archives. Three speeds. 20 min. 30 sec. (JP)

Symphony No. 4 (large orchestra). 1964–1968. Three movements. 15 min. (Incomplete parts at PM; computer sound recording and printed score edited by Helen Walker-Hill and Chris Hahn at AMRC/CBMR, PM)

Symphony No. 5 (small orchestra). 1966–67. "Integration." Two movements. (1) Slow, desolate; (2) Very fast. (JP)

Symphony No. 6. See *Band.*

Symphony No. 7. See *Chorus, Symphony U.S.A.*

Symphony No. 8. 1968–69. (JP, etc.)

Symphony No. 9. 1965–70. May be *A Suite Symphony?* (JP, etc.)

Symphony No. 10. 1972. "Soul Symphony."[93] Four movements. 20 min. (Score for movements I and II and parts for movements II and IV at Fisk; parts for movements I and II, and score for movements II and IV at PM; computer sound recording and printed score of all movements edited by Helen Walker-Hill and Chris Hahn at AMRC/CBMR, PM)

Symphony No. 11. See *Band.*

Symphony No. 12. 1973. Also titled "Simple Symphony" and "Children's Symphony." Two movements.[94] 10 min. (parts at Fisk; JP, de Lerma)

Symphony No. 13. See *Ensemble.*

Three Spirituals for Orchestra. 1956? 1965–67? (1) Roll Jordan, Roll; (2) Not identified; (3) Dere's No Hidin' Place Down Dere. (Parts from memorabilia, printed score edited by Chris Hahn in AMRC/CBMR)

Vivaldiana. 1959. Same as *Homage to Vivaldi.*

(About 10 additional arrangements of Negro spirituals for large orchestra are mentioned in Perry's correspondence as having been composed between 1965 and 1967.)

Band

Marching Band Symphony. 1972. Four movements: (1) Marching Band Salute; (2) Venus Moon; (3) Fireworks on Mars; (4) Theme, Variations, and Finale. (PM; JP)

Panorama. 1972. One movement for concert band. 3 min. (JP)

Soundout (3 trumpets, 2 trombones). 1970–1971. Formerly *Fanfare.* Five movements: (1) Salute, in 1 part, 30 sec.; (2) Let's Score, in 2 parts, 30 sec.; (3) Shake Those Shakers, in 3 parts, 1 min.; (4) Pep Up, 4 parts, 1 min.; (5) Game's Over, 5 parts, 30 sec. (JP[95])

Space Symphony. 1975. Four movements for concert band. Possibly the same as *Marching Band Symphony.* (JP[96])

Splash Down. Same as *Marching Band Symphony* fourth movement. (PM)

Symphony No. 6. 1966. New York: Carl Fischer, 1968 (rental). Same as *Symphony No. 6 for Winds.* Four movements.

Symphony No. 11. 1972. For concert band.[97] Possibly *Space Symphony*? (JP, de Lerma)

Theme Song: "Gimme That Ole Time Religion" (mini-marching band). 1973. (PM)

Tom Thumb Series (snare drum, cymbal, high and low block). 1972. Two pieces employing patterns from *Twelve Rudiments for Snare Drum and Cymbal Block* woven into a composition. (PM; JP)

Vocal Music

Solo voice (with piano, orchestra, or other instrumentation)

Alleluia (medium voice, organ). N.d. (1950s?). Text: Matthew 28: 1, 2, 5, 6. "For Virginia Shuey." Courtesy of Patricia Sides. (AMRC/CBMR)

Bicentennial Reflections (tenor, 2 clarinets, 3 percussionists, electric bass). 1977. 1 min. (Fisk)

By the Sea (high voice, piano). 1948.[98] New York: Galaxy, 1950. Text: Julia Perry. "To Ellabelle Davis." See discography. 2 min. (AMRC/CBMR)

Deep Sworn Vow. 1947. First performed 26 May 1947 by James McKeever at Westminster Choir College. (JP, Green)

Five Negro Spirituals for Mezzo-soprano and Orchestra. 1956–64. Includes *Three Negro Spirituals for Soprano and Orchestra.* 11 min. (JP[99])

Five Songs (mezzo-soprano and string quartet). Ca.1977. (IDBC, de Lerma)

Five Songs for Soprano and Piano. 1963. Possibly the same as *Five Songs* (mezzo-soprano and string quartet). 5 min. (JP[100])

Frammenti dalle lettere di Santa Caterina (SATB, soprano solo, small orchestra). See *Chorus*.

Free at Last (high voice, piano). 1950. New York: Galaxy, 1951. Spiritual. In *Art Songs and Spirituals by African-American Women Composers*, edited by Vivian Taylor (Bryn Mawr, Pa.: Hildegard Publishing Co., 1995). See discography. 2 min. (AMRC/CBMR)

How Beautiful Are the Feet (med. voice, piano/organ). 1951. New York: Galaxy, 1954. Text: Isaiah 52:7. See discography. 3 min. 40 sec. (AMRC/CBMR, IU)

I'm a Poor Little Orphan Girl (medium voice, piano). 1950. New York: Galaxy, 1952. Spiritual. In *Art Songs and Spirituals by African-American Women Composers*, edited by Vivian Taylor, (Bryn Mawr, Pa.: Hildegard Publishing Co. 1995). See discography. 2 min. (AMRC/ CBMR, IU)

King Jesus Lives. 1947. First performed 26 May 1947 by Lillian Hall and Julia Perry at Westminster Choir College. (JP, Green)

Lord, What Shall I Do? (high voice). Boston: McLaughlin and Reilly, 1949. "A Spiritual by Julia Perry." "To my mother." First performed 26 May 1947 by Julia Perry at Westminster Choir College. Sung by Nan Merriman of the Metropolitan Opera. (AMRC/CBMR)

Parody (baritone). 1954. Text by Patricia Sides. Composed at MacDowell Colony. Courtesy of Patricia Sides. (AMRC/CBMR)

Prayer (soprano, piano). Performed by Jacquelyn Chandler, soprano, and L. Douglas Brockington, piano, on 10 February 1991 at Florida State University School of Music.

Quinary Quixotic Songs (bass baritone, flute, B-flat clarinet, viola, baritone horn, piano). 1976. Formerly *Triptych*. Text by Julia Perry. 11 min. (AMRC/CBMR, PM; at Fisk as *Triptych*; sound tape and printed score edited by Helen Walker-Hill and Chris Hahn at AMRC/CBMR, PM)

Resurrection. Ca. 1959. Text: Patricia Sides.[101]

Seven Contrasts (baritone, chamber ensemble). N.d. (Green, etc.)

A Short Service from "The Mystic Trumpeter" (tenor/soprano, trumpet). 1954. Text: Walt Whitman. Four movements: (1) Prelude; (2) Ricercar; (3) Scherzo; (4) Postlude. Composed at the MacDowell Colony. Courtesy of Patricia Sides. (AMRC/CBMR)

Stabat Mater (contralto, string quartet/string orchestra). 1951. New York: Southern, 1954.[102] Text: 13th-century Latin sequence by Jacopo da Todi. First performed in the summer of 1951 by Julia Perry and student orchestra conducted by Piero Bellugi at Tanglewood, Mass. See discography. 18 min. (AMRC/CBMR, PM)

Three Negro Spirituals for Soprano and Orchestra (large/small). 1956. Written for and performed by Gloria Davy and the Rome Chamber Orchestra of Santa Cecilia.[103] Possibly recorded on Decca Italiana. 8 min. See also *Five Negro Spirituals for Soprano and Orchestra*.

To Elektra. 1947. First performed 26 May 1947 by Jack DeLon at Westminster Choir College. (JP, Green)

Triptych. See *Quinary Quixotic Songs*.

Chorus

Be Merciful unto Me (SATB, soprano and bass solos, organ). New York: Galaxy, 1953. Text: Psalm 57: 1, 2. 7 min. (AMRC/CBMR, IU)

Carillon Heigh-Ho. (SATB a cappella). New York: Carl Fischer, 1947. Text: Julia Perry.

"To Lo Rean Hodapp". First performed 26 May 1947 at Westminster Choir College. See discography. (AMRC/CBMR)

Chicago (SATB, baritone solo, narrator, orchestra). 1948. Text: Carl Sandburg. Westminster Choir College master's thesis. 4 min. 30 sec. (Ammer, Green, JP)

Contrasts. See *Seven Contrasts.*

Four Anthems. 1950. (JP)

Frammenti dalle lettere di Santa Caterina (SATB, soprano solo, small orchestra). 1953, revised 1957. New York: Southern, 1957 (rental). There may have been plans by Hugh Ross to perform it with the Schola Cantorum in New York.[104] 10 min. (AMRC/CBMR)

Hymn to Pan (SATB, organ/piano). 1963. Text: John Fletcher (1579–1625). Commissioned by the University of Akron-Firestone Conservatory Choral Society. (AMRC/CBMR, Fisk)

Is There Anybody Here? (women's voices). 1947. First performed 26 May 1947 at Westminster Choir College. (Cohen, Green, JP)

The Lord Is Risen Today (men's voices). 1947. First performed 26 May 1947, at Westminster Choir College. (Green, JP)

Missa Brevis (SATB, organ). November 1950.[105] (Cohen, Green, JP)

Our Thanks to Thee (SATB, contralto solo, organ). New York: Galaxy, 1951. Text: Julia Perry. "To Virginia Shuey." 4 min. (AMRC/CBMR).

Ruth (SATB, organ). 1950. Sacred cantata. Text: Chapter 1 of book of Ruth. Performed 16 April 1950 at Riverside Church, New York City. (Cohen, JP, etc.)

Song of Our Savior (SATB a cappella). New York: Galaxy, 1953. Composed for Hampton University choir. (AMRC/CBMR, IU)

Symphony U.S.A. (chorus and small orchestra). 1967. Same as *Symphony No. 7.* Five short movements. (JP, etc.)

Ye Who Seek the Truth (SATB, tenor solo, organ). New York: Galaxy, 1952. 3 min. 14 sec. (AMRC/CBMR, IU)

Dramatic Music

The Cask of Amontillado. 1953. New York: Peer-Southern, 1954. Rental from Presser. One-act opera. Same as *The Bottle.* Story by Edgar Allan Poe, adapted by Julia Perry and Virginia Card. May have been performed as *The Bottle* in December 1953 at the Academy of Music in Vienna[106]; performed on 20 November 1954 by Harold Bertelsen, baritone; Richard Edwards, tenor; and Alice Wieland, soprano, with the Columbia University Orchestra, conducted by Howard Shanet, in the McMillin Academic Theater at Columbia University. 30 min. (AMRC/CBMR, PM)

The Selfish Giant. 1964. Subtitled *A Sacred Musical Fable.* From a story by Oscar Wilde, adapted by Julia Perry. Three-act opera. (Piano reduction by Perry at AMRC/CBMR, PM)

The Symplegades. Ca. 1960–74.[107] Three acts. Same as *Mary Easty* and *Gallows Hill.* (Fragments: Act II and Scene 2 of Act III from memorabilia, AMRC/CBMR; Ammer)

The Three Warnings. 1950. Dramatic cantata. (JP,[108] etc.)

Other

"Compendium in Musical Perspective."[109] 1969. Essay. (Cohen)
Fisty-Me. 1969. Original play/libretto without music. (Same as "contemporary American
play"? JP) (From memorabilia, AMRC/CBMR)
"Forty Studies for Classroom Musical Composition." 1969–70. (Cohen)
"Generation Gap in Popular Music." 1969. Essay. (Cohen)
Graves of Untold Africans. 1965. Poem. (From memorabilia, AMRC/CBMR)
Music dictionary. 1966–67. (JP[110])
Seventy-eight African fables translated from Italian to English. 1966–1967. (JP, etc.)
Three-act dramatic ritual. 1969. (Cohen, etc.)

NOTES

I am grateful to Patricia Sides and Kermit Moore for their careful reading and advice on this chapter, and to Sides as well as to Piero Bellugi and Dominique-René de Lerma for permission to quote from their letters. Sources for this chapter include interviews, conversations, and correspondence with some 20 people who knew Perry, among them her sister Alycia Berry, Patricia Sides, Kermit Moore, Piero Bellugi, and Howard Shanet; Perry's correspondence in the archives at the PeerMusic Publishing Company, Composers Recordings Inc., the Library of Congress, the American Music Center, Westminster Choir College, Fisk University, and the Center for Black Music Research (abbreviated PS, CRI, LC, WCC, Fisk, and CBMR, respectively, in the notes); the small box of memorabilia loaned to me by her sister Alycia; and the research shared with me by Angela Hammond.

Full references for written sources are given in the selected bibliography at the end of the chapter.

1. Perry, quoted in Rogers.
2. Kermit Moore, interview with the author in New York, 11 December 1995.
3. She was a passenger on a single-car commuter train, called the "Doodle Bug," from Cleveland to Hudson (near Akron) when the gasoline engine exploded (Moore).
4. In Perry's letter of 29 June 1974 to James McKeever she asks if they still choose someone for this "unique yet secretive position." (WCC)
5. Perry, letter of 6 August 1946 to Dr. and Mrs. Williamson (WCC).
6. She won the award a second time the next year. (Perry letter of 13 November 1950 to Ted Cronk at WCC).
7. Piero Bellugi, E-mail to the author, 4 April 2000.
8. Bellugi, E-mail.
9. She was seen off by her mother. A photo dated 1951, taken of both of them on board the ship, is in the box of memorabilia loaned by her sister Alycia.
10. Smith, "Julia Perry Acclaimed."
11. Patricia Sides, interview with the author, New York, 19 May 1994.
12. Quoted in Smith, "Julia Perry Acclaimed."
13. Illegible, but possibly "Student," or "Scholar" (memorabilia).
14. Reel-to-reel tape of both performance and interview at Columbia University Archives (see discography).
15. In Italian, *La Botte d'Amontillado*. This fulfilled her proposal to the Guggenheim

Foundation, to study Italian opera in order to write a full-length opera of her own (letter from Thomas Tanselle of the Guggenheim Foundation to Angela Hammond, 11 December 1997). It is possible that as *La Botte* it was performed in late 1953 at the Academy of Music in Vienna (Smith, "Awaits Playing").

16. Letter of 12 December 1955 from Perry at Corso Italia, Florence (LC).

17. Her proposal for her second Guggenheim was to write a ballet for orchestra based on one of the tales from Washington Irving's *Sketch Book* (Tanselle letter to Hammond). This may be *Portraits* for orchestra from the ballet *Crossroads*, which appeared in a list of pieces proposed for a recording (Perry letter of 8 August 1961 to CRI).

18. Roberto Lupi (1908–71) was a conductor, composer and theoretician who devised a new harmonic system, *armonia di gravitazione*, (harmony of gravitation), which he discussed in two books. He conducted the first performances in Italy of Perry's *Stabat Mater* in 1951–52.

19. According to a biographical sketch from 1962, she was also "chosen to participate in the International Orchestral Conducting Competition in Liverpool, England." (CRI)

20. Brinkley.

21. St. Catherine of Siena (1347–80), known for her service to the poor and sick, was also influential on political affairs of her time through her prolific letter writing. She was subject to mystical experiences, including the stigmata on her hands and feet.

22. Patricia Sides, interview with the author, New York, 17 January 1996; Howard Shanet, interview with the author, New York, 13 February 1996.

23. Note added in parentheses to her typed analysis of her *Symphony No. 3* (memorabilia).

24. William Steinberg, letter to Perry 12 January 1964 (CRI).

25. Perry, letter of 31 July 1967 to David Hall (CRI).

26. David Hall, letter of 10 May 1967 to Perry, saying he wrote to Walter Hendl on her behalf (CRI).

27. Other authors, both black and white, were writing surrealistic plays in the 1960s, notably Adrienne Kennedy. Her *Funnyhouse of a Negro* features unusual characters: Patrice Lumumba, Queen Victora Regina, etc.

28. This announcement was among papers at Carl Fischer; a copy was sent to me by Angela Hammond.

29. This approximate date is confirmed in her letter of 29 June 1974 to James McKeever, in which she says she is recuperating after a four-year paralytic stroke (WCC). Confusion resulted from contradictory statements by Perry to other people. In correspondence to Nancy Van de Vate, she wrote that her last three symphonies were composed after her paralytic stroke in 1971 [sic] (Van de Vate).

30. Perry wrote a note to Patricia Sides around 1972 saying she "still couldn't talk," but was feeling much better and had started to use "a 'quad' cane" (Patricia Sides, letter to the author, 9 May 2000).

31. Now her symphonies numbered 11, including those for symphonic band and concert band, etc.

32. Perry, letter of January 1975 typed in crooked slanting lines, to Professor de Lerma; Perry, letter of 3 August 1977 to de Lerma (CBMR).

33. Exchange of letters in April 1973 (LC). Quoted by permission.

34. Professor de Lerma informed me that Perry "was not omitted from the Columbia

set. She was just not included" before Columbia brought the project to a premature close. (De Lerma, E-mail to the author, 15 March 2000).

35. De Lerma, letter of 21 January 1975 to Perry (Fisk). Quoted by permission.

36. Perry, letter of 5 January 1979 to Corbett Evans (PM).

37. Corbett Evans, letter of 18 April 1979 to Perry (PM).

38. In an undated letter to the author in the summer of 1994, Perry's younger sister Alycia speculated that the lost works had been deemed unworthy by her older sister Lucie and destroyed even before Perry died. She described Lucie as a severe and jealous person.

39. Perry, letter from Birmingham, Ala., to Mr. and Mrs. Williamson, summer of 1947.

40. Patricia Sides, telephone conversation with the author, 7 May 2000.

41. Patricia Sides, letter to the author, 9 May 2000. Quoted by permission.

42. I am grateful to Christopher Hahn for his invaluable assistance, and to the Thanks Be to Grandmother Winifred Foundation for funding the reconstruction of five works, including *Symphonies Nos. 4* and *10*, and *Quinary Quixotic Songs*.

43. A solo piano *Miniature* appeared in *The New Scribner Library*, vol. 11, in 1972 (out of print). Her *Prelude for Piano* was included in *Black Women Composers: A Century of Piano Music* ed. by Walker-Hill, (1992). Two solo spiritual arrangements were reissued in *Art Songs and Spirituals by African American Women* ed. by Vivian Taylor (1995). Publication, commercial performance, and recording of Perry's unpublished music is blocked at present because her heir and copyright holder has not responded to requests for permission.

44. *The Cask of Amontillado* may have been first performed as *La Botte* in December 1953 at the Academy of Music in Vienna (Smith, "Awaits"). It was performed at Columbia University in 1964 (see list of works for performers) and at the University of Delaware in the summer of 1955 on a double bill with Lehman Engels' *Malady of Love*, with Wieland replaced by Adelle Sardi (Shanet). Piero Bellugi remembers conducting *Homunculus*, perhaps in 1961. It was also performed in 1965 by the Manhattan Percussion Ensemble, and in 1980 by members of the Brooklyn Philharmonic conducted by Tania León. Performances of Perry's works since her death have been sparse but persistent. Her solo spiritual arrangements have received some exposure, on stage and in recording. *Stabat Mater* was performed in 1982 at a Clarion "Recall" Concert at Alice Tully Hall of Lincoln Center in New York, sung by Katherine Ciesinski and conducted by Newell Jenkins. In 1988 portions of it were sung on a Celebration of Black Women Composers program at the Smithsonian Institution by Elvira Green and the Tigot String Quartet. *Prelude for Piano* was performed several times in the 1990s by Theresa Bogard. *Short Piece* has proved the most durable, as its performance history indicates.

45. *Black Perspective in Music* 7, no. 2 (Fall 1979): 282; Edwards, *International Dictionary*, pp. 918–19.

46. On the copy of *Prelude* at Fisk, she wrote in parentheses "a slight revision in 1962."

47. Taylor.

48. Oteri.

49. *Free at Last* was reviewed by Robert Sabin, "Julia Perry Sets Negro Spiritual," *Musical America*, 71, no. 7 (May 1951): 26, "set with taste and appropriate simplicity . . . accompaniment transparent."

50. Quoted in Smith, "Julia Perry Acclaimed."

51. Quoted in Smith, "Julia Perry Acclaimed."

52. Salzman. However, not all reviews were favorable. A critic of a 1970 performance reported that "the piece fell to pieces under stress of its simple sectional construction" (Jacobson, "Fine Arts Quartet").

53. Boroff. Detailed and informative analyses can be found in Green and Edwards, *International Dictionary.*

54. Kamien

55. Strongin. *Musical America*'s reviewer found the opera "rather forbidding; the vocal style is declamatory and lacking in lyric inspiration, and with two male protagonists, there is little contrast in texture . . . The characters themselves are grimly unappealing and fail to stimulate much interest, mainly because they are so barely provided with motivation or interior illumination of any sort."

56. *New York Herald Tribune; New York Times.*

57. A detailed analysis is provided in Green.

58. *New Records*; Jacobsen, "New Works."

59. In a letter of 12 May 1976, Perry tells Southern Music that Italian dynamics may be used instead of American.

60. Mike Moss characterizes this symphony as "largely built of overlapping ostinati. The harmonic tension seems consistent with Perry's style, but the near total absence of melody is an extraordinary turn, especially as it is carried out through the entire four movements of the Symphony" (Moss). He reports that this work has never been performed, due at least in part to a discrepancy between parts and score, and some erroneous transpositions.

61. The program notes for *Symphonies Nos. 3* and *4* were in the archives at Carl Fischer Publishing Company and were sent to me by Angela Hammond.

62. These fragments are undated and unreliable as evidence of its style, which must have evolved in the 14-year course of its composition. Patricia Sides remembered that Perry discussed this ongoing project with her in the early 1960s when it was *Mary Easty*, and asked her for advice on the libretto (Sides, telephone conversation with the author, 24 April 2000).

63. In an undated letter Perry wrote to Professor de Lerma that the first movement contained a "slight reminiscence" of a spiritual (CBMR).

64. In a letter to James McKeever at Westminster Choir College in 1974, Perry rejects that term and asserts that the only compositions which she would call "ethnic" are the spiritual arrangements for orchestra and for voice.

65. Parmenter.

66. Schonberg.

67. Duguay.

68. *Hi-Fidelity; American Record Guide.*

69. Other performances are Savannah Symphony Society, 31 January 1987; Richmond Philharmonic, 15 January 1990 and 24 March 1995; Columbus (Indiana) Philharmonic, February 1990 and 1991; Sacramento's Camellia Symphony Orchestra, 13 April 1991; Philadelphia Orchestra, 13 January 1997; Albany Symphony Orchestra, 27 February 1999; and African American Chamber Music Society, 14 March 1999.

70. Kozinn.

71. *Chicago* (1948) included orchestra; Harold Rogers reported that she was working on a "rhapsody for full orchestra" in 1949 (Rogers).

72. Edwards, *International Dictionary* p. 920. See Edwards for detailed analyses.

73. Perry program notes at Carl Fischer, courtesy of Angela Hammond.

74. Perry, letter received 16 March 1973 (PM).

75. Perry made six partial lists of her compositions between August 1961 and some-time in 1964 or 1965 (not all were dated), some for CRI and some for AMC. The January 1963 list for CRI includes detailed instrumentation and durations. The 1962 list indicates publishers and recording companies, most of which never offered contracts.

76. Mentioned in Smith, "Awaits Playing."

77. This item, plus several titles of songs and choral pieces dated 1947 which are lost, are taken from the Composition and Dramatics recital program Julia Perry gave on 26 May 1947 at Westminster Choir College (WCC).

78. Deduced from undated letter from Julia Perry to CRI in which she mentions the release of *Homunculus C.F.* by Southern (which was 1968), then reports that she has completed three short pieces for oboe, clarinet, and viola, with piano.

79. The copy at Fisk is slightly different, and includes the missing bass clef notes in measure 2. It does not mention the arrangement for strings.

80. Perry letter of 8 August 1961 to CRI, with list and times.

81. Instruments from de Lerma. According to the 1953–54 Guggenheim report on grantees, this was performed at the Berkshire Music Center in 1951.

82. Instrumentation and time for *Portraits* on 8 August 1961 list are same as for *Ballet for Orchestra* in 6 January 1963 list (CRI).

83. Two lists, 9 October 1964 and undated, list this as a separate composition (AMC).

84. This date appears on the first page of the second speed. The score of this move-ment is the same as *Concerto No. 2*, with some revisions.

85. In a letter of 5 May 1975 from Julia Perry to Southern, she says they already have the second and third movements of the "2nd [sic] Piano Concerto" (lasting approx. 11 min.) and asks if they would be interested in a first movement (6 min.) she has just composed. However, even earlier she wrote the American Music Center informing them that the title was changed from *Piece for Piano and Orchestra*, and that it had been lengthened to three movements (note, undated, from Perry to American Music Center).

86. Letter of 14 May 1964 from David Hall to Perry, saying the tape of *Equations* arrived. It must have been *Contretemps* performed by the Akron Symphony Orchestra.

87. "Addenda for Julia Perry Since 1964" lists "15 orchestral arrangements for large orchestra of Negro folk melodies" (WCC).

88. The times for many of these works come from Perry's list sent to CRI ca. 1964–65.

89. Dated by Perry in letter of 4 August 1967 to CRI saying she is sending *Module* under separate cover; letter of December 1975 to Southern saying she has made deletions and additions, and that it has taken seven more years to see its completion. She explains that the title stems from Le Corbusier's "architectural unit."

90. The score is undated; IDBC lists date as 1976, but the manuscript with titles for all seven movements is in her own handwriting before her stroke. At some point *Suite Symphony* was in five movements (Perry, letter of 26 May 1976 to De Lerma [CBMR]). She also listed *Slums* and *Global Warfare* as two "short oeuvres" for orchestra in a letter to de Lerma of 10 October 1978 (CBMR).

91. De Lerma says that a third movement, a rondo, was unfinished at her death.

92. De Lerma says it was revised in 1970.

93. *Black Perspective in Music* 1, no. 1 (Spring 1973) lists under Orchestral Music: "Soul Symphony," No. 10, 1972; N.Y.: Southern Music [*sic*]."

94. *Black Perspective in Music* 2, no. 1 (Spring 1974) lists *Simple Symphony, No. 12*, 1973, as two movements, for strings, three clarinets, three trumpets, and percussion. 10 min. De Lerma adds a title for the second movement: "Miniature."

95. Perry, letter of 5 February 1971 to Southern describes *Soundout* as very brief brass pieces corresponding to the various "cue music" pieces played by the college band during a football game (PM).

96. Perry, letter of 14 November 1975 to Southern asks for its return. In their reply of 11 December 1975 they say they do not know of the piece or have it in their possession. It is possible that Perry was referring to the *Marching Band Symphony*, which is in four movements with names like "Venus Moon" and "Fireworks on Mars."

97. *Black Perspective in Music* 1, no 1 (Spring 1973) lists under Band Music: *Symphony No. 11* for concert band, 1972, and *Venus Moon* for marching band, 1971, both Southern Music [*sic*], 1973.

98. Several of these dates of early compositions are from the Guggenheim *Report*, 1954; others, from the WCC recital program of 1947.

99. Perry list of compositions, ca. 1964–65 (CRI).

100. *Five Songs for Soprano and Piano* in Perry list of compositions, ca. 1964–65 (CRI).

101. Patricia Sides, letter to the author, 9 May 2000. Sides visited Perry at MacDowell Colony in the summer of 1959: "She probably played and sang it to me, because I can still hear parts of it in my head."

102. Ammer, Green, and Patricia Sides all state the work is dedicated to Perry's mother, but this dedication does not appear on the published score.

103. Perry, letter of 29 June 1974 to James McKeever. Here she says there were six spirituals in that set (WCC).

104. Smith, "Awaits Playing."

105. Described by Perry in a letter of 13 November 1950 to Ted Cronk as an extended but simple work with much two-part writing (WCC).

106. Smith, "Awaits Playing."

107. Perry, letter of 3 February 1964 to Harold Spivacke, Library of Congress, inquires about changing the title of her copyrighted libretto for "Mary Easty" to "Gallows Hill" because it is a symbol of panic—and an Aristotelian idea of resolved catharsis.

108. Perry, letter of April 1950 to Dr. Williamson (WCC) says *Three Warnings* was written for Columbia Opera Workshop.

109. A letter of 30 January 1970 from the Copyright Office to Julia Perry says the manuscript is incomplete.

110. Also listed with date in "Addenda for Julia Perry since 1964" (WCC). Her memorabilia collection contains a partial bibliography for this dictionary.

SELECTED BIBLIOGRAPHY

Not all the sources consulted in this study are listed, only those useful to readers or cited in notes.

American Record Guide: Review of Short Piece for Orchestra. Vol. 28, no. 7: 572.

Ammer, Christine. *Unsung: A History of Women in Music.* Westport, Conn.: Greenwood Press, 1980.

The Black Perspective in Music. "Orchestral Music. Band Music." Vol. 1, no. 1 (Spring 1973).

———. "Orchestral Music." Vol. 2, no. 1 (Spring 1974).

———. "Obituaries." Vol. 7, no. 2 (Fall 1979).

Boroff, Edith. "Black Women Composers (Julia Perry and Undine Smith Moore)." Unpublished paper presented at the Black American Music Symposium, Ann Arbor, Mich., 10 August 1985.

Brinkley, William. "Look at the American Signora—Our Women Abroad." *Life,* 23 December 1957, p. 72.

Brooks, Tilford. *America's Black Musical Heritage.* Englewood Cliffs, N.J.: Prentice-Hall, 1984.

Cohen, Aaron. "Perry, Julia Amanda." In Cohen, *International Encyclopedia of Women Composers.* 2nd ed. New York: R. R. Bowker, 1987.

Duguay, Robert E. "Records. Review of CRI *Short Piece for Orchestra.*" *Hartford Times,* 27 July 1968.

Edwards, J. Michelle. "Perry, Julia Amanda." In *International Dictionary of Black Composers.* Edited by Samuel A. Floyd, Jr. Chicago: Fitzroy Dearborn, 1999.

———. "Perry, Julia (Amanda)." In *New Groves Dictionary of Music and Musicians.* Edited by Stanley Sadie and John Tyrrell. New York: Macmillan, 2000.

Green, Mildred Denby. *Black Women Composers: A Genesis.* Boston: Twayne, 1983.

Guggenheim Memorial Foundation. *Reports—1953 and 1954, of the Secretary and Treasurer.* New York: The Foundation, 1955.

Hammond, Angela. *An Annotated Bibliography: Julia Amanda Perry.* Web site: http://www.uky.edu/Libraries/NilesCenter/perry.html.

Hi-Fidelity. Review by A. F. of CRI *Short Piece for Orchestra.* January 1962: 77.

Jacobson, Bernard. "New Works. Review of *Homunculus C.F.*" *Music Journal* 13, no. 3 (March 1965): 74.

———. "Fine Arts Quartet at Peak." *Chicago Daily News,* 14 March 1970.

Kamien, Roger. "Lion About Music: A Composer of Originality." *Columbia Daily Spectator,* 23 November 1954.

Kozinn, Allan. "Some Like It Straight, Some Like It Hot." *New York Times,* 15 February 2000.

Moss, Mike. "Concert Band Music by African-American Composers 1927–1998." D.M.A. diss., University of Michigan, 2000.

Musical America. "Julia Perry Opera Has Premiere at Columbia." Vol. 74 (December 1954): 32.

New Records. Review of CRI *Homunculus C.F.* (Vol. 3, no. 1 March 1970): 6–7.

New York Herald Tribune. "Howard Shanet Conducts Works of 5 Composers." 14 March 1959.

New York Times. "2 World Premieres Played at Concert." 14 March 1959.

Oteri, Frank J. "Another Century List." *Chamber Music,* 8, no. 1 (June 2000): 47.

Parmenter, Ross. "Music: Little Orchestra in Concert." *New York Times,* 22 February 1955.

Pendle, Karin. *Women and Music: A History.* Bloomington: Indiana University Press, 2001.

Perry, Julia. Post-concert interview, 20 February 1954, at Columbia University. See discography.

————. Liner notes for *Homunculus C.F.* Composers Recordings, Inc. CRI-SD 252, 1969.

————. Correspondence in archives at Composers Recordings, Inc., PeerMusic Publishing Company, Fisk University, Center for Black Music Research, Westminster Choir College, Library of Congress Music Division, and American Music Center.

Roach, Hildred. *Black American Music, Past and Present.* 2nd ed. Malabar, Fla.: Krieger, 1992.

Rogers, Harold. "Promising Negro Composer Lauds Peace Role of Music." *Christian Science Monitor,* 4 August 1949.

Salzman, Eric. Review of CRI *Stabat Mater. New York Times,* 8 October 1960.

Schonberg, Harold C. "Music: Van Cliburn Is Soloist." *New York Times,* 6 May 1965.

Scott, Sandra Cannon. "Perry, Julia Amanda (1924–1979)," in *Black Women in America: An Historical Encyclopedia.* Edited by Darlene Clark Hine. Brooklyn, N.Y.: Carlson, 1993.

Smith, Oscar. "Julia Perry Acclaimed in Europe for Music." *Akron Beacon Journal,* 6 July 1952.

————. "Awaits Playing of New Work." *Akron Beacon Journal,* 27 September 1953.

Southern, Eileen. "Perry, Julia Amanda." In Southern, *Biographical Dictionary of African and African-American Musicians.* Westport, Conn.: Greenwood Press, 1982.

Strongin, Theodore. "Columbia Orchestra." *New York Herald Tribune,* 22 November 1954.

Taylor, Vivian, ed. *Art Songs and Spirituals by African American Women Composers.* Bryn Mawr, Pa.: Hildegard Publishing Co., 1955.

————. "Kaleidoscope: Music by African-American Women." *IAWM Journal* 2, no. 3 (October 1996): 33.

Thieme, Darius. "Perry, Julia." In *Notable Black American Women.* Edited by Jessie Carney Smith. Detroit: Gayle Research, 1992.

Van de Vate, Nancy. "The American Women Composer: Some Sour Notes." *High Fidelity/Musical America,* June 1975: MA 18–20.

Walker-Hill, Helen, ed. *Black Women Composers: A Century of Piano Music 1893–1990.* Bryn Mawr, Pa.: Hildegard Publishing Co., 1992.

————. "Music by Black Women Composers at the American Music Research Center." *American Music Research Center Journal* 2 (1992): 23–52.

————. *Piano Music by Black Women Composers: A Catalog of Solo and Ensemble Works.* Westport, Conn.: Greenwood Press, 1992.

————. *Music by Black Women Composers: A Bibliography of Available Scores.* CBMR Monographs no. 5. Chicago: Center for Black Music Research, 1995.

DISCOGRAPHY

Carillon Heigh-Ho. Performed by Morgan State University choir, Nathan Carter, conductor. Silver Crest MOR 111977, n.d.

Homunculus C. F. Performed by the Manhattan Percussion Ensemble, conducted by Paul Price. Composers Recordings Inc. CRI-S252, 1969.

Prelude for Piano. Performed by Helen Walker-Hill on *Kaleidoscope: Music by African-American Women.* Leonarda Records CD LE 139, 1995.

A Short Piece for Orchestra. (1) Performed by the Imperial Philharmonic Orchestra of

Tokyo, conducted by William Strickland. Composers Recordings Inc. LP, CRI-145, 1961. (2) A limited edition, live sound recording on reel of the performance under the title *Study for Orchestra* by the New York Philharmonic Orchestra, conducted by William Steinberg, at Lincoln Center, New York, on 7 May 1965. Recorded and distributed by the Recording Guarantee Project, American International Music Fund, Koussevitsky Music Foundation. New York Public Library Division of Recorded Sound (Rogers & Hammerstein) at Lincoln Center. Call no. LT-5 186.

Stabat Mater. (1) Performed by Makiko Asakura, mezzo-soprano, with the Japan Philharmonic Symphony Orchestra, conducted by William Strickland. Composers Recordings, Inc. LP, CRI-133, 1960. (2) A sound recording of a performance on 20 February 1954 by Virginia Shuey with the Columbia University Orchestra, conducted by Howard Shanet. Reel-to-reel tape at Columbia University Archives, New York. Call no. CF 21a, 1954.

You Can Tell the World: Songs by African-American Women Composers. Performed by Sebronette Barnes, soprano; Elise Auerbach, piano. Senrab Records, 2001. Includes *How Beautiful Are the Feet* and *By the Sea*.

Watch and Pray: Spirituals and Art Songs by African-American Women Composers. Performed by Robert Honeysucker, baritone; Ruth Hamilton, contralto; and Vivian Taylor, piano. Koch International Classics CD, 1994. Includes *Free at Last* and *I'm a Poor Little Orphan Girl*.

Margaret Bonds. Photographs and Prints Division, Schomburg Center for Research in Black Culture, The New York Public Library, Astor, Lenox and Tilden Foundations.

4

MARGARET BONDS

(1913–72)

CHRONOLOGY

1913   Born Margaret Jeanette[1] Allison Majors on 3 March in Chicago, to Dr. Monroe Majors and Estella C. Bonds.

1917   Parents divorced; Margaret's last name changed to Bonds.

Ca. 1925   Attended Parker High School; studied piano with Tom Theodore Taylor at Coleridge-Taylor Music School; became charter member of National Association of Negro Musicians' (NANM) Junior Music Association.

1926   Studied composition and piano with Florence Price, composition with William Dawson.

1929   Entered Northwestern University; studied piano with Emily Boettcher Bogue, composition with Arnie Oldburg and Carl Beecher.

1931   *A Dance in Brown* for piano won Honorable Mention in Rodman Wanamaker Competition.

1932   Song *Sea Ghost* won First Prize in Wanamaker competition; also composed *Sleep Song*.

1933   Performed John Alden Carpenter's *Concertino* with Chicago Symphony Orchestra; completed B.M. at Northwestern University; won Rosenwald Scholarship for graduate study; composed *Piano Quintet in F Major*, songs *Down South in Dixie*,[2] *To a Brown Girl Dead* (early version).

1934   Completed M.M. at Northwestern University; performed Florence Price's *Concerto in D Minor* with Chicago Women's Symphony.

1934–35   Composed children's musical *Winter Night's Dream*, produced at Goodman Theater.

1935   Composed songs *I'm Going to Reno, Love Ain't What It Ought to Be.*

1936   Met Langston Hughes; composed musical *Romey and Julie*, produced by Negro Theater Project (NTP) in Chicago; toured as pianist with singer Katherine Van Buren in Wisconsin and Iowa; played for Elsie Roxborough's show in Detroit; studied orchestration with Dr. Albert Nölte; attended NANM convention in Detroit; worked at YWCA Workers' Conference at Camp Gray, Saugatuck, Mich.; composed Hughes songs *The Negro Speaks of Rivers, Joy, Love's Runnin' Riot, Park Bench, Poème d'Automne, Winter Moon.*

1937   Played for dancer Muriel Abbott at Palmer House; more shows with Elsie Roxborough; worked with choreographer Katherine Dunham on William Grant Still's ballet *La Guiablesse*; composed songs *Playing with Fire, That Sweet Silent Love.*

Ca. 1938 Founded and directed Allied Arts Academy; composed Hughes musical *Don't You Want to Be Free*, produced by NTP; composed songs *The New York Blues, West Coast Blues.*

1939   Recital at Allied Arts Academy in April; moved to New York in August; editor at Clarence Williams publishing company; published *Twelve Easy Lessons and Exercises for the Piano*, composed piano pieces *Composition for the Dance, A Spanish Mother, Waltz from the Notebook of an Accompanist*; composed songs *Lady by the Moon I Vow, Peach Tree Street, Georgia, Bound.*

1940   Worked for Leonard Harper at the Apollo Theater; published choral *Children's Sleep* from *Winter Night's Dream*; married Lawrence Richardson in summer; moved to 240 E. 106th St.; began two-piano team with Frances Kraft Reckling; composed Hughes musical *Tropics After Dark*, songs *Three Sheep in a Pasture, Radio Ballroom.*

1941   Performed Carpenter *Concertino* with the WNYC orchestra for broadcast; *Negro Speaks of Rivers* sung by male chorus at Town Hall on 25 May; *Spring Will Be So Sad* heard on radio; composed songs *The Moon Winked Twice, Empty Interlude, You're Pretty Special, The Blues I'm Playing.*

1942   *Five Creek-Freedmen Spirituals* performed by Hortense Love at Town Hall; two-piano partner now Calvin Jackson; studied with Roy Harris; composed song *T'ain't No Need.*

1945   Two-piano partner now Gerald Cook (until 1948).

1946   Grandmother Margaret Bonds died in April; daughter Djane born on 23 October.

1949   Visit to Hollywood; concert tour; composed song *Be a Little Savage.*

1950   Performed as first Negro soloist with Scranton Philharmonic Orchestra; served as chair of the concert series at Community Church of New York for eight years during the 1950s; composed song *Supplication.*

1952   Town Hall debut 7 February; composed *Peter Go Ring Dem Bells* for chorus and orchestra, vocal spiritual setting *Swing Low, Sweet Chariot*, and *Spiritual Suite* (early version) for solo piano.

1953   *My Kind of Man* sung by Alberta Hunter at Bon Soir on 4 August 1953;
        composed vocal duet *African Dance*.

1954   Music director for Spring Shows 1954–60 at East Side Settlement House;
        cantata *Ballad of the Brown King* premiered 12 December 1954 at East Side
        S.H.

1955   Composed songs *Young Love in Spring, Summer Storm, Minstrel Man*.

1956   Organized Margaret Bonds Chamber Music Society; premiere of *Songs of the
        Seasons* by Lawrence Watson on 25 March at Town Hall.

1957   Moved to 123rd St.; worked for Harlem Cultural Council, organized Harlem
        Jazzmobile; mother, Estella Bonds, died 6 February in New York; composed
        song *The Price of a Love Affair*.

1958   Production of musical *Midtown Affair* in February; composed song *The Pas-
        ture*.

1958–59 Worked with Hughes on *Shakespeare in Harlem*; worked at the American
        Theater Wing; took composition course in Juilliard Extension Division for
        two semesters.

1959   *Kyrie* from *Mass in D Minor* performed at St. Phillip's Episcopal Church, 15
        March; premiere of *Three Dream Portraits* by Lawrence Watson in Colum-
        bus, Ohio; publication of spirituals *Ezek'l Saw the Wheel, I Got a Home in
        That Rock*.

1960   *Shakespeare in Harlem* opened in New York in February; father, Dr. Monroe
        Majors, died in Los Angeles on 10 December; *Ballad of the Brown King*
        orchestrated, performed, broadcast by NBC in December; served as chair of
        Afro-American music for the Eastern Region of NANM; composed songs *Cue
        10, When the Dove Enters In, Note on the Commercial Theater, Stopping by
        the Woods on a Snowy Evening*; publication of spiritual arrangement *Sing
        Aho*.

1961   *Ballad of the Brown King* published by Fox; composed song *Hyacinth*, mu-
        sical *Clandestine on the Morning Line*.

1962   *Spiritual Suite* performed by Joan Holley at Town Hall, 12 April; all-Bonds
        concert in Detroit, 2 June; appointed chairman of the music committee for
        the establishment of a Harlem Cultural Community Center; publication of
        spiritual *Go Tell It on the Mountain* and orchestrations of *Sit Down Servant,
        Hold On* and *Joshua fit da Battle of Jericho*.

1963   Traveled to the Bahamas, Bermuda, and Los Angeles for performances of
        Ballad of the Brown King; on Honor Roll of Outstanding Negro Women;
        composed spiritual *He's Got the Whole World in His Hands*, and *Fields of
        Wonder*, a cycle for men's chorus.

1964   Received Woman of the Century Award and first of three ASCAP awards;
        organized Brooklyn Museum birthday party for Langston Hughes; production
        of ballet *Migration*; composed cello arrangements *I Want Jesus to Walk with*

Me, and *Troubled Water*, choral *Freedom Land, Montgomery Variations* for orchestra, and completed Easter cantata *Simon Bore the Cross*.

1965   Composed cantata *Credo*, songs *Feast* and *What Lips My Lips Have Kissed*, choral *The Night Shall Be Filled with Music* and *Praise the Lord*.

1966   African premiere of *Ballad of the Brown King* at University of Ibadan (Nigeria) in March; choir mistress at Mt. Calvary Baptist Church; took class in choral conducting at Juilliard Extension Division with Abraham Kaplan in fall; composed choral *I Shall Pass Through This World*.

1967   Northwestern University Alumni Merit Award 29 January; 31 January declared Margaret Bonds Day in Chicago by Mayor Richard Daley; all-Bonds program with premiere of *Credo* in Washington 12 March; Langston Hughes died 22 May; attended NANM convention in Los Angeles in August; moved to Los Angeles; taught at Inner City Institute; music director at Inner City Repertory Theater; published solo vocal *Didn't It Rain*.

1968   Composed songs *Bright Star, Diary of a Divorcee, Don't Speak, Pot Pourri* [*sic*] a set of six songs.

1970   Composed musical *Burlesque Is Alive*, solo piano *He's Got the Whole World in His Hands*, songs and spirituals *Every Time I Feel the Spirit, Hold the Wind, Run Sinner Run*, choral work *No Man Has Seen His Face*; arranged spirituals for voice and SATB for RCA recording by Leontyne Price and Rust College Choir: *I Wish I Knew How It Would Feel to Be Free, Standin' in the Need of Prayer, Sinner Please Don't Let This Harvest Pass*.

1971   Honored by NANM Golden Gate Branch; *Scripture Reading* performed by Little Symphony, San Francisco, in October.

1972   Died on 26 April in Los Angeles, at the age of 59; *Credo* excerpts performed by Los Angeles Philharmonic on 21 May.

> I realized, very young, that I was the link ... between Negro composers of the past. You see, my mother was friends with all of them. So I realized that I was the link between these older people and the contemporaries. And now when I sit in Philharmonic Hall or any of those places, I hear the young Negroes today. Many of them are trying to reconcile atonality with the Negro idiom and they just don't go together. I think, if anything, if I deserve any credit at all, it's that I have stuck to my own ethnic material and worked to develop it.[3]

Margaret Bonds was a dynamic, outgoing woman, a mover and shaker with an active interest in the social, political, and cultural events of her times. She had a strong sense of her racial cultural heritage and a clear vision of her own role as intermediary and composer. In early childhood she met the leading Negro figures in art, music, and literature at her mother's salons, and observed her mother's activities as a charter member of the newly formed National Association of Negro Musicians (NANM). In high school she participated in founding its Junior Music Association and was active in NANM throughout her life. Through her father she inherited a legacy of race consciousness and activism. She worked tirelessly to awaken public awareness to the rich musical heritage of her race and chose to cultivate it in her own compositions. In doing so she won fame and admiration in the world of music at large. At the turn of the twenty-first century she was recalled as "the legendary Margaret Bonds."

BIOGRAPHY

Bonds' family background was a significant shaping force in her life and work. Her mother, Estella C. Bonds, was born in 1882 in New York City, the oldest of five children of Margaret's grandparents, Edward W. Bonds, a railroad dining car cook, and Margaret A. Bonds, a musician. The family moved from New York to Chicago in the 1890s. By 1910 they lived in the house at 6652 Wabash Avenue that was to become so familiar to Chicago's black cultural community. Margaret's grandmother, after whom she was named, was recalled as a strong matriarchal figure, affectionately nicknamed "Mima." She ran the house and prepared the meals while Margaret's mother, Estella, and her aunts, Victoria and Helen, who were elementary school teachers, pursued their careers and provided the income.

Estella Bonds received her musical training at Chicago Musical College and was a member of the Choral Study Club under the direction of Pedro Tinsley.[4] She was a highly respected piano teacher, and served for many years as organist and choir director at the Berean Baptist Church. Her home often housed musicians in need, and older Chicagoans recalled her Sunday afternoon musicales as one of the few places where aspiring young black students could gather and meet famous creative artists: the singers Abbie Mitchell, Lillian Evanti, and Roland Hayes; the composers Will Marion Cook, William Dawson, and Noble Sissle; the poets Countee Cullen, Arna Bontemps, and Langston Hughes; the artists Charles Sebree and Richmond Barthé; and many others.

On Margaret's father's side, her background was no less illustrious. Her father, Monroe Alphus Majors, was born in 1864 in Waco, Texas, and attended West Texas College, Tillotson College, and Central Tennessee College, and graduated in 1886 from Meharry Medical College in Nashville, Tennessee. He practiced medicine in Texas, California, and Illinois; contributed research on diabetes; lectured at medical schools; founded and later administered a hospital for Negroes in Waco; and, because of exclusion from the American Medical Association, organized the Lone Star Medical Association for black physicians. His success as a physician and his political activities won him enemies and threats on his life by the Ku Klux Klan. He was also a poet and journalist, serving as editor of numerous black newspapers. He published one of the earliest books for Negro children, *First Steps to Nursery Rhymes*, and wrote *Noted Negro Women: Their Triumphs and Activities*, published in Chicago in 1893.

This book provides valuable information on black women composers of the nineteenth century.

Estella Bonds, whom he married in 1909, was his second wife. Their marriage was a stormy one, and by 1915 the couple separated, divorcing in 1917 when Margaret was four years old. Estella resumed her maiden name and also gave it to her young daughter, who would be known as Margaret Bonds for the rest of her life. Dr. Majors tried to remain close to Margaret and to involve her in his political interests. When she was in her teens, they collaborated on a campaign song, "We're All for Hoover Today."

Margaret's musical abilities were evident even as a toddler, and her mother immediately started her on piano lessons. When she turned five, she was entrusted to the piano teacher Martha B. Anderson. According to a family friend and music teacher, Ruby Clark, it was about this time that she composed her first piano piece, "The Marquette Road Blues." At the age of eight, she began lessons with Tom Theodore Taylor[5] at the Coleridge-Taylor Music School, where her mother was on the faculty. Until she entered Northwestern University, Taylor and Florence Price were her principal piano teachers.[6]

This was the period of the Harlem Renaissance, and many of its literary and artistic personalities visited Chicago, dropping in at the Sunday afternoon musicales at the Bonds home. Years later, Margaret's childhood friend Nematilda Ritchie Woodard vividly recalled these elegant afternoons of tea and crumpets and polite, cultivated conversation. "Lillian Evans Tibbs [opera singer Lillian Evanti] was there, wearing black velvet and a long string of pearls. She spoke in a rather affected manner of her various trips to Europe, her studies in 'Paree with Madame—' and put on such airs that we [Nematilda and Margaret] began giggling, and our mothers put us out on the back porch."[7]

Nematilda, called Nell, was Margaret's partner in more than mischief. Margaret would play for Nell's violin performances at NANM conventions in Indianapolis or Detroit, always held in August when it was hot and fans were blowing. One summer, the fans blew Margaret's music pages off the grand piano and under it. Somebody was sent to scramble after them, but meanwhile Margaret played on without interruption. NANM and other black music organizations brought Margaret not only opportunities to perform as soloist and accompanist but also scholarships enabling her to continue music studies through her high school and undergraduate university years. While a student at Parker High School, she became a charter member of the Junior Music Association, which she represented at NANM conventions.

Estella's dreams of her daughter becoming a concert pianist caused increasing conflict with Margaret's growing interest in composition, which was supported by her grandmother. Margaret told how "my grandmother used to talk to me about songwriting. I think she put that bee in my bonnet.' . . . She was crazy about Carrie Jacobs Bond . . . the lady who made all that money."[8] In 1926 the composers Florence Price and William Dawson moved to Chicago, and Margaret studied composition with both of them. Price's example and encouragement played an important part in Margaret's development, and Dawson's expertise in both European forms and jazz may have provided the groundwork for her style.

When Bonds entered Northwestern University in 1929, at the age of 16, she was one of a handful of black students there. Because the university had no accommodations for African Americans, she had to take the long trip by train from Wabash Avenue to Evanston every day.[9] She used this time to compose and jot down her ideas. At Northwestern she continued piano study with Emily Boettcher Bogue while pursuing composition studies with Arnie Oldburg. She also took vocal composition classes with Carl Beecher, then dean of the School of Music, who had been an accompanist for the famous singer Amelita Galli Curci and had an excellent knowledge of song literature.

Meanwhile, the Great Depression was under way and the Bonds' home on Wabash Avenue sheltered not only the Bonds family but also the husband and wife singing team of Helen and Lewis White, as well as Florence Price and her two young daughters. Bonds related, "[My mother was] a true woman of God, she lived the Sermon on the Mount. Her loaves and fish fed a multitude of pianists, singers, violinists, and composers."[10]

Mother took her [Price] into our house . . . she had two children and she had trouble with a second marriage. She was very down and out, and mother moved her into our house. We had . . . a tremendous kitchen, and the weather in Chicago was so cold. . . . Florence and I would sit in that kitchen, and I was trying to help her with her extractions of orchestration parts. . . . When Florence had something that she had to do, every black musician in Chicago who could write was either scratching mistakes, or copying, or extracting, or doing something to get Florence's work done.[11]

This was Price's *Symphony in E Minor*, which won the Rodman Wanamaker Competition in 1932. That year Bonds won a first prize in the song category with her *Sea Ghost*. The year before, *A Dance in Brown* for solo piano had received Honorable Mention. Even before completing her undergraduate degree, Bonds was winning honors that would have gratified many older musicians. In 1933 she received a Rosenwald Fellowship, which enabled her to finish her master's degree at Northwestern University.[12] When the Century of Progress was celebrated at the Chicago World Fair that year, Frederick Stock, conductor of the Chicago Symphony Orchestra, programmed both Price's award-winning symphony and John Alden Carpenter's *Concertino* with Bonds as pianist.[13] This was the first appearance by a Negro pianist as soloist with the Chicago Symphony Orchestra. The reviews of Bonds' playing were unanimously favorable. Eugene Stinson, in the *Chicago Daily News*, reported, "Margaret Bonds, a brilliant and dependable pianist, gave an admirable performance."[14] Edward Moore, in the *Chicago Tribune*, referred to her "brilliant, well-developed technique, with a tone tending toward modern brittleness rather than old-fashioned suavity, and she played with much composure and a good sense of the lines of construction of the work."[15] Glenn Dillard Gunn, for the *Herald and Examiner* found that "Miss Bonds' vivid style and able technique . . . made Mr. Carpenter's work glow with a fire more experienced pianists well might envy."[16] In Chicago's black newspaper, the *Chicago Defender*, Maude Roberts George quoted these reviewers, noting approvingly that "Miss Margaret Bonds . . . reached the heights expected of her."[17]

In October, following completion of her master's degree, Bonds performed Price's *Piano Concerto in D Minor* with the Women's Symphony Orchestra of Chicago, conducted by Ebba Sundstrom. Glenn Dillard Gunn had good things to say about Price's concerto and Margaret's performance: "The piano part is expertly set upon the keyboard and was brilliantly played by Margaret Bond [*sic*]." A widely published photograph of the occasion shows this concert being broadcast by CBS.[18]

Margaret entered the working world during these depression times. The Harlem Renaissance had given way to a more serious, politicized stage of the New Negro Movement that would later be called the Chicago Renaissance. Margaret worked variously as a pianist for dancer Muriel Abbott at the Empire Room of the Palmer House Hotel, for Elsie Roxborough's show touring in Michigan, and with singer Katherine Van Buren touring in Wisconsin and Iowa. She also accompanied singers Etta Moten and Abbie Mitchell,[19] both close friends of the family. With Abbie Mitchell, she continued the exploration of song literature. She recalled the excitement of these sessions:

She was a very dynamic woman, you know. She'd been in the theater. She did all the shows . . . I would just sit there and drink in what Abbie had to tell me. She would take me to the piano and say, "Let's go excursioning." And she would take out these German Lieder and French songs. . . . I remember one song . . . she said, "Now that down there, that's the cello section." She would make me express, you know, not just play notes.[20]

Mitchell had been married to Will Marion Cook, famous for his musical comedies.[21] Margaret also worked for Cook and other composers, extracting instrumental parts from their scores. She stressed the importance of these experiences in her education. "In that day, in Chicago, we were constantly apprenticing . . . we did our boot training in Chicago, and then . . . went to New York."[22]

These educational experiences were not only musical. Margaret formed close friendships with artists and writers.

Richmond Barthé, the great sculptor, studied in Chicago. . . . I remember Richmond used to take his paintings up the North side to deliver them. He'd take me with him. He was much older than I, and one of the things he told me was so sweet . . . "Remember, your talent was given you by God, and you are accountable to God for what you do with it." Then there was Charles Sebree . . . One time during the depression, a group of us . . . were worried about him because he didn't have any food. So we put our pennies together and we bought him a big salami, and watched him paint Posie Flowers, a dancer.

Margaret first met Langston Hughes in 1936 at the home of a mutual friend. She had already connected with him on a spiritual level through his poetry while a student at Northwestern. "I actually met him . . . after I came out of the university. The first time I saw Langston was at Tony's house in Chicago, Tony Hill, the ceramicist. Finally he came to my house. My family rolled out the red carpet. We were like brother and sister, like blood relatives." She also met Hughes' close friend, the writer Arna Bontemps, and the poet Countee Cullen and his companion, Harold Jackman. Her association with these writers continued throughout their lives.

After Hughes left Chicago later in 1936, Margaret continued to keep in close touch with him.[23] Her letters to him speak of her other activities in those years: serving on the summer staff of the YWCA worker's conferences at Camp Gray in Michigan; studying orchestration with Dr. Albert Nölte; composing musicals for the Negro Theater Project of the WPA: Robert Dunsmore's *Romey and Julie* (1936) and *Winter Nights' Dream* for children, and Hughes' *Don't You Want to Be Free?* (1938); and composing one song after another to Hughes' lyrics, sometimes with popular shows and movies in mind.[24] In his travels, Hughes was able to promote their songs; in New York he showed their art songs to Harry Burleigh, and *Love's Runnin' Riot* to Duke Ellington. Cab Calloway performed their *Love Ain't What It Ought to Be* at the Cotton Club, and Jimmie Lunsford was "supposed to make a record of another song" (18 February 1937). Margaret became restless and envious, wishing she could go to New York or Los Angeles, where William Grant Still was working on music for films.

For a while Bonds persevered in Chicago, freelancing, composing, and teaching piano. Among her students was Ned Rorem, who was to become a prominent American composer and a prolific diarist. She had met the Rorems when she received the Rosenwald Fellowship. Ned's father, Rufus Rorem, dean at the University of Chicago, was on the board of the Rosenwald Fund. The Rorem family took an interest in Margaret, inviting her to their home and taking her to concerts. Bonds recalled, "Ned was 10 . . . he wanted to play all contemporary music and he didn't want the classics. . . . They sent him to me. I guess it was the blind leading the blind. I was still in my twenties."[25] Ned Rorem acknowledged her influence many years later, and told the story in his memoirs:

Every Saturday morning I boarded the streetcar for her house in the ghetto of South Wabash . . . for a white child to have a black teacher was not standard practice in Chicago during the 1930s, and is there a reason not to be proud of it? . . . At our first lesson she played me some ear-openers: *The White Peacock* by Griffes, and Carpenter's *An American Tango*. . . . Fired by my enthusiasm, she assigned these pieces on the spot, with no talk of scale-and-trill practice. . . . Margaret, ten years older than I, played with the authority of a professional. An authority I'd never heard in a living room, an authority stemming from the fact that she too was a composer and thus approached music from the inside, an authority that was contagious. . . . She also showed me how to notate my ramblings . . . hoisting the ephemeral into the concrete.[26]

Some time in the 1930s Bonds opened the Allied Arts Academy, a school for ballet, art, and music, at 6407 South Parkway.[27] In January 1939 Bonds wrote to Hughes about the academy's concert series and the "spiffy students" she had playing for it. Among them was Anna Louise de Ramus, who went on to study at Northwestern University and with Robert Casadesus in France. Another of her students, Gerald Cook, also continued studies at Northwestern, where Nadia Boulanger heard him and invited him to study with her at Harvard. On 23 April 1939 Bonds gave a recital at the academy that consisted of works by Bach, Handel, Brahms, Ravel, Carpenter, Florence Price, Coleridge-Taylor, and four of her own pieces. This is the last documented appearance by Bonds in Chicago. The hard financial situation of the Great Depression took its toll on the Allied Arts Academy and Margaret's Chicago endeavors. In August she moved to New York.

The early months in New York were also difficult, but Margaret was at last in the city of her dreams. "No job was too lousy; I played all sorts of gigs, wrote ensembles, played rehearsal music and did any chief cook and bottle washer job just so I could be honest and do what I wanted."[28] She wrote to Hughes, now back in Chicago, that she was discouraged and needed him in New York because he knew "the ropes." Despite her discouragement, her composing was going well. "I know definitely that I want to devote all of my time to writing . . . I write all day long as usual and I still don't have enough time to get it all down. . . . My art songs are nearly all completed and a stack of popular songs done, and I'm ready for a good theater production" (9 April 1940). She was writing the music for a Hughes show in Chicago, *Tropics After Dark*, while playing piano for Leonard Harper at the Apollo Theater in Harlem. She "knocked out" one of the songs, *Lonely Little Maiden by the Sea*, while waiting for Harper to arrive at a rehearsal, and pronounced it a "swell tune" (27 May 1940). She also composed for the Apollo shows: "My second show there is going in this week with Cab Calloway. I'm doing lyrics and everything" (27 May 1940). She created the music for a show called *Wings over Broadway* at the Hurricane Restaurant and served as audition pianist for a number of Broadway shows: *Street Scene, Carmen Jones*, and *Happy Hunting*. She got a job as editor with songwriter Clarence Williams' publishing company, thus gaining entree to Tin Pan Alley, New York's popular music industry. This led to songs like *Spring Will Be So Sad*, a World War II song of loss and longing written with Harold Dickinson, which would soon be performed and recorded by the bands of Glenn Miller, Charley Spivak, and Woody Herman. With lyricist Andy Razaf she wrote *Empty Interlude, Georgia*, and *Peachtree Street*.

That winter Bonds met a New York probation officer named Lawrence Richardson, possibly through Langston Hughes, with whom Richardson had attended Lincoln University in 1928–29. In the summer of 1940 they were married, and moved to an apartment on 106th Street where they would spend the next 17 years. She wrote to Hughes, "We moved here because we wanted to be alone. The rent is cheaper, the air cleaner, the Italian food is good, and it's quieter:

Italians go to bed earlier than Harlemites. We can walk to the river from here" (22 July 1940).

Soon after, Bonds received a scholarship to study composition with the noted American composer Roy Harris, and began to take piano lessons from Djane Herz at the Juilliard School of Music. She formed a two-piano duo, first with Frances Kraft Reckling, then with Calvin Jackson, whom she met while working on a show called *Priorities*, and finally with her former student Gerald Cook. Ned Rorem heard Cook and Bonds improvising together on the two grand pianos at Bonds' 106th Street apartment and was impressed by how well they matched; both had perfect pitch and a natural expertise in many styles. Their two-piano repertoire included popular and classical music, from Bach to her arrangements of spirituals. They played in New York nightclubs—Café Society, Spivey's Roof, the Ritz Tower Hotel, Roger's Corners, Cerutti's, and others—and toured other cities including Philadelphia, Cleveland, and Columbus, Ohio. They also presented a series of concerts on radio station WNYC in 1944.[29]

In September 1946 Margaret's daughter was born, and she named her Djane after her piano teacher at Juilliard. Although Margaret complained about her multiple duties, motherhood did not check her professional activities. Her solo concerts were even more frequent in the late 1940s. She hired a personal representative to manage her affairs and made a tour of Southern black colleges in 1947. In 1950 she made a solo appearance with the Scranton Philharmonic Orchestra, the first Negro to do so. For her Town Hall debut on 7 February 1952, she played Beethoven's *Sonata Opus 2, No. 2*, Franck's *Prelude, Chorale, and Fugue*, works by C.P.E. Bach, Liszt, Roy Harris, and Coleridge-Taylor, a sonata by a Dutch woman composer recommended to her by Hughes, and two of her own arrangements of spirituals. Reviews were mixed at best: in the *New York Times* Harold Schonberg called her "a diligent workman, [who] conscientiously applied herself to her music." He complained of a lack of finish and technique but conceded that "her grounding, however, was obvious in the basically musical manner with which she approached each piece."[30] The critic for *Musical America* also was ambivalent: "Miss Bonds demonstrated an appreciable, attractive musicality; generally, however, her playing lacked the technical finish or interpretive originality to make the performances really interesting."[31] Undaunted, Margaret changed her management to Norman Seaman and increased her concert schedule, touring St. Louis, Cleveland, Toledo, and Chicago in February and March 1953.

Bonds was described by many of her friends as warm, generous, and hospitable. The salutations of her letters were often effusive. Ned Rorem was greeted as "Ned, my dear, dear Ned"; Langston Hughes as "My dearest poet," or "My dear Schiller (Longfellow, Goethe, etc.),", or, in some letters written in French, as "Mon ange"; and just about everybody was addressed as "Beloved." The cellist Kermit Moore, who met her soon after moving to New York in the 1950s, said, "Margaret and I hit it off immediately. She tried to become a second mother to me. It worked." Kermit's wife, the composer Dorothy Rudd Moore, remembered, "When I met Margaret before we were married . . . she was very encouraging to me. We would go up to her house for dinner, or musical evenings." According to Kermit, "Margaret loved to entertain . . . she loved having her friends around her. And she could sight-read so well at the piano that if anyone had a score they had written, she would play through it without any problem." In addition to her strong Christian spirituality and religious outlook, Bonds was very interested in astrology and would arrange parties by horoscope signs. One dinner party consisted of Kermit, Hall Johnson, McHenry Boatright, and others born under the sign of Pisces.[32] She often referred to the horoscope in her letters and would consult a psychic before going on a trip.

In the 1950s, Langston Hughes' sojourns in New York became longer and more consistent. Djane remembered, "Uncle Langston was always coming over to the house. He was completely at home with us and was nearly always around to spend the Thanksgiving or Christmas holidays with the family. He was really just part of the family."[33] When in New York, Hughes lived with his close friend Emerson Harper and his wife Ethel (nicknamed Toy, who had been a friend of Langston's mother). The close, familial relationship Bonds had with Hughes extended to the Harpers as well. She took some composition lessons with Emerson Harper, and arranged accompaniments for some melodies Toy wrote for Hughes' poems. Bonds kept up a steady stream of settings of Hughes' poems, adding *Summer Storm* and *Young Love in Spring* to two earlier songs to form the cycle *Songs of the Seasons*, commissioned and performed by the tenor Lawrence Watson at Town Hall in 1955. *Minstrel Man* (1955) was the first of *Three Dream Portraits*, which became the most famous of her art songs. She wanted to set Hughes' works for theater, and sometimes she had to be forceful. In late 1959 she wrote to him, "The producer has another composer for 'God's Trombones.' I accept that graciously, but I would be ready to shoot someone in the event that another composer even touches 'Shakespeare in Harlem' " (4 December 1959). She got her wish, and her music was used for Robert Glenn's dramatization of Hughes' *Shakespeare in Harlem*, produced at the White Barn Theater in Westport, Connecticut, and at the 41st Street Theater in New York.

Margaret's mother, who had lived with her in New York off and on, died in her home in February 1957.[34] Margaret took refuge from her grief in work, writing to Carl Van Vechten, "Since my mother's illness and passing . . . my mind has been fuzzy, and it is through sheer willpower that I do three-quarters of the chores I have to do . . . Each year at this time I am Music Director of a delightful show performed by underprivileged children . . . I had scheduled the Countee Cullen Memorial for April 14 and so in spite of grief and shock I carried on with it."[35]

Bonds was tireless in a variety of musical endeavors. In 1956 she formed the Margaret Bonds Chamber Music Society, with many prominent supporters. Their inaugural concert on 3 November 1956 at Carnegie Recital Hall featured the works of Harry Burleigh in the first half, and works by other black composers in the second half. Margaret's activities during the 1960s included organizing a concert of Bach's *B Minor Mass* by Harlem choirs, serving on the music committee to establish the Harlem Cultural Community Center, organizing the Harlem Jazz Mobile, and lecturing on Negro music at Long Island University, Fairleigh Dickinson University, and Columbia University's Teachers College. She worked in various capacities at the American Theater Wing, Paper Mill Theater, White Barn Theater, Fifty-Two Association, and Stage for Youth.

Bonds never stopped her efforts to improve her craft. She had hoped to study composition with Nadia Boulanger, but Boulanger refused to take her as a student. "She said that 'I had something' but she didn't know what to do with it. She added, however, that whatever it was I was doing felt right to her and that I should continue to do it, but I shouldn't study with anyone."[36] Boulanger probably recognized Bonds' stubborn independence. Bonds enrolled in a composition course in the Juilliard Extension Division for two semesters in the fall of 1958, expecting to be taught by Vittorio Giannini, who was replaced by noted composer Robert Starer. "Starer was fine and I stayed at the Juilliard School. Then I went to his house for private lessons . . . [after a while] I did my own scoring for an RCA recording with Leontyne Price and told him 'I don't need you anymore.' "[37] In 1966 she consulted Ned Rorem on her *Montgomery Variations* for orchestra. He called her orchestration "shimmering and foolproof," but objected to the lack of variety and suggested she "shrink" the whole thing into a one-movement rhapsody. She replied, "I admire your frank evaluation. However, I'm certain that I handled this traditional Negro spiritual theme only to the extent that it should be 'handled.' "[38]

In December 1960 Bonds' Christmas cantata with a text by Hughes, *Ballad of the Brown King*, received a gala performance at the Clark St. YWCA and was televised by CBS. This event was remembered by many. Dorothy Rudd Moore joined the effort. "I went up to Morningside Heights to help with the parts and we would sit there in her kitchen working. It was so great for me as a young composer to be included."[39] Her daughter, Djane, recalled how she and her teenage friends served as ushers, and how her mother led the orchestra and at the end had to bow to a standing ovation. "The place was jam-packed. People from Harlem could be depended upon to attend black cultural events and support their own."[40] The choir was from the Church of the Master in Harlem. Bonds related, "It's a colored church; it's Presbyterian. Those staid little ladies sat up there and sang that thing—it's really jazz, you know. And they didn't bat an eye, they just . . . sang it."[41]

Ballad of the Brown King was published by Fox in 1961 and subsequently performed throughout the United States and abroad. Inspired by this success, Bonds developed plans for another cantata, *Simon Bore the Cross*, and invited Hughes to supply the text. This work was completed and pronounced by Bonds to be even "better musically [than *Ballad of the Brown King*]." Henry Switten at Hampton Institute eagerly awaited the score for a premiere performance, and it was seriously considered for publication by Fox. Inexplicably, it was never published, and the score almost disappeared.[42]

Performances of Bonds' other works occurred with increasing frequency. After Ricordi published her *Three Dream Portraits* in 1959, they were performed by numerous concert artists. Her songs to texts by Robert Frost and Edna St. Vincent Millay were premiered, and *Songs of the Seasons* was programmed by Charlotte Holloman and others. Leontyne Price commissioned orchestral arrangements of spirituals for her RCA recordings, and Bonds also arranged several for Betty Allen. A special all-Bonds concert was given in Detroit in 1962, and in 1963 she traveled to the West Indies for premieres of *Ballad* in Nassau, Bahamas, and Bermuda.

Margaret longed to go to Africa for the premiere of *Ballad of the Brown King* at the University of Ibadan, Nigeria, in March 1966. Her music was being performed with increasing regularity in Africa, largely through the efforts of her friends Fela Sowande and Langston Hughes—who traveled to Nigeria, Ethiopia, Kenya, and the first World Festival of Negro Arts in Dakar, Senegal, in the summer of 1966. Moreover, the pianist Armenta Adams played *Troubled Water* throughout Africa that June. Although Bonds was invited, she never did go to Africa.[43]

In the summer of 1966, at Mt. Calvary Baptist Church, Bonds began a new job that was deeply satisfying to her. It involved supervising and conducting five different choirs at that church, including the senior choir and the gospel chorus. That fall she enrolled in a conducting class at Juilliard with Abraham Kaplan, indicating how completely she immersed herself in her new role. She began a program to teach choir members to read music so that they could perform more challenging music. That Christmas, her senior choir joined the Brooklyn Antioch Baptist Church choir under Alfred Cain for a program presented in both places, called "Christmas in Harlem" and "Christmas in Brooklyn." In the spring of 1967, she described a "fabulous Palm Sunday. When five choirs marched in, the sound shook me so. Picture me sitting at the organ with the tears streaming down my face" (21 March 1967).

The year 1967 must have been one of emotional highs and lows for Bonds. Among the highs was the Alumni Merit Award from Northwestern University in January. She was one of twenty-two alumni to receive awards, including Arthur Goldberg, U.S. Ambassador to the United Nations, Senator George McGovern, and the actress Patricia Neal. At the ceremony the University Men's Glee Club sang her arrangement of *You Can Tell the World*. It meant a great deal to Bonds to be honored at the institution where she had experienced hurt and prejudice many years before. There was also an all-Bonds concert at the Berean Baptist Church, at which a representative of Mayor Richard Daley presented a proclamation declaring 31 January 1967 Margaret Bonds Day in Chicago. After this stirring event, Bonds returned to the east coast to prepare for another all-Bonds concert in Washington, D.C., on 12 March, arranged by an old friend, Frederick Wilkerson, at which her major opus, *Credo*, received its first performance.

Langston Hughes died in New York on 22 May 1967. The rich record of Bonds' life through her letters to him came to an end. It is difficult to imagine the psychological effect of the death of Hughes, who had been her "soul mate," her "blood brother." She was ready to be persuaded to leave New York. She attended the annual NANM convention held in Los Angeles that summer and visited a number of friends who insisted that there were jobs available in the film industry.[44] When these jobs did not materialize, she accepted Bernard Jackson's invitation to join the Los Angeles Inner City Cultural Center and Repertory Theater, formed after the Watts riots. The move came as a shock to her friends in New York, who were astounded at the suddenness of her decision. According to Djane, Margaret wanted her and her father to come to California, too, but Lawrence Richardson's work as a probation officer would not permit it.

Bonds worked on productions such as *The Fantasticks, Street Scene*, and *West Side Story* at the Inner City Repertory Theater, and started a music school in the basement of the Cultural Center. Her students inspired her characteristic enthusiastic and dedicated response. "Every morning when those little kids come in . . . we do our little finger exercises. . . . I don't say where any of them are going . . . some may end up scoring in Hollywood, or some may just end up with personal enjoyment."[45] One particularly rewarding student was Gary Osby, a young man who toured Europe as accompanist for Albert McNeil's Jubilee Singers and was, in Margaret's view, "on his way to being an important concert artist."[46]

That Bonds' normally ebullient disposition was subject to mood changes and depressions was well known, and she herself alluded to it when she wrote to Hughes that "I would be a liar if I told you all is well."[47] Another time she wrote to him, "You know once I was on a tour and had a nervous breakdown (after Aunt Helen's passing)" (4 September 1964). Hughes periodically expressed concern about her depressions in his letters. The depressions were compounded by her tendency to drink too much, which she acknowledged in a letter to Ned Rorem after reading portions of his memoirs: "Never again will I reproach myself for imbibing. However, new interests are causing me to put the bottle aside."[48] After she moved to Los Angeles in 1967, the depression and alcoholism both worsened, and were blamed by some for leading to her death.[49] Her student Gary Osby was the last person to see Bonds alive. On the evening of 25 April 1972, he brought her home from a reception attended by a number of well-known Los Angeles musicians. The next day she did not appear for her appointments, nor the following day. The third day, friends became concerned and broke into her apartment. She had died of a heart attack at the age of 59.

Several memorial services were held after Bonds' death. There were two in Los Angeles, two in Chicago, and one in New York at the Community Church. Her body was sent to Chicago for burial in Mount Glenwood Memorial Cemetery, next to her mother. On 21 May 1972, almost a month after her death, parts of her cantata *Credo* were included in a "Tribute to Black Music" concert by the Los Angeles Philharmonic, conducted by Zubin Mehta.

SOCIAL ISSUES

In their recollections of the 1910s and 1920s in Chicago, Nematilda Ritchie Woodard and the singer Hortense Love described the neighborhood where they and the Bonds lived, and the schools they attended, as mostly white at that time, although their families belonged to black churches and social groups. Within Chicago's black community, the strength of the churches, social clubs, and political structure gave its members security and self-respect in the face of segregated restaurants, theaters, and concert halls elsewhere in Chicago. Despite the horrendous race riots in the "Red Summer" of 1919, as children they were insulated from these events by their families and communities. They were too young and carefree to pay attention. "We didn't have enough sense to have a reaction."[50]

Northwestern University in Evanston provided Margaret's first prolonged experience with discrimination, and it was hard for her to endure. In the 1930s the university swimming pool was closed to black women, and Northwestern didn't have accommodations for the handful of black students.

I was in this prejudiced university, this terribly prejudiced place. . . . I was looking in the basement of the Evanston Public Library where they had the poetry. I came in contact with this wonderful poem, "The Negro Speaks of Rivers," and I'm sure it helped my feelings of security. Because in that poem he [Langston Hughes] tells how great the black man is. And if I had any misgivings, which I would have to have—here you are in a setup where the restaurants won't serve you and you're going to college, you're sacrificing, trying to get through school—and I know that poem helped save me.[51]

As she found more poems by Hughes, and had discussions with the artists and writers who were her friends in those years, Bonds realized how important it was to value and preserve her Negro heritage. She promoted the music of black musicians and composers in whatever ways she could, organizing concerts and exhibits in churches, schools, YMCAs, and museums, and she continued to contribute her services to the National Association of Negro Musicians throughout her life. Years later, Langston Hughes wrote to her, "All of them [African Americans in the late 1960s] are intent on performing 'our own' now, but we've been at it for years and years!"[52]

Bonds gratefully acknowledged those who had supported black culture through the years. She felt strongly about black performers' obligation to include black composers ("brothers," as she called them) on their programs when performing in white venues. "God bless Betty [Allen] for taking us all out of the ghetto and not one of us will be completely out of it until all American singers start thinking this way" (4 March 1966).

In her choice of texts for two of her major works, Bonds picked stories with a message. For her Christmas cantata, she wanted to highlight Balthazar, one of the three kings who was black, and for her Easter cantata, she found Simon, the dark man who bore Christ's cross. In this way she passed on the affirmation of black identity she had received from "Negro Speaks of Rivers" in her time of need. Of *Ballad of the Brown King*, she wrote, "I honestly want the propaganda of this piece spread all over the world" (7 July 1961). Her deliberate use of black musical idioms in these works made a statement about the value of African Americans and their culture.

Bonds' consciousness of gender discrimination was just as acute, although expressed less often. She had grown up with strong women, and this conditioning gave her confidence. But when asked about the drawbacks of being a woman in the music business, she replied, "People don't think that a woman can really compete in this field . . . I could write a book about it all."[53]

There were the obstacles presented by domesticity and motherhood. Shortly after the birth of her daughter, Margaret lamented that she was "as busy as sixteen people: mother, laundress, pianist, wife, composer, etc. etc. . . . I have found an excellent nursemaid for Djane. I weaned her and took a job" (14 May 1947). In a letter to Ned Rorem, she said, "I am not planning any blazing career as a pianist—marriage and Djane don't permit."[54]

Bonds was more forceful in an interview in 1964 when she said, "Women are expected to be wives, mothers and do all the nasty things in the community (Oh, I do them). And if woman is cursed with having talent too, then she keeps apologizing for it. . . . It really is a curse in a way because instead of working 12 hours a day like other women, you work 24."[55]

Margaret Bonds said very little about social class, but her life and work were affected by it. It was an issue for her family even before her birth, as indicated by the 1910 U.S. Census. There were separate categories of "black" for her grandfather Edward and her foster great-grandmother Mary Curtis, and "mulatto" for her grandmother Margaret, and their children. Her mother, Estella, and her aunts were members of a small elite social group in which light-skinned women were preferred as marriage partners. This must have been a tremendous advantage to Estella in attracting the remarkable circle of talented and famous friends, acquaintances, and visitors who gave Margaret such a head start in her musical development and career. It certainly attracted the attentions of Margaret's brilliant father and the gene pool she inherited. Dr. Majors was dark-skinned, a disadvantage compensated for by his distinguished educational background and many accomplishments.[56] In her mother's social class at that time, manners, education, and good taste were important. The class implications of different kinds of music were obvious; for many, jazz and blues were not acceptable.

Thanks to the New Negro Movement, these upper-middle-class values expanded to include pride in African and African-American folk and popular culture. Jazz became the emblematic music of the Harlem Renaissance, and the subject of much poetry and art. Bonds could not help but be aware of the meaning of class, influenced by Hughes' sympathy for the leftist workers' movement. She was also actively involved, serving on the summer staff of the YWCA workers' conferences at Camp Gray in Michigan, and requesting Hughes to write lyrics for labor songs.[57]

Nevertheless, this awareness did not change the class Margaret moved in, or the privileges that came with it. While she was moved by the simplicity of the spirituals as sung "originally in Mississippi and way down there" (14 July 1966), she also deplored the "children who are not culturally developed from the parents ... I had that happen in New York where I was working in a church in Harlem. I had children who came out of farms in Mississippi, and they didn't have any feeling for the instrument [piano]."[58] But for Bonds this was a challenge; she believed that it was her duty to open up a new world for these children, and to give them an opportunity to enter a different cultural class.

THE MUSIC

Bonds is best remembered for her arrangements of spirituals because many celebrated singers, including Betty Allen and Leontyne Price, performed them all over the world and recorded them commercially. In his definitive work *Black Song: The Forge and the Flame*, John Lovell, Jr. named Bonds, along with Will Marion Cook and Harry T. Burleigh, among the composers whose arrangements widened public appreciation of spirituals. Almost 30 years after her death, her arrangements are still found on recordings of spirituals by Kathleen Battle, Jessye Norman, and Leontyne Price.

While these arrangements are significant in her output, they are not the only important works Bonds composed. Her known compositions number roughly 200, many of which are arrangements of the same works for different media. The list of works includes titles of about 75 scores located and verified in collections and archives, plus more than 125 other titles mentioned by Bonds and listed in reference books. Margaret did not keep very good track of her manuscripts; she was in the habit of giving her music to the people for whom she wrote it, so many works survive only in the personal libraries of the recipients. After her death, Bonds' personal effects and all her scores and manuscripts (which had been sent to her in California when she moved there) were found by her daughter, Djane Richardson, in boxes in the basement of the Los Angeles Inner City Cultural Center, where she worked. Richardson thinks it is possible that some manuscripts may have been removed from these boxes before she could have them shipped back to New York.

Spiritual arrangements account for more than 50 titles, although only some 22 different spirituals were set. These include works that are considerably more than arrangements, such as *Troubled Water* for solo piano, *Peter Go Ring Dem Bells* for orchestra and chorus, and the orchestral *Montgomery Variations* on "I Want Jesus to Walk with Me." Most of the spirituals were originally set for solo voice and piano, and these were the most frequently published of her works. Her songs are by far the most numerous, comprising at least 77 compositions (not counting the 21 spirituals for solo voice, and 2 duets). Although it is hard to differentiate without seeing all the scores, about 37 of these are art songs,[59] and another 40 are popular in style.

Forty-seven of Bonds' works were published during her lifetime,[60] and, as the discography shows, recordings were fairly numerous, especially of a few works. Probably no other black woman composer has been as widely performed. Her Christmas cantata, *Ballad of the Brown King*, was a yearly event at black churches for many years. Bonds listed in her autobiographical information some 30 concert artists who performed her compositions. It is therefore astounding that so little critical comment has been published. Critics often listed her works in their reviews of the performers without comment, or favorably noted them with a half sentence or so. One wonders if they did not take her fusion of styles seriously, or if it was beyond their capability to judge.

The assessments of Bonds' music by friends, colleagues, and scholars are fairly consistent. Several refer to her nineteenth-century or neoromantic style, ethnic identification, and jazz-infused style. Some echo Raoul Abdul's judgment that "Her musical ideas are not particularly original," while praising her "high degree of musicality and fine craftsmanship."[61] In all, they do not do justice to her extraordinary skill, range of expression, and richness of detail.

It is hard to say what kind of evolution Bonds' composition went through. Unfortunately, her earliest works, two of which won Wanamaker Prizes—*Dance in Brown* for piano (1931) and the song *Sea Ghost* (1932), have been lost. She acknowledged the early influence of Harry T. Burleigh, whose songs she first heard from Abbie Mitchell. She recalled, "In my teens and highly impressionable, I began unconsciously to copy Harry T. Burleigh . . . [his] *Ethiopia Saluting the Colors* became [my] *The Negro Speaks of Rivers*." Burleigh, like Bonds, expanded his basically late-nineteenth-century vocabulary with extended and augmented chords, occasional dissonance, and tonal ambiguity. Another strong influence was Will Marion Cook, whose music she transcribed. "When I write something . . . jazzy and bluesy and Tchaikovsky all rolled into one—that is Will Marion Cook."[62]

Bonds referred to a kind of evolution in her progressive revisions of *To a Brown Girl Dead* (1935, revised 1956). "Now this music I set when I was very young—in my teens. I had a whole lot of movement in it. When we're very young we overdo. Then in later years I decided to use it as an experiment in economy. I pared down to write as little as I could write."[63]

She expressed her concern about her compositional maturity when she wrote to Hughes, "Perhaps I could study with Still. . . . His work will be lasting because it belongs to the twentieth century. I worry about myself sometimes because I'm still nineteenth century. But time and study will take care of that. Gradually I become more modern" (12 May 1937). She never did study with William Grant Still.[64]

More useful than an attempt to trace an evolution in Bonds' composition is a consideration of the ingredients of her style, and of the different genres she favored. The trademarks of her musical language included extended and doubled "tall" chords—quartal chords, ninths, elevenths, and thirteenths—and parallel chord progressions, cadences of roots moving by thirds (III–I, VI–I, etc.) instead of the traditional V-I, chords on modal degrees of the lowered second and lowered sixth, modal ambiguity (major, minor, and other modes), and syncopated rhythms, all of which are found in jazz.[65] She combined these ingredients with classical principles: balance and proportion, traditional forms, contrapuntal textures, and careful notation.

Since Margaret herself was a superb pianist, one would expect her to have composed many more piano works than the ones listed. There is evidence that she did, in programs for her recitals and in Gerald Cook's reference to two-piano arrangements of spirituals for their duo. Given her skill at improvising and her long experience playing in shows and nightclubs, it is understandable that she may have had many of these compositions in her head without writing them down. Her three-movement *Spiritual Suite* is the only solo piano work available to us. Jazz harmonies are prominent, as are rocking gospel rhythms and a virtuoso improvisatory piano style, all precisely notated. The piano writing is often orchestral in its layered masses of sound emanating from different registers of the keyboard, simultaneously in counterpoint, or alternating in a kind of call and response, or interjecting and filling rests or long notes. Bonds' pianistic skill is also revealed in the piano parts to her arrangements and songs, many of which are challenging. They are full and separate parts, commenting upon and illustrating the words of songs in a dialogue of equals.

Bonds' pop song enthusiasm probably started with her grandmother's encouragement to produce hits, like Carrie Jacobs Bond. The title of Margaret's legendary first piece, *Marquette Road Blues*, indicates an early interest. Later, the Harlem Renaissance spirit of the 1920s and 1930s stimulated her interest in blues and jazz. By the time she began to collaborate with Andy Razaf, Roger Chaney, and Harold Dickinson, her skill was well honed. Several of her songs were performed by popular black entertainers—Cab Calloway, Jimmy Lunceford, and white bandleaders—Glenn Miller and Woody Herman. *My Kind of Man* was performed by legendary blues singer Alberta Hunter at the Bon Soir nightclub in New York in 1953. In the 1960s Bonds was still writing pop songs for Nina Simone.

Of the 10 or more stage works for which she wrote music, parts of only two scores are available at present. The unpublished songs for a Chicago production called *Tropics After Dark*, with lyrics by Langston Hughes (1940), show a graceful musical wit and simple, well-shaped melodic lines. The extant incidental music cues for *Shakespeare in Harlem* (also by Hughes, 1958) include brief "fast boogie" interludes and a couple of lovely songs in jazz style. In his *New York Times* review, Brooks Atkinson made a brief reference to the music: "a subdued but stirring musical score."[66] While remuneration may have had a lot to do with the production of her theater and popular music, Bonds was also genuinely attracted to the genres.

It was in her art songs that Bonds achieved her greatest depth and originality. The simplicity of vocal lines, the independence and complexity of the piano part, the modal shifts and ambiguity, the extended and augmented chords and subtle shifts in rhythmic patterns are used with confidence and economy. Every note and chord counts; a new rhythm of just half a measure is enough to paint a word. Bonds gave credit for her skill to her many hours exploring the great European song literature with Abbie Mitchell: "From her I learned the importance of the marriage between words and music."[67]

In *The Negro Speaks of Rivers* (1936), the rivers' flow is depicted with undulating parallel sixth chords in eighths and triplet eighths, the depth of the murky water is conveyed by the underlying steady half-note chords in the very lowest register, blurred by long pedals. The Euphrates River in the light of early morning is evoked by expansive, arpeggiated augmented chords, and the melodious rippling of the Mississippi in New Orleans is accompanied by dancing, syncopated staccato eighth notes evoking the plucked banjo of early ragtime.

The ability to communicate meaning with subtle musical details continues in *To a Brown Girl Dead* (1935, revised 1956) in the frozen immobility of the piano's steady, half-note chords. The harmonies expand to ninth and eleventh chords briefly as the poet imagines the pleasure the young girl would have taken in dancing and singing in her funeral finery. This understatement and restraint is also characteristic of Bonds' setting of Hughes' poems in *Songs of the Seasons*. This set of four songs, although never published, ranks with her best art songs, displaying her trademark modal and tonal ambiguity, unusual chromatic chords from the jazz idiom, and extravagant modulations verging on atonality. The jazz inflections that mark Bonds' art song settings of poems by black authors are more rare in her settings of poems by Robert Frost and Edna St. Vincent Millay, of which she was justly proud.

The many spiritual arrangements for which Bonds is most famous are fullfledged compositions in their own right. Unlike composers such as Undine Smith Moore, who set spirituals with great skill and musicality but wished to retain their simplicity, Bonds enveloped the words and lines in a complex musical world, transforming them into something new. The *Five Creek-Freedmen Spirituals*, commissioned by Hortense Love for her New York debut in 1942, contain all the ingredients present in later settings: active and independent accompaniments around the simpler, slower-moving vocal lines, obvious black idioms, word painting, and daring harmonies, with much less restraint than in her art songs. In *I Got a Home in that Rock* she begins the piano introduction with a stride-type bass of wide tenths alternating with chords, and an easygoing syncopated melodic motive derived from the spiritual melody. The final verse, in which "God gave Noah the rainbow," slows the tempo and expands the harmonies in a series of shifting chromatic ninth chords that illustrate the many colors of the rainbow.[68] Bonds' setting of *He's Got the Whole World in His*

Hands is less complex than many of her others, employing a simple, four-part hymn style. This may account for the popularity it has sustained with concert artists through the years. Bonds arranged it for many different media, including solo piano.

It was orchestral writing that most intrigued Bonds. Perhaps spurred by a comment from Florence Price that she would never be able to write good orchestration (which she still remembered years later), she worked hard at it all her life. After completing her master's degree at Northwestern, she continued to study orchestration with Albert Nölte and remarked that she was "writing all the time, and studying orchestration furiously" (21 October 1938). Years later, she fretted over *Ballad of the Brown King*: "I want the orchestration to be so fine that I can show it to the most distinguished conductor with no apology" (27 December 1955). In the late 1950s, Bonds took private lessons in orchestration with Robert Starer. By 1960 she could describe her orchestration for the *Ballad* as "shimmering and fabulous" (24 August 1960). That was a word Ned Rorem later used to describe her orchestration for *Montgomery Variations*: "Perhaps the best thing is the orchestration which looks shimmering and foolproof."[69] The orchestrations for *Ballad* and *Credo* show a masterful and creative command of the resources, with especial fondness for the bassoon and for instrumental timbres useful in word painting. Her orchestral arrangements of spirituals for commercial recordings are lush and sleek, typical of the style of her era. In *He's Got the Whole World in His Hands*, which is otherwise a simple transcription of the piano part for instruments, she added a part for the celesta to accompany "the sun and the moon." In *Joshua Fit da Battle of Jericho* she illustrates "ram sheep horns" and "trumpets beg to sound" with horns, trumpets, and trombones. In some orchestral arrangements, the presence of instrumental resources inspired whole new parts, as in the last chorus of *Sit Down Servant*, where flutes, violins, and oboes add a high ostinato in 16th-notes.

Bonds wrote four large, multimovement choral works, two of which were orchestrated and survive complete: the Christmas cantata The *Ballad of the Brown King* (1954–1960), with text by Hughes, and *Credo* (1965), with text by W.E.B. Du Bois. The other two were an Easter cantata, *Simon Bore the Cross* (1963–64), with text by Hughes, and a liturgical Latin *Mass in D Minor* (1959). Bonds referred to the Mass in her letters and lists of works, sometimes as for chorus and orchestra, and other times for chorus and organ. It was commissioned by St. Phillip's Episcopal Church in Harlem, and on 15 March 1959 the *Kyrie* was performed by the St. Phillip's choir with organ. The *Kyrie* is the only surviving evidence of this work, and shows a conservative style with no real ethnic influence.[70]

As has already been noted, *Ballad of the Brown King* was possibly Bonds' most frequently performed work. The premiere of a shorter version was given at the East Side Settlement House in New York in December 1954 by the George McClain Choir. Bonds set the work aside for several years until, inspired by the civil rights movement, she dedicated the work to Martin Luther King,

Jr., and asked Hughes to write two more poems for it. The enlarged and orchestrated version was performed on 11 December 1960 at the Clark Street YMCA by the Westminster Choir of the Church of the Master, conducted by Theodore Stemp, and the New York City College Orchestra, led by Bonds, and televised by CBS in a program *Christmas U.S.A.* The complete version of *Ballad* comprises nine movements forming a cycle by means of thematic and key relationships.[71] The movements display a wide variety of African-American musical styles ranging from four-part hymn and gospel to calypso. The fourth movement, *Mary Had a Little Baby*, for soprano solo and mixed chorus, proved to be so popular that it was later published in a solo voice arrangement as well as for women's voices.

The Easter cantata, *Simon Bore the Cross*, was completed in 1964. Only the last four of the eight movements of the cantata have been located (in the Hampton choir archives), all of them for chorus. Of the other movements, the first is a piano/organ prelude, the second is a solo by Pilate, the third is a choral fugue, and the fourth, a solo by Mary. The work is darker in tone than *Ballad*, befitting the somber subject. The spiritual "And He Never Said a Mumblin' Word" is employed in the last two movements.

Margaret Bonds' career extended from the 1930s through the early 1970s, a period in which many black composers swung with the intellectual currents of the times, from the deliberate and self-conscious use of black American folk idioms in the 1930s and 1940s, to a rejection of racial references and an embrace of mainstream international modernism's atonality and serialism during the 1950s and 1960s, and back to race-consciousness in the Black Arts Movement of the late 1960s and 1970s. Through it all, Bonds never wavered in her pride in her racial musical heritage, her loyalty to the common humanity of a Harlem or a Chicago's south side, or in her concern with the social implications of her art.

Five Creek-Freedmen Spirituals (1942)

The *Five Creek-Freedmen Spirituals* were commissioned by soprano Hortense Love for her Town Hall debut in 1942 and were published in 1946. Love was born in Oklahoma of Native American and African-American ancestry. Her family moved to Chicago when she was a child, and attended Berean Baptist Church together with the Bonds family. Hortense was one of the few Negroes to attend Northwestern, in the class two years ahead of Bonds. During their years at Northwestern they explored arrangements for the *Five Spirituals*, dating the inception of this cycle to around 1930, while Bonds was still a teenager.[72]

In the preface to the published score, Love wrote,

In the Southwest of the United States lies a wildly beautiful and fabulous strip of land, once called the "Indian Territory" but now known as Oklahoma. Dwelling there near Muskogee is a group of people called "Creek-Freedmen" or "Natives" who are a mixture of Creek Indian and Negro. The fusion of these two races has produced a culture that is highly intelligent and artistic. The five songs collected here are excellent examples of the musical moods of these people who are deeply religious. The difference between these spirituals and others lies in the fact that the Negro's exuberance is tempered by the Indian's seriousness. . . . From early childhood I have heard my grandmother, a "Native," sing these songs in both Creek Indian and English.

The spirituals are often sung separately, and several have been arranged for other media. The cycle is out of print at this time, but *Dry Bones* and *Lord, I Just Can't Keep from Cryin'* appear in *Art Songs and Spirituals by African-American Women Composers* (Hildegard, 1995).

The first spiritual, *Dry Bones*, begins with a section in minor in which the singer laments "Dese ol' bones o'mine." The vocal range is narrow and repetitive until the words "shall rise together in the morning." The accompaniment stays sparse, dry, and static in the desolate "valley of the bones," until at "rise together" it expands into widely spaced doubled triad chords moving by thirds. After that, "Dese bones," become "Dem bones" the key changes to major, and the melody is enlivened by an exuberant octave leap on "dry bones." The middle section is the famous catalog, "From the toe bone—to the foot bone, etc." repeated some 26 times until the head bone is reached, all on the same hypnotic, three-note repeated figure. As the catalog commences (marked "Slow—decisive beat"), the accompaniment plays a blues bass ostinato, first very softly in single notes, then in octaves, then adding ornamental notes and broken octave bass, gathering momentum, becoming louder and more inspired in its improvisatory embellishments, until it coalesces into bare, parallel open fifth chords in half notes. One can almost hear the shuffled steps of the religious congregational dance known as the "ring shout" thudding between the chords. In the climactic reprise of "Dem bones" the "rise together" chord progression expands even further into polychords. This setting is the jazziest of the five, with the possible exception of *You Can Tell the World*.

It is followed by *Sit Down Servant*, a dialogue between the Lord, ordering, "Sit down servant," and the servant protesting, "My soul's so happy Lord I can't sit down." Oddly, these upbeat words are sung "Andante con moto" to a lugubrious, repetitive minor melody. The introductory piano accompaniment begins with ambiguous tonality, the left-hand open fifths establishing A minor while the right-hand melody outlines the Lydian mode on F. As the voice begins the refrain's dialogue, a repeated A minor seventh chord confirms the key until, at the words "My soul's so happy," the piano breaks away with jazzy A-sharp seventh and E-flat eleventh chords. In later refrains a right-hand passage features the piano blues effect of neighboring keys struck together. In the verses, a conversation in heaven is accompanied by harplike arpeggiated chords in the high register of the piano. As in *Dry Bones*, the steady beat and repetitive intervals have a hypnotic quality that suggests the congregational "ring shout."

The setting of the third spiritual, *Lord, I Just Can't Keep from Cryin',* is the most unusual of the cycle. The three verses in E minor have identical melody and accompaniments, and almost the same words. "Lord, I just can't keep from cryin' some time," becomes "Lord, I fold my arms and cry some time," then "Lord, I hum a tune and cry some time" while the alternating phrase remains "When my heart is full of sorrow and my eyes are full of tears." Bonds accompanies these heartbreaking words with impressionistic major ninth and added-sixth chords, alternating and swaying in languid syncopation, perhaps in the spirit of a solitary person crooning and comforting herself. She fills in the long word "time" with a left-hand echo of the vocal melody as the swaying right-hand chords continue. The major quality of the chords is incongruously serene, yet mysteriously dissonant, against the melancholy minor vocal line. At the conclusion, the piano sweetly arpeggiates a very soft E major ninth chord. This is a daring conception, and creates out of the spiritual a highly original composition.

With *You Can Tell the World*, the mood changes to exuberant joy, from the introductory wide, swinging G major half-note chords, marked "Maestoso" to the frisky contrapuntal piano accompaniment with stridelike left hand. The words alternate between the speaker's joyful witness and the group responding, "Yes, He did." The verse culminates in ecstatic treble repeated-eighth tone clusters on the long, high "You—" that brings back the refrain. Then the piano changes to a rocking, syncopated bass pattern in parallel open fifth chords. At the first statement of "He brought joy, joy, joy to my soul," the piano forms parallel seventh chords with the voice. On the last statement, this changes to a dramatic augmented doubled B-flat chord, before concluding fff with the opening exultant chords. This spiritual was published separately and is the most frequently performed of the set. It was arranged for soprano and orchestra, and for various choral combinations.

The final spiritual, *I'll Reach to Heaven*, remains the least known and performed. In many ways it is the most interesting. The words of the refrain mix patient optimism with intimations of suffering: "King Jesus will be mine, I'm mos' done working with the crosses, King Jesus will be mine, I'll reach to heaven bye and bye." The refrain alternates with three verses: A B A B A B A. The words of the third and fourth refrains change, substituting the closing line of the previous verse for "King Jesus will be mine." As in the melodies of many spirituals, including the others in this set, the interval of the falling third predominates, a characteristic traced to Africa by way of the field holler. The key is minor and the mood is somber. The accompaniment is not repeated for each refrain and verse, but continuously provides new material, although it incorporates a brief recurring motive, a haunting pair of fragments alternating F minor and D-flat minor seventh chords. The movement of chord roots by thirds and the use of the modal lowered sixth degree recall Bonds' favorite harmonic devices. A detail in the piano part, a recurring two-measure eighth-note melody in unison two octaves apart, played very softly with a hollow and mysterious effect, accompanies the ominous words, "The moon run down in a purple stream." At the first appearance of "I'll reach to heaven bye an' bye," a series of simple major triads rise by thirds outlining an augmented triad. The effect is both reassuring and mysterious at the same time. In the penultimate refrain, the bass line moves down chromatically in half notes for one octave from F to F. On the last verse this descending chromatic device is repeated, emphasizing the agony of "My knee bones' a-achin', an' my sides a-rackin' wid a pain." In the concluding refrain this device is used a third time, now in octaves growing in volume, while the right-hand chords double the vocal line in a triumphal last statement of "And heaven is my aim." After a last, jubilant, rolled eleventh chord, the spiritual closes softly with the haunting motive of alternating F and D-flat seventh chords.

These descriptions can convey only a few of the imaginative details of the settings. These spirituals equal the skill, inventiveness, and daring of the art songs and are at least as profound. They are less restrained than the art songs, and more abundant in their harmonic and contrapuntal richness, their rhythmic vitality, and their variety of black idioms.

Spiritual Suite (1950s)

The *Spiritual Suite* for solo piano grew out of Bonds' expressed need:

When I was a little girl I never missed a concert of Marian Anderson, Roland Hayes, and Abbie Mitchell. I was always thrilled by their singing of spirituals at the end of each concert. . . . So I felt cheated and wanted some spirituals at the end of my concerts, too. I learned some settings of African folk songs of Coleridge-Taylor and some of his spirituals, but they didn't have enough of the "American Gospel" feeling. I began to experiment for myself and set several for piano.[73]

The only other piano arrangement of a spiritual for which there is evidence is the arrangement she made of *He's Got the Whole World in His Hands* for Gary Osby in Los Angeles.

At least two of the three movements of *Spiritual Suite* were taking shape by 1952 when Bonds included them on a program: "She closed the recital with two of her own compositions, *Peter Go Ring Them Bells* and *Group Dance.* . . . She asked her audience to receive the renditions as 'beginnings.' "[74] By 1962 the entire suite was performed, not only by Bonds but also by pianist Joan Holley in her Town Hall recital. The review in the *New York Times* described them as "a charming setting of three spirituals in a light, quasi-jazz idiom."[75] In 1967, the third movement, now renamed *Troubled Water*, was published by the Sam Fox Publishing Company, and in 1992 it was reprinted in *Black Women Composers: A Century of Piano Music 1893–1990* (Hildegard). The other two movements are still unpublished, and were obtained for this study through the generosity of the pianist Frances Walker.

The first movement, *Valley of the Bones*, is based on the vocal arrangement of *Dry Bones* from the *Five Creek-Freedmen Spirituals*. The musical material of the vocal *Dry Bones* setting is still there, with some important differences. The basic form, A B C B, is retained with some extensions and new passages. The slow introduction by a steady quarter-note melody in 4/4 meter doubled in octaves shifts back and forth between the lowered and raised seventh degree in modal ambiguity. This melody continues in the right hand as the refrain melody enters mournfully in the left hand. The refrain then shifts to the right hand over a faster ostinato in parallel fourths, breathing more life and motion into the desolate landscape. The widely spaced chord progression which accompanies the spiritual words, "rise together in the morning," in the vocal setting is retained here with its distinctive root movement by thirds (E, C, A-flat, C). After a pause, the B section begins, now in major in a jazzy dotted rhythm and piano-blues effect of neighboring keys struck together, over a familiar blues bass pattern, ascending G, B, D, E, G. In the C section, the famous catalog of the bones, repetitions are reduced to 17, and variety is introduced by a change in the left-hand pattern, leading to a different boogie ostinato. Meanwhile, the repeated "catalog" motive has begun to swing in triplet rhythm, and is spaced farther apart to allow insertion of triplet-eighth fill-ins, with increasing momentum. As the bones come to life, the piano version breaks into a raucous new riff. The final "rise together" progression is extended into a climactic series of seventh chords before closing with a tremolo tone cluster on G.

The slower middle piece, *The Bells*, based on *Peter Go Ring Dem Bells*, provides a suitable contrast to the outer two movements. Its jazz harmonies are smoother than the earthy *Valley of the Bones*, but less sophisticated and complex than the last piece, *Troubled Water*. Bonds set this spiritual in two other ways: a choral-symphonic work and a solo voice setting. The latter uses the same harmonies and layered spacing as the outer sections of the piano version.

The form of *The Bells* is a combination of variation and three-part ternary form. The refrain (A) and verse (B) of the spiritual alternate in variations A B A B[1] in C major and 2/2 time in the first section; then A[1] B[2] B[3] in E-flat major in 3/4 time in a contrasting middle section; then a return to A B[4] B[5] in C major and 2/2 time in the last section. The texture is the most impressionistic of all her works. The widely spaced layers or planes of activity written on three staves; the very high, parallel open fifth chords of the melody; and the tolling, bell-like octaves are unmistakable references to Debussy's piano piece *The Sunken Cathedral*. In a lecture-recital to students at the University of California at Davis, Bonds explained that a middle section had been added, with changes in texture and time-signature, "to create new interest," because of the absence of a singer.[76] In this contrasting middle E-flat major section, the tempo relaxes into a swirling Viennese waltz and the spiritual melody almost disappears, suggested only in the long left-hand bass notes. Here the spirit, texture, and harmonies are lightly romantic rather than impressionistic. The harmonies gradually evolve into poly-chords building to a cadenza consisting of an arpeggiated ninth chord on D, then a very soft D-flat seventh chord. The opening section with its layered impressionistic texture returns before the final verse B is stated fortissimo in unison octaves, in call and response with phrases of big rolled chords.

The last movement, *Troubled Water*, has been frequently performed by, among others, Frances Walker, Armenta Adams, and Joan Holley. This success led to arrangements for other media. In her notes Bonds informs us that "It was used in a ballet entitled 'The Migration,' . . . was performed [on cello] by Kermit Moore, and next summer is to be performed at the Watergate in Washington, D.C. by a symphony orchestra. The Fiske [*sic*] Jubilee Singers performed it with voices and piano on . . . concerts throughout Europe."[77]

The spiritual from which it comes, "Wade in the Water," consists of a refrain (A) containing the words "God's gonna trouble the water" (whence the title), and verses (B). Bonds uses this material in a modified variation form: Intro., A, A^1, B, A^2, A^3, B^1, Intro., A, A^4, and a coda combining B and A. She changes the meter of the spiritual refrain from 4/4 to 3/4 time and introduces it with a rapid, syncopated rhythmic ostinato in E minor. The layers or planes of activity are introduced one by one from one variation to the next, becoming farther apart and more independent. In the first brief B section the mood is more relaxed and lyrical. The middle two A sections shift from minor to major, slow down to a more languid tempo, and introduce adventurous jazz harmonies. The music in A^3 becomes more agitated and nervous, with a syncopated background of parallel fourths, fifths, then parallel sevenths, expanding to doubled chords marked "forte" and "espressivo," and leading to the next B section. This time the B section is harsh and hard-driving. It subsides to the return of the initial Intro, and A section beginning as it did before, then expanding to very full doubled chords of major sevenths and elevenths. After a dramatic pause, the coda enters in very fast 2/2 time. It closes with climactic chords descending by thirds and resolving in a triumphant E minor arpeggio racing "rapidamente" from the bottom to the top of the keyboard.

Three Dream Portraits (1959)

In December 1955 Bonds wrote to Langston Hughes, "I did a setting of your 'Minstrel' with which I'm quite pleased—the music marries the poem." *Minstrel Man* became the first in a trilogy of songs on texts from Hughes' 1932 collection *The Dream Keepers and Other Poems*. *Three Dream Portraits* has remained the most frequently performed of Bonds' art songs, along with *The Negro Speaks of Rivers*. Originally published by Ricordi in 1959, the set has been reprinted in anthologies in 1977 and 1995.

The whole set was first performed by Lawrence Watson in May 1959 at a NAMN concert in Columbus, Ohio, then again in Chicago that month, before the songs were off the press. This was followed by numerous other performances; however, opera baritone Lawrence Winters, to whom she dedicated the first and last songs, and soprano Adele Addison, the dedicatee of the second song, are not known to have performed them. The songs have often been sung separately.

The text of the first song, *Minstrel Man*, contrasts the singer's stereotypical minstrel mask with the reality hidden underneath: "Because my mouth is wide with laughter, and my throat is deep with song, You do not think I suffer after I have held my pain so long . . . you do not hear my inner cry. Because my feet are gay with dancing, you do not know I die." The memory of minstrelsy is evoked in the mournful syncopated rhythm of the piano introduction. The shifts from the façade of laughter to the inner suffering are reflected in the alternation between major and minor, while the minstrel's "throat, deep with song" is suggested by a ninth chord on the lowered second degree, and "song" is illustrated by a mini piano solo.[78] The climactic desperation of feet "gay with dancing" while "you do not know I die" is conveyed by the high vocal notes, the climactic piano octaves, and intensified triplet ornamentation.

The second song, *Dream Variation*, is a gentle contrast to the anguish of *Minstrel Man*. In a bright major key, its meter is a lilting 12/8. The expansiveness of the words, "To fling my arms wide in some place in the sun, To whirl and to dance till the white day is done," is conveyed by the long notes on "wide," "sun," "dance," etc., and the widely spaced chords beneath them. On each of the long vocal notes, the piano fills in with word painting or imitation of the previous vocal line. The accompaniment is further distinguished by parallel quartal chords; their dissonance, rather than sounding harsh, creates an impressionistic, dreamy, bell-like effect. The exuberance of "dance," and "whirl" is illustrated by brief, subtle dance rhythms in the piano part. The second appearance of the "tall, slim, tree" is accompanied by Bonds' favorite progression of chords descending by thirds. The change to rest at evening and night is denoted in the major chords on the darker, more "restful" lowered second degree. The dissonant sevenths and quartal chords shift to consonant parallel octaves in the last line, and the final repeated line, "Night coming tenderly," is accompanied by chords on the modal lowered sixth and seventh degrees, while the affirmation of "black like me" is conveyed by the major tonic seventh chord.

The third portrait, *I, Too*, returns to *Minstrel Man*'s confrontation with the pain of racism, but with more hope. *I, Too* begins and ends with the same six-measure piano solo; at the beginning it suggests a patriotic march, and at the end it is played more slowly and softly, in a nostalgic mood. The voice opens with "I, too, sing America" in a declamatory manner. At "I am the darker brother," the piano alternates chords on the "darker" lowered seventh degree. At "They send me to eat in the kitchen when company comes," the harmony drops in distress to the lowered tonic chord. The left hand's staccato octaves laugh heartily at "But I laugh," and repeated staccato fifths by both hands sound sturdy and vigorous for "grow strong." The next lines, "Tomorrow I'll sit at the table when company comes, Nobody'll dare say to me 'Eat in the kitchen' then," are accompanied by a chordal blues progression repeated over and over, perhaps indicating patience, then shifting a half-step higher in growing expectation. Suddenly the pattern stops on "then" and the key changes to a peaceful major. The left hand begins a continuous descending scale as the voice wistfully affirms, "Besides they'll see how beautiful I am and be ashamed." Bonds omits the last line of Hughes' poem (a repeat of the first line "I, too, am America)," choosing instead to let the piano solo postlude fulfill that function as it repeats the opening measures.

Dream Portraits exhibits all the best characteristics of Bonds' art songs: an expressive melodic line that follows the rhythms of the words, an independent piano part that intimately and subtly responds to the meanings of the words, an extended harmonic palette, and subtle rhythmic changes, all employed with economy and understatement. African-American idioms are used sparingly and tellingly, in jazz harmonies, syncopations, and imitative responses by the piano.

Credo (1965)

Credo, for chorus, soprano and baritone soloists, and orchestra,[79] was Bonds' major opus, the work she had wanted to write for several years. In May 1960 she wrote to Hughes, "Some day we must do that really profound piece of work. I'd like the texture of the music to be similar to the *Mass in D minor*." Since Hughes never delivered the hoped-for libretto, she turned to W.E.B. Du Bois. In November 1964 she wrote to Hughes that she was in seclusion to finish her "largest symphonic score to date." After it was finished, she expressed her concern about the U.S. government's response to Du Bois' affiliation with the Communist Party:

I'm happy we didn't do "Credo." Every day on the radio I hear news of W.E.B. Du Bois Clubs and I hear rumor that the government will crush them. I'm not despondent or hurt, or disappointed. I live so much under the guidance of the divine, I know there had to be a reason for me to set those words, so in time, something good will happen with "Credo," and sometimes in my own mind I hear it. (20 October 1965)

The music remains unpublished; the score exists in piano reduction as well as full score for orchestra. The orchestral manuscript bears the dedication "In memory of Abbie Mitchell and Langston Hughes." *Credo* had its premiere on 12 March 1967 in Washington, D.C., on an all-Bonds concert arranged by her friend Frederick Wilkerson.[80] The performance on 21 May 1972 by the Los Angeles Philharmonic, conducted by Zubin Mehta, is the only known performance with orchestra. On that occasion the critic for the *Los Angeles Times* noted: "The late Margaret Bonds was represented with four excerpts from her "Credo and Darkwater"—simple, lush, and lyrical."[81]

Since then a number of performances have been given with piano reduction by the Albert McNeil Jubilee Singers, and in November 1997 the first four movements were performed by the combined glee clubs of Agnes Scott, Spelman, and Morehouse colleges, conducted by Lynn Schenbeck, at Agnes Scott College in Atlanta.

The work can be divided into seven sections or movements. The first section, in A minor, sets the text beginning "I believe in God who made of one blood all nations." The words "I believe in God" are introduced by the choir in stark parallel open fifths in a syncopated rhythm, a motive that reappears throughout the work. On the words "I believe that all men, black and brown and white, are brothers," the voices enter in a fugato, one by one from the lowest part to the highest, before the section closes with the opening unifying motive on "and alike in soul." The next section, a soprano solo marked "Largo" and "Grazioso," sets the words "Especially do I believe in the Negro race" in A major with a modal lowered seventh degree. The 6/8 meter and rhythms are gentle and lilting, and when the chorus joins the soprano, their parallel thirds provide a sweet contrast to the block fifths of the previous movement.

The third section, in D minor, is marked "Declamando" and scored for basses and baritones. It sets the words "I believe in pride of race and lineage and self." The last passage, "All distinction not based on deed is devilish and not divine," returns to the parallel open fifths and fourths, ending with the "God" motive in diminution by the brasses.

The fourth and central section is marked "Very Dry—Tempo giusto." The words begin "I believe in the devil and his angels." It is scored for five choral parts and a reduced instrumentation: bassoon, contrabassoon, timpani, cellos, and basses. Over a drummed pedal point on D with ominous tremolos in the bassoons, the words are set in rapid, syllabic movement of parallel diminished seventh chords in very close harmony, in winding chromatic melodic intervals.

The fifth section is labeled in the score, in large letters, "Darkwater."[82] It is scored for sopranos and altos, thus balancing the second section for men's voices. In F major, it is marked "Andante" and written in the sweet, close harmony of gospel style, to the words "I believe in the Prince of Peace." A more agitated middle section for full chorus, winds, and strings sets the words beginning "I believe that war is murder" with dissonant chromatic harmonies and tritones.

The sixth section, in D major, marked "Quick," features a long baritone solo accompanied by a syncopated ostinato figure and delivering the text "I believe in liberty for all men." The movement closes with the full choir singing "Thinking, dreaming, and Ah! I believe in liberty," with a long melisma on "Ah!" over slowly changing seventh chords and triplets by the bassoon, then cellos, and harp. The final movement, marked "con fuoco" (with fire) recalls the rhythmic motive, the open fifths, and the A minor key of the first movement, and also features a (different) fugato passage. The whole work closes with the strident open fifths of the opening phrase, declaring "Finally, I believe in patience with God," accompanied by a climactic orchestral tutti.

These seven movements present a symmetrical whole with an arch form, most clearly seen when diagrammed.

Credo: "I believe in . . ."				*Darkwater*		
God	Negro race	Pride of race	Devil	Prince of Peace	Liberty	Patience
Section I	II	III	IV	V	VI	VII
	Grazioso	Decla-mando	Very dry, tempo giusto	Andante	Quick	Con fuoco
A minor	A major	D minor	D minor	F major	D major	A minor
Choral/ fugato	Sop. solo	Men	5 pt. choral	Women	Barit. solo	Choral/ fugato

Diagram: *Credo*

This masterful work exhibits vivid word painting and compelling expression in its details, and strong organization in its overall form. The writing style is more conservative and the chromatic harmonies and modulations are less frequent than in most of Bonds' compositions, befitting the large number of musicians and a wider public. Bonds wished to reach as many people as possible with this work, as she made clear: "I'm sure every line contains a Universal Truth—and with my Universal Language—music—the Public will hear" (23 November 1966).

LIST OF WORKS

Archives holding scores (reference citations will also be listed only if they give more information)

(AH) Azalia Hackley Collection in the Detroit Public Library (eight published scores).
(AMRC/CBMR) The Helen Walker-Hill Collection of scores by black women composers, in duplicate at the American Music Research Center at the University of Colorado at Boulder and the Center for Black Music Research at Columbia College, Chicago (33 published, 39 unpublished scores).
(Yale) James Weldon Johnson Collection in the Beinecke Library of Rare Books and Manuscripts at Yale University (20 unpublished scores).
(IU) Indiana University Music Library (13 published scores).
(Schomburg) Schomburg Center for Research in Black Culture, New York (four published, six unpublished scores).

References (complete information is in the selected bibliography)

(Cohen) *International Encyclopedia of Women Composers.*
(Green) Mildred Denby Green, *Black Women Composers.*
(IDBC) *International Dictionary of Black Composers.*
(MB biog.) Margaret Bonds, autobiographical sketches.
(MB corresp.) Margaret Bonds, letters.

(MB interv.) Margaret Bonds, interview with James Hatch.
(Tischler) Alice Tischler, *Fifteen Black American Composers*.

Unless a publisher is indicated, scores are unpublished. If no archive or library is listed, the work has not been located for this study.

Instrumental Music

Cello

I Want Jesus to Walk with Me. 1964. Performed 10 September 1964 in Maryland by Kermit Moore. (Green, IDBC, Tischler)
Troubled Water. 1964. Transcribed for cello by the composer for Kermit Moore. (AMRC/ CBMR; IDBC, Green, etc.)

Piano

Clandestine on the Morning Line. See Dramatic Music.
Composition for the Dance. Performed by Margaret Bonds, 23 April 1939, at Allied Arts Academy, Chicago. (program in MB corresp.)
A Dance in Brown. 1931. Received Honorable Mention in Rodman Wanamaker Music Competition in 1931. (IDBC, Green)
He's Got the Whole World in His Hands. Ca.1970. Solo piano arrangement for Gary Osby. (MB interv.)
Marquette Road Blues. Ca. 1918. (IDBC, etc.)
Mary Had A Little Baby. New York: Fox, 1962. (Green)
A Spanish Mother. 1930s. Performed by Margaret Bonds, 23 April 1939, at Allied Arts Academy, Chicago. (program in MB corresp.)
Spiritual Suite. 1950s. Contents: (1) The Valley of the Bones (based on "Dry Bones"); (2) The Bells (based on "Peter Go Ring Dem Bells"); (3) Troubled Water (formerly Group Dance, based on "Wade in the Water"). (AMRC/CBMR; Cohen, Green, IDBC, MB biog., etc.).
Three Sheep in a Pasture. Ca. 1940. (IDBC, Tischler)
Twelve Easy Lessons and Exercises for the Piano. 1938. Chicago: Bowles Music House, 1939. Composed, edited, and compiled by Margaret Bonds. (AMRC/CBMR, Yale; IDBC, MB corresp.)
Troubled Water. 1950s. New York: Sam Fox, 1967. Also in *Black Women Composers: A Century of Piano Music 1893–1990*, edited by Helen Walker-Hill. (Bryn Mawr, Pa.: Hildegard Publishing Co., 1992). "To Toy Harper." From *Spiritual Suite*. Also arranged for several other media: see Cello, Orchestra, Chorus, Dramatic Music: *Migration*. See discography. (AMRC/CBMR, MB note on manuscript, etc.)
Waltz from the Notebook of a Ballet Accompanist. 1930s. Performed by Margaret Bonds, 23 April 1939, at Allied Arts Academy, Chicago. (program in MB corresp.)

Ensemble

Piano Quintet in F Major. 1933. One movement. (IDBC, Tischler)

Orchestra

Montgomery Variations. 1965. Written for the March on Montgomery, Ala., and dedicated to Martin Luther King, Jr. Variations on spiritual "I Want Jesus to Walk
with Me." Sections titled Prayer Meeting, March, One Sunday in the South, Dawn
in Dixie. Copy in collection of Ned Rorem. (IDBC, MB interv. and corresp.,
Tischler)

Nile Fantasy (piano, orchestra). Not by Bonds. This work is by Philippa Duke Schuyler
and was arranged by Bonds for a memorial service for Schuyler at Town Hall,
New York, on 24 September 1967. (erroneously listed in Cohen, IDBC, etc.)

Peter and the Bells. See *Orchestra and Solo Voice or Chorus.* (Cohen, Green, IDBC)

Scripture Reading (chamber orchestra). 1971. A medley incorporating four spirituals
based on the biblical characters Ezekiel, King David, Peter, and Joshua. Commissioned and first performed 22 and 29 October 1971 by the Little Symphony
of San Francisco Symphony Orchestra, Nicklauss Wyss, conductor. (Tischler, MB
corresp.)

Troubled Water. 1966. Arrangement for orchestra in collection of Albert McNeil.

Vocal Music

Solo Voice

April Rain Song. N.d. Arrangement of a melody by Toy Harper. Text: Langston Hughes.
(AMRC/CBMR, Yale)

Available Jones. N.d. Text: Ted Persons, Russ Smith. (Tischler)

Be a Little Savage with Me. 1949. Text: Langston Hughes. (AMRC/CBMR, Yale; MB
corresp.)

Beyond the End of the Trail. N.d. Text: Roger Chaney. (Tischler)

Birth. N.d. Text: Langston Hughes. (Tischler)

The Blues I'm Playing. 1941. Text: Langston Hughes? (MB corresp.)

Bound. 1939. Text: Margaret Bonds. "To my Larry." (AMRC/CBMR, Schomburg; Tischler)

Bright Star. Sherman Oaks, Calif.: Solo Music, 1968. Text: Janice Lovoos. Christmas
music. See also *Pot Pourri.* (Green, Tischler)

Chocolate Carmencita. 1940. See Dramatic Music: *Tropics After Dark*

Cowboy from South Parkway. N.d. Text: Langston Hughes. (AMRC/CBMR, Yale)

Cue 10. Ca. 1960. Text: Langston Hughes. Alternate title: *Down and Out.* (Tischler)

Diary of a Divorcee. Ca. 1968. Text: Janice Lovoos. (Tischler)

Didn't It Rain. New York: Beekman, 1967. Spiritual. See discography. (AH, AMRC/
CBMR, IU; Tischler)

Don't Speak. Ca. 1968. Text: Janice Lovoos. Recorded by Peggy Lee. (Green, Tischler)

Down South in Dixie. Ca. 1933. (Tischler)

Dream Variation. See *Three Dream Portraits.*

Dry Bones. In *Art Songs and Spirituals by African-American Women*, compiled by Vivian
Taylor (Bryn Mawr, Pa.: Hildegard Publishing Co., 1995). See *Five Creek-
Freedmen Spirituals.* See discography.

Empty Interlude. New York: Robbins, 1941. Text: Roger Chaney, Andy Razaf. (AMRC/
CBMR, Schomburg; Tischler)

Every Time I Feel the Spirit. 1970. Spiritual. (Cohen, Green)

Ezek'el Saw the Wheel. New York: Mercury, 1959. Spiritual. "For Betty Allen." (AH, AMRC/CBMR, IU, etc.)

Fantasy in Purple. 1937. (MB corresp.)

Fate Is a Funny Thing. N.d. Text: Roger Chaney and Ted Persons. (Tischler)

Feast. 1965. Greenville, N.C.; Videmus, in progress, 2002. Edited by Louise Toppin. Text: Edna St. Vincent Millay. Sung by Muriel Beck, 7 February 1965, Corcoran Gallery, Washington. (AMRC/CBMR, MB corresp.)

Five Creek-Freedmen Spirituals. 1942. New York: Mutual, 1946. See separate listings. Contents: (1) Dry Bones; (2) Sit Down Servant; (3) I Just Can't Keep from Cryin'; (4) You Can Tell the World; (5) I'll Reach to Heaven. Commissioned and first performed by soprano Hortense Love in 1942, at Town Hall, New York. (AMRC/CBMR, etc.)

Footprints on My Heart. N.d. Text: Marjorie May. (Tischler)

Freedom Land. 1964. Text: Langston Hughes. (MB corresp.)

Georgia. New York: Georgia Music, 1939. Text: Andy Razaf, Margaret Bonds, Joe Davis. (AMRC/CBMR, Schomburg, etc.)

Go Tell It on the Mountain. Bryn Mawr, Pa.: Mercury, 1962. Spiritual. (AH, AMRC/CBMR, IU, etc.)

He's Got the Whole World in His Hands. New York: Beekman, 1963. Spiritual. In *Art Songs and Spirituals by African-American Women Composers*, edited by Vivian Taylor (Bryn Mawr, Pa.: Hildegard Publishing Co., 1995). See discography. (AH, AMRC/CBMR; Cohen, Green, Tischler)

Hold On. Ca. 1960. New York: Beekman, 1962. Spiritual. (AH, AMRC/CBMR, IU; Green, Tischler)

Hold the Wind. 1970. (Green, IDBC)

Hyacinth. Ca. 1961. Text: Edna St. Vincent Millay. Sung by Joyce Bryant. (MB corresp.)

I Got a Home in That Rock. New York: Beekman, 1959, reissued 1968. Spiritual. "For Betty Allen." (AH, AMRC/CBMR, IU, Schomburg, etc.)

I Shall Pass Through This World. New York: Bourne, 1966. (Green, IDBC)

I, Too. See *Three Dream Portraits*.

I Want to Be Ready. N.d. Spiritual. (ASCAP list)

I'll Make You Savvy. N.d. Text: Langston Hughes. (AMRC/CBMR, Yale)

I'll Reach to Heaven. New York: Mutual, 1946. From *Five Creek-Freedmen Spirituals*. (AMRC/CBMR)

I'm Going to Reno. Ca. 1935. A "fox trot song." (Tischler)

I'm So in Love (only melody). Ca. 1937. Text: Margaret Bonds, Leonard Reed. (Tischler)

Joshua Fit da Battle of Jericho. New York: Beekman, 1967. (AH, AMRC/CBMR, IU, Schomburg)

Joy. 1936. Text: Langston Hughes. (Green, IDBC, MB corresp.)

Just a No Good Man. See *No Good Man*.

Lady by the Moon I Vow. Ca 1939. Text: Robert Dunsmore. (Tischler)

Let's Make a Dream Come True. N.d. Text: Roger Chaney. (AMRC/CBMR, Schomburg; Tischler)

Let's Meet Tonight in a Dream. N.d. Text: Roger Chaney. (Tischler)

Little David, Play on Your Harp. N.d. Greenville, N.C.: Videmus, in progress, 2002. Edited by Louise Toppin. Spiritual. First performed by Lawrence Watson, tenor,

25 March 1956, at Town Hall in New York. See discography. (AMRC/CBMR; Tischler)

Lonely Little Maiden by the Sea. See Dramatic Music: *Tropics After Dark.*

Lord, I Just Can't Keep from Crying. New York: Chappell, 1946. Spiritual. From *Five Creek-Freedmen Spirituals.* In *Art Songs and Spirituals by African-American Women Composers,* edited by Vivian Taylor (Bryn Mawr, Pa.: Hildegard Publishing Co., 1995). See discography. (AMRC/CBMR)

Love Ain't What It Ought to Be. Ca. 1935. Played by Cab Calloway at the Cotton Club. (MB corresp., Tischler)

Love's Runnin' Riot. 1936. Text: Langston Hughes. (IDBC, MB corresp.)

Market Day in Martinique. See Dramatic Music: *Tropics After Dark.*

Mary Had a Little Baby. New York: Sam Fox, 1962. Text: Langston Hughes. From *Ballad of the Brown King.* (AMRC/CBMR, IU)

Minstrel Man. See *Three Dream Portraits.*

The Moon Winked Twice. Ca.1941. Text: Margaret Bonds, Dan Burkey, Dorothy Sachs. (Tischler)

My Kind of Man. 1953. Text: Roger Chaney. Sung by Alberta Hunter in 1953 at the Bon Soir in New York City. (MB corresp.)

The Negro Speaks of Rivers. 1936. New York: Handy Bros., 1942. Also known as *I've Known Rivers.* Text: Langston Hughes. Written for Marian Anderson. In *Art Songs and Spirituals by African-American Women Composers,* edited by Vivian Taylor (Bryn Mawr, Pa.: Hildegard Publishing Co., 1995). See discography. (AH, AMRC/CBMR, MB interv. and corresp.)

The New York Blues. Ca. 1938. Text: Malone Dickerson. (Tischler)

Night Time. Ca 1937. Text: Langston Hughes (MB corresp.)

No Good Man. N.d. Text: Langston Hughes. (AMRC/CBMR, Yale, Schomburg).

Note on the Commercial Theater. 1960. Text: Langston Hughes. "For Betty Allen." (MB corresp.)

Park Bench. 1936. Text: Langston Hughes. (MB corresp.)

The Pasture. 1958. Greeneville, N.C.: Videmus, in progress, 2002. Edited by Louise Toppin. Text: Robert Frost. First performed by soprano Marjorie McClung on 8 August 1959 at Stanford University. See discography. (AMRC/CBMR; Tischler)

Peachtree Street. New York: Georgia Music, 1939. Text: Andy Razaf, Margaret Bonds, Joe Davis. Recorded by Glenn Miller, Charley Spivak, Woody Herman; used in film *Gone with the Wind.* See discography. (AMRC/CBMR, Schomburg; Tischler)

Peter Go Ring Dem Bells. N.d. Spiritual. (AMRC/CBMR)

Playing with Fire. 1937. Text: Langston Hughes. (MB corresp.)

Poème d'Automne. See *Songs of the Seasons.*

Pot Pourri. [*sic*] Ca. 1968. Text: Janice Lovoos, Edmund Penney. Contents: (1) Will There Be Enough; (2) Go Back to Leanna; (3) Touch the Hem of His Garment; (4) Bright Star; (5) No Man Has Seen His Face; (6) Animal Rock 'n Roll. (Green, Tischler)

Pretty Little Flower of the Tropics. See Dramatic Music: *Tropics After Dark.*

The Price of a Love Affair. Ca. 1957. Text: Ernest Richman. (Tischler)

Radio Ballroom. Ca. 1940. Text: Andy Razaf. (Tischler)

Rainbow Gold. New York: Chappell, 1956. Text: Roger Chaney. (AH, AMRC/CBMR, IU)

Run Sinner Run. 1970. (Green)

Sea Ghost. 1932. Won Wanamaker Prize, 1932. (Green, Tischler)

Silent Love. 1937. Same as *That Sweet Silent Love.* Text: Langston Hughes. (MB corresp.)

Sing Aho. New York: Chappell, 1960. Spiritual. "For Betty Allen." (AH, AMRC/CBMR, IU)

The Singin' Mouse (melody only). Ca. 1937. Text: Henry Douté. (IDBC, Tischler)

Sin Weary (melody only). Ca. 1938. Text: Robert Dunsmore. From *Romey and Julie.* (Tischler)

Sinner, Please Don't Let This Harvest Pass. 1970. (Cohen, Green)

Sit Down Servant. 1942. See *Five Creek-Freedmen Spirituals.*

Sleep Song. 1932. Text: Joyce Kilmer. (Green, IDBC)

Songs of the Seasons. Greenville, N.C.: Videmus, in progress, 2002. Edited by Louise Toppin. Text: Langston Hughes. Contents: (1) Poème d'automne (1936); (2) Winter Moon (1936); (3) Young Love in Spring (1955); (4) Summer Storm (1955). Commissioned and first performed by tenor Lawrence Watson, 25 March 1956 at Town Hall in New York. See discography. (AMRC/CBMR, Yale; Tischler)

Spring Delight (melody only). (AMRC/CBMR, Yale; IDBC)

Spring Will Be So Sad. 1940. New York: Mutual, 1941. Text: Margaret Bonds, Harold Dickinson. Performed by Glenn Miller, Charley Spivak, Woody Herman, and others. See discography. (AMRC/CBMR, IU; Tischler).

Stopping by the Woods on a Snowy Evening. 1960. Text: Robert Frost. (AMRC/CBMR; MB corresp.)

Summer Storm. See *Songs of the Seasons.*

Sweet Nothings in Spanish. See Dramatic Music: *Tropics After Dark.*

Swing Low, Sweet Chariot. 1952. Spiritual. Performed 22 May 1952 in New York. (Tischler)

T'ain't No Need. 1942. Text: Roger Chaney. (AMRC/CBMR,[83] IDBC)

That Little Sugar I Had Last Night (or *Twice a Week*). 1961. For Nina Simone. (MB corresp.)

That Sweet Silent Love (melody only). 1937. Text: Langston Hughes? (MB corresp., Tischler)

This Little Light of Mine. 1970. (Green)

Three Dream Portraits. New York: Ricordi, 1959. In *Anthology of Art Songs by Black American Composers,* edited by Willis Patterson. (New York: E. B. Marks, 1977). Also in *Art Songs and Spirituals by African-American Women Composers,* edited by Vivian Taylor (Bryn Mawr, Pa.: Hildegard Publishing Co., 1995). Text: Langston Hughes. Contents: (1) Minstrel Man (1955); (2) Dream Variation; (3) I, Too. First performed by Lawrence Watson in May 1959 at a NAMN concert in Columbus, Ohio. See discography. (AMRC/CBMR, MB corresp.)

Three Sheep in a Pasture. New York: Clarence Williams, 1940. (Green)

To a Brown Girl Dead. 1933, revised 1956. Boston: R. D. Row, 1956. Text: Countee Cullen. Commissioned by Etta Moten. First performed by tenor John Miles. (AH, AMRC/CBMR; MB interv., Tischler)

Trampin'. New York: Galaxy, 1931. Spiritual. (Tischler)

Voo Doo Man. N.d. Words and melody only. Text: Langston Hughes. (AMRC/CBMR, Yale)

The Way We Dance in Chicago (*Harlem*, etc.). N.d. Text: Langston Hughes. (AMRC/
     CBMR, Yale)
West Coast Blues. Ca. 1938. (Tischler)
What Lips My Lips Have Kissed. Ca. 1965. Greenville, N.C.: Videmus, in progress, 2002.
     Edited by Louise Toppin. Text: Edna St. Vincent Millay. First performed by Mary
     Beck, 7 February 1965 at Corcoran Gallery, Washington, D.C. (AMRC/CBMR;
     Green, MB corresp.)
When the Dove Enters In. Ca. 1960. Text: Langston Hughes. (Green, Tischler)
When the Sun Goes Down in Rumba Land. See Dramatic Music: *Tropics After Dark.*
Who Is That Man? (melody only). 1963. From *Simon Bore the Cross.* (AMRC/CBMR,
     Yale; IDBC)
Winter Moon. See *Songs of the Seasons.*
You Can Tell the World. New York: Mutual, 1946. Spiritual. *Five Creek-Freedmen Spir-
     ituals.* See discography. (AH, AMRC/CBMR)
Young Love in Spring. See *Songs of the Seasons.*
You're Pretty Special. Ca. 1941. Text: Dorothy Sachs. (Tischler)
(Also an illustrated book of children's songs published in 1939, title unknown—MB
     corresp.)

Vocal Duet

African Dance. 1953. Text: Langston Hughes. Written for and first performed by Adele
     Addison and Lawrence Winters. (MB corresp., Tischler)
Joy. 1966. Text: Langston Hughes. Arranged for Adele Addison and Lawrence Winters.
     (MB corresp.)

Orchestra and Solo Voice or Chorus

Ballad of the Brown King (SATB, soloists, orchestra). 1960. New York: Sam Fox, 1961
     (rental from Presser). Orchestrated version first performed on 11 December 1960
     by New York City College Orchestra, conducted by Margaret Bonds, with Church
     of the Master choir, conducted by Teddy Stemp, at the Clark Street YMCA,
     broadcast by NBC television. See Dramatic Music for contents. (AMRC/CBMR;
     MB interv.)
Credo (SATB, soloists, orchestra). 1966. See Chorus for contents. "In memory of Abbie
     Mitchell and Langston Hughes." Four excerpts first performed 21 May 1972 by
     Los Angeles Philharmonic, conducted by Zubin Mehta. (AMRC/CBMR, Univer-
     sity of Illinois at Urbana; MB corresp., Tischler).
Ezek'el Saw the Wheel (solo voice, orch.). New York: Mercury Music, 1968 (rental from
     Presser). "Dedicated to Betty Allen." Spiritual. (AMRC/CBMR; Tischler)
Five Creek-Freedman Spirituals. Only two were orchestrated. *Sit Down Servant* (voice,
     chorus, orch.). Bryn Mawr, Pa.: Mercury, 1962. Spiritual. Arranged for Leontyne
     Price. See discography. *You Can Tell the World* (voice, orch.). New York: Chap-
     pell, 1960. Spiritual. Orchestration by Mark Fax. (CBMR, AMRC/CBMR; MB
     corresp.; see bibliography: Dillon)
He's Got the Whole World in His Hands (voice, orch.). Bryn Mawr, Pa.: Mercury, 1962
     (rental from Presser). Spiritual. Arranged for Leontyne Price. See discography.
     (AMRC/CBMR; MB interv., Tischler)
Hold On (voice, orch; also SATB, orch.). New York: Mercury, 1962 (rental from
     Presser). Spiritual. (AMRC/CBMR; Tischler)

I Got a Home in That Rock (voice, orch.). New York: Mercury, 1959, reissued 1968
(rental from Presser). Commissioned by Betty Allen. Spiritual. (AMRC/CBMR;
Tischler)

I Wish I Knew How It Would Feel to Be Free (voice, chorus, orchestra?). (Tischler.
Probably an error. See *Chorus*.)

Joshua Fit da Battle of Jericho (voice, orch.) 1962. New York: Mercury, 1962 (rental
from Presser). Spiritual. (MB corresp., Tischler; see bibliography: Dillon)

Mass in D Minor (chorus, orchestra). 1959. (Cohen, Green, IDBC, MB corresp.)

The Negro Speaks of Rivers. 1964. Orchestrated for Betty Allen. (MB corresp.)

Peter, Go Ring Dem Bells (chorus, strings/orchestra). 1952. Performed by Luxembourg
Symphony Orchestra with the Fisk Jubilee Singers, 30 September 1952. (score
and parts at Fisk University)

Sing Aho. 1962. Performed by Charlotte Holloman with Dayton Symphony Orchestra.
(MB corresp.)

Sinner, Please Don't Let This Harvest Pass (voice, chorus, orchestra?). (Tischler. Probably an error. See *Chorus*.)

Sit Down Servant. See *Five Creek-Freedmen Spirituals.*

Standin' in the Need of Prayer (voice, chorus, and orchestra?). See discography. (Tischler. Probably an error. See *Chorus*.)

This Little Light of Mine (voice, SATB, orchestra?). 1962. Spiritual. (Tischler. Probably
an error.)

You Can Tell the World. See *Five Creek-Freedmen Spirituals.*

Chorus

The Ballad of the Brown King. See Dramatic Music.

Children's Sleep (SATB, piano) 1940. New York: Carl Fischer, 1942. Text: Vernon
Glasser. From *Winter Night's Dream.* (AMRC/CBMR, Yale; Tischler)

Credo (SATB, soloists, piano score). 1965. Text: W.E.B. Du Bois. Contents: Credo—
(1) I Believe in God; (2) I Believe in the Negro Race; (3) I Believe in Pride of
Race; (4) I Believe in the Devil and His Angels; Darkwater—(5) I Believe in the
Prince of Peace; (6) I Believe in Liberty; (7) I Believe in Patience. First performed
12 March 1967 in Washington, D.C. (AMRC/CBMR, Schomburg; MB corresp.)

Ezek'el Saw the Wheel. New York: Mercury, 1966. (Cohen, Green)

Fields of Wonder (men's chorus). 1963. Text: Langston Hughes. Contents: (1) Heaven;
(2) Snake; (3) Snail; (4) Big Sur; (5) Moonlight Night; (6) Carmel; (7) New
Moon. First performed by the Lincoln University men's glee club, February 1964,
at the Brooklyn Museum in New York City. (Cohen, MB corresp., Tischler)

Freedom Land (SATB). 1964. Text: Langston Hughes. (MB corresp.)

Go Tell it on the Mountain (SATB a cappella). Bryn Mawr, Pa.: Mercury, 1962. Spiritual.
(Tischler)

He's Got the Whole World in His Hands (TTBB). Ca. 1966. "In memory of Estella
Bonds." (AMRC/CBMR, Schomburg; MB corresp.)

Hold On (SSA/SATB). New York: Presser, 1968. (SSA version at Schomburg, AMRC/
CBMR.)

I Shall Pass Through This World (SATB a cappella). 1966. New York: Bourne, 1967.
Text: Etienne Grellet. "In Memory of Aunt Victoria." (AMRC/CBMR, IU,
Schomburg; MB corresp., Tischler)

I, Too (male chorus). 1967. Text: Langston Hughes. Performed by Wyatt Logan Choir, May 1967, at Town Hall in New York. (MB corresp.)

I Wish I Knew How It Would Feel to Be Free (SATB, soprano solo). 1970. Arranged for Leontyne Price. See discography. (Cohen, Green)

If You're Not There (SATB). 1939. Text: Andy Razaf. (Tischler)

I'm Gonna Do a Song and Dance (unison chorus). N.d. Text: Bill Cairo. (Tischler)

Joy (6-part choral arrangement/SATB/SAT, string quartet, piano). 1954, 1966. Text: Langston Hughes. First performed by George McClain Chorale. (Tischler)

Kyrie Eleison. See *Mass in D Minor*. (AMRC/CBMR)

Mary Had a Little Baby (women's chorus). New York: Sam Fox, 1963. From *Ballad of the Brown King*. (AMRC/CBMR; Tischler)

Mass in D Minor (SATB, organ). 1959. Only *Kyrie Eleison* found. (Tischler; see bibliography: Thomas)

The Negro Speaks of Rivers (SATB). 1940. New York: Handy Bros., 1942. Text: Langston Hughes. Dedicated to Albert J. McNeil and the Sanctuary Choir. First performed by the Belmont Balladiers, conducted by Fritz Weller, 25 May 1941, at Town Hall in New York. (CBMR; MB interv., Tischler)

The Night Shall Be Filled with Music. 1965. Text: Longfellow. First performed by Cain Choristers, conducted by Alfred E. Cain, on 29 May 1965 for the sixth Annual Arts Festival in Yonkers, N.Y. (MB corresp.)

No Man Has Seen His Face (SATB). 1970. (Green, IDBC)

Oh, Sing of the King. New York: Fox, 1961. From *Ballad of the Brown King*.

Peter, Go Ring Dem Bells (men's choir). 1952. Spiritual. First performed by the Uptown Men's Chorale, 9 September 1956, at Town Hall in New York. (Tischler)

Praise the Lord (SATB). 1965. Written for and first performed by Cain Choristers, conducted by Alfred Cain, at the sixth Annual Arts Festival, 29 May 1965, Yonkers, N.Y. (MB corresp., Tischler)

Simon Bore the Cross. See Dramatic Music.

Sinner Please Don't Let This Harvest Pass (SATB, soprano solo). 1970. Arranged for Leontyne Price. See discography. (Tischler)

Standin' in the Need of Prayer (SATB, soprano solo). 1970. Arranged for Leontyne Price. (Cohen, Green)

St. Francis' Prayer. N.d. In collection of Albert McNeil.

Supplication (SSAATTBB and piano). 1950s. Text: Roger Chaney. "To Harry Revel and George Marion, Jr." (Tischler)

Troubled Water. 1952. Sung by Fisk Jubilee Singers on European tour. (MB corresp., MB note on manuscript of *Troubled Water* at CBMR)

When the Dove Enters In (SATB). 1962. (MB corresp.)

You Can Tell the World (TTBB, SSA, SATB). New York: Mutual Music, 1957, 1964. (Cohen, Green, Tischler)

(Also a choral work, title unknown, published in High School Series in 1939 by Aschenbrenner—MB corresp.)

Dramatic Music

The Ballad of the Brown King (SATB, soloists, piano score). 1954–60. New York: Sam Fox, 1961. Text: Langston Hughes. Christmas cantata. Contents: (1) Of the Three

Wise Men; (2)They Brought Fine Gifts; (3) Sing Alleluia; (4) Mary Had a Little
Baby; (5) Now When Jesus Was Born; (6) Could He Have Been an Ethiope? (7)
Oh, Sing of the King Who Was Tall and Brown; (8) That Was a Christmas Long
Ago; (9) Alleluia. See also Orchestra and . . . Chorus. (AMRC/CBMR, IU,
Schomburg; MB interv. and corresp.).

Burlesque Is Alive. 1970. Music for stage work at Inner City Repertory Co., Los Angeles.
(Green)

Clandestine on the Morning Line (piano score). 1961. Incidental music for a stage play
by Josh Greenfield, performed October 1961 in New York. (Tischler)

Don't You Want to Be Free? 1938. Text: Langston Hughes. Produced by Negro Theater
Project of the WPA, Chicago. (MB corresp.)

*Happy Hunting.*1956. Not by Bonds. (erroneously listed in IDBC, etc.)

Midtown Affair. 1958. Text: Roger Chaney. Contents: (1) You Give Me a Lift; (2) Mist
over Manhattan; (3) I Love the Lie I'm Living; (4) My Kind of Man. (MB
corresp., Tischler)

The Migration (piano, instrumental ensemble). 1964. For Talley Beatty. Performed 7
March 1964 at YM-YWHA in New York. Uses *Troubled Water*, according to a
note by MB on manuscript of *Troubled Water* at CBMR. (MB interv., Tischler)

Romey and Julie (incidental music for the stage play). 1936. Text: Robert Dunsmore.
Produced in Chicago by Negro Theater Project of the WPA. (MB corresp., Tischler)

Shakespeare in Harlem (incidental music for the stage play). 1958. Text: Langston
Hughes. Produced and directed by Robert Glenn, August 1959, at White Barn
Theater, Westport Conn.; and February 1960, at 41st Street Theater, New York.
(incomplete music cues at AMRC/CBMR, Yale; MB corresp., Tischler)

Simon Bore the Cross. 1963–64. Easter cantata. Contents: (1) Jesus in the Garden (piano/
organ prelude); (2) He Is a Good Man (solo by Pilate); (3) The Trial (choral
fugue); (4) Who Is That Man? (Mary's recit. and solo); (5) Don't You Know,
Mary? (chorus); (6) Simon and Jesus (chorus); (7) Crucifixion (chorus); (8) The
Resurrection (piano/organ and chorus). (movements 5, 6, 7, 8 at AMRC/CBMR;
MB corresp.)

Tropics After Dark. 1940. Text: Langston Hughes, Arna Bontemps. For canceled production in July 1940 at the American Negro Exposition, Chicago. Contents: (1)
Chocolate Carmencita; (2) Lonely Little Maiden by the Sea; (3) Market Day in
Martinique; (4) Pretty Little Flower of the Tropics; (5) Sweet Nothings in Spanish; (6) When the Sun Goes Down in Rumba Land. Only Pretty Little Flower of
the Tropics, sung by Rubel Blakly, was used in that production. (AMRC/CBMR,
Yale; Green, MB corresp.)

Troubled Island (incidental music for the stage play). 1938. Text: Langston Hughes.
Produced as benefit for the Allied Arts Academy, Chicago. (Green, MB biog. and
corresp.)

U.S.A (incidental music for the stage play). N.d. Text: John Dos Passos. Produced by
ANTA Theater. (Cohen, MB biog., Tischler)

Wings over Broadway (ballet). Ca. 1940. Produced at the Hurricane Restaurant in New
York. (Cohen, Green)

Winter Night's Dream. 1934–35. Text: Robert Dunsmore. Children's operetta performed
in Chicago. (Green, MB biog.)

NOTES

My thanks go to Djane Richardson for permission to quote from Bonds' letters and interview, and to Ned Rorem for permission to quote from his letters. Sources for this chapter include Bonds' taped interview with James Hatch in Los Angeles; the Margaret Bonds letters at the Yale University Beinecke Library of Rare Books and Manuscripts; the Bonds files in the archives of Northwestern University Deering Library; interviews and conversations with fifteen people who knew Bonds, including her daughter Djane Richardson, Theodore Charles Stone, Helen White, Nematilda Ritchie Woodard, Gerald Cook, Albert McNeil, Ned Rorem, and Kermit and Dorothy Moore. Langston Hughes' letters are quoted by permission of Harold Ober Associates; W.E.B. Du Bois' "Credo" is quoted by permission of David Graham Du Bois.

Full references are given in the selected bibliography at the end of the chapter.

1. Jeanette is used in early Chicago city directories. Most references only use Allison.

2. The dates given in the chronology for some works are the earliest references to them in Bonds' correspondence.

3. Margaret Bonds, interview with James Hatch, Los Angeles, 28 December 1971 (abbreviated: Bonds interview).

4. Pedro Tinsley (1856–1921) was a noted black musician and choral conductor who founded the Choral Study Club in Chicago in 1900.

5. Tom Theodore Taylor (1885–1965) was a well-known choir director and accompanist for the singers Patti Brown and Abbie Mitchell, the violinist Joseph Douglass, and others.

6. Florence Price dedicated her *Fantasie negre* for solo piano to "my talented little friend, Margaret A. Bonds," just before Margaret's sixteenth birthday. The *Fantasie* is a formidable work requiring strength, agility, and stamina, and no doubt Margaret was able to play it well even at that age. It is published in Walker-Hill, *Black Women Composers*.

7. Nematilda Ritchie Woodard, interview with the author in Chicago, 8 July 1989.

8. Bonds interview. Carrie Jacobs Bond (1862–1946), a white Midwesterner, became famous for her commercially successful popular songs.

9. In her last years at Northwestern, Margaret roomed in Evanston with a black woman who catered parties and meetings for white women's clubs. Among Bonds' black classmates were Nell Ritchie and Hortense Love.

10. Bonds, "Reminiscence," p. 191.

11. Bonds interview.

12. The Rosenwald Fund, established by Julius Rosenwald, sponsored fellowships for Negroes in the arts and sciences. Other recipients were Katherine Dunham, Marian Anderson, and Howard Swanson.

13. This historic program, given 15 June 1933 at the Auditorium Theater, also included tenor Roland Hayes singing Berlioz, Coleridge-Taylor, and spirituals.

14. Stinson.

15. Moore.

16. Gunn.

17. George.

18. Quoted in Price publicity flyer; see Southern, *The Music of Black Americans*, p. 426.

19. Etta Moten (b. 1901) sang in Eva Jessye's choir and in films in the 1930s. In

1939 Bonds and Moten toured schools and colleges all over the United States. Abbie Mitchell (1884–1960) performed in Will Marion Cook's Broadway show *Clorindy: The Origins of the Cakewalk* in 1898. She was a concert singer and a member of the original cast of *Porgy and Bess* in 1935.

20. Bonds interview.

21. Will Marion Cook (1869–1944) studied violin at Oberlin and in Berlin, but turned to stage work in the 1890s. It may also have been around this time (ca. 1934) that Margaret studied with the organist Walter Gossette (1879–1965), then in Chicago, who is often listed among her teachers.

22. Quotes in this paragraph and the two that follow are from Bonds interview.

23. Bonds' letters to Hughes, which continued until his death in 1967, provide many details of her life. Quotations from them will be cited by date only, in parentheses following the quote.

24. Bonds once asked Hughes for more lyrics because De Menna from MGM was in town to make colored movies and wanted to use their songs (10 January 1936).

25. Bonds interview.

26. Ned Rorem, *Knowing When to Stop*, p. 64

27. Theodore C. Stone, who taught music history at the Allied Arts Academy, thought it was in the early 1930s. Helen White, whose husband, Lewis, taught voice there, remembered it lasting only a year or two.

28. Demaitre.

29. After a term at Harvard with Boulanger and three years in New York as Bonds' duo piano partner, Cook became accompanist for blues singers Libby Holman and Alberta Hunter. There is an excellent publicity photo of Bonds and Cook in Ned Rorem's "Beyond Playing," p. 121.

30. Schonberg.

31. *Musical America.*

32. Dorothy and Kermit Moore, interview with the author in New York, 11 December 1995.

33. Quoted in Harris, p. 12.

34. The year before her death, Estella went to Los Angeles and remarried Monroe Majors, then in his nineties, and blind for many years (Djane Richardson, interview with the author, New York, 8 October 1990). The marriage lasted only a month or two, but it may be the reason why, after Margaret's death, obituaries referred to her as the daughter of Dr. and Mrs. Majors.

35. Bonds letter to Carl Van Vechten, 29 April 1957.

36. Bonds, "Reminiscence," p. 191.

37. Bonds interview.

38. Rorem, letter to Bonds, 4 July 1966; Bonds' reply, 7 July 1966.

39. Dorothy Rudd Moore interview.

40. Richardson interview.

41. Bonds interview.

42. Switten planned it as early as Easter 1963, but by 1967 it still had not been performed.

43. According to Djane Richardson, Bonds' only trips outside the United States were to Canada and the West Indies.

44. Bonds had also kept in touch with the Los Angeles family of her older half sister, Grace Majors Boswell.

45. Bonds interview.

46. Bonds interview.

47. Bonds, letter to Hughes, 5 July 1960, just after the funeral of the composer Clarence Cameron White.

48. Bonds, letter of 21 June 1966.

49. Albert McNeil, in an interview with the author, 29 December 1989, in Los Angeles, voiced this opinion, reiterated by other friends and acquaintances. Her Los Angeles nephew thought that Margaret was "like her father, unhappy and frustrated with life" (Robert Boswell, telephone interview with the author, 29 December 1989).

50. Woodard interview.

51. Bonds interview.

52. Hughes, letter to Bonds, 4 March 1966.

53. Demaitre. Feminists could easily question Bonds' gender sensitivity, not to mention Langston Hughes', in some of the texts she set for popular songs, such as "You're a no good man (but you do me good somehow)" and "Be a little savage with me." These songs used typical themes of the female blues singers of the 1920s and also catered to the popular tastes of the 1940s.

54. Bonds, letter of 15 September 1952.

55. Demaitre.

56. The only known photograph of Estella is in her obituary in the *Chicago Defender*. A photograph of Monroe Majors is the frontispiece of his book *Noted Negro Women*.

57. Undated letter to Hughes, ca. 1936.

58. Bonds interview.

59. Only 15 of her art songs have been located, and of those, 5 were published.

60. Published works still available in 2000 are *Ezekiel Saw the Wheel* (voice and piano, SATB, voice and orchestra; rental), *Go Tell It on the Mountain* (voice and piano, SATB a cappella), *He's Got the Whole World in His Hands* (voice and piano, voice and orchestra; rental), *Hold On* (voice and piano, SATB, voice and orchestra; rental), *I Got a Home in That Rock* (voice and piano, voice and orchestra; rental), *Joshua Fit da Battle* (voice and piano, voice and orchestra; rental), *Ballad of the Brown King* (SATB and piano), *Troubled Water* (solo piano), *Didn't It Rain, Dry Bones, I Just Can't Keep from Cryin', Three Dream Portraits*, and *The Negro Speaks of Rivers* (voice and piano).

61. Abdul, p. 54.

62. Bonds, "Reminiscence," pp. 191–192.

63. Demaitre; Bonds interview.

64. By that time (1930s) Still had rejected the atonal, dissonant harmony of his teacher Edgar Varèse in favor of what he called "the racial idiom," a more accessible and conservative style. His style (infusing classical forms with jazz and vernacular idioms) and philosophy (affirming African-American identity) were very like her own.

65. While she absorbed the harmonic language of French Impressionism through jazz, in which it had been common for years, Bonds was also directly influenced by her knowledge of French literature, as her piano piece *The Bells* demonstrates.

66. Atkinson.

67. Bonds, "Reminiscence."

68. The scholar Rosalyn Floyd believes that it was this passage that Boulanger was referring to when she told Margaret that Puccini had already written it (see Floyd, p. 32).

69. Ned Rorem, letter to Bonds, 4 July 1966.

70. See Thomas.

71. Detailed analyses are given in Green and Hawkins.

72. See Dillon.

73. Bonds' note, dated 31 January 1965, attached to a manuscript of *Troubled Water* donated by Cheryl Wall to CBMR.

74. *New York Amsterdam News*, 27 September 1952.

75. Rich.

76. Homann.

77. Bonds' note on the CBMR ms. The cello version includes all the notes of the piano music but distributes them differently and adds such a complex layer of embellishment and counterpoint that it is virtually another composition.

78. See Green for a detailed analysis.

79. The standard instrumentation: strings, pairs of woodwinds, contrabassoon, brass, harp, timpani, side drum, cymbals, and woodblock.

80. The first performance of *Credo* was with piano reduction.

81. Bernheimer. The inclusion of *Credo* in this concert was suggested to Mehta by Albert McNeil, whose Jubilee Singers had been invited to participate, along with Gerald Wilson and his big band, the pianist Natalie Hinderas, the gospel choir Operation Breadbasket Chorus, and Oliver Nelson's combo. Four excerpts from *Credo* were inserted among other numbers. The haphazard programming was soundly criticized by Bernheimer.

82. Bonds' reason for the label "Darkwater" is not known. Du Bois' "Credo" was published in his collection titled *Darkwater: Voices from Within the Veil*.

83. *T'ain't No Need* was sent to the Library of Congress from the papers of Roy Harris found at the University of Colorado at Boulder.

SELECTED BIBLIOGRAPHY

Not all written sources consulted in this study are listed, only those useful to readers or cited in footnotes.

Abdul, Raoul. *Blacks in Classical Music*. New York: Dodd, Mead, 1977.

Ammer, Christine. *Unsung: A History of Women in American Music*. Westport Conn.: Greenwood Press, 1980.

Atkinson, Brooks. "Theater: 'Shakespeare in Harlem.' " *New York Times*, 10 February 1960.

Bernheimer, Martin. "Zubin Mehta Leads 'Tribute.' " *Los Angeles Times*, 23 May 1972.

Berry, Faith. *Langston Hughes Before and Beyond Harlem*. Westport, Conn.: Lawrence Hill, 1983.

Bonds, Margaret. Correspondence in the Langston Hughes Papers, James Weldon Johnson Collection. Beinecke Library of Rare Books and Manuscripts, Yale University.

———. "A Reminiscence." In *The Negro in Music and Art*. Edited by Lindsay Patterson. New York: International Library of Negro Life and History, 1967, pp. 190–193.

———. Interview with James Hatch, Inner City Cultural Center, Los Angeles, 28 December 1971. Tape in the Division of Recorded Sound, Schomburg Center for Research in Black Culture, New York.

———. Margaret Bonds File in the archives of Deering Library, Northwestern University, Evanston, Ill.

Brown, Rae Linda. "Florence B. Price and Margaret Bonds: The Chicago Years." *Black Music Research Bulletin* 12, no. 2 (Fall 1990): 11–14.

Chicago Defender. "Mrs. Bonds, Musician, Dies in New York City," 2 March 1957.

———. "Famed Chicago Composer's Rites Set for Tuesday." 2 May 1972.

Cohen, Aaron. *International Encyclopedia of Women Composers.* 2nd ed. 2 vols. New York: R. R. Bowker, 1987.

Demaitre, Christina. "She Has a Musical Mission: Developing Racial Harmony; Heritage Motivates Composing Career." *Washington Post,* 14 August 1964.

Dillon, Alice. "The Orchestral Arrangements of Spirituals by Margaret Bonds." D.M.A. diss., University of Missouri at Kansas City, 1998.

Du Bois, W.E.B. *Darkwater: Voices from Within the Veil.* New York: Schocken Books, 1969.

Floyd, Rosalyn Wright. "Afro-American Piano Music: Two Black American Female Composers." D.M.A. diss., University of South Carolina, 1990.

George, Maude Roberts. "Noted Tenor and Miss Margaret Bonds Star with Symphony." *Chicago Defender,* 17 June 1933.

Green, Mildred Denby. *Black Women Composers: A Genesis.* Boston: Twayne, 1983.

Gunn, Glenn Dillard. "Roland Hayes Is Soloist at Auditorium." *Chicago Herald and Examiner,* 16 June 1933.

Harris, Charlene Diane. "Margaret Bonds, Black Woman Composer." M. M. thesis, Bowling Green State University, 1976.

Hawkins, Deborah. "Bonds, Margaret." In *International Dictionary of Black Composers.* Edited by Samuel A. Floyd, Jr. Chicago: Fitzroy Dearborn, 1999.

Hughes, Langston. *The Dreamkeeper.* New York: Alfred A. Knopf, 1932.

Homann, Leonard G. "Bonds' Hour Is Entertaining." No source, no date. (from Schomburg microfilm files)

Jackson, Barbara Garvey. "Bonds, Margaret Allison." In *New Groves Dictionary of Music and Musicians.* Edited by Stanley Sadie and John Tyrrell. New York: Macmillan, 2000.

Majors, Dr. Monroe A. *Noted Negro Women: Their Triumphs and Activities.* Chicago: Author, 1893.

Moore, Edward. "City Assured Symphony Season." *Chicago Tribune,* 16 June 1933.

Musical America. "Margaret Bonds, Pianist Town Hall Feb. 7 Debut," February 1952, p. 218.

New York Amsterdam News. "Poetry Joins Music for Delightful Eve." 27 September 1952.

———. "Margaret Bonds, Composer Dies, Noted Arranger of Spirituals." 13 May 1972.

Rich, Alan. "Joan Holley Plays Works by Dohnanyi." *New York Times,* 19 March 1962.

Roach, Hildred. *Black American Music: Past and Present.* 2nd ed. Malabar, Fla.: Krieger, 1992.

Rorem, Ned. "Beyond Playing: A Composer's Life with the Piano." In *The Lives of the Piano.* Edited by James R. Gaines. New York: Holt, Rinehart, and Winston, 1981.

———. *Knowing When to Stop: A Memoir.* New York: Simon & Schuster, 1994.

Schonberg, Harold C. "Debut Piano Recital Given by Miss Bonds." *New York Times,* 8 February 1952.

Scott, Sandra Cannon. "Bonds, Margaret Allison Richardson (1913–1972)." In *Black Women in America.* Edited by Darlene Clark Hine. Brooklyn, N.Y.: Carlson, 1993.

Southern, Eileen. "Bonds, Margaret." In her *Biographical Dictionary of Afro-American and African Musicians.* 2nd ed. Westport, Conn: Greenwood Press, 1982.

————. *The Music of Black Americans.* 3rd ed. New York: W. W. Norton, 1997.

Spearman, Rawn Wardell. "A Study and Performance of Selected Settings for Solo Voice and Piano of the Poetry of Langston Hughes." Ed.D. diss., Columbia University Teachers College, 1973.

Stephenson, JoAnne. *"Tropics After Dark, Songs of the Seasons* and Other Unpublished Works of Margaret Bonds to the Poetry of Langston Hughes as Found in the James Weldon Johnson Collection." D.M.A. diss., University of Illinois at Urbana-Champaign, 1995.

Stinson, Eugene. Review of Chicago Symphony Orchestra concert. *Chicago Daily News,* 16 June 1933.

Stone, Theodore Charles. "Mayor Proclaims Margaret Bonds Day as Musicians Salute Her." *The New Crusader,* 11 February 1967.

Sullivan, Lester. 1992. "Margaret Bonds (1913–1972)." In *Notable Black American Women.* Edited by Jessie Carney Smith. Detroit: Gayle Research, 1992.

Taylor, Daryl. "Margaret Bonds 1913–1972." Http://www.uni.edu/taylord/bonds.bio.html

Thomas, Andre Jerome. "A Study of the Selected Masses of Twentieth-Century Black Composers: Margaret Bonds, Robert Ray, George Walker, and David Baker." D.M.A. diss., University of Illinois at Urbana-Champaign, 1983.

Tischler, Alice. "Margaret Bonds." In *Fifteen Black American Composers: A Bibliography of Their Works.* Edited by Alice Tischler. Detroit: Information Coordinators, 1981.

Walker-Hill, Helen. "Black Women Composers in Chicago: Then and Now." *Black Music Research Journal* 12, no.1 (Spring 1992): 1–24.

————. "Music by Black Women Composers at the AMRC." *American Music Research Center Journal* 2 (1992): 23–52.

Walker-Hill, Helen, ed. *Black Women Composers: A Century of Piano Music 1893–1900.* Bryn Mawr, Pa.: Hildegard, 1992.

————. *Piano Music by Black Women Composers: A Catalogue of Solo and Ensemble Music.* Westport, Conn.: Greenwood Press, 1992.

————. *Music by Black Women Composers: A Bibliography of Available Scores.* CBMR Monograph no. 5. Chicago: Center for Black Music Research, 1995.

DISCOGRAPHY

Ah, Love, but a Day—Songs and Spirituals of American Women. Louise Toppin, soprano; Jay Pierson, baritone, and John O'Brien, piano. Albany Record #385, 2000. Album includes *Songs of the Seasons, The Pasture, Little David Play on Your Harp.*

Didn't it Rain, He's Got the Whole World in His Hands. Performed by Stephen Salter, voice, and Sheila Kibbe, piano. Musica Numeris, CYP 9602 CD, 1996.

The Essential Leontyne Price. RCA Victor Gold Seal CD, BMG Classics 09026–68157–2, 1997. Contains all the items by Bonds from the LP albums *Swing Low Sweet Chariot,* performed by Leontyne Price and the Leonard DePaur Orchestra, RCA-LSC 2600, 1962, and *I Wish I Knew How It Would Feel to Be Free,* performed by Leontyne Price and the Rust College choir, directed by Lassaye Van Buren Holmes, RCA-LSC 3183, 1971. Album includes *He's Got the Whole World in*

His Hands, Sit Down Servant, I Wish I Knew How It Would Feel to Be Free; Sinner Please Don't Let This Harvest Pass, and Standin' in the Need of Prayer.

He's Got the Whole World in His Hands. Performed by Daisy Jackson, voice, and Buckner Gamby, piano, on *The Lois J. Wright Memorial Concert Series*, vol. 1. Phase II Recording Services LP, Baltimore, 1977; other recordings of this spiritual have been made (see *Essential Leontyne Price* above, etc.).

Minstrel Man (from *Three Dream Portraits*). Performed by Neva Pilgrim, voice, and Steven Heyman, piano, on *Women's Voices: Five Centuries of Song*. Leonarda CD, LE 338, 1994; Richard Heard, voice, and Pamela Howland, piano, on *Ain't That Good News: African-American Art Songs and Spirituals*. HM Classics CD, 1998.

The Passion of Christ in Spirituals. Performed by Veronica Tyler, soprano, and Ernest Ragogini, piano. BRC Productions LP, n.d. Album includes *You Can Tell the World, He's Got the Whole World in His Hands.*

Spirituals. Performed by Wilhelmenia Fernandez, voice, and George Darden, piano. Tioch Digital Records TD 1009 LP, 1982. Album includes *You Can Tell the World, He's Got the Whole World in His Hands.*

Spring Will Be So Sad (When She Comes This Year). Performed by Glenn Miller and his orchestra. BS-060916–1 Bluebird B-11095-B, recorded 20 February 1941 in New York City.

Three Dream Portraits. Performed by Claritha Buggs on *Art Songs by Black American Composers*, University of Michigan School of Music LP, 1981; Odikhiren Amaize, voice, and David Korevaar, piano, on *The Negro Speaks of Rivers: Art Songs by African-American Composers*. Musicians' Showcase CD 1011, 2000. (see also *You Can Tell the World and Watch and Pray* below).

Troubled Water. Performed by Ruth Norman on Opus One LP #39, n.d. Althea Waites on *Black Diamonds*, Cambria Records CD 1097, 1993; Helen Walker-Hill on *Kaleidoscope: Music by African American Women*, Leonarda CD LE339, 1995; Debra Torok on *Through and Within This Century Past.* Verra Classics CD, 1997.

You Can Tell the World: Songs by African-American Women. Performed by Sebronette Barnes, soprano and Elise Auerbach, piano. Senrab Records, 2001. Includes *You Can Tell the World* and *Three Dream Portraits.*

Watch and Pray: Spirituals and Art Songs by African-American Women Composers. Performed by Videmus: Pamela Dillard, soprano; Ruth Hamilton, contralto; Robert Honeysucker, baritone; Vivian Taylor, piano. Koch International Classics CD, 1993. Album includes *Dry Bones, Lord I Just Can't Keep from Cryin', The Negro Speaks of Rivers, He's Got the Whole World in His Hands,* and *Three Dream Portraits.*

5

IRENE BRITTON SMITH
(1907–99)

CHRONOLOGY

1907   Born 22 December in Chicago; youngest of four siblings.

1913–17   Attended Ferron Grammar School; studied piano with V. Emanuel Johnson.

1917   Parents separated; attended Catholic boarding school for one year.

1918   Attended Doolittle Grammar School (seventh and eighth grades).

1919   Chicago race riots; father escorted to and from work by a company bodyguard.

1920–24   Attended Wendell Phillips High School.

1924–26   Attended Chicago Normal School.

1930   Began teaching in primary grades in the Chicago public schools.

1930s   Attended Berean Baptist Church.

1930–31   Played violin in the Harrison Farrell Symphony Orchestra.

1931   Married on 8 August to Herbert E. Smith.

1932–43   Part-time student at the American Conservatory; studied with Stella Roberts.

1938   Composed *Fugue for String Trio.*

1940   Composed *Psalm 46* for SATB and baritone, *Invention in Two Voices* for piano, *Passacaglia and Fugue in C-sharp Minor* for piano.

1941   Composed *Reminiscence* for violin and piano, performed in recital May 1942 by Adele Mdjeska; studied form and analysis with Leo Sowerby 1941–43 at American Conservatory.

Irene Britton Smith. Helen Walker-Hill Collection, Center for Black Music Research Library and Archives, Columbia College, Chicago.

1943   Received Bachelor of Music degree from American Conservatory of Music.

1945   Separated from husband for next 10 years; took entrance exam at Juilliard
         that summer; composed choral anthem *Fairest Lord Jesus*, published 1946 by
         G. Schirmer.

1946–47 On sabbatical from Chicago school system; graduate student at Juilliard,
         where she took courses in song forms, larger forms with Vittorio Giannini;
         composed *Dream Cycle* for voice and piano, *Variations on a Theme by Mac-
         Dowell* for piano, and *Sonata for Violin and Piano*.

1948   Attended summer school at Eastman, studied composition with Wayne Bar-
         low; composed solo vocal arrangement *Let Us Break Bread Together*.

1949   Attended summer school at Tanglewood Music Festival, studied composition
         with Irving Fine.

1950s   In residence at the Rosenwald Building where Florence Price also lived;
         Price's grandson was in her first-grade class.

1952   Composed *Born Anew* (SATB).

1953   Composed *Two Short Preludes for Piano*.

1954   Composed song *Trees of the Night*.

1956   Completed Master of Music degree at De Paul, studied with Leon Stein;
         master's thesis was *Sinfonietta* for full orchestra.

1957   Attended demonstration of phono-visual reading method and began using it
         in her classes.

1958   Moved to 501 East 32nd St. in Chicago; transferred to Pershing Elementary
         School; attended Fontainebleau Summer School in France, studied composi-
         tion with Nadia Boulanger.

1960   Her monograph *Methods and Materials for Teaching Word Perception in
         Kindergarten Through Grade Three* published by University of Chicago
         Press.

1962   Stopped composing.

1969   Trip to Europe, visited Beethoven's grave in Vienna.

1971   Performance of *Sunset* from *Dream Cycle* by soprano Lolla McCullough
         Shavers.

1972   Performance of *Let Us Break Bread Together* by baritone Theodore Charles
         Stone.

1975   Husband, Herbert E. Smith, died 28 December.

1977   Performances of songs from *Dream Cycle* by soprano Jo Ann Pickens at the
         Chicago Public Library Myra Hess Concerts and other venues.

1978   Retired from teaching in the Chicago public schools in June; became a docent
            for the Chicago Symphony Orchestra at Schiller and Beidler elementary
            schools.

1983   Performance of Smith's songs by soprano Jo Ann Pickens on 9 January.

1984   Performance of *Let Us Break Bread Together* by Theodore Charles Stone at
            Second Presbyterian Church on 4 November.

1989   Performance of *Fairest Lord Jesus* at Second Presbyterian Church on 26
            March.

1990   Performances of *Prelude No. 1* by Helen Walker-Hill at Stanford University
            and the University of Colorado; premiere of *Sonata for Violin and Piano* by
            violinist Gregory Walker and pianist Helen Walker-Hill at Denver Public Li-
            brary.

1994   Moved to Montgomery Place Retirement Home in Chicago.

1995   *Sonata for Violin and Piano* released by Leonarda Records on album *Kalei-
            doscope: Music by African-American Women*.

1996   *Sonata for Violin and Piano* published by Vivace Press.

1999   Died on 15 February in Chicago, at the age of 91.

> Sometimes I say I am limited,
> I will never be able to write my song,
> Then from within a voice reminds me,
> That this thought is wrong.
> I must not think of limitations
> If I would achieve this goal . . .
> He will impart the notes
> And I will write His song.[1]

Because she was reported to have known the composers Florence Price and
Margaret Bonds, I contacted Irene Smith in the summer of 1989 and asked for
an interview. She replied that, yes, she had known Margaret Bonds and Florence
Price, and she would be willing to talk about them. Only in passing did it emerge
that she herself composed. As she brought out her meticulously copied compositions, it became evident that hers was a highly trained and sensitive talent.
She had learned her craft in relative obscurity during years of dedicated study
with some of the leading musicians and teachers of the twentieth century. Although music and composing may have been the love of her life, most of her
energy was required in her profession of teaching in the public schools. Time
for composing was stolen during her spare hours, summer vacations, and rare
sabbatical leaves. A few of her compositions had been performed, and one choral
piece had even been published, but most of her music, including some of her
most ambitious works, had never been heard.

Despite the affirmation and encouragement of her teachers, Smith was reluctant to promote her music, saying, "I have not really tried [to publish]. I'm too critical of my compositions, so I'm my own worst enemy." She was hesitant to call herself a "real" composer, certainly "not like Margaret Bonds."[2] Not surprisingly, Irene Britton Smith was little-known among her contemporaries, and her name did not appear in any of the reference books on black music. Not only were there few outside sources of information about her, but she was reluctant to talk about herself, and her memory suffered many gaps. She is representative of the unknown women who compose for their own satisfaction, with little thought of public recognition.

BIOGRAPHY

Smith was born in Chicago on 22 December 1907 and grew up on the city's south side near the location of the modern apartment building where she spent most of the last 42 years of her life. She attended Ferron Grammar School, then completed the seventh and eighth grades at Doolittle Grammar School, two blocks away. For her secondary education she went to Wendell Phillips High School.

Her father had moved to Chicago from Kentucky, where he grew up on a farm near Maysville and attended Louisville College. He was of Crow and Cherokee as well as African-American descent; his Crow grandmother lived with his family until she died at age 93. This ancestry is evident in photographs from his straight hair and prominent cheekbones. Irene recalled that as a child she liked to stand behind his chair and comb his hair. In Chicago he held a position as a clerk in a manufacturing company. Irene could remember that during the race riots of the "Red Summer" of 1919, his company sent an escort to protect him on the way to and from work.

Her mother, who came to Chicago from Detroit, was musical and loved to play hymns by ear, "favoring the black keys." She had acquired a piano before Irene was born, and as a small child, Irene began composing little pieces on it. There were two brothers who died in infancy and an older sister who survived until the 1980s. When Irene was 10, her parents separated and she was sent to a Catholic boarding school for a year. Later she and her sister took piano lessons from V. Emanuel Johnson, who made them play duets. "He was the kind who hits you on the fingers." When Irene accompanied her high school orchestra, she became fascinated with the violin section and started to teach herself on her sister's violin. She was then given lessons, and attended her first symphony orchestra concert at Orchestra Hall as a guest of her public school violin teacher when she was 14 years old.

Irene had ambitions to study music at Northwestern University but her parents couldn't afford it, so she turned instead to the two-year course at Chicago Normal School to prepare herself to teach in the elementary grades. After being assigned to teach primary grades in the Chicago public schools, she decided to take a course in music theory, which she had longed to study for many years.

She took one course a year at the American Conservatory, beginning with theory and harmony for two years, then progressing through form and analysis, and counterpoint.

During the 1930s, Irene attended the Berean Baptist Church along with a good number of other musicians who were well-known in the black community. These included Estella Bonds, church organist, and her daughter, Margaret. Smith knew the Bonds family well, and was good friends with Estella's sister Helen. Irene played violin in the all-black Harrison Ferrell Symphony Orchestra, which rehearsed at the church and gave yearly concerts at Kimball Hall.[3] She was later a member of the student orchestra at the American Conservatory.

In 1931 Irene married Herbert E. Smith, an employee of the postal service. Smith had greater ambitions, and returned to school for a master's degree in chemistry at Bradley University in Peoria. But after he finished his degree, he found that it was still very difficult for qualified blacks to get jobs in Illinois. For a period of 10 years during the 1940s and 1950s, Irene and her husband lived apart while they both pursued their degrees. She recalled that he would send her a dozen roses on their anniversary, even during their years of separation. They later reunited, and he eventually worked for the U.S. Department of Agriculture on such projects as the development of gasohol. The couple remained childless, and in December 1975 her husband passed away.

In 1936 Smith wrote to Florence Price, already well-known as a composer, after hearing her give a talk. Price responded with a letter saying,

It was very kind of you to say you enjoyed my little talk at Lincoln Center, and it makes me happy indeed to know that you received encouragement from it. That you find the study of composition such a pleasure indicates that we may expect to hear from you some of these days. I should be very glad to see some of your work if you care to call a few days ahead of time and make an appointment.[4]

Smith was too shy to accept Price's invitation. But Price's words encouraged her, and she decided to work toward a degree in theory and composition at the American Conservatory, with the approval of her instructor, Stella Roberts, and Dean Charles Haake. She continued to take one music course each year, including violin and voice (she was also proficient in piano and organ), and in her last two years she studied composition with Leo Sowerby. She distinguished herself in these studies, receiving an Honorable Mention in theory and analysis at the 1938 commencement exercises of the American Conservatory of Music. Years later, she wrote to Roberts thanking her for her inspiration and encouragement: "I will never forget that story you told me about the hare and the tortoise—the folk who won the competitions and were never heard from again and the girl who tried but although she lost was building up a repertoire. Sometimes I equate myself with the tortoise."[5]

Smith's composition gathered momentum in 1940–41, the years in which she wrote several ambitious works: *Passacaglia and Fugue in C-sharp Minor*, and

Invention in Two Voices for piano, *Psalm 46* for chorus and baritone, and *Reminiscence* for violin and piano, which was performed in May of the following year by violinist Adele Mdjeska. In 1943, after 11 years of study, she completed her bachelor's degree in composition at the American Conservatory.

Further impetus came in 1946 when *Fairest Lord Jesus*, her choral work for women's voices and organ on the words from the Crusader's Hymn, was accepted for publication by the prestigious New York publishing firm of G. Schirmer. That year she was on sabbatical leave from the Chicago public school system and went to New York for graduate study at the Juilliard School of Music. She chose two courses taught by Vittorio Giannini, one in song forms and the other in larger forms of composition. Smith recalled that when she brought her setting of the Paul Laurence Dunbar text "Why Fades a Dream?" to Giannini, he exclaimed, " 'Who is this poet?' He went out and bought a whole book of Dunbar poetry. He liked it [the song] and he's the one who suggested to me that I write a cycle." For her class in larger forms, Smith completed her *Sonata for Violin and Piano*. She was living at International House and did not have access there to a piano, so her composing was done away from the piano. She recalled working on the third movement of the sonata all one night and being late to class the next day, but with the movement finished.

Upon returning to Chicago and her classroom teaching, Smith resumed studies in composition with Leon Stein at De Paul University. She spent several summer vacations away from Chicago, studying with well-known composers and teachers. In the summer of 1948, she studied contemporary harmony at the Eastman School of Music with Wayne Barlow.[6] In 1949 she was at Berkshire Music Festival in Tanglewood, working with Hugh Ross in choral conducting and studying composition with Irving Fine. She recalled Tanglewood as a "marvelous place in '49. Koussevitsky was 75 years old that summer." There was a big birthday celebration for Koussevitsky, and at the end of the summer Smith participated in the performance of a new choral/orchestral work in his honor by Benjamin Britten, *Spring Symphony*. She met Julia Perry and showed her some of her compositions. "In addition to Julia Perry, Elayne Jones, Mattiwilda Dobbs, and I were the only black women attending. I will never forget those wonderful, marvelous, six weeks."[7]

Smith completed her master's degree in theory and composition at De Paul University in 1956. In the summer of 1958 she fulfilled a dream to study with the famed teacher Nadia Boulanger at the American Conservatory at Fontainebleau, France. Boulanger praised her compositions and told her, "You are a born musician. Follow your ear."[8]

Smith continued to be a dedicated teacher in the public schools for more than 40 years. Her last position was at Pershing Elementary School, from 1958 to her retirement in 1978. She adopted the phono-visual method of teaching reading after attending a demonstration at Northwestern University in 1957. It was remarkably successful, enabling her students to consistently leave first grade with third, fourth and even higher grade reading levels. For the next decade, her energies went into giving workshops, and promoting and using this teaching technique. She wrote to the publishers that the method worked "like magic." They asked if they could quote her in their catalogs and invited her to attend their training sessions free of charge. In 1960 she delivered a talk on this method at the University of Chicago. Her monograph *Methods and Materials for Teaching Word Perception in Kindergarten Through Grade Three* was published by the University of Chicago in 1960, and was subsequently reprinted in Albert J. Mazuriewicz' book *New Perspectives in Reading Instruction*. Although she might have accepted a position training teachers to use the method, she felt an obligation to stay in the classroom. She lamented that many teachers did not care for the challenge of teaching well in all subjects in the primary grades. Many of her former students remained in their old neighborhood close to Smith's home, and she was able to watch them grow up. A number of Irene's outstanding students went on to graduate from Harvard and the Massachusetts Institute of Technology, and several completed their Ph.D. degrees.[9] They continued to keep in touch with their grade school teacher, sending her news of their accomplishments and photos of their children. She called them her "Golden Apples."

Besides her classroom teaching, Smith started several rhythm bands in the schools where she taught and at the Cosmopolitan Community Church, where her children's rhythm band presented annual concerts. Smith's concern for young people was also evident in her volunteer work as a docent for the Chicago Symphony Orchestra in the Chicago public schools, which she began soon after her retirement from classroom teaching in 1978. This involved visiting classrooms several times a year, bringing recordings, pictures of instruments and composers, discussing the music, and preparing the children to listen to the concerts; then going to the concerts to meet them (often over 200 at a time) and distribute programs. She remarked that she was always proud of the children's behavior. Her first schools were in the inner city: Schiller School, located in the Cabrini-Green area, where she taught 100 students, and Beidler School, with 120 children under her charge. Later she worked at Doolittle School, which she had attended as a child, and she was still active there in 1990. She particularly emphasized to these young people the importance of learning to read notes, and of becoming aware of their classical musical heritage.

Irene Smith was a short, compact, light-skinned woman with a kind face and lively, intelligent eyes. Her orderliness and serenity were reflected in her lovely, sunlit apartment, decorated with African-American art objects, overlooking Lake Michigan. On a coffee table stood a small-scale reproduction of black sculptor Augusta Savage's famous piece *Lift Every Voice*, depicting black choir singers grouped in the form of a harp.[10]

After her death, a perusal of Smith's papers at the Center for Black Music Research revealed that, in addition to art, Smith collected poetry, typing out her favorites and saving them in a folder. Among them were Paul Laurence Dun-

bar's "We Wear the Mask," Langston Hughes' "I Dream a World," Sara Teasdale's "What Do I Care," and Lillian Whiting's "The Mystery." Most
significantly, there were also some two dozen poems of her own that provide a
glimpse into her otherwise hidden emotional life. She avoided sentimentality in
her conversation, responding matter-of-factly to questions in her sensible schoolteacher voice. But through her poetry we learn that she missed her husband
deeply during their long separation, something that did not come across in her
account of those years: "When you're away the days are long, /My heart grows
heavy—so still my song. /I wonder if you think of me, /And wish this world
could be, /A magic carpet of dreams come true, /and I could suddenly be with
you."

Smith loved to travel, and she was proud of having visited 18 countries,
including Japan and Mexico. On a particularly memorable trip in the summer
of 1969 she took a 46-day tour of Europe and was thrilled to visit Beethoven's
grave in Vienna. Among the musical events she attended that summer was a
chamber concert in Salzburg at which, to her amazement, all the musicians
except the cellist played standing up.

From the 1970s on, Smith's music received increasing numbers of performances. Her spiritual arrangement for baritone and piano, *Let Us Break Bread
Together*, was sung in 1972 by Theodore Charles Stone, noted concert artist and
music critic for the *Chicago Defender*. In 1984 it was performed again, at the
Second Presbyterian Church, where her *Fairest Lord Jesus* was later programmed (1989). Songs from her Paul Laurence Dunbar *Dream Cycle* were
performed by several noted artists and broadcast over WFMT, drawing a con-
gratulatory letter from Cyrus Colter, chairman of the African-American studies
department at Northwestern University.

Smith never joined the black music groups in Chicago, nor did she belong to
the National Association of Negro Musicians. When questioned about this, she
replied that she was not a "joiner," partly because she was afraid to go out at
night on the dangerous streets. In later years, her only outside activity was
attending the Chicago Symphony Orchestra music appreciation classes and concerts. She never stopped expanding her knowledge of music. In the mid-1970s
she wrote to Stella Roberts, "I haven't written any music for 15 years. However,
I do not regret one minute of learning about music and composition, and I still
continue to learn. I read current periodicals and books on music."

For the last few years of her life, Smith lived in the Montgomery Place
Retirement Home on Chicago's South Shore Drive. During this time her *Sonata
for Violin and Piano* was published and issued on a CD recording, but she had
difficulty recognizing her own music because she suffered from Parkinson's
disease and Alzheimer's disease. On 15 February 1999, at the age of 91, she
died of complications from these diseases. Services were at the Griffin Funeral
Home, and she was buried in Lincoln Cemetery, where Florence Price is also
buried. In accord with her wishes, her papers and music scores were given to
the Center for Black Music Research (CBMR) at Columbia College Chicago.

SOCIAL ISSUES

Smith's attitude toward race seemed ambivalent, and her remarks were often contradictory. She claimed that race was never much of an issue for her, either in daily life or as a composer. She had always avoided any situations that might cause a "race problem."[11] She was often critical of the ignorance of black people: "People of my race can't read music." She was disappointed in most black poets: "They're all worrying about being black and being trod upon." But she also complained about prejudice: "There are people who think black people can't interpret white people's music." And she did recall with considerable feeling some unpleasant racial encounters during her early years at Chicago Normal School, where she was one of 11 blacks among a graduating class of 600. Observations were sprinkled through her conversation about the limitations that qualified blacks faced in employment and in the musical life of Chicago during her lifetime.

Smith's compositional style displayed no trace of black idioms. She didn't think that her experiences as a black person had any bearing on her composition, yet her use of poems by Paul Laurence Dunbar and her arrangements of spirituals indicate her sense of racial identity. She had no objection to being categorized as a black woman composer for this study, and said, "I think that's good. That's the only way we're going to get known."

It was in her poetry that Smith revealed her loyalty to and identification with her race. Two of her poems in the archives at CBMR celebrate the strengths of African Americans and her sense of belonging to "my people." Smith ends one of them with these words: "This is my life, a song—because I am me. I am my people." In another, she proclaims,

> My people laugh,
> Merry, happy laughter,
> Repressed in sorrow,
> Sometimes in despair. . . .
> My people long
> Not for self
> But for their children
> What to them was denied, Not by God but by man.
> My people long for one nation undivided
> With freedom and justice for all. . . .
> My people pray,
> Within them is depth,
> That others cannot understand. . . .

Like Bonds, Smith had grown up in an integrated neighborhood. She deplored the increasing isolation of Chicago's black south side, first around the time she graduated from grammar school in the 1920s and 1930s, in the aftermath of the migrations from the South and the race riots, and again in the 1970s, under the influence of the Black Power movement, "when black got so black." In 1950 she moved into a lakeside apartment in a privately owned complex which was then integrated, though by the late 1980s it was mostly black. When I mentioned I was going to look for the elementary school named after Florence Price, she insisted on going with me because the trip involved several bus changes, and that area was no longer safe.[12] She said that if she were with me, I'd have less trouble (as a white person) and would be "more legitimate."

When she began work as a docent for the Chicago Symphony Orchestra, Smith asked to be assigned to inner-city schools. She wrote to Stella Roberts, "I asked to be sent into the so-called ghetto. I had been assigned to a Jewish Day School, they wanted someone "qualified." However . . . it was changed. I was needed more in the north and north-west ghetto." She told me, "I want these black kids to hear a little more than just rock and roll and gospel music. . . . I hope the exposure these children have will be remembered and [will affect] their lives and decisions."

Smith avoided churches where gospel music was sung, saying, "I used to go to Cosmopolitan Church, but now there's a young minister who does gospel music which I can't abide—all that stomping and screaming—it's just bribery." In these preferences, she reflected a generational as well as a class conditioning. Smith remarked that in her youth, spirituals were not sung in some churches because they were reminders of slavery and degradation.[13] She expressed a desire to work more with spirituals as a statement of pride to younger generations, a sentiment at odds with her professed musical detachment from her racial heritage. She said, "A good spiritual—you don't have to jazz it up. It's going to be syncopated, but you don't have to do all this shouting and whatnot. I'm going to work more with spirituals!"

Smith was not conscious of difficulties she faced in her work or daily life because of her gender. Like other young black women, she had taken it for granted that she would need to earn a living, and she saw nothing unusual in continuing to teach throughout her marriage. She spoke only indirectly of the reasons for her 10-year separation from her husband, but it is possible that her ambitions were incompatible with her role as a wife: "It was during that time I did my traveling, and my work." As a composition student, however, Irene did report experiencing more difficulty as a woman than as an African American. When she applied to summer school at the Tanglewood Music Festival in 1949, she was admitted to the school but not to Aaron Copland's composition class. When he recognized her on the campus one day, she expressed her disappointment, and he arranged for her to have lessons with Irving Fine. She felt sure that she would have had no problem entering his class had she been male. "I didn't know until years later that Copland didn't think women could write music. . . . And you think you're rejected because you're not good enough." Even though she did not pursue a professional career in music herself, she was aware of the practical difficulties faced by women composers. "I really and truly think it will be a long time before men will accept women as composers . . . they

figure women are worried with the house and whatever other chores: they have
the idea that women don't have time for it. . . . [Also,] it costs a lot of money
to put these things on [musical performances of one's works] and women don't
get those chances . . . [because] they believe we can't write music."[14]

Smith's class identity played an important although largely unconscious role
in her upbringing, aspirations, and choices. On the one hand, Irene regretted her
inability to attend Northwestern University because her family could not afford
it. On the other hand, her father's education and semi-professional occupation
placed her family in a class that owned pianos, gave its children private music
lessons, and educated them to become schoolteachers. In the 1950s, both Smith
and Florence Price lived in the fashionable Julius Rosenwald Building at 46th
and Michigan, named after the Sears Roebuck founder and designed by the noted
black architect Robert Taylor. A beautiful building intended specifically for
black residents in the professions, it was self-contained, with its own nursery
school and activity center, making it almost unnecessary to leave the building.

Class considerations were inextricably enmeshed in Smith's comments on
black musical idioms (for instance, her dislike of churches where gospel is sung)
and her complaints about black people's ignorance of classical music. A phrase
she used repeatedly, "When black got so black," and her descriptions of some
of her students as "black black" (especially in view of her own light skin and
wavy hair) indicated her absorption of the color consciousness that so often
accompanies class distinctions among African Americans.

THE MUSIC

Smith considered only 15 of her compositions worthy to be listed as her body
of work, out of the 36 or so that have been preserved.[15] Most of her small body
of music was composed between the ages of 30 and 50 (1938–56). There is no
doubt that she had been composing before then, as the 1936 letter from Florence
Price indicates, but no works survive from before that date. She must have still
been composing during the summer of 1958 while studying with Nadia Boulanger at Fontainebleau, but she completely stopped writing music in 1962.[16]
Her surviving compositions begin with her *Fugue for String Trio* (1938) and
end with her *Sinfonietta*, her master's thesis, in 1956.

Seventeen of the total of 36 compositions, a little less than half, are purely
instrumental works, and 19 are vocal. Of the vocal works, seven are choral,
while 12 are for solo voice or voices. Ten instrumental works are for solo piano
(including two arrangements of Bartók), two are for violin (surprisingly little,
since she was a violinist), one is for string trio, and four are for orchestra
(including an arrangement of *Three Fantastic Dances* by Shostakovitch). Spiritual arrangements account for six of the vocal pieces.

Smith had one choral anthem published by G. Schirmer (1946), the Crusader
Hymn *Fairest Lord Jesus* for women's voices, but it is now out of print and
the copyright was returned to her. Vivace Press published her *Sonata for Violin*

and Piano in 1996 and four of her solo piano works in 2001. The *Sonata for Violin and Piano* is the only work available on recording (see discography).

Smith's music does not employ African-American idioms or espouse the "racial" loyalties and characteristics typical of the music of William Grant Still, Florence Price, William Dawson, and other black composers of the 1920s and 1930s.[17] She knew the music of Margaret Bonds and admired her craft, but she did not share her social concerns or her enthusiasm for popular traditions. Her attitude was closer to the international modernist sensibility of the 1950s and 1960s, which governed the work of Julia Perry, George Walker, Hale Smith, and other black composers. During those years, the pendulum of artistic fashion swung away from racialism toward an aesthetic of art in itself, independent of social or cultural conditioning. This aesthetic included atonalism, serialism, and pointillism, and a series of "isms" introduced by such twentieth-century European innovators, as Stravinsky, Hindemith, Schoenberg, Berg, and Webern. But although Smith studied those techniques in her classes, she was never interested in writing atonal or serial music. "I had to write serial music—I know serial music. But it was hurting me all inside, not because it was atonal but because it was just numbers—take this out, put that in, invert the other . . . and so on and so forth. . . . It wasn't really music."

Smith's process of composition usually began with a melodic idea. Then a countermelody would immediately suggest itself. She said, "I think and compose linearly," that is, in horizontal melodic lines rather than vertical harmonies. She preferred to compose away from the piano, and was aided in this by perfect pitch. She did not need to play her music or hear it played, because she could hear the entire work in her head.

In harmonic style, Smith's oeuvre varies from conservative and tonal to sharply dissonant. Smith's favorite composers were Tchaikovsky and Brahms, and she was also fond of the French composers Gabriel Fauré and César Franck.[18] It was in the music of Franck that she first discovered augmented sixth chords: "When I found what an augmented sixth chord would do—I marvelled!" Much of her own music is reminiscent of early twentieth-century French neoclassical music in its transparent texture, linear writing, and modal harmonies. Smith's works display an elegant simplicity, overall formal balance, discreetly placed harmonic color, subtle contrapuntal details, wide pitch range, and open textures. She attributed her mastery of composition to her excellent training, as she commented in a letter to her former teacher Stella Roberts: "I can listen to music and evaluate it mentally whether it be traditional, contemporary or avant-garde, and all of this I can do because of the thoroughness of the theory I received from you at the American Conservatory. . . . This development of the composer's mind is necessary and in the act of composition one knows what one is doing—retaining the techniques taught or discarding them and knowing why."[19]

Smith had little use for much of contemporary music. She wrote to Stella Roberts:

I also attend Contemporary Concerts which are very Avant Garde, and through the years have had [heard?] both European and American composers using many "gimmicks," but they get their music played and I guess that is the thing! Some of it you would not call "music" just "sound" pieces and that could be hitting a pipe, or walking around and playing from a circular-revolving score. However, I listen with an open mind, and [am] sympathetic with those who can't get their compositions performed because they ARE music.[20]

Smith's many years studying the compositional techniques of different historical periods resulted in study pieces that go beyond a demonstration of her mastery of these techniques. The scores of such works as the *Passacaglia and Fugue in C-sharp Minor* (1940) retain telltale labels indicating their original function as exercises in eighteenth-century counterpoint. Smith doubted their appeal to others, asking, "Who would want to hear them?!" Upon examination of the *Passacaglia*, however, one leaves the academic classroom far behind, and becomes absorbed in expressive, meditative counterpoint over the inexorably repeated ground bass. Voices are added one by one, and parts pile up, gradually increasing in momentum as the note values progress in each variation from slow quarter note values to eighth notes, 16th-notes, and dotted rhythms.[21] A low, triple octave pedal point is introduced as the voices solidify into chords in mounting tension. A momentary lull allows the ground bass to be heard inverted (upside down), following itself closely in imitation, before the texture thickens and the momentum builds up again. Soon all four voices are interlaced, each in a different rhythmic pattern, doubled in octaves, then thirds, before the overburdened structure gives way to a free fantasia of arpeggios and passage work in double thirds. One has become lost in a vista reminiscent of the architectural etchings by the eighteenth-century Italian artist Giambattista Piranesi, a fantasy of grandeur, vast heights, towering arches, parapets and ledges, and stairways disappearing into nowhere. Smith's love of the baroque contrapuntal technique as well as its grandiose late-romantic transformation, her skill, and her talent have transcended the exercise to create an original work in its own right, just as she does in her virtuoso exploration of the late-romantic harmonic language in *Variations on a Theme by MacDowell*.

Her *Psalm 46* for mixed chorus and baritone solo (1940) also shows the influence of her studies in counterpoint with its choral fugal section following an introductory baritone solo. But the *Reminiscence* for violin and piano of 1941 leaves behind the elaborate contrapuntal technical studies of the previous year. A short, simple piece in D major and unchanging 4/4 meter, it is marked "Andante" and "espressivo." The texture is transparent and open, with widely spaced four-part harmony accompanying the violin solo. Both violin and piano cover a wide pitch range, with expansive leaps and arpeggiation in the violin part. The opening melody outlines a questioning E minor ninth chord, repeated and sustained until its resolution to D major in the fourth measure. The piano then repeats the violin's melody, the main departure from its basically homophonic accompaniment. While not as linear as some of Smith's works, and not as modally ambiguous, the broadly lyrical style is unmistakably hers.

In *Fairest Lord Jesus* for women's voices and organ, composed in 1945, both texture and melody are very economical. The organ introduction presents the opening notes of the choral theme in bare octaves, and is repeated by the voices, also in octaves. This spare opening is followed by four-part organ harmony, but the texture remains very simple, with frequent returns to unison octaves. For the comparisons of various beautiful things, "Fair is the sunshine, fairer still the moonlight," etc., the tonality modulates from F major to D-flat major, changing key again to G-flat major at "but Jesus shines brighter."

The works dating from Smith's graduate studies at Juilliard with Vittorio Giannini (1946–47) are large-scale, ambitious projects displaying a lyricism similar to *Reminiscence*, with long phrases, wide range, and open texture, but with a more piquant modal ambiguity and a more chromatic harmonic language (see the essays on *Dream Cycle, Sonata for Violin and Piano*, and *Variations on a Theme by MacDowell*).

Smith's arrangement of the spiritual "Let Us Break Bread Together" for solo baritone (or mezzo-soprano/soprano) and piano demonstrates her unconscious loyalty to her racial roots. It was composed in 1948 and merits a closer look. The setting employs contrapuntal devices and harmonic color so unobtrusively that the simplicity of the spiritual melody is enhanced. Unusual chromatic chords are used rarely and discreetly, for mild expressive emphasis on words like "on your knees," or "rising." The steady half-note harmonic rhythm maintains a stately, dignified pace throughout. The second verse, "Let us drink wine together on our knees" is sung "pianissimo" (very softly) while the piano introduces another melody above it, a descant in a high register, as the steady half-note harmonic pace continues. This descant melody is the familiar hymn "Break Thou the Bread of Life" by William Sherwin. The combination creates a beautifully placed (although unspoken, since the descant has no words) dialogue between the spiritual's "drinking wine" and the hymn's "breaking bread." It is also a dialogue between a traditional black spiritual and a traditional white hymn. It is immediately followed by the repeated interjection "Let us praise God together on our knees," with increasing strength and urgency, in unison with the piano. The piece concludes quietly with the repeated phrase "O Lord have mercy on me." This arrangement illustrates Smith's elegant simplicity, her exquisitely placed harmonic color, and her subtle use of counterpoint, combined with a tribute to her racial musical heritage.

The choral work *Born Anew* (1952) again shows a richer harmonic palette, with a contemporary harmonic vocabulary. It begins with a low E-minor organ chord, followed by an unaccompanied baritone solo, marked "molto espressivo," declaiming "Truly, truly I say unto you" on shifting chromatic pitches. The tonality settles down to E minor as the chorus enters with "You must be born anew," to prepare for the dramatic change of color at "anew" to a D minor seventh, then a B minor seventh chord. In the passage "There is one body and one spirit . . . One God and Father of us all" the voices begin in unison, then follow each other in imitation at the unison. It was this passage that Boulanger particularly admired when Smith showed *Born Anew* to her at Fontainebleau in 1958.

Smith explored mixed modes and bitonality, dissonance and quartal harmonies in her *Two Short Preludes for Piano* (1953), rebelling, as she said, against the strict voice-leading rules of her conservative training. She also honed her instrumentation skills in several preliminary orchestral exercises, including transcriptions of works by Arensky, Shostakovitch, and Grieg before composing her master's thesis, a three-movement work for full orchestra modestly titled *Sinfonietta*.[22] Her skill in orchestration is apparent, as is her mastery of large forms. All three movements are unified by a three-note motive consisting of a whole step down and back up, sometimes shortened to a two-note falling whole step, and sometimes lengthened by incorporation into longer themes. In the middle movement this motive is inverted to a rising whole step. Despite its brevity, the motive is prominent and clear in all three movements, and does not become monotonous. The standard movement sequence of fast, slow, fast is followed. Although key signatures are absent, each movement is tonal with references to conventional key relationships: the first is oriented to the natural minor mode on E, the second centers on C-sharp, and the third returns to E minor, closing the whole work with an E major "tierce de Picardie."[23] The first movement's introductory "Moderato tranquillo" erupts into a fugal "Allegro con moto" by the string section. The fragmented, agitated subject is six measures long, with a pattern of one 5/8 measure followed by five 4/8 measures. Two more sections with new themes and mixed meters follow, each with much imitation and development of themes by extension and fragmentation. The most distinguishing feature is the over-all mirror structure that governs the movement. The same fugue appears in the winds the second time, with the "Moderato tranquillo" returning for a quiet close. The second movement, marked "Adagio" remains serenely in 3/4 meter, opening with a long melody handed from oboes, to muted trumpets, to clarinets, and flutes. In succeeding sections, more themes are introduced, resulting in an over-all A B A C A D form. After a close, marked ppp (extremely quiet), the concluding movement, "Energico," is launched. It is characterized by sharply rhythmic themes with motivic similarities, a pervasive 5/4 meter, much imitation, and a roughly A B A structure. Smith called her *Sinfonietta* "very original," and was disappointed that De Paul University's music department did not arrange a performance or reading of it.

Taken all together, Smith's music shows her love of order, restraint, and precision, and her understanding of traditional European musical styles of many periods. In her compositions Smith reveals her true stature, one that transcends her modest life and demonstrates strength of intellect and breadth of imagination.

Dream Cycle (1947)

This set of four songs on poems by Paul Laurence Dunbar was composed in 1946–47 while Smith was studying composition with Vittorio Giannini at the Juilliard School of Music in New York. The poems Smith chose are "Over the Hill," "By the Pool," "Sunset" (Smith's favorite), and "Why Fades a Dream?" She selected them to describe a life cycle: the rapture of young love, followed by the sunset of life, and concluding with the disillusionment of the fading dream. She spoke highly of Dunbar's poetry and said, "I don't know why I'm led to earlier black poets. I've gone through the anthologies and can't find more recent poems [that I like]."[24]

Two songs from the Dream Cycle have received several performances, notably Sunset, performed by Lolla McCullough Shavers in April 1971 at the Colonial House on East 79th Street in Chicago, and Sunset and Why Fades a Dream?, performed by Jo Ann Pickens in October 1977 on the Dame Myra Hess Memorial Concert series at Chicago Public Library and broadcast over WFMT. The songs received high praise from a number of prominent musicians who heard them, including Professor Ellen T. Harris of the University of Chicago's department of music, who admired the vocal lines and marveled at the striking declamation of the last song.[25]

The first song, Over the Hill, begins serenely in F major with a flowing 16th-note piano introduction evoking rolling hills. The two four-line verses are set syllabically, with pitches and rhythms reflecting the rhythms and inflections of the words. At the words "Down through the dales and the bowers of loving, Singing, singing I roam afar," the tonality "roams" through D major and other keys, an instance of word painting.

By the Pool, in A major and 6/8 time, is marked "In reflective mood." The poem is in the form of six couplets plus a concluding line. In her setting, the first, third, and fifth couplets begin with a similar melody but on different pitches, and the alternate couplets introduce new melodic material (ABA^1CA^2DE). The harmonic language is more chromatic in this song, particularly on the words "But Oh, I've a wish in my heart, dear love, The wish of a dreamer it seems, That I might wash free of my sins."

A tranquil flowing eighth-note accompaniment in double thirds and sixths sets the mood of Sunset. This steady motion continues until the words "the first faint star lifts to the night its silver face, and twinkles to the moon afar across the heavens graying space, low murmurs reach me from the town, as Day puts on her somber crown." Here, alternating recitative, speechlike phrases between voice and piano create a dialogue between star and moon.

In the final song, Why Fades a Dream? Dunbar's treatment of the dream subject presents an unsentimental, even disillusioned interpretation: "Lest men should learn to trust the things that seem, So fades a dream." Smith sets this in a chromatic harmonic language and a fluid vocal line interwoven with the piano part. Thematic unity is provided by the return of melodic material, particularly the return of the piano's introductory melody at the end, and by the repetition of the intervallic motif on the recurring phrase "Why fades a dream?" The three verses introduced by this recurring phrase each receive a different setting. In the first, piano and voice alternate in a kind of dialogue, the "tryst of night and day." In the second, the piano accompanies a recitative-like vocal line with simple half-note chords, the "shade wrought out . . . upon life's stream." And in the third verse, which answers the repeated question, the voice takes on a more continuous melodic flow while retaining the speech rhythms, and the piano accompaniment gains momentum in triplet movement, then 16th-notes, to underscore the words "thrive," "grow," and "glow."

Sonata for Violin and Piano (1947)

When Smith was asked which of her works she most wished she could hear played (she had never heard most of them), I assumed she would say her *Sinfonietta* for full orchestra. She replied, "Yes, but I would like to hear the violin work [*Sonata for Violin and Piano*], too. I think your son [violinist Gregory Walker] would like it." She continued to refer to it as "your son's piece," and dedicated the sonata to him. It received its premiere performance by Walker at the Denver Public Library in February 1990, and although she could not attend, she was at last able to hear it on tape. It was recorded by Walker and myself on the Leonarda Productions CD, *Kaleidoscope: Music by African-American Women* (1995). The reviewer for the *American Record Guide* complained that it was "incessantly melodic but dull and tensionless,"[26] but *Strings* magazine gave it a glowing review as "an outgoing and elegantly designed work in the American neoclassical tradition, and deserves further listening."[27] Other reviewers also were favorably impressed. Barbara Harbach pronounced it "an exciting contribution to the violin and piano literature, rewarding not only to its performers, but also its listeners," and found it "immediately appealing . . . [with] long expressive lyrical melodies, careful and intriguing placement of unexpected harmonies, playful and imaginative interaction between the violin and piano, touches of chromaticism, and alternating moods and tempos."[28] Rae Linda Brown considered it a "highlight of the CD . . . a substantial (almost fifteen minutes) work in the late nineteenth-century romantic tradition. Tonally conservative, it is not without technical demands. The work requires complete balance between the two instruments."[29] In 1996 it was published by Vivace Press.

Smith began the *Sonata for Violin and Piano* just before receiving her Bachelor of Music degree from the American Conservatory of Music in Chicago in 1943. She resumed work on it in 1947 while at the Juilliard School, in Vittorio Giannini's class in larger forms of music.

When she later showed the work to Irving Fine at the Berkshire Festival at Tanglewood, the first movement reminded him of Fauré. Indeed, this work, more than any of her others, captures the combination of lyrical gravity and whimsy, modal ambiguity and transparent contrapuntal texture so typical of French neo-classicism. The work is in the standard three movements, fast, slow, and fast. This conventional format defines the basic neoclassical spirit of the work, and also serves to frame some unexpected departures in each of the movements. The juxtaposition of the predictable and unpredictable gives the sonata its unique character and charm.

In the first movement, after the presentation of the broadly lyrical first theme in B-flat minor, with its stately, steady half-note accompaniment combined with flowing eighth-notes, the sprightly, playful second theme, marked "Allegro di molto," suddenly enters in the key of A major, a half-step lower rather than the more usual relative major or dominant key. In place of development there is a contrasting section, marked "espressivo," in E minor. This section gradually quickens its pace, creating the expectation of a grand reentry, only to settle quietly into the stately measures of the opening theme. Balance and order are confirmed when the second theme returns in the original key.

Unexpected key relationships, unusual modal shifts, and chromatic modulations enhance the shifting moods, alternately mysterious and mischievous, in each movement of the work. Even the serene second movement, which starts off well-grounded in the relative D-flat major, soon starts to undergo subtle "sea changes," mysterious ambiguities in key and mode, even before interjecting an astonishing shift of key to G major, a tritone relationship to D-flat, in its Viennese waltz-like middle section. The waltz vacillates between major and minor, finally returning to the opening theme in D-flat major before settling to a sublimely peaceful close. This movement was a favorite of Smith's.

The last, "Vivace," movement carries this modal and tonal ambiguity the farthest, transforming it from a mystery into a lighthearted joke. The opening theme begins with a lowered seventh, casting doubt on whether it is in B-flat major or minor, but after some playfully shifty racing about, it settles demurely into a contrasting lyrical second theme in the completely predictable dominant key of F major. The next episode in this ABACABA rondo form is a freely composed imitative canon in G minor, juxtaposing erudite solemnity with the surrounding mischievous activity. After a last reappearance of the lyrical second melody, the main theme returns for the final time, with one last naughty tweak of our ears.

Variations on a Theme by MacDowell (1947)

The *Variations on a Theme by MacDowell* (1947) for solo piano was completed the same year as the *Sonata for Violin and Piano*, while Smith was studying composition at the Juilliard School of Music. It was always a favorite of hers, and she was still revising portions of it as late as 1989.[30]

The theme she chose by the nineteenth-century American composer Edward MacDowell (1861–1908) is from his *Air*, Op. 49, No. 1 (1894), less known than its companion piece, *Rigaudon*, Op. 49, No. 2. The harmonies are typical of the

German late-romantic school in which MacDowell was trained, highly chromatic and replete with augmented sixth chords resolving irregularly to the tonic. Smith took the first 16 measures of the *Air* in A minor, its four regular four-measure phrases moving in stately half notes, supported by somber chords. She states these in her theme just as MacDowell wrote them, "Nobilmente e Largo," without any changes or additions.

She then proceeds to explore the theme in 10 variations, the first nine in A minor and the climactic tenth in A major. One could consider them as three sets of three variations, grouped by certain similarities. Variations I through III are derived from the melody of the theme, while variations IV through IX contain little or no reference to the melody, and are based instead on the bass line and harmonies of the theme. The tenth variation turns our attention back to the melody, set in chorale-like four-part major harmony, and enlarged with an introduction and an extended conclusion.

The first variation includes the most complete statement of the theme in half notes, with flowing eighth-note counterpoint in both right and left hands, moving for the most part in parallel sixths but also at times in contrary motion. The original harmonies are altered only slightly, the subdominant chord in measure 3 replaced by a Neapolitan chord in root position. This serene variation is followed by a more playful one in dancing 6/8 dotted rhythms. Only the first two phrases of the theme's melody appear in the bass line, with a new counterpoint in the treble. Again the original harmonies are followed fairly closely, with a Neapolitan chord substituting for a dominant late in the variation. The third in this subset of three variations, marked "poco piu animato," picks up the pace further. Its melody in running triplets begins by incorporating the notes of the first phrase of the original theme as the first note of each triplet, but soon abandons the theme entirely to roam freely. It expands in rising contours, the left hand joining the triplets in arpeggiated figuration bringing the set of three variations to an exuberant cadenza-like close.

The fourth variation employs the bass line of the theme in half notes in the left hand, alternating with chords, while the right hand provides a quietly flowing eighth-note melody. The melody features slurred, falling four-note stepwise groups across the bar line, stressing the offbeats against the steady half-note motion in the bass. Harmonies remain close to the original theme. In the fifth variation, the falling eighth-note melodic figuration inverts to rising 16th-note groups. These alternate with broken 16th-note arpeggiated figurations in the left hand in which the original theme's bass line remains as the first note of each group. The sixth variation eliminates the theme's bass line, retaining only the theme's harmonies. It is characterized by dotted rhythms and vigorous chordal leaps. The last subset of three variations begins serenely again, the tied right hand eighth notes producing a syncopation against the beat, reminiscent of the fourth variation's cross rhythms. The left hand moves in widely spaced triplet eighths, the first note of each triplet again tracing the bass line of the theme. This focus on motion and meter is continued in the 5/8 meter of the next (eighth) variation, in which the left hand moves in flowing eighths, each group of five beginning with the theme's bass line. The right hand maintains a rhythm of 2+2+1 (eighth values) as its melody thickens from single notes, to double sixths, to chords. The ninth variation shifts to 6/4 meter, with the right hand melody in a steady rhythmic pattern of 3+2+1 (quarter values). The bass line and harmonies follow the original theme while the right-hand melody expands in ever more richly expressive contours and thickening chords.

The last variation provides an effective finale to the entire work, beginning with an extended introduction of grand flourishes, runs leading to massive chords, and extended triplet figuration gradually slowing quietly to a half-cadence on the dominant in preparation for what follows. The melody of the theme then reappears in a four-part chorale, harmonized in even more richly chromatic chords than its original statement. The first and third phrases retain their four-measure structure, but the second phrase is extended by several measures of sequences over a pedal point. The fourth and last phrase is also prolonged and expanded by cadenza-like flourishes and octave doublings.

Smith displays a dazzling command of the melodic and harmonic vocabulary of MacDowell and the late-Romantic style. Her use of this vocabulary is never obtrusive or excessively flamboyant, showing restraint while demonstrating a complete comfort with and mastery of the style. Only faint traces of her more modern harmonies and progressions can be discerned, and the originality of the set lies in its unself-conscious and completely natural unfolding within its own idiom.

Two Short Preludes for Piano (1953)

Smith's *Two Short Preludes for Piano* are in contrasting styles, with the second one predominantly lyrical and contrapuntal. She said she "really wrote it first, but it's going to be number two" because it was not completed at the time of her interview and, as it turned out, was never finished by her. I completed the prelude, and the pair was published by Vivace Press in a collection of Smith's solo piano works (2001). The second prelude incorporates many of her signature characteristics—linear counterpoint and modal ambiguity—and combines them by stages with an increasingly dissonant harmonic palette. The meter remains stable in 4/4 time, with very few changes. The prelude begins with a gently flowing right-hand melody in the Phrygian mode on G, some 15 measures long. The melody moves mostly by steps with very few leaps, the largest a descending fifth, and its range lies within an octave. A second voice enters one measure later, imitating the melody in a strict two-part canon at the octave for its full duration. At that point the two-part texture is enlarged into five-part quartal parallel harmonies under the same melody, increasing in volume and becoming more dissonant. The lowest parallel fourths expand to martial-sounding fortissimo parallel fifths as the section reaches a climax, then subsides. After a pause, the gentle melody returns in the left hand, inverted this time and marked "tranquillo." The tonal center has changed to B-flat, and the mode is ambiguous, the seventh degree shifting back and forth between A-flat and A-natural, sometimes sounding both simultaneously in different voices. The section closes quietly on a G major chord, reaffirming the original key. A middle section begins with octaves in both hands in a marchlike canon (imitated this time six beats later) building in a crescendo. Then, instead of the expected climax, it shifts into a development of the eighth-note upbeat motif that opens the piece. This repeatedly interrupted two-note upbeat motive builds in tension and volume, enhancing the relief when the opening melody finally reappears, now in triumphant five-part quartal harmony. The dissonance is intensified by combining the modal shifts against each other. The recapitulation continues with the left-hand inversion, gentle and serene for a brief time. Abruptly the octave doubling returns in the left hand, departing farther and farther from the original key as the volume increases, to bring the piece to a clangorous, bitonal ending.

In the original order, this bitonal ending effectively leads up to the following prelude. That prelude (now number one) is more dissonant and angular than many of Smith's other works, but with the same natural, spontaneous sense of rhetorical gesture. She says that she wrote it in defiance of all the rules she had to learn prohibiting tritones and parallel fifths. The overall shape of this short piece is achieved in a total of four phrases. The first phrase, a 12-measure gesture, begins with the interval of an open fifth on middle C alternating tightly with the major triad a half-step higher on C-sharp. The tightness of the half-step is gradually stretched, as the interval and chord move from a half-step apart to a whole step, then a major third apart, and finally to fifths on C and triads on G-sharp alternating in a crescendo of flurries up and down the keyboard, ending fortissimo on an open perfect fifth on low C.

The second phrase, nine measures long, begins again with the alternating open fifth and major triad but diminishes to quiet, meditative half- and whole-note open fifths, ending again in the lowest register, but now quietly on E. It is as if the piece is searching for its tonal center (tonic-dominant relationship or a similar polarity), trying C in the first phrase, then E in the second phrase.

In the third and longest phrase of 18 measures, this groping for balance and resolution continues, the vocabulary of open fifths and triads enlarging to include second inversion chords, opening up to octaves and finally expanding in contrary motion to the farthest reaches of the keyboard to reiterated simultaneous octaves on fortissimo F-sharps in both hands.

The fourth and final phrase of nine measures begins again with the triads alternating half-steps apart like the opening, but it immediately combines all the preceding intervallic relationships among the triads in a cascade, ending in widespread octaves on C. The piece thus ends firmly on the C tonal center with which it opened, providing a kind of resolution from the earlier reiterated octaves on F-sharp. The highly dissonant interval of the tritone between F-sharp and C (dividing the octave exactly in half) has finally assumed the function of the dominant-tonic relationship.

The changing meters of 2/4, 3/4, 4/4, and 5/4, and the irregular lengths of phrases convey a sense of dramatic and rhetorical gesture that is spontaneous and unpredictable. One does not miss a regular pulse, for the pacing of tension and release is so satisfying. The conflict of consonant perfect fifths with dissonant minor seconds and tritones, the groping for tonal balance and center, and the culmination in the tonal symmetry and polarity of the F-sharp and C combine to create a marvelously expressive work which is at the same time abstract and cerebral.

LIST OF WORKS

Archives Holding Scores

(CBMR) Unpublished manuscripts in the Irene Britton Smith Collection in the archives of the Center for Black Music Research, Columbia College, Chicago.

(AMRC/CBMR) The Helen Walker-Hill Collection, located in duplicate at the American Music Research Center at the University of Colorado and at the Center for Black Music Research, Columbia College, Chicago.

(Smith list, Smith interview) Compositions mentioned by Smith but not located.

Instrumental Music

Violin

Reminiscence (violin, piano). 1941. Performed sometime in 1942 by Irene Britton Smith at the American Conservatory, and 17 May 1942 by Adele Mdjeska in Kimball Hall at the American Conservatory. (AMRC/CBMR, CBMR)

Sonata for Violin and Piano. 1947. Pullman, Wash.: Vivace Press, 1996. Three movements: Allegro cantabile, Andante con sentimento, Vivace. First performed February 1990 by violinist Gregory Walker and pianist Helen Walker-Hill at the Denver Public Library. See discography. (AMRC/CBMR, CBMR)

Piano

Fugue in A Flat Major. N.d. (CBMR)

Invention in Two Voices. 1940. (Smith list)

Nocturne. 1945. Composed in New York when she came to take her entrance exam for the Juilliard School of Music. (Smith interview)

Passacaglia and Fugue in C-sharp Minor. 1940. *Passacaglia* published: Stevens Point, Wis.: Vivace Press, 2001. (AMRC/CBMR, CBMR)

Prelude. N.d. (CBMR)

Preludes I and II. N.d. Béla Bartók, arranged by Smith. (CBMR)

Two Short Preludes for Piano. 1953. Stevens Point, Wis.: Vivace Press, 2001. First performed by Irene Britton Smith "years ago" at an International Society of Contemporary Music meeting. Prelude No. 1 performed by Helen Walker-Hill in January 1990 at Stanford University, etc. (AMRC/CBMR)

Variations on a Theme by MacDowell. 1947. Stevens Point, Wis.: Vivace Press, 2001. (AMRC/CBMR, CBMR)

Instrumental Ensemble

Fugue in G minor (violin, viola, cello). 1938. Performed by student trio at the American Conservatory in 1938. (CBMR, Smith interview)

Orchestra

Autumnal Reverie (piccolo, flute, oboe 1 & 2, clarinet 1 & 2, bassoon 1 & 2, trumpet 1 & 2, trombone, bass trombone, violin 1 & 2, viola, cello, bass). N.d. (CBMR)

Sinfonietta (flute 1 & 2, oboe 1 & 2, clarinet 1 & 2, bassoon 1 & 2, horn 1–4, trumpet 1 & 2, trombone, bass trombone, timpani, drums, triangle, violin 1 & 2, viola, cello, bass). 1956. Three movements: Moderato tranquillo, Adagio, Energico. (AMRC/CBMR, CBMR)

Sonata No. III for piano by Edvard Grieg, arranged and orchestrated by Smith (flute 1 & 2, oboe 1 & 2, clarinet 1 & 2, bassoon 1 & 2, horn 1–4, trumpet 1 & 2, trombone 1 & 2, timpani, snare, triangle, harp, glockenspiel, violin 1 & 2, viola, cello, bass). N.d. (CBMR)

Three Fantastic Dances by Dmitri Shostakovitch, arranged and orchestrated by Smith (piccolo, flute 1 & 2, oboe 1 & 2, clarinet 1 & 1, bass clarinet, horn 1–4, trumpet 1 & 2, trombone 1 & 2, bass trombone, tuba, timpani, xylophone, violin 1 & 2, viola, cello, bass). N.d. (CBMR)

Untitled—Variations on a Theme (piccolo, flute, oboe 1 & 2, clarinet 1 & 2, bassoon 1 & 2, horn 1–4, trumpet 1 & 2, trombone 1 & 2, tuba, celeste, violin 1 & 2, viola 1 & 2, cello, bass). N.d. (CBMR)

Vocal Music

Solo Voice

The Angel Roll the Stone Away (voice, piano). N.d. Spiritual. Incomplete. (CBMR)

Dream Cycle (soprano, piano). 1947. Text: Paul Laurence Dunbar. Contents: (1) Over the Hill; (2) By the Pool; (3) Sunset; (4) Why Fades a Dream? Sunset performed by Lolla McCullough Shavers, 27 April 1971, at the Colonial House on E. 79th Street in Chicago. Sunset and Why Fades a Dream? performed by Jo Ann Pickens, 19 October 1977 in Dame Myra Hess Memorial Concert series at Chicago Public Library and broadcast over WFMT. (AMRC/CBMR, CBMR)

Let Us Break Bread Together (baritone/soprano/mezzo). 1948. Spiritual. Performed by Theodore Charles Stone, 20 February 1972, at Jones Commercial High School, Chicago. (AMRC/CBMR)

Psalm 121 (voice, piano). N.d. Incomplete. (CBMR)

Trees of the Night (soprano, piano). 1954. Text: Irene Britton Smith. (AMRC/CBMR, CBMR)

Vocal Ensemble

Born Free (two voices). N.d. Spiritual. (CBMR)
Let Us Break Bread Together (mezzo, soprano, baritone). N.d. Spiritual. (CBMR)
Not a Word (solo voice and four male voices). N.d. Spiritual. (CBMR)
Panis Angelicus (three female voices). N.d. (CBMR)
Psalm 25 (three female voices). N.d. (CBMR)

Swing Low and *Were You There* (three female voices). N.d. Combined spirituals. (CBMR)

Chorus

Born Anew (SATB, solo baritone, organ). 1952. Text: The New Testament. (AMRC/ CBMR, CBMR)

Fairest Lord Jesus (SA, organ). 1945. New York: G. Schirmer, 1946. Crusader Hymn. Copyright returned to Smith, now belongs to CBMR. (AMRC/CBMR, CBMR)

God Is Our Refuge/Psalm 46 (SATB, solo baritone, piano). 1940. (AMRC/CBMR, CBMR)

Good Morning (unison voices, piano). N.d. (CBMR)

It's Me, O Lord (SSA). N.d. Spiritual. (CBMR)

Psalm 130 (SATB, organ). N.d. (CBMR)

The Story of Crosspatch (SATB). N.d. (CBMR)

Other

Methods and Materials for Teaching Word Perception in Kindergarten through Grade Three. Chicago: University of Chicago Press, 1960. Reprinted in Albert J. Mazuriewicz, *New Perspectives in Reading Instruction* (1964).

NOTES

I wish to express my appreciation to Eva Butler and Jeanne Ellis, Irene Smith's sisters-in-law, and to Leon Despres, her attorney, for their kindness and cooperation. I would also like to thank Suzanne Flandreau, archivist at the Center for Black Music Research, for her invaluable assistance with this chapter, and the Center for Black Music Research for permission to use photos and quotations from Smith's letters and poetry in the Irene Britton Smith Collection.

Full references are given in the bibliography at the end of the chapter.

1. "My Song Is His" (1947), unpublished poem in the Irene Britton Smith Collection at the Center for Black Music Research at Columbia College, Chicago, quoted by permission. From now on, this collection will be abbreviated CBMR.

2. Irene Britton Smith, interview with the author, 7 July 1989, in Chicago. All Smith quotations not otherwise identified come from this interview.

3. A photo of the Harrison Ferrell Orchestra taken in 1931 appears in Handy (Picture Gallery).

4. Florence Price, letter to Smith of 27 January 1936 (CBMR). Quoted by permission.

5. Smith, undated letter (ca. 1978) to Stella Roberts (CBMR).

6. This was not a happy experience. She felt "out of the loop," up against classmates who were composers with more experience, studying a method foreign to her. The texts were by Dallin and Hanson.

7. *CBMR Digest*, p. 7, with Smith's snapshot of Julia Perry at Tanglewood. Elayne Jones was later timpanist with the San Francisco Symphony, and Mattiwilda Dobbs sang with the Metropolitan Opera Company. In her interview, Smith added that composers Olivier Messiaen and Easley Blackwood were also there that summer.

8. Smith, telephone interview with Scott Schlegel in August 1990 for a National Public Radio *Horizons* program broadcast on 10 October 1990.

9. One of her students, Judith Anderson, graduated magna cum laude from Harvard University and was active in improving conditions at Harvard for black students.

10. This large-scale outdoor sculpture was commissioned by the New York World's Fair in 1939 and destroyed by bulldozers at the end of the fair. Augusta Savage (1892–1962) was a pioneering black artist who struggled against racism to study art in Europe and to open opportunities to black artists.

11. Unconsciously, however, Smith displayed fears originating in old patterns of injustice, such as the appropriation of black music and ideas by white musicians and publishers without acknowledgment or remuneration. She would not give permission to include her compositions in an anthology of music by black women because she was afraid of losing "her children," as she called them.

12. Florence Price Elementary School, built and dedicated in 1964, is located on South Drexel Blvd. near 43rd Street.

13. Smith, telephone conversation with the author, 9 February 1990.

14. Smith, interview with Scott Schlegel.

15. In addition to the 36 works, her composition exercise books contain a *Sonata, Two-part Invention, Suite*, and *Three-part Invention*, as well as sketch books for her *Sinfonietta* and other works.

16. Smith stated this in the interview with Schlegel and an undated letter to Stella Roberts (CBMR).

17. Her composition notebooks include a resource list for African-American and calypso music. Her collection of scores also contains works by black composers Florence Price, Margaret Bonds, Clarence Cameron White, and Julia Perry, as well as Lili Boulanger, Ravel, Delius, and Paderewski.

18. Especially Tchaikovsky's fifth and sixth symphonies, and Brahms' first, second, and fourth symphonies. Her composition notebooks include a transcription for piano of Franck's *Symphony in D Minor*. The music books in her library lean heavily to French treatises and exercise books by Théodore Dubois, Marcel Dupré, Andre Gedalge, Olivier Messiaen, Marcelle Soulage, and Georges Dandelot.

19. Smith, undated letter to Roberts (CBMR).

20. Ibid.

21. Obviously demonstrations of "species counterpoint," as it is called in traditional counterpoint studies.

22. Composition exercise books in IBS Collection. They include at least three orchestration notebooks, as well as several each for counterpoint, harmony, and composition.

23. A final major chord in minor works, beloved of J. S. Bach and other baroque composers, said to have originated in the Picardy region of France. It gives a dramatic effect of triumphant resolution.

24. Her personal collection of poetry included several by Countee Cullen, and she may have set his "Leaves" (if so, the setting is lost). Her papers included correspondence from Cullen concerning her request to use the poem. Other favored sources were the Bible, especially the Psalms. She felt that recent poetry by blacks was "too complaining." She herself wrote the text for *Trees of the Night*.

25. Ellen T. Harris, letter to Smith, 10 April 1989 (CBMR).

26. Raymond.

27. *Strings.*
28. Harbach, p. 16.
29. Brown, p. 117.
30. She practiced the form in several "theme and variation exercises" in her composition notebooks.

BIBLIOGRAPHY

Brown, Rae Linda. "Recording Reviews: *Kaleidoscope: Music by African-American Women.*" *American Music* 16, no. 1 (Spring 1998): 116–118.

CBMR Digest. "From Our Photo File." Vol. 4, no. 1 (Spring 1991): 7.

Dunbar, Paul Laurence. *The Complete Poems of Paul Laurence Dunbar.* N.Y.: Dodd Mead, 1913.

Handy, D. Antoinette. *Black Women in American Bands and Orchestras.* Metuchen, N.J.: Scarecrow Press, 1981.

Harbach, Barbara. "Review of *Kaleidoscope: Music by African-American Women.*" *Women of Note Quarterly* 4, no.2 (May 1996): 15–26.

Mackey, Jocelyn. "Recordings: *Kaleidoscope: Music by African-American Women.*" *Pan Pipes* 88, no. 2 (Winter 1996):17.

Raymond, David. "Kaleidoscope: Black Women." *American Record Guide* 59, no. 5 (September/October 1996): 253.

Smith, Irene Britton. Correspondence and poetry in the Irene Britton Smith Collection at the Center for Black Music Research at Columbia College, Chicago.

Strings, 11 (July/August 1996): 115.

Struzzi, Diane. "Irene Britton Smith, Composer." *Chicago Tribune,* 17 February 1999.

Walker-Hill, Helen. "Black Women Composers in Chicago: Then and Now." *Black Music Research Journal* 12, no.1 (Spring 1992): 1–24.

———. *Piano Music by Black Women Composers: A Catalog of Solo and Ensemble Works.* Westport, Conn.: Greenwood Press, 1992.

———. *Music by Black Women Composers: A Bibliography of Available Scores.* CBMR Monographs no. 5. Chicago: Center for Black Music Research, 1995.

———. "Chicago Composer Irene Britton Smith." *Women of Note Quarterly* 5, no. 1 (February 1997): 5–8.

———. "Smith, Irene Britton." In *International Dictionary of Black Composers.* Edited by Samuel A. Floyd, Jr. Chicago: Fitzroy Dearborn, 1999.

DISCOGRAPHY

Sonata for Violin and Piano. Performed by Gregory Walker, violin, and Helen Walker-Hill, piano, on *Kaleidoscope: Music by African-American Women.* Leonarda Productions CD, LE 339, 1995.

Dorothy Rudd Moore. Courtesy of the Composer.

6

DOROTHY RUDD MOORE
(b. 1940)

CHRONOLOGY

1940 Born 4 June in Wilmington, Del., to James Monroe Rudd and Rebecca L. Ryan Rudd; oldest of six siblings.

1950s Studied piano privately with Naomi Roberts in New Castle, Del.

1955–58 Attended Howard High School in Wilmington, studied clarinet with Harry Andrews; studied piano at the Wilmington School of Music.

1956 Composed *Flight* for solo piano; began writing popular songs.

1958–63 Attended Howard University, studied piano with Thomas Kerr, voice with Louise Burge, and composition with Mark Fax.

1962 Composed *Reflections* for symphonic wind ensemble, which won competition at Howard, and *Songs from the Rubaiyat* for voice and oboe.

1963 Wrote music and libretto of musical, *Race for Space*, and performed lead role at Howard; *Symphony No. 1* completed, one of 10 selected by National Symphony Orchestra for performance at Constitution Hall in Washington, D.C.; graduated magna cum laude with B.A. in theory and composition from Howard University; received Lucy Moten Fellowship to attend the American Conservatory in Fontainebleau, France, that summer, studied with Nadia Boulanger; *Songs from the Rubaiyat* premiered at Fontainebleau.

1964 Composed *Ballad of the Winter Soldier* for benefit concert for Congress of Racial Equality, performed by Howard Roberts Chorale at Philharmonic Hall, New York, in September; married Kermit Moore in New York in December.

1965 Studied composition with Chou Wen-chung; taught theory and piano at Harlem School of the Arts; completed *Baroque Suite for Unaccompanied Violoncello*, premiered by Kermit Moore in 1965.

1966–67   Composed *Three Pieces for Violin and Piano*, premiered by Richard Elias in
           1967.

1968   Cofounded Society of Black Composers; began to teach piano and voice pri-
           vately; composed *Modes* for string quartet, premiered in 1968.

1969   Taught music history and appreciation at New York University; composed
           Moods for viola and cello, and *Lament for Nine Instruments*, both premiered
           in 1969.

1970   Completed *Trio No. 1* for violin, cello, and piano, and song cycle *From the
           Dark Tower* for voice, cello, and piano, both premiered in 1970.

1971   Taught music history and appreciation at Bronx Community College; com-
           pleted *Dirge and Deliverance* for cello and piano, premiered by Kermit Moore
           and Zita Carno at Alice Tully Hall, New York, in 1972.

1972   Began vocal studies with Lola Hayes (until 1993); received American Music
           Center grant; orchestrated four songs of *From the Dark Tower*, premiered that
           October; composed *Weary Blues* for baritone, piano, and cello.

1974   Composed *Dream and Variations* for solo piano, premiered by Zita Carno in
           February 1975.

1975   "Salute to Dorothy Rudd Moore" concert of works by Moore in Carnegie
           Recital Hall, New York, 23 February, with U.S. premiere of *Songs from the
           Rubaiyat* sung by Moore.

1976   Completed song cycle *Sonnets on Love, Rosebuds, and Death* for voice, vi-
           olin, piano, premiered by Miriam Burton and Sanford Allen in 1976.

1977   Composed *In Celebration* for chorus, soloists, and piano, premiered by Triad
           Chorale at Alice Tully Hall, New York, in 1977.

1978   Composed *Night Fantasy* for clarinet and piano, premiered in 1994 by Keith
           King, clarinet, and Daniel Michalak, piano, at Indiana University; composed
           A Little Whimsy for piano.

1978–85   Composed opera *Frederick Douglass*, premiered by Opera Ebony in 1985.

1980   Presented vocal recital at Wilmington School of Music, 18 May.

1985   Received grant from the New York State Council on the Arts.

1986   Served on panel for the National Endowment for the Arts 1986–88; completed
           Transcension for chamber orchestra, premiered by the Brooklyn Philharmonic
           Orchestra at the Brooklyn Museum of Art in 1986.

1987   Served on Illinois Council for the Arts.

1988   Served on New York State Council for the Arts 1988–91.

1989   Composed song cycle *Flowers of Darkness* for tenor and piano, premiered in
           1990 by William Brown and Philip Morehead.

1990   Visiting guest composer at Oberlin College in February; served on Wisconsin Arts Council; *Modes* for string quartet performed by members of Atlanta Symphony Orchestra at Spelman College.

1992   Served on panel for the Detroit Symphony Orchestra's Unisys African-American Composers Competition.

1995   Concert of music by Kermit Moore and Dorothy Rudd Moore presented at Greenwich House Music School, New York, on 11 May.

1996   Served as judge for the Detroit Symphony Orchestra's Unisys African-American Composers Competition.

1997   Composed *Voices from the Light* for girls' choir, oboe, string quartet, and piano, premiered in 1997 by Girls' Choir of Harlem at Alice Tully Hall, New York.

2001   Completed novel *Pieces of Moon* (begun in 1968, revised 1980s).

> The most gratifying experience of all is the writing itself. Of course, I want my music to be liked, but I must first be true to my own ideas. I want to communicate. I think the best way to do that is to be honest.[1]

Ever since the beginning of her career in the early 1960s, the music of Dorothy Rudd Moore has been highly respected for its communicative power, integrity, intelligence, and impeccable craft. While she was still an undergraduate, her symphonic wind ensemble work, *Reflections*, won a Howard University competition, and a year later (1963) her *Symphony No. 1* was one of ten finalist compositions (the only one by a woman among the anonymous contestants from area colleges) for a National Symphony Orchestra performance at Constitution Hall in Washington, D.C. Her works have been commissioned and premiered by top artists in their fields. She was one of the founders of the Society of Black Composers in 1968, and her works were regular features of the society's concerts in New York City. She has received fellowships and grants from Meet the Composer, American Music Center, Opera Ebony, and the New York State Council on the Arts.

Despite this recognition, Moore has never pursued fame or pandered to audience tastes. She has gone her own way without regard to what has been considered fashionable, writing only those works she felt compelled to write. Her reputation is based on a small body of solidly crafted works in a variety of forms including songs, choral works, instrumental pieces, chamber music, extended song cycles, orchestral music, and an opera.

BIOGRAPHY

Moore was born on 4 June 1940 in Wilmington, Delaware, five miles from the small town of New Castle, Delaware, where she grew up. Now almost merged with Wilmington, New Castle still retains reminders of the idyllic Americana of Moore's childhood: its cobblestone streets, village green, grand old New England-style houses on the Strand, and Battery Park with its wharf from which a ferry used to cross the Delaware River to Stanhope, New Jersey. The Rudd family home was about a mile out of town, across the road from an apple orchard and flower farm. At that time, the 2,000 or so white and black residents lived together harmoniously. Many of the black residents were related to Moore's family, the Bungys and the Rudds. Pastor Bungy, Moore's maternal great-grandfather, was born in New Castle, and served as minister of one of the two black churches in town, Mt. Salem Methodist Church, where they still celebrate Bungy Day on the third Sunday of September.

Although some spirituals were heard at Mt. Salem, the choir and congregation usually sang Methodist hymns, and cantatas on special occasions. Its ministers were well educated, and their sermons were delivered with restraint and decorum. Classical music was part of the social fabric of the black community, and there were many opportunities to perform at church musicales, Easter services, church breakfasts, and teas. Moore's mother, a fine soprano, was often called upon to sing at these functions, and at weddings and funerals.

Dorothy began singing at an early age, and she received her first piano lessons from her mother. At age 10 she began piano lessons with Naomi Roberts, a local music teacher. She would often practice in the Mt. Salem Church, next door to her grandparents' house, and liked to amuse herself by making up tunes to children's poems. While growing up, she was frequently taken to performances of the Philadelphia Symphony Orchestra, conducted by Eugene Ormandy, and recalls assuming that all orchestras must sound as polished as they did.

Dorothy's father worked for the U.S. government in Philadelphia, and served on the Board of Education for the New Castle School District. Her parents wanted her to have the same excellent education they had enjoyed. They sent her to elementary school in nearby Millside, and then to Bancroft Junior High School and Howard Senior High School in Wilmington. She also studied piano at the Wilmington School of Music with a teacher of German background. To get to school from her home in New Castle, she had to rise very early in the morning and take three different buses. She was a member of the choir, the orchestra, and the band, and also did artwork for the school yearbook. Moore is proud of the fact that her early teachers were African Americans of outstanding ability and experience. Her English teacher, Miss Sadie Jones, introduced her to great literature and encouraged her love of reading, and also coached her on her valedictory speech. A particularly influential teacher in high school was Harry Andrews, who would later become superintendent of music for Wilmington's schools. He formed a music theory class especially for Moore and a fellow student, the pianist Robert Jordan, and taught her to play the clarinet so that she could integrate the all-boys school band. By the time she entered college she had a thorough musical grounding.

Moore was the oldest of six siblings, having four sisters and one brother.[2] Her sister Simone studied voice and flute at Chatham College, and continued to sing in choirs and give piano lessons, but she chose a career in banking, along with her other sisters. The immediate family also included a favorite uncle, Walter S. Ryan, who taught Humanities at Morgan State College in Baltimore. A graduate of Howard University, he also attended McGill University in Canada. He completed a graduate degree at Harvard University when Dorothy was 10, and she and her grandmother traveled to Cambridge to attend his graduation. This experience inspired dreams of some day attending college in Boston.

Moore remembers being something of a snob as a teenager, avoiding the hangouts, dances, and the music favored by her contemporaries. She preferred to listen to symphonic music on the radio. Nevertheless, she enjoyed writing popular and love songs (which she continued to do in the 1960s, in Paris and New York). At age 16 she wrote her first serious piece of music for solo piano, called *Flight*. It was inspired by Duke Ellington, who, along with Bach, was (and still is) her favorite composer. Two years later she met Ellington when he appeared at the Brandywine Music Box in Pennsylvania; he invited her and three of her friends who also attended the concert to his suite at the Dupont Hotel in Wilmington afterward, an unforgettable experience. (He would not permit her and her young friends to order alcoholic drinks, suggesting some ice cream instead.) Ellington was very interested in Dorothy's desire to be a composer, and she renewed contact with him after moving to New York.

Moore has always been grateful to her parents for not placing any limits on her aspirations and allowing her to explore as many avenues as possible. A particularly important experience for her during her high school years was her membership in the Civil Air Patrol, an auxiliary of the U.S. Air Force, which she joined because she loved airplanes and wanted to fly. The cadets attained rank (Dorothy became a lieutenant), marched in Memorial Day parades, and were flown to other northeastern Air Force bases for encampments with their counterparts in other states. With her identification card, Dorothy could go to the Du Pont air base and request airplane rides on the "two seaters," a privilege which must have greatly impressed her schoolmates. She was particularly proud to be one of two female cadets chosen from Delaware to attend an all-girl national encampment at Lackland Air Force Base in Texas, where she jumped from the parachute tower and went through regular airmen's training. There were few African-American young people in the organization, and when they stopped at an airfield in Mississippi on the way to Texas, the black workers in the officers' canteen were amazed and apprehensive for her.

Although Dorothy had been accepted at the Boston Conservatory, her uncle convinced her to attend his alma mater, Howard University, in Washington, D.C. At first she planned to major in music education and to write music as an avocation. Later she decided that composition was more than a side interest and changed her major, a decision that was supported by her teachers, Warner Lawson, dean of the fine arts department, and Mark Fax, her theory and composition teacher.[3] She minored in piano, studying with Thomas Kerr, and took voice lessons from Louise Burge. She soon produced music of high quality and sophistication, winning competitions and receiving public performances of her work. In her senior year she wrote the libretto and music for a musical, *Race for Space*, and starred in the production at Howard University's Crampton Auditorium.

Her experiences at Howard expanded Dorothy's world in more than musical directions. A three-month tour of South America and the Caribbean by the Howard University Concert Choir, directed by Warner Lawson, exposed her to places, people, and social conditions she had never known in her protected youth in New Castle. Her appetite was whetted for travel abroad. In 1963 she graduated magna cum laude and received a Lucy Moten Fellowship for study at the American Conservatory at Fontainebleau, France.

She left for France planning to stay indefinitely, and even asked her parents to ship all her belongings to her. She had romantic notions of living in a garret, washing dishes by day and composing by night, until she discovered that she would need a work permit. In any case, by summer's end she was thoroughly homesick and decided that she would rather try to live in New York, where her parents would be only a few hours away.

Her time in France was well spent, however. Among the students she met at Fontainebleau was the pianist Philip Morehead, who would later perform several of her works in the United States. She studied composition privately with Nadia Boulanger, sang in her madrigal choir, and took her class in form and analysis. While still a student at Howard, Moore had heard Boulanger speak at the U.S. State Department and was already in awe of her. At Fontainebleau, Boulanger was won over by Moore's playing of the Bach *B Minor Prelude* from *The Well Tempered Clavier*. She refused to look at her *Symphony* saying, "You're too young to write symphonies." Boulanger was so impressed with her *Twelve Songs on the Rubaiyat of Omar Khayyám*, for mezzo-soprano and oboe, however, that she chose it for performance in a regular evening concert in the Jeu de Paume hall at the Palace of Fontainebleau. Moore never forgot the rigor of Boulanger's analysis, nor the pristine pitch and pronunciation she demanded of her madrigal singers.

The decision to return to the United States was fortuitous, because soon after, her uncle was discovered to have cancer and she was able to spend time with him during his last years. Moore settled in New York and found employment, first with First National City Bank and later as a receptionist in the famous Brill Building on Tin Pan Alley, for a singing group called The Tokens. Perhaps those surroundings inspired her to continue to write popular songs. One of them, *I'm Gonna Beat My Drum Tonight*, was sung by Joyce Bryant in her nightclub routine. In the fall of 1964 Moore left The Tokens and was hired as an assistant director for a benefit program and reception for the original Congress of Racial Equality. It was a major event held at Philharmonic Hall at Lincoln Center with many celebrity guests including Dick Gregory, Ossie and Ruby Davis, Shelley Winters, and Robert Ryan. For that occasion she wrote text and music for a choral piece, *Ballad of the Winter Soldier*, which was orchestrated by Hale Smith and performed by the Howard Roberts Chorale.[4] At a reception following the concert at the home of Arthur Krim, head of Orion Pictures, and his wife, the well-known biologist Matthilda Krim, she met her husband-to-be, cellist/composer/conductor Kermit Moore. He had returned to New York after living in Paris and Brussels for seven years and concertizing throughout Europe.[5] The attraction must have been immediate and intense, because Dorothy began to compose the *Baroque Suite* for unaccompanied cello a few days after she met him, and presented it to him as a wedding gift at their marriage just three months later. Theirs has been a partnership of mutual inspiration and support; they have presented joint programs of their music, and both were founding members of the Society of Black Composers in 1968.

The society lasted until 1976 and had a membership of more than 25 composers, including Stephen Chambers, Noel DaCosta, Carman Moore, and Hale Smith. It established an information center, published a newsletter, gave readings of members' works, and presented public concerts at the Harlem School of the Arts, the Brooklyn Academy of Music, and various colleges. Moore, who served as its vice president, described it as an important self-affirming organization. It played a significant role in bringing African-American composers together and performing their compositions.

During the 1960s Moore studied composition with the well-known composer Chou Wen-chung,[6] a professor at Columbia University. She taught theory and piano at the Harlem School of the Arts (1965), founded by singer Dorothy Maynor, who recruited the Moores to be two of the first teachers at the school. She also taught music appreciation at New York University (1969) and Bronx Community College (1971). She returned to serious voice study and enrolled in the Lola Hayes voice studio, singing operatic roles and participating in recitals. Her performance of her *Songs from the Rubaiyat* in Carnegie Recital Hall in 1975 received a glowing review: "Ms. Moore's voice is mellow and clear, her diction flawless, and her presence angelic."[7] In a "homecoming" solo vocal recital at the Wilmington School of Music in 1980, she sang Bach, Mozart, Schubert, Wolf, Fauré and Puccini in addition to her own *Sonnets on Love, Rosebuds, and Death*, and drew this critical praise: "The voice has a penetrating quality that soared well beyond the confines of the hall. Stylistic taste and know-how were always present."[8] Moore taught, and still teaches, voice privately, along with piano, ear training and sight singing for singers.

In January 1978, tragedy struck Moore's family. Her brother Jimmy died at the age of 31, frozen to death in a blizzard as he tried to dig his car out at Fort Devon in Massachusetts. He had enlisted with the U.S. Marines at the age of

17, with his parents' reluctant permission, and immediately saw action in Vietnam at Danang. Fortunately he returned from the war, and several years later he became a medical technician in the army. He was later diagnosed to have pancreatic cancer, probably as a result of his exposure to Agent Orange in Vietnam. Her brother's death was a devastating blow to Moore.

She had long written poetry as a way to respond to personal and world events, but never set these poems to music because she felt they were too complete as entities. (Her husband Kermit, however, did set five of them in *Five Songs for D.R.M.*) The titles and words of her poems are indicative of her concerns: "To My Brothers" (about the black Americans serving in Vietnam); "The Uninvited" (about the absence of black guests at White House receptions); and "Night Wanderer" ("The heavy fabric of quiet late is woven with threads of deeds undone"). Many of her poems reveal her despair and rage at the human condition. She feels that she is "condemned to always see the glass as half empty." When asked what inspires her to create, despite her views on the world's injustices, Moore said, "There is a little part of me that doesn't want to be defeated, doesn't want to become like 'them,' whoever 'they' are." She chooses to focus instead on her good fortune in having a close family, friends, and a life that is full and rewarding.

Several of her poems ponder human foibles from the perspective of the moon. "Moon Message" and "This Eternal Sphere" are about humans landing on the moon: "Albeit cluttered with Apollo's waste, it speaks to me, And reaffirms my worst fears." In her poem called "Mooning," she asks, "How many times have I seen the moon? . . . We take for granted all the moons; But there are limits to our sighs." Moore had always been fascinated by the moon's beauty and remoteness. This continuing fascination is revealed in the title of her novel, *Pieces of Moon* (which, however, has nothing to do with the moon).

For Moore, music is another way to respond to the world, and with transforming power and energy. Most of her chamber, instrumental, and vocal compositions, all of them substantial works, were written during the turmoil of the late 1960s and 1970s. During the mid-1970s Moore was preparing to compose an opera, a setting of the Greek myth of the unhappy and treacherous Phaedra, portrayed as a young mulatto girl in nineteenth-century New Orleans. But when she received a commission from Opera Ebony in 1978, she abandoned that opera and began historical research for an even larger and more ambitious project, an opera on the life of the great abolitionist Frederick Douglass. She had always been fascinated by Frederick Douglass the man, and this subject gave her the opportunity to deliver in her own libretto "a series of musical meditations on love, death, religion, political oppression and eventual deliverance,"[9] themes which were close to her heart. The opera was a labor of eight years, lasting until its premiere performance in Aaron Davis Hall at City College in New York on 28 June 1985.

With the completion of *Frederick Douglass*, Moore turned to other activities, serving as judge for competitions and participating on panels for several state arts councils and the National Endowment for the Arts. She was commissioned by the Brooklyn Philharmonic to write *Transcension*, a work commemorating Martin Luther King, Jr. (1986), and composed the song cycle *Flowers of Darkness* on a commission from tenor William Brown (1989). In 1990 she had another project in mind, an antiwar piece for orchestra and three singers, with her own text inspired by the Civil War. This project was placed on hold when her inspiration returned to the writing of a novel, another long-term project begun in 1968, revised in the 1980s, and nearing completion at the end of 2000, the aforementioned *Pieces of Moon*.

Moore finds her life full, with teaching, writing, and composing. She has said that she does not care about personal fame, although she is pleased that her music is recognized. One of her fondest memories is being brought to the stage, deeply moved, to acknowledge the enthusiastic audience response to her songs with the premiere of the orchestral version of *From the Dark Tower* at Philharmonic Hall in 1972. Other premieres were also emotional experiences: *Dirge and Deliverance*, written for her husband, and first performed by him in 1972 at Alice Tully Hall, and the premiere of her opera *Frederick Douglass* in 1985.

SOCIAL ISSUES

When Moore was asked how she felt about being categorized as an African-American woman composer, she responded, "That's what I am. I am a composer who is female and who is African-American. Others [composers] are identified by ethnicity, geography, and even religious affiliation. Bach was a German Lutheran." Although she recognized that a composer's music is influenced by everything in his or her life—cultural history, family, life experiences—she was adamant that she didn't write "black music," a term that reminded her of "race music" of an earlier era. Besides being inappropriate, the term, she believes, is used to further segregate—if not belittle—the musical expression of people of African descent. She has a dislike of labels, and elaborated on this subject in an interview with the author Wallace Cheatham: "We are all different . . . no composer that I know of would permit 'typecasting.' . . . It is important that black composers not be ghettoized. Unfortunately certain forces are intent on polarizing our society. . . . There are many black artists in all disciplines and each is an individual with his or her unique experiences."

Moore feels strongly about the multiplicity of African-American experiences: "The 'African-American experience' is a narrow and limiting term. We must not allow others to dictate what we should create nor succumb to the notion that black artists have legitimacy only when dealing with the pathology of what politicians and bureaucrats like to call 'the inner city.' Such myopia deprives people of their humanity and unique vision. . . . African-Americans, like any other group, are vast and various in their musical tastes and appreciation."[10]

Moore's opinions on racism are radical and passionate. With the civil rights struggles and uprisings of the 1960s, and the rise of the Black Panther movement, this passion turned into rage and helplessness at the intractability of human behavior. At that time she wondered if the legal profession would have provided her an opportunity to fight injustice more directly. She supported the Black Panthers, "whose efforts were constantly criticized and vilified in the American Press and by the U.S. government." She would have liked to join them, but since she couldn't do that, she expressed her solidarity through her poetry and music. In 1970 she wrote the song cycle *From the Dark Tower*, an impassioned setting for mezzo-soprano, cello, and piano of texts by eight African-American poets of the Harlem Renaissance, as her "own black power statement," idealistically hoping that "the composition would contribute to enlightenment and understanding." She later realized that works of art have limited influence, and that the world does not change. However, the response of a reviewer in 1972 to *From the Dark Tower* contradicted her pessimism: "All the ranting and raving on the boob-tube in recent years put together haven't equaled the power of those few moments . . . in conveying the message 'We were not eternally made to weep.' It hurt."[11]

For Moore, racism is inextricably bound up with American history, colonialism, and militarism. The Civil War public television series in 1990 reinforced her contention that "Everything redounds to the Civil War. . . . Things aren't worse—they were always bad . . . the South and its northern allies really won that war." She adheres to her conviction of the futility of war, any war, and believes there is no such thing as 'a good war,' since war is based on greed and hate despite the ideological explanations used to justify it. She remembers that she was politicized even as a little girl, acutely aware of the Korean War. She became convinced during her student days at Howard, when the Vietnam War was heating up, "of the futility of war and its destructive consequences." In her poem "Sins of the Fathers," she writes,

> What grievous sins, Almighty One, from dusty centuries hence
> Decreed the wretched misery behind the Auschwitz fence,
> Directed blood to lap the lovely Perfume River's banks,
> And flesh to burn by Napalm from a land that gives you thanks?

She sees no hope of progress, despite all the lessons of history. "Maybe this is the only way the species knows how to act. Maybe war is the way human nature controls population." However, she believes one must continue to hope, and to strive to live out one's ideals, for, as she says in a poem, "Dreams unfurled are dreams no more."

Moore became acutely conscious of the connection between racism and colonialism when she toured South America and the Caribbean with the Howard University Choir: "What I saw there really . . . turned me on the road to seeing the world in a different light. . . . We were wined and dined in American embassies, some of which had signs posted warning the indigenous people to keep off the grass, or to not cross the road unless they were domestics or worked in the garden." She saw similar patterns of discrimination toward the indigenous people and blacks in all countries in the Americas. "This is one person who does not celebrate Columbus's birthday!"

What discourages Moore most is the prevailing political indifference of many Americans, and the willingness to be controlled by news media. "News is selective—orchestrated, controlled. Even the wording is the same from one news channel to the next. . . . The United States government's true Middle East policy, for example, is not publicized." She was irate that when 1,800 people gathered at Cooper Union in New York to protest the U.S. Middle East policy, it was not mentioned in the *New York Times* or any other news source. This mind control is possible, she feels, "because 'feeling good' is too important. The Super Bowl is more important than world suffering, and we casually step over homeless people on the street."

Moore doesn't like to discuss the issue of class and refuses even to use the word. She is aware that the term has cultural and economic implications that are used to judge one's 'station' in life. Regarding her own background, she acknowledges only that her father had a responsible government job and was highly respected, that she knew both sets of grandparents (her maternal great-grandfather was still alive when she was born), and that all of her relatives lived in their own homes.

Moore's distress at the injustice of class distinctions was revealed in her concern for the indigenous people in South America and for the homeless people in New York. She was also disillusioned in Paris. "I had thought that all French people were intelligent, suave, sophisticated. . . . Then I saw these very poor children playing in the street in some less than lovely section of Paris. . . . I always had this feeling that if intelligence prevails, we won't have any [social] problems." Moore's privileged small-town upbringing did not desensitize her to economic and social injustice.

Her awareness of sexism was awakened when she was in high school. She was insulted when an adviser told her that she should learn to type. "That was the worst thing—like taking home economics. I refused. I wasn't using the word 'feminist.' That wasn't even it. All I knew was I didn't want whatever I was going to be proscribed by someone else." She knew that if she took typing, she would probably be good at it and wind up getting a dead-end job. "No secretary for this 'chick,' " she said with a wry reference to sexist labels. Of course, she has no quarrel with the profession of office work or housekeeping. She eventually taught herself to type, and indeed, after marriage, became a "homemaker."

Although she remembers thinking that composers were "all male, white, and dead," she knew by the time she was a teenager that she wanted to be a composer. There were few role models; a guest appearance at Howard by Julia Perry was her first exposure to a female composer. She was never discouraged from composing because of her sex, either by her family or by her teachers (although her mother had hoped she would study law). Her sense of solidarity with women is shown in her use of black female poets in her song cycles: Georgia Douglas Johnson in *From the Dark Tower*, and Alice Dunbar-Nelson, Clarissa Scott Delaney, Gwendolyn Bennett, and Helene Johnson in *Sonnets on Love, Rosebuds, and Death*. Two of her song cycles are focused on women's lives and issues: the eight *Sonnets* reveal aspects of a woman's inner life—rekindled love, joy, intimacy, and loss—and all the songs in the cycle *Flowers of Darkness* are devoted to African-American male poets' appreciation of African-American women—the "flowers of darkness."

THE MUSIC

Dorothy Rudd Moore is not a facile or prolific composer, but her output is consistent in quality. Her body of work consists of less than 35 compositions, (besides her popular songs and her arrangements for voices of works by Purcell, Brahms, and other composers, made in response to requests). Fifteen of her serious compositions are substantial—either extended or multimovement works. They are almost equally divided between vocal and instrumental media, and include music for orchestra, band, chamber groups, and solo instruments. Her vocal works combine the solo voice with various solo instruments: oboe, cello and piano, violin and piano, and also with orchestra and chorus. Most of her works may be obtained in facsimile from the American Composers' Alliance, and a few have been anthologized. Commercial recordings are available on CD of her *Three Pieces for Violin and Piano*, and her *Modes* for string quartet. *From the Dark Tower* and *Dirge and Deliverance* were issued on Performance Records LPs in the 1980s.

In style, her music is highly individual and contemporary, with almost no traces of African-American idioms. Her powerful, dissonant settings of poetry express a deep spiritual response to the African-American condition, even if they do not usually employ a black idiomatic language.

Moore's early and enduring influences were Johann Sebastian Bach and Edward Kennedy ("Duke") Ellington. She admired the organization and logic of Bach, and the structure and inventiveness of Ellington, who inspired her first serious composition for solo piano, titled *Flight*, written when she was 16. She was attracted to the mathematical aspects of music and enjoyed the study of counterpoint and harmony. This regard for underlying structure and detail is expressed in her comparison of composing with sewing: "If the seams are done right, it will fit well and look good," and if the structural details of composition are carefully executed, it will sound good.

Moore's compositional process is deliberate and methodical. She prepares her compositions painstakingly with extensive study of similar works by other composers. When setting poetry, she first absorbs the text at length, writing it out in longhand and then memorizing it. Each work is approached with a fresh outlook in terms of its function, its text, or its instrumentation. She has no preconceived notions of how it will sound, and each work suggests and assumes its own form. Despite the identifiable characteristics of her music, she does not know "what her style is," and avoids listening to her own music when composing something new. She thinks through what she is going to do before writing anything down, but trusts her initial ideas. "My mother used to say, 'My first mind leads me right.' Whatever you think first. It's another way of saying instinct, I guess."

She does have strong opinions on trends such as minimalism, considering it the "narrowing of the American mind." She says, "Unfortunately, 'less' often equals less," and declares that her music will not "evolve" in the direction of minimalism, nor toward electronic or chance/improvisatory experiments. It will remain strictly in her control. While a student at Howard, she attended a concert of Luciano Berio's avant-garde music at American University and was fascinated by the sounds and combinations. But the novelty wore off, and left her wondering "then what?" She sees no need to abandon the musical language and resources of the twentieth century. "The orchestra is not 'dead' yet, and there are still challenges to be met in dealing with [traditional] instruments. The whole book has not been written on Western music."

In its maturity and style, Moore's music seems to have sprung, fully formed, displaying her skill, serious intent, and musical characteristics from her earliest works. *Songs from the Rubaiyat*, composed while she was still an undergraduate at Howard, shows the mixed meters, dissonant counterpoint, attention to structure, and motivic cohesiveness of much later works. The unusual instrumentation of mezzo-soprano and oboe, and the two-part texture of lines curling intimately and sinuously around each other, lend an oriental sound and atmosphere to the settings of twelve quatrains chosen from the *Rubaiyat* by the twelfth-century Persian astronomer and poet Omar Khayyám. The gentle, melancholy texts about nature, the pleasures of love, and the fleeting sweetness of life are given tonal expression in the pervasive whole-tone scale and its inherent tritone. It is an open-ended scale with an elusive tonal center, suited to the transitory meaning of the words, but with a dissonant bite. The quatrains are differentiated and grouped through musical continuity, tempo, and texture (legato and staccato), and unified by similar melodic contours and cyclic recall of specific themes.

Although Moore enjoyed writing both vocal music and instrumental string music, she did not write for voice again until seven years later. Her early instrumental works each have their own style while continuing many traits first seen in the *Rubaiyat* songs. Both the *Baroque Suite* (1965) for solo cello and the string quartet *Modes* (1968) were intentional tributes to Johann Sebastian Bach, one of Moore's two acknowledged influences. The three movements of *Modes* are based on modal scales, as the title indicates. In the first, a serenely flowing melody is introduced by the cello, then imitated in a canon by the viola, the second violin, and finally the first violin; at the end, the same melody is imitated in the same order, this time overlapping in a stretto. In the slower second movement, pairs of instruments wind mournfully around each other in

close, dissonant counterpoint. A lively, dancelike third movement in cross meters brings the work to a vigorous close. *Modes* was described by a critic as
"sounding like Bach and . . . [getting] no further than Hindemith. It gave off the
unmistakable air of a musical mind trying to reach other musical minds."[12]
Moods for viola and cello, written in 1969, has no connection with *Modes* and
is in a very different style. Critics described it as "excellent, intense, chromatic,"
and "modest, intense . . . it convinces."[13] The *Three Pieces for Violin and Piano*
(1967) place less emphasis on counterpoint, contrasting graceful playfulness
with spare, stark dissonance.

The three movements of her *Trio No. 1* (1970) for piano, cello, and violin,
are strongly defined and rhythmic, each with a different emotional point of
departure. One reviewer compared it with other works on the program as
"spunkier. . . . Tonal, but there was enough dissonance to add tension and
strength to the musical fabric."[14] Another listener found it "Of more interest . . .
[with] simple compositional techniques to offer intermittent but strong images
of alienation and deep feeling."[15] In *Dirge and Deliverance* (1971) for cello and
piano, Moore abandons the three-movement format for a two-movement
antecedent-consequent relationship, as she does again in *Night Fantasy* (1978)
for clarinet and piano.

Song cycles are particularly significant in Moore's body of work. She wrote
four cycles, each of them a lengthy and major work. In the cycles after the
Rubaiyat, Moore no longer set poems by a single author, but rather texts by
different authors. *From the Dark Tower* (1970) for mezzo-soprano, cello, and
piano, presents eight poems by black poets of the Harlem Renaissance. Despite
its use of the female voice, many elements combine to present a somber tone
and masculine point of view: the title, the recurring theme of militant protest
against racial injustice, the cello range and timbre, the predominantly male poets
(only one is female), and the austere, dissonant sonority. The lighter sound of
the violin complements the gentler, more graceful tone of the eight poems in
the *Sonnets on Love, Rosebuds, and Death* (1976), in which Moore returns to
the subjects of the *Rubaiyat*: love, beauty, and death as part of life's continuum.
These themes are presented here from the woman's point of view, and five of
the eight texts are by black women poets. The songs are prevailingly tonal, often
clearly major or minor, and the dissonance is rarely obtrusive. The title itself is
feminine, and the unifying theme is "a woman's inner life . . . rekindled love,
joy, intimacy, premonitions, and loss."[16]

Within these unifying parameters among the *Sonnets*, there is much contrast
of mood, from pensive, to rhapsodic, to ominous, to angry, to mournful, to
nostalgic. Among the most powerful is Langston Hughes' "Song for a Dark
Girl," a young girl's heartrending outcry for her lynched lover. Her anger and
grief are conveyed by pounding octaves, jabbing syncopations, and the violin's
swirling 16th-note figuration. Equally affecting is the setting of Gwendolyn Bennett's "Some Things Are Very Dear to Me." Its slow, measured pace, winding

chromatic melodies, and hollow sonority of voice and piano in unison against the floating counterpoint of the violin all combine to recall the myriad beautiful details that constitute a life well lived. The *Sonnets* received praise from one critic for their "wistful, bittersweet . . . chromaticism and gentle dissonances."[17] Another reviewer commented on the "unusual sensitivity to the mood and underlying sense of each poem, captured through long lyric lines and effective dramatic contrasts. Mrs. Moore's music is couched in a conservative idiom, but within that context, it almost always strikes a tone of expressive originality."[18]

Moore's fourth song cycle, *Flowers of Darkness*, composed in 1989, explores the many facets of black womanhood through the eyes of six black male poets. For tenor and piano, it was commissioned and first performed in 1990 by William Brown, who is known especially for his remarkable performances of twentieth-century works. The recurring themes of sensuality, poignant tenderness, loss and longing, and yearning for Africa are expressed in a variety of styles, from jazzy (marked "laid back and cool)" in Hughes' mouthwatering *Harlem Sweeties*, to languid and sensual in Binga Dismond's *At Early Morn*, straightforwardly tonal and triadic in James Weldon Johnson's *The Glory of the Day Was in Her Face*, and an almost primitive atonality in Robert Hayden's fantastical and mythical *O Daedalus Fly Away Home*. The harmonic language alternates from one song to the next between consonant triadic harmonies and more dissonant quartal structures, and the many shifts in tonal center are used to highlight significant words. A reviewer in Jacksonville, Florida, described the work as "eclectic in mood and color—running the gamut of emotional response—rich in tonal imagery."[19]

Perhaps Moore's best-known work is her *Weary Blues*, a setting of the Langston Hughes' poem for baritone, cello, and piano, commissioned by the noted baritone Rawn Spearman in 1972.[20] The melancholy mood of the subject, a black man playing blues on an old piano by gaslight, is conveyed by the cello's opening solo, before the voice and piano enter in a 12-bar blues, each part with its own distinct melodic material. The jazz harmonies, flatted "blue" thirds, syncopation, and sliding, melismatic melodies may be Moore's most overt use of black idioms, but the independent parts, dissonant counterpoint, and changing meters keep *Weary Blues* within her characteristic style.

Night Fantasy, Moore's last composition for solo instruments, was composed in 1978.[21] Six years later, clarinetist Keith King and pianist Daniel Michalak gave its premiere at Indiana University. The two-movement work is nine minutes long. Both movements are atonal and rhythmically irregular, and exploit the full range of each instrument; both leave behind Moore's characteristic contrapuntal lyricism for short, abrupt phrases in a kind of gruff, argumentative dialogue. The second movement is faster and more continuous than the first, but slows down to an almost pensive mood midway through. Moore calls the whole work "virtuosic, fanciful, and colorful" and describes the opening movement, *Largo*, as "episodic and pointillistic"; the following *Allegro* is "energetic and driven. . . . It evokes the image of spritely spirits that furtively appear on a moon-lit lawn, and then, with playful abandon, dance a revelry."[22]

In Moore's opera *Frederick Douglass*, her ability to fuse music and words into a dramatic whole was extended into a three-act, three-hour-long opera. Moore began research in 1978 and wrote three drafts of the libretto before starting to compose the music. She did all the orchestration from March through June 1985, often working all night. Moore has said that opera writing requires strong desire; hard work; a knowledge of the voice, theater, and orchestration; a sense of drama; and thorough research into the subject matter. She credits her training as a singer with giving her an understanding of how to write for the voice, how to set texts and develop thematic material. These skills were noted by reviewers of the opera, who called it "an ambitious and important work by a composer of great gifts," in which "drama and music coalesced brilliantly."[23] They also commented on Moore's "rare ability to wed musical and dramatic motion, graceful lyric inventiveness, and a full command of the orchestral palette."[24] Moore's libretto (based on Douglass's *Narrative* and other accounts) spans 18 years of the protagonist's life, and its grand design unfolds in a series of representative scenes or tableaus. It calls for a large cast of black and white characters, mixed chorus and orchestra. Since its premiere in June 1985, Opera Ebony has performed excerpts from it in the United States, Europe (Germany, Iceland, etc.), and the Caribbean (Martinique).

After a hiatus of nine years (since *Flowers of Darkness* in 1989), Moore returned to composition when commissioned by Walter Turnbull, director of the Boy's Choir of Harlem, to write a work for the debut of the Girls' Choir of Harlem in 1997. This was *Voices from the Light* for female chorus, oboe, string quartet, and piano, on a text by the composer in which a voice narrates to a sleeping child the hopes and struggles of African-Americans through history. The premiere of the 20-minute work by the Girls' Choir of Harlem drew warm praise from Raoul Abdul: "This is, without question, a major work. The vocal and instrumental writing is first class."[25]

Moore's music has been called "essentially conservative,"[26] and while this description is true in relation to various twentieth-century trends, it inadequately describes the challenges for both listeners and performers. Moore's vocal and instrumental lines are often combined in highly dissonant counterpoint, requiring an unfailing ear and accurate pitch. Her works have a complex and cohesive underlying structural organization; one hallmark is her use of small motivic cells to provide thematic material for entire works. Some of these cells, such as a major or minor third followed by the interval of a second, are often encountered in different permutations in several works. Moore also makes extensive use of the intervals of the perfect fourth and the augmented fourth (tritone). These intervals pervade her music in both melodic lines and harmonic structures.

Critics have commented that dissonant elements "add tension and strength to [Moore's] musical fabric,"[27] and do not obscure the "most arresting feature of her music, an original and often intense lyricism that pervades even the most complex harmonic and contrapuntal textures."[28] This combination of intellectual complexity with deep emotional intensity results in the compelling power of expression so characteristic of her music.

Three Pieces for Violin and Piano (1966–67)

This work was commissioned by Richard Elias and first performed by Elias with David Garvey at the piano in Carnegie Recital Hall, New York, on 2 March 1967. In his *New York Times* review, Theodore Strongin noted that each of the three pieces was "short, musical, strongly melodic and idiomatic for the violin." The work was recorded by Gregory Walker, violin, with Helen Walker-Hill, piano, for Leonarda Records in 1995.

This relatively early composition illustrates the timeless quality of Moore's output. Unlike less "conservative" music of the twentieth century, it sounds fresh and undated; and it is neither experimental nor reactionary in its idiom and expression. Its three short movements—"Vignette," "Episode," and "Caprice"— are, all together, six minutes in duration. The first and last movements are animated by humor and whimsy, and the middle movement provides a stark contrast of almost paralyzed anguish. This work contrasts consonant major/minor triadic harmony with more dissonant quartal harmony.

"Vignette" opens with a languidly seductive dancelike piano accompaniment in undulating 6/8 time. Complex chords built on thirds are joined by the slyly playful violin, skipping in consonant intervals (thirds and fifths) and flirting impishly with the more dissonant fourths. When the instruments exchange material in the tenth measure, fourths have won out. With this added stringency, each instrument grows in aggressiveness and urgency, changing to 5/8 meter with faster note values and sharply accented, irregular rhythms, until they are suddenly reined in by the piano's "subito p" (suddenly soft) ninth chord. The piece closes with a brief and wry recall of the opening playful dance motives.

In the second piece, marked "Molto adagio," the struggle of thirds versus fourths has turned from playful to deadly serious. The piano's opening major third on E-flat, far from carrying its traditional sunny implication, hangs and dies away for what seems like an eternity, before being repeated wearily. It is joined with more energy as other pitches (the clashing D-flat below it, then B-natural and D-natural) slowly repeat and gather momentum, until the violin enters. Piano and violin surge to a chord built on fourths, completing the 12-tone spectrum. The violin's long sustained notes and labored leaps of wide intervals are accompanied by the piano's dryly hammered commentary, only to die away again. In a burst of agitated energy, piano and violin together cry out another chord of fourths. After the violin's agonized bitonal double stops, played solo, they attempt one last joint surge to the chord of fourths, before closing with the piano's long-held major third on D against the violin's high C, recalling the intervallic motif from the beginning. An infinity of suffering is contained in this 22-measure "Episode."

Fourths reign supreme in the concluding "Caprice," marked "Presto." Both perfect and augmented fourths frolic unhampered by traditional tonality. The violin's jaunty theme is accompanied first by staccato chords built in fourths, then by running whole-tone scales and tritone skips, before both instruments shift suddenly into a bizarre, ungainly waltz marked "dolce." The violin leaps wildly from one register to the next while the piano's fourths pile up with ever more atonal insistence. Both instruments return just as suddenly to the opening jaunty theme, then toss it away blithely at the end.

From the Dark Tower (1970)

This cycle of eight songs for mezzo-soprano, cello, and piano was commissioned by Moore's husband, the cellist Kermit Moore, and written for Moore and the mezzo-soprano Hilda Harris, who gave its premiere performance with Alan Booth at the piano on 8 October 1970 at Norfolk State University in Virginia. The 34-minute cycle has been performed many times since then, and was recorded by Moore and Harris with Wayne Sanders, pianist, on Performance Records in 1980. In 1972, Hilda Harris commissioned four of the songs (the first, third, sixth, and eighth) to be arranged for mezzo-soprano and orchestra; this version was first performed on 29 October 1972 in New York City at Philharmonic Hall by members of the Symphony of the New World, with George Byrd conducting. The orchestrated songs are 22 minutes in length.

The eight poems by African-American poets of the Harlem Renaissance, are (1) "O Black and Unknown Bards," by James Weldon Johnson; (2) "Southern Mansions," by Arna Bontemps; (3) "Willow Bend and Weep," by Herbert Clark Johnson; (4) "Old Black Men," by Georgia Douglas Johnson; (5) "No Images," by Waring Cuney; (6) "Dream Variation," by Langston Hughes; (7) "For a Poet" by Countee Cullen; and (8) "From the Dark Tower," also by Countee Cullen.[29] These poems are unified by themes of affirmation of black creativity and anger at its frustration. Moore has said that at the time she composed this music, she needed a way to express her support for the struggle toward a black nationalist identity, and to vent her anger at events of the late 1960s. She described this work as her "black power statement," and notes its "constant vocal and instrumental involvement with the wonder, irony, agony, militancy, and pride characteristic of the Black American experience."[30]

In preparation for the composition of this work, Moore studied Schubert's song cycle Die Winterreise, paying especial attention to the treatment of the words, the use of key relationships, and how the ideas and emotions of the poems were conveyed. A comparison of the two works shows both obvious and subtle similarities: the predominance of freely strophic forms, the use of instruments to provide essential pictorial and coloristic elements, dialogue between the voice and instruments, unison passages, similar syllabic vocal treatment, and the association of contrasting lighter songs with the dream motive. Perhaps the most interesting parallel is between Moore's use of less dissonant tonality in the dreamlike songs and Schubert's use of major keys for similar purposes in his predominantly minor-key cycle.

Besides their poetic themes, the songs in *From the Dark Tower* are unified by the distinctive sound of the instrumentation (voice, cello, and piano) and by the consistently dissonant counterpoint of the instruments' interaction. The recurrence of the theme of the first song toward the end of the last song contributes to the closure of the cycle.

The first song, "O Black and Unknown Bards," opens majestically with octave-doubled pedal points in the piano, followed by a noble and eloquent statement of the cycle's theme by the cello. The voice enters with its own straightforward and independent melodic line, and the resulting dissonant clashes with cello and piano serve to heighten the mood of protest. The vocal contour and rhythmic inflection give powerful expression to the words, and later manipulation of the melodic materials also serves the poetic meaning. The first question, "How came your lips to touch the sacred fire?" begins with the interval of the rising fifth; the second question, "Who first from midst his bonds lifted his eyes?" inverts this to a falling fifth; and the third question, "Heart of what slave . . . ?" has the voice and cello exchanging melodies. The last question, "Who heard great Jordan Roll?," employs the vocal melodic line of the first question, but in diminution (faster note value) emphasizing the "rolling Jordan." This economy of musical materials lends a powerful cohesion to the setting. Particularly effective are the references to spirituals: the phrase "Steal Away to Jesus" breaks the prevailing dissonance for just a moment with the indescribably sweet consonance of the traditional harmonies, while "Swing Low" echoes the rising and falling thirds of its tune. "Nobody Knows the Trouble I See" is sung mournfully on repeated notes, while the piano softly plays the familiar melody as if from a great distance.

Thematic unity and the independence of each instrumental part provide meaningful resonance to the words of "Southern Mansions." The response of the cello, then the voice, to the piano's graceful undulating melodic ostinato introduction and accompaniment is at first independent and contrasting, conveying the distance between the gentlemen and their ladies walking together at leisure under the poplar trees, and the bondsmen dragging their chains. The cello's theme is a four-bar rising, then falling, stepwise progression that is stated six times in the song. This pattern is broken only at the words "Chains of bondmen dragging on the ground," when the cello exchanges thematic material with the piano.

In the third song, "Willow Bend and Weep," the image of poplar trees shifts to willow trees which also have endured and witnessed the change in years and fortunes. But instead of a musical painting of gracefully swaying willows, the piano enters with stark, block chords, changing to a more flowing accompaniment only with the words "Let river tears wash out land grief." At that point the cello and voice sound in unison, a rare occurrence in the entire cycle. They return to their independent parts when the singer commands the willow to weep, and to submit to the axe.

Each of the four lines of "Old Black Men" is treated vocally with similar melodic material. The piano's robustly rolling 6/8 accompaniment supports a lilting reiterated four-bar snatch of melody in octaves in the right hand, with the cello underscoring the piano melody. Only at the end, when the "young men's dream of glory" changes to "And they have learned to live it down, As though they did not care," does the piano's virile accompaniment become subdued, with the octaves broken, evocative of diminished lives and shattered dreams. The cello wistfully repeats an elongated, mournful version of the voice's opening hopeful melody.

That melody is further transformed in Moore's setting of "No Images." With the piano silent (imitating a drum when it does enter), the solitary cello declaims a mournful monologue as though reflecting on the sentiment expressed at the end of the previous song, oddly meandering and arhythmic in a 5/4 meter. When the voice sings of the black woman who does not know her own beauty, the cello answers in similar intervals and durations. Then the pace changes and the piano enters with low cluster drumbeats, joined by the cello "col legno" (played with the wood side of the bow to suggest an African instrument), transforming this meter into a primitive and pulsating dance. The voice, bearing the indication "earthy," sings, "If she could dance naked under the palm trees and see her image in the river." The drumbeats fade, and the cello reenters with its lost and searching melody while the voice laments the absence of palm trees in the city streets, and the river vanishing into dishwater.[31]

"Dream Variation" provides the cycle with a welcome contrast of carefree gaiety, and this mood is set by the uncomplicated tonal strumming by piano and cello, swirling to the "Dance, Whirl" of the text. The vocal part is likewise consonant and direct, and the same melody is employed for both stanzas. But the composer's indication at the beginning of the song—"Dream-like"—cautions that the joyful celebration of carefree days and nights "coming tenderly, Black like me," is not reality; it is only the poet's dream.

The dream motif is also linked to the seventh poem, "For a Poet," whose dreams "have been wrapped in a silken cloth, and laid away in a box of gold." After a brief, quiet introduction by the piano, the solo cello spins out a winding melody, which is then taken up by the voice as the cello continues intertwining and the piano accompanies with a pedal-point pattern based on the weaving lines of the voice and cello. This repetition of melodic material reinforces and builds upon the opening theme. Stark chords interrupt to underscore the bitterness of the poet, for whom this world is hostile and cold. After this brief, impassioned outburst, the opening mood returns. The cello mirrors the vocal line, ending in a searing dissonance. The piano darkly repeats its patterns to an inconclusive end.

The cycle closes with Cullen's title song, "From the Dark Tower," a dramatic statement of protest against the injustice of incessant labor without reward, exclaiming, "We were not made eternally to weep!" The music employs vigorous rhythms in 5/4 and 5/8 meters, and the melodies incorporate strongly marked, repeated patterns matching the rhythms. The slower middle section refers to the broadly lyrical melody of the opening song before returning to the vigorous protest of the first lines, to bring the cycle to a triumphant close.

A review of the 1972 New York premiere of the orchestrated version of four of these songs lauded the "expressive and strongly contoured vocal lines, pungent harmonies," and the "vibrant Romantic idiom yet one free of clichés," summing it up as a "luscious cycle of songs."[32] In a later report on the entire cycle, the same reviewer observed: "The texture is . . . reminiscent of the French impressionists in its gestural clarity and telling use of dissonance."[33] Repeated hearing does not dull the impact of this powerful set of songs, a worthy companion to Schubert's *Die Winterreise*.

Dirge and Deliverance (1971)

This work for cello and piano was commissioned by Kermit Moore, and premiered by Moore with pianist Zita Carno at Alice Tulley Hall in May 1972. It was later recorded on Performance Records by Kermit Moore with Raymond Jackson, pianist. A little less than 16 minutes long, its two movements correspond to the two parts of its title. This work was one of Moore's favorites, because she identified so closely with its themes of struggle with despair and progress toward hope. She found it a challenge to compose because she does not play the cello, and both cello and piano have difficult virtuoso parts.

Dirge opens with a piano introduction of stark chords and a slow ostinato of low, falling half-note octaves, somewhat reminiscent of the piano openings of *From the Dark Tower* (1970) and *Dream and Variations* (1974). All three works establish at the outset a mood of serious portent through slowly repeated octaves in the low register of the piano. The repetition also establishes a tonal center (F minor), which is abandoned in the sections that follow. According to Moore's program notes, this chordal and rhythmic pattern embodies a force enchaining the spirit and intensifying its despair.

The main theme, played by the cello, is intended to represent the human spirit longing to be free. The opening triplet motif of rising half-step and falling whole step (A, B-flat, A-flat) is used throughout the work in various rhythmic and pitch permutations. This three-note cell has, in fact, already been heard in the piano introduction, in whole-note chords outlining C, D-flat, C-flat. The cello theme continues with a second motif, a stepwise descending figure interrupted by a leap up a diminished fourth, only to repeat its stepwise descent. The rhythmic variations of these motives—in diminution and augmentation—make their presence felt but not always recognized. In addition, the intervals are sometimes turned upside down, and sometimes expanded to larger intervals. In its close chromatic steps and circling motion, this theme conveys the imprisonment of the human spirit longing to be free. (It is also reminiscent of the theme on the name of BACH spelled in pitch names—B, A, C, B-flat—so rich in its thematic and emotional implications and so often used by composers. This may even have been a conscious reference, given Moore's admiration for Bach.)

The *Dirge* consists of several large phrases or sections, all but one of them characterized by a steady rhythmic motion in the accompaniment, first in half-notes, then quarter-notes, then eighths. In the penultimate section the muted cello is accompanied by an ostinato of more varied rhythms. The *Dirge* closes with the three-note cell in the piano (a long-held G, G-sharp, F-sharp).

Deliverance is marked "Allegro" and begins with solo cello repeating the triplet motif in energetic 16th-notes. This movement is based on the same three-note motif of the *Dirge*. Its character has become angry and determined, fighting to be free. The piano struggles with the cello; they play the triplet 16th-note pattern together in rapid figurations, leading to an extended cadenza by solo cello. The quasi-improvisational, recitative-like solo exploits ponticello and other techniques, exploring the range and expressive possibilities of the cello. The two motives of the main theme are embedded in this solo in both diminution and augmentation. A mysterious new (and liberating?) theme in harmonics (overtones) ushers the piano back in, and both instruments build to a climactic and satisfying close. At the end, the cello's suspenseful long-held trills on E-flat, then E natural, instead of leading to the motif's expected D natural, leaps up to high A accompanied by reiterated A major chords. The work thus ends with a triumphant "deliverance" from the prison of its motivic cell, and closes as it opened, with a firm sense of tonal center.

Dream and Variations (1974)

This 20-minute, one-movement work, composed for Ludwig Olshansky, was first performed by Zita Carno at Carnegie Recital Hall on 23 February 1975, and is Moore's major work for solo piano.[34] Her shorter piano pieces are *Flight*, composed when she was 16, and a children's teaching piece, *A Little Whimsy*, composed in 1978 (part of an unfinished set of teaching pieces) and published by Hildegard Publishing Company in the anthology *Black Women Composers: A Century of Piano Music 1893–1990*. Both *Dream and Variations* and *A Little Whimsy* are available in facsimile edition from the American Composers Alliance, as are her other compositions.

The title of this piece reminds one of Langston Hughes' poem "Dream Variation," which has been set in song very often by composers, including Moore herself, but this work is unrelated to the Hughes poem and brings a heavier, nightmarish interpretation to the dream idea. It consists of an introduction, a theme, and six variations. Although no programmatic indications are included in the score, the composer provides separate program notes. Her program for the work begins with the introduction: the "chiming" of midnight bells and the drifting off to sleep of the dreamer. Next, a "dream" theme tenuously unfolds, followed by Variation I, sharply falling back and forth from sleep to awakening. Variation II is filled with "disjointed, psychedelic images" both heavy and bright. This variation is witty and funny in its sudden contrasts of dynamics and mood, suggesting the "plodding elephant comically dancing in a brightly colored costume." Variation III is "seductive in its transparent, formless quality," representing the sensual dream. Variation IV is "fleeting and elusive," providing thematic material for Variation V, in which "former playfulness is transformed into a foreboding heaviness, presaging the 'nightmare.' " Variation VI is "a fantasia, an amalgamation of the theme and the preceding variations" in which "there is a frenetic quality, the nightmare realized, now intensified by fear and torment." The work ends with an awakening, recalling the "chimes" of the introduction.

This program would lead one to expect an easily followed musical narrative, but the piece is much more than that. *Dream and Variations* is a major interpretive challenge for the pianist as well as for the audience. On the more obvious and audible level, the thematic variations are not easily distinguishable, and require many hearings to unravel. In large part, this is due to the extraordinary compositional economy and recombination of motivic cells, so that "variation" has become development. More than a story of a particular dream, the composition is "about" the nature of this development, an altogether more engrossing and mentally demanding plot.

Almost all the motivic material in the introduction is repeated and expanded in later variations, from the deep chimes to the chromatically falling and rising fragments of the dreamer. But it is the three-note motivic cell of the dream theme that undergoes the most permutations. These begin even before the variations, within the theme statement itself, as the rising minor third and falling major third is stretched to rising major third and falling tritone. In Variation I, the three-note cell has become a rising fourth and falling tritone, and its rhythm has been reversed. In Variation III, the languidly sensual version of the cell has it rising a major third and falling chromatically in half-steps. The fourth variation reintroduces the dreamer's falling chromatic half-steps from the introduction in a distinctively playful rhythm before combining it with the first variation on the dream theme.

In Variation V, the falling chromatic figure is barely recognizable as it changes its character to a tortured outcry, and is recombined with other motives from the introduction. The apotheosis of Variation VI brings back all the previous motives in both recognizable and not so recognizable forms, such as the reappearance of the dream theme inverted and in retrograde. In addition to the three-note cell described above, other intervallic cells, from the most vestigial two-note fragments to combinations of linking motives, are reused, expanded, and transformed into major thematic materials.

The resulting homogeneity makes thematic differences difficult to distinguish, and other parameters provide audible shape, most obviously contrasts in tempo, rhythm, thickness of texture, and dynamics. A sense of drama, forward motion, and direction is also provided by several less obvious devices: rhythmic foreshortening, rhythmic diminution, elaboration of motives by the addition of notes, and repetition of material at rising pitch levels. The rhythmic shortening and elaboration can be seen right from the introduction, as the melodic fragments are repeated with shorter rests between them, and extended with added notes. The repetition of similar motivic material at rising pitch levels occurs on both small and larger structural levels, most notably the climactic moment just before the awakening, when the theme appears a full step higher than its previous occurrence two pages earlier.

Dream and Variations is the kind of work that reveals new clues and twists to its plot at each rehearing. In this respect, as well as in the subtle nature of its variations, it reminds one of Anton Webern's landmark 12-tone *Piano Variations*, Op. 27 (1936), which also provides the performer and the serious listener with endless emotional and intellectual pleasure and satisfaction.

LIST OF WORKS

Sources of Information

Publisher: Dorothy Rudd Moore's music may be purchased in facsimile from American Composers Alliance, 73 Spring St., Room 506, New York, NY 10012. (212) 362–8900. It may be rented from University of Maryland, Performing Arts Library, Special Collections, College Park, MD 20742.

Archives Holding Scores

(AMC) American Music Center, 30 West 26th Street, New York, N.Y. 10010 (nine scores)

(AMRC/CBMR) The Helen Walker-Hill Collection of scores by black women composers, housed in duplicate at the American Music Research Center at the University of Colorado and the Center for Black Music Research at Columbia College, Chicago (10 scores)

(Oberlin) Oberlin Conservatory Library, Oberlin College, Oberlin, Ohio 44074 (12 scores)

References (for complete citation, see the bibliography at the end of the chapter)

(IDBC) *International Dictionary of Black Composers*

(McGinty) Doris Evans McGinty, *The New Grove Dictionary of American Music* (cited only if works are not listed elsewhere)

(Moore) Dorothy Rudd Moore unpublished list of works, and correspondence with the author

(Tischler) Alice Tischler, *Fifteen Black American Composers*.

Instrumental Music

Violin

Three Pieces for Violin and Piano. 1966–67. New York: American Composers Alliance, 1967. Contents: (1) Vignette; (2) Episode; (3) Caprice. Commissioned and first performed by violinist Richard Elias with David Garvey, 2 March 1967, at Carnegie Recital Hall, New York. See discography. 10 min. (AMC, AMRC/CBMR, Oberlin; IDBC, Moore, Tischler)

Cello

Baroque Suite for Unaccompanied Violoncello. 1964–65. New York: American Composers Alliance, 1974. Three movements. Written for and first performed by Kermit Moore, 21 November 1965, at Harlem School of the Arts. 15 min. (AMC; IDBC, Moore, Tischler)

Dirge and Deliverance. 1970–71. New York: American Composers Alliance, 1972. Two movements. Commissioned and first performed by cellist Kermit Moore with Zita Carno, Alice Tully Hall, 14 May 1972. See discography. 16 min. (AMC, AMRC/CBMR, Oberlin; IDBC, Moore, Tischler)

Clarinet

Night Fantasy. 1978. New York: American Composers Alliance, 1979. Two movements. First performed by Keith King, clarinet, and Daniel Michalak, piano, in 1994 at Indiana University Art Museum. 12 min. (AMRC/CBMR, Oberlin; IDBC, Moore, Tischler)

Piano

Dream and Variations. 1974. New York: American Composers Alliance, 1979. Composed for Ludwig Olshansky. First performed by Zita Carno, 23 February 1975 at Carnegie Recital Hall, New York. 20 min. (AMC, AMRC/CBMR, Oberlin; IDBC, Moore, Tischler)

Flight. 1956. (IDBC)

A Little Whimsy. 1978. New York: American Composers Alliance, 1978. Also in *Black Women Composers: A Century of Piano Music* 1893–1900, edited by Helen Walker-Hill (Bryn Mawr, Pa.: Hildegard, 1992). A teaching piece, part of an uncompleted set. Performed by Elena Mirazchiyska, 12 November 2000, at the third annual American Music Week festival in Sofia, Bulgaria. 2 min.(AMRC/CBMR, Oberlin; IDBC, Moore)

Ensemble

Adagio (viola, cello). 1965. This became the middle movement of *Moods*. First performed by Selwart Clarke, viola, and Kermit Moore, cello, February 1965 in Town Hall, New York. (McGinty, Moore)

Lament for Nine Instruments (flute, oboe, clarinet, trumpet, trombone, percussion, violin, viola, cello). 1969. New York: Composers' Facsimile Editions, 1969. First performed in reading session by Society of Black Composers Ensemble conducted by Kermit Moore, 16 August 1969, in New York. 8 min. (IDBC, Moore, Tischler)

Modes (string quartet). 1968. New York: American Composers Alliance, 1968. Three movements. First performed by Clarmore Quartet: violinist Sanford Allen, violinist Selwart Clarke, violist Alfred Brown, cellist Kermit Moore, 28 May 1968, at the Harlem School of the Arts. See discography. 12 min. (AMC, Oberlin; IDBC, Moore, Tischler)

Moods (viola, cello). 1969. New York: American Composers Alliance, 1974. Contents: (1) Agitated and Erratic; (2) Melancholic (see *Adagio*, 1965); (3) Frenetic. Won grant from the Society of Black Composers. First performed by violist Selwart Clarke and cellist Kermit Moore, 20 May 1969, at Intermediate School No. 201, New York. 15 min. (Oberlin, IDBC, Moore, Tischler)

Trio No. 1 (violin, cello, piano). 1969–70. New York: American Composers Alliance, 1970. Commissioned and first performed by the Reston Trio, 26 March 1970, Carnegie Recital Hall, New York. 15 min. (AMC, AMRC/CBMR, Oberlin; IDBC, Moore, Tischler)

Orchestra

Symphony No. 1. 1962–63. One movement. One of 10 finalist works selected and performed by the National Symphony Orchestra in May 1963 at Constitution Hall. 15 min. (IDBC, Moore, Tischler)

Transcension ("I Have Been to the Mountaintop") (chamber orchestra). 1985–86. New York: American Composers Alliance, 1986. Commissioned and first performed by Brooklyn Philharmonic, conducted by Tania León, in honor of Martin Luther King, Jr., January 1986. 7 min. (IDBC, Moore)

Band

Reflections (symphonic wind ensemble). 1962. Won Howard University competition. First performed by Howard University symphonic wind ensemble, conducted by William Penn, at Howard University in May 1962. 10 min. (IDBC, Moore, Tischler)

Vocal Music

Voice, Solo and with Instruments

Flowers of Darkness (tenor, piano). 1988–89. New York: American Composers Alliance, 1989. Contents: (1) Flowers of Darkness (Frank Marshall Davis); (2) Creole Girl (Leslie M. Collins); (3) Harlem Sweeties (Langston Hughes); (4) At Early Morn (Binga Dismond); (5) The Glory of the Day Was in Her Face (James Weldon Johnson); (6) O Daedalus Fly Away Home (Robert E. Hayden). Commissioned and first performed by tenor William Brown with Philip Morehead, piano, at an American Women Composers conference on 11 February 1990, at Ganz Hall, Roosevelt University, Chicago. 13 min. (AMRC/CBMR; IDBC, Moore)

From the Dark Tower (mezzo-soprano, cello, piano). 1970. New York: American Composers Alliance, 1974. Contents: (1) O Black and Unknown Bards (James. W. Johnson); (2) Southern Mansions (Arna Bontemps); (3) Willow Bend and Weep (Herbert. C. Johnson); (4) Old Black Men (Georgia D. Johnson); (5) No Images (Waring Cuney); (6) Dream Variation (Langston Hughes); (7) For a Poet (Countee

Cullen); (8) From the Dark Tower (Cullen). Commissioned by Kermit Moore. First performed by mezzo-soprano Hilda Harris, cellist Kermit Moore, and pianist Alan Booth on 8 October 1970 at Norfolk State University, Virginia. See discography. 34 min. (AMRC/CBMR, Oberlin; IDBC, Moore, Tischler)

From the Dark Tower (mezzo-soprano, orchestra). 1972. Songs nos. 1, 3, 6, 8 from cycle of the same title. Commissioned and first performed by Hilda Harris and the Symphony of the New World, conducted by George Byrd, on 29 October 1972, at Avery Fisher Hall, Lincoln Center, New York. 22 min. (IDBC, Moore, Tischler)

Songs from the Rubaiyat (mezzo-soprano, oboe). 1962. New York: American Composers Alliance, 1974. Text: Omar Khayyám. First performed by soprano Janet Lytle and oboist Sandra Fischer in August 1963 at the American Conservatory at Fontainebleau, France. American premiere by soprano Dorothy Rudd Moore and oboist Harry Smyles, 23 February 1975, at Carnegie Recital Hall, New York. 15 min. (Oberlin; IDBC, Moore, Tischler)

Sonnets on Love, Rosebuds, and Death (soprano, violin, piano). 1975–76. New York: American Composers Alliance, 1976. Contents: (1) Sonnet: I Had No Thought of Violets of Late (Alice Dunbar-Nelson); (2) Joy (Clarissa Delaney); (3) Sonnet: Some Things Are Very Dear to Me (Gwendolyn Bennett); (4) Sonnet: He Came in Silvern Armour (Bennett); (5) Song for a Dark Girl (Langston Hughes); (6) Idolatry (Countee Cullen); (7) Youth Sings a Song of Rosebuds (Arna Bontemps); (8) Invocation (Helene Johnson). Commissioned and first performed by soprano Miriam Burton, violinist Sanford Allen, and pianist Kelley Wyatt, 23 May 1976, at Alice Tully Hall, New York. 21 min. (AMC, AMRC/CBMR, Oberlin; IDBC, Moore, Tischler)

There Never Was a Finer Day (soprano, piano). 1975. Aria for proposed opera *Medea*. (Moore)

Weary Blues (baritone, cello, piano). 1972. New York: American Composers Alliance, 1972. Also in *Anthology of Art Songs by Black American Composers*, edited by Willis C. Patterson (New York: E. B. Marks, 1977). Text: Langston Hughes. Commissioned and first performed by baritone Rawn Spearman with cellist Kermit Moore and pianist Kelley Wyatt, 20 November 1972, at Horace Mann Auditorium, New York. 5 min. (AMC, AMRC/CBMR, Oberlin; IDBC, Moore, Tischler)

Weary Blues (baritone, chamber orchestra). New York: American Composers Alliance, 1972. Commissioned and first performed by baritone Benjamin Matthews (founder of Opera Ebony) with Buffalo Philharmonic Orchestra, conducted by Michael Tilson Thomas, 2 February 1972, at Kleinhaus Hall, Buffalo, N.Y. See discography. 8 min. (IDBC, Moore, Tischler)

Choral Works

Ballad of the Winter Soldier (SATB, piano). 1964. Text: Dorothy Rudd Moore. Orchestrated by Hale Smith for the first performance by the Howard Roberts Chorale, at a benefit for the Congress of Racial Equality, September 1964, at Philharmonic Hall, Lincoln Center, New York. (Moore)

In Celebration (SATB, soprano and baritone solos, piano). 1977. New York: American Composers Alliance, 1977. Text: Langston Hughes. Dedicated to Howard Swanson on his seventieth birthday. Commissioned and first performed by the Triad

Chorale, conducted by Noel DaCosta, with soprano Carol Joy, baritone Andrew Frierson, and pianist Marjorie de Lewis, on 12 June 1977, at Alice Tully Hall in New York. Orchestrated in 1994 and performed at Schomburg Center, conducted by Kermit Moore. 5 min. (AMC; IDBC, Moore, Tischler)

This Little Light of Mine (SATB a cappella). 1973. Spiritual. (Tischler)

Voices from the Light (girls' choir, oboe, string quartet, piano). 1997. Commissioned by Dr. Walter Turnbull, director of the Boys' Choir of Harlem, for the debut performance of the Girls' Choir of Harlem. First performed in November 1997 under the direction of Lorna Myers at Alice Tully Hall. 20 min. (IDBC)

Dramatic Music

Frederick Douglass (opera in three acts). 1978–85. New York: American Composers Alliance, 1985. Libretto by Dorothy Rudd Moore. Commissioned and first performed by Opera Ebony, directed by Ward Fleming and conducted by Warren George Wilson, 28 and 30 June 1985 at Aaron Davis Hall, City College of New York. Douglass was portrayed by James Butler, and his wife, Anna, by Hilda Harris. 3 hours. (Moore)

Race for Space (musical). 1963. Text and music by Dorothy Rudd Moore. Performed at Crampton Auditorium, Howard University, in 1963, with Moore in lead role. (Moore)

Popular Songs

Written between 1955 and 1963; words and music by Dorothy Rudd Moore (Moore)

As Time Goes By (Remembered Love). See discography

Billy

But I Love You

Camp Meetin'. See discography

Farewell, My Darling

Hello, Heart

Ice Blue

I Know You're Not an Ordinary Cat

I Never Knew Love

I'm Gonna Beat My Drum Tonight. 1963. Performed by Joyce Bryant. See discography

Love Gone Bad. 1963. Composed in Paris

Love's a Sometime Thing

Night of Splendor

Odyssey

A Sad Song

Silly Guy

Arrangements

Vocal Solos, Duets and Trios

Charity (SA). 1973. New York: American Composers Alliance, 1973. Adaptation of song
   by Richard Hageman with text by Emily Dickinson. 3 min. (Tischler)
Deep River (SA). See *Choral Arrangements.*
He's Got the Whole World in His Hands (soprano, baritone, piano). 1991. Adaptation of
   spiritual setting by Margaret Bonds. (Moore)
I, Too (tenor, cello, piano). 1982. Adaptation of song by Margaret Bonds. Text: Langston
   Hughes. (Moore)
If Music Be the Food of Love. See *Choral Arrangements.*
Life and Death (tenor, cello, piano). 1982. Adaptation of song by Samuel Coleridge-
   Taylor, who also wrote the text. (Moore)
Little Black Boy (tenor, cello, piano). 1982. Adaptation of song by Virginia Lowe Carter.
   Text: Morton. (Moore)
Lullaby (SS duet, piano). 1974. Adaptation of song by Cyril Scott, text by Christina
   Rossetti. (Tischler)
Lullaby from opera *Jocelyn.* See *Choral Arrangements.*
Minstrel Man (tenor, cello, piano). 1982. Adaptation of song by Margaret Bonds. Text:
   Langston Hughes. (Moore)
Nymphs and Shepherds. See *Choral Arrangements.*
On Wings of Song (SS, piano). New York: American Composers Alliance, 1973. Ad-
   aptation of song by Felix Mendelssohn. 3 min. (Tischler)
Praise Be to Thee (soprano, baritone, piano). 1991. Adaptation of song by Handel.
   (Moore)
Songs to the Dark Virgin (tenor, cello, piano). 1982. Adaptation of song by Florence
   Price. Text: Langston Hughes. (Moore)
Thanks Be to Thee (SST). 1973. Adaptation of aria by George Frideric Handel. (Tischler)
Wiegenlied. See *Choral Arrangements.*

Choral Arrangements

Ave Maria (SSA, piano). 1973. Adapted from the prelude by J. S. Bach in the Charles
   Gounod vocal arrangement. (Tischler)
Deep River (SA chorus or duet, piano). 1974. Spiritual adapted from arrangement by
   H. T. Burleigh. (Tischler)
He's Got the Whole World in His Hands (SATB, piano). Spiritual adapted from Margaret
   Bonds' arrangement. (Tischler)
If Music Be the Food of Love (SA chorus or duet, piano). New York: American Com-
   posers Alliance, 1973. Adaptation of song by Henry Purcell. 5 min. (Tischler)
Let My Song Fill Your Heart (SSA, piano). Adaptation of song by Ernest Charles. (Tis-
   chler)
Lullaby from opera *Jocelyn* (SA chorus or duet, piano). New York: American Composers
   Alliance, 1974. Adapted from opera by Benjamin Godard. 4 min. (Tischler)
Nymphs and Shepherds (SSA, piano). Adaptation of song by Henry Purcell. (Tischler)
Passing By (SA, piano). 1973. Adaptation of song by Henry Purcell. (Tischler)
Ride On, King Jesus (SATB, piano). 1973. Spiritual adapted from arrangement by Hall
   Johnson. (Tischler)

Wiegenlied (women's chorus or trio SSA, piano). 1973. Adaptation of song by Johannes Brahms. (Tischler)

Other

"A Linguistic Dilemma" (poem). *Dasein: The Quarterly Review*, 2, no.1 (1969):9.
Pieces of Moon (novel). Begun in 1968, revised in the 1980s, completed in 2001. (Moore)
"To a Vase in a Second Hand Antique Shop" (poem). *Dasein: The Quarterly Review*, 1, no.4 (1968): 25.
Many unpublished poems.

NOTES

I am grateful to Dorothy Rudd Moore for her careful reading, corrections, and additions to this chapter, and for her permission to quote from her poetry.

Full references are given in the bibliography at the end of the chapter.

1. Dorothy Rudd Moore, interview with the author in New York, 27 September 1990. Unless otherwise indicated, all quotes are from interviews and telephone conversations on 27 September 1990, 8 April 1991, 11 December 1995, and 3 December 2000.

2. Moore's siblings are Jacqueline, Rosalyn, Jimmy, Simone, and Carolyn.

3. Mark Fax (1911–74) was a native of Baltimore who studied at Syracuse and New York universities and completed his M.Mus. at the Eastman School of Music. He wrote in a variety of forms, but his operas and piano pieces were best-known.

4. The title, *Ballad of the Winter Soldier*, came from the text of a book by Lufton Mitchell and John O. Killens, written for the event and read by actors.

5. Kermit Moore also attended the American Conservatory at Fontainebleau, as well as the National Conservatory in Paris for three years, where he studied cello with Paul Bazelaire and theory with Nadia Boulanger.

6. Chou Wen-chung (b. 1923) was a student of Varèse, and completed Varèse's piece *Nocturnal*. His works fused Chinese tradition with a sophisticated Western vocabulary and style.

7. Cumming.

8. Kozinski.

9. Page.

10. Cheatham, pp. 72–73.

11. Phraner.

12. Henahan.

13. Snyder; T.M.S. in the *New York Times*. These reviews were of *Adagio*, the middle movement of *Moods*, composed in 1965, before the other two movements, and performed by violist Selwart Clarke and cellist Kermit Moore.

14. Hughes.

15. Rothstein.

16. Moore's program notes.

17. Senzel.

18. Davis, "Moore Song Cycle."

19. Grant.

20. Rawn Spearman was writing his doctoral dissertation on solo voice settings of

Hughes' poetry at Columbia University's Teachers College, and invited Moore to add to that literature.

21. All Moore's subsequent works are vocal except *Transcension*, for chamber orchestra (1986).

22. Moore's program notes.

23. Page.

24. Schmidgall.

25. Abdul, "Harlem."

26. Page.

27. Hughes.

28. Davis, "Concert is Salute."

29. All of the poems are from *The Poetry of the Negro 1746–1949*.

30. Moore, unpublished program notes for *From the Dark Tower*.

31. This song drew especial mention from one reviewer: "the music is particularly successful on "No Images," a song of frustration" (Buckley).

32. Davis, "Moore Song Cycle."

33. Davis, "Five Black Artists."

34. *Dream and Variations* has been performed several times by Theresa Bogard.

BIBLIOGRAPHY

Abdul, Raoul. *Blacks in Classical Music*. New York: Dodd, Mead, 1977.

——. "Musical Event at Aaron Davis Hall." *New York Amsterdam News*, 6 July 1985.

——. "Harlem Opera and Girls Choir of Harlem Make Grand Debut." *New York Amsterdam News*, 27 November–3 December 1997.

Belt, Byron. "Coming Back Strong." *The Jersey Journal* (Jersey City, N.J.), 30 October 1972.

Buckley, Daniel. Record review of *From the Dark Tower* and *Dirge and Deliverance*. *Newsreal* (Tucson, Ariz.), 12 February–11 March 1982.

Cheatham, Wallace McClain, ed. *Dialogues on Opera and the African American Experience*. Lanham, Md.: Scarecrow Press, 1997.

Cohen, Aaron. *International Encyclopedia of Women Composers*. 2nd ed. 2 vols. New York: R. R. Bowker, 1987.

Cumming, Robert. "Carnegie Recital." *The Music Journal* 33, no. 4 (April 1975): 36.

Davis, Peter G. "Moore Song Cycle Heard in Premiere." *New York Times*, 30 October 1972.

——. "Concert Is Salute to Dorothy Moore." *New York Times*, 25 February 1975.

——. "Violinist and Soprano Offer Dorothy Moore's 'Sonnets.' " *New York Times*, 24 May 1975.

——. "Five Black Artists Are Featured on a New Label." *New York Times*, 6 September 1981.

Fossner, Alvin. "Rare Viola Concert by a Master." *The Jersey Journal* (Jersey City, N.J.), 7 December 1965.

Grant, Rick. "UNF's American Music Week Highlighted by William Brown and Gerson Yessin's Ethereal Artistry." *First Coast Entertainer* (Jacksonville, Fla.), 17 November 1990.

Henahan, Donal. "Concert Honors Black Composers." *New York Times*, 29 May 1968.

Horne, Aaron. *Woodwind Music by Black American Composers*. Westport, Conn.: Greenwood Press, 1990.

―――. *String Music by Black American Composers*. Westport, Conn.: Greenwood Press, 1991.

Hughes, Allen. "Reston Trio Offers First of Two Concerts." *New York Times*, 27 March 1970.

Kozinski, David B. "Homecoming Displays Singer's Talents." *Evening Journal* (Wilmington, Del.), 19 May 1980.

McGinty, Doris Evans. "Moore, Dorothy Rudd." In *The New Grove Dictionary of American Music*. Edited by Stanley Sadie and John Tyrrell. New York: Macmillan, 2000.

Middleton, Norman. "Black American Composers Series." *Washington Post*, 18 May 1988.

Morris, Mellasenah. "Moore, Dorothy Rudd." In *Black Women in America: An Historical Encyclopedia*. Edited by Darlene Clark Hine. Brooklyn, N.Y.: Carlson, 1993.

New York Times. T.M.S., "Viola Debut Made by Selwart Clarke." 6 December 1965.

Page, Tim. "Opera: World Premiere of 'Frederick Douglass.' " *New York Times*, 30 June 1985.

Patterson, Willis C., ed. *Anthology of Art Songs by Black American Composers*. New York: E. B. Marks, 1977.

Perry, Frank, Jr., ed. *Afro-American Vocal Music: A Select Guide to Fifteen Composers*. Berrien Springs, Mich.: Vande Vere Publishing, 1991.

Phraner, Leighton. Review of *From the Dark Tower*. *The Music Journal*, 30, no. 1 (January 1972): 51.

The Poetry of the Negro 1746–1949. Edited by Langston Hughes and Arna Bontemps. New York: Doubleday, 1949.

Rothstein, Edward. "Concert: Harlem Piano Trio."*New York Times*, 29 April 1982.

Schmidgall, Gary. Review of *Frederick Douglass*. *Opera News* (October 1985): 77.

Senzel, Alan J. "Violinist Xiao-Lu Li Stimulating at Stewart." *News and Observer* (Raleigh, N.C.), 11 November 1989.

Snyder, Louis. "Weekend Concert Roundup." *New York Herald Tribune*, 6 December 1965.

Southall, Geneva Handy. Program notes for concert "In Celebration of Black Women Composers." National Museum of American History, Smithsonian Institution, 15 May 1988.

Southern, Eileen. "Moore, Dorothy Rudd." In her *Biographical Dictionary of Afro-African and African Musicians*. 2nd ed. Westport, Conn.: Greenwood Press, 1983.

―――. *The Music of Black Americans*. 3rd ed. New York: W. W. Norton, 1997.

Strongin, Theodore. "Richard Elias Gives Bold Violin Recital." *New York Times*, 7 March 1967.

Tischler, Alice, ed. *Fifteen Black American Composers: A Bibliography of Their Works*. Detroit: Detroit Studies in Musical Bibliography, 1981.

Walker-Hill, Helen, ed. *Black Women Composers: A Century of Piano Music 1893–1990*. Bryn Mawr, Pa.: Hildegard Publishing Company, 1992.

―――. *Piano Music by Black Women Composers: A Catalog of Solo and Ensemble Works*. Westport, Conn.: Greenwood Press, 1992.

―――. *Music by Black Women Composers: A Bibliography of Available Scores*. CBMR Monographs no. 5. Chicago: Center for Black Music Research, 1995.

———. "Moore, Dorothy Rudd." In *International Dictionary of Black Composers*. Edited by Samuel A. Floyd, Jr. Chicago: Fitzroy Dearborn, 1999.

White, Evelyn. *Selected Bibliography of Published Choral Music by Black Composers*. 2nd ed. Lanham, Md.: Scarecrow Press, 1996.

Who's Who Among Black Americans. 2nd ed. Detroit: Gale Research, 1977–78.

Williams, Ora. *American Black Women in the Arts and Social Sciences*. 3rd ed. Metuchen, N.J.: Scarecrow Press, 1994.

The World Who's Who of Women. 4th ed. Cambridge: International Biographical Centre, 1976.

DISCOGRAPHY

Dirge and Deliverance. Performed by cellist Kermit Moore and pianist Raymond Jackson on *Cellist Kermit Moore*. Performance Records CR 77001, 1981.

Dorothy Rudd Moore demonstration recording, singing her popular songs *As Time Goes By (Remembered Love), Camp Meetin'*, and *I'm Gonna Beat My Drum Tonight*, arranged and conducted by Harold Wheeler. Early 1970s.

From the Dark Tower. Performed by mezzo-soprano Hilda Harris, cellist Kermit Moore, and pianist Wayne Sanders on *Hilda Harris*. Performance Records CR-77003, 1980.

Modes (string quartet). Performed and recorded at Oberlin College by Meaux Quartet: Nora Carter and Rebecca McFaul, violin; Sharon Neufeld, viola; Rebecca Thornblade, cello. Opus One CD169, 1991.

Three Pieces for Violin and Piano. Performed by violinist Gregory Walker and pianist Helen Walker-Hill on *Kaleidoscope: Music by African-American Women*. Leonarda Productions CD, LE 339, 1995.

Valerie Capers. Courtesy of the Composer.

7

VALERIE CAPERS
(b. 1935)

CHRONOLOGY

1935   Born 24 May in New York City to Alvin and Julia (Auld) Capers; one younger sibling, Bobby (Robert) Capers.

1941   Blinded by misdiagnosed viral streptococcal infection, attended New York Institute for the Education of the Blind.

1946   Began formal piano study at the institute with Elizabeth Thode.

1953   Graduated as valedictorian from New York Institute for the Education of the Blind.

1954   Offered full scholarships at Barnard College and Juilliard School of Music; chose Juilliard.

1959   Completed B.S. degree, first blind graduate of Juilliard.

1959, 1960   Taught at Hunter College, department of special education, during summers.

1960   Completed M.S. degree at Juilliard.

1960–67   Served on faculty of Bronx Neighborhood School of Music.

1960s   Composed numerous jazz pieces, several of which were recorded by Mongo Santamaria: *El Toro, La Gitana, Chili Beans, Ah Hah*, etc.

1967   Debut album, *Portrait in Soul*, produced by Atlantic Records, including her piece *Odyssey* and other original compositions.

1968–75   Served on the faculty at Manhattan School of Music; instituted its first jazz workshop.

Commissioned by John Motley of the All-City Chorus to write a short Christmas choral piece, *Sing About Love*, for national television.

1970s   Became interested in the music of Wagner.

1971   Hired at Bronx Community College of the City University of New York as adjunct professor; composed *Christmas Is Love* for the Bronx Community College Chamber Choir.

1972   Promoted to assistant professor at Bronx Community College.

1973   Conducted student jazz ensemble from the Manhattan School of Music at the Newport Jazz Festival at Carnegie Hall in July.

1974   Bobby Capers, brother and musical mentor, died; expanded *Sing About Love* into a 2-hour, 15-minute Christmas cantata funded by a Creative Artists Public Service grant and premiered in 1974 at Central Presbyterian Church, also performed in 1975 in Cleveland, Ohio.

1975   Began to compose *Portraits in Jazz* for piano.

1976   Received grant from National Endowment for the Arts to write a work on Sojourner Truth; composed *In Praise of Freedom*, a bicentennial celebration for chorus and instrumental jazz ensemble, premiered at Avery Fisher Hall by All-City Chorus.

1978   Promoted to associate professor at Bronx Community College; conducted fourth performance of *Sing About Love* at Carnegie Hall, produced by George Wein (Festival Productions).

1981   Premiere of *Sojourner* at St. Peter's Lutheran Church, New York City; *Jazz in America* television performance with Dizzy Gillespie and Ray Brown.

1982   Issued second jazz album, *Affirmation*, including her piece *Organum*.

1983   Received CUNY Research Foundation grant for research on Paul Laurence Dunbar.

1984   Commissioned by All-City Chorus to write *Duke Ellington Medley* for chorus and jazz ensemble, commemorating tenth anniversary of Ellington's death.

1985   *Sojourner*'s first staged performance, produced by Opera Ebony; commission from New Music Consort for *Escenas Afro-Cubanas* for percussion ensemble; served as panelist and performer for the Black Music in America Conference at the University of Michigan.

1986   Promoted to full professor at Bronx Community College; performed with Billy Taylor on Meet the Composer program at the Whitney Museum in January; *Sojourner* performed by Opera Ebony at Aaron Davis Hall, City College, in February; completed a set of five choral pieces, *The Gift of Song*, setting the poetry of Dunbar.

1987   Elected chairman of the department of music and art, Bronx Community College; commissioned by Smithsonian Institution to write *Song of the*

Seasons cycle for voice, piano, and cello; received Woman of Essence Award from *Essence* magazine, presented on TV.

1988–89   Served as NEA Jazz Performance panelist; performed at Grande Parade du Jazz festival, Nice, France.

1992   Performed Mozart's *Piano Concerto No. 23 in A Major* with Bronx Arts Ensemble chamber orchestra and at the Strawberry Arts Music Festival in Malibu, California; attended Wagner Festival in Bayreuth, Bavaria; received Bronx Borough President's Award for outstanding artistic contributions to the community.

1993   Appeared with Kathleen Battle at Riverside Church; composed jazz instrumental works *The Ring Thing*, and *Winter's Love*; performed at North Sea Jazz Festival, The Hague, Holland.

1994–95   Received NEA Special Projects Award; performed at Mellon Festival, Philadelphia.

1995   Retired as chair of the department of music and art, became artist-in-residence at Bronx Community College; released third jazz album on CD, *Come on Home*, as part of Legendary Pioneers of Jazz series issued by Columbia/Sony (including compositions *Odyssey* and *Out of All He's Chosen Me* from *Sing About Love*).

1996   Received honorary Doctor of Fine Arts degree from Susquehanna University.

1997   Performed at Mary Lou Williams Festival, Kennedy Center, Washington; received Jazz Heritage Award; inducted into International Women in Jazz; featured composer at first Symposium of Black Women Composers at Hampton University in February.

1999   Recorded fourth album, CD *Wagner Takes the A Train* (Elysium Records), including her arrangements/compositions *Wagner Takes the A Train, Always You, Organum*, and *Winter's Love*; featured composer at second Symposium of Black Women Composers at Hampton University in February.

2000   Artist-in-residence, Doan College, Crete, Nebraska; concert at Russian Consulate, New York City.

2001   *Portraits in Jazz* published by Oxford University Press with CD; appearance at Half Note Club in Athens, Greece; featured jazz composer and artist at sixth Annual Festival of Women Composers at Indiana University of Pennsylvania in March; performed at music festival in Nantes, France, in August.

I love playing. I'll always play, but . . . if I'm lucky enough to make a difference in the lives of other people . . . if I'm fortunate enough to leave something behind that will be significant, it will be in the area of composing. And I feel now that my work in that area is always going to be related to my African-American heritage in one way or another, whether it's symbolism, or musical textures (joined of course with Western European musical techniques) or it may be black subjects.

Some people describe me as an eclectic composer. I like that idea. . . . I
like to call on musical colors and textures, regardless of where they come
from, and it works for me. It doesn't sound disjunctive. . . . One piece
sounds baroque and another piece sounds like the blues—I think of all those
approaches as sound textures. It's the way in which you coordinate the
musical textures.[1]

Valerie Capers' melding of musical traditions and her triumph over physical
limitations drew this comment from violinist Maxine Roach, daughter of drummer Max Roach, "She's breaking down barriers—musically and personally. . . .
This is a woman who hired a string section that played with a jazz band and a
choir."[2] A critic for the *New York Times* lauded her "sure-handed mixture of
musical idioms" that reminded him of "some of the extended compositions of
Duke Ellington."[3] Such critical high praise is routinely given to the performances
of her music, which is admired by musicians as diverse as the soprano Kathleen
Battle, with whom she shared a program at Riverside Church in 1993, and
Wynton Marsalis, who collaborated with her on her third jazz album, the 1995
CD *Come On Home*. She has appeared as soloist playing Mozart piano concer-
tos, and has performed with jazz greats Dizzy Gillespie, Billy Taylor, Marian
McPartland, Mongo Santamaria, Donald Byrd, Slide Hampton, Max Roach, and
Ray Brown, to mention only a few. Her jazz trio has performed at the Monterey
Jazz Festival, the Newport Jazz Festival, the Kool Jazz Festival, the North Sea
Jazz Festival in The Hague, Holland, and the Grand Parade de Jazz in Nice,
France. She has taught music at the Manhattan School of Music, Hunter College,
and the Bronx Community College of the City University of New York, where
she served as chair of the department of music and art from 1987 until her
retirement in 1995. The New Music Consort, the All-City Chorus of New York
City, the Smithsonian Institution, the City University of New York Research
Foundation, and the National Endowment for the Arts are among the organizations from which she has received grants and commissions.

BIOGRAPHY

Valerie Gail Capers was born in New York City on 24 May 1935. Her father,
Alvin Capers, was a professional stride jazz pianist until the Depression, and a
close friend of Fats Waller. He was employed by the federal postal system at
the Morgan Annex in New York for 36 years, and before he retired, he became
one of the first African-American postal supervisors. Her mother, Julia, who
worked in the civil service for the New York Department of Hospitals, liked to
play piano, and there was always a large stack of sheet music on the piano.

Valerie's parents grew up in Harlem in the 1920s and 1930s, during the
Harlem Renaissance. At that time, people in Harlem entertained themselves at
home; they did not go downtown to concerts at Carnegie Hall or to Broadway
shows, even though black stars like Ethel Waters and Bert Williams were picked

up by limousines and taken to the theaters where their hits were playing. Her parents had a huge record collection; they would listen to *Porgy and Bess*, or Beethoven's *Fifth Symphony*, or Duke Ellington, Bing Crosby, the Inkspots, Ella Fitzgerald, or early Connie Boswell records. For Christmas, Valerie would receive records of the Grieg *Piano Concerto*, or Tchaikovsky's *Nutcracker Suite*, or Rachmaninoff's *Rhapsody on a Theme of Paganini*. She was always exposed to all kinds of music. She began to play piano by ear almost as soon as she could reach the keys.

Valerie was close to her paternal grandmother, who was a staunch member of the Salem Methodist Church. She felt her grandmother's religious fervor was probably a good influence on her, and years later, Salem Methodist's Phillis Wheatley Club sponsored her first concert. Her father was a Sunday school teacher in the Presbyterian church, and as a little girl, she would go to St. Augustine's Presbyterian Church in the Bronx. But that changed in 1941, when Valerie became ill and a sore throat was misdiagnosed. A streptococcal viral infection entered her bloodstream and damaged her optic nerve, leaving her blind. The last thing she remembers seeing through the window was "snowflakes as my father carried me up the stairs of our brownstone on East 168th Street."[4] After she lost her sight, her father stopped going to church, and she recalls that the church had little influence on her from then on.

Capers has said:

I am very grateful that I didn't lose [my eyesight] earlier because I do have visual memory. I can remember what stars look like, and the beach, the city streets . . . I remember when my grandmother took me to Poughkeepsie, and I remember riding along the Hudson and how beautiful the river was, the mountains. And I remember seeing a horizon and asking my grandmother, "Why is it that the mountain touches the sky when I know that the sky's got to be higher up?" She described it to me and I've never forgotten. In that play *Children of a Lesser God*, when he's telling the deaf woman how wonderful Bach is—he said there's no way to explain it. . . . If I had to bring a horizon in focus to one of my friends who had never seen one, it wouldn't have the same impact. . . . We have to use our imagination. . . . Many things in my life are not visual . . . people will describe things and I'll try to imagine. . . . To compensate, if I want a real sense of what things look like, my tactile sense is important.[5]

When Capers first conducted her cantata *Sing About Love*, she encountered another difficulty. "She found that one of the major problems was that she had no visual frame of reference to the music [or the musicians]. To her it was all sound. [This] led her to put a string across her doorway while she practiced [conducting] so that her arm would hit the string if her motion was too broad."[6]

Ironically, her blindness provided Valerie with a quality of education she might not otherwise have received.

I grew up in a situation where I had a marvelous education, the kind of education that my very hardworking parents could not have afforded if I had not lost my sight. . . . The

New York Institute for the Education of the Blind here in the Bronx was an extraordinary school. It no longer exists. I lived in that school during the week and came home on the weekends. I had a wonderful balance of magnificent teachers and a loving family.

The institute campus took up a large block on Pelham Parkway, with the earlier grades at one end and sixth grade through high school at the other end. When she was 11, she graduated to the upper level, and began classical piano lessons with Elizabeth Thode, an exacting but inspirational teacher. Valerie was still playing by ear, and her previous teachers warned Thode not to play for her, so that she would be forced to learn to read. Braille is a very difficult and cumbersome music system, and Valerie tried to get out of it by writing a letter to her teacher, saying, "Maybe I'm not really good enough to study with you." The ploy didn't work, and terrified as she was, she learned to read music well.

Braille music requires both hands to read, making it impossible to sight-read in the usual manner. Valerie had to take each little section and memorize it, then piece it all together. In later years at Juilliard, she would memorize all her repertory for the following year during the summers. She could never participate in the yearly concerto competitions because the required concerto would be posted only at the beginning of the school year, and there was never enough time to learn it.

Under Thode's tutelage, Capers blossomed as a pianist, and by the time she was 12 she was practicing five or six hours a day. At age 15, she experienced a live concert for the first time when Mary Weir, one of her teachers, took her to hear a piano recital by Dame Myra Hess at Carnegie Hall. (They would become friends years later, and Capers still treasures her letters and a framed handkerchief.) Valerie soon gave solo recitals which were supported by her grandmother's church and by her father's colleagues at the post office, who would bring their families to hear her.

Her love of classical music grew as she was exposed to different genres. An older schoolmate at the institute, Dorothy Wright, loved opera and introduced Valerie to the Braille librettos in the school library and to the Saturday afternoon radio broadcasts of the Metropolitan Opera with Milton Cross. In her senior year, she heard her first live opera at the Met, Puccini's *Tosca*, sung by Zinka Milanov.

After graduating from the institute in 1953 as valedictorian of her class, she was advised by her teacher to take a year to prepare for college, during which she practiced eight to ten hours a day. She was offered scholarships at both the Juilliard School of Music and Barnard College. Capers chose to attend Juilliard, and Thode, who remained involved in Capers' career all her life, helped her to pick out teachers. Among her memories from her six years at Juilliard are her analyses of Moussorgsky's *Boris Godunov* and Tchaikovsky's *Eugene Onegin*, the several miniature Singspiele she composed for her class in history of the theater, and the compositions she was required to write in different classical forms for her theory class. Capers was the first blind student to receive the bachelor's degree from Juilliard and went on to obtain her master's degree there in 1960.

Capers was urged by her brother Bobby to explore her African-American musical roots in the jazz idiom. Because the jazz discipline is so different from the classical, she found it necessary to put aside classical playing for two years. "I was coming out of the Bach and Brahms tradition. . . . The ambience and mental set and the discipline is just not the same. [This] discipline is geared to spontaneity. I finally realized that if I was in earnest about learning jazz, I wasn't going to be able to balance it with classical. . . . I had to step back and start crawling again. . . . It was a very long process." Her brother and other jazz musicians, such as Art Jenkins, taught her chord changes. "Jenkins played at a local club, The Blue Morocco on Boston Road in the Bronx. He would come over and play, and every time I heard a chord I liked, I'd stop him and say, 'What's that?' He would play [it] and I'd play back to him. I had a good ear." She systematically made up exercises for herself, and played long-playing records at slow speed, memorizing the music, then transposing it. It was a couple of years before she tried her first gig at Kenny's on Boston Post Road, where her brother knew the owner. "I was terrible! It was just awful! I was nervous and scared, and that blocks the mind." But Capers persevered, and in 1967 she recorded her first jazz album, *Portrait in Soul*.

During these years, it was almost impossible for Valerie to find employment. She remembered:

For years I couldn't get a job. . . . Maybe one of the lesser reasons might have been that I'm a woman, certainly [because I'm] a black woman; but the primary reason was that I was blind. I had all sorts of things thrown up at me, like . . . I might be an insurance risk, I might get hurt, there might be students who would be affected by having a physically disabled person teaching them. . . . I finally got a little job in a neighborhood music school in the Bronx making $2.50 an hour with no sick benefits. But I was very grateful just to start. That little band of people—they were really brave, because they were sort of concerned about whether the students would react in a positive way—how their parents would react. The students were wonderful! The director was so pleased that she sent a letter to Helen Keller telling her about my work, and Keller wrote back. That was special!

Valerie was able to supplement her teaching at the Bronx Neighborhood Music School with a job at the Brooklyn School of Music, where she started a jazz department. In two years her class of 10-to-14-year olds doubled in size. They held monthly jazz sessions at the school, played, criticized each other's performances, and drifted into discussions on the emerging African states and social problems at home.

From 1968 to 1975 Valerie worked at the Manhattan School of Music in an advisory capacity. Six blind and partially sighted students were enrolled full-time in the music curriculum, and Valerie assisted the faculty in dealing with the academic and music problems of these special students. This opportunity and her reputation led to the establishment of the Manhattan School of Music jazz workshops. At this time, jazz was just starting to be accepted in music schools and departments, and the jazz curriculum developed by Capers eventually served as a model for schools nationwide. By 1973, the Manhattan School Contemporary Jazz Ensemble, a group of 15 instrumentalists and 11 singers, was participating in a Carnegie Hall jazz series during the Newport Jazz Festival, earning critical praise for its "surprisingly high level," its "big-band smack," and its "attractive and stimulating approaches . . . to the standard . . . jazz lexicon." Capers' own jazz piano style was lauded for her "strong, positive attack" and "big, brash chords that swung with tremendous force."[7]

For one semester, in the fall of 1971, Capers taught at the High School of Music and Art. That year Bronx Community College of the City University of New York became interested in her and decided to take a chance if Capers felt she could teach there. She was hired part-time as an adjunct professor for one semester before being promoted to assistant professor in the spring of 1972. Her academic career there was one of steadily increasing rank and responsibilities. When the chair of the department of music and art retired in 1987, she was elected to that position.

Capers' composing career had two main instigators: her brother Bobby, and the choral conductor John Motley. She had composed theory assignments at Juilliard and knew it was something she could do easily. But she was never motivated until, around the time she was learning to play jazz, Bobby asked her to write pieces for Mongo Santamaria's band, in which he played tenor saxophone and flute.[8] She started with the Latin jazz piece, *El Toro*, recorded on Santamaria's *Live at the Village Gate* album in 1963 and performed on television. This led to more pieces: *La Gitana, Chili Beans*, and *Ah Hah*, which was used for a dance sequence in the movie *Made in Paris*, starring Louis Jourdan and Ann-Margret.

The next impetus came through a course in vocal techniques she took at the Manhattan School of Music in 1969 as part of the requirements for a teaching certificate. The instructor was John Motley, the first African American to be appointed director of the All-City Chorus of New York, a world-class group that received much exposure during Mayor John Lindsay's administration. Motley had been a protégé of Hall Johnson, and had coached and accompanied Marian Anderson in her last tours. He was an impressive and inspiring teacher. Motley asked her to write a Christmas piece for his chorus that December, the first of several commissions by Motley for the All-City Chorus, and the nucleus of the 2-hour, 15-minute cantata she composed several years later under a Creative Artists Public Service grant, *Sing About Love*.

In February 1974, her brother Bobby died unexpectedly. His death was the biggest crisis in her life. Capers says, "In the last analysis he really died from alcohol. He didn't deal with frustration very well—pressures of the business, a marriage that didn't go well."[9] She and Bobby had sometimes talked about death, and he would say, "I don't want a lot of sorrow [when I die]. If I die before you, put all that energy into something creative." That summer, Capers was working on *Sing About Love* while adjusting to Bobby's death. "It was terribly hot and terribly sad. A lot of grief that I had about my brother was private. I had two parents that were really suffering something terrible . . . and I had to be very strong for them, so a lot of what I felt had to be private and personal. . . . Many times I would be crying and writing at the same time, hearing him say 'Sit down and do something! Music is what counts!' " *Sing About Love* was composed under his guiding spirit. "I felt that extra push. There was something I had to do for Bobby's memory, and for me, and for Mother and Daddy. I was the only one left. Whatever I do now is what my family was all about—Mother, Daddy, Bobby, and myself. . . . That work is the closest to my heart." *Sing About Love* was premiered in December 1974 at Central Presbyterian Church to critical acclaim. That year was the watershed year in Capers' life. There would be other crises in her life, but nothing to equal the loss of her brother.

Capers' love affair with the music of German composer Richard Wagner (1813–83) had its origins in the appreciation of opera acquired in her teens at the Institute for the Education of the Blind. She studied his opera cycle, *The Ring of the Nibelungen*,[10] in music history class at Juilliard, but her instructor did not like Wagner. It was not until the early 1970s, when one of her students made tapes for her of his works, that she truly "discovered" him: "Richard Wagner really, absolutely, turned my life around. . . . I have a Walkyrie hat [helmet with horns] that I wore at the Ring Cycles in Bayreuth in 1992." During that visit she met Wolfgang Wagner, Richard's grandson, through Walfredo Toscanini, Arturo Toscanini's grandson, who was a fan of hers and arranged the meeting. The New York Wagner Society contacted the curator of the Wagner home at Wahnfried, where she was permitted to play his piano and to touch the statues of Tannhauser and Tristan, and the busts of Cosima Wagner and Wagner himself. They allowed her to sit on the couch on which Wagner had died in Venice. She brought home two handfuls of pebbles from the garden where Wagner was buried and keeps them in a glass dish on her coffee table. "I can run my fingers through it every day. . . . I soaked up all that atmosphere, and became spiritually attuned."[11] Capers wanted to reciprocate in some way, and informed the Wagner Society in New York that she wished to present a little musical offering based on the themes from the *Ring of the Nibelungen*. They invited her to play it at a year-end party in 1993.

With the completion of her cantata *Sing About Love* and its critical success, Capers had the confidence to apply for an NEA grant to write a work about Sojourner Truth, and received it in 1976. This work, in a form that Capers called "operatorio" (longer than an oratorio and shorter than an opera), also was well received. More grants and commissions came in, one of them from Motley's All-City Chorus for a choral piece on the tenth anniversary of Duke Ellington's death (1984), and another from the City University of New York Research Foundation to write a work on the black poet Paul Laurence Dunbar (1872–1906). For this project she traveled in 1984 to Dayton, Ohio, where Dunbar grew up. Like her visit to Bayreuth, this was a memorable experience.

I wound up spending a whole weekend in his house, and they allowed me to touch everything. I went up to his study and touched all the books that he loved—Keats, Shelley, Byron—with torn covers from use, and I actually took his pipes out of their holder and put them to my heart for the vibrations. He went to school with the Wright brothers, Wilbur and Orville. They were his classmates and . . . they had a poetry club at school, and he loved to recite poetry. . . . I saw his bicycle. . . . He had a paper route and Reverend Wright gave him an old bicycle to help with his route. . . . I went into his closet and touched the cutaway suit that he wore at President Theodore Roosevelt's inauguration . . . the vibrations were incredible.

These commissions were followed by others, among them one for a nonjazz work from the Smithsonian Institution in 1987. This came through D. Antoinette Handy, then head of NEA music division, who said, "Everyone knows that you work as a jazz musician, but I want them to know that you are a composer."[12] The resulting song cycle, *Song of the Seasons*, received rave reviews and was later performed at the Marlboro Festival and in Europe.

The 1980s were productive in many other ways. The Valerie Capers Trio performed widely in the United States and abroad, and recorded a second album in 1982, *Affirmation*, hailed by Dizzy Gillespie as "sheer delight."[13] She performed with Gillespie on his video *Jazz in America*, and with Billy Taylor in a program for the Meet the Composer series at the Whitney Museum. She was promoted to full professor at Bronx Community College in 1986, the same year that *Sojourner* was staged by Opera Ebony. In 1987 she received the Woman of Essence Award from *Essence* magazine, the first ever awarded to a musician, and the presentation was televised.

After she was elected chair of the department of music and art at Bronx Community College in 1987, Capers had very little time to compose. Budget cuts eliminated release time for creative work, and her academic duties exerted tremendous pressures: administering, dealing with personalities, and teaching courses in music history, class piano, introduction to jazz improvisation, Latin jazz ensemble, jazz history, and songwriting. She continued to perform with her jazz trio at clubs, festivals, and symposia, and recorded two more jazz CDs: *Come on Home*, with a stellar group of musicians including Wynton Marsalis, produced in 1995 as part of Columbia/Sony's Legendary Pioneers in Jazz series, and *Wagner Takes the A Train* in 1999, which was ranked among the top ten by jazz radio stations.

In these CDs her rich, supple contralto voice can be heard, a new element in her jazz performances. She had sung in choirs and knew she had a voice, but felt it lacked control and authority. She now began systematic training with the noted baritone Andrew Frierson, and worked hard at it, singing art songs and spirituals as well as her jazz ballads.

In 1992 she was excited to have the chance to play Mozart's *Piano Concerto No. 23 in A Major* with the Bronx Arts Ensemble chamber orchestra and again at the Strawberry Arts Music Festival in Malibu, California. It had been a long time since she had performed classical music. "People who have known me over the past 20 years do not associate me with classical music, and of course that's all I played at one time." After that success, she returned to a heartbreaking personal situation. In her absence her niece, Bobby's daughter, the mother of a little baby, had begun forging checks in her name. It was some time before this betrayal was discovered, and by then almost $30,000 was gone from Capers' retirement savings. These were funds earmarked for the care of Capers' 82-year-old mother, who lived in the same apartment building. Capers mourned, "She was given probation. We have not talked to each other for a while. The baby hasn't been here for more than a year, and I miss the child, but I am still angry. Can you imagine how violated I felt? I had opened up my home to her. Blind people have to trust others more than the sighted, and this kind of betrayal hurts terribly."[14]

Capers retired from Bronx Community College in 1995, but returned as artist-in-residence, and is also kept busy by numerous engagements to present workshops and give concerts with her jazz ensemble. She established her own company, Valcap Music, to publish her compositions. She continues to live in her spacious apartment on the Grand Concourse in the Bronx, where she enjoys cooking gourmet meals, often with regional themes from France, Italy, and the Caribbean, while listening to opera. Her home is filled with mementos of her rich and varied life; the celebrities she has known; and her travels to Puerto Rico, Europe, Canada, and many states in the United States. In the entry hall hang portraits of John Coltrane and Richard Wagner, whom she calls her great mentors. Bobby's picture hangs above her piano, and Duke Ellington, Beethoven, Puccini, and Martin Luther King, Jr. round out her pantheon of heroes. A tall, dark, beautiful woman with commanding presence, she moves confidently and speaks with warmth and authority, whether one-on-one in her home or to a group of student musicians in a workshop.

Occasionally, a hint of regret creeps into her conversation when she talks about the fame she wishes she had received, and her dreams of performance of *Sing About Love* becoming an annual event. "I really thought that I'd have a chance, that this would take off, but I guess maybe it wasn't the right thing at the right time." And to a reporter in 1999 who remarked that few outside of jazz circles had heard of her, she said, "I can't blame anybody. I think it's just fate. Sometimes you strike gold, sometimes you don't."[15]

Hopes were revived in 1999 when her CD, *Wagner Takes the A Train*, was ranked among the top ten by jazz radio stations. Its title piece quotes themes from Wagner's *The Ring of the Nibelungen* in a high-spirited satire. It is just one of the many ways—as composer, performer, and teacher—Valerie Capers creates a bridge between the European classical and the African-American jazz traditions. As exhilarating as a "hit" would be, Capers' contributions will be more lasting.

SOCIAL ISSUES

Capers' experiences of and views on race, gender, and class have been shaped and overshadowed by her experience as a blind person. Since race is usually registered visually first, it cannot help but be experienced differently by someone who doesn't see skin color and features. Although Capers did not comment on that aspect, she considered her early schooling at the New York Institute for the Blind to be a factor. "There weren't a lot of black kids there. I was not really aware of anything." She also believed that the attitude of the times, and the protection she received at home, insulated her from having to think about race.

My parents were very conscientious. They grew up in Harlem. My father maybe knew a little bit more about black history than my mother did. I have to admit it's not something we discussed in our home. When I was growing up, nobody ever taught me anything about anybody other than George Washington Carver who did wonderful things with peanuts. . . . I had to read later about the others. I didn't know anything about black artists . . . painters . . . architects. I was a grown woman before I heard about them.

Her brother Bobby was responsible for awakening her strong sense of racial identity and motivating her to learn to play jazz. "I really have my brother to thank for that. . . . He felt that we as African Americans are responsible for one of the greatest art forms ever to come out of mankind, and we had a responsibility to carry it on. It was kind of like an ethnic pride."[16] "He felt that as a black woman I should direct my talents to areas that are related to my culture and my background."

Since then, Capers has demonstrated her racial awareness in music not only by mastering the art of jazz but also by absorbing Afro-Cuban musical idioms and culture, and immersing herself for a time in gospel traditions "at the source," attending Church of God in Christ and other holiness churches. Capers referred to her jazz compositions as her "African-American" music. Along with many jazz traditions—ragtime, New Orleans, stride piano, Afro-Cuban—she consciously incorporated African-American folk materials. In describing the closing chorus of her *Wagner Takes the A Train*, she said, "The shout chorus is always the last chorus. . . . It is a jubilant celebration of the individual improvisations that went before and has its roots in the religious services, the hands-on Holy Ghost kind of religious service, so it's very emotional."[17]

She has chosen black subjects and authors for the texts of major works. The poems she selected for her choral cycle of Dunbar songs include poignant expressions of racial suffering, such as "We Wear the Mask." Her libretto for *Sojourner*, assembled from various historic accounts and speeches, speaks eloquently: "This great nation of ours can be the promised land for all its people. . . . We must rise to the challenge of justice and stand solid as a rock. And in the course of time we shall gather the harvest of love and respect and touch a chord of truth."

Her strong sense of racial identity emerged in her response to questions about her inclusion in a book about African-American women composers.

I'm very proud to be a part of that. I'm not always that enthusiastic about being part of a survey. . . . However, this is a special case. . . . We are still struggling as African-American artists, musicians, men and women, to not only be recognized in society but for us to know one another. I think this is sorely needed. I want to know about the wonderful women that are out there composing and doing things. It's stimulating, it's wonderful to hear them, because as a composer you should always be open. . . . I think this book is very much needed, not only for the educator, but for those of us who are in the creative, composing community and don't have a chance to know about one another. . . . I think that we're in a stage at this particular time where these things have to be more specifically identified and categorized.

Some of Capers' feeling about women's issues is expressed when she has Sojourner say, "We eat as much, work as much, and want as much as any man. Men have been having our rights for so long, they think like a slave master— that they own us. If rights more than you got is what you want, then honey, it's time to stop talkin' and start takin'!" Her passionate speech in which she exclaims, "See these arms—they have plowed and planted and gathered into barns, and no man could head me, and ain't I a woman??" is a climactic point of the whole work. Capers brought Sojourner's point into the present when she objected to studies exclusively about women in jazz: "In many senses I resent it because it's often one of the limited avenues in which women have an opportunity to gain attention or recognition. I feel that we should be able to get that . . . on an equal level with men who do what we do."

Despite her awareness of racial and gender issues, Capers considered her own struggles to have been a result of prejudice against the physically disabled. She said that being a woman was one of the lesser reasons for not getting a teaching job in the 1960s. The overriding reason was that she was blind, and the excuse was just as false and insulting: that she would traumatize the students and/or their parents. She resented that categorization most of all.

I had to fight a long time to keep people from using the word "blind" every time I did something. My blindness had nothing to do with what ability or lack of ability I had. But people felt for the longest time it was something immediate that they could put a hook on. Now they'll maybe say it in a sentence, maybe that I'm sightless. . . . That's what we're looking for—the African-American person to be written about, accepted, presented, without that label, maybe just coming up incidentally, but unfortunately we're not there yet.

While not commenting directly on class, Capers also speaks to this issue through Sojourner: "As I travel the countryside I see those privileged to live in comfort and oft-times luxury and it is a painful reminder of those who still struggle in squalor, poverty, oppression, and lives of frustration." In Valerie's family background she observed both privilege and sacrifice. Her parents worked tirelessly and selflessly to provide the best possible education and opportunities for her and her younger brother, Bobby.

Every cent they had went into my growing up and my brother's growing up. . . . Their relatives, my aunts, uncles, and cousins, had homes, jewelry, investments. My mother and father never had anything. Daddy saved up and bought me a grand piano. . . . When my brother went to the High School of Music and Art and had to have a clarinet, Daddy got the best and he had to have insurance for it because we lived in a bad part of the Bronx.

Capers' affluent relatives, hardworking parents, and Bronx neighbors acquainted her at a young age with a full range of economic circumstances. And she was, of course, conscious of hardship and differences in privilege through her association with jazz musicians from all backgrounds, as well as her counseling and encouraging a broad spectrum of students. All these experiences inspired her desire "to make a difference in the lives of other people" through her teaching and through her music.

THE MUSIC

Valerie Capers' compositional output falls into two main groups: pieces for jazz ensemble, numbering about 20, most of them written for the Valerie Capers Trio, and other instrumental, choral, and vocal works, of which there are 10, most of them commissioned by individuals and groups. They begin in the early 1960s with *El Toro*, written for Mongo Santamaria's band. The first choral piece, *Sing About Love*, was commissioned by John Motley for the All-City Chorus in 1969. Her works appeared at regular intervals in the 1970s and 80s, and a few were composed in the 1990s. All have been performed, and a few are published by her company, Valcap Music (see list of works). Her most important large-scale works are *Sing About Love* (1974), a Christmas cantata *Portraits in Jazz* (1976), a set of 12 solo piano teaching pieces, and *Sojourner* (1981), a dramatic work on Sojourner Truth lasting almost an hour. Half a dozen of her jazz ensemble pieces have been recorded on her own albums, and *Portraits in Jazz* is available on a CD included with the score, published by Oxford University Press. A song cycle for voice, cello, and piano, *Song of the Seasons*, also has been recorded (see discography).

The size of Capers' body of work is directly related to the difficulty of notating her music. She writes it down in Braille, reads it out loud on tape, and then has someone transcribe it for her. The reading is slow and tedious because she literally dictates note for note.

Braille music notation is quite primitive; it is not based on line and space notation at all—they have a different reference for sound. They have the piano divided into different octaves. . . . [For instance] middle C on the piano is called fourth octave C because it's fourth highest from the bottom. Everything from that note up to the next C is named fourth octave. . . . If the flute is playing G above the treble clef, I would say "That's fifth octave G," or "in bar so and so the violins have such and such a note, tied over to the next bar while the trumpets play such and such a note." That's a lot of talking. That's why I'm sort of anxious about the new technology and getting advice and availing myself of it so that I will be able to write my own scores. I'm worried that all that technology is so expensive, we're talking thousands and thousands of dollars which I don't have.

At a conference in Washington, D.C., on access technology for the disabled, Capers heard about a machine advertised by Stevie Wonder, called a personal reader, that cost over $12,000. "I told them I was very upset—this machine would turn my life around and I can't afford it! They said, 'Get a bank loan'!" That is not an option she can consider, and if she applied for a grant at the college, the equipment would have to stay on the premises.

With such discouragement, it is a wonder that Capers composes at all. Her process starts with an idea—a melody, or sound, or even just a feeling. "I start with whatever the inspirational force pumps into me. . . . How do I want people to feel when they hear it? . . . Many times it's just a vague concept. I don't write necessarily spontaneously. I have to be pushed." Perhaps that is why she admires Beethoven so much. "The greatest [composer] was Beethoven—a man who had vision beyond his time. He was the single greatest innovator. After the third symphony, the Eroica, the symphonic concept was never the same. But he didn't write with divine ease—he reworked his ideas over time—he worked! I guess that is what endears him to me."

Although most of her jazz pieces are instrumental, Capers prefers vocal writing, and only two of her "serious" works are just for instruments. Her enthusiasm for the voice began with the vocal techniques class she took from John Motley: "I got hooked on writing for the voice. . . . I'd rather write something with words than a purely instrumental composition. The union of music and words is powerful." After her brother Bobby, it was Motley who provided the "push" she needed, by commissioning choral works for his All-City Chorus. The *Duke Ellington Medley* was composed for the tenth anniversary of the death of Ellington; it was choreographed and performed at Alice Tully Hall with great success, and later done by other choruses and by Opera Ebony. It is a choral suite based on five Ellington compositions: *I'm Beginning to See the Light, Satin Doll, Sophisticated Lady, Take the A Train,* and *It Don't Mean a Thing.* She added other Duke Ellington songs to interchange and insert between the last two, making the work more versatile.

Another choral jazz piece composed for the All-City Chorus was her setting of the 150th Psalm. When it was performed at the premiere of *Sojourner* in 1981, a reviewer noted that it "almost upstaged her operatorio . . . [and] floated on an enticing melody that had the appealing qualities of a superior popular song."[18]

Capers' earliest creative efforts were in Afro-Cuban jazz, inspired by Mongo Santamaria, and this idiom continues to influence her works. An Afro-Cuban dance, the mambo, holds a pivotal position in the auction scene of her operatorio *Sojourner*. She developed a particular fondness for the bossa nova, which she described thus to Walter Rudolph: "The bossa nova is one of the most wonderful rhythms ever created. When you apply that rhythm, it gives the music a certain swing, a certain grace, a movement that is unique, very special. It lends itself to lyricism. Antonio Carlos Jobim was probably the greatest bossa nova writer; he was known for the lyricism and beauty of his melodies." A bossa nova figures prominently in her major work, *Sing About Love*, in the lovely movement *No Room at the Inn*. Her *Portraits in Jazz* includes a bossa nova and a *Canción de Havana* dedicated to Mongo Santamaria.

In 1985, Capers featured the Afro-Cuban idiom in a percussion work commissioned by the New Music Consort for its tenth anniversary, and dedicated it to Santamaria. The three movements of *Escenas Afro-Cubanas* are basically folk and ethnic in character, and the first movement is played on traditional instruments: log drums, congas, bongos, timbales, and numerous hand rhythm instruments with various colors and sounds. The middle movement, *Homenaje*, evokes three African gods worshiped in Cuba—Elegua, Chango, and Obatala—and "because of this, I have expanded the instrumentation of this piece with a five-foot rain stick and Japanese temple bowls as a symbol of the common bond shared by all of mankind with nature and the supernatural."

As Capers' jazz piano style evolved, it became a part of her compositional style. It shows the influence of several of her idols: Oscar Peterson, Ahmad Jamal, Hank Jones, and Art Tatum, the blind jazz pianist whose virtuoso pyrotechnics are echoed in her lightning-fast technical passagework. But the greatest influence was John Coltrane (1926–67). According to one reporter who remarked on her early struggle to find her jazz "voice," "Ms. Capers can point to the day in 1962 when she found it—with the release of John Coltrane's critically acclaimed *Giant Steps*."[19] That she had, indeed, found her voice was confirmed by a critic who wrote, "[She has] come up with a commanding style all her own. . . . the bristling density of Miss Capers' chordal passages and her habit of materializing melody lines out of lush tremolos are notably original. Her ballad playing . . . was remarkable for its control of dynamics and depth of feeling."[20]

Her jazz work, *Organum*, gets its name from the use of melodic ideas in parallel fourths, fifths, and tritones.[21] In the middle section, the piece hurtles freely from one musical texture to another, at one time driving and rhythmic, at another arhythmic and tonally meandering; here the bass bows a lyrical melody, there the piano bashes huge chords like arm clusters.

Capers pays homage to Coltrane in the last piece of her *Portraits in Jazz,* titled *Cool-trane.* Capers has also dedicated a work-in-progress called *Celebration* to Coltrane. "It's going to be an orchestral work in one movement based on the first four notes of [Coltrane's] *A Love Supreme.* . . . with a [narrated] text that is a combination of little quotes he put on some of his later albums and my own way of putting things together. . . . Coltrane got very metaphysical in his later life—his whole concept of brotherhood and our connection with the infinite."

While Bobby Capers and John Motley gave Capers the motivation to compose, her greatest musical inspiration came from John Coltrane and Richard Wagner. In an article she wrote on John Coltrane, she said, "As a devotee of Richard Wagner, I find a striking set of aesthetic parallels between his music and that of John Coltrane. . . . with Wagner or Trane, you cannot separate the man from his art. Coltrane, like Wagner, exalts the artist to the highest calling in society, possessing the most powerful and positive forces for good and love in the world."[22]

Capers felt her mission to be the reconciliation of African-American jazz and European classical musical styles. Maxine Roach considers this an "ability to successfully combine unthinkable musical elements. . . . This is a woman who hired a string section that played with a jazz band and a choir. She's just so fluent on both disciplines. . . . She's breaking down barriers."[23] Capers likes to say, "Once I was a classical pianist, then I was a jazz pianist, but now I'm a pianist—no label. And in my writing, I'm not concerned with any particular style. I've found that if you have musical groundwork and some idea of the emotional impact the music should have, the musical style will hang together."[24]

In the 1970s, when she fell under the spell of Richard Wagner, his music inspired Capers to tackle large projects and to experiment with orchestration. "Wagner did for me in composition what John Coltrane did for me in developing my jazz . . . I learned more about the relationship of drama to music than from anyone, more about the use of instruments. When I wrote *Sing About Love,* the second half opens with this dark, brooding clarinet. . . . I never would have thought of that morose, evil scene if it hadn't been for Wagner." Wagner's influence can also be heard in the instrumentation and continuous melodic lines of *Sojourner.*

While *Sing About Love* and *Sojourner* put jazz at the service of classical forms, classical music was placed in the service of jazz in her compositions *Wagner Takes the A Train, Winter's Love,* and *The Ring Thing.*

Wagner is such a natural for the whole concept of jazz and improvisation. His motives create a germ of an idea that you as a musician or performer can put into a musical life of its own; you can develop it, you can create a whole metamorphosis, you can do what

Wagner does so masterfully in his operas. . . . We took motives, ideas, and themes [from Wagner's *Ring of the Nibelungen*] and used them in strategic places as jumping off points for developing improvisational lines. . . . The Rhine maidens' melody from the first act of *Das Rheingold* worked very well over the harmonic progression of the middle section of *Take the A Train.*[25]

In *Winter's Love*, which uses the bossa nova rhythm, Siegmund's aria provides the melody. In the coda, Wagner's Magic Fire or Fate Theme is heard, and a quote from Siegfried's Funeral Music by her bassist John Robinson closes the piece.

Capers' purely nonjazz works lie at the other end of her range of styles. These include *In Praise of Freedom*, a choral work based on the March on Washington speech of Martin Luther King, Jr., and her *Song of the Seasons*, four songs on her own texts for soprano, cello, and piano, composed in the late-Romantic idiom. *Sing About Love*, an extended jazz work, is more eclectic in nature. In addition to the African-American, Latin, and jazz styles, the composer found some of her resources in traditional European styles, ranging from the serene baroque string Interlude to the twentieth-century dissonance of the Prologue.

Another eclectic work that includes nonjazz movements is the choral setting of five Dunbar poems, *The Gift of Song* (1986). Scored for SATB, flute, a rhythm section, and percussion, it includes a "warm and lyrical" bossa nova (*You*) as well as a hymnlike setting (*Farmchild's Lullaby*), and closes with a rousing gospel number (*Gift of Song*).

One of Capers' big goals is to write a grand opera on the ancient Greek myth of Medea, the sorceress whose story was dramatized by Euripides. "It's an extraordinary story—it's got everything you ever wanted—vengeance, drama, love, politics, and two very strong women: Medea, of course, and the nurse who has known her ever since she was a little girl. And then the story of Jason and the Golden Fleece and how Jason and Medea met, and her murdering her children—it's an incredible story."

The opera is still in the thinking stage, but Capers already has ideas. One of them was inspired by the parade that greeted Nelson Mandela on his visit to New York.[26]

When Nelson Mandela was here, he spoke at Riverside Church. He was going from there to 125th Street in Harlem, and lining the streets were these various African percussion ensembles, all the way to 122nd Street and Riverside Drive up Broadway to 125th Street. They were in their colorful ceremonial robes and [played] all types of African drums, but also the shakers, the bells, the gongs. It was the most glorious-sounding thing you'd ever want to hear. As they went up the street, it was almost like listening to Charles Ives.[27] You would hear one group recede into the airwaves as another one approached with different rhythms and different sonority. . . . I thought to myself, I'm going to get in touch with Olatunji[28] and ask him to talk to me about the traditions of celebratory percussion and also funeral percussion, because I thought they would be very dramatic in the opera.

It is to be hoped that the dream of this opera will be realized, and that Capers will be inspired to produce more of the remarkable jazz compositions which have brought a fresh, imaginative approach to the standard jazz forms and instrumentations. In her jazz cantata and operatorio she has carried on and expanded the legacy of Duke Ellington's and Mary Lou Williams' large-scale sacred jazz works in classical forms.[29]

Sing About Love (1974)

In 1969, Valerie Capers was invited by John Motley, conductor of the All-City Chorus of New York, to compose a Christmas piece for his choir. Sing About Love, a five-minute work in semi-gospel style, was performed that Christmas. A year later Capers received a Creative Arts Public Service grant to write a larger composition suitable for community presentation. Sing About Love was expanded to a 2-hour, 15-minute cantata and first performed in 1974 at Central Presbyterian Church in New York City, with a 20-voice chorus and 22-piece orchestra conducted by Capers. The following two seasons the work was performed at Cuyahoga Community College in Cleveland, Ohio. A fourth performance of Sing About Love occurred at Carnegie Hall on 18 December 1978, by the New York Jazz Repertory Company, conducted by Capers. Guest performers were Slide Hampton on trombone, Mongo Santamaria on congas and Donald Byrd and Nat Adderly on trumpet. The work has received other performances, at Symphony Space in New York City in 1985, at Clark Atlanta University in Georgia in 1991, and at the College of New Rochelle (New York) in 1993.

Of all her compositions, Sing About Love is closest to the composer's heart. While completing the work in 1974, she was mourning the death of her beloved brother and mentor, Bobby. She resolved to compose music that would be connected to her African-American heritage and would make a difference in the lives of other people. As she worked on the cantata, she was also inspired by the universal and enduring popularity of Handel's Messiah, composed at a time when he was losing his sight.

Sing About Love tells the biblical Christmas story with a combination of traditional biblical texts and the composer's words. To ensure historic accuracy, Capers did extensive research at Union Theological Seminary. She also attended a variety of pentecostal churches for a year—prayer meetings, healing services—in order to "go to the source," to absorb the authentic flavor of gospel music for the big church/gospel sequences. The cantata's movements are in a variety of forms and styles: classical European, blues, swing, Latin jazz, jazz solos, and gospel. Mary's solo Out of All He's Chosen Me is in popular song style. Each One to His Own City employs salsa and blues. Herod's councilor sings a gospel solo full of fiery preaching and testifying. The chorus God of Ancient Israel is in Lutheran chorale style (with a slight blues inflection). No Room at the Inn is a bossa nova. A meditative instrumental Interlude evokes Bach's Air on a G String. The original chorus Sing About Love concludes the work in joyous gospel style. Capers is masterful in her juxtapositions of these seemingly incompatible idioms. The various styles are well suited to the mood of each particular episode, and the sequence of contrasting styles and instrumentation contributes to the overall dramatic structure of the work.

The instrumentation, both the choice of instruments and how they are used, is equally skillful. When combined, the orchestral strings and jazz ensemble enhance one another. Instrumental solos and small groupings, vocal and choral sounds and textures are alternated to optimal effect. In *No Room at the Inn* the bossa nova is introduced by piano, bass, Latin percussion, and three flutes, a totally unexpected and original sound.

When Herod sings his *Soliloquy*, the bass clarinet accompanies him in a dark and sinuous duet. Then the chorus, strings, and timpani improvise eerie unpitched and glissando sounds to echo his delusions, and the bass drum builds tension. Capers says the instrumentation of this episode was inspired by Wagner's orchestration, portraying inner psychological drama.

The tonal language varies according to stylistic idiom. The *Prologue* begins with a movement for full orchestra with biting contemporary dissonances, in which the angel Gabriel announces her future to Mary in declamatory vocal style. In the following number, the brass and rhythm sections open a duet between Gabriel and Mary in jazz vocal style with jazz harmonies. The final section of the Prologue, the solo *Out of All He's Chosen Me*, sung by Mary in popular song style, simplifies the harmonies still further. The remaining movements continue to vary their tonal language to reflect the psychological development of the narrative. Herod's fevered *Soliloquy* is the most atonal movement of the cantata. It begins with a long, tonally ambiguous solo for bass clarinet, followed by a duet between Herod and the bass clarinet which becomes progressively more dissonant, and culminates with unpitched sounds at his decree that all male children two years and under must die. The movement ends in an atonal cluster by the winds, and screams by the chorus. After this climactic and violent moment the consonant diatonic harmonies of the following unaccompanied chorale, *God of Ancient Israel*, provide a stunning contrast and emotional consolation. Later on the work *Quiet Night*, with its soothing jazz harmonies and alto saxophone solo (written with her brother Bobby in mind), and the following haunting *Interlude* for strings in baroque aria style, supply similar contrast after the chromatic dissonance of the choral and instrumental *Glory*. The audience is thereby given an opportunity to meditate upon the events of the narrative. This, in turn, prepares and contrasts with the upbeat gospel rhythms and harmonies of the joyful Finale, *Sing About Love*, in which audience joins with clapping.

Each performance of the cantata has met with enthusiastic critical acclaim. After the 1978 performance at Carnegie Hall, the critic for the *New York Times* stated, "Miss Capers proved her talent as an adept writer in several idioms, but more importantly, she demonstrated a rare ability to make disparate elements cohere compositionally.... 'Sing About Love' was first-class jazz writing ... it should be performed every Christmas."[30]

Portraits in Jazz (1975–76)

The twelve piano pieces in Capers' collection *Portraits in Jazz* were begun in 1975, while Capers was convalescing from back surgery and completed in 1976. Three of them appear in the anthology *Black Women Composers: A Century of Piano Music 1893–1990*, published by Hildegard Publishing Company in 1992. Two were included on the 1995 Leonarda Records CD *Kaleidoscope: Music by African-American Women*, performed by Helen Walker-Hill, and the entire set performed by Valerie Capers is on a CD included with the Oxford University Press publication of the work (2001).

Capers intended the set to be pedagogical in the spirit of Robert Schumann's *Album for the Young*, or Bartók's *Mikrokosmos*. The technical difficulty varies from slight to considerable. The pieces are meticulously fingered and marked by the composer. Further instruction is provided by prefaces with remarks on construction or style, and by the dedication of each piece to a great jazz musician whose spirit it evokes. All together, they last approximately 20 to 25 minutes. They can also be effectively used in small groups.

The first piece, *Ella Scats the Little Lamb*, marked "Bright and Spirited," arranges the familiar nursery tune "Mary Had a Little Lamb" in Ella Fitzgerald's improvisatory style of scat singing over a steady left-hand basso continuo in half notes. *Waltz for Miles* is a simple melody paying tribute to Miles Davis's sensitivity of phrasing and warm, impressionistic harmonies. *Sweet Mister Jelly Roll* pays homage to Jelly Roll Morton in ragtime style. The left hand plays a simplified stride bass with typical oom-pah skips and repeated chords.

The Monk, written in the keyboard style of Thelonius Monk, features open fifths and sevenths, biting seconds, off-balance accents, and cluster chords, and a quote from Monk's blues, *Straight No Chaser*. *Blues for the Duke* is reminiscent of Duke Ellington's early style. In traditional 12-bar blues form, the harmonic structure is based on chords on the first, fourth, and fifth notes of the key. According to the composer's preface, this blues can be thought of as a theme with two variations and a return to the opening theme.

A Taste of Bass is dedicated to the bassist Ron Carter, whose solos and rhythm work influenced the next generation of bass players. The first section is a miniature bass solo by the left hand, followed by a quarter-note walking bass line characteristic of the supportive rhythmic and harmonic role of the bassist in a jazz ensemble. The seventh piece, *Billie's Song*, is a simple, one-page ballad dedicated "in fondest memory" to Billie Holiday, and evokes the warmth and poignancy of her style.

In *Mr. Satchmo*, the right-hand interjections imitate Louis Armstrong's early trumpet playing. The piece is in the style of the New Orleans street bands in which Armstrong began his career. *Canción de Havana*, dedicated to Mongo Santamaria, is an example of the Afro-Cuban idiom. It includes a passage of *guaguançó* music, a combination of flamenco and Western African influences that is part of the heritage of Cuba and Puerto Rico. *Bossa Brasilia* is a variant of the Brazilian bossa nova, which strongly influenced American popular music and jazz during the 1960s. It is characterized by a two-measure rhythmic pattern in 4/4 time. The combined rhythms in this piece are tricky for inexperienced pianists. *Blue-Bird* is also challenging for the student, with its subtle rhythmic complexities and extended bebop melodic line with offbeat accents characteristic of the saxophonist Charlie "Bird" Parker. The form is a modern "chromatic blues," including frequent chord changes and expanded harmonies.

The last piece, *Cool-trane*, is the most difficult and the most harmonically adventurous. Less than a minute long, it consists of a dazzling shower of melodic 16th-notes imitating Coltrane's saxophone style, interspersed with parallel chords built on fourths, their roots climbing by minor thirds. The title is a word play on Coltrane's name, and the piece closes with a quote from his *Cousin Mary Blues*.

Song of the Seasons (1987)

This song cycle for soprano, cello, and piano, commissioned by the Smithsonian Institution specifically to demonstrate Capers' versatility as a composer in the nonjazz idiom, is dedicated to D. Antoinette Handy. It was premiered 3 May 1987 at the Smithsonian Institution in Washington, D.C., by soprano Mereda Gaither-Graves with Capers as pianist and John Robinson on cello. The 10-minute work has subsequently been performed at the Bronx Community College by soprano Beth Farnum, with Sylvia Eversole, pianist, and John Robinson, cellist. In 2000, two CDs were released that included performances of *Song of the Seasons*: Charsie Randolph Sawyer's on *The Unknown Flower* and Anita Johnson's on *Sence You Went Away* [*sic*] (see discography).

These songs are not in the jazz or popular song idioms usually associated with Capers, but rather in a late-Romantic art song style. The harmonic language is tonal, with lush harmonies and florid piano figuration. The influence of Wagner is heard not only in the unexpected shifts of key and evasions of resolution, but also in the freely floating, semi-declamatory vocal melodic line. The cello functions as a partner with the voice, in contrapuntal duet or imitative dialogue, and also as the melodic solo line in introductions and transitory interludes. When played pizzicato, it shares the accompanying role of the piano, whose arpeggiations and repeated chords provide harmonic color, sustain motion, and fill out the texture. In the third song, *Autumn*, and part of the last, *Winter*, the cello is silent and the piano takes over the function of melodic counterpoint with the voice.

The text is by the composer, and was inspired by the economy and imagery of haiku, the Japanese poetic form. The work is divided into four songs, *Spring, Summer*, followed immediately (*attaca*) by *Autumn*, then *Winter*. The second and last songs each change mood before they end, in anticipation of the next season. The lyrics to the first song extol typical spring emblems—melting snows, cherry blossoms, returning birds, and hope "of splendid dreams and things to be." In 6/8 meter, vocal and cello lines lilt in predominantly quarter-eighth rhythm, with large, expansive melodic contours and a wide pitch span. Its three sections are centered on E-flat major, A-flat major, and D-flat major, respectively.

Summer begins with a short cello introduction in A minor. The indication is "Moderato ed espressivo," and the chordal piano accompaniment is gently pulsated. The song explores several tonalities before ending in A-flat major. In the course of this love song, the mood shifts from the fulfillment of "warm days," "hot summer skies," and "two people but a single heart," to the "fading summer days" that "whisper of what used to be" . . . and "just a memory." Just before the change to anticipation of *Autumn*, the piano shifts to a static, whole-note chord progression, foretelling the opening of the last song, *Winter*.

Although *Summer* ends with a conclusive cadence on A-flat, the next song begins *attaca*, without a break, and it maintains the same tempo and the same gently syncopated accompaniment. Its lyrics depart, however, from the love theme to a depiction of fall colors, the fruits of harvest and labor's rest, for "autumn is the promise kept." The cello is absent, not to return until the melting of the snows of winter. *Autumn* concludes in B-flat major, setting up the relative G minor opening of the next song.

Winter changes mood radically, with a piano introduction of slow, static, whole-note chords, inspired, according to the composer, by the hollow open chords in Schubert's *Der Doppelganger* from his song cycle *Die Winterreise*. When the voice enters, it intones the first phrase on one note in its low register: "Late at night as I peer into the dark and endless winter sky." The starkness of this initial statement sets up the next breathtaking phrase, "I listen to the rain," with its soaring leap to high A. Recollections of times past summon motives of previous songs in the accompaniment, and in a transitional passage of almost atonal suspended time, the stage is set for the triumphant return of *Spring*.

Unity in the song cycle is established by the obvious anticipations of following seasons in *Summer* and *Winter*, and by the recall of previous material in the concluding song. Key relationships also tie the songs together, as they cadence first in D-flat major, then A-flat major, B-flat major, and finally again D-flat major. A less perceptible unity is provided by similar rhythmic and melodic motives among the songs. The first and last songs end with climactic, thrice-repeated short motives separated by rests and accompaniment figures: " 'tis spring" three times in the first, and "tomorrow" three times in the last. A short melodic motif of four rising scale notes is found in all four songs: in *Spring* at "My heart cries out"; in *Summer* at "The fields were green"; in the opening phrase of *Autumn*, in almost the same words: "The fields of green"; and at the close of *Winter* in "The time has passed." In addition, the opening melodic line of *Summer* recurs in *Autumn*. These melodic and rhythmic recalls are not obvious, but operate on a subliminal level to unite the songs.

The cycle is a worthy and very accessible addition to the growing repertory of songs for voice with cello and piano. The reviewer for the *Washington Post* called its premiere at the Smithsonian Institution the "high point of the afternoon.... This is music rooted in the tradition of Debussy, endowed with a lovely feeling for melody and a nice sense of texture."[31]

Sojourner (1981)

While her Christmas cantata, *Sing About Love*, may be closest to the composer's heart, she considers her most innovative work to be her "operatorio" on the life of Sojourner Truth. She coined the name to indicate a form that is more concise than an opera and employs elements of both oratorio and opera. She emphasizes that it is primarily music rather than theater, and should not be considered an opera. Nonetheless, it has been staged by Duane Jones for Opera Ebony in 1985 and again in 1986, with Loretta Holkam in the title role; by Hope Clark for Opera Ebony in 1988, with soprano Elvira Green; and by Von Washington at Calvin College Fine Arts Center in Grand Rapids, Michigan, in 1990, with soprano Claritha Buggs.

The work was commissioned in 1976 by the National Endowment for the Arts for the bicentennial year, but due to illness, Capers was not able to finish it until several years later. Its premiere was a concert performance at St. Peter's Lutheran Church in New York City in February 1981, with Elvira Green in the title role, Capers at the piano, and John Robinson conducting. One reviewer lauded its "strong dramatic sensibility, not only in the inherently dramatic slave-auction scene.... Miss Capers' music uses jazz elements very skillfully and perceptively. When jazz was intrusively effective, it intruded. But it was also an unobtrusive and very effective element when an alto saxophone wound through the background of Sojourner's monologue of challenges."[32]

The 55-minute work for chorus, soloists, and jazz ensemble is organized into three parts, and built around episodes in the life of Sojourner Truth, the nineteenth-century freed slave who became a powerful and eloquent orator in the struggle for emancipation and the rights of blacks and women. The narrative takes place on two time levels: actual time, and remembered or disjunct time. Actual time corresponds to the setting in a small Midwestern town which frames the work in the first and last sections. Remembered time includes previous events and recollections, and reflections by Sojourner on her past, in nonsequential order.

In the story on the actual time level, the arrival of Sojourner in the small town is awaited by the townspeople, some of whom object "We don't want her here!" and others who eagerly welcome her. Before she appears in the town, however, we are taken back to several episodes from her life. The first event is from her childhood in New York, when she was sold at the age of seven, as a throw-in with an auction of sheep. In the next section she remembers her parents, Papa Baumfree and Mama Betts, and the man she loved and lost, as well as the man she married.

In the third part, the New York law freeing slave children born after 1799 is proclaimed, and she prays for guidance. The Lord instructs her to travel the countryside with the message of freedom, and gives her the name Sojourner Truth. She arrives in the small Midwestern town of the opening scene, and speaks her message despite confrontations and a near riot.

This story unfolds in a variety of musical sections, some of them transitory and connected through the narrative flow, and others set off as fully developed, independent units. The scenes in the town flow continuously from solo voices in declamatory style to choral interjections to instrumental interludes. Part I culminates in an extended and energetic choral and instrumental jazz number, marked "swinging," in which the townspeople welcome Sojourner.

Part II, in which Sojourner is sold, begins with an instrumental piece in Latin-Caribbean style marked "mambo." The Caribbean rhythms and instrumentation are carried over into the auction scene, where each bid is delivered in the mambo rhythm. Part II continues with Sojourner's recollections of her past, in which her parents appear and sing to her. The vocal lines are partly declamatory and partly arioso, with interjections by solo instruments—string bass and alto saxophone. A striking effect is achieved by the inclusion of the Lord's Prayer sung by Sojourner: each of its phrases is intoned on one note and followed by questions and further recollections in combinations of melody and speech. The final phrase of the prayer concludes Part II.

In Part III, the law freeing slaves in New York is proclaimed, and is explained by the chorus. The vocal lines are delivered in speech, supported by instrumental background. Then the instruments fall silent and a piece in the style of a spiritual for chorus and soloist begins, in which Sojourner laments her confusion and calls upon the Lord. An unusual element in this piece is a section in which four members of the chorus improvise overlapping independent lines in "a moaning and beseeching manner." Sojourner's plea is answered by the Lord in a classical recitative replete with traditional declamation, harmonies, cadences, and instrumental punctuation. Part III has been done separately, notably by Elvira Green on a program at the Smithsonian Institution, where a reviewer called it "the apex of the concert. . . . One longed for a complete performance, for the excerpt was riveting. . . . Truth's compassion, nobility and bitterness was spellbinding."[33]

The Finale returns to the small town, with the town band playing a Salvation Army-style march and the crowds challenging Sojourner in half-spoken shouts and cries. She delivers a monologue consisting of passages from her most memorable speeches, underscored by an instrumental background including an eloquent and poignant single melodic line by the alto saxophone. The last instrumental accompaniment in chorale style leads into the choir's concluding phrase of the work, "Truth is eternal and truth is love."

Sojourner, while continuing Scott Joplin's legacy, in his opera *Treemonisha*, of combining classical operatic and African-American elements, does indeed represent a new form in its brevity, its combination of traditional and novel formal elements, classical and African-American idioms, and real and remembered time. It broadens the possibilities for dramatic expression while avoiding the necessity of a large and expensive stage production, and is a welcome model for the many other composers drawn to the opera genre.

LIST OF WORKS

Works are available from Valcap Music, P.O. Box 1509, Bronx, NY 10451. Phone and fax: (718) 993–7428.

Archive

(AMRC/CBMR) Helen Walker-Hill Collection of scores by black women composers housed in duplicate at the American Music Research Center at the University of Colorado School of Music and the Center for Black Music Research at Columbia College, Chicago (five scores).

References

(Capers) Valerie Capers, unpublished list of works.
(IDBC) *International Dictionary of Black Composers*—see bibliography.

Instrumental Music

Piano

Portraits in Jazz. 1976, revised 1998. New York: Oxford University Press, 2001. Contents: (1) Ella Scats the Little Lamb; (2) Waltz for Miles; (3) Sweet Mister Jelly Roll; (4) The Monk; (5) Blues for the Duke; (6) A Taste of Bass; (7) Billie's Song; (8) Mr. Satchmo; (9) Canción de Havana; (10) Bossa Brasilia; (11) Blue-Bird; (12) Cool-trane. Nos. 5, 6, 7 in *Black Women Composers: A Century of Piano Music 1893–1990*, edited by Helen Walker-Hill (Bryn Mawr, Pa.: Hildegard, 1992). See discography. 20 min. (AMRC/CBMR; Capers, IDBC)

Percussion Ensemble

Escenas Afro-Cubanas. 1985. Contents: (1) Canción Callejera; (2) Homenaje; (3) Descarga. Written for New Music Consort. Dedicated to Ramon "Mongo" Santamaria. (Capers, IDBC)

Jazz Ensemble

Ah Ha. 1960s. Mongo Music. (Capers, IDBC)
Blue Monday. 1960s. Valcap Music. (Capers, IDBC)
Chili Beans. 1960s. Mongo Music. (Capers, IDBC)
La Gitana. 1960s. Mongo Music. (Capers, IDBC)
Hey Stuff. 1960s. Valcap Music. (Capers, IDBC)
Kenne's Soul. 1960s. Valcap Music. (Capers, IDBC)
Little David Swings. 1960s. Valcap Music. (Capers, IDBC)
Odyssey. 1960s. Valcap Music. See discography. 6 min. 28 sec. (Capers, IDBC)
Organum. 1960s. Valcap Music. See discography. 9 min. 14 sec. (Capers, IDBC)

The Ring Thing. 1993. Based on Wagner's *Ring of the Nibelungen.* (Capers, IDBC)

Ruth. 1960s. (Capers)

Sabrosa. 1960s. Valcap Music. (Capers, IDBC)

Sarai. 1960s. Mongo Music. (Capers, IDBC)

Thelonius Assault. 1960s. (Capers)

El Toro. 1960s. Mongo Music. See discography. (Capers, IDBC)

Wagner Takes the A Train. 1993. See discography. 6 min. 23 sec. (Capers)

Waltz Pierrot. 1960s. Valcap Music. (Capers)

Winter's Love. 1993. Valcap Music. Bossa nova based on Wagner love themes. See discography. 5 min. 42 sec. (Capers, IDBC)

Vocal Music

Solo Voice with Instruments

Always You (voice, jazz ensemble). 1995. Text: Valerie Capers. See discography. 5 min. 53 sec. (Capers)

Song of the Seasons (voice, piano, cello). 1987. Greenville, N.C.: Videmus, in progress, 2002. Edited by Louise Toppin. Text: Valerie Capers. Contents: (1) Spring; (2) Summer; (3) Autumn; (4) Winter. Commissioned by the Smithsonian Institution. Dedicated to D. Antoinette Handy. First performed by Mereda Gaither-Graves, soprano; Valerie Capers, piano; and John Robinson, cello, on 3 May 1987 at Smithsonian Institution, Washington, D.C. 10 min. (AMRC/CBMR; Capers, IDBC)

Chorus

Christmas Is Love (SATB). 1971. Text: Valerie Capers. Performed by the Bronx Community College chamber choir. (Capers, IDBC)

Duke Ellington Suite (SATB, jazz trio). 1984. Commemorating the tenth anniversary of the death of Duke Ellington. Commissioned and first performed in May 1984 by the All-City Chorus of New York, conducted by John Motley, at Avery Fisher Hall. (Capers, IDBC)

The Gift of Song (SATB). 1986. Text: Paul Laurence Dunbar. Contents: (1) You; (2) A Love Letter; (3) Farmchild's Lullaby; (4) We Wear the Mask; (5) The Gift of Song. Commissioned by CUNY research grant. First performed at Wesleyan University, 1987. (AMRC/CBMR; Capers, IDBC)

He's There. 1972. Text: Valerie Capers. Composed for and performed by Bronx Community College chamber choir. (Capers)

In Praise of Freedom (SATB, jazz ensemble). 1976. Setting of Martin Luther King, Jr.'s March on Washington speech. Commissioned and first performed in 1979 by the All-City Chorus of New York, conducted by John Motley, at Avery Fisher Hall. (Capers, IDBC)

Psalm 150 (SATB, jazz ensemble). 1980. Commissioned and first performed by the All-City Chorus of New York at Avery Fisher Hall, and again in 1981 at St. Peter's Lutheran Church, New York. (Capers, IDBC)

Sing About Love (SATB, soloists, jazz ensemble, orchestra). 1974. Text: Valerie Capers. Commissioned by the New York City Creative Artists Public Service. First per-

formed with ensemble and orchestra conducted by Valerie Capers in 1974 at
Central Presbyterian Church, New York. 2 hrs. 15 min. (AMRC/CBMR; Capers,
IDBC)

Dramatic Music

Sojourner (SATB, jazz ensemble). 1981. Operatorio. Text: Valerie Capers. Composed
on NEA grant. First performed with Elvira Green, soprano; Valerie Capers, piano;
John Robinson, conductor, in February 1981 at St. Peter's Lutheran Church, New
York. 55 min. (AMRC/CBMR; Capers, IDBC)

Other

"Tenor Madness: John Coltrane: Bringing Verismo to Jazz." *Village Voice*, 24 June 1986.

NOTES

I thank Valerie Capers for her patience and generosity in granting me interviews,
answering questions, checking this chapter for accuracy, and permitting me to quote from
her poetry and her libretto of *Sojourner*.

Full references are given in the bibliography at the end of the chapter.

1. Valerie Capers, interview with the author, New York, 12 October 1990. Quotations
by Valerie Capers are from this interview or a later interview with the author on 8
November 1995, unless otherwise cited.

2. Maxine Roach, quoted in AP.

3. Palmer.

4. Baiocchi.

5. Valerie Capers, interview with Walter Rudolph, New York City, 22 June 1995.

6. Wilson, "Valerie Capers."

7. Wilson, "Imaginative Approach."

8. Bobby Capers had also written a piece, *Don't Bother Me No More*, which was
recorded on the flip side of one of Santamaria's biggest hits, *Watermelon Man*, and was
sharing in the royalties.

9. Bobby married twice, the last time a year or so before his death. He had two
daughters from his first marriage.

10. *Der Ring des Nibelungen* comprises four operas (Wagner preferred the term "music dramas") based on Norse and Teutonic mythology: *Das Rheingold* (1854), *Die Walk-
üre* (1856), *Siegfried* (1871), and *Götterdammerung* (*The Twilight of the Gods*, 1874).

11. Rudolph interview.

12. Quoted by Capers, interview with the author, 12 October 1990.

13. Endorsement on cover of album *Affirmation*.

14. Kaufman.

15. AP. These remarks are reminiscent of Margaret Bonds' hopes in the 1960s for hit
songs and a commercial success with her Christmas cantata *Ballad of the Brown King*.

16. Quoted in AP.

17. Rudolph interview. See also note 29.

18. Wilson, "Jazz."

19. AP.

20. Palmer.

21. "Organum" refers to a type of medieval church music in which thirds and sixths were forbidden and voices moved in parallel fifths and fourths, imparting a hollow sound ideally suited to the acoustics of Gothic cathedrals.

22. Capers, "Tenor Madness" (see list of works).

23. AP.

24. Wilson, "Valerie Capers."

25. Rudolph interview.

26. Nelson Mandela (b. 1918) visited New York in 1990 shortly after his release from prison, having served 28 years for his opposition to apartheid in South Africa. A Nobel Peace Prize winner, he was president of South Africa from 1994 to 1999.

27. Charles Ives (1874–1954) was an American composer who pioneered many modernist techniques, some of them inspired by watching parades in which the music of different passing bands was heard simultaneously.

28. Babatunde Olatunji, world-famous drummer, was born in 1927 in Nigeria and educated in the United States at Morehouse College and New York University.

29. Capers is not entirely comfortable with labeling her works "jazz compositions," preferring to call them "African-American derived." The works of Mary Lou Williams, on the other hand, she considers true jazz compositions because of their basis in blues and jazz band traditions.

30. Palmer.

31. Reinthaler.

32. Wilson, "Jazz."

33. Middleton.

BIBLIOGRAPHY

Anekwe, Simon. "Students Pack Blind Teacher's Jazz Class." *New York Amsterdam News*, 16 June 1962.

Associated Press (AP). "Jazz Pianist Takes Wagner for a Ride on 'A' Train." *Jefferson City (Missouri) News Tribune*, 4 July 1999. http://www.newstribune.com/stories.

Baiocchi, Regina A. Harris. "Capers, Valerie." In *Facts on File Encyclopedia of Black Women in America: Music.* Edited by Darlene Clark Hine. New York: Facts on File, 1997.

Claghorn, Charles Eugene. *Biographical Dictionary of Jazz.* Englewood Cliffs, N.J.: Prentice-Hall, 1982.

Dahl, Linda. *Stormy Weather: The Music and Lives of a Century of Jazz Women.* New York; Limelight, 1984.

Edwards, Audrey. "Valerie Capers." *Essence*, May 1987, 39.

Gourse, Leslie. *Madame Jazz: Contemporary Women Instrumentalists.* New York: Oxford University Press, 1995.

Handy, D. Antoinette. *Black Women in American Bands and Orchestras.* Metuchen, N.J.: Scarecrow Press, 1981.

Kaufman, Michael T. "When a Life of Music Nearly Went Sour." *New York Times*, 16 March 1994.

Knowlton, Ellen. Liner Notes. *Affirmation.* KMArts Record, 1982.

Middleton, Norman. "Performing Arts: Black American Composers Series." *Washington Post*, 18 May 1988.

New York Times. "Valerie Capers: Composer Plans Piano Performances." 22 January 1986.

Palmer, Robert. "Concert: Valerie Capers." *New York Times*, 20 December 1978.

Perlmutter, Nick. "Bronx Song Composer Won't Sing the Blues." *Bronx Beat*, 1 May 1995.

Reinthaler, Joan. "Music of the Black American Composer." *Washington Post*, 4 May 1987.

Routes. Review of *Sing About Love*. (December 1978/January 1979): 38.

Southall, Geneva. Program notes for "In Celebration of Black Women Composers," concert at Smithsonian Institution, 15 May 1988.

Southern, Eileen. *Biographical Dictionary of Afro-American and African Musicians*. 2nd ed. Westport, Conn.: Greenwood Press, 1983.

Walker-Hill, Helen, ed. *Black Women Composers: A Century of Piano Music 1893–1900*. Bryn Mawr, Pa.: Hildegard, 1992.

——. *Piano Music by Black Women Composers: A Catalog of Solo and Ensemble Music*. Westport, Conn.: Greenwood Press, 1992.

——. *Music by Black Women Composers: A Bibliography of Available Scores* CBMR Monographs no. 5. Chicago: Center for Black Music Research, 1995.

——. "Capers, Valerie." In *International Dictionary of Black Composers*. Edited by Samuel A. Floyd, Jr. Chicago: Fitzroy Dearborn, 1999.

Wilson, John S. "An Imaginative Approach." *New York Times*, 2 July 1973.

——. "Valerie Capers to Conduct Her Jazz-Based Cantata." *New York Times*, 17 December 1978.

——. "Jazz: By Valerie Capers." *New York Times*, 28 February 1981.

DISCOGRAPHY

Billie's Song, Cool-trane from *Portraits in Jazz*. Performed by Helen Walker-Hill, piano, on *Kaleidoscope: Music by African-American Women*. Leonarda Records CD LE339, 1995.

Capers, Valerie. *Affirmation*. Valerie Capers, piano; John Robinson, bass; Al Harewood, drums. KMArts, KMA 1907-B, 1982. Includes *Organum*.

——. *Come On Home*. Valerie Capers, piano; Terry Clarke, drums; Wynton Marsalis, trumpet; John Robinson, bass; Mongo Santamaria, congas; Paquito D'Rivera, alto sax; Bob Cranshaw, bass. Legendary Pioneers of Jazz series, Columbia/Sony CK 66670, 1995. Includes *Odyssey, Out of All He's Chosen Me* from *Sing About Love*.

——. Interview with Marian McPartland. On radio program *Marian McPartland's Piano Jazz*, season 4, no. 8, Station WBGO (National Public Radio), 1985. Reel-to-reel recording at Rodgers and Hammerstein Archives of Recorded Sound, New York Public Library, Lincoln Center, New York City.

——. *Portrait in Soul*. Valerie Capers, piano; John Daley, bass; Charlie Hawkins, drums; Frank Perowski, reeds; Vince McEwen, trumpet; Robin Kenyatta, Richie Landrum, percussion. Atlantic Records, 1967. Includes *Odyssey*.

——. *Portraits in Jazz*. Valerie Capers, piano. Oxford University Press, CD included in score, 2001.

————. *Wagner Takes the A Train.* Valerie Capers, piano; John Robinson, bass; Earl Williams, drums; Alan Givens, sax and flute; and Mark Marino, guitar. ERI Elysium Recordings GRK 715, 1999. Includes Capers' *Always You, Wagner Takes the A Train, Winter's Love.*

Song of the Seasons. Performed by Anita Johnson, soprano; Susan Keith Gray, piano; Timothy Holley, cello, on *Sence You Went Away.* [*sic*]. Albany Records #387, 2000.

Song of the Seasons. Performed by Charsie Randolph Sawyer, soprano; Karen Krummel, cellist; and Susan Keith Gray, piano, on *The Unknown Flower.* Calvin College, 2000.

El Toro, by Mongo Santamaria's band on *Live at the Village Gate,* 1963; reissued on *Mongo at the Village Gate.* Fantasy/Original Jazz Classics OJCCD-490-2, 1990.

Mary Watkins. Courtesy of the Composer. Photo by Phillip Brey.

8

∽

MARY WATKINS
(b. 1939)

CHRONOLOGY

1939	Born 9 December in Denver, Colo.
1941	Adopted by Benjamin and Evelyn Maloney, named Mary Maloney, and taken to Pueblo, Colo.
1943	Began piano lessons with Edith Johnson in Pueblo, Colo.
1945	Entered Columbia Elementary School in Pueblo, Colo.
1953	Entered Central High School.
1954	Began piano lessons with Miss Page in Pueblo, Colo.
1957–60	Attended Pueblo Junior College (later University of Southern Colorado); studied theory and piano with James Duncan.
1962–63	Father, Benjamin Maloney, passed away April 2, 1962; attended Adams State Teachers College in Alamosa, Colo.
1963	Married Edward Dawkins on 17 February in Pueblo; moved to Washington, D.C.; daughter Sharron born.
1970–72	Attended Howard University, studied composition with Mark Fax and Russell Woollen.
1971–72	Musical director and resident composer for theater group Ebony Impromptu in Washington, D.C.; composed piece for flute and piano, and five woodwind quintets.
1972	Completed Bachelor of Music degree cum laude at Howard University; began freelance work as performer (keyboards), arranger, composer.

1974   Divorced from Edward Dawkins; composed *Illusions* and *Introspection* for flute and piano, a piece for single reed instruments, and *Potomac Park* for full orchestra.

1975   Attended University of Colorado at Denver; studied with Bill Fowler and coached with jazz musician Joe Keel; *Potomac Park* performed by the Pueblo Civic Symphony Orchestra.

1976   Moved to Los Angeles; changed name to Mary Watkins; did freelance work; joined staff of the Olivia Records Collective.

1970s, 1980s   Keyboardist, arranger for albums by Stephanie Mills (1976), Teresa Trull (1976, 1980), Linda Tillery (1977), Meg Christian (*Face the Music*, 1977), Cris Williamson (*Blue Rider*, 1982), Holly Near (*Fire in the Rain*, 1981; *Speed of Light*, 1982), and Gayle Marie (*Rainbow at Night*, 1982); performed at jazz festivals including Monterey Jazz Festival, Kansas City Women's Jazz Festival, Alewives Jazz Festival in Milwaukee, U.C. Berkeley Jazz Festival Symposium, Universal Jazz Coalition Salute to Women in Jazz in New York City, Midwest Women's Music Festival, Michigan Womyn's Music Festival, West Coast Women's Music and Cultural Festival, Women's Jazz Festival in Boston, New England Women's Music Retreat.

1977   Moved to Oakland, Calif.; established her own jazz group; performed at the Monterey Jazz Festival, Russian River Festival, and major jazz clubs.

1978   Composed jazz fusion pieces *Back Rap, Brick Hut, A Chording to the People, I Hear Music, Witches' Revenge, Yesterday's Children*; released album *Something Moving* (Olivia Records); nominated for Best Debut Album, Bay Area Music Awards.

1980   Received National Endowment for the Arts grant for tour of women's prisons.

1981   Received NEA Jazz Performance grant to produce record *Winds of Change*; located birth mother; two concerts at Herbst Theater in San Francisco with small jazz combo and 42-piece jazz orchestra, recording her jazz orchestra pieces *The Street Merchant, Samba Orleans, Waterwheel, Billie's Barb, Woman Messiah, Winds of Change, Changin' Times*, in October 1981.

1982   Composed songs: *The Way You Smile, Sweet Refrain, The Meaning of Love, and You'll See When You See*; produced second album, *Winds of Change*, for small combo and 42-piece jazz orchestra.

1983   Composed piano pieces *Mirrors, Playground, Manhattan Mist, Changing Seasons*, and *Spiritsong*; pieces for cello and for flute, *Patrick the Dancer, Braziltown USA*; two instrumental quartets; and two trios.

1984–85   Composed songs *A Little Closer, Love's Sweet Song, I Suppose*; flugelhorn work *A Matter of Urgency*.

1985   Produced third album, *Spiritsong*; nominated for Best Composer/Arranger and Best Keyboardist, Bay Area Jazz Artist Music Awards; music director for the Oakland American Jazz Theater; mother, Evelyn Maloney, passed away.

1985–89   Participated in California Arts Touring Program.

1986   Commission from Bay Area Women's Philharmonic orchestra, *One Episode of an Inner Journey*, for piano and orchestra, premiered April 1987; received Oakland Redevelopment Agency Jazz Performance Award; composed film score for *Ethnic Notions* (winner of several awards); also composed a piano quintet.

1986–88   Received Zellerbach Family Fund Award.

1987   Received NEA Jazz Composers fellowship to write *The Sword That Heals*; six-week residency at the Djrassi Foundation arts colony; composed score for film *Valuing Diversity*.

1987–88   Received Clorox Foundation grants; *The Sword that Heals* premiered 20 November 1988; composed jazz ensemble score for Lorraine Hansberry Theater production of *The Resurrection of Lady Lester*; scores for films *Fighting for Our Lives* and *The Coming Ice Age*.

1987–96   Annual performances of her jazz adaptation *The Revolutionary Nutcracker Sweetie* for 13-piece ensemble by the Dance Brigade of Oakland.

1988   Birth mother passed away.

1989   Commission from the Gerbodi Foundation for score for Lorraine Hansberry Theater production of *The Bluest Eye*; composed score for film *Out in Suburbia*.

1990   American Jazz Theater commission for a 50-minute work for 12-piece jazz ensemble (*Suite Convulsions*), funded by the Meet the Composer Commissioning Program; composed *Elusion* for full orchestra; score for film *Diversity Among Japanese American Women*.

1991   Received California Arts Council Award; City of Oakland Composer Fellowship Award; composed oboe piece *Chablet*, and *Hide and Seek*, and *Rag* for clarinet, *A Desert Storm* for full orchestra; completed *Suite Convulsions* for jazz orchestra, and *River* for women's chorus; scores for films *Color Adjustment, Ein Stehauf Männchen, Faces of Aids*.

1992   Commission from consortium for composition of *We Are One* in six movements, premiered by Vocal Motion from the Oakland Youth Chorus, 27 November; produced record album, *The Soul Knows*; composed suite for piano duet, *The Burning Hills*, scores for film *World of O'Brien-Kreitzberg*, and six documentary films on black authors.

1992–94   Received Meet the Composer Commissioning Program awards.

1993   Commission by Sacramento's Camellia Symphony Orchestra and a grant
                from Meet the Composer for *Five Movements in Color*, premiered in
                1994; composed scores for three films, *Valuing Relationships*, parts I, II,
                and III.

1993–95   Toured as pianist and co-composer of score for the earliest known full-
                length black silent film (1919) by Oscar Micheaux, *Within Our Gates*,
                performed at the Mill Valley Film Festival, the Kennedy Center in Wash-
                ington, D.C., the Philadelphia International Film Festival, and the Smith-
                sonian Institution.

1994–96   Taught at Holy Names College, Oakland; composed *Mount Cathedral* for
                flugelhorn, *The Gallery* for flute, clarinet, bassoon, viola, cello, and *Party
                Line*, a woodwind quintet; arranged *Hide and Seek* and *Rag*! for chamber
                orchestra; scores for films *Straight from the Heart, Complaints of a Du-
                tiful Daughter, Out for a Change, Black Is . . . Black Ain't.*

1995   Composed *The Emperor's New Clothes* for the Berkeley Youth Orches-
                tra; scores for films *Skin Deep, Family Values.*

1996   Composed piano pieces *Moods of Color, Raging Rapids, The Sleuth.*

1997   Composed viola piece *The Sand Dancer*, piano pieces *Ancient Visions* and
                Passing Lights, an instrumental quartet for piano, flute, clarinet, and cello.

1998   Composed *Royal Holiday* for two flugelhorns, horn, trombone, tuba, and
                flute; and wind trio.

1999–2000   Concerts and CD *Dancing Souls* with composer/flutist Kay Gardner; con-
                certs with violinist India Cooke; revisited Pueblo, Colo.; composed three
                pieces for cello: *Focus, The Medium*, and *Bus Stop*, and opera *Queen
                Clara: Fields of Glory, Rivers of Blood*; excerpt of opera premiered in
                workshop in San Francisco in July 2000.

> When the performers and the audience come together for the collective
> musical experience, whether we are conscious of its deeper meaning or not,
> the Creator becomes manifest. It is at these times that I glimpse the truth
> of our being—our being as one with another and with the Creator.[1]

Mary Watkins was aware of the link between music and spirituality early in her
life. As a child, secretly experimenting with "colors, shades and the effects of
melody and harmony on emotion," she felt the music lead her deeper into herself, "to this place I believe might be what we call 'home.' "[2] Mary felt disapproval from her elders toward this "exhilarating and empowering experience.
. . . The message was clearly that certain power belongs only to God . . . producing something from an unseen source might very well be dangerous or evil.
. . . There was a taboo against seeing oneself as powerful in ways that could not
be monitored and therefore controlled by authority figures."[3] So Mary was very
careful to do all her musical exploring in private. Music brought her the healing
and wholeness she had sought from her earliest childhood: "In this way I was

coming to use music as a tonic for my own mental and emotional well-being. . . . I was finding a kind of healing balance within me."[4]

In the 1970s Watkins brought this emotional and spiritual depth to the women's music movement in her work with the Olivia Records Collective. She was credited with shaping the growth and development of women's music, "single-handedly making the most valuable contribution" to this genre, transforming it into "full, rounded *music*."[5] By the 1980s Watkins had made the transition to jazz, winning kudos for her album *Winds of Change*: "For those who know what real jazz is, Watkins' latest album is an affirmation."[6] She composed music for many documentary films and videos, three of which received Academy Award nominations. She received numerous commissions, awards, and fellowships from the National Endowments for the Arts, becoming "one of the Bay Area's most successful composers and jazz pianists."[7]

BIOGRAPHY

Mary was born in Denver, Colorado, on 9 December 1939. Fourteen months later she was adopted by Benjamin Maloney and Evelyn Moman Maloney, a childless black couple who lived in Pueblo, Colorado, a steel mill town about 100 miles south of Denver. Mary knew she was adopted as early as she can remember, and she assumed everybody was, until she was about four or five. Then she began to learn the facts of life and it dawned on her that someone else was her biological mother. Because her adoptive mother did not talk about the circumstances of her birth, Mary received the distinct impression that her origins were shameful and inferior, and that she should feel grateful for having been rescued.

Despite her mother's secrecy, her parents were well-meaning and loving. They adopted another child, Charles, when Mary was four, in part because of her repeated entreaties for a little brother. Just before that time, when she was three years and nine months old, her mother began taking her to a family friend, Edith Johnson, for piano lessons. Although Mary had no idea what these lessons were about, and had not asked for them, she later acknowledged the importance of this early start and the unlikelihood that she would have received it from her birth parents.

Evelyn Maloney was spurred to start her tiny daughter on piano lessons by the precocity of her sister's little girl, who started to play piano at two years old and was showing remarkable musical talent. She was also vicariously fulfilling her own desire to be a musician. She had taught herself how to play the piano and to read notes, key signatures, and time signatures, and she even played for church services for a time, but she wanted Mary to learn piano the correct way, from a real teacher.

The family background and early experiences of her mother were to have much influence over Mary's perception of herself and her world. She loved to hear her mother reminisce about growing up in Kansas. Evelyn was born in

Abilene, and spent her childhood in rural central Kansas. After losing both parents, one through death and the other through abandonment, she was separated from her siblings and sent to live with an aunt and uncle. When she began school, "colored" children were not allowed to join Brownies or Girl Scouts, or to participate in extracurricular activities, social functions, or sports. Evelyn was a good student and graduated in the top tenth of her high school class, but "colored" students could not be awarded scholarships, no matter how excellent their academic performance. When she married and moved to Colorado, Mary's mother had to find work as a domestic, the only type of work available to Negro women. A proud woman who held her head high, Evelyn denied the pain and humiliation she endured in her job.

Mary's father was a native of Colorado, born in Denver. He went to college for four years, but never graduated. When Mary was eight years old, he contracted severe rheumatoid arthritis and had to quit his job as a laborer at a local air base (now the Pueblo Ordnance Depot). By the time she was 13, he was unable to walk. He died in April 1962.

Mary's piano teacher, Edith Johnson, lived on the edge of town and taught many children from the black community, as well as some Latino and white children who lived nearby. She was a thorough teacher: "all business, making sure her students learned the correct way of doing everything. . . . and gave us oral and written tests to make sure we understood the fundamentals of music theory."[8] When she realized Mary was playing by ear, the long battle began over how to play music. Mary was told that playing by ear was bad, and she must follow the notes on the printed page, and nothing but the notes. This puzzled her, especially when it was discovered that she had perfect pitch and her parents delighted in testing her ability. She was supposed to use her ears, yet not use them. Nevertheless she memorized quickly and made good progress, and her mother and teacher were proud to show her off on every occasion.

Mary's family, which included aunts, uncles, and cousins on both sides, attended St. Paul's African Methodist Episcopal Church (now First African Methodist Episcopal Church). The music program there was well developed, and Mary had the opportunity to hear and observe good musicians. She particularly admired Melba Wheeler, the daughter of a minister and a graduate of Oberlin, who came to direct the church music when Mary was about 10. Mary paid close attention to all the church musicians, thus receiving an important part of her early music education. One of them played in clubs—pop and blues—and had her own style of playing gospel at church, a style that Mary promptly absorbed. When she was eight, she was asked to play piano for the Sunday school and junior choir, and as she got older, she was given more musical responsibility at the church. The fact that Mary was receiving attention for her musical ability caused problems with her peers, some of whom were jealous.

Perhaps because of this, she did not relish practicing, and for a while she resisted the pull of music. During those years she was a tomboy, interested more in sports. At the age of 12 or 13, she began listening more intently to music on the radio and television, and for the first time heard jazz, as well as classical music. The music of Tchaikovsky and other composers of the Romantic era awakened emotions that almost frightened her with their intensity. When she heard other students in her school who had progressed during the time she was avoiding music, she felt the competitive drive to prove she could play as well as they. Besides piano, she played violin in the school orchestra, as well as the cornet and tuba. She played trumpet in the school band and sometimes did solos in assemblies. Pueblo had many community activities for its size, many of which included school music groups, in which she was usually involved.

Although she still took lessons from Miss Johnson, she began to be aware of the limitations of her musical background, her lack of sophistication, and her ignorance of the basic repertory. Nevertheless, when she was 15, she and her teacher decided she should enter a piano contest. Her selection was Schubert's *Ave Maria*, and when the day arrived, she sat down at the huge concert grand Steinway piano and began filling the room with sound, dazzling the audience with her own special version of the classic. The puzzled judges must have thought they had the wrong music. To her great disappointment she did not win first place. She was told her piece was not suitable for a competition, and she could have been disqualified for taking such license with the notes. She did receive a second prize of a season ticket to the Pueblo Civic Symphony, and the assurance that she had a fine musical sensibility and creative ability. She was advised to learn to play what the composer wrote, and to look for a professional teacher. Both chastened and encouraged, she determined to persevere, and began studies with a Miss Page, a classical pianist in Pueblo. The season ticket to the Pueblo Civic Symphony proved to be an education in itself. It was the first time she was able to hear live symphonic music, and she knew immediately that that was what she wanted to create.

Meanwhile, she was enduring the pressures of adolescence and the stresses at school. She excelled not only in music and sports but also in art, for which she won prizes in contests. While her talents enabled her to be accepted by some of her white schoolmates as "normal," she knew they didn't recognize her whole self. She suppressed and protected her black heritage and the gospel music at her church, not wanting it to be misunderstood. Her black schoolmates saw her music as "uppity" and pretentious, and they made her school days uncomfortable with teasing and ridicule. Mary's time with other African-American kids was limited; she saw them at church and once a month at parties sponsored by the junior choir, of which she was president. She didn't live in their neighborhood, and her mother kept a strict rein on her activities. She hated being an outsider, and longed to go to the movies and have fun, like everyone else.

In her first year at Pueblo Junior College (later University of Southern Colorado), Mary heard more Haydn, Beethoven, and Mozart in her music history class, and her desire to create such music was confirmed. She began in music education with piano as her applied major. When her mother suggested that she change to something practical, like business skills, typing and shorthand, she reluctantly did so for a semester.

Mary wanted more than anything to escape from Pueblo, so she transferred to Adams State Teachers College in Alamosa, Colorado. Before finishing her degree, she met Edward Dawkins, who was stationed in the army at Fort Carson in Colorado Springs. She married him in Pueblo in February 1963 and they moved to his home area, Washington, D.C., where their daughter Sharron was born.[9] It was a new experience to live among so many black people. She had never before met black composers, or seen "successful" black role models. Although Washington was the scene of intense turmoil in 1963, with the March on Washington in August, the beginning of greater involvement with the Vietnam War, and President Kennedy's assassination on 22 November, Mary was preoccupied with her own struggles and felt disconnected from current events. She and Ed separated, and she had to work hard to make ends meet and to care for her infant daughter. She took jobs playing organ in churches and doing temporary work to keep food on the table. Then she enrolled in Howard University as a composition student, and sent her daughter to be cared for by her mother in Pueblo. Although she felt guilt at the separation from her daughter, she was the happiest she had been in a long time, "because it was the first time in my life that I was able to sit down and compose music . . . without having to apologize for the time spent doing it." Her teachers were the renowned Mark Fax and Russell Woollen, and her earliest written works date from that time.[10] After graduating cum laude in 1972 with her Bachelor of Music degree, Mary stayed in Washington for several years, refining her jazz skills, arranging, songwriting, playing gigs, and working as musical director and resident composer for the theater group Ebony Impromptu. In 1974 she was divorced from her husband. She considered teaching, but she was turned off by the ivory tower remoteness. "The more I listened to teachers the more I thought I didn't want to stand up in front of a class and talk about music. I wanted to do music! I wanted to write scores for movies, for high school bands, for orchestras, whatever."[11]

Watkins returned briefly to Colorado, where she studied for a semester with Bill Fowler at the University of Colorado at Denver, and coached with jazz pianist and composer Joe Keel. It was here that she composed *Potomac Park* for full orchestra. It received a reading by the Pueblo Civic Symphony Orchestra, but unfortunately she was not able to go to Pueblo to hear it.

The major turning point in her career came in 1976, after she met the singer Holly Near at a music workshop and was exposed for the first time to women-oriented music. That year she moved to Los Angeles and took the professional name Mary Watkins. After freelancing as a copyist and transcriber, she began working for the newly formed women-owned and-operated Olivia Records Collective. At first she packed records in the shipping department, but was soon participating in the production of records by Linda Tillery, Holly Near, Meg Christian, Cris Williamson, and others. She and Linda Tillery were bringing the black woman's viewpoint and music from soul, gospel, and jazz, into a largely white women's realm. The group of women at the Olivia Collective released a new creative energy in Watkins, and she was soon composing her own music, forming her own jazz combo, touring with Linda Tillery and June Millington, and appearing regularly at women's music festivals. When the collective moved to Oakland, California, in 1977, Watkins moved, too. In 1978 she recorded her own jazz fusion album, *Something Moving*, on the Olivia Records label. This recording received critical acclaim and considerable air time, earning her a position on the "most-played" radio charts. She received a National Endowment for the Arts Jazz Performance grant, enabling her to make a second album, *Winds of Change*, for small combo combined with a 42-piece jazz orchestra. The project was an enormous challenge, from writing the grant proposal, to marshaling the performing forces and arranging the venue and recording facilities, writing and arranging the music, performing and recording, and mixing the album. She recorded it live in two evening concerts at San Francisco's Herbst Theater in October 1981, employing her own jazz septet,[12] the Los Angeles-based all-women Maiden Voyage big band, and a 19-piece string section. The album was released in 1983 on the Palo Alto label, a newly established record company with a commitment to presenting jazz.

If *Something Moving* had been well received, *Winds of Change* brought Watkins, in the words of one reviewer, to "fame's doorstep." It was reviewed in *Down Beat, Ms.*, and *Keyboard* magazines, and *Jazz Forum* placed it among the ten recordings most played on jazz stations. This album marked a shift in Watkins' targeted audience and a clarification of some of her goals. Although she continued to identify with the feminist movement and to appear at women's music festivals (one of the works on this album was *Woman Messiah*), she now wanted to appeal to a wider audience. She said, "It [her music] may be feminist in that it's my experience in life and I am a woman. But ultimately I'm a humanist."[13] Leaving behind the women-only policy of the Olivia Collective, she now featured men as well as women in her jazz combo.

Watkins remained in Oakland, stimulated by its lively theater and music scene, the intellectual atmosphere created by its many colleges and universities, and its ethnic diversity. During the years from 1978 to 1982 Mary was undergoing intense personal developments. In 1981, the search for her birth mother and family finally met success. The reunion in Denver was a mutually gratifying one that resolved a lifelong need. This inward focus showed itself in the gospel hymnlike solo piano piece *Mother's Song* in *Winds of Change* and in the more introverted and reflective solo piano music of her next album, *Spiritsong*.

One music critic who had been following her career noted that after the release of *Spiritsong* in 1985, she had "disappeared from public view."[14] In fact, she was accomplishing some of the very goals she had spelled out in an interview in 1982: "I'd like to do some things with modern dance. Maybe a movie score. Those are things I would find challenging."[15] In 1986 she composed the first of a long series of scores for important, social-consciousness-raising documentary videos and films: the award-winning *Ethnic Notions*, followed in the next years by *Valuing Diversity, Fighting for Our Lives, Out in Suburbia, Color Adjustment*, and many more. The next year she adapted Tchaikovsky's *Nut-cracker Suite* for the Oakland Dance Brigade's satirical production, *The Revolutionary Nutcracker Sweetie*, which became an annual Christmas event for the next ten years. The music for the Lorraine Hansberry Theater productions of *The Resurrection of Lady Lester* and *The Bluest Eye* followed in 1988 and 1989. In order to expand into these new musical contexts, Mary had to shift from playing clubs with her combo and recording albums, to the more solitary pursuits of composing theater music behind the scenes, of writing grant proposals, and conceptualizing and carrying out grand compositional designs. She worked self-sufficiently in her apartment surrounded by electronic equipment. By 1992 she had became conscious of her isolation. Always a loner, she remarked, "I'm one of those private people. I get in my room and start experimenting and playing around and I don't want to go out."[16] The commissions and grants kept coming: fellowships from the City of Oakland, the California Arts Council, Meet the Composer; commissions from the American Jazz Theater, the Redwood Cultural Works, Boy's Choir of Harlem, and Sacramento's Camellia Symphony Orchestra. They enabled her to write the large-scale jazz, orchestral, and choral works she loved. But she considered commercial success "a double-edged sword. I've gotten many grants and done a lot of film work and been paid. That was real important. But on the other hand it's not enough because what I do ultimately is not about making money. It's about the art itself. Sometimes a composer can find herself between a rock and a hard place if not fully employed, i.e. teaching in a school or some other full-time job with a steady income."[17] Mary no longer felt as negative about teaching as she had in her twenties. She taught piano at Holy Names College for a couple of years, and thought about pursuing an advanced degree in order to teach practical harmony and theory. "I'd like to write up my own course for integrating traditional 'Theory 101' with a more relevant and demystifying approach for the students."[18]

In the late 1990s Mary was still playing concerts with her group, appearing frequently in the Bay Area with the violinist India Cooke. She began a series of concerts improvising with flutist/composer Kay Gardner, performing at the National Women's Festival in Muncie, Indiana, the Michigan Womyn's Music Festival, and other places nationally. Together they put out a CD, *Dancing Souls*, much of which was recorded live at these festivals.

She returned to Pueblo in 1999 to find old family connections, and to face the demons of the place she once wanted to leave so badly. After the visit she said, "Pueblo has not really changed. It has only spread out a little more. . . . Going there made it very clear why I was always so desperate to get away. I saw cousins and friends and that was wonderful. I also saw my theory and piano teacher, James Duncan, who is still teaching at USC."[19]

In 2000 she was satisfied with the goals she had met, and hoped to stay focused. "Now of course, it's taking on bigger and better things. I want to move forward. Momentum can easily get lost when you get caught up in the mundane."[20]

SOCIAL ISSUES

Watkins sees race as an external thing, like the clothes she wears. She considers herself

a child of the universe. It's almost like Paul said—neither Jew nor Gentile, male nor female—I just am. I think that being adopted has something to do with this. . . . For a long time I felt like I'd never really been born, just appeared. . . . Racial differences don't matter to me, though racism does. A lot of things don't matter. . . . I'm not one who feels it is that necessary to identify myself as black since that should be quite obvious.[21]

At the same time, she acknowledges the importance of race in her life: "I have lived the black experience and it has shaped and affected me in all ways." She had no hesitation in claiming her identity as a black woman composer. "Well, I'm a black woman, and I'm a composer . . . people do need to know that black women compose, and they compose all kinds of music." She believed Tania León's objections to a book on African-American women composers were because "her experience is not that of one growing up African-American. That could be very much why [she thinks that way]."[22]

Watkins writes about her racial heritage extensively in her memoirs. "Among Negroes in the days before the civil rights movement of the '60s, there really was such a thing as a black community. We were 'colored people' and there was a great deal of pride in our ability to have created a community for ourselves and all of the accomplishments within that community. We had a sense of dignity as a people."[23] Of course, in those days, people called themselves "colored people" or "Negroes"; the terms "black" and "African" were insulting. In Pueblo, the Negro population was small, and lived mostly in Bessemer, on the south side of town. That's where most of the men worked, at the steel mill of the Colorado Fuel and Iron Company. The other place in Pueblo that employed black people was the Colorado State Mental Hospital. At that time there were few black churches: two African Methodist Episcopal churches, the Bethlehem and Eighth Street Baptist and one other Baptist church, and a Pentecostal church whose members "kept to themselves." Churches were very important in Pueblo, as they were in other black communities. They were located close to each other, so people visited other churches often and their choirs collaborated in concerts.

They were the center, the social center of the community . . . until I was much older people had a lot of dinner parties in their homes, because they couldn't rent hotels or things like that. Finally that got changed, of course, but the church was where you met and where you got all your news. . . . It was also the center of musical activity, where you heard concerts and recitals of touring black artists.[24]

I liked church. It seemed the most natural thing in the world when all the people around me were black like me! There was always a great deal of laughter and a great deal of pride in our ability to make the best out of what we had to work with. Without humor we could not have survived.[25]

But as she began to enter the larger world around her, and to go to the neighborhood school, which was 98 percent white, Mary encountered a different world.

I found it very difficult to feel proud of myself as a 'colored person' when in the presence of whites, which was every day, all day. . . . At school I would catch a classmate staring at me for no reason I could think of, and when we read aloud about Africans or "Negro slaves," I just wanted to disappear on the spot, because everybody would noisily turn in their seats and look at me. At recess when we played the game, Red Rover, which required holding hands, nobody wanted to stand next to me, and sometimes after holding my hand, little "Miss Anne" would look at her hand, then at me, squinting her eyes in the bright sunlight, and wipe her hand on her dress—as if to wipe away my touch.[26]

Outside of school, the message was the same. Discrimination in the North was as hurtful, if not more, than segregation in the South. Jobs available to blacks were menial; she never saw a black person wait on someone in a store or teach in the schools. They would have had to move to the South in order to teach in black schools. Negroes were generally invisible, working in kitchens, sweeping floors, cleaning, lifting and transporting loads of goods. Until she was in her teens, neither Mary nor her parents attended public concerts unless the artists were very special, like Marian Anderson, because in Pueblo colored people were allowed to sit only in the back of the balcony. White racism, current events, the early U.S. Supreme Court rulings on desegregation, and the begrudging changes they caused in Pueblo were subjects often discussed in her home after dinner or when the relatives got together on Sunday evenings. She felt grief and rage when 14-year-old Emmett Till was murdered in Mississippi. In the smaller towns of the North, the black population wasn't large enough to effectively segregate into a ghetto. "One of the drawbacks of not growing up in the South under segregated rule was that from day one, most of us in the North had to face and deal with racism head on. Most black kids in the South didn't meet the 'devil' until older when they had to venture outside their own community—which is [not] to say it was better or worse . . . just different. . . . Every day those of us in the North were living and interacting for many hours of our lives among whites who were either blatantly racist, mildly so, or totally unconscious . . . as they shared the latest racial joke or stereotype with one of us."[27]

The internalized negativity was more damaging than the external insults and dangers. "There's something that often goes on in the black community . . . a lot of times people don't want to admit they've been affected, that it's hurt them. It's too shameful and too painful. . . . Your parents want to shield you, they want you not to be hurt by this, but they haven't dealt with their own hurt about it, and they give you double messages that are really bad. And it's coming from people that you love, the people that are trying to protect you."[28] A phrase that turned up in their conversations over and over again, "the trouble with black folks is—," revealed the fear that there was something wrong with being a Negro. Other phrases she grew up hearing confirmed this suspicion: "Don't make a nuisance of yourself." "People don't want to be bothered with you." "Don't ask for anything." "You can't trust people." "Don't let them know what you really think."[29]

Many of Mary Watkins' observations on gender show a connection to race. She said, "You can't write about black women without addressing the racial issues. And there are so many nuances, so many offshoots of that, like our relationships with the men in our lives. It [race] is tied up with gender."[30] One of the offshoots had to do with skin color and the advantage enjoyed by light-skinned women. This advantage was especially true in male-female relationships. Another offshoot had to do with the perception of black female leverage with the white male. "Black men and black women have special stuff going on. I think that a lot of black men feel black women have gotten a better deal than they have, and this isn't true at all. . . . It is argued all the time today that black men get first place for victimization."[31] But in Watkins' experience, this was not true. She observed that members of her own extended family openly and admittedly valued the lives of boys more than the lives of girls. She envied male privilege and vainly attempted to earn her family's respect by playing football, baseball, and basketball, and roughhousing with her brother and his friends. They taught her to throw a solid punch, which got her into trouble in school. The issue of gender came up there, too. Her behavior was seen as "un-ladylike." "Being angry was not nice—according to adults. So I would often end up feeling ashamed for fighting . . . [but] to behave like a 'lady' was totally defeating, only making me feel more vulnerable."[32]

The specter of guilt and shame as a woman followed her into marriage and motherhood. When she had to separate from her daughter in order to go to Howard University, she suffered "a lot of guilt . . . a lot of energy was expended in trying to deal with not being with my daughter, worrying about not being the right mother—the perfect mother, worrying about not feeling the way I was told I was supposed to feel and be." How she was "supposed to be" was, basically, not a composer, certainly not a person with a vision and purpose beyond family. She "would hear things and read things that definitely negated women as composers, as creators of anything but children." This conflict over being a composer was one of the main reasons behind the failure of her marriage. Her husband would talk about how "crazy" she was to want to write music. The conflict between family and creative work remained heartfelt and painful for her. "I'm glad I had a daughter and love my grandsons. It's not like I don't think those things are important. They're very important. [But] that's not my focus." Her relief upon meeting the women in the Olivia Collective in California was profound. "It was the first time I'd seen women like myself—both playful and purposeful. They had goals and ideas, and it wasn't about husband and family. . . . I met other women who were aggressively involved in music. So I began to see myself doing this and not feeling like a freak."[33]

For Watkins, class issues are even more bound up with race. Class is a controversial subject, and many composers would not discuss it. Watkins had the most to say, yet she also was reluctant. Where class is concerned, a kind of racial solidarity takes over, a sense that "dirty linen" should be kept in the family. Watkins empathized with the vulnerability that black women feel around the issue of class, and their fear of possible ostracism from the black community. But she said, "In many ways I'm feeling more angry than vulnerable these days."[34]

For Watkins, class touches on aspects of African-American life with which she does not want to be connected. "Parts of black culture I love; it's in my soul, it's who I am. . . . Some [parts] I don't want to be a part of: the skin color issue, the elite clubs that used to have color codes."[35] In the community in Pueblo, there may not have been enough African Americans to develop the elite clubs and color codes so prevalent in bigger cities. But feelings and attitudes about skin color are pervasive in the black community, wherever it is. Watkins observed, "Dark skin and black hair were not an advantage for me in black society." Watkins' aversion to elitism among blacks was strengthened by the messages she received as a child: her fright about her possible birth origins, her mother's anger at Negroes who exemplified the kind of stereotypical behavior the whites attributed to all blacks. "She didn't want her kids to be like that. . . . She didn't want us to reflect badly on the family or the race. God forbid we do that. And believe me, growing up, that became an all important thing, because it always came down to 'the race.' "[36] The borderline between race pride and class prejudice was very thin. "Colored folks who were uneducated were often an embarrassment to those who were. Those who refused to inhibit themselves in laughter and speech were an embarrassment because they were acting out the stereotype of the loud and uncouth Negro."[37]

The educated black middle class frequently worked at jobs that would have been considered working-class in other contexts. But there were other standards for worth and class; ownership of property was one. Mary's father was highly regarded in the community because he owned his own home, and therefore demonstrated a sense of solidity and responsibility. Another standard was church attendance. "There tended to be two kinds of people. There were those people who went to church and those that didn't. And we were a little leery of the ones who didn't. . . . And I think the AMEs tended to be a little more . . . they had a higher level of education in general, and probably, money. They seemed a little more flashy, like in their dress, more affluent." Membership in social clubs was also a measure of status. "These things were important. They met every month and planned things and had rummage sales, took food to the poor, and sponsored and presented shows and concerts."[38]

Some black people were driven to excel, like Mary's mother, who believed herself to be "somebody," the extraordinary individual who might have a chance to be respected by the white majority. "But to many blacks, thinking big was foolishness. Dangerous. To varying degrees within the community thinking big was getting 'uppity.' 'Uppity' was thinking you were better than other Negroes."[39] But to Mary's mother, "uppity" Negroes were

right on the money . . . particularly if it meant being better educated and enjoying a higher standard of living. If it meant mimicking the mannerism and lifestyle of white folks, so be it. . . . The black community, cut off from its African roots, accepted and saw themselves as Americans . . . with only the larger white majority to pattern itself after, since very few of us in those days looked to Africa as a source of prideful identity. . . . As Americans we were bound to the rules of the game that all Americans were expected to play.[40]

The standards of ambitious Negroes like Mary's mother did not include anything outside of the "nice," conforming, middle-class, conservative white lifestyle. Artists, independent thinkers and doers, liberal progressives, intellectuals who went against the conventional wisdom were irregular, "strange," "eccentric," "arrogant," and even "crazy."

For Watkins, the ramifications of this conformity became more confusing as she grew up. Her mother had not anticipated that her gifted child would also be a "maverick": dreamy, moody, concerned with the reality behind appearances, "backward" in social situations, often a subject of ridicule among her friends. She was unprepared to deal with a sensitive, artistic child who was not just "uppity" but "different." In Watkins' life, the circumstances of race, class, and gender were exacerbated by the fact of being adopted, and by the coping patterns of her adoptive mother. It was her gift of musical talent that saved her. "[My music] was the way I could buy [my mother] off, and everybody else."[41] Music was the ticket to acceptance, whether by her own mother and family, in school, her community, or the world at large.

THE MUSIC

The approximately 100 written compositions in Watkins' body of music span 30 years to date, encompassing the years 1971 to 2001. Most of her creative output was improvised and never written down. Her written works cover a wide range of genres and mediums. At this point in her career, the majority of her written compositions are instrumental. Stylistically they are a mix of many traditions: classical, jazz, gospel, folk, and popular works stand side by side, and many works incorporate or blend more than one style.

Most of her music has been performed because Watkins plays her own works and knows a network of musicians who also have performed them. About 37 percent of her works are published, and the majority of those are available through her own company, Shotsky Publishing Company, in Oakland, California. Morning Sky AQEI Publishing in Minneapolis brought out several of her works, then went out of business and returned the rights to her. Only 20 percent of her compositions have been recorded, even though she has produced six albums that include her own music.

The development of her musical style began long before her earliest written compositions. In her childhood, she was exposed to and absorbed the hymns, spirituals, and gospel music in church, and it was there her improvisational style developed.

I would hear something that sort of turned me on, but then it went somewhere else . . . and that's how I started improvising . . . so that it would do what I wanted it to do. I was discovering on my own . . . that certain patterns of notes in the melody, certain chord patterns voiced in a certain way could induce flashes of absolute bliss. . . . [it] was nothing all that complex . . . I was simply playing familiar chord patterns in ways I wanted to hear them. . . . Harmony was absolutely fascinating to me. While melody was the guiding logic of a piece of music, harmony was its soul.[42]

In Watkins' music, the harmonies and colors certainly do induce emotionally charged states, and when one tries to pin them down at the keyboard, they turn out to be fairly familiar chords, but voiced and ordered in unusual ways.

Her description of the way she "improved" Schubert's *Ave Maria* at the piano competition comes to mind as one listens to her album *Spiritsong*, or to any of her piano solos: "I began filling the room with . . . rich, arpeggiated Schumannesque chords accompanying that familiar melody of sweet, longing adoration and flowing poignancy gently stated with the right hand in octaves."[43] Her piano style is, indeed, characterized by elaborate ornamentation in sweeping scale or arpeggio passagework, and melodies doubled in octaves contribute to its orchestral sound. She said that when she heard Mozart, Haydn, and Beethoven symphonies in her college music history class, she was entranced with the sound of the orchestra and knew she wanted to write such music. Later she was to comment that she had "always thought in orchestral terms even in the smaller group things. I liked the colors, the access to textures, being able to work with strings."[44]

The mystery of her late but spectacularly successful arrival in jazz is also illuminated by early anecdotes. As a teen she would listen late at night, her ear to the radio, to the music of the bebop era. The pyrotechnics of Charlie Parker and Dizzy Gillespie dazzled her with their lightning speed, darting melodies, jabbing rhythms, and constant modulations. It struck her as very masculine music, while the jazz singers she heard—Billie Holiday, Ella Fitzgerald, and others—were less intimidating. Later on, "at [Adams] State some of the guys would get together in one of the music rooms and play jazz. Now jazz was a no-no at that time; it was not respected at all. . . . So students kind of did it on the sly, or they did it out of outright rebelliousness. I was fascinated by the music but not involved."[45] She may not have been "involved", either in her earlier dis-

covery of bebop, Billie Holiday, and Ella Fitzgerald on late-night radio, or in
these later exposures, but she was passively absorbing enough so that when the
time came to play gigs in Washington, D.C., she was ready. "By the time I was
a young adult I still hadn't heard much jazz, but I absorbed what I heard like
a sponge. . . . I knew I had what it took to hold my own in jazz. I could swing;
nobody taught me; I just sort of picked it up."[46] When she freelanced in Washington, she often played with musicians who imitated John Coltrane, Herbie
Hancock, and Miles Davis, and fused jazz with rock instrumentation. She was
also influenced by Motown and its change of style in the 1960s; she liked the
"Handelian" sound of their orchestral arrangements.[47]

Watkins' music education at Howard University in the early 1970s emphasized the twentieth-century classical composers Hindemith, Stravinsky, and Bartók, and developed her tolerance for dissonance and polytonality. The
nineteenth-century Romantic composers she had loved were out of favor. Her
earliest written compositions (for flute, and for woodwind quintet, and her first
work for full orchestra) date from this time. In keeping with her training at
Howard, they were more astringent and dissonant than sweet and tonal. But they
also showed the influence of African-American idioms and the currently popular
"soul" music.

Her move to California marked a pivotal point in her evolution as a composer
as well as in her personal life. The arrangements and instrumentations she did
for the musicians at the Olivia Collective gave free rein to her musical imagination while affording her the psychological protection of working behind the
scenes. With the resources that the Olivia Collective was able to provide, she
could "work with other people's music—enhance other people's music in a
creative way."[48] Larry Kelp wrote, "Her arranging ability is mature and awesome
in its ability to display a great range of very personal emotions." He found her
string and horn arrangements for Holly Near's *Fire in the Rain* album "a near-
cathartic experience."[49]

In the first album of her own music, *Something Moving*, the band included a
string section of four violins, viola and cello as well as the more usual jazz
fusion instruments.[50] In Watkins' hands, all these instruments blend unobtrusively, producing orchestral colors, textures, and layers of sound. Her performing on the keyboard is especially effective in *A Chording to the People* and
Witches' Revenge (an answer to Miles Davis's *Bitches Brew*), both of which
stand out for their originality and innovation. *Something Moving* was judged by
some to be "the best thing to come out of Olivia Records. . . . For a change,
someone has used the fusion medium as a means of expression . . . the all-
woman band plays and sings with so much feeling and depth of expression that
in many ways this is the best electric jazz album of the year."[51]

In *Winds of Change*, recording with a live audience was essential to the
concept, and it worked. For one reviewer, "The album really captures the spirit
of the audience."[52] Another critic said, "Watkins responds [in her solos] to the
orchestra and to the audience. She plays as though she is thanking every being

present for creating the music with her."[53] Watkins dedicated the album to jazz greats Mary Lou Williams, Helen Humes, and Hazel Scott. Her own authority was demonstrated in her "knack for balancing the interplay among combo, soloists, and sections. Watkins' arranging trademark is the way she slowly builds a crescendo. . . . In the tune *Winds of Change*, she builds a crescendo from the sax section through the brass behind a flute solo. . . . the super brass sections peek out thrillingly under Watkins' arranging hands. . . . The timing of the strings' entrance . . . spurs the alto solo to great intensity."[54] The energy and lightness of this album were noted by many, and one reviewer heard something more: "Her music projects a positive, intrepid spirit with strong jazz harmonies that convey a certain toughness."[55]

For many, the highlight of the album was Mary's gospel-flavored piano solo, *Mother's Song*. This may have had some role in determining Mary's next direction, her solo piano album *Spiritsong*, written in 1983 and recorded in 1985. The music of *Spiritsong* is mostly quiet and meditative, a bit reminiscent of New Age music and George Winston, but more substantial and interesting. When she presented these numbers at her concert in Anchorage, Alaska, the reviewer was impressed by her musical ideas and orchestral sound: "Watkins exhibited a first-class piano technique, making the piano sing and shout by turns . . . she made no effort to use the piano for display; technique served only the necessity of musical ideas . . . music that stretches the confines of classical and jazz tradition."[56] In El Paso, Texas, as the headliner for the League of Academic Women's fourth annual Women in the Arts program, she provided a "transcendental experience . . . [converting her material] into a mesmeric, largely improvisational workout, and stirring into these musical tempests a great blending of accessible linear melodies."[57] The material ranges from gospel hymnlike melodies and harmonies in *Comin' Home*, to a mechanical merry-go-round waltz and teasing children's tunes in *Playground*. One of the most interesting is *Changing Seasons*, with its opening parallel thirteenth chords, daring tonalities, and a declamatory melody including a three-note motive that is developed extensively.

Having retreated, in a sense, to the more intimate format of solo performing, Watkins was now ready to return to the large canvas of the orchestra. Recording interested her less and less, as synthesizers took the place of strings in the recording studios and as the cost of live recordings of large ensembles became prohibitive. In 1986 she was commissioned by the Bay Area Women's Philharmonic Orchestra to compose a symphonic work for piano and orchestra, *One Episode in an Inner Journey*, a dissonant twentieth-century classical work with minimal jazz inflection, which was premiered the following year. In her next work, *The Sword That Heals*, Watkins brought together all of the expertise developed in her previous projects—orchestral, classical, jazz ensemble, and jazz piano—as well as her personal spiritual growth, into one harmonious and grand design.

In the 1990s Watkins introduced some new elements into her music: programmatic incorporation of current events, exploration of musical church roots, and composition for chorus. In response to a commission from the Cincinnati Women's Choir in 1991, Watkins wrote her first choral work, *River*, to a text by Jill Rose. Watkins had really never left her church roots, evoking the gospel spirit in pieces such as *Mother's Song* and *Comin' Home*. In 1992 she was commissioned by a consortium including the Harlem Boys' Choir of New York, the Redwood Cultural Works of Oakland, and MUSE and Friends of Cincinnati, to compose a work for a "new spirituals" project. She responded with a six-movement choral work, *We Are One*, premiered in November 1992 by Vocal Motion, the touring ensemble of the Oakland Youth Chorus. Traditional religious music was also featured in her next record album, *The Soul Knows*, released by Wenefil Records in 1992. Concern with current events is evident in *A Desert Storm* for full orchestra, inspired by the Gulf War, and a set of three pieces for piano duet titled *Terror on the Mountain*, prompted by the fierce Oakland fires of November 1991. The impetus to respond programmatically to real-life situations may also have been stimulated by the many scores for films and videos that she produced during these years.

In the years 1991 to 2000 Watkins composed a number of works for chamber ensemble and solo instruments, many of them in a more astringent, purely twentieth-century classical style that served for the expression of her ideas as comfortably as jazz. In these she enjoyed combining different instruments, especially winds, for the coloristic effects. A commission for a large orchestral work from Sacramento's Camellia Orchestra brought Watkins back to her favorite medium in a big way: *Five Movements in Color* was premiered in 1994, and very well received. It returned to the fusion of styles with which Watkins was most associated. Together with *The Sword That Heals*, it ranks among her most important works and among her own favorites.

Watkins' next phase was in the area of opera. Many years earlier she had played piano for rehearsals of Menotti operas, and had become fascinated by the way composers treated musical ideas in the service of drama. She enjoyed writing the music for the stage adaptation of Toni Morrison's *The Bluest Eye*, and wanted to do more with texts while utilizing the dramatic potential of purely musical language. In 1999 she began collaborating with the librettist Lance Belville on an opera about Clara Barton, the Civil War nurse who founded the American Red Cross. *Queen Clara: Fields of Glory, Rivers of Blood* consists of the traditional numbers of grand opera—recitatives, arias, choruses, and instrumental interludes. Its harmonic language is basically tonal, with Watkins' characteristic sudden dramatic modulations and emotionally affecting harmonies. The vocal lines are natural and flowing. There are some atonal passages, but no discernable jazz elements. A portion of the opera was presented in a workshop in July 2000 at the Goat Hall Productions theater in San Francisco.

Whatever her musical direction, Watkins will be living most fully through her music. In 1998 she said, "The more I do music, the longer I live, my experiences all seem to say that what I am trying to do with my music is experience God. I am not trying to convert anyone, I just want to share the bliss."[58]

The Sword That Heals (1987)

This 54-minute work for symphony orchestra, solo piano, and jazz combo is one of Watkins' most ambitious projects and occupies a central position in her oeuvre. The original idea came from a shorter piece, created several years earlier. "But at that time it was just one movement. The audience loved it and I didn't want it to die."[59] Watkins came up with a proposal to expand the work, and received a National Endowment for the Arts Jazz Composer's fellowship. While on a six-week residency in 1987 at the Djrassi Foundation arts colony in Woodside, California, she added the first three movements. Watkins wrote the work in commemoration of the 1960s civil rights movement. "I was growing up in Colorado when it started, then was in Washington, D.C. when it got serious. . . . The music isn't really based on the movement, but it is inspired by it. . . . It draws on music you hear today that didn't exist in the '60s, like jazz-fusion."[60] She has also said that in this work she deals with emotional and spiritual struggle and healing. "My music is often about triumph and it's about pain, about healing—'The Sword That Heals' . . . out of the love that heals, that touches people and binds you."[61]

It was premiered in 1988 by members of the Oakland Symphony Orchestra and a specially assembled jazz ensemble at the First Presbyterian Church in Oakland, California.[62] Reviewer Sarah Cahill of the *East Bay Express* found it "a powerful blend of upbeat, fairly mainstream jazz and [classical symphony orchestra]—an actual marriage, rather than a situation in which one part overwhelms the other. . . . Watkins managed to work the two ensembles into the mix without actually having themselves cross into each other's territory. . . . she had written out the parts for the orchestra, without expecting them to take up jazz-like riffs, while the jazz quintet mainly improvised."[63] These different forces and styles are often imperceptibly blended, sometimes smoothly combined while still clearly differentiated, and at other times separated by a complete and sudden break for special effect. Opportunities abound for good improvisational solos, and Watkins later provided optional written solos to make the work easier to program.

The mammoth work shapes its grand design through layers of sound, long lines, and slowly building, long-sustained climaxes. The form is delineated by sections of different instrumental groupings and timbres, dynamic contrasts and shifts, rhythm and tempo changes, shifts from tonal or modal to dissonant harmonies, and textural contrasts between sustained chordal and contrapuntal passages, thick and sparse scoring, and narrow and wide ranges. Especially effective are the passages which combine more rapid, irregularly moving foreground activity by solo instruments or ensembles with slowly moving banks of powerful background sound by strings and/or winds.

The first movement, some 14 minutes long, begins with a very soft roll of the timpani that swells and recedes, fading into a sustained C and G pedal point by the low strings. The bassoon enters slowly with a low, mournful theme in C minor. The lowered fifth degree of the melody is the only trace of jazz for the first eight minutes of the work. The cellos replace the bassoon, the upper strings provide a second melody in counterpoint, and the winds a third, before the bassoon returns with its original theme. The other orchestral groups imitate this theme, and as the pace picks up, the activity becomes more complex and dissonant. A shift to triple meter casts the theme in a bizarre, eerie light, leading up to a total change, a cheerful waltz in major in which motives from the theme are combined in a circular tune turning and turning within a narrow range, like a merry-go-round. The tune is passed from one instrumental group to another until a crescendo signals a return to the minor, mournful melody of the beginning with its sustained pedal point. This time high chimes added to the low winds and strings lend distance and mystery to the theme. A big crescendo by a timpani roll ushers in an even more startling shift as the jazz combo suddenly kicks in with a cheerful swinging version of the theme in major. Solos are improvised as the piano adds punctuating chords and the rhythm section with its cymbals and bass provides a steady walking beat. Then the meter shifts to 5/4 and the orchestra strings unobtrusively join in the background, preparing a return to the orchestral texture and somber mood of the beginning.

The piano and percussion of the jazz combo open the 12-minute second movement. Against a fast-driving rhythm with an underlying triple pulse, the brass instruments enter (doubled at the dissonant major seventh interval) with a slowly moving melodic figure, a falling three-note motive combining a minor third and minor second, answered with its rising inversion by the woodwinds. (This three-note cell is frequently found in Watkins' music, a kind of "signature" motive.) Improvised solos are heard from the alto saxophone, then the trumpet. Suddenly the orchestra strings and winds shift to a passage of carol-like tunes in counterpoint. Then the brass choir alone delivers solemn, sustained chords in square hymnlike phrases, alternating with quiet string passages. This orchestral interlude gradually becomes more dissonant and rhythmically irregular, building suspense. A melodic ostinato by the cellos and basses emerges more and more prominently (joined by the tuba, then the piano), eventually effecting an almost imperceptible return to jazz by the combo's rhythm section. Here the jazz brass are superimposed on the orchestral strings and brass, with a return of the opening three-note motive.

After the exhilaration and adventurousness of the second movement, the third returns to a steady walking pace and consonant harmonies, opening with a pensive solo piano melody doubled in sixths. The gentle eighth-note accompaniment outlines a G minor chord, alternating with an E-flat major triad, then settles on an E-natural minor harmony, an example of Watkins' subtle yet effective tonal ambiguity. The melody is passed from flutes and soprano saxophone to the piano and strings, then to the flutes, oboes, and sax joined by a clarinet countermelody.

After an improvised solo by the alto saxophone, there is a change of pace with a section marked "Marcato." The snare drum sets a martial mood, and the flowing eighth-note background is replaced by a steady quarter-beat chromatic ostinato in the piano, trombones, and bassoons. After an ad lib solo by the flugelhorn, the percussion drops out, leaving a lyrical contrapuntal conversation among strings, piano, and woodwinds. The movement ends as it began, with the piano's pensive song in G minor, and comes to a quiet close on the E-natural minor triad.

The fourth movement had been sketched out in an earlier version that was given a reading by the Pueblo Civic Symphony Orchestra in 1974. A jazz version was performed at the Herbst Theater *Winds of Change* concert in San Francisco in 1981 (but not included on the album). Some of the ideas had an even earlier origin. The hymnlike sequence at the end was heard in some form by Mark Fax at Howard in the early 1970s. He was impressed by the emotional power of this passage.

Eighteen minutes long, this movement opens with a catchy, syncopated marching band solo by snare drum and bass, joined by strings in a sinuous, circling chromatic ostinato, echoing the ostinato of the Marcato section in the third movement. The music segues smoothly to the jazz combo's rhythm section, soon rejoined by orchestral strings. The horns and piano quote the initial theme of the first movement, then build to a tutti in the sinuous chromatic figure. At this point, four minutes into the movement, the piano begins a five-minute unaccompanied cadenza as the instruments fade out. (An alternative orchestral section was later provided to substitute for the improvised piano cadenza.) It starts with a rambling improvisation on the main theme of the first movement (the minor melody) in a free, unmetered rhythm. The improvisation becomes highly ornamented, with runs, arpeggios, and lush, orchestral piano flourishes. A new section of the solo, with the steady chromatic motive in the left hand, brings in punctuating right-hand fragments, dry and staccato. The right hand returns gradually to the free, lush texture, now superimposed on the regular left-hand bass. As the piano cadenza comes to a close, the electric bass guitar enters with a solo passage ending in dominant chords played softly together with the strings.

Changes of mood and pace follow, with the jazz combo and piano in the foreground against a muted trumpet solo in the background. The strings bring back the chromatic sinuous pattern, which dissolves into a walking bass as the piano improvises with the combo, gradually building in force and intensity. The chromatic walking bass becomes more emotionally charged, with more and more dissonance, piano arm clusters, and huge doubled thirteenth chords. A long, sustained climax subsides into low piano ninth chords and chimes.

In a deeply moving dramatic resolution, the strings begin an intense, sustained, gospel-like melody. The harmonies are tonal but modally ambiguous, combining the minor scale and the jazz scale with its lowered fifth and seventh degrees. Winds join in a hymnlike countermelody in major. The comforting harmonies, together with the clash between major and minor modes, deliver a powerful emotional charge. The passage incorporates a brief reference to the chromatic motive, now imbued with this emotional tension. The counterpoint of simultaneous activity among the different instrumental forces, triumphal and anthem-like, builds gradually to a big ending.

The four movements of this large cyclic work achieve an overall balance and variety. The moods and speeds change and alternate, not only from one movement to the next, but also within the movements. In the first movement, sections with full orchestra frame a faster middle section by the jazz combo. The second movement reverses this order, beginning and ending with the jazz combo, with a slower, solemn middle section by the orchestra. The piano is given a progressively bigger role in each movement. It is imperceptible in the first movement, more prominent in the second, and featured in a solo for the first time in the third movement, a welcome change of sound and pace. In the last movement, the piano has the most spectacular, virtuoso role; this movement ties the whole work together, quoting and developing themes from the other movements and using all the instrumental combinations. It is the longest and most intense, providing the healing emotional catharsis and release.

Five Movements in Color (1993)

In 1993, Watkins was commissioned by the Sacramento-based Camellia Orchestra to write a five-movement orchestral work. The composition was funded by the Meet the Composer, Rockefeller, and Ford foundations. It was premiered by the Camellia Orchestra, conducted by Nan Washburn, in February 1994 to celebrate Black History Month. The program consisted of jazz-influenced twentieth-century music by Leonard Bernstein, Igor Stravinsky, Darius Milhaud, Duke Ellington, and Watkins. According to William Glackin of the *Sacramento Bee*, "Watkins' 'Five Movements in Color' . . . provided the best example of fusion that works."[64] The 26-minute work received a long ovation, and was repeated the following year by the Camellia Orchestra at Sacramento's Westminster Presbyterian Church. This time Kirk Edward Smith of the Iowa State music faculty was the guest conductor, and the work was programmed with twentieth-century music that was not jazz-influenced (Zoltan Kodaly, Jeffrey Prater, and Linda Robbins). On his second hearing, Glackin pronounced the Watkins work "substantial, complex, often eloquent music, challenging to conduct and play."[65] Radio critic Clark Mitze declared, "This is remarkable music written by one of the Bay area's most successful composers and jazz pianists. There are long, sweeping phrases. The changes in mood are direct and effective with great use of unison violins and violas, and a moving flugelhorn solo."[66]

In a preconcert interview, Watkins called the work a statement about the African-American experience, and gave a description of each movement. The first, titled *Once Upon a Time*, "starts with African drums, then the strings begin to tell a story that moves from peaceful to active to violent." In the second movement, *Soul of Remembrance*, "a melody floats over a march. It's bittersweet and nostalgic, a song of sorrow and a song of hope." The third movement, *Urban Suave and Dance Survivalist*, is "plain fun; it mixes swing and ragtime." The fourth, *Slow Burn*, is "based on a slow funk, this is more esoteric than anything before." *Drive by Runner*, "the final movement, is fast and energetic, action-packed. It says something to me, but I don't want to spell out what. I prefer to let the listeners draw their own conclusions."[67]

The African drums of the first movement enter softly, one by one, each with its own ostinato and rhythmic pulse. The first instrument, a xylophone with the sound of the African balafon,[68] plays a seven-note melodic pattern in 5/4 time. Soon a low drum enters in a cross rhythm, followed by a higher-pitched, drum. Underlying the polyrhythms is a slow, steady, hypnotic pulse. The high strings join with a melody of slowly shifting pitches; the wood block begins to play, then the low strings enter with a countermelody in a different key. All in all, some ten different instrumental parts are introduced separately, each with its own layer of activity. The xylophone drops out as the chimes and low winds enter with ominous, slowly shifting dissonant intervals. The growing complexity and volume mount in tension up to the entrance of timpani and snare drum, and a change to a more military rhythm. All the instrumental groups now build to a dissonant climax, then subside and drop out until only the bells and brass bring the movement to a quiet, unresolved close with a low augmented triad.

Soul of Remembrance, the second movement, is clearly in a D major tonality, in contrast to the polytonal first movement. Soaring melodies in long notes float above a slow, steady quarter-note chordal accompaniment. The first melody, 12 measures long, is played by the clarinets and violins, while the harp and bass pluck the chords. A serene spaciousness is effected by the broad melody, the steady beat, and the lush, widely spaced, seventh and ninth harmonies. In the next 12-measure phrase, the flutes, oboes, and strings sustain the melody above the chordal accompaniment, now joined by the bass clarinet, bassoons, and tuba, played very softly. The third phrase runs on continuously to the end, and combines the first phrase of the melody played by strings and horns with countermelodies in the clarinets and the cellos. This long phrase builds in intensity, then subsides and fades away to a long, high D in the flutes and violins, against a softly reiterated A major ninth chord, leaving it, like the first movement, open and inconclusive. Each of the movements could stand on its own, but none more than this ode to sorrow and hope. Critic William Glackin called this movement "powerful, affecting music . . . a solemn beautiful melody, with harmonies of increasing richness . . . [and a] processional pulse."[69]

In the third movement, the mood changes drastically. With "urban suave," the swinging jazz theme is handed from oboe and clarinets to trumpets, as the cellos and bass provide a walking bass. The score calls for ad lib solos by the clarinet, and later the trumpet, first in "any key or no key," then in D minor and F minor at the same time. The trumpets impudently splat their riffs in dissonant seconds, and flutes tease with snatches of "Pop Goes the Weasel."

The high fun is left behind with *Slow Burn*, a hypnotic dirge with slowly shifting harmonies including eleventh and thirteenth chords. Four-bar phrases of half notes by the winds, doubled in hollow-sounding parallel fourths and fifths, are heard against a persistent African drumbeat on the third beat of each measure. The snare drum begins a funereal rhythmic pattern while strings sustain melancholy, dissonant counterpoint. The harp introduces an ostinato, later joined by piano, while the flugelhorn plays an improvised solo. Critic Glackin found this movement "eerie, even ghostly music, amply dissonant, superbly put together, dying away effectively."[70]

The last movement, *Drive by Runner*, provides an action-packed finale. There are the propulsive eighth-note ostinatos in the bassoons and cellos, frenetic interjections of coloristic layers of sounds from the brass and woodwinds, and the tension-building sustained notes in the high strings against the rapid, agitated percussion. One reviewer found it "compelling and contemporary, a juxtaposition of disparate elements. . . . The tension Watkins intended was indeed extreme."[71] Another described it as "hectic, threatening, full of skittering trumpets . . . coming to a violent, sudden end."[72]

This work demonstrates once again Watkins' virtuoso mastery of orchestration in her vivid, coloristic palette and her combinations of instruments for blended banks of sound. In *Five Movements in Color*, in contrast to *The Sword That Heals*, the virtuoso solo piano is missing, the cyclic element that ties together themes from different movements is absent, and the movements do not end decisively, but rather drift away, open and inconclusive. Here the combination of the standard orchestra with the sound and style of the jazz combo is even more fused and seamless than in *The Sword That Heals*, with no startling shifts within movements.

Raging Rapids (1995, revised 1997)

Raging Rapids, for solo piano, was at one time titled *Rafting*. As the opening indication, "Feroce," implies, this was too mild a word, and it was subsequently changed to the more violent *Raging Rapids*. An earlier version was performed by Sarah Cahill in March 1995 at Old First Church in San Francisco. Watkins commented, "It's about a certain kind of struggle . . . not like the emotional, spiritual struggle in *The Sword That Heals*. . . . There are other sides of me, other needs."[73] This piece is more about physical struggle, a struggle with nature.

Only four minutes long, the piece is built on two technical ideas which it exploits in the manner of an etude or a prelude. One of these is the arpeggiated chord of the augmented fifteenth. This chord contains bitonality, because the top three notes form a triad in a different key than the bottom triad. The augmented triad also carries within it the implication of a whole-tone scale because of the augmented fifth outlining four whole steps. The whole-tone scale has no inherent tonic center. Altogether, the whole-tone scale, augmented triad, and fifteenth chord create extreme instability. It is easy to see the association with the image of raging rapids. The augmented fifteenth chord is one of the two contrasting harmonic ideas in this piece. The other is the chromatic scale, which, although it also does not have an inherent tonic center, contrasts its close half-steps with the expansiveness of the fifteenth arpeggio. These two ideas are used simultaneously in *Raging Rapids*, so that dissonance and instability are both heightened to the maximum.

The piece begins with four measures of left-hand 16th-note arpeggiation of the fifteenth chord in 3/4 time, setting up a pulse and growing in volume to forte until the right hand enters in octaves on high E, cascading down to low A in a chromatic figuration in slower triplet eighth-notes. This chromatic figuration in the right hand is immediately repeated in more rapid triplet 16th-notes, starting an octave higher on the keyboard. The wide range enhances the expansiveness already established by the arpeggiation. The left-hand accompaniment pattern is raised a half-step higher, increasing the tension. The right hand also begins its descending chromatic octaves on a higher pitch. Because of the contrast to the very rapid 16-notes, the slower right-hand octaves, which recur at pivotal points in the piece, take on the function of a theme, albeit a rudimentary one. Sections of vehemently repeated octaves with added seconds, or repeated augmented seventh chords in both hands, alternate with sections of swirling arpeggiation and figuration. After a climactic tremolo, the arpeggiation slows down and gets softer, shifting to the right hand against sustained augmented seventh chords in the left, as the piece comes to a calm close.

Raging Rapids is an effective concert piece. It requires good technique, agility and strength, and a temperament equal to its wild and tempestuous mood.

Dancing Horses (1999)

Dancing Horses for string quartet was completed in October 1999 and to date has yet to be performed. It is a one-movement work about five minutes long. There are no obvious jazz elements. It is atonal; although tonal centers are occasionally suggested, they are immediately canceled by contradictory pitches.

Its most arresting features are the propulsive rhythm and the timbre—the drumming hoofbeats of its "dancing horses." Marked "Energico" and "forcefully driving," the piece is reminiscent of Stravinsky's *Rite of Spring* in its additive, irregular rhythms and meter changes, and its use of strings combined in chord clusters to create thudding drum sounds. The primitive percussive quality and its length and formal cohesiveness also bring to mind Bartók's *Allegro Barbaro* for piano. Here, however, the strings lend a strident muscularity rather than the sharp, clean percussiveness of the piano hammer in the Bartók piece.

The continuous propulsive eighth-note stream is produced by interlocking layers of rhythmic ostinatos in two or more instruments. The listening ear superimposes a half-note pulse on the changing meters of 5/4, 6/4, and 7/4, so that when the quarter note is displaced or the meter changes, it is heard as a syncopation, an offbeat that eventually corrects itself. In the last half of the piece, repeated 16th-notes are added to the eighth-note ostinatos, creating an increase in speed and excitement.

The striking timbre of the drumlike chordal clusters results from the repeated double stops in a low register. The double stops form a diminished triad with superimposed seconds, creating the distinctive brutal sound. Despite only four string instruments, the pervasive double stops produce a thick five- or six-part texture. In the introductory six measures, it is very dense and close, the double stops superimposed on one another within a narrow range.

The pitches presented vertically at the outset in the drum cluster are the source for subsequent melodic material. They give rise to a recurrent melodic three-note motive or cell consisting of a minor third plus minor second, Watkins' "signature" motive, used in inversion and retrograde (upside down and reversed). The chains of falling and rising alternating minor thirds and minor seconds produce a winding, chromatic, oriental-sounding melodic line, resonating with the sound of the diminished triad in the vertical chord clusters.

After seven measures of the low drumming ostinato, a melodic theme of 12 notes (nonserial) is added in a high register by the violins in slower-moving note values. The theme is stated twice over 12 measures, and then the drumming suddenly ceases. A variant of the theme in diminution (shorter note values) becomes the subject of a fugato in which each successive entry is less recognizable, recombining the intervallic cells in different ways. For these nine measures of counterpoint the ostinato is silent, and when it re-enters, rhythmic ostinatos and melodic activity are combined. Later, 16th-note figuration is introduced and passed back and forth among the instruments. More melodic fugatos follow, with even more concentrated versions of the main theme. When the piece ends as it began, with six measures of ostinatos, the thudding double stops accompany a winding melodic ostinato of 16th-notes.

The form is through-composed and highly concentrated. There is no repetition of sections, and the combinations of melodic motives are ever-changing. Yet it is powerfully unified by the continuous interlocking rhythmic ostinatos and the underlying harmonic and melodic cells.

LIST OF WORKS

Source of information is Mary Watkins' checklist of scores.

Publisher: Shotsky Publishing Company, 5337 College Avenue #425, Oakland, CA 94618.

Archive Holding Scores

(AMRC/CBMR) Helen Walker-Hill Collection of music by black women composers in duplicate at the American Music Research Center, University of Colorado at Boulder, and the Center for Black Music Research, Columbia College, Chicago (20 scores).

Instrumental Music

Viola

The Sand Dancer (viola, piano). August 1997. Shotsky. First performed by Barbara
    Houser, viola, and Mary Watkins, piano, at Michigan Womyn's Festival, August
    1997. (AMRC/CBMR)

Cello

Bus Stop (cello, piano). 2000. Shotsky. In *Black Women Composers: Twentieth-Century
    Music for Piano and Strings*. Edited by Gregory Walker and Helen Walker-Hill.
    Bryn Mawr, Pa.: Hildegard Publishing Co., 2002. 2 min. 32 sec. (AMRC/CBMR)
Focus (cello, piano). 2000. Shotsky. 2 min. 14 sec. (AMRC/CBMR)
The Medium (cello, piano). 2000. Shotsky. 4 min. (AMRC/CBMR)
Piece for Cello (cello, piano). 1983.

Flute

Braziltown USA (samba for flute and piano). 1983. Morning Sky AQEI Publishing.
Illusions (flute, piano). 1974.
Introspection (flute, piano). 1974.
Patrick the Dancer (flute, piano). 1983. Morning Sky AQEI Publishing.
Piece for Flute and Piano. 1971.

Oboe

Chablet (oboe and piano). September 1991. Shotsky. 1 min. 30 sec. (AMRC/CBMR)

Clarinet

Hide and Seek (clarinet and piano). September 1991. Shotsky. 2 min. 30 sec. (AMRC/
    CBMR)
Rag (clarinet and piano). September 1991. Shotsky. 2 min. (AMRC/CBMR)

Trumpet

A Matter of Urgency (flugelhorn, piano). 1984.
Mount Cathedral (flugelhorn, piano). 1994. Shotsky.

Piano

Ancient Visions. August 1997. Shotsky. 2 min. 58 sec. (AMRC/CBMR)
Breakfast Tea (duet). January 1992. Originally first movement of a suite, *Terror on the
    Mountain*. 1 min. (AMRC/CBMR)
The Burning Hills (duet). January 1992. Shotsky. Originally second movement of *Terror
    on the Mountain*. First performed by Theresa Bogard and Helen Walker-Hill in
    February 1993 at the Sonneck Society annual conference, Asilomar, Calif. 5 min.
    (AMRC/CBMR)
Changing Seasons. 1983. Recorded on *Spiritsong*. 8 min.
Comin' Home. 1983. Recorded on *Spiritsong*. 4 min. 56 sec.
Manhattan Mist. 1983. Recorded on *Spiritsong*. 5 min. 47 sec.
Mirrors. 1983. Shotsky. Recorded on *Spiritsong*. 5 min. 29 sec. (AMRC/CBMR)

Moods of Color. April 1996.

Moonlight Chapel. 1983. Recorded on *Spiritsong.* 6 min. 22 sec.

Passing Lights. March 1997. Shotsky. 7 min. 18 sec. (AMRC/CBMR)

Playground. 1983. Shotsky. Recorded on *Spiritsong.* 4 min. 12 sec. (AMRC/CBMR)

Raging Rapids. 1995; revised 1997. Shotsky. Formerly titled *Rafting.* First performed by
    Sarah Cahill in August 1996 at Old First Church in San Francisco. 4 min.
    (AMRC/CBMR)

Rebirth (duet). January 1992. Originally third movement of *Terror on the Mountain.*

The Sleuth. June 1996. Shotsky. 3 min. 8 sec. (AMRC/CBMR)

Spiritsong. 1983. Recorded on *Spiritsong.* 6 min. 47 sec.

Instrumental Trios

Piece #1 for Flute, Oboe, and Piano. 1983.

Piece #2 for Flute, Oboe, and Piano. 1983.

Wind Trio (bassoon, flute, clarinet). 1998. Shotsky. Four movements. Contents: 1) Mid-
    week; 2) TGIF; 3) Blue Sabbath; 4) Monday Morning. Total 15 min.

Winter Solstice (viola, cello, piano). 1999.

Instrumental Quartets

Dancing Horses (string quartet). 1999. Shotsky. 5 min. (AMRC/CBMR)

Piece #1 for Piano, Flute, Oboe, and Cello. 1983.

Piece #2 for Piano, Flute, Oboe, and Cello. 1983.

Quartet for Piano, Flute, Clarinet, Cello. 1997. Shotsky. Three movements. Contents:
    (1) Grand Fury, 4 min. 30 sec.; (2) Dream/Solitude, 5 min. 30 sec.; (3) Discharge,
    3 min. Total 13 min.

Instrumental Quintets

The Gallery (flute, clarinet, bassoon, viola, cello). 1994.

Party Line (woodwind quintet). 1994. Morning Sky AQEI Publishing.

Royal Holiday (2 flugelhorns, horn, trombone, tuba, and flute). January 1998. Shotsky.

Woodwind Quintet #1. 1971. (lost)

Woodwind Quintet #2 (Dance of the Trolls). 1971. (lost)

Woodwind Quintet #3 (Hopscotch). 1971. (lost)

Woodwind Quintet #4. 1971. (lost)

Woodwind Quintet #5. 1971. (lost)

Jazz Ensemble

Back Rap (jazz ensemble). 1978. Recorded on *Something Moving.* 5 min. 51 sec.

Brick Hut (jazz ensemble). 1978. Recorded on *Something Moving.* 4 min. 30 sec.

A Chording to the People (jazz ensemble). 1978. Recorded on *Something Moving.* 6 min.
    40 sec.

Fleeting Moments (jazz trio). 1999. Recorded on *Song for My Mother.*

I Hear Music (jazz ensemble). 1978. Recorded on *Something Moving.* 7 min. 48 sec.

Leaving All the Shadows Behind (jazz ensemble). 1978. Recorded on *Something Moving.*
    5 min.

Mom's Blues (jazz trio). 1999. Recorded on *Song for My Mother.*

Remember the Love (jazz trio). 1999. Recorded on *Song for My Mother.*

Suite Convulsions (jazz ensemble). April 1991. Seven movements. Contents: (1) The Rap
    Files; (2) Death of an Illusion; (3) Uptown Express; (4) The Dispossessed; (5)
    Desert Watch; (6) Goodbye Yesterday; (7) Stagflation. Commissioned by the
    American Jazz Theater and funded by Meet the Composer.
Witches' Revenge (jazz ensemble). 1978. Recorded on *Something Moving*. 7 min. 39 sec.
Yesterday's Children (jazz ensemble). 1978. Recorded on *Something Moving*. 3 min. 57
    sec.

Jazz Orchestra (42-piece)

Billie's Barb. 1981. Shotsky. Recorded on *Winds of Change*.
Changin' Times. 1981. Shotsky. Recorded on *Winds of Change*.
Samba Orleans. 1981. Shotsky. Recorded on *Winds of Change*.
The Street Merchant. 1981. Shotsky. Recorded on *Winds of Change*.
Waterwheel. 1981. Shotsky. Recorded on *Winds of Change*.
Winds of Change. 1981. Shotsky. Recorded on *Winds of Change*.
Woman Messiah. 1981. Shotsky. Recorded on *Winds of Change*.

Chamber Orchestra

The Emperor's New Clothes. 1995. Shotsky. Commissioned and first performed by the
    Berkeley Youth Orchestra.
Hide and Seek. 1994. Shotsky. For Berkeley Chamber Symphony. 2 min. 30 sec.
One Episode of an Inner Journey (arranged for chamber orchestra). 1986. Three move-
    ments.
Piece for Single Reed Instruments. 1974. (lost)
Rag! (arranged for chamber orchestra). 1994. Shotsky. For Berkeley Chamber Symphony.
    2 min.
Soul of Remembrance (arranged for chamber orchestra). 1993. See Full Orchestra: *Five
    Movements in Color*. Morning Sky AQEI Publishing. Performed by the Rohnert
    Park Chamber Orchestra. 4 min.

Full Orchestra

A Desert Storm. March 1991.
Elusion. December 1990. 9 min. (AMRC/CBMR)
Five Movements in Color. 1993. Morning Sky AQEI Publishing. Contents: (1) Once
    Upon a Time; (2) Soul of Remembrance (also adapted for chamber orchestra);
    (3) Urban Suave and Dance Survivalist; (4) Slow Burn; (5) Drive by Runner.
    First performed in February 1994 by the Camellia Orchestra of Sacramento.
    Funded by Meet the Composer. 26 min. (Movements 2, 3, 4 at AMRC/CBMR)
One Episode of an Inner Journey (full orchestra, piano). 1986. Three movements. Com-
    missioned by the Bay Area Women's Philharmonic.
Potomac Park. 1974. Performed by the Pueblo Civic Symphony in 1975–76.
The Sword That Heals (full orchestra and jazz ensemble). 1988, revised and provided
    with written solos in 2000. Four movements. Commissioned by the National
    Endowment for the Arts Jazz Composer's fellowship and first performed in 1988
    by Watkins with members of the Oakland Symphony Orchestra and specially
    assembled jazz ensemble in Oakland, California. 54 min. (Movement 3 at AMRC/
    CBMR)

Vocal Music

Voice

I Suppose. 1985. Shotsky.
A Little Closer. 1984. Shotsky.
Love's Sweet Song. 1984. Shotsky.
The Meaning of Love. 1980. Shotsky.
Sweet Refrain. 1985. Shotsky.
The Way You Smile. 1982. Shotsky.
You'll See When You See. 1980. Shotsky.

Chorus

River (women's chorus, piano). April 1991. Shotsky. Text: Jill Rose. Commissioned by
    the Cincinnati Women's Choir. (AMRC/CBMR)
We Are One (solo voice, SATB, piano). 1992. Shotsky. Contents: (1) In the Morning;
    (2) A People Without Vision Perish; (3) A Change Will Come; (4) We Are One;
    (5) God Is All There Is; (6) Happy, Joyous, and Free. Commissioned by consor-
    tium of Redwood Cultural Works (Oakland), MUSE and Friends (Cincinnati),
    and Harlem Boys' Choir (New York). First performed November 1992 by Vocal
    Motion, touring group of the Oakland Youth Chorus. 20 min. (AMRC/CBMR)

Dramatic Music

The Bluest Eye (6 singers, piano). 1989. Shotsky. Music for the play. Text: Toni Mor-
    rison. Contents: (1) Quiet as It's Kept; (2) Rosemary; (3) The Family; (4) Pecola's
    Prayer, 2 min; (5) We Got a Case Comin'; (6) Little White Girls; (7) Moma's
    Tirade; (8) Winter; (9) Fluffy Sweaters; (10) Her Pain; (11) Cholly/The Rape of
    Pecola; (12) The Miracle I; (13) The Miracle II; (14) I See the Baby; (15) The
    Mirror; (16) Finale. Composed for Lorraine Hansberry Theater Productions, San
    Francisco. (The Rape of Pecola at AMRC/CBMR)
Queen Clara: Fields of Glory, Rivers of Blood (soloists, chorus, orchestra/2 pianos).
    2000. Full-scale opera. Libretto: Lance Belville. Portions performed in workshop
    17 July 2000, with two-piano score, by singers Ruthann Lovetang, Aurelio Vis-
    carra, and Douglas Mandell, and pianists Steve Cosgrove and Keisuke Nakagoshi,
    at Goat Hall Productions, San Francisco.
The Resurrection of Lady Lester (bass, drums, piano). 1988. Music for the play. Text:
    OyamO. Contents: (1) The Resurrection of Lady Lester; (2) Blue Racer; (3) A
    Poem for Lester; (4) Earlybird; (5) Younghawk; (6) It's Over; (7) A Prayer for
    Lester; (8) Lesterbird; (9) 'Nuther Dance; (10) Carnival Music; (11) The Curse
    of Mora; (12) On the Road; (13) Travelin' Light; (14) The Last to Know; (15)
    G Minor Riff. Lorraine Hansberry Theater, San Francisco.
The Revolutionary Nutcracker Sweetie (13-piece chamber orchestra). 1987. Contempo-
    rary version of Tchaikovsky's *The Nutcracker* ballet. Commissioned and per-
    formed by the Oakland Dance Brigade and American Jazz Theater each year from
    1987 to 1997.

Video and Film Scores

Ethnic Notions. MTR Productions. 1986. Winner of Emmy and other awards.

Valuing Diversity. Parts I, II, and III (3 films). Copeland and Griggs Productions, 1987.

Fighting for Our Lives. Seidler Productions, 1988.

The Coming Ice Age. Ephron Productions, 1988.

Out in Suburbia. Pam Walton Productions, 1989.

Diversity Among Japanese American Women. The American Japanese Historical Society, 1990.

Color Adjustment. Signifyin' Works Productions, 1991. Peabody Award winner.

Ein Stehauf Mannchen. Vivian Kleiman Productions, 1991.

Faces of Aids. Iris Films, 1991.

World of O'Brien-Kreitzberg. Koppelman & Associates, 1992.

Conversations with Alice Walker, Charles Johnson, Toni Morrison, Gloria Naylor, August Wilson, John Wideman. 6 documentary films. California Newsreel, 1992.

Valuing Relationships. Parts I, II, and II (3 films). Griggs Productions, 1993.

Freedom on My Mind. Clarity Productions. Sundance Award Winner, Academy Award nomination. 1994.

Straight from the Heart. Woman Vision. Academy Award nomination. 1994.

Complaints of a Dutiful Daughter. Hoffman Productions. Academy Award nomination. 1994.

Out for a Change. WomanVision, 1994.

Black Is . . . Black Ain't. Signifyin' Works Productions, 1994.

Dream Horse. Shaffer Travis Productions. 1994.

Skin Deep. Iris Films, 1995.

Family Values. Pam Walton Productions, 1995.

Different Colors. 1999. KQED public radio.

Other

Memoirs. 1997. Unpublished. Contents: (1) Beginnings; (2) Little Musician; (3) School Daze; (4) Early Performance; (5) Teenage Daze; (6) Career Beginnings; (7) Perceptions of African American Life.

NOTES

I wish to thank Mary Watkins for giving her time and spirit in many interviews, telephone calls, and E-mail messages; for reading and checking the accuracy of this chapter; and for her permission to quote her memoirs, which are cited by the titles of chapters.

Full references are given in the bibliography at the end of the chapter.

1. Quoted in Pearson.
2. Watkins, unpublished memoirs, 1997.
3. Watkins, "Little Musician," p. 7.
4. Watkins, "Early Performance," pp. 5–6.
5. Thurber.

6. Lee.

7. Clark Mitze, review on KXJZ, 5 December 1995.

8. Watkins, "Little Musician," p. 3.

9. Sharron Dawkins Tatum is the mother of two sons and is employed as a finance officer at the World Bank in San Lorenzo, California.

10. Cuffie. Dorothy Rudd Moore studied composition with Fax at Howard a few years earlier. See chapter 6, n. 3.

11. Cuffie.

12. In 1981 the personnel of Watkins' band included Ray Obiedo on guitar, Arnie Barruch on sax and flute, Paul van Waganinen on drums, and Rich Girard on bass; in 1988 she had Oscar Williams on trumpet, Reggie Oliver on sax, bassist David Belove on bass, and Eddie Marshall on drums.

13. Lynch.

14. Kelp, "Watkins Is Back."

15. Bloom.

16. Watkins, interview with the author, Oakland, Calif., 23 February 1998.

17. Watkins, letter to the author, 2 April 1999.

18. Watkins, letter to the author, 2 April 1999.

19. Watkins, E-mail correspondence with the author, 13 October 1999.

20. Watkins, conversation with the author, San Francisco, 21 February 2000.

21. Watkins, interview of 23 February 1998.

22. Watkins, interview of 23 February 1998.

23. Watkins, "Perceptions of African American Life," p. 11.

24. Watkins, interview of 23 February 1998.

25. Watkins, "School Daze," p. 1.

26. Watkins, "School Daze," pp. 1–3.

27. Watkins, "Perceptions," p. 9.

28. Watkins, interview of 23 February 1998.

29. Watkins, "Perceptions," pp. 13, 8.

30. Watkins, interview of 23 February 1998.

31. Watkins, interview of 23 February 1998.

32. Watkins, "School Daze," pp. 3–4.

33. All the quotations in this paragraph are from Watkins' interview of 23 February 1998.

34. Watkins, E-mail to the author, 1 March 2000.

35. Watkins, conversation with the author, Evergreen, Colo., 1 October 1999.

36. Watkins, "Perceptions," pp. 13–14.

37. Watkins, "Teenage Daze," p. 4.

38. Watkins, interview of 23 February 1998.

39. Watkins, "Perceptions," p. 5.

40. Watkins, "Perceptions," p. 6.

41. Watkins, interview of 23 February 1998.

42. Watkins, "Early Performance," p. 5.

43. Watkins, "Career Beginnings," p. 6.

44. Lynch.

45. Cuffie.

46. Cuffie.

47. Watkins, interview with the author, Oakland, Calif., 21 February 2000. Motown

Records, founded by Berry Gordy, Jr. in Detroit in 1959, employed a large studio orchestra including strings, producing a lush, sophisticated mainstream sound.

48. Thurber.

49. Kelp, "Watkins Plays."

50. Watkins on keyboards and synthesizers, backed by Linda Tillery and Vicki Randle on percussion, Jerene Jackson on electric and classical guitar, Bonnie Kovaleff on trumpet, and Joy Julks on electric bass and French horn.

51. Kelp, "Moving Up."

52. Thurber.

53. Pearson.

54. Lee.

55. Lynch.

56. Spellens.

57. Pullen.

58. Watkins, interview of 23 February 1998.

59. Kelp, 1988.

60. Kelp, "Watkins Is Back."

61. Watkins, interview of 23 February 1998.

62. On that occasion the jazz ensemble consisted of Watkins, drummer Eddie Marshall, trumpeter Oscar Williams, saxophonist Reggie Oliver, and bassist David Belove. When one movement was performed by the Women's Philharmonic in 1991, the jazz ensemble was saxophonist Jean Fineberg, flugelhornist Ellen Seeling, drummer Hilary Jones, bassist Karen Horner, and pianist Ellen Hoffman.

63. Cahill.

64. Glackin, "Classical Meets Jazz."

65. Glackin, "The Camellia."

66. Clark Mitze, review of Camellia Orchestra concert, Radio station KXJZ, 5 December 1995.

67. Masullo.

68. The balafon is a wooden xylophone with resonating open gourds suspended underneath.

69. Glackin, "Camellia."

70. Glackin, "Classical Meets Jazz."

71. Mantay.

72. Glackin, "Classical Meets Jazz."

73. Watkins, interview of 23 February 1998.

BIBLIOGRAPHY

Bloom, Mike. "New Horizons for Mary Watkins." *Music Calendar* (San Francisco.) October 1982.

Cahill, Sarah. "Women at Work." *East Bay Express*, 29 March 1991.

Cuffie, Lionel. "Oakland Jazz Artist Knocks on Fame's Door." *The Montclarion*, 3 May 1983.

East Bay Express. Review of *Revolutionary Nutcracker Sweetie*. 21 December 1990.

Felciano, Rita. "African Beats and Radical Treats." *East Bay Express*, 9 December 1995.

Glackin, William. "Classical Meets Jazz, and It's a Fine Match." *The Sacramento Bee*, 15 February 1994.

————. "The Camellia Takes a Cue from the News." *The Sacramento Bee*, 4 December 1995.

Gere, Dave. "Local Scene." *Oakland Tribune*, 23 March 1991.

Hertelendy, Paul. "Datebook." *San Jose Mercury News*, 25 March 1991.

Kelp, Larry. "Moving Up: From Piano to Her Own Band." *Oakland Tribune*, 7 February 1979.

————. "Watkins Plays to a Packed Crowd." *Oakland Tribune*, 20 March 1981.

————. "Watkins is Back Wielding 'Sword' of Chords." *Oakland Tribune*, 16 November 1988.

————. "Critic's Choice: Mary Watkins & Friends." *East Bay Express*, 20 January 1994.

Kosman, Joshua. Review of *The Sword That Heals*. San Francisco Chronicle, 23 March 1991.

Lee, Cathy. "Swingin' Along with Mary." *Equal Times*, 30 January 1983.

Lindner, John. "Record Talk: Mary Watkins—*Winds of Change*." *IAJRC Journal* (October 1984).

Liske, Jim. Concert review. *Billboard* magazine, September 1981.

Lynch, Kevin. "Jazz Pianist Watkins a Late Bloomer." *Milwaukee Journal*, 18 September 1983.

Mantay, Marilyn. "Music of the People Inspires Program."*The Davis Enterprise*, 5 December 1995.

Masullo, Robert A. "Premiere for Oakland Composer." *The Sacramento Bee*, 12 February 1994.

Pearson, Yaniya. "Watkins at Her Very Best." *Sojourner: The New England Women's Journal of News, Opinions, and the Arts* 8, no. 8 (August 1983): 41.

Pullen, Doug. "Watkins Gives Magic." *El Paso Herald-Post*, 9 April 1986.

Richmond, Dick. "Jazz Albums: Establishment to Experimental." *St. Louis Post-Dispatch*, 14 January 1983.

Spellens, Larry. "Pianist Blends Jazz, Classical Traditions for a 1st-Class Recital." *Anchorage Daily News*, 26 January 1987.

Thurber, Martha. "Mary Watkins: Passion for Music." *Sojourner: The New England Women's Journal of News, Opinions, and the Arts*, 7 (October 1982): 40.

Walker-Hill, Helen. *Black Women Composers: A Bibliography of Available Scores*. CBMR Monographs no. 5. Chicago: Center for Black Music Research, 1995.

Watkins, Mary. Unpublished memoirs. 1997.

Weiner, Bernard. "Datebook: The Resurrection of Lady Lester." *San Francisco Chronicle*, 22 May 1988.

————. "*Lady Lester* Sings the Blues." *San Francisco Chronicle*, 17 May 1988.

DISCOGRAPHY

Something Moving. Mary Watkins, keyboards, synthesizers, vocals; Jerene Jackson, electric and classical guitar; Joy Julks, electric bass, French horn; Linda Tillery, vocals, percussion; Vicki Randle, vocals, congas; Donna Dickerson, vocals; Gwen Avery, vocals; Colleen Stewart, clarinet; Bonnie Kovaleff, trumpet; Priscilla Andrews, violin; Sabrina Berry, viola; Stephanie Harice, violin; Melian Eldalin, violin; Hilda Lakewood, violin; Kirsten Wickham, cello. Olivia Records, 1978. *Yesterday's Children, Back Rap, Brick Hut, A Chording to the People, Leaving All the Shadows Behind, Witches' Revenge, I Hear Music.*

Winds of Change. Mary Watkins, piano; Ray Obiedo, guitar; Arnie Barruch, sax and flute; Paul van Waganinen, drums; and Rich Girard, bass; Maiden Voyage big band; and a 19-piece string section. Recorded live at the Herbst Theater, October 1981. Produced under a Jazz Performance grant from the NEA. Palo Alto Jazz, 1981. *Billie's Barb, Changin' Times, Samba Orleans, The Street Merchant, Waterwheel, Winds of Change, Woman Messiah, Mother's Song.*

Spiritsong. Mary Watkins, piano. Redwood Records, 1985. *Comin' Home, Mirrors, Playground, Manhattan Mist, Spiritsong, Moonlight Chapel, Changing Seasons.*

The Soul Knows. Mary Watkins, piano. Wenefil, 1992. Traditional hymns, gospels, spirituals.

Peace for a Warrior. Mary Watkins, synthesizer. Meditation tape. 1995.

Song for My Mother. Mary Watkins jazz trio. High Tide Music CD, 1999. Includes *Fleeting Moments, Remember the Love, Mom's Blues.*

Dancing Souls. Improvisations by Mary Watkins, piano, and Kay Gardner, flute. Ladyslipper LR120CD, 2000. *Midnight Velvet, Beloved, Sweet Thing, Caprice, A Rose Remembered, Dancing Souls, Sacred Embrace, Dreamscape.*

9

REGINA HARRIS BAIOCCHI
(b. 1956)

CHRONOLOGY

1956 Born 16 July to Elgie Harris, Sr. and Lanzie Mozelle Belmont Harris in Chicago; third of eight siblings.

1961–65 Attended Burnside and Hardigan elementary schools; studied guitar at age nine.

1966–70 Attended St. Elizabeth's Elementary School.

1971 Attended Richards Vocational High School, Chicago; studied recorder with Judith Cammon Rogers.

1971–74 Attended Paul Laurence Dunbar Vocational High School; studied counterpoint and chorus with Nathaniel Green, and trumpet, theory, arranging, and composition with Dr. Willie A. Naylor.

1975 Married Gregory Baiocchi 12 July.

1975–79 Attended Roosevelt University/Chicago Musical College; studied composition with Robert Lombardo, Sergei Tipei, and Don Malone, theory with Lucia Santini, and piano with Ludmilla Lazar.

1978 Completed Bachelor of Music in composition at Roosevelt; continued for a year of graduate study, 1978–79; composed *Two Piano Etudes*.

1979 Instructor at Dunbar Vocational High School (theory) in summer; composed *Chasé* (clarinet sextet and *Realizations* (string quartet).

1979–81 Teacher at St. Bride's Junior High School (math, social studies, religion, etc.).

1980s Poets and Patrons awards for poetry "Teeter Totter" and "Ghetto Child"; "Teeter Totter" published in *Chicago Tribune Magazine*.

Regina Harris Baiocchi. Courtesy of the composer. Photo by Pete Thurin.

1980–82   Reporter for *Technology News*, Chicago.

1982–86   Teacher at St. Thomas the Apostle Junior High School (math).

1984–86   Studied design at Illinois Institute of Technology, Institute of Design; composed *Send Your Gifts* and *Who Will Claim the Baby?* (SATB).

1986–89   Writer and quality control analyst, Telaction Corporation, Chicago; composed *Father, We Thank You* for SATB in 1986; *Two Zora Neale Hurston Songs* in 1989.

1988   Story "Mama's Will" won McDonald's Literary Achievement Award and was read in New York at Douglas Fairbanks Theater.

1989–94   Public relations director at Catholic Theological Union, Chicago.

1990   *Two Zora Neale Hurston Songs* premiered at American Women Composers concert at Roosevelt University on 11 February; solo trumpet work *Miles per Hour* premiered at Chicago Symphony Orchestra concert 19 May; also composed *We Real Cool* for jazz ensemble.

1990–92   Studied journalism and public relations at Northwestern University; Composer-in-residence at Mostly Music, with support from Arts Midwest.

1991   *Two Zora Neale Hurston Songs* performed at Sumner Museum, Washington, D.C.; earned public relations certificate from New York University in summer; recital of works at Roosevelt University 18 October; composed *Autumn Night* for flute, *Foster Pet* (vocal/instrumental), and *Crystal Stair* (song).

1992   *Orchestral Suite* premiered by Detroit Symphony Orchestra, with interview on Detroit's WDET radio, also performed in Los Angeles by the Southeast Symphony Orchestra; wrote vocal/instrumental pieces *Shadows, Legacy*, and *A Few Black Voices* for Mostly Music children's music education program; also composed *Sketches for Piano Trio, Bwana's Libation* (ballet); joint recital of compositions with Michael Adams at Roosevelt University 30 October.

1993   "Variations in Black" composition recital at Chicago Cultural Center 23 February; interview on BBC (in Chicago) on contemporary black American composers and her own work; *Two Zora Neale Hurston Songs* performed at Oberlin College; composition workshops at Wayne State University, University of Florida, Columbia College; composed vocal works *Mason Room, Much in Common*, and *Ain't Nobody's Child*; joint composition recital with Michael Adams 29 October by Chicago Brass Quintet.

1993–98   Grants from the Chicago Department of Cultural Affairs.

1994   Graduate work at De Paul University; studied composition with George Flynn; commentator and featured composer in concert by American Women Composers/Midwest at Harold Washington Library 26 February; performance of *Teddy Bear Suite* by Marsha Mabry conducting a youth orchestra in Pennsylvania; *QFX* performed by Milwaukee Brass Quintet at University of Wisconsin at Milwaukee in June; received AT&T grant; also composed *Liszten, My Husband Is Not a Hat* (piano) and *Three Pieces for Greg* (orchestra);

performances of *Deborah, Best Friends, Ancestor's Medley, Much in Common, After the Rain,* and *Say No to Guns* at Harold Washington Library on 22 October.

1994–95   Public workshops at Northwestern University.

1995   Completed Master of Music degree at De Paul University; began composition studies with Hale Smith, jazz piano studies with Alan Swain; received grant from the Illinois Arts Council for children's programs; received Chicago Music Association (NANM) music award; compositions performed in two concerts: "Composers' Forum" at De Paul University and "Sounds from the Motherland," 20 and 26 February at Harold Washington Library; received grant from the NEA's Regional Artist Program; Patricia Morehead's setting for soprano and orchestra of her poem *Good News Falls Gently* performed at Festival Incontri Musicali di Musica Sacra in Rome; guest composer/lecturer at Columbia College and Northeastern Illinois University; composed *Darryl's Rose* (voice) and *Friday Night* (jazz combo).

1996   *Friday Night* included in "Jazz Sisters" concert at Harold Washington Library 3 February; composition workshop at Indiana University; guest composer at Northwestern University.

1996–97   Support from the NEA Regional Arts Program at Randolph Street Gallery to compose hand drum concerto *African Hands*; performance of *African Hands* by Ruben Alvarez with Seattle Philharmonic Orchestra under Marsha Mabry; performance of *Dreamhoppers* (drama with incidental music) at Harold Washington Library 24 October; participant in "Crossing Over," a program presented by the Three Arts Club of Chicago, 13 November; award from Art Institute of Chicago and the Lila Wallace/Reader's Digest Fund for performances of opera *Gbeldahoven: No One's Child.*

1997   Composer/music director for Steppenwolf Theater, Chicago, collaborating with poet Nikki Giovanni; wrote incidental music for *Nikki Giovanni*; also composed *Skins* (percussion), *Muse* (orchestra), *Message to My Muse* and *Dream Weaver* (songs); artistic director of Ravinia Music Festival children's music program, December 1997–January 1999.

1999   Panelist for American Composers Forum in St. Paul, Minn.; panelist for the Mid-Atlantic Arts Foundation in Baltimore, November; composed *Communion* (marimba concerto).

2000   Adjudicator for Illinois High School Orchestra and Band Competition; concert 30 April at St. Elizabeth Seton Church in Naperville, Illinois, with performances of *Communion, Liszten, Azuretta, Ask Him, Cycles, Dream Weaver, HB4A, Lovers & Friends, Psalm for a Cat,* and *Litany for Hale Smith.*

2001   Taught African-American literature at East-West University in Chicago.

When I was seven or eight years old I became a writer, and I probably became a composer by age nine or ten. . . . It just never dawned on me that I could not be either, or both.

> It's not wise to tell people you're a composer. When people think of a composer, they often think of Bach, Beethoven, Mozart. People are afraid of these big giants. . . . Being a composer is a big thing. . . . It is important that people know that I'm black because . . . [they] often don't know that there are black composers.[1]

This combination of optimistic self-confidence and cautious realism has enabled Regina Harris Baiocchi to establish herself as a leading African-American composer of the younger generation in Chicago. She is also active as a writer (under the pen name Ginann) of novels, plays, short stories, and poems, and believes that words, visual imagery, and sound work together.

Largely "self-made" as a creative artist, she struggled to learn her craft and to promote her artistic career while supporting herself with a series of demanding jobs. Yet she is acutely aware of her indebtedness to others. She says, "Whenever I give a concert, when people see me standing on stage, they're looking at my family, my high school teachers, my college professors—the whole list of people I've come in contact with. . . . It's important not to forget from whence we came."

Baiocchi's self-confidence, her ambition, and her faith in limitless possibilities were nurtured by a large, loving, musical family, supportive black Catholic church, and excellent black schools and teachers. Her realism, determination, and resilience were tempered by growing up in the rough projects of Chicago's south side, and the charged, confrontational atmosphere of that racist, hostile city. She said, "You either become stronger or you're defeated."

BIOGRAPHY

Regina's parents moved to Chicago (from Kentucky and Tennessee, respectively) before she was born, and her earliest memories are of living with them and two older sisters (two older brothers died in infancy) in a duplex at 93rd and South Park Drive (later Martin Luther King Drive). Her mother received her teaching certificate and taught school before retiring to raise her family of eight children. She was very organized, kept them all busy, required them to help keep their home spotless, put them in summer schools and children's choirs, made sure they all had hobbies, and encouraged them to develop a passion for what they loved best. Regina's early poems and songs were met with delight and praise. (Her first song was titled *Listen*, and her sisters still sing it to tease her.) Her mother sang in the church choir and liked to listen to jazz on Chicago's WSDM (whose tag line was "The station with the girls and all that jazz") because all the disc jockeys were female.

Regina's father was a high school graduate who had taken some college courses and studied art and creative writing. He worked as a truck driver for a snack distributor, and often brought outdated candy and chips home for the children. He read novels voraciously, subscribed to many newspapers and magazines, and wrote fiction and autobiography. He was good at painting, whittling, and photography, developing his pictures on equipment behind a curtain on their washing machine, and he loved to play harmonica and bluegrass fiddle, activities that embarrassed his children among their inner-city friends. He was, and still is, an ordained church deacon with many connections, which later became particularly useful to Regina when she was looking for jobs.

When Regina was quite young, her parents converted from the African Methodist Episcopal denomination to Catholicism and joined St. Elizabeth's Church, the oldest black Catholic church in Chicago. Soon after, Vatican II changed the liturgy from Latin to the vernacular, and Gregorian chant was replaced by folk Masses. Regina attended grades four through eight at St. Elizabeth's Elementary School, where the nuns were members of the Sisters of the Blessed Sacrament, whose mission was to educate African Americans and Native Americans. Black history was an important part of the curriculum. Regina took guitar lessons from Sister Elizabeth Dismas and played guitar for the services. Regina formed close relationships with the nuns, and still corresponds with her fourth and seventh grade teachers. The school engaged Mr. Larney J. Webb, a classically trained musician who was also minister of music at Metropolitan Methodist Church, to form a girls' gospel choir. He trained the girls to sing in three and four parts, classics as well as gospel music, and they became well-known as the Grand Boulevard Community Girls' Choir.

Regina was close to her paternal grandmother, who lived in South Bend, Indiana. She was an organist at Notre Dame Chapel, and later at Roberts Temple Church of God in Christ. Until Regina was 13 years old, she often visited her and, at her father's insistence, accompanied her to church, which was just across the street. Services there were long and lively, and Regina became familiar with the enthusiastic singing of spirituals and gospel songs, the improvisation and rich harmonies of her grandmother's organ playing, and the fervent, energetic preaching.

Regina's family was one of the first to move into the Robert Taylor Homes in 1961.[2] A massive project that stretched from 39th Street to 55th Street on Chicago's south side, it was initially a safe and pleasant place to live. Regina, then five years old, liked to go with her sisters from their apartment on the third floor to the roof above the 16th floor, to see Lake Michigan and the city stretched out below them. They sometimes had forbidden picnics on the roof. At first, the project housed hardworking families while they saved up for homes of their own. But it gradually became a refuge for the very poor, a rough and dangerous place called the " 'jects" by its inhabitants. The discipline in the Harris household had always been strict, but now Regina and her siblings were not allowed to go out unsupervised, and had to be home before the streetlights came on. Young hooligans would deal drugs, harass residents, and hurl heavy objects from the roof, endangering anyone below.

This environment and the severe restrictions imposed to counteract it took a toll on the Harris family. Regina has four sisters and three brothers. Her youngest brother became so frustrated by the conflict between his angry feelings and the parental and religious requirements to love and forgive his enemies that he joined an underground network of gangsta rap musicians. Along with another brother, he became a member of the Nation of Islam, and changed his name from John to Raheem. While still a teenager, Regina's older sister had two children who were raised by her mother and her sisters. She was a talented musician who had been invited to join the Johnny Mathis band as a backup singer, but her father forbade her to leave home until she was 21. But much as Regina's father might disagree with his children's choices, he rarely stopped or limited them, and even tried to support her brother Raheem's gangsta rap activities. The large, extended family was a tremendous bulwark during times of tribulation; grandparents and aunts and uncles frequently visited or lived with them for periods of time. A rebellious or hurting member could always find support and sympathy.

All the Harris siblings inherited a love for reading and knowledge, and for music. Most attended college, and two besides Regina completed degrees. All of them sang in choirs at one time or another, two siblings studied guitar, two others studied piano, a brother and a sister were drummers, and another brother formed a gospel duo with his wife, which they call "Anointed Voices."

When Regina moved out of St. Elizabeth's supportive atmosphere into secondary school, she tried two high schools briefly and unhappily before settling on all-black Paul Laurence Dunbar Vocational High School. The music faculty there was excellent; the curriculum included theory, harmony and counterpoint, and a wide variety of performance ensembles. Regina played trumpet and French horn in the concert and jazz bands. She carried the various mouthpieces for these instruments in a leather pouch, which could be swung with considerable force and came in handy for protection as well. Weighing in at around 70 pounds, she would have been "mincemeat" without it because the hallways could be rough, with special abuse for initiating newcomers and asserting rank.

A vital formative influence was Dr. Willie Naylor, a former basketball star who started late in music but earned a doctorate and became a professional musician and teacher. He taught composition and directed the bands at Dunbar High School, and encouraged Regina to arrange and compose for them. She could "turn in a piece on Monday, and hear it performed on Thursday," a valuable learning experience. Naylor's influence was both musical and personal; he taught trust, cooperation, and friendship both inside and outside school musical ensembles. He invited a group of students to travel with him to his parents' home in rural Louisiana, where they slept on the floor, experiencing a totally different way of life from Chicago.

When Regina was 14 years old, she attended a Fourth of July party given by a friend from her days at St. Elizabeth's school. There she met Greg Baiocchi, a 15-year-old who lived with his Italian-American family near Wrigley Field on Chicago's north side. Despite the difference in their backgrounds, they formed a close attachment that stood the test of time. They were married five years later, and have sustained and encouraged each other through the years as they each pursued their careers, Greg in computer systems design engineering, and Regina in teaching, public relations work, writing, and composing.

The strength of their relationship was forged through some severe trials. As a teenager, Greg would often travel on the elevated train to her home in the " 'jects." White people so rarely entered these neighborhoods that he would routinely be stopped and detained by the gangs or by the police, until they recognized him and gave up, warning that they could not protect him. On one visit, he was accosted by a group of men who robbed him and forced him to the roof of one of the high-rise buildings. They dangled him over the edge by one ankle, ready to drop him, relenting only when a girlfriend of one of the gang members recognized him and protested. He ran barefoot at 1:30 in the morning to Regina's apartment, pounding on the door until her father answered. Fortunately, the Harrises moved out of the housing project soon after, to a home near Wabash and 40th Street.

After graduation from high school, Regina decided to enroll at Roosevelt University (which had absorbed Chicago Musical College, where so many early black composers were trained). In doing so, she left behind the affirmation she received in high school to enter an academic musical world that had little tolerance for the kinds of music she enjoyed writing. She pursued a double major in music and psychology, and studied piano, horn, and flute. Her composition teachers there insisted that she compose atonal music using serial techniques, so she learned to prepare that kind of music for class while continuing to write "real" music for herself. In doing so, she expanded her skills and range of styles, and several compositions from that period are worthy additions to her body of work. When she began to compose a string quartet, she received encouragement from Professor Adia Gierdovici, who taught violin, viola, and string ensemble. He astonished her by including her piece as required repertory on his string ensemble syllabus, alongside works by Beethoven and Ravel. As he taught the work to his students, he deepened her own understanding of writing for strings. Unfortunately, the public performance of this piece, called *Realizations*, was also the occasion for conflict with her other professors, who could not accept the poetry and program cover artwork she designed to accompany it as a part of the composition, a holistic creative concept that was very important to her.

Upon entering the workforce after graduation, Baiocchi was helped to find teaching jobs by her father's many connections as a church deacon. She taught theory at Dunbar High School for a summer, then spent two years at St. Bride's Junior High School, teaching mathematics and assorted other subjects. Her students there included many Haitian children who did not speak English. Such challenges forced her to overcome her inherent shyness and to develop confidence. In 1982 she transferred to St. Thomas the Apostle Junior High School, where she taught mathematics and social studies for four years. Meanwhile she also took classes at the Illinois Institute of Technology's Institute of Design. She composed some religious choral pieces, and wrote poems and short stories, several of which won prizes and were published. While teaching at St. Thomas, she met a fellow teacher, Darryl Green, who became a close friend until his death from sarcoidosis in 1995. Green was a talented artist, calligrapher, and literary editor who shared her philosophy of the interconnectedness of the arts. Baiocchi took calligraphy lessons from him, developing the elegant manuscript that characterizes her handwriting and her music scores. He encouraged her to keep writing and composing, and was an honest and relentless critic of her work. Like Margaret Bonds' relationship with the poet Langston Hughes, they were "soul mates" who nourished each others' dreams.

In 1986 Baiocchi left the classroom: "I just had this horrible fear that I was going crazy in slow motion." After working for three years as a writer and quality control analyst at the Telaction Corporation, she took a job as public relations director for the Catholic Theological Union in Chicago. This was demanding work that involved writing, editing, and producing newsletters, brochures, news releases, and videos; delivering speeches; organizing banquets for hundreds of guests; and founding and managing the Courtyard Gallery, through which she met many visual artists, including Lillian Brulc, with whom she would later collaborate. At the same time she was able to study journalism and public relations at Northwestern University, complete her public relations certificate at New York University, and serve as composer-in-residence for Mostly Music, an organization that sponsors hundreds of concerts and children's music education programs. This grueling regimen was hard on her health, and for several years she suffered from a series of severe ailments. But it also convinced her that public relations was the missing link in her composing career. "I don't know why [music schools] don't have a promotional curriculum in conjunction with any sort of fine arts degree . . . musicians can't just sit and practice and expect to have an audience." Baiocchi combined her public relations knowledge, her work experience, and her training in photography and design to promote her own career as a composer. She began in 1991 by giving a concert of new music every fall, which grew to twice a year, in spring and fall. Some of these concerts were shared with other composers, such as Henry Heard and Michael Adams, and her works also appeared on programs of American Women Composers/Midwest.

She left her job at Catholic Theological Union in 1994 to concentrate on her promotional efforts and to complete her master's degree in composition at De Paul University. Commissions, grants, and invitations from colleges to be guest composer or lecturer began to come in. She received awards from the National Endowment for the Arts to write and produce a concerto for African hand drums and orchestra. She gave guest composer and public relations workshops at schools including Northwestern University, Northeastern Illinois University, and Indiana University. Best of all, commissions for and performances of her music by established musicians grew more frequent year by year, from members of the Chicago Symphony Orchestra, the Detroit Symphony Orchestra, the Milwaukee Brass Quintet, the Seattle Philharmonic Orchestra, and many others. She has connected her music to art by combining performances with exhibits of paintings by the Chicago artist Lillian Brulc, whose work inspired *QFX* for brass quintet; *Deborah* for marimba, percussion, and piano; and *Communion* for marimba and string quartet. Her vision of the interconnectedness of the arts was given form in a group she founded called SUSAAMI—Sisters and Brothers United to Support African American Music, Inc.—a performing arts ensemble of musicians, actors, and visual artists which had its origins in the concerts she shared in the early 1990s. She herself is also an artist, painting in oils and acrylics, and a collector of paintings by such artists as Marcya Veeck, Abrom Salley, and the Nigerians Dayo, and Bayo Iribhogbe. In 1997 she was composer and music director for the Steppenwolf Theater, collaborating with the poet Nikki Giovanni, and in 1998 she became composer and artistic director at the famous Ravinia Music Festival, developing their outreach to inner-city children. Although Baiocchi's dream is to "earn my living as a composer writing full-time," control over performances of her music is more important to her than commercial success ("it's not going to happen").

She continues to polish her craft, and since 1995 has been studying jazz piano with Alan Swain and composition with the renowned composer Hale Smith, professor emeritus at Connecticut State University. Her association with Smith was a major turning point in her life; he has been a mentor who understands her need to grow as a writer as well as composer. She continues to write articles, poems, and stories, and has completed a collection called *Sankofa Twin*. Along with fascinating stories filled with unforgettable characters and unusual plot twists, it includes a brief poetic essay which illustrates her belief in the interconnectedness of the arts:

Mystics say the world is organized in octaves. A repeated series of seven different units. Digits, Notes, Colors. All in accordance. Each energy vibrates in time. In turn. None repeating itself until each is heard and seen. Yet each flowing, splitting from the root.

One splits into two, three-four-fivesixseven. Red splits into orange. Orange into red. Yellow into green, into blue. . . . The C-note flows into D, E, F, G, A, Be. . . .

> All in accordance with the ebbing of
> Lake Michigan as she seduces the beach
> with silent strokes of virile
> brumalsperm.[3]

SOCIAL ISSUES

There is no question that the most important issue to Baiocchi, next to belief in God and herself as a child of God, is her racial identity. She has said, "Being a woman is important but not as important as being black,"[4] and she refers to being an African American as "a bottomless well."[5] When questioned on her preference for identification for this book, she responded, "I consider myself an

African American (no hyphen or dash between African American). While 'black woman composer' is an OK category title, it does not clearly describe who I am. There are many people of color in the world, we may all be categorized as 'black.' "[6]

Baiocchi's experience of being an African American has been greatly shaped by growing up in Chicago, which she calls a "racist, hostile city." She remembers the hurt she felt when she first experienced prejudice and rejection. "I thought I was a nice person and fun to be with. Why would anyone not want to be around me? It was hard to imagine the feeling was not mutual." The contrast between the nurturing black community of the south side and the harsh realities of the larger metropolis intensified her loyalty to her African-American roots, expressed in both her writing and her music. The subjects and titles of her stories and poems confirm that loyalty: the four black Chicago women in her musical drama *Dreamhoppers*; the complicated African-American rural family of "Hummingbird"; the African customs in *Sankofa Twin*. In *Dreamhoppers*, the psychiatrist, Doctor Du Bois, "believes in quality mental health care for African Americans. His Hippocratic addendum: 'It is the most and least I can do for my people: descendants of Mother Africa, whose birthmark I share."[7] In Baiocchi's rap piece, *A Few Black Voices*, the rapper chants "Yo! Listen up! Gotta rap about some poets and I think you oughta know it." He then lists historical figures: first women heroes and writers, then men. The piece ends with the audience joining in *Lift Every Voice and Sing*, often referred to as the *African-American National Anthem*.

In her vocal music, many of her choices of black poets and texts also reveal the importance to her of race: Chicago poet Gwendolyn Brooks's "We Real Cool," and Zora Neale Hurston's "I Am Not Tragically Colored" and "How It Feels to Be Colored Me." Her lyrics for the numbers in her opera, *Gbeldahoven: No One's Child*, about Harlem Renaissance writers Langston Hughes and Zora Neale Hurston, reveal much about her feelings on race. In one of the opera's numbers, *Black with Pride*, she says, "This is a story of the people standing tall, standing strong, standing Black with pride," etc. And in another, *But for the Grace of God*: "Tipping my hat with every bow . . . I aim to please . . . White folks think that Black folks dream that—White folks think of Black folks when they set the Welcome Table, but—I don't pay much never mind."

Baiocchi is fond of African garb, arts, crafts, and folklore, and often chooses African themes for her music, for instance, the African drums of *African Hands*. In *Bwana's Libation*, the first movement, *Ancestors' Medley*, proclaims: "Mother Africa welcomes you. Here are a few of our people. You should know their names."

Some of Baiocchi's need to affirm her racial identity may be due to her interracial marriage. She says that because of it, she often feels "dichotomized": not black enough for black people and too black for white people. The solidity of her relationship with her husband, Greg Baiocchi, along with the support of their immediate families, has alleviated the strain of the inevitable difficulties.

Greg's parents, first-generation Italians, were apprehensive at first, and Regina's mother warned her not to "take any mess from his family." But each is now warmly included as a member of the other's family. Baiocchi writes with wry humor about the complications of her Italian name in her autobiographical short story "What's in My Name," in which she enrolls in an Italian language class. When Luce, the somewhat flamboyant teacher, calls attendance and says, " 'Regina Baiocchi. Now that's a good, strong Italian name! Where are you?' I struggled not to blurt out in my most affected 'hood accent, 'Here I is!' Instead I raised my hand and said, 'Here.' Luce stared at my nappy locks. Her face turned molto rosso. She dropped her attendance pencil, and lost her place in roll call."[8] It turns out that the teacher's best friend, Bettina Baiocchi, is Regina's aunt by marriage; "Judging from the look on Luce's face, an outlaw is easier to digest than some in-laws."

Baiocchi understands the objections to categorizing black women composers voiced by Tania León, but she doesn't agree with them. She feels that it is important to record information before it's lost, and to get living composers' input. She also feels strongly about giving a voice to the unheard. "I think it's important to look for people who are not so obvious, because sometimes people who have a high profile may not be long-distance runners. They may not be the people who actually have the lasting effect on music, and sometimes, somewhere, buried in a church, or school, or in her basement or someplace, is someone who's toiling along and no one really knows who she is, and she might be the person you might be interested in, as opposed to someone who has a very public career."

Although this kind of neglect may be the lot of women composers, Baiocchi views black women in general as empowered rather than weakened. She credits the cultural patterns of African Americans with this empowerment. In her community women did all kinds of things, raised their families alone, and held a variety of jobs. She sees her mother as the "stereotypical strong black woman," despite being outwardly quiet and unassertive.

Where Regina's composing is concerned, she feels her gender has affected it very little. Her family and her husband have taken her work seriously, attending her concerts and giving honest criticism. They usually complain when her music isn't easily accessible, and Greg refers to her more dissonant, random-sounding works as "Ping-Pong music." Since they are childless, she has not had to deal with raising a family, but her demanding jobs have proved to be at least as distracting. She says that working outside the home made it difficult to find time to compose, but never affected the size or complexity of her composition projects. In fact, she feels that working taught her how to juggle many different things, and helped writer's block by shifting her attention around. And she has turned those work experiences (in public relations, etc.) to her advantage in promoting her music.

Although gender takes second place to race for her, it still is important, and she cherishes her relationships and solidarity with other women. When the composer Patricia Morehead was looking for a woman-centered text to set for soprano and orchestra, she commissioned Baiocchi's poem "Good News Falls Gently": "We saw a gathering of women young and old, sure and wise—many pairs of dancing feet—shuffling in clouds of soft, red dust."[9] In *Dreamhoppers*, Baiocchi's text explores the lives of four African-American women who have attempted suicide and treats them with care, insight, sensitivity, and dignity.

The issue of social class did not seem relevant to Baiocchi's experiences. She said that as children, she and her siblings were very sheltered and just not aware of it. Along with churches, social clubs were important in the African-American community—Girl Scouts, Ladies Auxiliaries, the Grand Boulevard Community Girl's Choir. Her mother belonged to several clubs, and Regina's first performance on the guitar, at age 10, was for a meeting of one of her clubs in the Tiki Room. The Girls' Choir and Dunbar High School instrumental groups were often called upon by these clubs to provide music for special occasions.

Some of the residents of the Robert Taylor Homes where they lived were teachers or semi-professionals, but their economic class was low, like their less educated neighbors. Class considerations were replaced with a distinction between those families who supervised their children, attended church, or observed Afrocentric family customs and holidays, and those whose children were latchkey kids, the parents too tired or discouraged to care. There were many unfortunate stories of children who drifted into crime or even became murderers, and her reaction to these tragedies was "There but for the grace of God go I."

The issue of violence, both as urban crime and as national policy, is important to Baiocchi. At the time she was composing the ballet *Bwana's Libation*, a former student of hers was murdered. She gave voice to her grief and concern in the lyrics of the last movement of the ballet, *Say No to Guns, Yes to the Future*: "There was a time when I could walk the streets alone. There was a time when every neighbor's house was home. And now we're living in fear." She protested the Gulf War in her *Orchestral Suite* of 1991. The first movement is titled *Against the O.D.S.* (Operation Desert Storm), and in the second movement, *Mother to Nique*, "a husband discovers his wife singing a lullaby to a photo of their baby daughter, now grown and serving in the Gulf War." The genocide in Rwanda inspired *Rwanda's Prayer*, the second movement of *Deborah* (1994). *Bosnia's Tear*, the second movement of the brass quintet *QFX* (1993; the letters stand for quintet and special effects), was her response to the tragedy in Bosnia. It was performed in collaboration with an exhibit of paintings by Lillian Brulc titled, "Storms of War, Dreams of Peace."

Musical composition for Baiocchi is inextricably entwined with her life, her interests in art and literature, and her concerns for mankind. The difficulty of discussing the music of composers in a compartmentalized, separate section is particularly acute in the case of Baiocchi's compositions, which are so explicitly related to social issues.

THE MUSIC

In 2001 Baiocchi's oeuvre comprises more than 60 works, not counting the arrangements and pieces she composed in high school. About a third of them are purely instrumental; almost a third are for solo voice(s) with piano or other instruments; and the other third are for chorus and stage. Virtually all of them have been performed, and many of them were commissioned.

Baiocchi has not pursued publication, feeling that she can supply any need for scores on her own. Her promotional efforts, which already take more time than she would like, are directed primarily toward performances and attracting audiences, and toward making her name known as a composer. As a result, her works have been performed by some stellar musicians: members of the Chicago Symphony orchestra, the Milwaukee Brass Quintet, the Detroit Symphony Orchestra, the Seattle Symphony Orchestra, and numerous individual artists of stature.

Critical response has generally been favorable. Joseph Cunniff pronounced her *Sketches for Piano Trio* "among the highlights of the concert,"[10] and Howard Reich described Baiocchi's *Friday Night* as "exquisite music."[11] Gavin Borchert of the *Seattle Weekly* thought that "Baiocchi's orchestral writing was finely wrought, aggressive and crunchy with still an edge to the lyrical passages."[12] In his review of the opera *Gbeldahoven* in the *Chicago Reader*, Ted Shen summed up Baiocchi's music: "Regina Harris Baiocchi is a talented though wildly uneven composer whose instinct-driven music veers between sophistication and naiveté. Her strength is vocal writing that borrows from a wide variety of idioms to evoke specific times and emotions; [but she] . . . often fails to elaborate on or sustain a musical idea. As a result, even the best of her works have the feel of pastiche."[13]

The unevenness and pastiche that Shen mentions may be a result of her penchant for juxtaposing differing elements in somewhat random fashion. Baiocchi composes in an amazing variety of styles and idioms—Negro spirituals, jazz, gospel, pop songs, rap, classical European models, and twentieth-century modern techniques—and is not afraid to combine these disparate elements in surprising ways, both between and within works. Indeed, the hallmarks of her style are whimsical unpredictability, melodic freshness, transparency, arresting sounds, and involvement with her listeners.

The compositions Baiocchi wrote before college were songs, solo guitar pieces, and choral pieces with religious texts influenced by Roman Catholic music. In high school, she would choose an interval or chord (dominant seventh, or tritone, etc.) and write pieces that exploited that chord. She was particularly fond of Motown groups like the Temptations and the Supremes because their songs told a story, and she listened to artists and composers as diverse as Betty Carter, Cassandra Wilson, Gerri Allen, and Dorothy Rudd Moore, whom she met when Moore visited Roosevelt University.

The earliest compositions Baiocchi lists were written during her years at Roosevelt in response to her teachers' requirements for the use of twentieth-century techniques. The *Two Piano Etudes* (1978) for solo piano are a combination of academic writing for her teacher and "real" writing for herself.[14] Subtitled "Equipoise by Intersection," after a poem by Paula McHugh, they are technical and conceptual studies in the transition from stable (standard, mainstream, nineteenth-century) to new (contemporary, living, innovative) styles, and can be performed in either straight classical or syncopated jazz style. The first etude is in A B A form and starts off with arm clusters in extreme high and low registers. Both etudes are atonal, and the second employs a 12-tone row beginning with a falling third: A, F, E, E-flat, B-flat B-natural, which became her "standby row," reappearing intermittently in such later works as *How It Feels to Be Colored Me, QFX, Azuretta*, and others. The second etude shifts back and forth among sections of languid arpeggiated clusters, imitative statements of the row, and four-part counterpoint in highly complex polyrhythms, and ends whimsically—"tongue in cheek," as Baiocchi says—with an incongruous E-flat major triad and very soft staccato octaves spaced widely apart.

In *Chasé* (1979), for clarinet, wind quartet and piano, the three movements appear to be independent of each other. In fact, the first movement is for clarinet and piano alone, and is sometimes listed separately as a clarinet sonata. This work is also atonal and dissonant. The relationship between the instruments is well balanced with some particularly fine idiomatic writing for the clarinet.

The next work is *Realizations* (1979), the string quartet accompanied by poetry and art that was used in Gierdovici's string ensemble class at Roosevelt University. It is a strong work: dissonant, 12-tone, with a vivid sense of dramatic gesture. The string writing is eloquent and expressive, alternating between solo or duet passages with sparse accompaniment, and rich, thick-textured four-part sustained or contrapuntal passages. Toward the end, the texture thins out, the parts spread out to the extremes of the pitch range, and the work closes with a lone, low cello pizzicato reminiscent of the ending of *Two Piano Etudes*.

During the 1980s, Baiocchi's energies were focused on working for a living. The only compositions of that period are religious choral pieces, often in gospel style, written for the choir at St. Elizabeth's Church. There are effective works among them, especially *Who Will Claim the Baby?*, for chorus, soloists, and piano, in which independent layers of musical activity build together slowly and powerfully.

By 1990, when she decided to seriously concentrate on composing and promoting her music, the dissonance and atonality of her early works had combined with folk and jazz elements in a truly eclectic style. She had found her "voice," her distinctive and characteristic sound and style, in the *Two Zora Neale Hurston Songs* (1989) for voice, cello, and piano. In these songs, style and texture change randomly almost phrase by phrase, from jazzy blues (she indicates "substitute playful hum quasi-scat") to 12-tone coloratura recitative-like passages, reflective piano solos, folk-song passages, and whispered words, in a whimsical, ironic interpretation of "I Am Not Tragically Colored" and "How It Feels to Be Colored Me" from Hurston's essays, by turns mischievous, defiant, and introspective. Both these songs were later used in Baiocchi's opera *Gbeldahoven: No One's Child*, and in his review of the opera, Ted Shen heard "Weillian confession"[15] in *How it Feels to Be Colored Me*, and a "bluesy lament" (certainly only part of its humorous intent) in *I Am Not Tragically Colored*.

The trumpet piece *Miles per Hour* (1990, dedicated to Miles Davis) is both jazzy and atonal, with "blue" flatted fifths and thirds in its expressive gestural phrases. *Autumn Night* for solo flute (1991) is mostly tonal, and produces percussive rhythmic effects by tapping the instrument. In these pieces Baiocchi thoroughly explores the instruments and exploits their resources to the fullest.

By now her compositional process had settled into a pattern. She described it in an interview: "Most of the time I work it out in my head. I go to the keyboard to check pitches. I do a lot of writing with my voice . . . with the idea if I can sing it, a trained jazz or opera singer can do it."[16] She is open to inspiration from any quarter, drawing on her memories of her father's bluegrass fiddle, Roman Catholic religious music, and the gospel music in her grandmother's Church of God in Christ church, in which "there is a very strict structure. You have to know that in order to deviate from it . . . like in the different blues forms and progressions in jazz. A lot of it has to do with the words. It's all based on what the minister's doing—the rhythm and cadences of his speech."[17] Besides the Motown music and heavy metal and soft country music she liked as a teenager, she also was influenced by the classical music she heard on the Columbia Records Black Composers Series. Her ongoing studies in jazz piano with Alan Swain and composition with Hale Smith provided important input and stimulation. As we have already observed, she draws strong inspiration from literature and art. In the case of the piano piece *Liszten, My Husband Is Not a Hat* which is discussed at length elsewhere, the literary element is combined with her ongoing interest in psychiatry.

To these sources of inspiration can be added the creativity of children. For *Foster Pet* (1991), her piece for voice, oboe, percussion, and piano, written for the children's educational program sponsored by Mostly Music, she collaborated with her five-year-old niece, Pebbles. The lyrics pose a guessing game about what animal is being described ("Her cool rock eyes are made for desert shade and her straw-like tongue for sipping cool ades"), and the instrumentation of oboe perfectly reflects the sinuousness of the snake while the casaba rattles and hisses.

Baiocchi's characteristic sound and style also result from several recurring devices or "fingerprints." The melodic contours of *Foster Pet* recall similar ones in the vocal duet *Crystal Stair* (1991) (the interval of a dropping major third followed by a larger skip up and step down—the scale degrees 3 1 5 4, or 3 1 7 6, etc.), as well as other contours in *Autumn Night* and *Sketches for Piano Trio* (a descending sequence of alternating thirds—degrees 7 8 6 7 5 6 4 and

8 6 7 5 6 4 3, etc.). Other recurring "fingerprints" are the abrupt final pizzicato or staccato endings (*Two Piano Etudes, Realizations, How It Feels to Be Colored Me, Pentasketch* from *Sketches*, etc.), minor seventh chords in second inversion resulting in an interior major second (*Two Piano Etudes, Sketches, Liszten*, etc.), use of chimelike glockenspiel and high piano effects (*Foster Pet, Shadows, Liszten*, etc.) and harplike, triplet arpeggiated clusters and chords (*Two Piano Etudes, Liszten, Crystal Stair*, etc.).

Baiocchi's favorite instruments are piano, double bass, percussion, and winds. Her experience playing all kinds of winds in high school and college contributes to her idiomatic writing for these instruments, and to the ease and flexibility of the solos in *Chasé* (clarinet), *Miles per Hour* (trumpet), and *Autumn Night* (flute). Percussion instruments of all kinds are used effectively in many ensemble works—*Foster Pet, Shadows*, etc., and are spotlighted in *Deborah, African Hands*, and *Communion*. Her fondness for double bass is evident in the orchestral opening of *African Hands* and in similar timbres evoked by the cello in the *Two Zora Neale Hurston Songs*. The piano writing in *Two Piano Etudes* and *Liszten* employs lots of octaves, pedal effects, occasionally thin textures, and contrasting high and low registers.

Deborah (1994), for marimba, piano, and percussion (including vibes, xylophone and traps), was supposedly written for instruments that would have been played by the Hebrew prophetess of the Old Testament, depicted in the paintings by Lillian Brulc which inspired this work. The timbres of marimba and piano are not particularly compatible, perhaps because they are too similar. The percussion is absent or sparse in the first two movements, and is suddenly featured in a march-like trap drum solo in the third movement, called *Percussing Up a Storm*. This instrumental imbalance is also present in the first movement of the wind sextet *Chasé* which is just for clarinet and piano, and the second and third movements of *Sketches for Piano Trio*, which omit violin and piano, respectively. This may be intentional, to produce contrast in texture and timbre. Prominent solos, reminiscent of solo turns in jazz, are provided for each instrument in the quartet *Realizations*, in *Sketches for Piano Trio*, in the piano solos in the Zora Neale Hurston songs, and in the first movement of the drum concerto *African Hands*, in which the drum alternates with the orchestra in solos rather than joining in ensemble.

Baiocchi's first work for orchestra appeared in 1992 with the *Orchestral Suite*, whose three movements all refer to the Gulf War. Unconventional instrumentation is present in the second movement, *Mother to Nique*, which includes voices delivering a text by Baiocchi, and instruments imitating voices. Unusual effects also appear in *African Hands* (1997), including the bent notes by both wind and string instruments, and added percussion instruments like a birdcalling device called the sea gull.

While not relinquishing songs and shorter pieces incorporating popular and jazz styles, such as *Darryl's Rose* and *Message to My Muse*, Baiocchi's compositions of the late 1990s gravitated toward large, multimovement orchestral/

instrumental projects—*African Hands* (1997) and *Communion* (1999), and dramatic/stage works—*Gbeldahoven: No One's Child* (1996), *Dreamhoppers* (1997), and *Nikki Giovanni* (1997). The continuing dichotomy between atonal and tonal language, as well as the variety of idioms within each, is shown in the portions of the opera *Gbeldahoven* that she composed in 1996. In these works she continues to expand her musical scope and give voice to her strong feelings on African-American identity in her inimitable, freewheeling style.

Sketches for Piano Trio (1992)

This work unmistakably bears Baiocchi's "fingerprints": her transparent sound, variety of instrumentation and instrumental techniques and sounds, upbeat yet wistful melodic idiom, and open-ended tonal and instrumental designs with possibilities in any direction. The absence of the full trio instrumentation in all movements has already been mentioned. In this case, the different combinations of the three instruments make it possible to use one or more movements separately depending on the instruments and talents available. This is the practical, utilitarian side of Baiocchi's creativity. The various combinations also give room for extended solos, interweaving contrapuntal textures, and open sonorities.

Sketches was commissioned by St. Mary's Episcopal Church in Philadelphia, to honor its artist/pastor, Miriam Pocevedo, and was completed in May 1992. It was performed at Roosevelt University on 30 October 1992 by Lori Ashikawa, violin, Elizabeth Anderson, cello, and Jane Kenas, piano. In a later performance, as part of an American Women Composers concert at the Harold Washington Library in 1994, Jane Kenas was replaced by Jamie Hagedorn. This performance drew the following comment from the critic Joseph Cunniff: "Her *Sketches for Piano Trio* is written in four movements'. . . . Collectively they make a strong impression . . . a work which also proved to be among the highlights of the concert."

Altogether, the four movements total 15 minutes. All of them are basically tonal and major in mode, with the clear, innocent, almost childlike sound of *Foster Pet* (1991). The melodies of both compositions employ major sixth intervals and thirds, intervals that lend a spacious, transparent sound. The instruments often play in the extremes of their ranges, which expands and thins the texture. Among the instrumental effects is the occasional use of the piano's high register in parallel octaves producing a bell-like sound similar to a glockenspiel (also used in *Foster Pet*). The harmonies are sweet, often jazzy, and even when they verge on the atonal, the dissonance is rarely jarring.

The first movement, *Sketches for the Ninth*, uses all three instruments. It opens with violin alone in an arching melodic gesture of four notes—the upward leap of a major sixth interval to D, then a third up and back down to D. This expansive phrase is followed in the second measure by the cello in a rapid, falling major scale passage repeated in octaves before coming to rest on D. When the piano enters in the ninth measure, we hear a sequence of slow parallel ninth and seventh chords, inverted with the prominent interior major second that lends a sweetness to the wistful lyricism of the melodies. The mood of reverie is soon broken by sharp, rhythmic piano chords and syncopated melodies in a quasi-jazz passage. The movement ends as it began with the arching four-note phrase.

The second movement, *Miriam's Muse*, was inspired by a sketch by Miriam Pocevedo. It is prefaced by Baiocchi's poem beginning "What if life is just make believe?" and ending with "Canvas stretched and ready to get set, blank paper waiting to unfold a life." The words reinforce the mood of reverie established in the first movement, and are continued here by the cello and piano in unmeasured, meandering improvisatory melodies. The familiar seventh chord inversion reappears, as well as strummed tone clusters in which the major second predominates. This major diatonic sound is interrupted by a fast, descending chromatic scale in the piano. A long solo by the cello passes through some atonal passages, before returning to the bland major melody of the beginning. The piano closes the movement with two very soft, staccato, dissonant sevenths, as if to undermine the bland consonance.

The violin and cello take over assertively in the third movement, *Variations on Two Puerto Rican Folk Songs*, based on two folk songs composed around 1924–26 by Rafael Hernandez: *Preciosa* and *El Boricano Lament*. Without the piano, they announce the first song in unison spiccato (bow bounces on string), in strongly marked rhythms, before expanding into four-part harmony with double stops that sound like a vigorously strummed guitar. A lyrical second theme provides contrast before the second dancelike folk song is introduced by the violin alone. The movement closes with the opening energetic melody.

In the closing movement, *Pentasketch*, all three instruments are combined, and the mood is reflective again. The long-breathed melodies, based on five-note gapped scales (hence the title), intertwine dreamily in a lilting 6/8 duet between cello and violin until the piano joins in with the familiar bland parallel seventh chord inversions. The winding melodic figures accelerate and become more agitated and dissonant before returning to the peaceful mood of the beginning. The piano then has an extended solo in which the agitated figures return, climaxing in wild and random leaps all over the keyboard. Suddenly the indication is "Placid dolce," and the piano recalls the sweet, bland seventh chords outlining the opening melody. The melodic motives from the first movement reappear as the piano sevenths expand into a sustained ninth chord on C. The piano is heard briefly in its bell-like high register, and closes the work with a staccato seventh chord.

Liszten: My Husband Is Not a Hat (1994)

In her title, Baiocchi refers to both the nineteenth-century Romantic composer Franz Liszt and to Oliver Sacks's book *The Man Who Mistook His Wife for a*

Hat and Other Clinical Tales (1987).[18] Sacks, a clinical neurologist, related the case of a voice professor who lost all ability to recognize faces and objects but could function in daily life when he heard music (mentally or otherwise). Music was therefore his only link to reality. Baiocchi is especially fond of this composition because it's connected to that part of her that might have become a psychiatrist (psychology was one of her majors at Roosevelt), and because she considers it a "peaceful marriage of different styles [tonal and atonal]."

Since it was originally requested as a piano sonata by George Flynn, her composition teacher at De Paul University, the piece is subtitled *Sonata*. It was given its premiere by Jamie Hagedorn at De Paul University in 1994–95, and was later performed by Esther Hanviriyapunt as part of the play *Dreamhoppers* on 14 October 1997 at the Harold Washington Library in Chicago.

The references to Lisztian Romanticism are easy to recognize in the lush lyrical and virtuoso passages. The psychological states of mind are more elusive, represented by "moving in and out of different areas," presumably different sections of contrasting musical activity. The piece shifts randomly from one passage to the next with little transition, coherence, or internal consistency. Fleeting tonal allusions occur in almost every measure, only to be canceled in the next. This musical instability could be understood to portray the operation of the irrational mind. These characteristics are also present in the *Two Piano Etudes* composed in 1978, along with many other similarities. Like the earlier work, it shifts from sections that are somewhat tonal and lyrical to others that are very atonal and mechanical; and it, too, ends tonally and very softly, in this case with a sustained low E-flat tonic and B-flat dominant. Both works open with languid triplet broken chords or clusters in a high register (sounding like a glockenspiel), and in both works the seventh chord in second inversion is prominent. Octave passages, familiar earmarks of the piano idiom, occur frequently in each piece.

In *Liszten*, a mildly atonal introduction with jazz-inflected parallel seventh chords leads to a triplet broken octave passage marked "quasi arpa." Some 11 measures of a somewhat tonal lyrical melody accompanied by left-hand solid chords are followed by a long section of harshly atonal virtuoso 16th-note figuration. This includes a quasi-fugal section beginning with the bass and imitated successively higher by three more parts, building in intensity until the 16th-notes break up into wildly leaping triplet octaves. Another climax is reached as rapidly sweeping upward grace-note groups are repeated insistently in a crescendo culminating in a long, descending glissando. At this point the "quasi-arpa" passage returns in a bell-like higher register. Another melodic section marked "dolce" (sweetly) balances the earlier lyrical passage, and the introductory sustained jazzy seventh chords return on the same pitches at the very end. This succession of sections and passages suggests a very loose A B A¹ form.

Gbeldahoven: No One's Child (1994–96)

Several numbers from this opera were performed as a cantata called *God-mother's Children* in February 1993 at the Chicago Cultural Center. The text for the completed opera was first written by Baiocchi as a novel, then a play, and finally as the libretto. She says that the strange, Dutch-sounding title came to her in a dream, and that it represents life's aspirations and positive possibilities. The full one-act chamber opera, Baiocchi's largest musical project to date, was first performed at the Harold Washington Library in October 1996 in its original two-hour version. A one-hour version was presented at the Art Institute of Chicago on 20 April 1997. The principal singers were soprano Marcya Danielle as Zora Neale Hurston, bass/baritone Timothy Graham as Langston Hughes, soprano Anisha McFarland as Charlotte Mason, and (first performance) alto Bobbi Wilsyn as Louise Thompson.

The real-life characters of the opera are the great Harlem Renaissance writers Zora Neale Hurston and Langston Hughes, their wealthy white literary patroness Charlotte van der Veer Quick Mason (who insisted they call her Godmother), the brilliant Marxist college professor Louise Thompson, who served as their stenographer, and Alain Locke, professor of philosophy at Howard and first African-American Rhodes Scholar, a cultural critic and author/editor of seminal books of the Harlem Renaissance, who first introduced Mason to African art and literature and served as her adviser. Baiocchi did extensive research for the libretto, even visiting at 499 Park Avenue in New York, where Mason lived in a penthouse. Several elements in the opera's plot are based in real life but altered in Baiocchi's libretto. Hughes and Hurston were really collaborating on a play at Mason's behest, a three-act folk play called *Mule Bone*, which ended up in a dispute over authorship. Because of copyright restrictions, Baiocchi changed the plot of the play-within-an-opera to a story about the importance of asserting one's individuality. She has given the 1930s subject and plot a new spirit of the 1990s. In her program notes she explains, "[*Gbeldahoven*] takes the political, religious, and social temperature of a nation weakened by the fever of fatal 'isms,' sexism, ageism, racism. [It] tells the story of how misunderstandings often separate People of Color from society." To this end, she exaggerates or alters some of the character traits in the service of her story. Hughes' personality as depicted by Baiocchi does not conform to the many biographical descriptions of him as a gentle, reflective man. The love scene between Hughes and Thompson also does not ring true, although he did have a long association with Thompson. In these respects the story is fictional, as Baiocchi acknowledges in her program notes.

In Baiocchi's libretto, the action takes place on one day in May in the 1930s, in three different rooms in Mason's penthouse, which are all revealed on stage at once: Mason's boudoir, the solarium/dining room, and Hughes' bedroom. Besides the five characters already listed, the cast includes a female servant and a male servant, as well as a chorus, chamber orchestra, and dancers. The numbers consist of a dozen arias, two choruses, and a dance. An intermission divides the one act into two scenes.

Several of the numbers were composed well before her work on the opera. Baiocchi's fascination with the characters goes back at least to 1989, when she composed the *Two Zora Neale Hurston Songs*, later absorbed as arias III and IV of the opera. Other portions composed separately were number VII, *The Mason Room* (1993); IX, *Ain't Nobody's Child* (1993); and X, *Friday Night* (1995). The 15 numbers present a wide array of styles and genres: dissonant and atonal, pop, jazz, blues, African chant, spirituals, gospel, and art songs. In most of the numbers, the styles are clearly differentiated rather than integrated, and seem to have been assigned by character in some instances: Langston Hughes gets the atonal, angular arias, Louise Thompson the jazz, and Zora Neale Hurston the sardonic, free lyrical numbers. All are placed to evoke specific emotions, places, and times, and to further the meaning of the drama.

The following synopsis deals mostly with the 15 numbers and does not provide the details of the story line. The opera opens with *Servant's Muse* (composed July 1996), sung by the female servant in jazz style accompanied by piano and drums: "What if we're just a writer's dream? And prose is Life that writers distill?"

The second number is Hughes' *But for the Grace of God* (1996). Marked "Dry" and "Recitativo Arioso," it is dissonant and angular, as he protests the perpetual mask that black Americans must wear: "Cup of coffee? Spot of tea? . . . I aim to please. I aim to please."

Hurston then sings aria number III, *How It Feels to be Colored Me* (1989), accompanied by piano and cello. It is more lyrical than *But for the Grace* but also dissonant at times, sung freely, with some words spoken. In an especially effective dramatic moment, a passionate coloratura passage with recitative-style piano chordal interjections sets the words comparing how it feels to be colored to the broken odds and ends of daily life.

Aria number IV is Hurston's *I Am Not Tragically Colored* (1989). More sardonic and humorous than the previous aria, it is delivered with a minor bluesy vocal line, with pizzicati and scooped pitches by the cello. The indications "Jazz feel" and "exaggerated syncopation" accompany the witty comments on the pleasures of life as a black woman.

The next aria V, Charlotte Mason's *Hell Hath No Fury* (1996), is more tonal, mostly in unaccompanied recitative style, as Mason rails against Hughes for betraying her and calling her "Guardmother" behind her back: "I can't believe a man would do this to his own Godmother, No!" A piano transition leads into the following aria, *Godmother's Lesson* (1996). Marked "reflectively," it is in tonal art song style with flowing accompaniment. As Mason wistfully sings "No wealth can buy me loyalty or make Godchildren of (grown) men. . . . Things will never be the same," her gradual understanding is expressed musically by expanding the range of the vocal line. This aria is among the most poignant and beautiful numbers of the opera, giving full human dimension to this basically unsympathetic character.

Hughes returns in number VII, *The Mason Room* (1993), in which he contrasts Mason's beautiful, bright drawing room with the reality of his sadness and loneliness. It is more lyrical, less angry and atonal than his previous aria, reflecting his more pensive mood.

A long interchange on folk superstition follows between Hughes and Hurston. Like other dialogue in the opera, it is spoken rather than sung. A love scene between Hughes and Thompson leads to aria VIII, the duet *Louise's Prayer* (1996), accompanied by cello and piano in which they sing, "Thank God Above for Our Love."

After more discussion of superstitions, the full cast and chorus sing number IX, *Ain't Nobody's Child* (1993, revised 1996). It is atonal and includes words spoken as well as sung, "Let's build our temples for tomorrow . . . We gotta raise that child so s/he ain't gotta be no one's child . . . no one's child, never: no more."

The first part of the one-act opera concludes with Thompson's aria X, *Friday Night* (1995). In an uptempo gospel/jazz style, it begins with a lyrical lament, "Someone's trying to take our jazz away," and closes exultantly with "We can scat where no one understands but us."[19]

After the intermission, the spoken dialogue of the play by Hurston and Hughes leads to aria XI, *Hold Out for Joy* (1996), heard on the radio. The radio voice sings a pop/gospel/ballad-style song based on Psalm 30:5: "Your heart may weep for a moment . . . but Joy's gonna come in the morning." The novelty of an aria "sung" by the radio is followed by another departure from conventional opera procedure. Number XII is not sung, but rather spoken and danced, accompanied by an African hand drum. The words of Baiocchi's poem, "Good News Falls Gently,"[20] describe and accompany the African dance titled *Rain*: "Each woman fanning a different skirt yet all sharing the same hem, their backs and elbows bending, rising and falling, casting one shadow."

The story calls for Thompson to tell the tale of her sister's rape, causing Hughes to become enraged and smash a mirror. He then sings aria XIII, *Hughes Man* (1996), in the angular, dissonant style of aria II, and rages, "Why can't you let me be a man? Can't you be strong without making me weak? . . . I'm not a Mason boy."

At this point, Alain Locke has his one aria, a commentary on the play Hughes and Thompson have been writing. He sings *Black with Pride* (1996) accompanied by chorus and chamber orchestra. The musical language is tonal, in gospel/jazz style, similar to number IX: "This is a story of a people standing tall." The opera ends with a reprise of *Hold Out for Joy*, the pop/gospel song previously heard on the radio, now sung by the chorus and cast.

A diagram of the distribution of the numbers among the cast is useful to see the whole design of the opera:

Cast	Beginning →			Intermission			→ End
Female servant:	I			/			
Hughes:	II	VII		/	XIII		
Hurston:	III, IV			/			
Mason:	V, VI			/			
Duet Thompson and Hughes:		VIII		/			
All and chorus:			IX	/			XV (reprise)
Thompson:			X	/			
Radio Voice:				/	XI		
Poem and Dancer (Rain):				/	XII		
Locke/chorus:				/		XIV	

The shape that emerges from this overview shows that the numbers before intermission are more individual, more in-depth psychological studies of character and relationships, while those after intermission are communal or abstract. Only one of the first ten numbers is a group expression, the choral number IX, *Ain't Nobody's Child*. After the intermission only one aria is solo, the defiant *Hughes Man*. The other numbers are less personal (the radio voice, dancers) or choral, expressing black solidarity and pride. A third of the numbers occur after intermission, a logical balance, considering diminishing audience attention spans.

In her notes, Baiocchi says that *"Gbeldahoven* illuminates a corner of the African American psyche." She also remarked that the opera may need a more knowledgeable listener, one acquainted with African-American history, and she related that one white audience member at the premiere thought the opera was racist. The corner of the African-American psyche that it explores is certainly angry as well as proud and affirming. For some listeners the tone may be too bitterly antiwhite.

The commentator Ted Shen apparently did not find it so, for he made no comment to that effect in his review. He was more impressed by other features, observing, "Her strength is vocal writing that borrows from a wide variety of idioms to evoke specific times and emotions . . . [*Gbeldahoven*] is quintessential Baiocchi: an amalgam of styles that includes blues, spirituals, and chant." He praised Baiocchi's careful research, and commented specifically on *Friday Night*'s "jazzy huzzah," and the vivid portrayals of "Mason's ambivalence toward blacks, Hughes' macho swagger, and Hurston's softer defiance and mild jealousy."[21]

African Hands (1997)

This concerto for African hand drums and orchestra was commissioned by the ethnomusicologist and master drummer Craig Williams of St. Louis, who performed Baiocchi's percussion piece, *After the Rain*, in 1994. The work was funded by a grant from National Endowment for the Arts and completed in 1997. The first movement received a performance in February 1997, in a version for orchestra without soloist, by the Detroit Symphony Orchestra under Leslie Dunner at the Unisys African-American Composers Forum. The full concerto was first performed by the drummer Ruben Alvarez on 24 October 1997 at the Harold Washington Library in Chicago. On that occasion the orchestra part was provided by a tape made by Kurt Tyler and Michael Adams. Two days later it was performed by Alvarez with the Seattle Philharmonic Orchestra, conducted by Marsha Mabry.

The solo instrumentation calls for the *ashiko*, a hand drum from Benin; the *bata*, a sacred Nigerian drum; congas from the Congo, and the *djembe* from Senegal. Each has different ranges and pitch possibilities, and can be stroked as well as struck. The orchestration is for the full complement, including the usual percussion plus rattan sticks, tom-tom, gong, temple blocks, claves, chimes, bell tree, and a birdcalling device called a seagull.

Before working on *African Hands*, Baiocchi had to learn the drums because she did not have any background in African music or instruments. There are entire families of *djembes, bata* drums, congas, and *ashikos*. There was no precedent for a concerto for hand drums; in fact, very little music for them had ever been written down. Although this work was one of her favorites because of the concept and challenge, she regarded it as a compositional failure in many ways, and regretted that the complete hand drum groups, their pitch and timbre possibilities, had not been utilized. "The hardest thing for nonpercussionists to accept is that percussion instruments are just like pitched instruments in the sense that they do play melodies." She also would have preferred more integration of hand drums with orchestra, especially in the first movement, in which drums and orchestra alternate. She considered that movement to be a better composition in its orchestral version without the solo drums.

The entire work is 16 minutes in length and consists of three movements: *Muse*, based on her composition *Message to My Muse; Mbira*, inspired by the African thumb piano; and *Oge*, which is Yoruban for "drummer." The first movement opens with call-like solos by the conga and *ashiko*. The drums roll as the cellos and basses enter with the main theme, a rapid vigorous melody in 16th-notes and dotted rhythms. They are joined by the winds, then all the instruments in an imitative variation on the theme. Another lengthy drum solo, seemingly unrelated in theme, by the *ashiko* features different strokes and polyrhythms, and leads back to the main theme developed in a lengthy passage by the strings. They first enter imitatively one by one, from bass upward, then continue in rapid, intricate counterpoint that mounts in agitation and force until the winds and other instruments take over in another tutti. A sustained chromatic rising line in the horns leads to a slower section in which a lyrical melody marked "Dolce" is passed by the flutes (or recorders) to the clarinets, then the violins. A series of flute trills and a new sustained horn melody bring the movement to a quiet close as basses and flutes quote from earlier themes in the background. As Baiocchi thought, the movement works better, has good continuity, and holds interest as an orchestral piece. The early drum solos are too unrelated; they are separate pieces in themselves.

In the second movement, *Mbira*, the sound of the thumb piano is suggested by the pizzicato strings, marimba, and temple block. The melodies are often pentatonic, with pitches established by the conga soloist and reiterated by the orchestra's pitched percussion instruments. There is good interaction by the soloist, first with the percussion section, then the whole orchestra, with lots of interlocking rhythmic and melodic figures. The conga drum plays continuously throughout the movement, ad-libbing some measures. Themes are passed around and imitated among the different sections in a complex polyphonic and polyrhythmic fabric. The instruments are often required to bend pitches, and a variety of unusual percussion instruments further enrich the sound. Combined with the lively pace set by the "Capricioso" indication, all this activity makes for an exhilarating movement.

The final movement, *Oge*, settles down to a more stately tempo, and begins with a soft, sustained F pedal point by the contrabass. The *bata* utters a reiterated "call," answered with a rising and falling interval of a fifth by the timpani and the winds. All these activities continue—the contrabass's organ point, *bata*'s call, and winds' answer—as four percussion instruments each commence their own ostinato patterns. These layers of activity suddenly stop, and the alto flute begins to play alone, a long-breathed melody marked "dolce." The cellos and basses resume the F pedal point, soon taken up by the other strings, while the tuba softly sounds the rising and falling fifth motive. Other sustained pitches are added by the instruments, with instructions to "play slightly flat" or "enter moaning with voice." These strange sounds crescendo until another sudden stop ushers in the solo *djembe*. A long cadenza by the *djembe* ensues, more than a third of which is extemporized. The other instruments finally return, each adding its own rapid ostinato pattern and all building together to a dramatic close.

The performance of *African Hands* by Alvarez and the Seattle Philharmonic Orchestra was warmly received by Seattle critic Gavin Borchert who wrote, "The all-too-brief work was a success, and I'd have been happy to have it twice as long. . . . The variety of timbres from his four drums easily cut through the orchestral texture, and more often spoke alone, providing sage and dignified utterances."

LIST OF WORKS

Music available from: Regina Harris Baiocchi, 40 East 9th Street #1816, Chicago IL 60605. (312) 922–3922 FAX: (312) 922–3978 E-mail: RHBwrites@aol.com

Archives

(AMRC/CBMR) Scores in the Helen Walker-Hill Collection of scores by black women composers at the Center for Black Music Research, Columbia College, Chicago, and in duplicate at the American Music Research Center at the University of Colorado (12 scores).

(CBMR) Scores in the archives of the Center for Black Music Research, Columbia College, Chicago (four scores).

Instrumental Music

Flute

Autumn Night (solo alto flute). 1991. Also arranged for jazz band. First performed by Darryl Pleasant, 18 October 1991 in Chicago. 3 min.

Trumpet

Miles per Hour (solo B-flat or C trumpet). 1990. Also called *Jazz Sonatina*. Dedicated to Miles Davis. Performed by George Vosburgh, 19 May 1990, at a Chicago Symphony Orchestra concert in Orchestra Hall. 6 min. (CBMR)

Piano

Azuretta. 2000. Dedicated to "my mentor and master composer, Dr. Hale Smith." First performed by Jamie Hagedorn, 30 April 2000, at St. Elizabeth Seton Church, Chicago. 5 min. (AMRC/CBMR)

Déjà Vu. 1999. First performed by Jamie Hagedorn, 10 October 1999, at Harold Washington Library, Chicago. 4 min.

Jazzed-up Circumstance. 1992. For Nique and Pebbles. (AMRC/CBMR)

Liszten, My Husband Is Not a Hat. 1994. First performed by Jamie Hagedorn at De Paul University, 1994. Received an AT&T grant. 7 min. (AMRC/CBMR)

Two Piano Etudes: Equipoise by Intersection. 1978. *Etude No. 2* published in *Black Women Composers: A Century of Piano Music 1893–1990*, edited by Helen Walker-Hill (Bryn Mawr, Pa.: Hildegard Publishing Co., 1992). First performed by Esther Hanviriyapunt, 18 October 1991, in Chicago. See discography. 5 min. (AMRC/CBMR)

We Real Cool. 1997. Jazz. See *Instrumental Ensemble, and Voice(s) and Instruments.*

Percussion

Communion. See *Instrumental Ensemble.*

Deborah (marimba, vibes, traps, xylophone, piano). 1994. Contents: (1) Jael; (2) Rwanda's Prayer; (3) Percussing Up a Storm. After the paintings of Lillian Brulc. Dedicated to Carroll Stuhlmueller. Received Chicago Department of Cultural Affairs Community Arts Assistance Program grant. First performed by Johnny Lee Lane, percussion, and W. David Hobbs, piano, 22 October 1994, at Harold Washington Library. 15 min. (CBMR)

Skins (2 hand drummers, 1 multipercussionist). 1997. 12 min.

Watoto's Kwanzaa (percussion). 1998–99. First performed by Roots and Wings Ensemble, 1999, at Ravinia Festival, Highland Park, Ill. 3 min.

Instrumental Ensemble

After the Rain (soprano sax, percussion, bass, piano). 1994. Bossa nova style. Commissioned and first performed by saxophonist Matthew Arau, 22 October 1994, at Harold Washington Library. 4 min.

B'Shuv Adonai (violin, piano, percussion). 1998. First performed by Roots and Wings Ensemble, 1998, Ravinia Festival, Highland Park, Ill. 4 min.

Chasé for Wind Sextet (flute/alto flute, oboe, B-flat clarinet, alto clarinet, bassoon, piano). 1978. Three movements: (1) B-flat clarinet and piano, commissioned by Richard Nunley Jr., and first performed by Deanna Hall, clarinet, on 18 October 1991 in Chicago. 4 min.; (2) and (3) for tutti. Altogether 20 min. (AMRC/CBMR)

Communion (5-octave marimba, string quartet/piano reduction). 1999. Concerto for marimba. Contents: (1) Canon; (2) Izat; (3) Ion. First performed by Yi Qian and the SUSAAMI String Quartet, 10 October 1999, at Harold Washington Library. 15 min.

Cycles (piano, bass, drums). 1998. First performed by Roots and Wings Ensemble, 1998, at Ravinia Festival, Highland Park, Ill.

HB4A (piano, bass, drums, sax). 1999. Title stands for "Hard Blues for Alan." Written for Alan Swain. First performed by SUSAAMI Ensemble: Diane Ellis, sax; Ben Willis, bass; Michael Adams, drums; and Esther Hanviriyapunt, piano, 1999, at Harold Washington Library. 10 min.

QFX (brass quintet). 1993. Title stands for "quintet, special effects." Contents: (1) March of the Impotent Ants; (2) Bosnia's Tear; (3) Brass Tacks. Inspired by Lillian Brulc's art exhibit, "Storms of War, Dreams of Peace." Received Chicago Community Arts Assistance Program grant from the city of Chicago Department of Cultural Affairs. First performed by Chicago Brass Quintet, 29 October 1993, at Roosevelt University, Chicago. 11 min.

Realizations (string quartet). 1979. 1 movement. 12-tone. First performed by Phyliss McKinney and Terence Gray, violins; Rene Baker, viola; and Ed Moore, cello, 18 October 1991, Roosevelt University. 5 min.

Sketches for Piano Trio (violin, cello, piano). 1992. Contents: (1) Sketches for the Ninth; (2) Miriam's Muse; (3) Variations on Two Puerto Rican Folk Songs by Rafael Hernandez; (4) Pentasketch. Commissioned by St. Mary's Episcopal Church in Philadelphia. First performed by Lori Ashikawa, violin; Elizabeth Anderson, cello; Jane Kenas, piano, 30 October 1992, at Roosevelt University. 15 min. (AMRC/CBMR)

Three Questions (violin, piano, percussion). 1998. First performed by Roots and Wings Ensemble, 1998, at Ravinia Festival, Highland Park, Ill. 3 min.

We Real Cool (solo trumpet/sax/voice, piano, bass, drums). Ca. 1992, revised 1995, 1997. Jazz.

Orchestra, Large and Small

African Hands (concerto for African drums: *ashiko, bata,* conga, *djembe,* and chamber or full orchestra). 1997. Contents: (1) Muse; (2) Mbira; (3) Oge. Commissioned by Craig Williams. Received grant from the National Endowment for the Arts Regional Artist Program and an ASCAP Special Awards grant. Premiere performance by Ruben Alvarez with the Seattle Philharmonic Orchestra, conducted by Marsha Mabrey, 19 October 1997. 16 min. (AMRC/CBMR)

Muse. 1997. First movement of *African Hands* for orchestra without African drums. First

performed by Detroit Symphony Orchestra, conducted by Leslie Dunner, at Unysis African-American Composers Competition, February 1997. 6 min.

Orchestral Suite. 1991. Contents: (1) Against the O.D.S. (Operation Desert Storm)—
based on drum cadence; (2) Mother to Nique—lullaby; (3) Thunder! First performed by Detroit Symphony Orchestra, conducted by Leslie Dunner, at Unysis
African-American Composers Competition, February 1992. 12 min. (AMRC/
CBMR, CBMR)

Teddy Bear Suite (chamber orchestra). 1992. Contents: (1) Ode to Her Child; (2) Legacy;
(3) Gwen's Cue. First performed by Pennsylvania Youth Orchestra, conducted by
Marsha Mabrey, 1994. 10 min.

Three Pieces for Greg. 1994. Contents: (1) Windows; (2) Best Friends; (3) Pentasketch.
Dedicated to Gregory Baiocchi. 15 min.

Vocal Music

Solo Voice

Darryl's Rose (piano, optional bass and rhythm). 1995. Text: Regina Baiocchi. First
performed by Barbara Farnandis, voice, with SUSAAMI Ensemble. 5 min.
(AMRC/CBMR)

Freedom Serenade (voice, piano). 2001. First performed by Elsa Harris, voice, with
SUSAAMI Ensemble, 3 March 2001 at Harold Washington Library.

Legacy (treble voice, piano, optional violin). 1992. Text: Regina Baiocchi. Commissioned
by Mostly Music. First performed by Roberta Thomas, soprano, and Esther Hanviriyapunt, piano, in 1992 at South Shore Cultural Center, Chicago. 2 min.

Mason Room (baritone, piano). 1993. Text: Regina Baiocchi. Part of opera *Gbeldahoven.*
First performed by Robert Sims, baritone; Esther Hanviriyapunt, piano; Ed
Moore, cello, 23 February 1993 at Chicago Cultural Center. 3 min.

Message to My Muse. 1997. Text: Regina Baiocchi. First performed by Michael Adams,
tenor, and Esther Hanviriyapunt, piano, in 1997 at Lunar Cabaret, Chicago. 2
min.

Vocal Duet

Best Friends (vocal duet, piano). 1993. Text: Regina Baiocchi. First performed by Roberta Thomas, soprano; Michael Adams, tenor; and Esther Hanviriyapunt, piano,
in 1993 at Roosevelt University. 3 min.

Crystal Stair (vocal duet, piano). 1991. Text: Langston Hughes, "Mother to Son." Gospel
style. First performed by Vita Scott Harris, alto; James Harris, baritone; Jukube
Felton, piano, 18 October 1991, at Roosevelt University. 3 min.

Much in Common (duet for soprano and bass, piano). 1993. Text: Gwendolyn Brooks.
First performed by Sandra Barnett-Davis and Alyce Claerbaut, sopranos in 1993
at Manchester Craftsmen Guild, Pittsburgh; Chicago premiere by Barbara Farnandis, soprano; Macea Leon Thomas, bass; and Esther Hanviriyapunt, piano, 22
October 1994, at Harold Washington Library. 2 min.

Voice(s) and Instruments

Ain't Nobody's Child (voice, piano, cello). 1993. Part of opera *Gbeldahoven.* First performed by Roberta Thomas, voice; Esther Hanviriyapunt, piano; and Ed Moore,
cello, 23 February 1993 at Chicago Cultural Center.

Ask Him (voice, piano, bass, drums). 1999. First performed by Jeanne Frank, voice, with SUSAAMI Ensemble: Michael Adams, drums; Ben Willis, bass; Esther Hanviriyapunt, piano, 1999, Harold Washington Library. 4 min.

Belize (voice, sax, piano, percussion). 2001. First performed by SUSAAMI Ensemble: Richard Nunley, baritone; Michael Adams, drums; John Whitfield, bass; John Goldman, sax; and Ann Ward, piano, 3 March 2001, at Harold Washington Library. 5 min.

Dream Weaver (voice, sax, piano, bass). 1997. Text: Regina Baiocchi. First performed by Susan Warmington, soprano; Matana Roberts, sax; Esther Hanviriyapunt, piano, in 1997 at Harold Washington Library. 5 min. (AMRC/CBMR)

A Few Black Voices (rapper, piano, percussion, optional tenor sax). 1991. Text: Regina Baiocchi. Rap style. Commissioned by Mostly Music. First performed by Runako Jahi, rapper; Michael Adams, drums; Esther Hanviriyapunt, piano, in 1991 at South Shore Cultural Center. 9 min.

Foster Pet (high voice, piano, oboe, percussion). 1991. Text: Regina Baiocchi. Children's piece. First performed by Roberta Thomas, soprano; Mee-Kung Yoon, oboe; Don Skoog, percussion; Esther Hanviriyapunt, piano, 18 October 1991, at Roosevelt University. Commissioned by Mostly Music. 5 min. (AMRC/CBMR)

Friday Night (voice, jazz ensemble). 1995. Text: Regina Baiocchi. First performed by Bobbi Wilsyn on American Women Composers Midwest program "Jazz Sisters," 3 February 1996, at Harold Washington Library. Part of the opera *Gbeldahoven*.

Koan #1 (voice, flute, piano, percussion). 2001. First performed by SUSAAMI Ensemble: Richard Nunley, baritone; John Goldman, flute; John Whitfield, bass; Michael Adams, drums; and Ann Ward, piano, 3 March 2001, at Harold Washington Library. 4 min.

Lovers and Friends (voice, piano, bass, drums). 1999. First performed by the SUSAAMI Ensemble with Susan Warmington, voice, and Tim Tobias, piano, at the Hot House, Chicago.

Psalm for a Cat (voice, bass, alto sax). 1999. First performed by SUSAAMI Ensemble with Jeanne Frank, voice, 1999, at Harold Washington Library. 5 min.

Shadows (medium voice, bassoon, percussion, piano). 1992. Text: Regina Baiocchi. Children's song. Commissioned by Mostly Music. First performed by Robert Sims, baritone; Joseph Urbinato, bassoon; Don Skoog, percussion; and Jane Kenas, piano, 30 October 1992, at Roosevelt University. 3 min.

Two Zora Neale Hurston Songs (mezzo-soprano, piano, cello). 1989, revised 1992. Part of the opera *Gbeldahoven*. Contents: (1) How It Feels to Be Colored Me; 2) I Am Not Tragically Colored. Commissioned by American Women Composers Midwest and first performed by Bonita Hyman, with pianist Philip Morehead and cellist Betsy Start, 11 February 1989, at Roosevelt University. (AMRC/CBMR, CBMR)

We Real Cool (voice, jazz combo). 1992. Text: Gwendolyn Brooks. Copyright difficulties; changed to instrumental ensemble piece.

Chorus (first performed by St. Elizabeth's Church Adult Choir in Chicago, unless otherwise indicated):

Ain't Nobody's Child (SATB). 1993. See opera *Gbeldahoven*.
Clear Out Your Mind (SATB). 1987. Gospel style.
Father, We Thank You (2-part choir). 1988.

Good News Falls Gently. See opera *Gbeldahoven.*

I Hear Voices (chorus/SAB soloists). 2001. Three-movement gospel suite. First performed by SUSAAMI Ensemble with Elsa Harris, Lucretia Jackson, Richard Nunley, voices, 3 March 2001, at Harold Washington Library. 6 min.

I've Got a Mother/Father (SATB/soprano/bass duet/ or both). 1985.

Litany for Hale Smith (SATB, optional percussion). 2000. First performed by SUSAAMI Ensemble, 30 April 2000, at St. Elizabeth's Church, Naperville, Ill. 8 min.

Open Your Eyes (SATB, solo voice, piano, percussion, bass, guitar). 1987. Easter song.

Psalm 138 (SATB). 1990.

Rainbows (SATB, soloist, piano). 1988.

Send Your Gifts (SATB, baritone solo, piano). 1984.

Who Will Claim the Baby? (SATB, soloists, piano). 1984. Christmas song. Gospel style. Received a CAAP Grant from the City of Chicago. First performed by choir at St. Elizabeth Church, Chicago in 1984. 5 min.

Stage Music, Opera

Bwana's Libation (voice, guitar, sax, percussion). 1992. Text: Regina Baiocchi. Four-act ballet. Contents: (1) Ancestors' Medley; (2) First Fruits; (3) Legends; (4) Say No! to Guns, Yes to the Future. Commissioned by Mostly Music. Choreographed and first performed by Darlene Blackburn Dancers in 1992 at South Shore Cultural Center, Chicago. 20 min.

Dreamhoppers (six-character drama with incidental music). 1997. One act. Text: Regina Baiocchi. Received an ASCAP Special Awards grant. First performed by SUSAAMI Ensemble at Harold Washington Library, 24 October 1997. 30 min.

Gbeldahoven: No One's Child (seven solo roles, SATB, chamber orchestra). 1996. One-act chamber opera. Forerunner was cantata *Godmother's Children.* Libretto: Regina Baiocchi. Contents: (1) Servant's Muse; (2) But for the Grace of God; (3) How It Feels to be Colored Me; (4) I Am Not Tragically Colored; (5) Hell Hath No Fury (recitative) Godmother's Lesson (aria); (6) The Mason Room; (7) Litany of Superstitions; (8) Louise's Prayer; (9) Ain't Nobody's Child; (10) Friday Night; (11) Hold Out for Joy; (12) Rain (Good News Falls Gently); (13) Hughes Man; (14) Black with Pride; (15) Reprise of Hold Out for Joy. First performed by tenor Timothy Graham as Hughes, soprano Marcya Danielle as Hurston, soprano Anisha McFarland as Mason, and alto Bobbi Wilsyn as Thompson, 6 October 1996, at Harold Washington Library. 2 hours (1 hour in shortened version). (piano/vocal score at AMRC/CBMR)

Nikki Giovanni. 1997. Incidental music for play based on poetry by Giovanni. First performed in 1997 at Steppenwolf Theater.

Other

"Black Curtains Up: A Peek at Opera Written by African Americans in the Twentieth Century." Master's thesis, De Paul University, 1995.

Entries on Valerie Capers, Gail Davis-Barnes, Geraldine de Haas, Danniebelle Hall, Hilda Harris, Margaret Harris, Patricia Prattis Jennings, Betty Jackson King, Marsha Mabry, Nkeiru Okoye, Kay George Roberts, and Gertrude Jackson Taylor in

Facts on File Encyclopedia of Black Women in America: Music (Vol. 5), and on Portia Maultsby, in *Facts on File Encyclopedia of Black Women in America: Education* (Vol. 6), edited by Darlene Clark Hine (New York: Facts on File/ Carlson Publishing, 1997).

"The Red Priest Still Shines." *Catholic Digest*, January 1998: 54–58.

Sankofa Twin, And Other Stories. 1997. 12 short stories. Unpublished.

"Sounds from the Motherland: African-Inspired Music by Women Composers." Program notes for tribute to Betty Jackson King by American Women Composers Midwest, 1994.

About 200 poems, 4 plays, 2 novels, unpublished.

NOTES

Regina Harris Baiocchi's time and attention in interviews, telephone conversations, and reading and correction of the chapter are greatly appreciated. She has kindly given permission to quote from her stories and essays.

Full references given in the bibliography at the end of the chapter.

1. Regina Harris Baiocchi, interview with the author in Chicago, 12 February 1998. Unless otherwise indicated, all quotes are from interviews and telephone conversations with the author on 10 March 1991 or 12 February 1998.

2. Robert Taylor Homes was named after the first black graduate from the Massachusetts Institute of Technology, who designed the Tuskegee Institute campus as well as the elegant Julius Rosenwald Building at 46th and Michigan, where the composers Florence Price and Irene Britton Smith once lived (see chapter 5).

3. "Chromatic Interpolations," copyright 1998 by Regina Harris Baiocchi.

4. Baiocchi interview, 12 February 1998.

5. Unpublished autobiographical statement, 1989.

6. Author's questionnaire, 1989.

7. Synopsis of *Dreamhoppers* in promotional brochure.

8. "What's in My Name," copyright 1997 by Regina Baiocchi.

9. The poem was commissioned by the composer Patricia Morehead and later translated into Italian, set for soprano and orchestra, and performed at Festival Incontri Musicali di Musica Sacra at Rome in 1995.

10. See Cunnif.

11. Reich.

12. Borchert.

13. Shen.

14. *Etude No. 2* is included in *Black Women Composers: A Century of Piano Music 1893–1990*, edited by Helen Walker-Hill (Bryn Mawr, Pa.: Hildegard Publishing Co., 1992). See also the discography.

15. An apt reference to Kurt Weill, the German-born composer of stage works (*Threepenny Opera*, etc.) which also use jazz and diatonicism for sardonic social commentary.

16. Herguth.

17. Baiocchi wrote a humorous short story about such sermonizing, "The Eleventh Commandment" (Thou Shalt Not Get Caught).

18. The title *Liszten* is also reminiscent of the title of her very first childhood song, *Listen*.

19. When *Friday Night* was performed independently by Bobbi Wilsyn on a program called "Jazz Sisters" at the Harold Washington Library, 3 February 1996, critic Howard Reich pronounced it "a terrific new work that deserves to be heard again."

20. See note 9.

21. Shen.

BIBLIOGRAPHY

Andre, Naomi. "Baiocchi, Regina Harris." In *International Dictionary of Black Composers*. Edited by Samuel A. Floyd, Jr. Chicago: Fitzroy Dearborn, 1999.

Borchert, Gavin. Review of *African Hands*: "Worldly World Music." *Seattle Weekly*, 29 October 1997.

Bruce, Robert C. "*African Hands*—a World Premiere." *sforzando* 2, no. 9 (October 1997): 32–33.

Cunniff, Joseph. "Black Women Composers Recognized at Library." *Hyde Park Herald*, 2 March 1994.

Herguth, Bob. "First Opera Is a Dream Come True." *Chicago Sun-Times News*, 6 October 1996.

Malitz, Nancy. "African American Composers Forum Aims for High Scores." *Detroit News*, 18 February 1992.

Pendle, Karin. "Baiocchi, Regina Harris." In *New Groves Dictionary of Music and Musicians*. Edited by Stanley Sadie and John Tyrrell. New York: Macmillan, 2001.

Reich, Howard. " 'Jazz Sisters'—a Good Idea Beset by Some Poor Execution." *Chicago Tribune*, 5 February 1996.

Shen, Ted. 1996. "Critic's Choice: *Gbeldahoven: No One's Child*." *Chicago Reader*, 4 October 1996.

Thompson, Kathleen. "Baiocchi, Regina Harris." In *Facts on File Encyclopedia of Black Women in America: Music* (Vol. 5). Edited by Darlene Clark Hine. New York: Facts on File/Carlson Publishing, 1997.

Walker-Hill, Helen, ed. *Black Women Composers: A Century of Piano Music 1893–1990*. Bryn Mawr, Pa.: Hildegard Publishing Company, 1992.

———. *Piano Music by Black Women Composers: A Catalog of Solo and Ensemble Works*. Westport, Conn.:Greenwood Press, 1992.

———. "Black Women Composers in Chicago: Then and Now." *Black Music Research Journal* 12, no.1 (Spring 1992): 1–24.

———. *Music by Black Women Composers: A Bibliography of Available Scores*. CBMR Monographs no. 5. Chicago: Center for Black Music Research, 1995.

DISCOGRAPHY

Etude No. 2 from *Two Piano Etudes: Equipoise by Intersection*. Performed by Helen Walker-Hill on *Kaleidoscope: Music by African American Women*. Leonarda Productions CD LE 339, 1995.

CONCLUSION

Spirituals to symphonies in less than fifty years! . . . The American Negro
is coming of age.[1]

Shirley Graham, 1936

Shirley Graham, composer, author, and second wife of W.E.B. Du Bois, wrote
these optimistic words in the popular music magazine *Etude* five years before
the United States entered World War II. In her article she applauded the remarkable progress made by composers William Grant Still, William Dawson,
Florence Price, and other black musicians, and described performances of their
works by major American orchestras as "typical of something which is to-day
happening in America." Unfortunately, that momentum was lost in the 1940s,
1950s, and 1960s, and Florence Price and many of her contemporaries were
nearly forgotten. More recent decades have seen progress in some areas. Jazz
is now recognized as an art form invented by African Americans, and is included
in college music curricula and discussed extensively in music textbooks. We
also have the advantage of national Black History Month and Martin Luther
King Jr. celebrations during which music by black composers can be heard in
community concerts along with jazz and gospel music. But for the remainder
of the year, African-American composers are rarely heard on the concert stage.[2]
Only in the mid-1990s did a few music history textbooks begin to mention the
existence of black art music or black composers.[3] Despite this marginalization,
concert music by both black men and black women has continued to thrive.

The fifty years estimated by Shirley Graham Du Bois is misleading, as the
survey in chapter 1 shows; black classical music (and black composers) existed
in the United States as far back as the eighteenth century. Composition by

African-American women began over a century ago, and much has changed in that time. Women, both black and white, did not gain access to higher education and public professional life until the last decades of the nineteenth century, and have had the right to vote only since 1920. Slavery was abolished in 1865, and many living black Americans have heard about its horrors firsthand from their grandparents or great-grandparents. At the beginning of the twentieth century, lynching was widespread and segregation was strictly enforced. Significant progress in racial justice has been made only since the 1960s.

A scan of the selected list of 89 composers in the appendix, however, shows a remarkable independence from those developments. Of the 70 or so composers for whom birth dates are known, 21 were born before 1900 and came from 13 different states, including Kansas and Arkansas, an indication of the breadth and longevity of the black upper middle class, and also of women's changing roles at the turn of the century. The number of composers born in the first two decades of the twentieth century dwindled, perhaps because of the hardships of World War I and the Great Depression, then averaged 10 in each of the decades from the 1920s through the 1950s. Only two composers from this sample are known to have been born in the 1960s, and one in the 1970s. This sudden decrease is surprising, even granting the length of time necessary to build a reputation as a composer. It may have been caused by the Black Power movement and a backlash against European art forms in the aftermath of the civil rights struggle.

Of the known birthplaces of all these composers, 34 states are represented, most of them (56 percent) in the north or west. Seven composers were born in New York City (Manhattan) and two in Brooklyn. Chicago, with nine, has the largest number of black women composers, explained in part by its large black population and its strong, independent black economic and social structure.

These composers received their advanced training from well over 70 different colleges, conservatories, and universities, about 20 percent of them historically black schools. The most frequently attended school was Howard University (nine composers), followed by Oberlin Conservatory of Music, the New England Conservatory, the Juilliard School of Music, Columbia University's Teachers College, and Fisk University.[4]

The occupations by which the composers most frequently earned their living were music teaching[5] and performing. It is hard to tell how many were also professional church musicians, because it was so often assumed that it was not even listed. A very few composers had careers outside the field of music.

The music they composed is predominantly vocal and choral, written to meet the needs of singers and choirs in churches and schools. But there is also a wealth of instrumental and orchestral works, as well as music for the stage. Much of this music has been lost, and most of the surviving music has not yet been published, though some can be obtained from the composers themselves or from archives (see appendix). There are hundreds of substantial works for voice(s) and all kinds of instrumental combinations among the approximately

750 scores by 110 songwriters and composers in the Helen Walker-Hill Collection of music by black women (see appendix).

The biographies of the eight featured composers illustrate how the experience of race, gender, and class is affected by geographical location and time period. The well-developed black community that provided protection and support for Undine Smith Moore in Virginia, and for Irene Britton Smith and Margaret Bonds in Chicago, was meager help for Mary Watkins growing up in Pueblo, Colorado. The transition from segregation to integration experienced in their youth by Watkins, Valerie Capers, and Dorothy Rudd Moore was a thing of the past by the time Regina Harris Baiocchi was growing up. The class distinctions taken for granted by earlier generations were anathema to those who matured during the 1960s and 1970s.

Out of the 38 composers on whom research was done, only two or three mentioned any reservations about classification by race or gender. Many spoke with pride of their identity as African Americans. Only one composer exhibited a negative attitude toward her race. Philippa Duke Schuyler identified primarily with the white world and briefly attempted to pass as a South American under the name Felipa Monterro, although her concert career in the United States was fostered by black audiences and she inspired innumerable young black women. Sixteen-year-old Florence Price was enrolled at the New England Conservatory as a Mexican in 1903 to protect her from racism far from home. But she later affirmed her identity in many ways, not the least of which was her deliberate use of African-American idioms in her music.

Their sense of pride in their identity as African Americans was nourished by their communities. When Price moved to Chicago in 1926 because of racial violence in her native Little Rock, Arkansas, she was welcomed by a close-knit musical community. As Margaret Bonds described it, "We were a God-loving people, and when we were pushed for time, every brown-skinned musician in Chicago who could write a note, would jump-to and help Florence meet her deadline."[6] Betty Jackson King confirmed this description of the black community in Chicago, where "all black musicians knew each other, went to each others' programs and church concerts."[7] According to Bonds' daughter Djane, the same was true of Harlem, where black people "could be depended upon to attend black cultural events and support their own."[8]

Mary Watkins wrote of her childhood experiences playing piano in her church in Pueblo, Colorado: "I liked church. It seemed the most natural thing in the world when all the people around me were black like me! There was always a great deal of laughter and a great deal of pride in our ability to make the best out of what we had to work with."[9]

While pride in their race and its accomplishments was almost universal, the impact of racism was also pervasive. Even when protected as children by their families and communities, these women inevitably felt prejudice and discrimination from the larger society, whether obvious or subtle. As she became older, Undine Smith Moore recognized that she and the other black students at Fisk were educated by a racist society to feel their "otherness," and to be limited in their aspirations. Margaret Bonds suffered at Northwestern University, to which she had to commute a long distance every day by train because there were no dormitory facilities for black students. Mary Watkins' sense of solidarity in church fell away at her almost entirely white school, where she "found it difficult to feel proud of myself as a 'colored person.' " Regina Baiocchi received a shock when she left her supportive schools on Chicago's south side to attend downtown Roosevelt University. But for many other black composers born in the 1950s, race was less of an issue. Patrice Rushen said, "I was so fortunate. By the time I was born [1954], a lot of the initial issues were being worked out. The impact is there, but I've seen us come out of it to a certain degree."[10]

An indirect but important effect of racism was the personal responsibility, ingrained over many generations, felt by these composers for protecting and raising the image of their race. Margaret Bonds told a reporter, "I want to . . . blot out the negative image. I want to show that the Negro is not. . . . ugly or stupid."[11] Echoes can be heard in Regina Baiocchi's remark in the 1990s, "It is important that people know that I'm black because . . . [they] don't know that there are black composers."[12]

Social class and the high value placed on education were of paramount importance in the formation of these women as composers. At least two-thirds of them grew up in families headed by educated professionals or semiprofessionals: doctors, dentists, college professors or schoolteachers, ministers, government officials, journalists, postal workers, and accountants. But many had less educated parents who worked hard as railroad brakemen, truck drivers, domestic workers, cooks, and other laborers to make better lives for their daughters. Only a couple of the fathers were professional musicians, but several were talented amateurs. The mothers were more likely to have been musicians, and some were music teachers.

The issue of class was difficult to discuss in interviews. It was rarely, if ever, voluntarily mentioned, and more than one composer requested that I not use the term to discuss her background. But older composers remembered the snobbishness of certain groups. Irene Britton Smith recalled that in her youth, spirituals were not sung in some churches because they were reminders of slavery and degradation, and she still avoided churches that did gospel music—"all that screaming and stomping!" She deplored the changes in her previously integrated neighborhood in the 1970s, "when black got so black," and referred to her darker students as "black black."[13] The class-related subject of skin color comes up in almost any gathering of black Americans. In *Our Kind of People* (1999) Lawrence Otis Graham confirms the importance of "the skin color, the hair texture, the family background, the education . . . that set some of us apart and made some of us think we were superior to other blacks."[14] When researching upper-class lifestyles in Detroit, he, too, encountered difficulty. "Many would speak with me only on background without being quoted. Others insisted that their names not be used. . . . And still others simply refused to talk to me at all."

He attributed this to the militant egalitarianism of the new black leadership, particularly mayors like Washington's Marion Berry and Detroit's Coleman Young, who "sent a clear message to the post-1970s black elite that they should keep quiet and stay out of the way."[15]

Yet the old distinctions did not disappear. For Mary Watkins, the subject of class opens old wounds: "Parts of black culture I love; it's in my soul, it's who I am. . . . Some I don't want to be a part of—the skin color issue. . . . Dark skin and black hair were not an advantage to me in black society."[16] Even in Pueblo, Colorado, the small black community where she grew up, "The borderline between race pride and class prejudice was very thin. . . . Colored folks who were uneducated were often an embarrassment to those who were."

The issue of gender also presented some problems. While many of the composers described the hardships and bravery of women in their families, there was a reluctance to identify themselves with the feminist movement. Tania León described the women of her family as "very strong, like sequoias. . . . We have been trained to portray ourselves as weak . . . We are servants through all our lives, first for our parents, then our husbands, our children, and grandchildren." But she spoke for many when she said, "I'm not a feminist, because feminism is very radical and doesn't include men. . . . I understand that men are raised [this way]. I feel sorry for them, too."[17]

The persistent professional difficulties for female composers were often mentioned. Margaret Bonds said, "People don't think that a woman can really compete in this field." She went on to complain, "Women are expected to be wives, mothers and do all the nasty things in the community (Oh, I do them). And if a woman is cursed with having talent too, then she keeps apologizing for it. . . . It really is a curse in a way because instead of working 12 hours a day like other women, you work 24."[18]

Lena Johnson McLin observed, "I think it's very hard for people to accept the fact that we as women write, especially if it's . . . forceful and dynamic and if it has the same ingredients of a Mozart, Beethoven, a Shostakovich or Stravinsky, people want to think that . . . maybe your husband wrote it."[19]

Irene Britton Smith was aware of the psychological and economic difficulties encountered by women composers competing in the public sphere. Commenting on her summer at Tanglewood in the late 1940s, she said, "I didn't know until years later that Copland didn't think women could write music. . . . And you think you're rejected because you're not good enough!" She also observed, "It costs a lot of money to put these things on [musical performances] and women don't get those chances."[20]

The professional difficulties experienced by Smith, Bonds, and McLin continue to plague other women composers, including those working in the popular entertainment industry. Patrice Rushen observed that there are very few female studio arrangers and composers. "I would have to say that [gender] was a factor. . . . The assumption [is] that you don't know your stuff. . . . When you're a woman, you get the 'surprised look.' They double-check your name. 'So do you actually do what it says you do here?' "[21]

As Margaret Bonds' complaint indicates, professional difficulties are amplified by domestic complications. It is significant that although about 70 percent of the composers were married, less than 30 percent had children. For Mary Watkins, the stress of her domestic life was severe. She felt guilt because she sent her daughter to live with her mother so she could attend Howard, and guilt again at the joy she felt at the freedom to do so. Her husband would talk about how crazy she was to want to compose.

Not all the women had to contend with unsupportive husbands, but all experienced the drain of domestic responsibilities, especially when they had children. Undine Smith Moore deplored that women "have been forced to deal with the minutiae of life," freeing men to be the creators, and felt this handicap in her own life: "A part-time typist or office assistant and cleaning assistant would seem ideal as ways of making composing more possible."[22] Florence Price wrote to a friend in the 1940s, "I found it possible to snatch a few precious days in the month of January in which to write undisturbed. But oh, dear me, when shall I ever be so fortunate again as to break a foot."[23]

Lena McLin described how "When my children were little . . . I'd write music when they went to sleep. And then I had a church job . . . so I would write the anthem and arrange the spiritual, the calls and the responses, and I did that every Sunday for three years and I couldn't imagine why I was so tired."[24]

Marriage and children are not the only gender issues faced by these composers. If discussions of class were difficult for black women composers, mention of nonheterosexual orientation was almost nonexistent. Nevertheless, two out of the more than 30 with whom I had conversations acknowledged being lesbian on condition that I not mention their names. As with other issues, the experiences of black lesbians vary with time and location. There is very little historical reference to lesbianism.[25] The importance of respectability required that public sexual orientation be restricted to chaste married life or single celibacy.

One composer said that lesbianism was considered a "white thing" in her black community, and told of her feelings of disloyalty to her race. This experience was confirmed by Barbara Smith, who wrote, "Lesbians [are reduced] to a category of beings deserving of only the most violent attack, a category totally alien from 'decent' Black folks. . . . Many Black people who are threatened by feminism have argued that by being a Black feminist (particularly if you are also a Lesbian) you have left the race, are no longer a part of the Black community."[26]

Another composer believed that black communities are no more homophobic than white ones. Church musicians are often gay, especially in the more emotional holiness churches, and this is understood but not openly discussed by the congregation. She had no apologies or feelings of disloyalty to her race. Author bell hooks observed that gays are quietly accepted in the black community if they are silent, although black preachers routinely harangue against homosexuality in church.[27]

The effects of being a lesbian are experienced in a variety of ways. One of the composers felt that a high percentage of women composers and other creative people are gay because it's about "a certain way of being in the world." "A lot of us wouldn't survive if we weren't lesbians. We would be dead—defeated by patriarchy—it's about belonging to myself."

She did not wish to be identified as lesbian in the context of this book because of the professional consequences in a field that depends on public perceptions. She said, "I don't want that attached to what I'm trying to do." But she acknowledged that fear of exposure affects her life, interferes with her decisions, and saps her creative energy. She said, "It's crazy-making. Life is too short. I spend too much time worrying about it. But ignoring it proliferates the problem."

Other life circumstances that were important to these composers' careers included the families in which they grew up. Seldom did the family of origin pose an obstacle to the creative impulse. There were occasional parental ambitions for their daughters in other directions: Margaret Bonds' mother hoped for a concert pianist, and Dorothy Rudd Moore's mother wanted her to be a lawyer. Mary Watkins' mother, along with other elders, disapproved of her daring to create music.

The positive influence of the home environment is illustrated in many anecdotes by these composers. In Lena Johnson Mclin's family, "Everyone sang, everyone played, everyone wrote music. . . . It was just natural."[28] As a child, she thought all families were like that. Regina Baiocchi told how she and her seven siblings were all expected to sing in choirs, and remarked on the importance of her mother's delight with her early poems and songs, her grandmother's playing gospel in church, and her father's pleasure in playing the mouth harp and the fiddle. Jeraldine Herbison, whose father played guitar in a jazz band and whose four siblings all were musical, said, "For company, we always had to put on a show. We had to come out and do a trio, maybe *You Are My Sunshine* in three-part harmony."[29] Diane White recalled, "I grew up in a musical family, and so music was just part of my environment. I have been performing ever since I can remember—singing with my sisters in church, composing since I was 10 or 11, conducting choirs since I was nine."[30]

For many composers, other issues had a great impact. For Mary Watkins, her adoption was the central fact of her life. She had always felt she needed to connect to her biological mother in order to give validity to her being. "I was paralyzed. I was too ashamed, . . . for me it was impossible to walk out on stage. I was a full-grown woman before I could stand up and take a bow."[31] When Mary was finally reunited with her birth mother, the resolution of this lifelong need was reflected in her music.

For Valerie Capers, it was her physical limitation, her blindness. "I had to fight a long time to keep people from using the word 'blind' every time I did something. My blindness had nothing to do with what ability or lack of ability

I had. But people felt for the longest time it was something immediate that they could put a hook on."[32]

For Julia Perry, as she struggled with paralysis during the last nine years of her life, composition was brought almost to a halt. But she learned to write laboriously with her left hand, and continued to compose and promote her music.

For Betty Jackson King, as for Valerie Capers and Dorothy Rudd Moore, the loss of a beloved sibling indelibly marked the rest of her life. After her gifted sister Catherine died in a car accident in 1958, the loss was "a cross that I carry. . . . It's been a peculiar force in my life: Why? What is my talent that I am still here?"[33]

Many factors affected, influenced, and motivated these composers. The death of a talented sibling was one; fulfilling family expectations was another; meeting the needs of students, colleagues, and church choirs provided impetus for many; and upholding the image of their race was important to others. But these motivations do not adequately explain why these women chose such a difficult, demanding, and solitary creative discipline rather than some other area of achievement. A remark made by Valerie Capers comes closer to an answer: "if I'm lucky enough to make a difference in the lives of other people . . . it will be in the area of composing."[34] This desire to give something enduring of themselves was expressed by other composers in various ways; Mary Watkins said, "I just want to share the bliss." The pure love of music and the inner necessity to be an active part of its creation were the most powerful motivations. Watkins was compelled to "take the music in a different direction so it would do what I wanted it to do,"[35] and Jeraldine Herbison knew she was a composer because "internally, a composer is a rebellious person. . . . They like to reorder things." The imperative to listen to the voice within, to take the road less traveled, is a lonely one. Herbison credited her mentor, Undine Smith Moore, with giving her the courage to follow that road. Moore told her, "Always write, just write; don't worry about where it's going, who's going to buy it, who's going to perform it. The writing is a part of you, so just do it because of yourself, and all the other things will fall into place."[36] Paradoxically, Lettie Beckon Alston found in this solitary calling a link to kindred souls: "We composers, we're hermits. . . . I enjoy people that are a part of the arts because we are a minority. The whole arts community—we are a minority." Alston echoed Moore's advice. "I tell my students, whatever your background is, just do it with love and a sincere heart and you'll be successful. If that's not the spirit of God, I don't know what is!"[37]

. . .

African-American women writers are now being celebrated, published, critiqued, and included in syllabi, and black women visual artists are also beginning to gain recognition. Black women composers have yet to receive comparable acknowledgment for their contributions. A very few have managed to participate successfully in the larger musical world. Florence Price received attention in the 1930s and is again becoming a well-known name (often the single representative name). Margaret Bonds was famous for her spiritual arrangements, still occasionally heard in recitals by prominent black singers. Julia Perry's star rose during the 1950s and early 1960s, when she received two Guggenheim awards, was published by Peer Southern Music Publishing Company, and was recorded by CRI. Her *Short Piece for Orchestra* is still programmed by symphony orchestras. Valerie Capers has a name among jazz lovers. For the last ten years Tania León has been in great demand. Other composers are well-known and respected in their local music communities and at universities, where their works are performed by top musicians.

The inertia and prejudice of the white musical establishment persists, albeit invisibly, for a variety of reasons. The concert world, besides being highly competitive, is very political. Connections are more important to success than musical worth. Also, concert subscribers are very conservative, yet at the same time fickle and prone to follow whatever is "in" at the moment. They pay for tickets to hear the established great composers and performers, tolerating only a limited amount of novelty, whether avant-garde or "ethnic." Even successful black concert artists rarely program any music by black composers, other than spiritual arrangements used by singers. As Antoinette Handy, formerly head of the NEA Music Division, observed, "Until you get an opportunity to have your music performed, to be seen, to get your name called, you're not going to get into the marketability status."[38]

Commercial recordings are almost as scarce as mainstream performances. A few companies, such as Albany Records, Koch International, Leonarda, and Opus One, include music by black men and women. Composers Recordings, Inc., a company devoted to works of American composers, now lists a few African Americans among its composers.

Publication remains a discouraging problem for black women, as it is for all struggling composers.[39] Betty Jackson King pointed out that the well-established white publishers usually accepted one token black (a male) on their roster of composers. This drove her to establish Jacksonian Press, perhaps the first of the women's self-publishing companies (followed by Mary Watkins' Shotsky and Valerie Capers' Valcap). Undine Smith Moore acknowledged that instrumental music is harder to sell than choral music and less likely to find a publisher. The steady market for choral music has given choral composers like Moore and Lena Johnson McLin an advantage in both publication and performance. PeerMusic (formerly Southern Music Publishing Company, then Peer Southern) publishes Julia Perry and Tania León along with a few black male composers and several other women composers. Some newer publishing companies now exist specifically to publish women's music, including some by black women: Hildegard, Vivace Press, and Clar-Nan.

It is significant that white women composers have made progress in overcoming this inertia and a few now exercise considerable power. The rise in the 1970s of women's studies classes and departments in colleges, feminist literary criticism, and feminist musicology gave encouragement to women currently composing and strong impetus to the discovery of women composers of the past, including a few black women. But with a few exceptions, their inclusion in women's music studies has been scant.[40] Predictably, within the field of African-American music, inclusion of women composers (at least by black women musicologists) has been more extensive.[41]

Black women have been, and still are, vastly more affected than either black men or white women by the combined effects of racism in the white musical establishment, sexism toward women composers, the scarcity of role models, and the consequent discouragement of aspirations.[42] African-American male musicians have traditionally had more contact with white audiences and have been more conditioned to challenge and circumvent their opposition. Until the 1960s, the protection and comfort of the black musical community afforded women a less threatening arena in which to express their talents. Long-standing patterns and memories are difficult to change. The singular success of Tania León may be due not only to her talent, hard work, and innate independence, but also to her freedom from the communal memory and experience of white discrimination in the United States. Other black American women are also composing music of skill and power. Their identification with their African-American heritage offers enrichment not only to the black community but also to the larger cultural world.

The Jamaican scholar Rex Nettleford wrote, "Black classicism is not for the benefit of black civilization exclusively, but for all of humanity. For excellence, whatever civilization produces it, becomes the stock and capital of all humankind. Black classicism is, in the end, human classicism . . . one that reflects the daunting and complex reality of humanity's richly diverse experience and cultural achievements."[43]

In the mainstream music world at the beginning of the twenty-first century it has become clear that the European-based concert tradition is in need of infusions of new blood. The music of the "great masters" will never cease to enrich us, but for concert music to continue to be viable, it will need to grow through new sound sources and tonal designs, new ways of presentation, new target audiences, and new and diverse ethnic traditions. Nettleford envisions music in the global civilization of the future as "seen not in terms of a rigid pyramid of cultural hierarchy, but rather as a dynamic phenomenon characterized by simultaneous modes of expression. . . . The classicism forged by the exiles of Africa and their offspring . . . has helped the twentieth century to prepare itself for a relatively smooth passage into the twenty-first."[44] African-American composers, both male and female, will have important contributions to make to concert music in whatever new forms it takes.

NOTES

1. Shirley Graham, "Spirituals to Symphonies." *Etude*, November 1936, p. 69.

2. The American Composers Orchestra could list only eight black American composers among the 421 whose works they have played. National Public Radio's *Perfor-

mance Today program presented one, William Grant Still, out of 46 composers programmed in the 13 months preceding 22 March 2001. Of 229 orchestral works premiered in the United States and Canada in the 2000–2001 season, three were by black American composers (*www.symphony.org, 22 March, 2001*). (See also n. 41.)

3. Joseph Machlis and Kristine Forney's *The Enjoyment of Music* (7th ed., 1995) and Robert Hickock's *Exploring Music* (5th ed., 1993) provide the best coverage of African-American art music. A few other textbooks discuss one or two token black composers without an attempt to indicate the scope of the field. The 2001 edition of *A History of Western Music* by Donald Grout and Jay Palisca mentions William Grant Still, Ulysses Kay, and Florence Price. The 3rd ed. (1987) of Gilbert Chase's *America's Music: From the Pilgrims to the Present* covers minstrelsy, blues, jazz, black Broadway, and Joplin's opera *Treemonisha*, and lists five early black composers including William Grant Still. Daniel Kingman's *American Music: A Panorama* (1990) covers the same territory but lists only Still, with no comment.

4. At least nine also attended schools abroad, and an additional six or seven studied with the famed pedagogue Nadia Boulanger at the American Conservatory at Fontainebleau, France: (possibly) Nora Douglas Holt, Maude Wanzer Layne, Julia Perry, Evelyn Pittman, Irene Britton Smith, Dorothy Rudd Moore, and Rachel Eubanks.

5. About 40 percent of the composers were employed at colleges; of the 53 known schools where they taught, 55 percent were historically black schools. Many maintained private studios or founded music schools, and several developed exemplary music programs in the public secondary schools.

6. Margaret Bonds, "A Reminiscence," p. 192. See bibliography to chapter 4.

7. Betty Jackson King, interview with the author, New York, 4 October 1990.

8. Djane Richardson, interview with the author, New York, 8 October 1990.

9. Mary Watkins, unpublished memoirs, 1997.

10. Marienne Uszler, "Patrice Rushen," *Piano & Keyboard* 197 (March/April 1999): 43.

11. Demaitre. See bibliography to chapter 4.

12. Regina Baiocchi, interview with the author, Chicago, 12 February 1998.

13. Irene Britton Smith, interview with the author, Chicago, 7 July 1989.

14. Lawrence Graham, *Our Kind of People* (New York: HarperCollins, 1999), p. 5.

15. Graham, pp. 296–97.

16. Watkins, conversation with the author, October 1990.

17. Tania León, interview with the author, New York, 24 September 1990. This concept of feminism appears to contradict that of the Black Feminist movement, in which support of black males is important.

18. Demaitre.

19. Lena Johnson McLin, interview with Scott Schlegel for NPR *Horizons* program, October 1990.

20. Irene Britton Smith, interview with Scott Schlegel for NPR *Horizons* program, October 1990.

21. Uszler, p. 43.

22. David Baker et al., p. 191. See bibliography for chapter 2.

23. Quoted in Barbara Garvey Jackson, "Florence Price, Composer," *Black Perspective in Music* 5, no. 1 (Spring 1977): 37.

24. McLin, interview with Scott Schlegel.

25. Exceptions are some lyrics by the blues women in the 1920s and 1930s, and some

unpublished poems and letters by writers such as Angelina Weld Grimké (1880–1958) and Alice Dunbar-Nelson (1875–1935).

26. Barbara Smith, "Introduction," in *Home Girls: A Black Feminist Anthology*, ed. by Barbara Smith (Latham, N.Y.: Kitchen Table Press/Women of Color Press, 1983), pp. xxii–xxx.

27. Cornell West and bell hooks, *Breaking Bread: Insurgent Black Intellectual Life* (Boston: South End Press, 1991), pp. 83–84.

28. Lena Johnson McLin, interview with the author, Chicago, 29 June 1989.

29. Panel discussion, "The Composers Speak," led by Helen Walker-Hill at second Symposium of Black Women Composers, Hampton University, 16 February 1999.

30. Ibid.

31. Mary Watkins, interview with the author, Oakland, 23 February 1998.

32. Valerie Capers, interview with the author, New York, 12 October 1990.

33. Betty Jackson King, interview with the author, New York, 4 October 1990.

34. Capers, interview.

35. Watkins, unpublished memoirs.

36. Herbison, panel discussion (see note 29).

37. Alston, panel discussion (see note 29).

38. Antoinette Handy, interview with Scott Schlegel for NPR *Horizons* program, October 1990. The NEA has provided significant support to several African-American women composers.

39. Music by early black composers was either self-published or published by a small number of black companies, including Handy Bros. in New York.

40. Christine Ammer's *Unsung: A History of Women in American Music* (1980) provides good coverage of Price, Bonds, Perry, McLin, and Pittman. The latest edition (2001) of Karin Pendle's *Women in Music* discusses five or six African-American composers. At the sixth International Festival of Women Composers at Indiana University at Pennsylvania in March 2001, at least 14 (16 percent) of the more than 85 composers whose works were performed were African Americans.

41. Maude Cuney-Hare's *Negro Musicians and Their Music* (1936) discusses Price, Camille Nickerson, Helen Hagan, the Afro-British Amanda Aldridge, and several other women composing at that time. Hildred Roach's *Black American Music, Past and Present* (1983, 2nd ed., 1992) does justice to the better-known women composers and also carries fragments of information on many obscure names. The third edition (1997) of Eileen Southern's *The Music of Black Americans* increased its coverage of women composers.

42. If the statistical proportions among composers were remotely similar to that of all college graduates in 1998, roughly 43 percent would be women (non-black) and 7.4 percent would be black (of whom more than half would be black women). In fact, based on statistics/averages from the rosters of the American Composers Orchestra, and *Symphony* magazine's annual list of premieres, no more than 15 percent are women, and less than 2 percent are black (of whom 0.25 percent are women). Of the 380 American composers listed by Composers Recordings, Inc., 13 (3 percent) are black (six of them appear only in Natalie Hinderas' *Piano Music by African-American Composers*), compared to 71 (17 percent) women composers.

43. Rex M. Nettleford, "Black Classicism and the Eurocentric Ideal: A Case for Integrative Inquiry into Black Expressive Arts?" *Lenox Avenue: A Journal of Interartistic Inquiry* 2 (1996): 32–33.

44. Nettleford, 28.

APPENDIX: SELECTED LIST OF COMPOSERS

The following African-American women composers were selected from a list of more than 700 names of black women composers and songwriters. They were chosen because sufficient information was available to indicate a body of written work. No gospel composers, and only a few of the hundreds of songwriters and jazz composers, are included here, because they lie beyond the scope of this study.

Sources of information are abbreviated in parentheses at the end of each entry. Only the most informative references are cited. If there is no reference, the source was the composer.

ARCHIVES

(AMC) American Music Center, 30 West 26th Street, New York, N.Y. 10010.

(AMRC/CBMR) Scores in the Helen Walker-Hill Collection of music by black women composers housed at the Center for Black Music Research at Columbia College, Chicago, and in duplicate at the American Music Research Center at the University of Colorado at Boulder.

(LC) Library of Congress card catalog of holdings.

(M-Sp) Guide to sheet music, Moorland-Spingarn Research Center, Howard University, Washington, DC.

(Schom) Sheet music at the Schomburg Center for Research in Black Culture in New York City.

REFERENCES (FOR FULL REFERENCE SEE SELECTED BIBLIOGRAPHY)

(BWiA) *Black Women in America: An Historical Encyclopedia.*

(Cohen) Aaron Cohen, *International Encyclopedia of Women Composers.*

(Facts) *Facts on File Encyclopedia of Black Women in America: Music*.

(IDBC) *International Dictionary of Black Composers*.

(Layne) Maude Wanzer Layne, *The Negro's Contribution to Music*.

(NBAW, NBAW II) *Notable Black American Women*.

(New Groves) *New Groves Dictionary of Music and Musicians*, 2nd ed.

(Roach) Hildred Roach, *Black American Music, Past and Present*. 2nd ed.

(W-H) Helen Walker-Hill, *Piano Music by Black Women Composers: A Catalog of Solo and Ensemble Works*.

(W-H Bib) Helen Walker-Hill, *Music by Black Women Composers: A Bibliography of Available Scores*.

SELECTED COMPOSERS

Allen, Geri. b. Detroit, 1959. Attended Howard, Univ. of Pittsburgh. Performed with Ornette Coleman, Betty Carter, etc. Taught at Howard. See selected discography. Jazz (*Silence and Song* 1991). (BWiA, Facts, Geri Allen on Windows-Media.com)

Alston, Dr. Lettie Beckon. b. Detroit, 1953. Attended Wayne State, Univ. of Michigan. Taught at Wayne State, Oakland Univ. See selected discography. Concert, electronic music (*Diverse Imagery* for dance and electronic synthesizers 1995). (6 scores at AMRC/CBMR, W-H, W-H Bib)

Armstrong, Lillian Hardin. b. Memphis, 1898; d. 1971. Attended Fisk, Chicago Coll. of Music, New York Coll. of Music. Jazz pianist for King Oliver's Creole Band and many others; bandleader. Married Louis Armstrong. Jazz (*After Tonight*). (BWiA, NBAW)

Austin, Lovie. b. Cora Calhoun in Tennessee, 1887; d. 1972. Attended Roger Williams Univ., Knoxville Coll. Performed in vaudeville, on recordings, etc. Influenced many musicians, including Mary Lou Williams. Hit songs, musicals (*Downhearted Blues* sung by Bessie Smith, musical *Sunflower Girls*). (Facts)

Bailey, Mable. b. Canton, Miss., 1939. Grew up in Oakland, Calif. Attended Univ. of New Mexico, Univ. of Denver, etc. Taught in Denver public schools. Sacred and secular concert music (*The Valentine Vendor* for soprano and baritone 1980). (8 scores at AMRC/CBMR, W-H, W-H Bib)

Baiocchi, Regina Harris. See chapter 9.

Baity, Judith M. b. Milwaukee, 1944. Attended Univ. of Wisconsin, Michigan State Univ. Church organist and choir director, freelance musician in Los Angeles. Sacred and secular concert music (*At Calvary* for string orchestra and solo clarinet). (2 scores at AMRC/CBMR, W-H Bib)

Barnwell, Dr. Ysaye Maria. b. New York City, ca. 1940. Attended Juilliard Prep. School, Howard, State Univ. of New York, Gallaudet Univ. Taught at Howard, performed with Sweet Honey in the Rock. Vocal, choral, symphonic works (*Suite Death* 2000). (See selected bibliography: Reagon)

Benjamin, Miriam E. (pseud. E. B. Miriam). b. Charleston, S.C.?, 1860s. Songs, marches for piano, band (*The Boston Elite Two-Step*, 1895). (See selected bibliography: Wright, "Black Women in Boston")

Blackwell, Anna Gee. b. Springfield, Ohio, 1928. Attended Sinclair Community Coll., Wright State Univ. Music teacher. Songs, piano pieces (*Ebony Waters* 1955). (Cohen, W-H)

Bonds, Margaret Allison. See chapter 4.

Bonner, Marietta or Marita. b. Boston, 1899; d. 1971. Graduated from Radcliffe in 1922. Teacher, playwright, author of the essay "On Being Young, A Woman, and Colored," etc. All-Bonner concert on Radcliffe Class Day 1922. Wanamaker prize in 1927 for song *Prestidigitation*. Concert music (*Imaginary Suite* performed in Boston 1920). (BWiA; see also *Crisis* [magazine], August 1920; *Crisis*, July 1922)

Busch, Marie Frances. b. Charleston, W.Va., 1908. Taught music at St. John's Settlement House; director of junior choir of St. Christopher's Church in Philadelphia. Piano pieces, songs (*Why Fades a Dream*). (1 score at AMRC/CBMR, LC, Roach, Layne)

Butler, Jean. b. Cleveland, Ohio. Attended Oberlin, Howard, etc. Taught at Levine School of Music in Washington, D.C. See selected discography. Jazz, concert music (*Maria's Rags* for two pianos, 1985). (W-H)

Capers, Valerie Gail. See chapter 7.

Carter, Yvette Moorhead. b. Alexandria, La., 1964. Attended Howard, Univ. of Virginia, Univ. of Frankfurt (Germany) on Fulbright. Taught in Richmond, Va., public schools; minister of music and church organist. Songs, choral works (*On the Dawn of Freedom*, 1993).

Clarke, Catherine K. b. Franklinton, N.C., 1932. Choral works (*The Prayer of a Saint*, 1984). (W-H Bib)

Coltrane, Alice McLeod. b. Detroit, 1937. Jazz harpist, pianist, percussionist. Married saxophonist John Coltrane. Chamber works (*Bliss the Eternal Now* for piano, harp, and guitar). (BWiA)

Cooper, Charlene Moore. b. Baltimore, ca. 1938. Attended Oberlin, Catholic Univ., Trinity Coll. Counselor, music teacher in Baltimore and Washington, D.C. public schools; music director at Municipal Opera Company of Baltimore (1990s); minister of music at several churches, including John Wesley AME Zion Church in Washington, D.C. Primarily sacred choral, organ, chamber music (*Meditation* for flute, clarinet and piano, 1978). (W-H Bib)

Corrothers-Tucker, Rosina Harvey. Late 19th cent. Songs, piano pieces (*Rio Grande Waltz*, 1902). (3 scores at AMRC/CBMR, W-H, W-H Bib)

Cummings-Taylor, Maude. b. 1897. Attended Columbia Univ. Choral and vocal music (*How Beautiful upon the Mountains*). (3 scores at AMRC/CBMR, W-H Bib)

Cuney-Hare, Maude. 1874–1936. Attended New England Conservatory. Pianist; music journalist for *Crisis*; author of *Negro Musicians and Their Music* (1936). Arranger of *Six Creole Folk-Songs* (incidental music for play *Antar of Araby*, Boston, 1926). (1 score at AMRC/CBMR, BWiA)

Curenton, Evelyn. See Simpson-Curenton, Evelyn.

Davis, Sharon "Rhapsody." b. Chicago. Winner of Chicago Heritage of Black Music Composers competition 1990. Jazz, concert music (*For You* for orchestra, 1990).

Davison, Harriette. b. Newark, N.J., ca. 1936. Attended Oberlin. Violinist. Vocal setting of Langston Hughes' *Fields of Wonder* (5 songs) performed at the 1977 New York celebration of Black Composers Week. (1 score at AMRC/CBMR, Schom)

Du Bois, Shirley Graham. See Graham, Shirley.

Evanti, Lillian. b. Washington, D.C., 1890; d. 1967. Attended Howard. Concert singer, first black American to sign contract with European opera company. Choral, vocal pieces (*Dedication*, 1948). (11 scores at AMRC/CBMR, LC, M-Sp, BWiA, NBAW, W-H Bib)

Eubanks, Dr. Rachel A. b. San Jose, Calif., 1922. Attended Univ. of California, Columbia Univ., Pacific Western Univ., etc. Founder and director of the Eubanks Conservatory of Music and Art in Los Angeles, 1951. See selected discography. Concert music (*Symphonic Requiem*, 1980). (11 scores at AMRC/CBMR, IDBC)

Forster, Estelle Ancrum. b. Wilmington, N.C., 1887. Attended Bennett, New England Conservatory. Founder and director of Ancrum School of Music in Boston 1922. Piano pieces, musical play (*Dream of Enchantment*, 1926). (Roach; see also *Who's Who in Colored America* 1942)

Freeman, Sharon Ahnee. b. Brooklyn, N.Y., 1949. Attended Manhattan School of Music. Arranger, conductor, performer (French horn) on radio and television, with Gil Evans, Charles Mingus, etc. Adjunct lecturer at Bennington Coll., Bronx Community Coll., etc. Received Rockefeller, NEA grants. Jazz, classical concert music (*War Sonata* for violin, cello, piano, 1968). (W-H Bib)

Gillum, Ruth Helen. b. St. Louis, 1907 or 1909. Attended New England Conservatory, Univ. of Kansas. Taught at Philander Smith, North Carolina College, etc. Piano pieces, choral music (*Roll Jordan Roll*). (2 choral scores at AMRC/CBMR, LC, Roach, W-H; see also *Who's Who in Colored America* 1950)

Goodwin, Anna Gardner. b. Augusta, Ga., 1874; d. 1959. Attended Univ. of Pennsylvania, Paine Coll. Taught at Paine, moved to Chicago 1919. Songs, piano pieces (*Cuban Liberty March*, 1897). (3 scores at AMRC/CBMR, LC)

Graham, Shirley. b. Indianapolis, 1904; d. 1978. Attended Oberlin. Taught at Morgan State. Author, stage director. Musicals, songs, opera (*Tom Tom* 1932). (2 scores in AMRC/CBMR, Schom, BWiA, NBAW)

Grant, Micki. b. Minnie Perkins in Chicago. Attended Chicago School of Music, Univ. of Illinois. Actress. Composed several Broadway musicals (*Don't Bother Me, I Can't Cope, Working*). (2 scores at AMRC/CBMR, NBAW II)

Greene, Diana R. b. Texas, 1956. Attended Baylor. Administrative assistant for Lincoln Center Institute in New York, etc. Concert music (*Rigorisms II* piano quartet, 1982). (2 scores at AMRC/CBMR, AMC)

Hagan, Helen Eugenia. b. Portsmouth, N.H., 1891; d. 1964. Attended Yale, Schola Cantorum in Paris, Columbia Univ. Teachers College, etc. Concert pianist. Taught at Bishop Coll. in Texas, etc. Concert music (*Concerto in C Minor* for piano and orchestra, 1912). (1 score at AMRC/CBMR, NBAW, New Groves; see also selected bibliography: Dannett)

Hairston, Jacqueline Butler. b. Charlotte, N.C., 1938. Attended Howard, Columbia Univ. Teachers College, etc. Taught at Johnson C. Smith Univ., Peralta Community Coll. in California, etc. Spiritual arrangements, sacred and secular concert music (song cycle *On Consciousness Streams*). See selected discography. (2 scores at AMRC/ CBMR, W-H, W-H Bib)

Harris, Ethel Hermina Ramos, or Ramos-Harris. b. Newport, R.I., 1908; d. 1993. Attended New England Conservatory, Carnegie Mellon, etc. Pianist for National Negro Opera Company. Songs, choral works, piano pieces (*Paquita Mia* for piano). (Cohen, LC, W-H, W-H Bib)

Harris, Margaret Rosarian. b. Chicago, 1943; d. 2000. Attended Curtis, Juilliard. Concert pianist, conductor, cofounder of Opera Ebony. Concert music (*Collage One* for piano at CBMR). (Cohen, Facts, W-H)

Herbison, Jeraldine Saunders. b. Richmond, Va., 1941. Attended Virginia State, Univ. of Michigan at Interlochen, etc. Violinist. Taught in secondary schools in Maryland, North Carolina, and Virginia. See selected discography. Concert music (*Sonata no. 2 for Cello and Piano*, Op. 19, no. 1). (12 scores at AMRC/CBMR, W-H, W-H Bib, Cohen, Roach, www.music-usa.org/nac_tw/ntw_jh.html)

Holt, Nora Douglas (Nora Lena James). b. Kansas City, Kans., 1885; d. 1974. Attended Western Univ., Chicago Musical Coll. Cofounder of NANM, entertainer, teacher, journalist for *Chicago Defender*, and *New York Amsterdam News*, publisher of *Music and Poetry*. See selected discography. Concert music (*Rhapsody on Negro Themes* for orchestra). (2 scores at AMRC/CBMR, BWiA, Facts; see also selected bibliography: Dannett)

Jessye, Eva. b. Coffeyville, Kans., 1895; d. 1992. Attended Western Univ., Langston Univ. Taught at Claflin, Morgan State, etc. Choral director for Virgil Thompson's *Four Saints in Three Acts* and Gershwin's *Porgy and Bess*, motion pictures, etc. Choral works, musical drama (*Chronicle of Job*). Her scores are located in the Eva Jessye Collection, University of Michigan Library. (2 scores at AMRC/CBMR, BWiA, NBAW, Facts, New Groves)

King, Betty Jackson. b. Chicago, 1928; d. 1994. Attended Chicago Musical Coll., Oakland Univ., etc. Taught at Roosevelt Univ. and Dillard, and in Wildwood, N.J., public schools. President of NANM 1979–1984. See selected discography. Sacred and secular concert music published by Jacksonian Press (*Saul of Tarsus*, oratorio). (25 scores at AMRC/CBMR, Facts, W-H, W-H Bib; see also *Crisis*, December 1979; and www.bettyjacksonking.com)

Layne, Maude Julia Wanzer. b. 1899. Author of *The Negro's Contribution to Music* (1942). Pageants, songs (*Dream Shadows*). (1 score at AMRC/ CBMR, Roach)

Latteta, Theresa (Brown). b. Washington, D.C., 1952. Musical dramas, flute compositions published by Alchemy Pub., Washington, D.C. (children's musical *When I Grow Up*, 1993).

Lee, Consuela. b. Snow Hill, Ala, 1926. Attended Fisk, Northwestern Univ., etc. Performer, musical director. Taught at Hampton, Norfolk State, etc. Established Springtree/Snow Hill Institute for the Performing Arts. Jazz, classical concert, and dramatic music (*The Chosen*, musical drama). (W-H Bib)

León, Tania Justina. b. Havana, Cuba, 1944. Attended National Conservatory in Havana, New York Univ. Cofounder and musical director of Dance Theater of Harlem, associate conductor of Brooklyn Philharmonic Orchestra. See selected discography. Concert music published by PeerMusic (*Concerto Criollo* for solo piano, percussion, and orchestra). (8 scores at AMRC/CBMR, IDBC)

Liston, Melba Doretta. b. Kansas City, Kans., 1926; d. 1999. Grew up in Los Angeles. Jazz trombonist with Gerald Wilson, Charles Mingus, etc. Papers and scores at the Center for Black Music Research. Jazz (*All Deliberate Speed, Melba's Blues*, etc.). (BWiA, Facts, NBAW)

Manggrum, Loretta. b. Gallipolis, Ohio, 1896. Attended Fisk, Royal Conservatory of Music in Toronto, Cincinnati Conservatory, etc. Taught in Cincinnati public schools, organist. Choral works, piano solos, 7 sacred cantatas (*Expression* for piano, 1984). (LC)

Mars, Louisa Melvin Delos. b. Providence, R.I., ca. 1860. Singer, pianist, organist. Five musical dramas, some produced in Boston area (*Leoni the Gypsy Queen*, 1889). (see selected bibliography: Wright, "Black Women in Boston")

Martin, Delores J. Edwards. b. Los Angeles, 1943. Attended Univ. of Southern California, Pepperdine, American Academy in Paris. Popular, concert music (*Circle of Dreams* for piano, 1974). (3 scores at AMRC/CBMR, Cohen, W-H, W-H Bib)

Maultsby, Portia. b. Florida, 1941. Attended Mt. Scholastica Coll., Univ. of Wisconsin, Mozarteum in Salzburg, etc. Taught at Colorado College, Swarthmore, Indiana Univ., etc. Concert instrumental music, popular songs (*Ceremonia Negra* for orchestra, 1969). (Facts, vol. 6)

McLin, Lena Johnson. b. Atlanta, 1929. Attended Spelman, American Conservatory, Roosevelt Univ. Taught in Chicago public schools, Kenwood Academy High School. Minister of Holy Vessel Christian Center. See selected discography. Concert music, operas, sacred choral music published by Neil J. Kjos, etc. (*Free at Last* cantata, 1973). (53 scores at AMRC/CBMR, Facts, IDBC, BWiA; see also selected bibliography: M. Green)

McSwain, Augusta Geraldine. b. Omaha, Neb., 1917. Attended Bishop Coll. (where she studied with Helen Eugenia Hagan), Northwestern. Taught at Bishop Coll. Choral works, songs, string quartet, piano pieces (*Passacaglia in E Minor* for piano, 1960). (3 scores at AMRC/CBMR, Cohen. W-H, W-H Bib)

Moore, Dorothy Rudd. See chapter 6.

Moore, Undine Smith. See chapter 2.

Moorehead, Consuela Lee. See Lee, Consuela.

Moorman, Joyce Solomon. See Solomon Moorman, Dr. Joyce.

Murray, Dierdre. b. Brooklyn, N.Y. Attended Manhattan School of Music, Hunter Coll. Performer, arranger, composer, and producer with jazz artists Henry Threadgill, Fred Hopkins, and others, for recordings, theater productions. Recipient of Rockefeller, Meet the Composer grants, etc. Jazz, classical concert music (*String Trio*). (AMC, W-H Bib)

Nickerson, Camille. b. New Orleans, 1888; d. 1982. Attended Oberlin. Concert singer as the "Louisiana Lady"; taught at Nickerson School of Music, Howard (1926–62).

Won 1931 Rosenwald Fellowship to collect Creole folk songs. Arrangements of Creole songs and original songs (*Death Song*). (8 scores at AMRC/CBMR, Facts, NBAW, BWiA, W-H Bib)

Norman, Ruth. b. Chicago, 1927. Attended Univ. of Nebraska, Eastman. See selected discography. Concert music (*Golden Precepts* for chamber ensemble, soprano). (19 scores at AMRC/CBMR, Roach, W-H, W-H Bib)

Okoye, Dr. Nkeiru. b. New York City, 1972. Attended Oberlin, Rutgers, etc. Taught at Norfolk State Univ. See selected discography. Concert music (ballet *Ruth*, 1998). (1 score at AMRC/CBMR, Facts, www.eden.rutgers.edu/~nokoye/)

Osterman, Dr. Eurydice V. b. Atlanta, 1950. Attended Andrews Univ., Univ. of Alabama. Taught at Oakwood Coll. Sacred and secular choral, instrumental music (*Serenitas* for band). (W-H Bib)

Perry, Julia Amanda. See chapter 3.

Perry, Zenobia Powell. b. Boley, Okla., 1914. Attended Tuskegee, Univ. of Northern Colorado, Univ. of Wyoming. Taught at Arkansas Agricultural, Mechanical, and Normal College, Central State Univ. See selected discography. More than 50 works in many genres (*Tawawa House*, opera, 1987). (28 scores at AMRC/CBMR, W-H, W-H Bib, BWiA, NBAW)

Pittman, Evelyn LaRue. b. McAlester, Okla., 1910; d. 1992. Attended Spelman, Atlanta Univ., Langston Univ., Juilliard. Taught in Oklahoma City public schools. Directed Evelyn Pittman Choir, taught at Woodlands High School in New York State. Choral works, operas (*Cousin Esther*, 1956). (4 scores at AMRC/CBMR, W-H Bib, see also selected bibliography: M. Green,)

Price, Florence Beatrice Smith. b. Little Rock, Ark., 1887; d. 1953. Attended New England Conservatory, Chicago Musical Coll., etc. Taught at Cotton Plant Arkadelphia Academy, Shorter Coll., Clark Coll. See selected discography. Scores are located in the Florence Price Archives at the University of Arkansas Library Special Collections, and at the Library of Congress. Published by G. Schirmer, Clar-Nan, etc. About 300 compositions in many genres (*Sonata in E Minor* for piano, 1932). (65 scores at AMRC/CBMR, Facts, IDBC, BWiA, NBAW, New Groves; see also selected bibliography: Brown, M. Green, etc.)

Robinson, Gertrude Rivers. b. Camden, S.C. 1927; d. 1995. Attended Cornell, Univ. of California at Los Angeles. Taught at Cornell, Loyola Marymount Univ. Ethnomusicologist, gamelan performer. See selected discography. Concert music (*Bayang Bayangan: Piece for Western Septet and Balinese Octet*, 1962). (2 scores at AMRC/CBMR, IDBC).

Rushen, Patrice. b. Los Angeles, 1954. Attended Univ. of Southern California. Classical and jazz pianist, arranger. See selected discography. Jazz, film, concert music (*Sinfonia* for symphony orchestra). (BWiA, Facts, www.patricerushen.com)

Schuyler, Philippa Duke. b. New York City 1931; d. 1967. Concert pianist, author. More than 60 works for voice, piano, orchestra (*Nile Fantasia* for piano and orchestra). Her scores are located at the Schomburg Center, Syracuse University Library, and the Library of Congress. (35 scores at AMRC/CBMR, Facts, IDBC, BWiA, NBAW, New Groves; see also selected bibliography: Talalay)

Scott, Hazel Dorothy. b. Trinidad, 1920; d. 1981. Attended Juilliard. Classical, jazz pianist, actress. Jazz piano pieces, spin-offs on the classics (*Caribbean Fete* in 3 movements for piano, ca. 1940). (1 score at AMRC/CBMR, Facts, BWiA, NBAW)

Sherrill, Barbara Geyen. b. Galveston, Tex., 1932. Attended CalArts, USC Teachers' Coll., California State Univ. Taught in Los Angeles schools. More than 50 vocal, choral, and dramatic works (*I Am Thomas!*, oratorio, 1989). (W-H Bib)

Simmons, Dr. Margo Nelleen. b. Nashville, Tenn., 1952. Attended Putney School, Antioch, Univ. of California at San Diego. Taught at Univ. of California at San Diego, Univ. of Ottawa, Hampshire College. Concert music (*Distant Images of Time and Voice* for orchestra, chorus, soloists, 1987). (2 scores at AMRC/CBMR, W-H, W-H Bib)

Simpson-Curenton, Evelyn. b. Philadelphia, 1953. Attended Germantown Settlement Music School, Temple Univ. Taught African-American sacred music at Westminster Choir College and lectured at Smithsonian Institution. Choral works and arrangements of spirituals for voice with instrumental ensembles, orchestra (*Is There Anybody Here That Loves My Jesus?*). (W-H Bib)

Smith, Irene Britton. See chapter 5.

Solomon-Moorman, Dr. Joyce. b. Tuskegee, Ala., 1946. Grew up in Columbia, S.C. Attended Vassar, Rutgers, Sarah Lawrence, Columbia Univ. Taught at Brooklyn Music School, St. Joseph's Coll., Queens Coll., Harlem School of the Arts, etc. Concert music (*Tone Poem* for orchestra). (10 scores at AMRC/CBMR, W-H, W-H Bib)

Taylor, Dorothy "Dotti" Anita. b. New York City ca. 1940. Attended Preparatory Division of Juilliard, Queens Coll., Syracuse Univ., Taught mathematics in New York public schools. Jazz flutist/pianist. Concert music (*String Quartet* 1989).

Temple, Maxine. b. Houston, Tex. Attended Wiley Coll., Illinois Wesleyan Univ. Taught at Rust Coll., Bethune-Cookman Coll., and Daytona Beach Community Coll., Saxophonist, clarinetist. Concert music for saxophone (*Arabesque* for sax and piano).

Thomas, Blanche Katurah. 1885–1977. Attended Juilliard, Westminster Choir Coll., etc. Music teacher, founder of Thomas Negro Composers Study Group in New York. Song *I Think of Thee* won 1928 Wanamaker First Prize; *I Am Troubled in Mind* won 1931 Wanamaker Honorable Mention. Songs, choral music, piano pieces (*Teddy Roosevelt March*). (2 scores at AMRC/CBMR, Schom, LC, W-H)

Thomas, Carlotta. b. New York City. Studied with Harry Burleigh. Organist. Songs, choral pieces (*Benediction*, 1932). (Roach, Carter, M-Sp)

Tilghman, Amelia L. b. Washington, D.C., ca. 1850. Attended Howard 1871, Boston Conservatory of Music. Concert soprano, teacher. Published first black music journal, *Musical Messenger* (1886). Vocal, piano pieces (*Come See the Place Where the Lord Hath Lain* for voice, violin, piano, 1903). (2 scores at AMRC/CBMR, LC, M-Sp, W-H)

Trice, Dr. Patricia J. b. Greensboro, N.C., 1939. Attended Oberlin, Univ. of Illinois, Univ. of North Carolina, Florida State Univ. Taught at North Carolina A&T State Univ., Hillsborough Community Coll., etc. Educational, vocal, choral, piano pieces (*Heaven Suite* for solo voice, 2000).

Tucker. See Corrothers-Tucker, Rosina Harvey.

Twine, Linda. b. Oklahoma. Arranger for Broadway shows, choral music for Boys' Choir of Harlem.

Watkins, Mary. See chapter 8.

White, Dr. Diane. b. Washington, D.C., 1964. Attended Washington Univ. in St. Louis, Ecole Normale de Musique in Paris, Univ. of California at Santa Barbara. Taught at Appalachian State Univ., Westmont Coll. See selected discography. Concert music (*Who Knows if the Moon's a Balloon* for soprano, flute, oboe, and cello).

White, Dolores. b. Chicago. Attended Oberlin, Cleveland Institute of Music, etc. Taught at Cuyahoga Community Coll., Wooster Coll. See selected discography. More than 50 works for instruments, orchestra, voice, chorus *Choral Triptych, 1976. (20 scores at AMRC/CBMR, W-H Bib)*

Williams, Mary Lou. b. Mary Elfrida Scruggs, Atlanta, 1910; d. 1981. Jazz pianist and arranger with Andy Kirk, Duke Ellington, and many others. Received Guggenheim grants, taught at Duke University. See selected discography. More than 80 works for piano, band, orchestra, voice, chorus (Mary Lou's Mass, 1971). More information can be obtained from Father Peter J. O'Brien, The Mary Lou Williams Foundation, 144 Grand St., Jersey City, N. J. 07302. (All scores at the Institute for Jazz Studies at the Rutgers University in Newark, 38 scores at AMRC/CBMR, Facts, IDBC, BWiA, NBAW, New Groves, W-H Bib)

Willis, Dr. Sharon J. b. Cleveland, 1949. Attended Clark Coll., Georgia State Univ., Univ. of Georgia. Singer, choral director. Taught at Agnes Scott Coll., Atlanta Metropolitan Coll., Morris Brown. See selected discography. Concert vocal and instrumental music, 3 operas (*The Opera Singer* 2000).

Winston, Dorothy Sims. b. Mississippi, 1897; d. 1967. Attended Tougaloo, Fisk, Wichita Univ. Founded and taught at Coleridge-Taylor Conservatory in Wichita (1920s, 1930s). Songs, choral and piano pieces (*Hymn of Freedom*, SATB, 1927). (Source: Dr. Linda Pohly, Ball State Univ., Indiana)

SELECTED BIBLIOGRAPHY/ DISCOGRAPHY

SELECTED BIBLIOGRAPHY

See also the bibliographies at the ends of chapters 2 through 9 for sources on the composers.

Ammer, Christine. *Unsung: A History of Women in American Music.* Westport, Conn.: Greenwood Press, 1980.

Baker, David, Lida M. Belt, and Herman C. Hudson. *The Black Composer Speaks.* Metuchen, N.J.: Scarecrow Press, 1978.

Berlin, Edward A. *King of Ragtime: Scott Joplin and His Era.* New York: Oxford University Press, 1994.

Black Women in America: An Historical Encyclopedia. Edited by Darlene Clark Hine. Brooklyn, N.Y.: Carlson, 1993.

Brooks, Tilford. *America's Black Musical Heritage.* Englewood Cliffs, N.J.: Prentice-Hall, 1984.

Brown, Rae Linda. "William Grant Still, Florence Price, and William Dawson." In *Black Music in the Harlem Renaissance.* Edited by Samuel A. Floyd Jr. Knoxville: University of Tennessee Press, 1993.

―――. "The Women's Symphony Orchestra of Chicago and Florence B. Price's *Piano Concerto in One Movement.*" *American Music* 11, no. 2 (Summer 1993): 185–205.

―――. *The Heart of a Woman: The Life and Music of Florence B. Price.* Urbana: University of Illinois Press, forthcoming, 2002.

Carter, Madison. *An Annotated Catalog of Composers of African Ancestry.* New York: Vantage Press, 1986.

Cohen, Aaron. *International Encyclopedia of Women Composers.* 2nd ed. 2 vols. New York: R. R. Bowker, 1987.

Cuney-Hare, Maude. *Negro Musicians and Their Music.* Washington, D.C.: Associated Publishers, 1936.

Dannett, Sylvia. *Profiles in Negro Womanhood.* New York: Negro Heritage Library, 1966. Reprint Da Capo Press, 1974.

Davenport, M. Marguerite. *Azalia: The Life of Madame E. Azalia Hackley.* Boston: Chapman and Grimes, 1947.

Du Bois, W.E.B. *The Souls of Black Folk.* 1903. Reprint New York: Gramercy Books, 1994.

Epstein, Dena J. "Black Spirituals: Their Emergence into Public Knowledge." *Black Music Research Journal* 10, no. 1 (Spring 1990): 58–64.

Facts on File Encyclopedia of Black Women in America: Music (vol. 5). Edited by Darlene Clark Hine. New York: Facts on File, 1997.

Floyd, Samuel A., Jr. *The Power of Black Music.* New York: Oxford University Press, 1995.

Franklin, John Hope, and Alfred A. Moss Jr. *From Slavery to Freedom.* 7th ed. New York: Alfred A. Knopf, 1994.

Gatewood, Willard B. *Aristocrats of Color.* Bloomington: Indiana University Press, 1990.

Green, Jeffrey. "Conversation with Josephine Harreld Love: Reminiscences of Times Past." *Black Perspective in Music* 18, no. 1 (1990): 179–213.

Green, Mildred Denby. *Black Women Composers: A Genesis.* Boston: Twayne, 1983.

Handy, D. Antoinette. *Black Women in American Bands and Orchestras.* Metuchen, N.J.: Scarecrow Press, 1981.

———. *International Sweethearts of Rhythm.* 2nd ed. Metuchen, N.J.: Scarecrow Press, 1996.

Handy, William Christopher. *Negro Authors and Composers of the United States.* New York: Handy Brothers, 1936.

Harrison, Daphne Duval. *Black Pearls: Blues Queens of the 1920s.* New Brunswick, N.J.: Rutgers University Press, 1988.

Holly, Ernestine. "Black Concert Music in Chicago, 1890–1930s." *Black Music Research Journal* 10, no. 1 (Spring 1990): 141–152.

International Dictionary of Black Composers. Edited by Samuel A. Floyd Jr. 2 vols. Chicago: Fitzroy Dearborn, 1999.

Jackson, Irene. V. "Black Women and Music: A Survey from Africa to the New World." *Minority Voices* 2, no. 2 (Fall 1978): 15–27.

Jones, Hettie. *Big Star Fallin' Mama: Five Women in Black Music.* New York: Viking Press, 1974. Rev. ed. 1995.

Layne, Maude Wanzer. *The Negro's Contribution to Music.* Philadelphia: Theodore Presser, 1942.

Locke, Alain, *The Negro and His Music.* 1936. Reprint. New York: Arno Press, 1969.

Majors, Monroe A. *Noted Negro Women: Their Triumphs and Activities.* Chicago: Author, 1893.

McGinty, Doris Evans. "Black Women in the Music of Washington D.C. 1900–1920." In *New Perspectives on Music: Essays in Honor of Eileen Southern.* Edited by Josephine Wright and Samuel A. Floyd Jr. Detroit: Harmonie Park Press, 1991.

New Groves Dictionary of Music and Musicians. 2nd ed. Edited by Stanley Sadie and John Tyrrell. London: Macmillan, 2000.

Notable Black American Women. Edited by Jessie Carney Smith. Detroit: Gale Research, 1992. Book II, 1996.

Pendle, Karin. *Women and Music: A History*. 2nd ed. Bloomington: Indiana University Press, 2001.

The Readers' Companion to United States Women's History. Edited by Wilma Mankiller, Gwendolyn Mink, Marysa Navarro, Barbara Smith, and Gloria Steinem. New York: Houghton Mifflin, 1998.

Reagon, Bernice Johnson, and Sweet Honey in the Rock. *We Who Believe in Freedom*. New York: Anchor Books, 1993.

Roach, Hildred. *Black American Music, Past and Present*. 2nd ed. Malabar, Fla.: Krieger, 1992.

Schenbeck, Lawrence. "Music, Gender, and 'Uplift' in the *Chicago Defender*, 1927–1937." *Musical Quarterly* 81, no. 3 (Fall 1997): 344–370.

Scruggs, Lawson. *Women of Distinction*. Raleigh, N.C.: Author, 1893.

Shockley, Ann Allen. *Afro-American Women Writers, 1746–1933*. New York: New American Library, 1988.

Smith, Catherine Parsons. *William Grant Still: A Study in Contradictions*. Berkeley: University of California Press, 2000.

Southern, Eileen. *Biographical Dictionary of Afro-American and African Musicians*. Westport, Conn.: Greenwood Press, 1983.

———. *The Music of Black Americans*. 3rd ed. New York: W. W. Norton, 1997.

Sterling, Dorothy. *We Are Your Sisters*. New York: W. W. Norton, 1984.

Talalay, Kathryn. *Composition in Black and White: The Life of Philippa Schuyler*. New York: Oxford University Press, 1995.

Walker-Hill, Helen. "Black Women Composers in Chicago: Then and Now." *Black Music Research Journal* 12, no. 1 (Fall 1992): 1–24.

———. *Music by Black Women Composers: A Bibliography of Available Scores*. CBMR Monograph no. 5. Chicago: Center for Black Music Research, 1995.

———. "Music by Black Women Composers in the American Music Research Center." *American Music Research Center Journal* 2 (1992): 23–52.

———. *Piano Music by Black Women Composers: A Catalog of Solo and Ensemble Works*. Westport, Conn.: Greenwood Press, 1992.

Ward, Andrew. *Dark Midnight When I Rise: The Story of the Jubilee Singers Who Introduced the World to the Music of Black America*. New York: Farrar, Straus and Giroux, 2000.

Williams, Ora. *American Black Women in the Arts and Sciences*. 3rd ed. Metuchen, N.J.: Scarecrow Press, 1994.

Williams, Ora, Thelma Williams, Dora Wilson, and Ramona Matthewson. "American Black Women Composers: A Selected Annotated Bibliography." In *All the Women Are White, All the Blacks Are Men, but Some of Us Are Brave*. Edited by Gloria T. Hull, Patricia Bell Scott, and Barbara Smith. Old Westbury, N.Y.: Feminist Press, 1982.

Wright, Josephine L. "Black Women and Classical Music." *Women's Studies Quarterly* 12, no. 3 (Fall 1984): 18–21.

———. "Black Women in Classical Music in Boston During the Late Nineteenth Century: Profiles of Leadership." In *New Perspectives on Music: Essays in Honor of Eileen Southern*. Edited by Samuel A. Floyd, Jr. and Josephine Wright. Detroit: Harmonie Park Press, 1992.

SELECTED DISCOGRAPHY

See also the discographies at the ends of chapters 2 through 9 for recordings of music by the composers.

Albums with Works by More Than One African-American Woman Composer

Ah, Love, But a Day—Songs and Spirituals of American Women. Louise Toppin, soprano; Jay Pierson, and John O'Brien. Albany record #385, 2000. Margaret Bonds, Florence Price, Betty Jackson King, Jacqueline Hairston, Undine Smith Moore.

Black Diamonds. Althea Waites, piano. Cambria Records CD1097, 1993. Margaret Bonds, *Troubled Water*; Florence Price, *Sonata in E Minor, Dances in the Canebrakes, Cotton Dance, The Boatman.*

Dark Fires: 20th Century Music for Piano. Karen Walwyn, piano. Albany Troy 266, 1997. Dolores White, *Toccata*; Lettie Beckon Alston, *Three Rhapsodies.*

Kaleidoscope: Music by African-American Women. Gregory Walker, violin, and Helen Walker-Hill, piano. Leonarda Records CD LE 339, 1995. Irene Britton Smith, Dorothy Rudd Moore, Undine Smith Moore, Regina Baiocchi, Valerie Capers, Betty Jackson King, Florence Price, Nora Holt, Margaret Bonds, Julia Perry, Dolores White, Lena McLin, Rachel Eubanks, and Lettie Beckon Alston.

The Negro Speaks of Rivers: Art Songs by African-American Composers. Odikhiren Amaize, voice; David Korevaar, piano. Musicians' Showcase CD 1011, 2000. Songs by Florence Price, Margaret Bonds, Undine Smith Moore.

Piano Portraits of the Seasons by Women Composers. Katherine Boyes, piano. Audio CD, 2001. Estelle Ricketts, *Rippling Spring Waltz*; Betty Jackson King, *Four Seasonal Sketches.*

Ruth Norman Plays Music by Black Composers. Opus One LPs #35, #39. Ruth Norman, *Molto Allegro* and *Preludes nos. 1, 4*; Margaret Bonds, *Troubled Water.*

The Unknown Flower. Charsie Randolph Sawyer, soprano; Karen Krummel, cello; Susan Keith Gray, piano. Calvin College CD, 2000. Song cycles by Lettie Beckon Alston, Valerie Capers, Betty Jackson King, Lena McLin.

Watch and Pray: Spirituals and Art Songs by African-American Women Composers. Videmus: Pamela Dillard, soprano; Ruth Hamilton, contralto; Robert Honeysucker, baritone; Vivian Taylor, piano. Koch International Classics CD, 1994. Florence Price, Margaret Bonds, Betty Jackson King, Julia Perry, and Undine Smith Moore.

You Can Tell the World: Songs by African-American Women Composers. Sebronette Barnes, soprano; Elise Auerbach, piano. Senrab Records, 2000. Margaret Bonds, Jackie Hairston, Jeraldine Saunders Herbison, Betty Jackson King, Lena Johnson McLin, Julia Perry, Zenobia Powell Perry, Florence Price, and Sharon Willis.

Albums with Works by Single Composers

Allen, Geri. *Gathering*, Polygram, 1998. *Eyes in the Back of Your Head*, Blue Note, 1997; *Some Aspects of Water*, Storyville, 1997; *Twenty-One*, Blue Note, 1994; *The Nurturer*, Blue Note, 1990; *Maroons*, Blue Note, 1992; *In the Middle/Open*

On All Sides, Polygram, 1986; *In the Year of the Dragon*, Polygram, 1989; *Segments*, DIW, 1989; *Twilight*, Verve 1989; *Homegrown*, Minor Music, 1985; *The Printmakers*, Polygram, 1984; *Etudes*, Soul Note, 1984; *Live at the Village Vanguard*, DIW, 1984.

Butler, Jean. *Maria's Rags, I, II.* On *Music by American Women Composers*, performed by duo pianists Leanne Rees and Stephanie Stoyanoff. Bravura recordings, BR 1001.

León, Tania. *Indigena.* CRI CD662, 1994; *Haiku* for narrator, 11-piece ensemble, and other works. Opus One #101.

Okoye, Nkeiru. *Movie Themes.* Produced by Nkeiru Okoye at Bloomfield College, 2000.

Price, Florence. *The Oak, Mississippi River, Symphony No. 3.* Performed by the Women's Philharmonic conducted by Apo Hsu. Koch International Classics 7518, 2001.

———. *The Deserted Garden.* On *Here's One.* Zina Schiff, violin; Cameron Grant, piano. 4-Tay 4005, 1998.

Robinson, Gertrude. *Moods.* On *Romantic Sax—Echosphere.* Performed by Paul Stewart, sax, and Deon Price, piano. Cambria Records CT-1047.

Rushen, Patrice. *Prelusion/ Before the Dawn*, 1974; *Patrice Rushen*, 1978; *Pizzazz*, 1979; *Posh*, 1980; *Straight from the Heart*, 1982; *Now*, 1984; *Watch Out*, 1987; *The Meeting*, 1990; *Update*, 1995; *Anything but Ordinary*, 1994; *Forget Me Nots*, 1996 Grammy Award; *Haven't You Heard*, 1996; *Signature*, 1997; etc.

Solomon, Joyce Moorman. *Tone Poem* for orchestra. On *Vienna Modern Masters New Music for Orchestra.* VNM 3045, 2000.

White, Diane. *In Stillness.* Bythax Records, 2000.

White, Dolores. *Crystal Gazing.* On *Cleveland Plays Music by African Americans.* Cleveland Chamber Orchestra, conducted by Edwin London. Albany Troy 303, 1998.

Williams, Mary Lou. *Zoning* (1974), Smithsonian Folkways SF CD 40811, 1995; *Zodiac Suite* (1945), Smithsonian Folkways SF CD 40810, 1995, etc.

SELECTED PUBLISHED MUSIC BY AFRICAN-AMERICAN WOMEN COMPOSERS

See also the appendix, and the lists of works for chapters 2 through 9.

Anthology of Art Songs by Black American Composers. Edited by Willis Patterson. New York: E. B. Marks, 1977. Includes songs by Margaret Bonds, Dorothy Rudd Moore, Undine Smith Moore, and Florence Price.

Art Songs and Spirituals by African-American Women Composers. Edited by Vivian Taylor. Bryn Mawr, Pa.: Hildegard Publishing Company, 1995. Margaret Bonds, Betty Jackson King, Undine Smith Moore, Julia Perry, Florence Price.

Black Women Composers: A Century of Piano Music 1893–1990. Edited by Helen Walker-Hill. Bryn Mawr, Pa.: Hildegard Publishing Company, 1992. Amanda Aldridge, Mable Bailey, Regina Baiocchi, Margaret Bonds, Valerie Capers, Anna Gardner Goodwin, Betty Jackson King, L. Viola Kinney, Tania León, Lena Johnson McLin, Dorothy Rudd Moore, Undine Smith Moore, Julia Perry, Zenobia Powell Perry, Florence Price, Estelle Ricketts, Philippa Duke Schuyler, Joyce Solomon, Mary Lou Williams.

Black Women Composers: Twentieth-Century Music for Piano and Strings. Edited by Gregory Walker and Helen Walker-Hill. Bryn Mawr, Pa.: Hildegard Publishing Company, forthcoming, 2002. Lettie Beckon Alston, Rachel Eubanks, Jeraldine Herbison, Zenobia Powell Perry, Mary Watkins, Dolores White.

Music by African-American Women series. Stevens Point, Wis.: Vivace Press:

Five Interludes for Piano by Rachel Eubanks, edited by Helen Walker-Hill, 1995.

Sonata for Violin and Piano by Irene Britton Smith, edited with Gregory Walker and Helen Walker-Hill, 1996.

Four Rhapsodies for Solo Piano by Lettie Beckton Alston, 2001.

Piano Music by Irene Britton Smith, edited by Helen Walker-Hill, 2001.

Negro Dance, Op. 25, no. 1, by Nora Holt, edited by Helen Walker-Hill, 2001.

We Shall Overcome: Suite for Organ by Sharon J. Willis, 2001.

Three Pieces for Violin and Piano by Dorothy Rudd Moore, forthcoming, 2002.

Soweto (piano, violin, cello) by Undine Smith Moore, forthcoming, 2002.

INDEX

About the Author

HELEN WALKER-HILL served on the piano faculty of the University of Colorado at Boulder, as well as on the faculties of Muhlenberg College and the University of Wyoming. She is the author of *Piano Music by Black Women Composers: A Catalogue of Solo and Ensemble Works* (Greenwood, 1992).